JAMES W. QUILLIN

D0095686

HUMAN DEVELOPMENTAL NEUROPSYCHOLOGY

HUMAN DEVELOPMENTAL NEUROPSYCHOLOGY

Otfried Spreen
David Tupper
Anthony Risser
Holly Tuokko
Dorothy Edgell

New York   Oxford
OXFORD UNIVERSITY PRESS
1984

Copyright © 1984 by Oxford University Press, Inc.

Library of Congress Cataloging in Publication Data
Main entry under title:

Human developmental neuropsychology.

Bibliography: p.
Includes indexes.
1. Pediatric neurology.   2. Developmental disabilities.
3. Neuropsychology.   4. Developmental neurology.
I. Spreen, Otfried.   [DNLM: 1. Child development dis-
orders.   2. Nervous system—Growth and development.
3. Nervous system diseases—In infancy and childhood.
WS 350.6 H918]
RJ486.H845   1984   616   83-23773
ISBN 0-19-503406-6
ISBN 0-19-503407-4 (pbk.)

Printed in the United States of America

Printing (last digit): 9 8 7 6 5 4 3 2 1

Preface

This book is addressed to neuropsychologists working with children as well as to students of psychology, education, and other child-care professions. We have attempted to write the book so that it poses no difficulties in understanding for the clinical psychologist without background in neurology or the pediatrician without background in psychology.

Developmental neuropsychology extends to many disciplines concerned with the development of the nervous system. These include developmental psychology, pediatrics, neurology, biology, and ethology as well as more specialized disciplines, such as behavioral embryology, developmental neurobiology, teratology, and many others. Much of the research basic to developmental neuropsychology can be found only in the highly technical literature of neurobiology, in exclusively disease-oriented medical publications, and in the many journals devoted to psychological development. This book attempts to integrate this information, rephrasing technical language or explaining studies as necessary, without trying to provide exhaustive, up-to-date coverage of background issues. Our main goal is an increased understanding of normal and abnormal development in early and middle childhood and adolescence as it relates to the development of the nervous system during the prenatal, perinatal, and postnatal periods.

The first part of the book attempts to provide the background essential to an understanding of the growth of the nervous system, information gathered in minute detail over many decades by neurobiologists, mostly from animal studies. The second part reviews some conceptual and methodological issues that deserve detailed treatment, such as the critical periods hypothesis, neural plasticity, and disconnection syndromes.

The third part enters the clinical arena. It deals with the information gathered by clinicians attending the human fetus, embryo or newborn and presents an overview of potentially damaging events and conditions that may affect the normal growth of the child. Of necessity, the tools of the clinician differ sharply from those available to the neurobiologist. Instead of dissection and experimentation, the results of clinical observation and measurement, or at best of radiological studies and other clinical procedures, have to be relied upon.

Part IV describes the functional disabilities frequently associated with damage to the developing nervous system. Once again the focus of interest and the tools of assessment differ. When functional disorders are discovered, the educator, psychiatrist, or clinical psychologist must focus on the problem and on the immediate environment of the child, how he or she is treated by peers and teachers, how achievement tests rank the child in the classroom and so forth. Compared with these questions, the problem of a difficult birth or a maternal infection during the first trimester seems rather remote. Although such remote events have been invoked as possible explanations of many functional disabilities in middle childhood, the relationships remain elusive and tenuous. Yet the exploration of such relationships remains the ultimate focus of this book.

No attempt is made to consider in detail social and other environmental conditions affecting the child after the postnatal and early infancy period, nor does the book deal with brain damage acquired later in the child's life unless it is necessary for the understanding of the topic.

While gathering material for this book, we were struck both by the rich detail of research in many areas and by the lack of integration. Research in basic developmental neurobiology proceeds largely in a field by itself; few attempts to relate the information to clinical research or long-term outcome of pathological conditions have been made. Studies of the clinical disorders of the perinatal period are usually designed to answer questions raised by the practicing obstetrician or pediatrician but pay little attention to long-term psychological sequelae except in their most severe form (e.g., mental retardation). The few follow-up studies that have been conducted usually are short-term and prospective; for example, the outcome of certain infections during pregnancy is assessed in the newborn or in early infancy and childhood. On the other hand, the disorders of psychological function discussed in Part IV are usually researched as current problems stressing how they affect the child's life at that time; the origin of such conditions during the pre- and perinatal period is often either assumed or researched retrospectively. For example, learning disorders or hyperactivity may be attributed to "minimal brain damage" of unspecified origin with or without a search of hospital records or a report from the parents.

Hence, a wide gap between our knowledge of specific adverse conditions at birth and of specific outcomes during later childhood and adolescence tends to be the rule rather than the exception. As is obvious from the discussion in this book, neither the prospective nor the retrospective research design has sufficient power to establish a clear causal relationship. If a significant relation can be demonstrated, it accounts for only a small portion of the variance. In other words, the effects of perinatal events are only to a very limited extent predictive: One likely reason for this is the large variability of outcome; another reason is the lack of precise measures of perinatal conditions; a third reason to be considered is the effect of "intervening" environmental conditions, including intervention and treatment.

With the rapid growth of neuropsychology as a discipline and the proliferation of neuropsychological explorations of many areas of applied psychology, including childhood disorders and especially educational problems, an integration of knowledge in the disciplines concerned with developmental issues is both timely and urgent. If successful, such an integration may well be fundamental to the application of neuropsychology to any developmental issue. Without such foundations, the neuropsychology of childhood must remain fragmentary and isolated from other approaches.

Throughout the text we provide brief definitions of terms that may not be readily understood by readers with little background in biology or medicine. Usually, the terms are defined the first time they are used and the page number indexed in italics. The index then can be used as a glossary to allow the reader to find the definition more readily if the term appears later in the text.

The authors are grateful to a number of people who have helped in the preparation of the manuscript: most of all, we appreciate the help of the students of 1981 and 1982 who worked with us through the course on developmental neuropsychology. Pamela Klonoff prepared the draft of Chapter 20 and Rosemary Wilkinson the draft of Chapter 26. We would like to acknowledge the careful reading of the manuscript and the many helpful comments provided by Arthur L. Benton, William H. Gaddes, and J. Kenneth Martin, as well as the assistance of Sonya and Georgia Spreen with both the manuscript and the references. We are grateful to Jeffrey House at Oxford University Press for encouragement and numerous valuable critical comments.

Contents

I
EARLY-LIFE NEURAL DEVELOPMENT

The normal development of the human nervous system is an orderly, sequential process. The principles governing this elaborate process are outlined in the first part of this book so that the effects of abnormal influences, to be discussed later, can be understood as deviations from the expected level of development for a particular individual at a given age.

1

Principles
of Neural Development

This chapter is devoted to theoretical issues, basic principles, and approaches to the study of nervous system development. First we discuss the role of the developmental neuropsychologist in understanding nervous system development, emphasizing difficulties that arise both in research and in practice when an attempt is made to correlate neuroanatomy and behavior. Then two basic approaches to the study of nervous system development—gross and microscopic—are presented. Finally, the role of specific neural elements in the building of the central nervous system is discussed in detail.

1.1 PROBLEMS IN CORRELATING ANATOMICAL AND BEHAVIORAL DEVELOPMENT

The first major difficulty in understanding the relationship between human anatomical and behavioral development arises from the variety of approaches used to study essentially the same subject matter (Birch 1974). Research fields have tended to become isolated, each growing so highly specialized that adequate communication with other disciplines is difficult. This often happens when different species are used for research. For several good reasons, developmental neurobiologists frequently use rats in their studies, and this limits generalizations to humans or other primates. We do not know, with regard to general principles and to the sequences involved, what inferences for humans can be made from animal research. However, research on nonhuman primates (Rakic's work with rhesus monkeys, for example) has often confirmed and extended findings from studies of lower vertebrates. Until more studies along these lines are done, pediatricians, neurologists, and psychologists will have trouble applying the results of animal research to the problems of their patients.

A second major difficulty in correlating anatomical and behavioral development is the definition of "development." The term "development" implies more of a search for relationships between processes than other terms, such as "maturation" (K. J. Connolly and Prechtl 1981, Rose 1980), "growth" (Trevarthen 1980), or "ontogeny" (Goldman 1976). It also puts the focus on the search for mechanisms underlying change rather than on just a description of change over time. As an organism develops neuropsychologically, many extrinsic influences create pressures that modify, through processes of their own, the mechanisms involved in the intrinsic differentiation of a unique, complex organism. Thus, the nervous system of an infant can be seen not as immature but rather as adapted to the specific functions necessary for survival at that age (K. J. Connolly and Prechtl 1981). At this point, however, researchers have only a glimpse of the underlying mechanisms and must rely heavily on descriptive analyses of changes over time in the nervous system and in behavior (Cooke 1980). Our search for "developmental" processes in this sense has just begun.

The third major difficulty we encounter is posed by multiple causes of any behavior. For example, numerous causes have been linked to cognitive deficit, delayed language development, and learning disabilities. On the other hand, the same antecedent conditions and events contribute to different behavioral outcomes; in some cases, many conditions are necessary to produce a particular outcome. Straightforward cause-effect relationships are not likely to be found with contemporary methods of developmental psychology (Baltes and Nesselroade 1970). When studying the relationship between anatomical and behavioral development, we have to be aware of this complicating pitfall and explicitly recognize the many possible antecedent events ("causes") that interact as mechanisms involved in development (see also the discussion in Hebb 1949).

A more theoretical caution put forth by Riesen (1971) concerns correlations between behavioral and anatomical changes. A proposed correlation, he suggests, may be misleading because, in early development, many changes are taking place in the organism that may or may not be directly related to the behavioral variable under study. Because many relatively independent processes may show a temporal relationship in a developing organism because they occur during the same short time period, it is better to use the suspected correlation as a general indicator of a relationship and to pose a new question, "What events and conditions produced the correlation?" (Riesen 1971, p. 60). For example, considerable progress has been made in specifying the conditions resulting in low birth weight, stressing contributing factors such as malnutrition, alcohol use, and smoking while distinguishing the "small for date" from the premature baby and from the baby who is small in relation to its actual gestational age.

TABLE 1-1   The Major Divisions of the CNS with the Principal Structures Associated with Each Division

Major division	Neural tube derivative	Major regions and nuclei	Major fiber tracts
Forebrain Telencephalon	Lateral ventricle	Cerebral cortex (neocortex) Hippocampal formation Septal nuclei Basal ganglia (striatum)	Corpus callosum Fimbria
Diencephalon	Third ventricle	Thalamus Hypothalamus	Internal capsule Medial forebrain bundle
Eye		Neural retina Pigment epithelium	
Midbrain	Aqueduct	Tectum (superior and inferior colliculi) Red nucleus Oculomotor and trochlear nuclei	Cerebral peduncle Cerebral-rubro-thalamic tract
Hindbrain	Fourth ventricle	Cerebellum Pontine nuclei Inferior olive Dorsal column nuclei Trigeminal nucleus	Cerebellar penduncles Pyramidal tract
Spinal cord	Central canal	Dorsal and ventral horns	Dorsal columns Pyramidal tract

Source: Lund 1978.

1.2 GROSS ASPECTS OF NEURAL DEVELOPMENT

The human nervous system can be divided into two major parts: the **central nervous system** (CNS), comprising the brain, brainstem, and spinal cord; and the **peripheral nervous system,** comprising the sensory and motor nerves branching from the CNS. Our emphasis is on the more complex CNS. Table 1-1 presents the major divisions of the CNS and the main structures within each. There are three major divisions of the brain: the forebrain, or **prosencephalon;** the midbrain, or **mesencephalon;** and the hindbrain, or **rhombencephalon.** Each of these areas is divided into several regions consisting primarily of either nerve cell bodies or nerve fibers. Regions that consist of cell bodies are called **gray matter** because the cells are that color, and regions that consist of **nerve fibers** are called white matter because the fatty sheath surrounding the fibers is white. Nerve fibers that connect different divisions of the nervous system are called **projection** fibers. Those that connect opposite areas in the two hemispheres are called **commissural** fibers, and those that travel only within a single division are called **association** fibers.

Figure 1-1 diagrams, in two views, some of the major structures in the

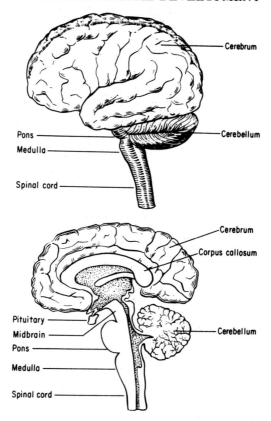

FIGURE 1-1   The lateral (above) and medial (below) aspects of the adult brain and their associated structures (R. F. Thompson 1967).

adult brain. More detailed information concerning the location of particular structures can be found in any neuroanatomy text. *Cytoarchitectonics* and *myelogenetics* are two approaches to the mapping of cerebral regions.

Cytoarchitectonics

Cytoarchitectonics refers to the arrangement of cells in a tissue and is commonly applied to studies of the location of different types of neurons in the cerebral cortex. Neurons are classified according to their structure; the classes are then charted on the brain. This yields a "map" of the cortex showing different zones for various cell types. Figure 1-2 portrays such a cytoarchitectural map with the numbering system of Brodmann and von Economo.

In the study of brain development, cytoarchitectonics has been used to establish the "birthdays" of cells in various CNS regions and to study changes in cellular areas during development (Rabinowicz 1979). The cytoarchitectural zone designation system implies a correspondence between cellular zones in the adult and in the child; changes in cellular zones during development have not been widely studied.

Myelogenesis

Myelogenesis (also "myelinogenesis") refers to the development of myelin, the fatty sheath surrounding the nerve fiber. We discuss the sequence of myelin formation in the CNS in conjunction with glial cell development (Sec. 1.3). It is assumed that the formation of myelin sheaths around an axon increases the conduction velocity, lowers the action potential threshold, and increases the neuron's ability to carry repetitive impulses, thus making it more functionally capable and efficient.

Flechsig (1901), a pioneer in the study of regions of myelin development, divided the cortex into what he termed "myelogenetic fields" and numbered them in the order of their progressive myelination. His developmental sequence of myelination consists of three general types of fields, called primordial, intermediate, and terminal zones.

Primordial, or premature, **fields** are those that myelinate before birth and include such areas as the somesthetic cortex, primary visual cortex, and primary auditory cortex. **Intermediate,** or postmature, **fields** myelinate during

FIGURE 1-2   Brodmann's areas. Cytoarchitectural map of the convex (lateral) surface of the adult brain (von Economo 1929).

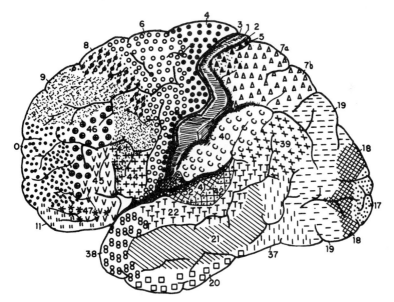

the first three postnatal months. These are generally considered to be **secondary association areas,** that is, areas that surround primary sensory or motor cortices. The **terminal fields** are the last to myelinate, between the fourth postnatal month and 14 years of age. They include the classical association areas, that is, areas assumed to subserve higher cortical functions.

In defining these myelogenetic fields, Flechsig conceived of what he called the **chronogenic hierarchy of myelogenetic zones.** Many other investigators have followed similar lines of investigation, attempting also to correlate myelination and behavioral development (e.g., Langworthy 1933, Yakovlev 1962, Yakovlev and Lecours 1967). P. Meyer (1981) reviewed Flechsig's original position in the light of more recent study and concluded that myelogenetics remains a valid approach to the study of structural neural development. Yakovlev and Lecours's (1967) work is presented in more detail when the chronology of postnatal development is discussed in Chap. 2.

1.3 NEURAL DEVELOPMENT AT THE MICROSCOPIC LEVEL

The light and electron microscopes are widely used in studies of the structural changes that occur in the CNS during development. These microscopic changes are often correlated with physiological changes in the developing organism. Recently, this approach has been extended to observations of biochemical and physiological changes in the microscopic structure and chemicals of the neurons during development (DiBenedetta et al. 1980). Changes at the microscopic level are almost always more difficult to correlate with specific developing behaviors but may, as in the case of nutritional disorders, be vital to an understanding of normal and abnormal neural development.

The subject of microscopic studies by neuroscientists is typically the nerve cell, or neuron (Fig. 1-3). A **neuron** consists of a cell body, a fiber that conducts impulses away from the body (axon), and an area of branching dendrites, which conduct impulses to the cell body from other neurons. Axons and dendrites are called the *processes* of the neuron. There are several types of neurons of various sizes and shapes in the CNS. A major structural classification is **Golgi** type I versus Golgi type II **neurons.** The former are usually large neurons with long axons and a large dendritic tree. They are thought to be formed prenatally and to serve as the major connections of the nervous system. They also act as part of the supporting structure of the CNS. Golgi type II neurons, also called **interstitial neurons,** are usually small cells with small axonal and dendritic expansions. It has been suggested that they are formed postnatally and may be important for higher cerebral functions (Hirsch and Jacobson 1975, Scheibel and Scheibel 1976, 1977). The nervous system also contains non-neuronal cells, called glial cells, which are thought to play a primary supportive and nutrient role in the CNS (Lund

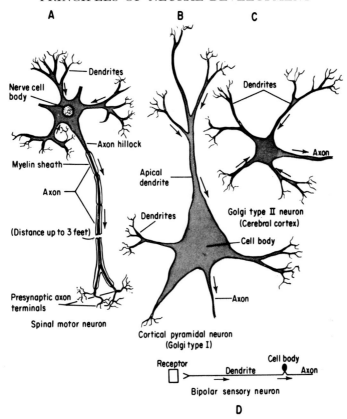

FIGURE 1-3 Some typical neurons and their associated structures. (*a*) Neuron. (*b*) Golgi type I neuron. (*c*) Golgi type II neuron from cerebral cortex. (*d*) Schematic drawing of a bipolar sensory neuron. (R. F. Thompson 1967).

1978); glial cells also form the myelin sheath that surrounds nerve fibers to aid conduction of electric nerve potentials.

Development and Placement of Neurons

The final location of a neuron in the nervous system is the result of many factors, both intrinsic and extrinsic to the organism, following the principles of specificity and plasticity but generally in a precise sequence (Cowan 1979). The terminology used here is that suggested by the Boulder Committee (1970).

PROLIFERATION   Cell generation by mitosis (cell division) is called *proliferation*. **Mitosis** occurs inside the neural tube (in the ventricular zone). The

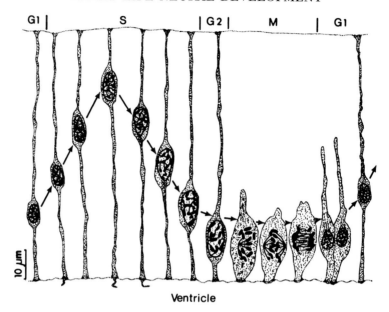

FIGURE 1-4   Schematic time-lapse diagram of the mitotic cycle of a neural germinal cell in the developing neural tube (Jacobson 1978).

mitotic cycle of each germinal cell follows a fixed sequence, as shown in
Fig. 1-4, and results in the production of **neuroblasts,** or nerve cell precursors, and **glioblasts,** or glial cell precursors. **Neurogenesis** is the term
used to describe nerve cell production.

The mitotic cycle begins as the nucleus of the germinal cell moves away
from the ventricle, enters the S phase of the cycle, and begins to synthesize deoxyribonucleic acid (DNA). As the cell moves into the premitotic, or
second gap (G2), period, the nucleus returns to the ventricular surface and
the cell becomes detached from the basal surface (top of Fig. 1-4). During
the mitotic (M) phase, the cell splits into two daughter cells, which begin
to extend their processes back to the surface before entering the presyn-
thetic, or first gap (G1), phase, prior to further DNA synthesis. The mitotic
cycle varies randomly for cells throughout the ventricular zone. It is repeated many times, the population of cells doubling roughly every eight to
24 hours (Cowan 1979), but at some point some of the daughter cells (those
destined to become neurons) become permanently arrested in the G1 phase
and never divide again.

MIGRATION   Upon completion of the mitotic, or proliferative, phase of neural
development but not before six weeks of gestation, the neuroblasts move
from the proliferative zone into their permanent locations (Moore 1977).
Sidman and Rakic (1973) have reviewed this process of migration in the hu-

man. Migration determines the ultimate destination of neurons and in so doing creates different cellular zones (Fig. 1-5). We shall use the developing cortex as the primary example of migration (Berry 1974, Sidman 1970), but the process also occurs in other brain regions.

The early neural tube consists only of a ventricular (V) zone of mitotic cells and a marginal (M) zone of the cellular processes. As proliferation continues and migration begins, an intermediate (I) zone of neurons forms. By eight to ten weeks after conception, the intermediate zone has enlarged to form the region from which cortex develops, i.e., the initial **cortical plate** (CP) of neurons, and a subventricular (S), or subependymal, zone, which is a secondary zone where cell proliferation may continue for several weeks. In fact, the smaller neurons (the microneurons, or Golgi type II neurons) of the brain as well as some glial cells are thought to be generated from this zone (Cowan 1979). The initial formation of the cortical plate occurs by migration of cells to the deepest (sixth) layer of the cortex, and subsequent migrations follow what has been described as an **inside-out pattern** (Marin-

FIGURE 1-5   Cellular zones in the developing cerebral cortex, cerebellum, and spinal cord (Jacobson 1978).

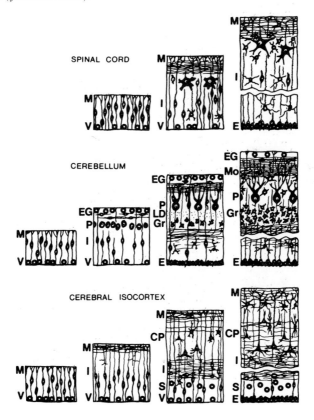

Padilla 1978, Rakic 1975a, 1979a, 1981). Thus the next layer to be formed is the next deepest layer; the top layer is formed last by neurons that must migrate past the cells of the deeper layers, over considerable distances, at later stages of development. A second migratory wave of cells occurs at 11 to 15 weeks of gestation and greatly thickens the cortical plate (Fig. 1-6).

Cell proliferation and migration vary from area to area and from stage to stage in the development of the nervous system. It appears that cell proliferation is generally complete in the human cerebral neocortex by six months gestational age but that glial cells may continue to be produced in the subventricular zone beyond that time.

It is still not known exactly what factors are responsible for the migration of neurons. Two possible explanations are (1) **mechanical guidance by radial fibers** and (2) **chemospecificity.** The latter hypothesis is discussed more fully later in this chapter in the context of axonal growth. The concept of mechanical guidance by radially oriented glial fibers has gained much sup-

FIGURE 1-6   Drawings of the developing cerebral cortex at various fetal ages with the two major waves of cell migration indicated by the curve below (Sidman and Rakic 1973).

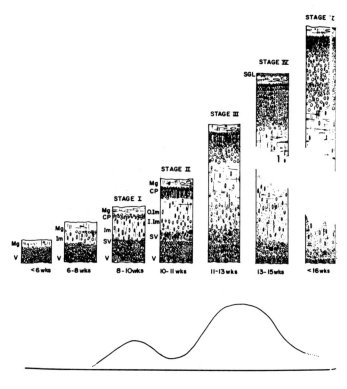

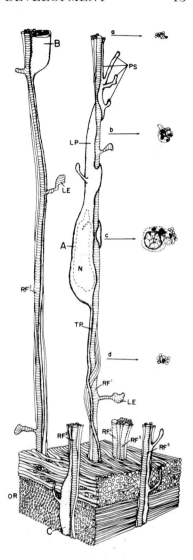

FIGURE 1-7 Relationship between migrating cells and radial fibers in the developing cerebral cortex of the rhesus monkey (Rakic 1972).

port from the work of Rakic (1975b, 1981). Fairly early in development, when it is difficult to distinguish cell types, a group of glial cells is radially oriented from the ventricular to the basal surface and appears to guide the migration of neurons from the site of their proliferation to their final destination in the cortical plate. These cells are called **radially oriented glia**. Figure 1-7 shows a neuron (N) that is migrating along a typical radial glia fiber (RF). Eventually, these radial glia disappear, transformed into astrocytes (Sidman and Rakic 1973). The discovery of radial glia as guides for migration is a major step in our understanding of the mechanisms of neural development, but many questions still remain unanswered.

In contrast to the course of events in the cerebral cortex and many other areas, migration in the cerebellum occurs in an "outside-in" fashion (Fig. 1-5). Between nine and 13 weeks of gestational age, germinal cells from the ventricular zone produce neuroblasts that migrate to the outermost layer of the cerebellum, the external granule (EG) layer, and proliferate. At the same time neurons from the ventricular zone continue to migrate into the Purkinje (P) layer, where they differentiate. External granule layer cell proliferation and migration continue throughout gestation. In the cerebellum the gray matter ends up external to the white matter, as is the case in the rest of the brain but not in the spinal cord. Particular radial glia (Bergmann glia) are thought to be responsible for this final migration of the granule cells in the external granule layer to their adult position beneath the Purkinje cell layer; this occurs in humans in the first year after birth.

Several **migratory defects,** termed **neuronal ectopias** (displacement or malpositioning), can occur in this sequence, resulting in abnormal structure and function of the neurons (Rakic 1975b). Three broad categories of defects can be distinguished: (1) complete failure of migration, (2) curtailment of migratory cells along the migratory pathway, and (3) aberrant placement of postmitotic neurons within the target structure. Anomalies may occur during normal development but are usually eliminated later in the process of selective cell death, described below (NINCDS 1979). Anomalies persisting into later development are infrequent, though they may result in certain types of mental retardation (Chap. 10). A study of genetic mutations in mice by Caviness and Rakic (1978) indicates that migrations may be under the control of a single or of several genes.

AGGREGATION   During their migratory cycle, neurons selectively aggregate to form the major cellular masses, or layers, in the nervous system. This process is called **lamination** (J. R. Wolff 1978) and precedes cell differentiation into distinctive types in each region. Cowan (1979) has specified two distinguishable events in this aggregation process. First the neurons come together and establish some form of mutual adhesion between the necessary cells; second, they align themselves preferentially with respect to their immediate neighbors. The aggregation process can be regarded as an aspect of neuronal specification or modification directed toward future functioning.

CYTODIFFERENTIATION   Following aggregation, neurons begin the process of differentiation (Pease 1971). Cellular differentiation, or cytodifferentiation, can be divided into four major concurrent aspects: (1) development of the cell body, or **perikaryon;** (2) selective cell death; (3) process formation, i.e., axonal and dendritic development; and (4) formation of synaptic connections (synaptogenesis).

Development   The morphological development of the cell body is a poorly understood process. Major influences on shape and function are thought to include genetic factors and mechanical pressures during migration and aggregation. LeDouarin (1980) has described one important factor in his work on neural crest tissue. In this tissue, environmental location helps determine whether neurons become adrenergic or cholinergic, i.e., whether upon stimulation they release noradrenaline or acetylcholine, two important neurotransmitters. A critical period of development (J. P. Scott et al. 1974) in the production of neurotransmitters, dependent upon environmental stimulation, has therefore been postulated.

Selective Cell Death The selective death of neurons during CNS development appears to be widespread and of sizeable magnitude. It has been estimated that 40 to 75 per cent of all neurons in the nervous system of birds die during development, although precise counts are difficult to obtain. Cell death could be a major determinant of the final cell number during development (NINCDS 1979, Oppenheim 1981). First, a population of neurons is generated; then, within a few days, this number is cut drastically by cell death. This pattern has led some investigators to suspect that it is programed to occur by genetic control, although little evidence has been found for this as yet. The most plausible hypothesis is that it occurs when synaptic contacts are made. Selective cell death may reflect the fact that only a limited number of neurons succeed in sending their axons to the correct targets. Others then degenerate.

Axonal and Dendritic Development Sperry (1951, 1959, 1968, 1971) put forth the theory of **chemospecificity,** or **chemoaffinity,** arguing that a biochemical specificity programed into each nerve cell determines the sequence of development and the contacts made by the cell. This theory of chemospecific contact guidance suggests that a neuron, as it forms an axon and dendrites, sends out an advance spray of cellular processes, termed **microfilaments,** that seek chemical attractions (Gazzaniga et al. 1979). A chemical correspondence between the growing filament and appropriate sites for connections on other nerve cells would help determine the functional development of that neuron. Thus far, however, there has been no direct evidence of specific chemicals involved in such a process.

Another hypothesis, the **synaptic and dendritic growth hypothesis** (Berry et al. 1980), is illustrated in Fig. 1-8. This is based on the extension of processes called **growth cones** and **filopodia.** Although this theory does not suggest the exact mechanism for the formation of specific contacts between cells, as Sperry's does, it has been supported by research (Lund 1978) and has been taken as a general model of process formation and elongation (Johnston and Wessells 1980).

The development of an axon begins soon after or concurrent with the differentiation and migration of the cell body. Once the axon is formed, two problems arise. The first is that the axon has to reach the proper place in relation to other cells. Secondary to the synaptic and dendritic growth hypothesis, mechanical constraints imposed by the developing nervous sys-

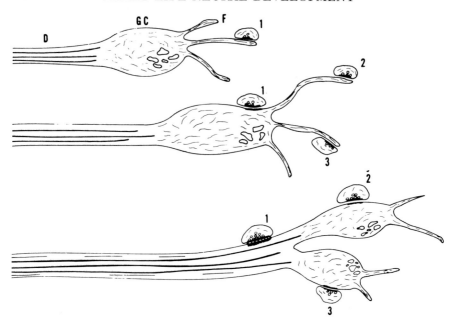

FIGURE 1-8   Sequence illustrating the synaptic and dendritic growth hypothesis with growth cone (GC) and filopodium (F) (Berry et al. 1980).

tem (rather than chemospecificity) guide the axon along a particular path to a particular terminal site (Cotman and Banker 1974). The length of axonal growth is presumably genetically determined.

The second problem is that of forming synaptic connections between axons and dendrites at specific sites. This is discussed below under synaptogenesis.

The development of dendrites has been extensively studied (Morest 1969). The major factor underlying dendritic growth and branching in the nervous system appears to be the presence and arrangement of the afferent (those leading to the neuron) axonal fibers. The dendrites of many types of neurons remain in a relatively primitive condition until the afferent axons arrive; many new processes then sprout, and gradually the dendritic tree is remodeled until the final form is established.

Growth of the dendritic spine is very important for both normal and aberrant neuronal development (Purpura 1975a, 1975b, 1977a). The dendritic spine is a recently discovered, very small appendage located on the individual dendrites of most neurons and showing a definite developmental progression. Purpura (1975b) found that there are well-developed apical dendritic spines on hippocampal pyramidal neurons at 14 weeks of gestation whereas more basilar dendrites showed dendritic spines later, at 18 to

22 weeks of gestation, and suggested that various forms of mental retardation can be related to abnormalities in dendritic spine development.

Synaptogenesis The final, and perhaps most intriguing, question in the study of neural development is how specific synapses are formed. Cotman and Banker (1974) emphasized that the formation of synapses in the human brain may not be under genetic control since the number of neurons and possible combinations among them are well beyond the amount of information carried in human genes. Therefore, at least some portion of these connections must be made by mechanisms other than genetic ones.

Synaptogenesis includes the termination of axonal growth, the selection of synaptic sites, which may require synapse degeneration (D. Purves and Lichtman 1980), and and finally the formation of the synapse. The appropriate formation of synaptic contacts requires that the neurons use positional information to organize themselves within a topographical field (Rakic 1981) and to find their way to the appropriate fields; axons and dendrites must also establish structural and functional connections with their mates. During normal nervous system development, these processes are closely related and dependent upon intrinsic and environmental influences (Goldman and Rakic 1979).

Glial Cell Development and Myelogenetic Cycles

Three types of glial cells are usually distinguished: (1) astrocytes, (2) oligodendrocytes, and (3) microglial cells. Timiras et al. (1968) have concluded that glial cells have several functions: they respond to injury by foreign agents; they regulate neuronal metabolism, contributing to the blood-brain barrier; and they play a role, through myelination, in the electric activity of the nervous system. Glial cells are relatively immature in the early stages of CNS development, as evidenced by the lack of a glial reaction (**gliosis**) to a penetrating wound in the newborn brain. The number of glial cells increases with the maturation of the CNS, and glia continue to proliferate throughout life.

The most important role of glial cells is believed to be in myelination, a process whereby the axon in the developing CNS becomes surrounded by a myelin sheath made of proteins and lipids. These sheaths are thought to result from the deposition of multilaminar spiral sheaths by surrounding oligodendrocytes (Fig. 1-9).

Myelogenetic cycles may give an indication of the sequence of glial cell development in different regions of the brain. The various regions myelinate at different times in a definite sequence. Figure 1-10 presents the results of the most recent large-scale study of myelogenetic cycles in humans (Yakovlev and Lecours 1967). In humans the myelin sheath begins to appear around many nerve fibers between the fourth month of fetal life and the end of the first year of postnatal life. Myelination starts in the spinal cord and then spreads to the medulla, pons, and midbrain and finally to

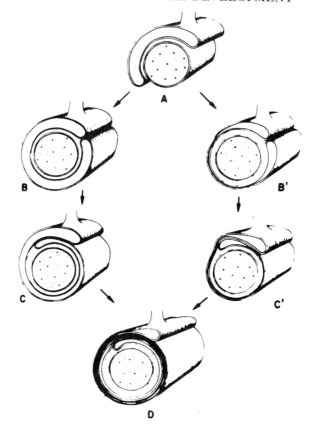

FIGURE 1-9   Formation of myelin in the CNS (Davison and Peters 1970).

the diencephalon and telencephalon. Many researchers have attempted to correlate these myelogenetic cycles with specific abilities (Jacobson 1975, Lecours 1975, Lenneberg 1976). It is assumed that myelination precedes functional ability; however, functional activity may occur without myelination, and in the adult nervous system some unmyelinated nerves are fully cabable of conducting impulses.

Metabolic and Biochemical Aspects

Many researchers have discussed in detail the relationship between nervous system development and biochemical maturation (Dodge et al. 1975; Himwich 1970, 1973, 1975; Paoletti and Davison 1971; Richter 1975). Only a brief overview can be presented here, and it is confined to the developmental changes in four major constituents of the brain: (1) the nucleic acids DNA and ribonucleic acid (RNA), (2) amino acids and proteins, (3) lipids (fats), and (4) neurotransmitters. Hormones, especially sex hormones and their relationship to brain development, are discussed later in the context of sex differences (Sec. 4.2).

The total brain content of RNA and DNA is high during the early phases of development but gradually decreases. Early proliferation of cells is reflected in the synthesis of DNA. As differentiation occurs, DNA replication is followed by increased translation (change) of DNA to RNA, then transcription of RNA to protein. DNA levels thus decline faster than RNA levels. DNA content is considered to be a reliable indicator of cell number. In humans two periods of cell proliferation have been detected by measuring DNA levels (Dobbing 1975). The first period begins at 15 to 20 weeks of gestation and corresponds to neuroblast proliferation. The second begins at 25 weeks and continues into the second year of postnatal life, representing the multiplication of glial cells.

Several behavioral disorders result from disturbances in nucleic acid metabolism. **Lesch-Nyhan syndrome,** for example, is a rare genetic defect in which there is mutation of a gene that affects the enzyme involved in the making of one of the nucleotide bases of the nucleic acids.

The amino acid composition of brain proteins changes during develop-

FIGURE 1-10 Myelogenetic cycles of regional maturation in the human brain (Yakovlev and Lecours 1967).

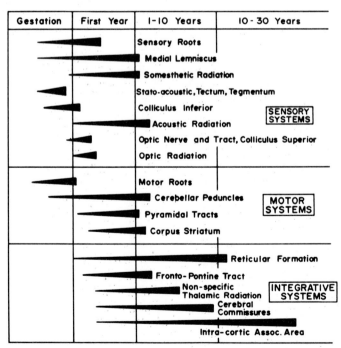

Gestation	First Year	1-10 Years	10-30 Years
		Sensory Roots	
		Medial Lemniscus	
		Somesthetic Radiation	
		Stato-acoustic, Tectum, Tegmentum	
		Colliculus Inferior	SENSORY SYSTEMS
		Acoustic Radiation	
		Optic Nerve and Tract, Colliculus Superior	
		Optic Radiation	
		Motor Roots	
		Cerebellar Peduncles	MOTOR SYSTEMS
		Pyramidal Tracts	
		Corpus Striatum	
		Reticular Formation	
		Fronto-Pontine Tract	
		Non-specific Thalamic Radiation	INTEGRATIVE SYSTEMS
		Cerebral Commissures	
		Intra-cortic Assoc. Area	

ment. Since the ratio of protein to DNA indicates cell size, an increasing ratio in development indicates protein increases. The absorption of amino acids from the blood is also much higher for newborns than adults; the rates of protein synthesis and turnover are much greater in the young organism. The rate of protein synthesis in the brain peaks during myelination since protein is a major component of myelin.

Many inborn errors of **amino acid metabolism** lead to developmental defects. One major amino acidopathy, as these defects are called, is phenylketonuria, a result of the absence of the enzyme phenylalanine hydroxylase, which breaks down phenylalanine. The consequent buildup of phenylalanine in the body often produces mental retardation.

A rapid increase in the lipid content of the brain begins after the peak periods for DNA and protein synthesis. In the fetal brain, little difference can be found between the composition of lipids in gray matter and the composition of those in white matter. The adult pattern is attained during myelination, with increase in three major lipids—cholesterol, cerebrosides, and sphingomyelin—especially in the white matter. The increased lipid content has been ascribed to myelin sheath development (Benjamins and McKhann 1976). Two representative disorders of lipid metabolism are Tay-Sachs disease (a lipid defect, specifically ganglioside) and Niemann-Picks disease (an intracellular accumulation of sphingomyelin).

The **neurotransmitters,** which mediate transmission between neurons at synapses, include acetylcholine, dopamine, epinephrine, and norepinephrine. Increases in their levels in the developing brain are functionally important (McGeer et al. 1978). A net increase in the concentration of neurotransmitters during development is accompanied by a simultaneous change in the enzymes that synthesize and degrade them (Lanier et al. 1976). Acetylcholinesterase activity, for example, has been used as evidence for the presence of the excitatory neurotransmitter acetylcholine. Other neurotransmitters showing similar increases include the monoamines serotonin and histamine, the catecholamines noradrenalin (or norepinephrine) (Moore et al. 1974) and dopamine, the prostaglandins, and the amino acids that are thought to have an inhibitory rather than a facilitating function (glycine and γ-aminobutyric acid).

2

Chronology of Gross Neural Development

Approximately seven days after fertilization of the ovum by a sperm, the ovum in the blastula, or hollow ball, stage attaches itself to the uterine endometrium (mucus membrane) and becomes implanted. On day nine the fertilized ovum is composed of two layers, a dorsal ectoderm and the inner endoderm. Later, during **gastrulation,** when the **blastula** invaginates (folds in), a third layer, called the **mesoderm,** develops between the ectoderm and the endoderm. Gastrulation is essential for **neural induction,** the ability of these early cell layers to initiate formation of the nervous system (Saxen 1980). Neural induction takes place on day 18 of gestation. The formation of the nervous system begins at the thickened surface ectoderm on the dorsal surface of the embryo. For general reviews of gross neural development, see S. R. Berenberg 1977, Marshall 1968, Minkowski et al. 1966, and Windle 1971.

Table 2-1 shows the stages of development traced in any chronological review of growth periods in the human. Two major periods are discussed here, the prenatal and the postnatal.

2.1 PRENATAL

The **prenatal period** in the human extends from fertilization of the ovum to approximately 280 days of gestational age. The prenatal period can be divided into various segments. Table 2-2 shows the sequential development of the nervous system.

Embryo

In what is termed the neurula stage of the developing embryo, during the third week of gestation, a pear-shaped neural plate appears from the **dorsal ectoderm.** In the center of this plate, the cells on the edge become narrower on their inner surface while those surrounding them become nar-

21

TABLE 2-1   Stages of Human Growth and
Development

Growth period	Approximate age
Prenatal	0 to 280 days
Ovum (pre-embryonic)	0 to 14 days
Embryo	14 days to 9 weeks
Fetus	9 weeks to birth
Premature infant	27 to 37 weeks
Birth	Average 280 days
Neonate	First 4 weeks after birth
Infancy	First year
Early childhood (preschool)	1 to 6 years
Later childhood (prepubertal)	6 to 10 years
Adolescence	{ Girls, 8 or 10 to 18 years / Boys, 10 or 12 to 20 years
Puberty (average)	{ Girls, 13 years / Boys, 15 years

Source: Adams and Victor 1981.

rower on their outer surface. This produces a longitudinal **neural groove** composed of **neural folds,** which gradually deepens and eventually folds over onto itself. It begins to close starting at the midpoint and extending in both the rostral (toward the head) and the caudal (tail) direction. As it closes (Fig. 2-1), there are temporarily two open ends, the **anterior and posterior neuropores,** which close at approximately day 25 of gestation. The resulting tube surrounding a fluid-filled central canal is called the **neural tube,** and the process of its conversion from open groove to sealed tube is termed

TABLE 2-2   Timetable for Normal Growth and Development of the Human Nervous System

Age days	Size (crown-rump length), mm	Nervous system development
18	1.5	Neural groove and tube
21	3.0	Optic vesicles
26	3.0	Closure of anterior neuropore
27	3.3	Closure of posterior neuropore; ventral horn cells appear
31	4.3	Anterior and posterior roots
35	5.0	Five cerebral vesicles
42	13.0	Primordium of cerebellum
56	25.0	Differentiation of cerebral cortex and meninges
150	225.0	Primary cerebral fissures appear
180	230.0	Secondary cerebral sulci and first myelination appear in brain
>180		Further myelination and growth of brain

Source: Lowrey 1978.

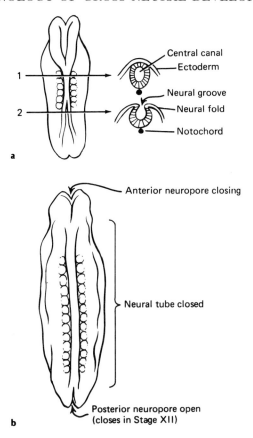

FIGURE 2-1   Beginning of development of the nervous system. (*a*) Start of neurulation, two cross-sectional views. (*b*) Late stage of neurulation, showing the anterior and posterior neuropores (Lemire et al. 1975).

neurulation (Levi-Montalcini 1964). Figure 2-2 shows the formation of the neural tube in cross-sectional views (see also Karfunkel 1974).

If neurulation is defective and the neural tube has difficulty closing, one of several possible anomalies can occur. Among these are anencephaly, in which the forebrain fails to develop properly because the anterior neuropore does not close, and **spina bifida,** which results from caudal difficulties (Chap. 10). These neural tube defects occur during the third and fourth weeks of gestation (Reinis and Goldman 1980).

Cells adjacent to the lateral margins of closure of the neural tube are called **neural crest cells.** They are free of the overlying ectoderm and form an irregular bundle of tissue surrounding the tube (Bronner-Fraser and Cohen 1980, LeDouarin 1980). These clumps of cells migrate and differentiate to form **ganglia** (or groups of peripheral sensory cells) in other parts of the

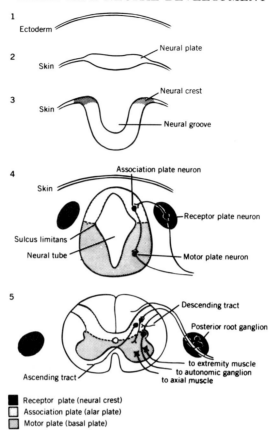

FIGURE 2-2   Stages in the development of a spinal cord segment. Note the development of the alar and basal plates into sensory and motor regions, respectively (Lemire et al. 1975).

nervous system, innervating glands and smooth muscle. An important derivative of the neural crest is the **dorsal,** or **posterior, root ganglion** (Fig. 2-2), a spinal ganglion whose cells become bipolar. **Bipolar cells** have only two processes, a dendritic and an axonal process. Spinal ganglion cells send dendrites to the skin and an axon back into the spinal cord, thus serving as sensory nerves.

Once the neural tube is formed, at about the fourth week of gestation, two events occur (Lund 1978): cells in the wall of the tube begin to proliferate and growth increases at the cranial end, where three **primary vesicles,** or outpouchings, appear, namely the **prosencephalic vesicle** (to become the forebrain), the **mesencephalic vesicle** (midbrain), and the **rhombencephalic vesicle** (hindbrain). The remaining portion of the tube becomes the **spinal cord,** maintaining its diameter and elongating.

During its development, the spinal cord keeps a remnant of the neural tube as the central canal. In the developing cord itself (Fig. 2-2), the neural tissue desegregates into two main bodies of neurons, the **dorsal,** or **posterior, horns** and the ventral, or **anterior, horns,** divided by the **sulcus limitans.** The dorsal horns (also called the **alar plate**) receive axons from the dorsal root ganglia, the derivatives of the neural crest, and are involved in sensory events. The **ventral horns (basal plate)** contain the cell bodies of axons that innervate muscles and are considered part of the motor system.

At the rostral end of the neural tube, the brain bends ventrally during the fourth week, forming two curves, termed the midbrain, or **mesencephalic, flexure** in the neck region and the **cervical flexure** (Fig. 2-3). These are followed later by a third bend in the opposite direction, the **pontine flexure** (Fig. 2-3). Otherwise, the brain has essentially the same cross-sectional structure as the spinal cord at this time, with dorsal alar and ventral basal plates.

During the fifth week of development, however, further divisions appear in the primary vesicles. The prosencephalic vesicle divides into the telencephalon and the diencephalon, and the rhombencephalic vesicle divides into the **metencephalon** and the **myelencephalon** (Table 1-1). Later, beginning at approximately the seventh week of gestation, the telencephalon is transformed into the cerebral hemispheres, the diencephalon into the thalamus and related structures, the metencephalon into the cerebellum and pons, and the myelencephalon into the medulla oblongata. In ves-

FIGURE 2-3   Embryological development of the human brain (Peele 1954).

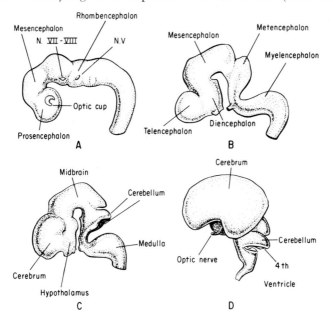

tigial form, the neural tube becomes the cerebral ventricles and the cerebral aqueduct (Windle 1971).

Fetus

The **fetal period** begins at about the eighth or ninth week of gestation as the embryo starts to develop into a recognizable human being. During this eighth week the head constitutes at least half of the fetus, but this ratio gradually decreases. In the fetal period there is little further differentiation of the tissues of the body, including the nervous system, and this lack of development decreases the vulnerability of the fetus to possible harmful effects of mechanical or chemical disruptions (**teratogens**) (Langman et al. 1975). It is during this period that myelin begins to form (Chap. 1). The **weight of the brain** rapidly increases from this stage on into adult life (Fig. 2-4) (Dobbing and Sands 1973).

Our discussion of changes in the brain during the fetal period concen-

FIGURE 2-4   Representative growth curve of the weight of the human brain into adult life (Lemire et al. 1975).

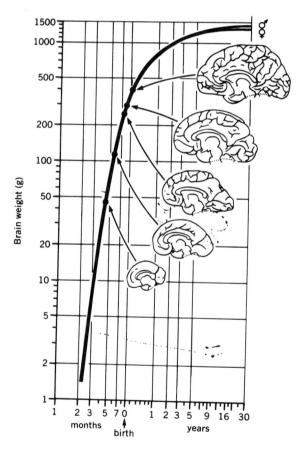

trates on the development of the cerebral hemispheres (**telencephalon**) since the higher functions are of primary interest in neuropsychology. The sensory, motor, and integrative systems are covered in Chap. 3.

The basal ganglia become visible in each hemisphere during the sixth week as swellings in the floor of the hemispheres. Later the internal capsule fibers from the developing cortex divide the basal ganglia into the caudate nuclei and the lentiform nuclei. The internal capsule then projects into the spinal cord as the pyramidal tract.

Microscopic studies of the developing cerebral cortex have shown that the early cortical plate forms from migrating cells during the first major wave of migration at eight to ten weeks of gestational age (Sidman and Rakic 1973). Four layers of cortex are visible at this time: ventricular, subventricular, intermediate, and marginal. As the cortical plate thickens due to migrating neurons, more layers are formed, giving the cortex its final six-layered composition by approximately the sixth prenatal month. A columnar organization within the cortex eventually develops (Goldman and Nauta 1977). Beginning in the fifth month, the increasing number of cortical cells causes the smooth surface of the developing brain to develop the typical pattern of convolutions and sulci. Much of this growth is the consequence of glial cell proliferation and axonal and dendritic differentiation (neuron production and migration cease at about this time). The development of the cerebral hemispheres progresses rapidly during the fetal period.

The developing convolutional and sulcal patterns in the brain follow a regular sequence. The primary sulci appear first, the hippocampal sulcus at 13 to 15 weeks and the parieto-occipital, calcerine, and olfactory bulb sulci at 19 weeks. The Sylvian (lateral) and Rolandic (central) sulci become visible at 24 weeks, when the calcarine and the parieto-occipital sulci join in a Y-shaped juncture. The secondary sulci, such as the first temporal sulcus and the superior frontal sulci, appear at 28 weeks (Larroche 1967, Turner 1948, 1950) (Fig. 2-5). The tertiary convolutions are not formed until the third trimester and continue to develop after birth (Chi et al. 1977, Rabinowicz 1964, 1974, 1979). Generally, the development of the convolutions is thought to depend upon the ratio of growth of the inner and outer cortical layers since, in two malformations of cortical development, **lissencephaly** (literally, smooth brain) and **mycrogyria** (small gyri), abnormalities in the layering pattern are also evident. Extent of convolution development is frequently used to judge the age of the fetus.

Closely related to the changes in the cerebral cortical layers during this time are changes in the intercerebral commissures, the major connections between the hemispheres. Their growth is rather slow and related to the maturation of association cortex (Trevarthen 1974). The first commissural fibers cross in the rostral end of the forebrain at approximately day 50 of gestation, creating the anterior commissure and the hippocampal commissure. The fibers of the corpus callosum cross the midline later. Hewitt (1962) points out that the fibers of the corpus callosum develop in parallel with

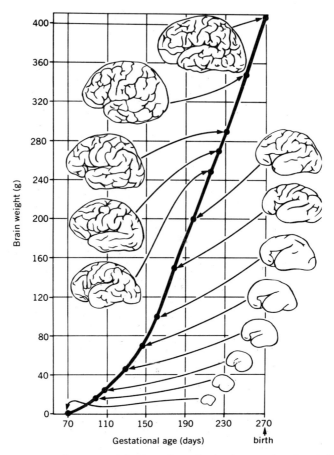

FIGURE 2-5   Development of the lateral cerebral sulci correlated with brain weight and gestational age (Lemire et al. 1975).

the various cerebral lobes and that this process is not complete until after birth. Failure of the commissures to cross the midline results in a variety of defects, most commonly **agenesis** of the corpus callosum, where this major structure is absent. This condition is discussed in Chapter 7 on the concept of disconnection syndromes.

2.2 POSTNATAL

Birth

At approximately 280 days of gestational age, the human fetus emerges from the womb and enters the **postnatal period.** The birth of even the most healthy organism can be a traumatic event. There are many possible traumatic factors, such as mechanical injury, that can disrupt the normal development of the nervous system. Some of these factors are discussed in Part III.

A newborn, or **neonate** (terms used for the first month of life) has a characteristic set of **reflexes** and behaviors (Humphrey 1964, 1970) that reflect the normal functioning of its nervous system (Chap. 11). Pediatricians often use a scoring system based upon the work of Apgar (1953, 1962) to evaluate general health after birth; the Apgar measures may have some predictive value for future development.

The brain immediately after birth weighs between 300 and 350 grams and continues to grow rapidly, increasing to 80 per cent of the adult weight of 1250 to 1500 grams in about four years. Much of this increase is due to an increase in the size, complexity, and myelination—rather than to an increase in number—of nerve cells following birth (Dodgson 1962). Conel's (1939–67) photographic series of stages of human neural development documents most of these changes.

Infancy

Infancy is the period from about one month to one year of postnatal age. As the infant becomes more mature in a variety of spheres—sensory, perceptual, motor, neurophysiological, and cognitive (Bower 1977)—more complicated and sophisticated behavioral patterns appear. The baby interacts more with the outside world through locomotion, learns how to manipulate its environment, and tries to make some sense out of the information that reaches its brain. As Dimond (1978) says, "It would be surprising if somehow this were not reflected by parallel changes in the workings and structure of the brain" (p. 115).

Along with an increase in brain size, as usually inferred from head circumference (Fig. 2-6), there is taking shape a **functional organization** of the nervous system that reflects its increasing responsiveness to stimulation from the environment (Goldman and Rakic 1979). Details of this growing functional organization are discussed in subsequent chapters. One of the major indices of the brain's increasing responsiveness is the elaboration of association fibers and tracts (Altman 1967, Altman and Bulut 1976). This increasing connectivity is often regarded as an indicator of information storage and processing. The plasticity to form connections in the young child's nervous system is reflected by postnatal increases in granule, or Golgi type II, cells, which aid in the ability to form connections (Hirsch and Jacobson 1975).

Neurophysiological changes are also evident during the first year of life, as reflected by changes in the electroencephalogram (EEG), a recording of the spontaneous electric activity of the brain, and in sensory-evoked potentials (Beck and Dustman 1975; Ellingson 1964, 1967; Hagne 1968, 1972; Spehlmann 1981). These measures, a summation of discharges from millions of neurons in many parts of the brain, give a picture of the brain's electric activity at a given stage of maturation. Just after birth EEG poten-

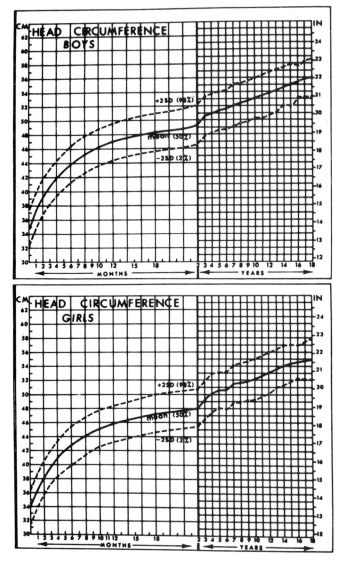

FIGURE 2-6   Head circumference charts, used for inferring brain maturation for both sexes (Nelhaus 1968).

tials are present but they are usually irregular and of low amplitude (Fig. 2-7). By approximately four months of age the first slow rhythm (three to four discharges per second) becomes evident, primarily over the occipital cortex, possibly reflecting maturation of the visual system. The frequency of EEG discharge gradually increases over time until a characteristic stable **alpha rhythm** (11 to 12 per second) is attained.

Early Childhood

Cellular patterning and increasing myelination in the CNS continue during early childhood, from years one to six (Dekaban 1970). Morphological and neurophysiological changes take place concurrent with the development of many abilities, such as language (Eeg-Olofsson 1970, Leary 1978). Table 2-3 summarizes some of the major postnatal changes. The biopsychology of childhood development has been described by Isaacson (1968), Tobach et

FIGURE 2-7   Awake EEG recorded from one child at six ages, showing changes in electric activity. Note appearance of a dominant frequency at four months (Hagne 1968).

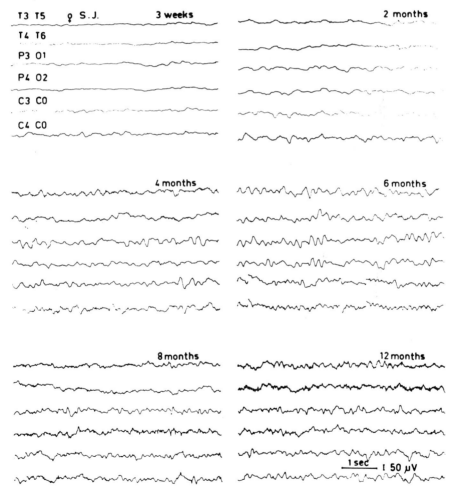

TABLE 2-3 Summary of Postnatal Human Development

Age	Visual and motor function	Social and intellectual function	EEG	Average brain weight, grams[a]	Total DNA, mg[b]	Degree of myelination[c]
Birth	Reflex sucking, rooting, swallowing, and Moro reflexes; infantile grasping; blinks to light	—	Asynchronous; low voltage 3–5 Hz; period of flattening; no clear distinction awake or asleep	350	660	Motor roots + + +; sensory roots + +; medial lemniscus + +; superior cerebellar peduncle + +; optic tract + +; optic radiation ±
6 weeks	Extends and turns neck when prone; regards mother's face, follows objects	Smiles when played with	Similar to birth records with slightly higher voltages; rare 14 Hz parietal spindles in sleep	410	800	Optic tract + +, optic radiation +; middle cerebral peduncle ±; pyramidal tract +
3 months	Infantile grasp and suck modified by volition; keeps head above horizontal for long periods; turns to objects presented in visual field; may respond to sound	Watches own hands	When awake, asynchronous 3–4 Hz, some 5–6 Hz; low voltages continue; sleep better organized and more synchronous; more spindles but still often asynchronous	515	860	Sensory roots + + +; optic tract and radiations + + +; pyramidal tract + +; cingulum + +; frontopontine tract +; middle cerebellar peduncle +; corpus callosum ±; reticular formation ±
6 months	Grasps objects with both hands, will place weight on forearms or hands when prone; rolls supine to prone; supports almost all weight on legs for very brief periods; sits briefly	Laughs aloud and shows pleasure; primitive articulated sounds, "ga-goo"; smiles at self in mirror	More synchronous, 5–7 Hz activity frequent; many lower voltages, slower frequencies; drowsy bursts can be seen; humps may first be seen in sleep	660	900	Medial lemniscus + +; superior cerebellar peduncle + +; middle cerebellar peduncle + +; pyramidal tract + +; corpus callosum +; reticular formation +; associational areas ±; acoustic radiation +

Age	Motor	Language	EEG	Brain weight (g)	Neuroanatomical development
9 months	Sits well and pulls self to sitting position; thumb–forefinger grasp; crawls	Waves bye-bye, plays patty cake, uses "dada," "baba"; imitates sounds	Mild asynchrony; predominant frequencies 5–7 Hz and 2–6 Hz, especially anteriorly; drowsy burst frequent; humps and spindles seen frequently in sleep	750	Cingulum + + +; fornix + +; others as previously given
12 months	Able to release objects; cruises and walks with one hand held; plantar reflex flexor in 50% of children	2–4 words with meaning; understands several proper nouns; may kiss on request	5–7 Hz in all areas; usually synchronous; some anterior 20–25 Hz; some 3–6 Hz; humps often seen in sleep and usually synchronous	925	Medial lemniscus + + +; pyramidal tracts + + +; frontopontine tract + + +; fornix + + +; corpus callosum +; intracortical neuropil ±; association areas ±; acoustic radiation + +
24 months	Walks up and down stairs (2 feet a step); bends over and picks up objects without falling; turns knob; can partially dress self; plantar reflex flexor in 100%	2–3 words sentences, uses "I," "me," and "you" correctly; plays simple games; points to 4–5 body parts; obeys simple commands	6–8 Hz activity predominates posteriorly with some 4–6 Hz seen especially anteriorly; humps in sleep always synchronous	1065	Acoustic radiation + + +; corpus callosum + +; association areas +; nonspecific thalamic radiation + +
36 months	Goes up stairs (1 foot a step); pedals tricycle; dresses and undresses fully except for shoelaces, belt, and buttons; visual acuity 20/20/OU	Numerous questions; knows nursery rhymes, copies circle; plays with others	When awake, synchronous 6–9 Hz predominates posteriorly; less 4–6 Hz activity seen; in sleep, spindles usually synchronous	1140	Middle cerebellar peduncle + + +

TABLE 2-3 Summary of Postnatal Human Development (*continued*)

Age	Visual and motor function	Social and intellectual function	EEG	Average brain weight, grams[a]	Total DNA, mg[b]	Degree of myelination[c]
5 years	Skips; ties shoelaces; copies triangle	Repeats 4 digits; names 4 colors; gives age correctly	When awake, some 9–10 Hz posteriorly; mostly 7–8Hz with occasional 4–6 Hz; synchronous; drowsy bursts less frequent and often limited to frontoparietal	1240	—	Nonspecific thalamic radiation + + +; reticular formation + +; corpus callosum + + +; intracortical neuropil and association areas + +
Adult	—	—	When awake, synchronous 9–12 Hz posterior frequencies; rare 7–8 Hz waves; 18–25 Hz waves and low voltage fast anteriorly; with drowsiness, flattening and low voltage theta; spindles and humps in sleep as before	1400	~1500	Intracortical neuropil and association areas + + to + + +

Source: Dodge et al. 1975.

[a]From Coppoletta and Wolbach 1933.

[b]From Winick 1968; adult value estimated from Dobbing and Sands 1973.

[c]From Yakovlev and Lecours 1967. Estimates are made from their graphic data (± = minimal amounts; + = mild; + + = moderate; + + + = heavy).

al. (1971), Van der Vlugt (1979), and S. H. White (1970) and is discussed in subsequent chapters.

2.3 GROWTH SPURTS

The importance of biological (intrinsic) and environmental (extrinsic) factors in determining CNS morphology and the relationship between the two have been mentioned (see also Hahn et al. 1979). A major conceptual development that bears on this relationship is that of **growth spurts.** In studies of nutritional deprivation and brain development, Dobbing and his colleagues (Dobbing 1975, Dobbing and Sands 1973, Dobbing and Smart 1974) have found that there are periods of development "when the brain is increasing its weight particularly rapidly" (Dobbing and Smart 1974, p. 164). The neural growth spurt does not begin until the number of neurons in the developing brain reaches the adult level. At that time (about 30 weeks of gestation) an enormous proliferation of glial cells occurs, and this marks the first growth spurt. The second growth spurt, which involves rapid myelination, begins in the second postnatal year and continues well into the third and fourth years.

Epstein's (1974) notion of correlated brain-mind growth spurts, called *phrenoblysis,* also serves as an explanatory principle for normal development. He found that head circumference and brain weight relative to the weight of other organs were related to mental growth. Several studies suggest that peaks and troughs occur at similar times in all these measures (Table 2-1). Epstein's review indicated peak growth periods between the ages of 6 to 8, 10 to 12, and 14 to 16 years.

If such periods of phrenoblysis could be confirmed, important implications for child-rearing and education practices would arise. If there is a trough of mind-brain growth at age four to six years, as Epstein (1978) claimed, then additional stimulation during those years might have little or no effect on the individual's total development. Even though little confirmation from other researchers has been provided as yet, Epstein even suggested that this trough may account at least in part for the failure of the Head Start program. Epstein (1978) and other authors (Thornburg 1982, Toepfer 1980) have, perhaps somewhat prematurely, attempted to relate the theory to Piagetian stages of development and other educational issues.

Unfavorable conditions during growth spurt periods can be expected to retard development, possibly with such lasting effects as small brain size, fewer cerebral cells, and lower brain lipid content. Disturbances during the growth spurt presumably reduce the extent of many, if not all, brain growth processes. Later discussions of sensitive periods and nutrition deal with this issue in detail.

3

Development of Functional Systems

When we discuss the disorders resulting from abnormal influences on nervous system development and on neuropsychological functioning (Chaps. 8 to 26), they will be seen as deviations from normal development in specific neurologically based systems of psychological functions. A functional system consists of those neural structures involved in the successful completion of an individual sensory, motor, or higher cognitive task, e.g., all parts of the visual system as well as structures mediating the response to visual stimuli (Anohkin 1964). It should be kept in mind that subtle disturbances in functional systems can occur without measurable change in neurological structure or function.

This chapter reviews the normal development of the functional systems that in later life regulate specific adult behaviors (Corner et al. 1978). Primary sensory and motor systems are discussed first, then the higher-order integrative systems. Because of the complexity of each system, only a brief description of structure and development can be provided.

3.1 SENSORY SYSTEMS

The Auditory System

The adult auditory system is illustrated in Fig. 3-1. Briefly, the external ear canal begins with the outer ear, or **pinna**, and ends at the eardrum (**tympanic membrane**). The eardrum connects to three small, interconnected bones of the middle ear (**ossicles**), then to a membrane covering the end of the coiled cochlea, which is part of the inner ear. Within this coiled tube lies a smaller tube, the cochlear duct, containing the **organ of Corti**, the sense organ of hearing.

Sounds, which consist of air vibrating at numerous frequencies, pass through the ear canal and cause the ossicles to vibrate. This movement is

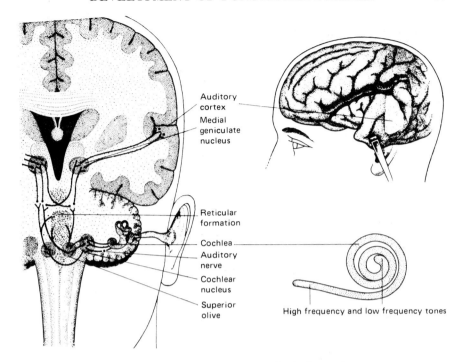

FIGURE 3-1 The human auditory system (Krech et al. 1969).

in turn transmitted to the fluid in the *cochlea*, thus producing vibratory movement of the **basilar membrane** in the inner ear. This bends the hair cells lying between the basilar and stiffer tectorial membrane. The particular frequency heard depends upon exactly which hair cells resting on the basilar membrane are activated. Fibers of the eighth, or auditory, nerve are stimulated by the hair cell receptors. Axons of the eighth nerve ascend into the CNS with synapses in the dorsal and ventral cochlear nuclei of the medulla. From here they are relayed through the superior olivary nucleus to the contralateral side of the brain or directly via the lateral lemniscus tract on each side of the brainstem. Auditory input is thus bilateral, with each ear transmitting impulses to both sides of the brain. The lateral lemniscus then synapses in the inferior colliculus of the midbrain and the medial geniculate body of the thalamus before projecting through the auditory radiation to the auditory area (transverse, or Heschl's, gyrus) of the temporal cortex.

The embryological development of the ear (Selnes and Whitaker 1976, C. A. Smith 1975) starts at around 22 days of gestational age with the emergence of the ectodermal auditory, or **otic placodes**, the precursors of the inner ear and the vestibular system. At four to five embryonic weeks the

placodes become the **otocyst,** which then divides into the cochlear and lab-
yrinth lobes (the latter forms part of the vestibular system). By about five
weeks the **external auditory meatus** (canal) originates from the first pharyn-
geal cleft by an invagination and reaches the future middle ear cavity. At
six weeks, the cochlea appears as a short, curved tube and the pinnae become visible and continue to grow rapidly through infancy and childhood.
At about seven weeks the middle ear ossicles appear and reach terminal
size by six to eight months.

The mechanical aspects of the human auditory system are therefore reasonably mature at birth. The hair cells in the organ of Corti develop at four
to five months of gestational age but are not fully differentiated until later.
At birth, the peripheral sensory aspects of the auditory system are functionally complete. Figure 3-2 summarizes some of these details (Clopton
1981).

The development of the eighth (auditory) nerve is also complete at birth,
and it is fairly well myelinated at that time (Hecox 1975). There is some
evidence that the brainstem development of the inferior colliculi and the
medial geniculate nuclei is also relatively complete at birth, but the myelination of projection fibers to the cortex is sparse and continues up to at
least four years of age. The slow myelination may explain the prolonged
latency and the diminished amplitude of **auditory-evoked response (AER)**

FIGURE 3-2   Development of the human inner ear, beginning at the age of 24
embryonic days *(a)* through adulthood *(e)* (Reinis and Goldman 1980).

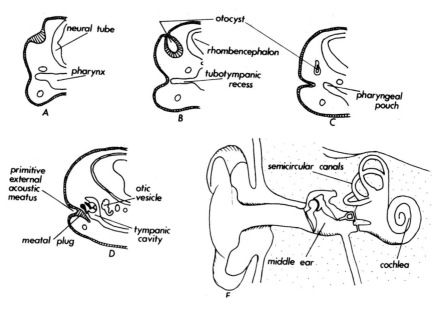

potentials in newborns (Ohlrich et al. 1978). AER potentials are a modification of the EEG technique used for assessing sensory systems by averaging several electrophysiological responses to time-locked stimuli over many trials. AER potentials indicate the efficiency of processing in the system as well as of differential lateralization, depending on the nature of the stimulus (Jeffrey 1980).

Within the first few days of life, auditory acuity improves as a result of the draining of amniotic fluid from the middle ear. Parts of the auditory system, such as the external auditory meatus and the tympanic membrane, do not reach adult dimensions until about one year of age; this may be the cause of relatively poor hearing sensitivity during infancy (Hecox 1975). Sensitivity gradually increases until about seven to ten years of age. Newborn infants have the basic ability to discriminate frequency and pitch (Selnes and Whitaker 1976). At birth, the auditory cortex is electrically active, but we do not know the extent of any active processing of auditory stimuli. The human auditory system requires a long time to reach adult capacity. At present, our knowledge of the physiological correlates of auditory development is still incomplete.

The Visual System

The visual pathways in the human adult (Fig. 3-3) are relatively simple and have been studied extensively. The visual image enters the eye via the cornea and lens and reaches receptors in the retina. Impulses from these receptors are then relayed through bipolar cells to ganglion cells, possibly modified on the way by two sets of interneurons (Lund 1978). The axons of the ganglion cells run across the surface of the retina (light passes through the fibers to reach the receptors), leave the back of the eye through the optic disk, creating a **blind spot** in the visual field, and then become the optic (or second cranial) nerve. In higher vertebrates, including humans, where some degree of binocular vision exists, part of each optic nerve goes to each side of the brain. Optic nerve fibers from the left half of the retina (stimulated by the right half of the visual field) project to the left lateral geniculate nucleus (in the thalamus), and fibers from the right half of the retina project to the right lateral geniculate nucleus. At the optic chiasm, where the two optic nerves come together, the other half of their fibers cross and project to opposite hemispheres. From the optic chiasm the fibers form the **optic tracts** entering the CNS and synapse at the respective lateral geniculate nuclei. Cells in these nuclei then send their axons to the middle layers of the primary visual cortex, **area 17** of the two occipital lobes. These pathways are the **primary projections for the visual system.** Another visual pathway, usually termed the **second visual system,** projects from the retina to the superior colliculus and thence to the pulvinar nuclei in the thalamus. These nuclei in turn project to secondary visual areas in the cortex (thought to be areas 18 and 19).

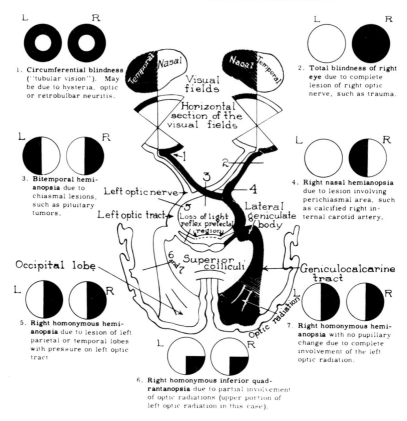

FIGURE 3-3 Primary visual pathways and major visual field defects (Noback and Demerest 1981).

The eye begins to develop, as the optic vesicle, about 30 days after fertilization. Between the second and fourth months of gestation the visual system, especially the retina, develops rapidly (Rakic 1979a). The retina differentiates gradually, the ganglion cells appearing first, the **rods** and **cones** (the receptor cells) last. In the sixth month the eyelids can open and the **fovea** (the central area of greatest acuity) begins to form, although it is not completely developed until after birth (Fig. 3-4). The laminated structure of the lateral geniculate nucleus also appears early in the prenatal period, although some relay interneurons may not develop until after birth (NINCDS 1979, Rakic 1979b). Hickey (1977) demonstrated that the geniculate cells increase rapidly in size during the first 6 to 12 months of postnatal life, suggesting a specific growth spurt for the development of this part of the visual system. Related to this rapid growth is the development of the visual cortex (Movshon and Van Sluyters 1981), which, as discussed in Chap. 1, develops in an inside-out pattern. Other cortical development also occurs after birth, including increases in the thickness of the visual cortex; in the number of glial cells, interneurons, and dendritic spines; and in the amount of myelination. These changes are related to the development of functional connectivity and depend to some extent on visual experience (Blakemore 1975, Imbert 1977). The development of visually guided skilled motor behavior later in the life of the infant has also been related to visual experience (Rosinski 1977). A more detailed discussion of the role of early experience on sensory development is presented in Chap. 6.

Although most senses are at least minimally functional at birth (Bower 1977), visual perception in early life relies on more than the primary visual system. Bronson (1974) proposed that early visual perception is mediated by components of the phylogenetically older second visual system, which develops earlier since it is primarily subcortical. At its receiving end, the

FIGURE 3-4   Sagittal sections through the human eye during embryonic and fetal periods (Lemire et al. 1975).

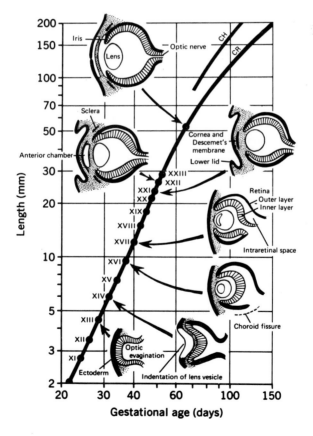

second visual system involves mainly the more peripheral areas of the retina. It transmits information regarding the location and orientation of visual stimuli, rather than highly resolved details, and relays this information via subcortical structures to different areas of the occipital lobes. Visual reactions to more complex visual information appear during the second and third postnatal months. Bronson suggested that this is a reflection of increasing participation by the primary visual system in the processing of visual input. The phylogenetically more recent primary system is concerned with the analysis and encoding of complex stimuli. Postnatal development of the visual system can be viewed as a progressive encoding of increasingly more complex aspects of visual information, calling upon different components of the visual network.

Many visual abilities increase during infancy. Binocular vision appears at about six weeks and is well established by about four months. Conjugate eye movements, necessary in binocular vision to prevent strabismus, are usually stable by six months. Color vision also develops in this period. Although all these functions are "wired in" prenatally, their development, refinement, and stabilization in terms of synaptic connectivity depend on information from patterned stimuli, which cannot be experienced until after birth (Trevarthen 1980).

The Somesthetic System

The **somesthetic,** or **somatosensory, system** relays thermal, tactile, and positional information to the brain. This system is not only crucial for the infant's early exploration of the world by touch but also interacts with the visual, motor, and other systems in the development of active tactile exploration, visually guided motor behavior, body movement, posture, walking, and many other activities of the developing organism. Generally, two subsystems are distinguished: (1) the lemniscal system, which is involved in the transmission of light touch and pressure stimuli, and (2) the **spinothalamic system,** which carries diffuse touch, pain, and temperature information.

The **lemniscal system** represents the more prominent cutaneous sensitivity. The lemniscal pathway of the adult begins as a peripheral process of the dorsal root ganglion, which sends axons into the spinal cord. The axons either end in the dorsal horns of the cord at the level of entry or run up the spinal cord in the white matter (the dorsal columns) and end in the dorsal column nuclei of the medulla. Fibers from these nuclei then cross and ascend in a tract called the **medial lemniscus** to synapse in the ventral posterior nucleus of the thalamus. From there, axons project through the internal capsule into the somatosensory areas of the **postcentral gyrus** in the parietal lobe. This major pathway is contralateral, left body surface to right hemisphere, since it crosses (**decussates**) in the brainstem.

Fibers entering the spinal cord from the spinothalamic receptors form synapses in the spinal cord with the dorsal horn cells. They then cross and ascend the spinal cord in spinothalamic tracts, relaying fibers to the reticular formation and synapsing again in the ventral nuclei of the thalamus before ascending to the somatosensory areas of the cortex. There is some evidence that this tract has some ipsilateral as well as contralateral connections (R. F. Thompson 1967).

The development of the somatosensory system in humans has not been studied thoroughly (Woolsey et al. 1981). Early development of one spinal cord segment, the sensory ganglia, is discussed in Sec. 2.1. The sensory nerves approach the skin of the fetus in the eighth week and make contact by the ninth week. However, no receptors have been described at this early stage.

Myelination of the tracts in the spinal cord begins by midgestation and continues until birth for the sensory roots and until one year after birth for the medial lemniscus (Yakovlev and Lecours 1967). Little direct evidence has as yet linked neural development to stages of behavioral development.

3.2 MOTOR SYSTEMS

Two systems operating semi-independently are involved in human motor activity. The **pyramidal system** is responsible for the initiation of voluntary, skilled movements involving precise and rapid control of the extremities. It is therefore regarded as the "executive" system concerned with motor control (Fig. 19-1). The **extrapyramidal system** is more concerned with alterations and adjustments in posture and with the modification and coordination of movements initiated by the pyramidal system. These two systems allow the developing organism to move around and, in humans and higher animals, to manipulate the environment directly. Any response of the organism, even if it is just a reflexive response to stimulation, involves the participation of some segment of the motor system.

Motor activity develops early during gestation. In 1885, Preyer (summarized by Espenschade and Eckert 1980 and Gottlieb 1976) established the developmental **primacy of the motor system** over the sensory systems; the embryo is capable of movement early in the second trimester, before responses to sensory stimulation can be demonstrated. Early motor behavior is generated spontaneously in the organism. As Humphrey (1970) suggested, such early movement may be necessary for the normal development of motility and leg structure. Reflexes also appear before regulated patterned movement and skills (Brandt 1979, Windle 1971). This prenatal and early postnatal activity may lead to neonatal movement representing the integration of earlier reflexes with responses to environmental demands.

Development of the milestones of motor abilities is sequential in most children, although much variability exists between individuals. The infant generally progresses from lifting the chin when lying on the stomach at one to two months of age to sitting at seven to eight months, creeping and crawling at nine to ten months, and standing and walking at about one year. The span for developing the ability to walk without assistance varies from 8 to 18 months.

Manipulatory abilities increase continuously during infancy. After the first two or three months the primitive grasp reflex disappears, and by 12 weeks voluntary grasping has begun. Reaching and grasping improve up to 20 weeks of age, and at 24 weeks the child may be quite competent at eating dry food.

Throughout early childhood the locomotor and manipulative abilities continue to improve steadily. By the age of two to three years, a child usually can dress and feed itself, has voluntary sphincter control, and can walk without assistance. The development of the two interacting motor systems forms the basis for these increasing abilities.

The Pyramidal System

The two motor systems "begin" at a different CNS level than sensory systems, and their neural signals move in the opposite direction. Sensory systems relay information up the spinal cord to the brain, and motor systems send information and instructions from the brain down the cord and out to the muscles involved.

The pyramidal tract begins in the cerebral cortex, in the area known as the motor cortex of the **precentral gyrus,** Brodmann's **area 4.** The neurons at the beginning of this tract, in layer 5 of the cortex, are called giant pyramidal cells (hence the name pyramidal tract) or, after their discoverer, *Betz cells.* The giant cells send their axons into the internal capsule forming the pyramidal tract and through the cerebral peduncles of the midbrain. At the level of the medulla, 80 per cent of the fibers cross to the other side. This decussation is responsible for the predominantly contralateral representation of the motor system from brain to body. The crossed fibers descend through the **lateral corticospinal tract** to their respective spinal cord level and synapse with large, anterior motor neurons. Uncrossed fibers (about 20 per cent) descend in the **anterior corticospinal tract** to their appropriate levels. The anterior motor neurons, located in the anterior horns, send axons out of the cord through motor nerves to innervate their respective muscles or muscle groups (see also Fig. 19-1).

Development of the pyramidal system and spinal cord is perhaps the most thoroughly studied aspect of CNS development (Coulombre 1970). The neural elements of the pyramidal system develop from embryonic ectoderm, and the effector (muscle) elements are derived from the embryonic mesoderm. During early prenatal development, these two types of tissue are in contact with each other (Hollyday 1980). The basal plate of the developing neural tube is the precursor of the developing pyramidal system; the system differentiates fully before birth. Myelination of the pyramidal tracts by Schwann cells in the spinal cord, however, occurs only later, in the first postnatal year (Yakcvlev and Lecours 1967). The late myelination is often associated with the onset of walking. The cortical connections of this tract also begin to develop early, but further maturation and differentiation of tissues and cells continue into early childhood. Maturation of corticospinal connections is thought to underlie the emergence and improvement of motor skills during normal development.

The Extrapyramidal System

Certain motor projections from several cortical areas are not part of the pyramidal tract. These projections have been called the extrapyramidal system, although the term has been criticized as inadequate. The pyramidal system proper and the spinal motor neurons are excluded from this second system, but parts of the cerebellum, the basal ganglia, and some brainstem areas, such as the red nucleus and the substantia nigra, are generally included. Developmental data for extrapyramidal structures are scanty and concentrate on the basal ganglia and the cerebellum.

At three to eight weeks of gestational age, the human cerebellum has three primary layers: the ventricular, intermediate, and marginal layers. At about 13 weeks, some neuroblasts migrate to the surface of the cerebellum to form the cerebellar cortex (Fig. 3-5) while others remain in place to form the deep cerebellar nuclei. Cells proliferate from two zones in the developing cerebellum, the ventricular and the external granular zone. Purkinje cells, which are derived from the ventricular zone, migrate outward using the Bergmann glia as guides and eventually form a middle layer between these two zones. The small, spherical granule cells originate in the external granular layer and migrate internally. In humans the number of granule cells at birth is only about 17 per cent of the final number; extensive neurogenesis occurs postnatally. In fact, the germinating external granular layer is present until about 18 months after birth (Minkowski et al. 1966). The importance of granule cells for later-developing cerebellar motor functions was shown by Brunner and Altman (1974), who reported locomotor deficits in rats after postnatal irradiation of cerebellar granule cells decreased their number. Balazs (1979) also stressed the sensitivity of postnatal granule cell generation to certain metabolic disturbances, suggesting that the "clumsy" child may be suffering from the persisting consequences of such insults.

Development of the **basal ganglia** (caudate nucleus and putamen) begins in the sixth week of embryonic life, when a prominent swelling called the ganglionic eminence develops along the floor of the lateral ventricles. However, the globus pallidus, a wedge-shaped structure at the side and near the end of the internal capsule, appears to develop in the diencephalon rather than in the telencephalon and originates in a proliferative zone of the third ventricle before being displaced to the telencephalon. How the globus pal-

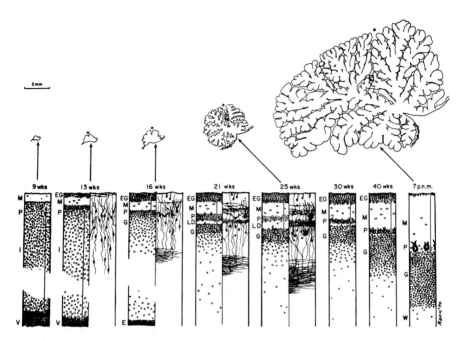

FIGURE 3-5 Development of the cerebellar cortex in the human from 9 weeks prenatal to 7 months postnatal (Sidman and Rakic 1973).

lidus is "welded" to the caudate and putamen is still unexplained (NINCDS 1979).

3.3 INTEGRATIVE SYSTEMS

Integrative systems of the brain oversee and coordinate several lower-order psychological and behavioral functions and are involved in such higher-order functions as learning, memory, attention, emotion, cognition, and language. Since they have such wide-ranging and complex functions, the integrative systems necessarily draw on large areas of the brain. It is generally agreed that their anatomical basis includes association areas of the cortex, the reticular formation and brainstem pathways, commissural connections between hemispheres, the limbic system, and language areas of the cortex.

Association Areas

Association areas are regions in the cortex where the information of various other parts is thought to be integrated. They are often referred to as the *silent areas* of the brain because they do not show sensory-evoked responses. They have also been called **tertiary areas** (Flechsig 1901) because they are the last to develop and myelinate. They are also the most sensitive to environmental influences (Goldman and Lewis 1978, Goldman and Rakic 1979). Several association areas of the cortex have been identified, specifically the parietal, temporal, and prefrontal areas. The prefrontal cortical association area has attracted much recent developmental research and is used as an example here.

As with all other cortical areas, the prefrontal cortex forms in an inside-out pattern of cellular layering, the neurons migrating through earlier layers to form new ones (Sidman and Rakic 1973). A distinguishing feature of the prefrontal cortex is the presence of many granule cells that develop postnatally. For this reason the area has also been called the **frontal granular cortex.** No specific projection fibers to other systems have been found. The axons within and leaving this area myelinate in the human from the sixth month after birth up to as late as the third decade of life (Flechsig 1901, Yakovlev and Lecours 1967). The late development supports the notion that higher, later-maturing functions are involved.

The developmental studies of the prefrontal cortex by Goldman-Rakic (Goldman 1972, 1974; Goldman-Rakic 1980, 1981) underline the importance of the age of the organism in the normal and abnormal development of functional connections in the prefrontal regions, as well as the importance of other variables, such as sex, and the interaction of these variables (Goldman 1975). Her work with monkeys indicates that the functional maturation of the dorsolateral prefrontal cortex extends over several years of postnatal life.

Various regions of the dorsolateral frontal cortex mature at different rates (G. E. Alexander and Goldman 1978). With the help of newer prenatal neurosurgical techniques in monkeys, Goldman-Rakic has been able to demonstrate that the effects of prenatal lesions in these areas differ depending on the rate of maturation. The major implication of this work is that, if disruptive influences impinge upon the primate brain before full functional maturation of a specific region (here, association cortex), they have little immediate impact on the development of the function subserved by that region. Goldman-Rakic's work is discussed further in relation to plasticity (Chap. 6) and sex differences (Chap. 4).

The Reticular Formation and Brainstem Chemical Pathways

The **reticular formation,** or, more specifically, the reticular activating system, consists of a number of nuclei and neuronal groups forming a ventral core of tissue in the brainstem ranging from the medulla to the midbrain. The name refers to the core network, or reticulum, of intermingled cell bodies and fibers surrounded by the ascending sensory and descending motor pathways. The importance of the reticular formation became clear in the late 1940s and early 1950s when a relationship between arousal and reticular formation activity was discovered (Moruzzi and Magoun 1949). Cur-

rent interest revolves around the role of the reticular formation in processes such as attention, alertness, habitation, and consciousness (McGuinness
and Pribram 1980). Despite the important role of the reticular formation in
many psychological functions, little research on its development has been
done.

The reticular formation nuclei arise from the dorsal plate of the developing brainstem and are among the first nuclei of the brain to form and
differentiate. The individual nuclei of the reticular formation have not been
studied in detail in humans but are known to consist primarily of four populations of neurons containing specific monoaminergic neurotransmitters:
dopamine, norepinephrine, epinephrine, and serotonin. The dopamine
system is located in the substantia nigra, norepinephrine and epinephrine
in the locus ceruleus in the dorsal pons, and serotonin in the midline nuclei
of the midbrain. In the human brain, most of the monoaminergic pathways
extending from these neuron populations develop by ten weeks of gestational age. Generally the development of serotonin-containing cells precedes that of the other monoaminergic neuron groups, but all have been
identified by 23 weeks of age. Since these neuron groups, especially the
norepinephrine and serotonin systems, have widespread projections to many
other areas in the nervous system, they may "modulate the cortical tone"
by exerting a general activational role or coordinate other areas, especially
the frontal lobes (Luria 1973). This is in accord with their presumed role in
attentional mechanisms and alertness (McGuinness and Pribram 1980).

Commissural-Interhemispheric Pathways

The **interhemispheric,** or **neocortical, commissures** are large fiber bundles
connecting the major portions of the cortex of the two hemispheres. Although these fibers reach their greatest relative size in humans, little is known
about their function. The largest commissure is the **corpus callosum,** which
connects most cortical areas of the two hemispheres. The smaller **anterior
commissure** connects primarily the anterior temporal lobes. The neocortical commissures are thought to transmit highly refined information from one
side of the brain to the other and to serve an integrating function for the
two sides of the body and perceptual space (Gazzaniga 1970).

The cerebral commissures do not myelinate until late in postnatal development. The corpus callosum in particular matures concurrent with other
cortical association areas and is therefore one of the last components of the
CNS to begin and complete myelination (Hewitt 1962).

It has been proposed that there is also a behavioral maturation of interhemispheric functions. Children aged one to three years act in a "**functional split-brain**" fashion, i.e., as if they were unable to transfer sensory
or motor information from one hemisphere to the other (Gazzaniga 1970).
Presumably, the efficiency of this transfer increases with anatomical maturation of the commissures. In a study of three- to five-year-old children

performing right-hand–left-hand tactile matching tasks, Galin and colleagues (1979) showed that five-year-olds are better able to transfer information between hemispheres. However, Tupper (1982) has been unable to replicate this finding. He stresses that intra- and cross-hemispheric functioning are so intimately related that they are difficult to seperate and quantify in young children.

The Limbic System

The **limbic system** is a ring of structures on the medial surface of and between the hemispheres. It includes the amygdala, the septal nuclei, the anterior thalamus, the cingulate gyrus, the fornix, and the hippocampus and dentate gyrus (Kappers 1971). Since the writings of Papez in the 1930s, the limbic system has been regarded as the morphological substrate of emotional behavior. More recently, it has been described as having a modulatory or attentional function (Wallace et al. 1977) or a role in memory, especially recent memory. The hippocampus and the related dentate gyrus have been most extensively studied from a developmental perspective.

During the third and fourth months of fetal development, the major nuclear groups of the limbic system form on the ventral aspect of the temporal lobe. The basal part of the temporal lobe differentiates into the **peri-amygdaloid area,** the hippocampal area, and the fornix. After the fourth month, the hippocampus area begins to differentiate into the hippocampus proper and the dentate gyrus (Cowan et al. 1980, Gall and Lynch 1980, Zimmer 1978). The **hippocampus** becomes a rolled structure inside the temporal lobe, surrounding the dentate gyrus. The overall shape of the hippocampus resembles a curve from which it gets its name, which means seahorse.

Neurogenesis occurs postnatally in the dentate gyrus region (Wallace et al. 1977). Some researchers, e.g., Altman et al. 1973, have postulated that the behavioral maturation of hippocampal functions also occurs postnatally. This interpretation is consistent with the proposed functions for this part of the limbic system, which are higher-order ones, such as memory. The prolonged postnatal hippocampal development makes the structure maximally sensitive to environmental events (Altman et al. 1973).

Language Areas

Communication with others through language is the most complex ability of humans. Speech requires the participation of many neurological and other structures (e.g., pharynx, larynx) and fully developed psychological abilities as well as the opportunity to learn how to use words.

The neurological mechanisms underlying speech and language abilities in the adult are fairly well understood because damage in specific brain regions produces disabilities such as **aphasia,** a loss or disruption of the ability to speak, **alexia,** inability to read, and **agraphia,** inability to write (Hécaen 1977, Lenneberg 1967). CNS structures thought to play a role in speech and language include Heschl's gyrus, the **primary auditory area** (Brodman's **area 41**) of the temporal lobe; **Wernicke's area,** located in the posterior part of the superior temporal gyrus and thought to be responsible for the analysis and comprehension of spoken language; and **Broca's area (area 44)** in the posterior part of the inferior frontal gyrus, responsible for the motor-output or expressive aspects of speech. Written-language abilities require good visuospatial and manipulative functioning, which involves other CNS regions, especially the third left frontal convolution. Reading also requires the participation of additional areas and abilities, notably visual abilities and correct perceptual analysis. The left angular gyrus of the parietal lobe has been singled out as particularly important for reading (Chap. 25).

These many regions and their connections undergo extensive changes during development. Growth and adaptation of the motor speech apparatus of the pharynx, larynx, and mouth continue through puberty (Bosma 1975). Many of the changes consist of enlargement of the various chambers, which affects the speech sounds since anatomical structure puts certain physical limitations on sounds. The sensory pathways (visual and auditory) necessary for speech mature relatively early in infancy (Lecours 1975). However, the maturation of the more specialized speech areas of the brain can be related to specific milestones in the development of language. For example, Lecours suggests that **babbling,** a phase of spontaneous production of sounds usually seen in two- to three-month-old infants, may be governed only by subcortical CNS structures because the connections between the cortex and the subcortical structures that carry sensory stimulation develop later in infancy. Echolalia (direct repetition of speech sounds) in the four- to seven-month-old infant is seen as a response to specific acoustic stimuli that is possible when the cortical connections of the auditory system become more active. Learning articulated systems of speech begins at 18 to 24 months and lasts until the age of five or six years.

In a recent review, Joseph (1982) made a case for the early "neurodynamic" influences of the limbic system on emotional speech, thought, and imagery. He proposed that the left hemisphere develops earlier than the right and "gains a competitive advantage in the acquisition of motor representation" while the later-maturing right hemisphere is assumed to have "an advantage in the establishment of sensory-affective synaptic representation, including that of limbic mediation" (p. 4).

4

Cerebral Organization

This chapter deals with two of the central issues of developmental neuro-psychology: differential lateralization of behavioral functions between hemispheres and sex-related differences in neural and behavioral development. Both topics have generated considerable dispute and discussion as well as mutually contradictory theories. A third section of the chapter addresses more general theories of neural development as they relate to behavioral development.

4.1 LATERALIZATION IN INFANCY

Few neuropsychological topics have stimulated as much interest as lateralization in hemispheric functioning. Although the left-right brain idea has been distorted and blown out of proportion, lateralized adult cortical control over handedness, language, and other less easily conceptualized behaviors, such as visuoperceptual ability, does raise some important developmental questions. Does hemispheric control over these functions develop with age? If so, what is their ontogenetic course? When is development most rapid and when does it level off?

Conceptual and methodological difficulties have limited the research that can be conducted during infancy and childhood. It is difficult enough to examine a given behavior in early life, let alone consider its possibly lateralized organization. However, an increasing number of studies of the first two years of life have appeared in recent years.

The neuropsychological findings in adults from which current developmental concerns arise began with the clinicopathological cases of Broca, Wernicke, and others in the nineteenth century. This work provided invaluable information leading to hypotheses about the relationship between language functioning and the left hemisphere of the brain and numerous other aspects of brain-behavior relations. Contemporary research on laterality was stimulated by Sperry's examination of patients undergoing split-brain surgery (commissurotomy) for the control of intractable seizures, which revealed stunning hemispheric differences not readily apparent in everyday activity (e.g., Sperry 1970, Sperry et al. 1969). Sperry's methods of examination included the selective tachistoscopic stimulation of one portion of the visual field to project to one or the other occipital cortex. This approach, together with Kimura's (1967) modification of the dichotic listening techniques of Broadbent, soon became a cornerstone of lateralization methodology and suggested left hemispheric specialization for recognition of speech and right hemispheric specialization for recognition of nonspeech sounds. The adult dichotic listening paradigm uses ear channels to deal with lateralized cortical processing as each ear predominantly, but not solely, sends sensory information to the contralateral hemisphere. Therefore, the left ear channel is assumed to relate to right hemisphere functioning and the right ear channel is assumed to relate to left hemisphere functioning.

If the cerebral hemispheres of the adult brain are so divergent in function, the important question arises as to how this specialization reaches normal adult levels. Developmental interest in lateralization was also stimulated by turn-of-the-century educational speculations about difficulties attributable to left-handedness and interventive strategies to correct a student's handedness "problem." Orton's (1925) ideas about the relationship between learning disabilities and poorly developed lateralization and left-handedness marked the onset of systematic work on this question, which has yet to find a definitive answer (Porac and Coren 1981).

Two theoretical positions dominate contemporary thought on the ontogeny of lateralized functioning. The first views lateralized functioning as a phenomenon that develops progressively during childhood, and the second sees it as an inherent property of brain-behavior relations present at birth. These two broad positions have been best articulated by Lenneberg and by Kinsbourne.

Based on clinical data concerning recovery from acquired aphasia in childhood (e.g., Basser 1962), Lenneberg (1967) proposed that the cerebral hemispheres of infants from birth until two years of age have an equal potential for serving as substrate for language functioning or other lateralized functions. From two years of age until the onset of puberty, the left hemisphere assumes increasing importance as the substrate for language. As the right hemisphere loses its ability to subserve language functioning to the increasingly more specialized left hemisphere, cortical plasticity for recovery of function following brain damage decreases. After puberty and throughout adulthood, the lateralization of language control in the left hemisphere remains relatively inflexible.

The second theory, nurtured by empirical data on early-life behavioral and anatomical asymmetries, holds that lateralized functioning "does not develop. It is there from the start" (Kinsbourne 1976, p. 189). The cerebral hemispheres are programed at the time of birth to function asymmetrically; the left hemisphere mediates language and motor function for the majority of the population.

Because laterality can be observed very early in life, the notion of early-life equipotentiality of hemispheric function was placed in serious doubt. However, the available data do not *completely* support or refute either position. A recent review by Satz and Bullard-Bates (1981) stressed that the risk of aphasia after left-hemisphere damage in children is the same as in adults, at least after infancy, hence narrowing the period of possible equipotentiality to the first year of life and rejecting the progressive lateralization hypothesis. Segalowitz and Gruber (1977) and Bryden (1982) provide a detailed examination of the key issues concerning lateralization through puberty. The various types of evidence are summarized by Lebrun and Zangwill (1981). The remainder of this section describes the major investigations of early-life lateralization with emphasis on the first years. Lateralization in neuroanatomical structure, speech perception, motor behavior, and electrophysiology are examined in turn.

Neuroanatomical Asymmetries

Normal brain structures show some variability in gross appearance among individuals, but the relationship of structures to one another remains relatively constant. Morphological examination of the brain to determine reliable differences between left and right hemispheres in weight, size, and density has a long history. Cunningham, for example, examined infant brains for differences in the length of left and right Sylvian fissures in 1892. However, most researchers felt that the observed anatomical differences were too small to explain the differences in hemispheric function (e.g., von Bonin 1962). Nonetheless, Geschwind and Levitsky's (1968) report that the left planum temporale (Fig. 4-1) was larger than the right in 65 per cent of their series of adult brains reawakened interest in the anatomical correlates of lateralized control over various functions.

Chi et al. (1977) studied several hundred sectioned fetal brains to establish the timing of gyral and sulcal development during fetal life. In some cases, gyri and sulci developed sooner in the right than in the left hemisphere. In two thirds of the series, the transverse temporal gyrus (Heschl's gyrus), known to be an essential region for language decoding and comprehension, was found to develop in the right hemisphere at 31 weeks of gestational age, one to two weeks before it developed in the left hemisphere. The calcarine fissure of the occipital lobe, the superior frontal gyrus, the angular gyrus, and the superior temporal fissure all developed earlier in the right than in the left hemisphere in most cases.

Despite the consistent reports of earlier development of right hemisphere areas, three studies of early-life neuroanatomical asymmetries indicate that even in fetuses as young as 29 gestational weeks, the left planum

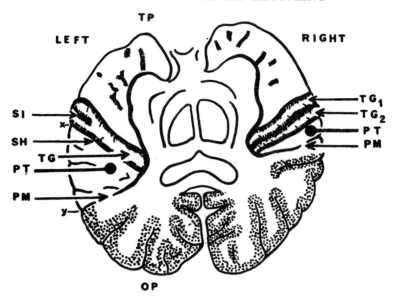

FIGURE 4-1   Upper surfaces of human temporal lobes exposed by a cut on each side in the plane of the sylvian fissure. Anatomical landmarks and typical left-right differences are shown. The posterior margin (PM) of the planum temporale (PT) slopes backward more sharply on the left than on the right, so that end y of the left Sylvian fissure lies posterior to the corresponding point on the right. The anterior margin of the planum formed by the sulcus of Heschl (SH) slopes forward more sharply on the left. In this brain there is a single transverse gyrus of Heschl (TG) on the left but two on the right (TG1, TG2). Other parts shown are temporal pole (TP), occipital pole (OP), and sulcus intermedius of Beck (SI) (Geschwind and Levitsky 1968).

temporale is usually larger than the right. Roughly 90 per cent of the 100 fetal, neonatal, and infant brains examined by Wada et al. (1975) had a larger left planum temporale. A less consistent anatomical asymmetry in the frontal operculum, the anterior region containing Broca's area of speech production, was also reported: the right frontal operculum was generally larger than the left. Witelson and Pallie (1973), examining 14 neonatal and infant brains, reported a larger left planum temporale in 75 per cent of their cases. Finally, Teszner et al. (1972) reported a larger left planum temporale in six of eight fetal brains. Interestingly, Cunningham had already determined in 1892 that the Sylvian fissure was generally larger in the left than in the right hemisphere, suggesting larger left temporal regions.

    These results admittedly deal only with gross aspects of the brain. More sophisticated morphological techniques, such as the cytoarchitectonic analyses by Galaburda et al. (1978) of adult brains, have yet to be used in developmental studies. It is not yet possible to relate these findings directly to functional lateralization. However, Taylor (1982, personal communication) reported that, based on sodium amytal tests (injected to obtain a temporary anesthesia in the ipsilateral hemisphere), left-hemisphere-damaged children below two years of age showed a change of speech lateralization to the right hemisphere; between two and six years of age such children showed evidence of bilateral speech representation, and above six years of age most had a permanent deficit consistent with speech lateralization in adults. The continued refinement of new imaging techniques, such as positron emission tomography (PET) and nuclear magnetic resonance (NMR), may provide additional direct evidence of the correlation between anatomical and functional asymmetries.

The origin of lateral asymmetries in brain development has been the subject of considerable speculation. Morgan (1977) proposed that lateralization depends solely on the orientation of the cytoplasm in the ovum. If this hypothesis proves true, lateralization would ultimately depend on genetic factors of the mother but not the father. In contrast, Annett (1970) proposed the action of a single "right-shift" gene responsible for lateralization; the action of this gene, however, would have to be modified by environmental factors to account for the variability found in the general population. J. Levy and Nagylaki (1972) proposed a two-gene model, each with two alleles, allowing for different variations in brain lateralization for speech and handedness. Finally, polygenetic models have also been considered (Porac and Coren 1981). None of the models have found general acceptance, nor do they explain published statistics on behavioral lateralization to everybody's satisfaction.

Perceptual Asymmetries

Examination of the functional lateralization of a given perceptual ability presupposes that the ability exists in the organism's repertoire and that it can be adequately measured. The abilities currently attributed to the infant are much more numerous, active, and nonreflexive than those listed 25 years ago. Since then, data on adultlike linguistic perception in the infant have accumulated almost concurrently with data on lateralization of this perception in adults. As a detailed discussion of developmental linguistics would lead too far afield, the reader is referred to reviews by Butterfield and Cairns (1974), Eimas (1974), Eimas and Tartter (1979), and Morse (1977) and to a critique by Trehub (1979).

The prime finding of this linguistic research is that the infant appears to be able to discriminate **phonemic differences** (e.g., /pa/ as opposed to /ba/) in the same categorical fashion as adults (e.g., Eimas et al. 1971). That is, when a speaker says /pa/ and then says /ba/, the difference between the two utterances crosses a phonemic boundary and therefore can be considered of *linguistic* importance. If two different speakers each say /pa/, the difference between the two utterances does not cross a phonemic boundary and is of acoustic, rather than linguistic, importance. If an individual can reliably discriminate changes in linguistically releveant utterances that cross phonemic boundaries, then he or she is able to make a *categorical discrimination* and identify phonemic utterances in their proper linguistic categories. Since this basic linguistic ability is similar in infants and adults, it is plausible to look for similarities in cortical substrate between infants and adults. While it is usually easy for adults to respond verbally to such tasks, however, such responses are not possible for infants. Special procedures have been developed to test infant speech perception so that comparisons across age can be attempted. Similarity in discriminative ability, however, does not necessarily imply the existence of similar cortical mechanisms in infants and adults. In fact, categorical discriminations similar to those made by human adults have also been reported in chinchillas (Kuhl and Miller 1975).

The procedure used most in examinations of speech perception by infants is the *habituation and dishabituation* of high-amplitude sucking (HAS) in response to linguistic stimuli. A particular language stimulus, e.g., the syllable /pa/, presented to the infant evokes a high frequency of strong sucking on a pacifier modified to serve as a recording instrument. Repeated presentation of the stimulus results in a gradual decrease in the intensity of sucking. When such habituation has occurred, a new speech stimulus that differs from the original one along a dimension that may or not be of linguistic relevance is presented. If the across-boundary (linguistically relevant) change elicits a dishabituation of the sucking response but the linguistically irrelevant change does not, one can infer that the infant has discriminated speech sounds in an adultlike, categorical fashion.

In general, results of perceptual studies do indicate that infants can distinguish linguistically relevant stimuli categorically along such basic dimensions as voice onset time and the transition of parts of the acoustical spectrum (formants) of a sequence of speech sounds (see, for example, Butterfield and Cairns 1974, Eimas et al. 1971, Morse 1972, Trehub 1973). Discrimination in infants is much the same as in adults. However, serious technical and interpretation questions have been raised about linguistic studies employing the HAS technique, as discussed by Pisoni (1977) and Trehub (1979). For example, performance on an HAS task appears to require both memory and linguistic ability, possibly confounding the interpretation of findings: the infant needs to remember the previous stimulus in order to be able to respond to the novelty of the current stimulus (Trehub 1979).

The habituation-dishabituation procedure has been adapted by neuropsychologists to examine hemispheric specialization in infants. The dichotic listening adaptation (Fig. 4-2) for examination of the lateralization of categorical discrimination involves the use of two independent stimulus channels, one directed into the left ear and the other into the right ear. Stimuli

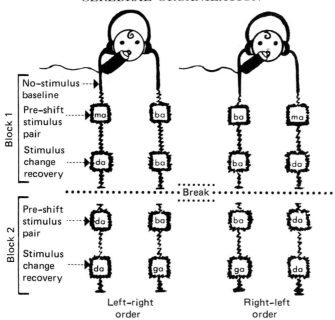

FIGURE 4-2 Schematic representation of the experimental procedure showing stimulus sequence and ear order for the dichotic listening adaptation of the habituation-dishabituation paradigm with high-amplitude sucking response in infants (Entus 1977).

are presented by headsets that allow projection of sound to a single ear. After the response (e.g., sucking) has habituated, the new stimulus is presented to one ear while the other continues to receive the original stimulus. If dishabituation occurs more readily in one ear than in the other, then inferences about the brain lateralization of that ability can be made.

Three studies of the **lateralization of categorical perception** in infants have been reported. Glanville et al. (1977) used a dichotic task to examine dishabituation of a heart rate (rather than sucking) response to auditory stimulation. Twelve infants ranging in age from three to four months were tested under four conditions: verbal or musical presentation with the stimulus change in the right or left ear. Eight of the infants showed more rapid heart rate dishabituation to verbal stimuli when the stimulus change was presented to the right ear. Ten of the infants showed greater dishabituation to changes in musical stimuli when the change was in the left ear, though both ears showed some dishabituation to musical stimulus change.

Both Entus (1977) and Vargha-Khadem and Corballis (1979) used a dichotic task in conjunction with habituation-dishabituation of the HAS response; however, their results conflict with one another. Entus examined dishabituation of HAS to verbal and musical stimulus changes as a function of ear channel in infants under four months of age. She found that 34 of 48 infants showed greater dishabituation to a change in verbal stimulation when the change was in the right ear channel; 38 of the 48 infants showed greater dishabituation to a change in musical stimuli when the change was in the left ear channel. Her results, along with those of Glanville et al., are strikingly similar to the adult right-ear advantage for verbal stimuli and left-ear advantage for nonverbal stimuli. Vargha-Khadem and Corballis failed to replicate Entus's verbal stimulus finding. Using a modified procedure to reduce possible experimenter bias, which they felt was present in Entus's original design, they interpreted her results as reflecting experimenter bias.

The finding of asymmetries in the perception of speechlike auditory stimuli in infants similar to those demonstrated in adults is striking. However, as the failure to replicate Entus's results suggests, the studies are fragile, exploratory efforts to examine lateralization of functions in the infant's repertoire of abilities.

The dichotic listening task, designed for adults, has been widely used throughout childhood. A relatively consistent right-ear advantage (REA) for verbal stimulation has been reported by most investigators from young childhood to adult age. Although some argue that the strength of the REA shows progressive lateralization, most recent studies have failed to find such an age effect (Bryden and Allard 1981, Hynd et al. 1979, Kinsbourne and Hiscock 1977). Van Duyne (1982) and Kinsbourne and Hiscock (1978) stress the fact that age effects in dichotic listening may be related to verbal and cognitive development dependent on the task demands and not to lateralization.

Motoric Asymmetries

Studies of laterality in motor performance and manual preference have a long history in neuropsychology. Two related aspects in infancy have been studied: the appearance of neonatal postural asymmetries, such as head position, and the development of handedness. Recent studies have addressed the relationship between these two aspects of motor asymmetry (Michel 1981).

HEAD POSITION   It has been a common observation by pediatricians, maternity-ward nursing staff, and parents that when newborn babies lie on their back their head usually remains turned in one direction. Because it can be observed easily, the direction of the neonate's head posture has been the most frequently examined aspect of neonatal lateralization. The results indicate two types of predominantly rightward lateral head position in the normal newborn: (1) an asymmetry in the attainment and maintenance of a rightward head posture and (2) a greater right-sided ipsilateral responsiveness to stimulation.

Turkewitz and his coworkers (e.g., Turkewitz and Birch 1971) observed spontaneous behavior and behavior subsequent to holding the baby's head in the neutral, body-midline axis position for a period of time. Similar studies have been done in a variety of hospitals with different patterns of early infant care (e.g., Cioni and Pellegrinetti 1982, Michel and Goodwin 1979, Risser 1981, Saling 1979). They indicate that, even when the baby's head is held in the midline position for as long as 15 minutes to minimize any asymmetric motor tone, most infants show a consistent rightward preference in head positioning. This preference shows a very rapid development: neonates under 12 hours of age are likely to turn right as often as left, whereas infants over 12 hours of age are much more likely to turn right. With few exceptions, full-term newborns maintain a strongly prevalent lateral head position soon after birth, rightward for most, leftward for some.

Rightward ipsilateral responsiveness to lateral stimulation has also been observed in newborns. The baby's head is held in the neutral midline position, and one or the other side of the face is quickly stimulated by touch. The neonate responds to right-sided stimulation with a rightward head turn much more frequently than to left-sided stimulation with a leftward turn.

The underlying mechanisms for these two very early lateralized behaviors remain obscure. There is some evidence that the first-appearing type of laterality, spontaneous tendency toward positioning the head to the right, contributes to the development of the second, stronger responsiveness to stimulation from the right side. There is also some evidence that the forced head position of the fetus as it grows in the uterus may contribute to the lateralized behavior after birth (Michel and Goodwin 1979). Liederman and Kinsbourne (1980) have attributed the lateralized response to stimulation directly to programed asymmetrical cortical control of motor behavior. This interpretation is strengthened by findings of an asymmetry of the stepping reflex in newborns.

Lateral head positioning has also been examined in relation to the development of handedness (Coryell and Michel 1978, Gesell and Ames 1947, Michel 1981). Michel tested babies at several points during the first 22 weeks of life with a task to elicit reaching by visual stimulation. Those who showed left-sided biases in neonatal head position used their left hand more than their right, and those who showed right-sided neonatal position preference reached with their right hand more than with their left. It must be remembered that head turning preference allows the infant to see the ipsilateral hand more often. Whether or not the experience of viewing the hand on the side of the neonate's head preference contributes to later handedness has been debated. It is plausible that "headedness" (i.e., the preferred side toward which the head is pointed) may represent the handedness of early life; alternatively, headedness may be the early-life manifestation of the same mechanism(s) that, in later life, leads to manual preference.

Evidence has been presented that premature infants and infants with low

Apgar scores fail to show these lateralities in head positioning (Turkewitz et al. 1968, Lewkowicz et al. 1979). In addition, a recent report noted that six-week-old infants with a history of perinatal complications lacked the rightward head-turning bias of infants without a history of perinatal trauma. The former also remained in the same posture longer than normal children after the tonic neck reflex had been elicited and showed less asymmetry of the reflex itself (Liederman and Coryell 1982).

MANUAL PREFERENCE   Despite the importance of handedness in adult neuropsychology, the development of preferences and consistencies of hand use and manual skills in infants has not been extensively examined. Historically, developmental research has focused on the observed types of manual skills per se rather than on their lateralization (Young 1977). Whether handedness is inherited has been an issue of lively debate. The development of handedness has also been related to fetal head position in utero, although the correlation is weak (Churchill et al. 1962).

Lateralized hand preference and efficiency in infancy and childhood are variable. Gesell and Ames (1947) concluded that, at different times during normal development, a child may show right-hand preference, left-hand preference, or apparent bilaterality. Gesell and Ames's studies agreed well with clinical thought at the time. Several studies since then have examined lateralization of gross movement, grasping, and reaching behaviors but, like the earlier research, are methodologically unsatisfactory. Caplan and Kinsbourne (1976) examined lateral consistencies in grasping behavior of infants and reported a possible asymmetry in holding an object with the hand. The results suggested a longer grasping time with the right hand but were ambiguous in that this might be interpreted either as an indication of hand preference or as evidence that the hand that grasps for the shorter time is dominant because it remains ready for active manipulation. E. Strauss (1982) failed to replicate the reported differences in grasping time.

Reaching ability has also been examined. Michel's (1981) study of visually elicited reaching, which indicated consistent lateralized reaching preferences in early infancy, is described above.

Electrophysiological Cortical Asymmetries

Electrophysiological recording methods have been used to study lateral hemispheric responsiveness to a variety of stimuli in early life. The techniques are described briefly in Chap. 1. One advantage of their use with infants is that the infant need not be an active and attentive participant in the experiment, an advantage that very few behavioral techniques for the study of developmental laterality offer (Molfese and Molfese 1979a). However, the frequency of recording artifacts from the infant's movements and the maturational changes observed in both the EEG and evoked potentials seem to cancel out these advantages (S. R. Butler and Glass 1974).

Davis and Wada (1977) examined the evoked responses of infants' brains by recording auditory-evoked responses (AER) to click stimuli, visual-evoked responses (VER) to flash stimuli, and power spectral transformations (a computer analysis of certain frequencies of the electrical recording) of both AER and VER. To study specific hemispheric contributions, recordings were made from right and left occipital and temporal scalp locations (01,02, T3, and T4 in the standard system). The results indicated a center of high-amplitude activity in the left temporal lobe for the auditory click stimuli and a center of high-amplitude activity in the right occipital lobe for visual flash stimuli. Thus, even in infants, lateralization of cortical activity in response to different types of stimulation is discernible.

Molfese and coworkers (Molfese 1977, Molfese and Molfese 1979b, Molfese et al. 1976) used electrophysiological recording techniques to examine language-related cortical mechanisms and their possible lateral asymmetry in a cross-sectional study of neonates, infants, adolescents, and adults. The general format was to record critical responses over both the left and right temporal regions of the scalp (i.e., recording areas T3 and T4) evoked by a variety of auditory stimuli that either were or were not speech-like. In an initial study, Molfese (1977) examined hemisphere-specific AERs to four speech stimuli, noise, and a C-major piano chord in small groups of infants, children, and adults. Most subjects of all ages showed greater amplitude in the left-hemisphere AER to speech sounds and greater right-hemisphere AER amplitude for music and noise. It is tempting to interpret this cross-sectional analysis of the AER as indicating a consistent electrophysiological asymmetry from infancy through adulthood. Later work by Molfese (1977), however, suggested that neonates were relying on acoustic rather than linguistically relevant phonetic cues when the AERs were recorded, whereas adult AERs were more cued by the phonetic aspects of the stimuli.

A factor analysis of neonatal AERs to speech and nonspeech sounds yielded four factors (Molfese 1977): a sex effect in the initial part of the AER (females showed a greater response amplitude), stimulus bandwidth, a greater amplitude for a specific stimulus, and a general hemispheric response difference across all stimuli. The absence of an interaction between hemispheric response and either stimulus transition or bandwidth suggested that no specific acoustic function was responsible for the differential hemispheric responsiveness reflected by this fourth factor.

Molfese (1977) described the AER habituation to repetitive stimulation for a small group of neonates and a small group of adults. The dishabituation stimulus sound differed from the original stimulus either across a linguistically relevant phoneme boundary or within a phoneme boundary (not linguistically relevant). The left-hemisphere AER in five of the six adults showed an increase in amplitude while the right-hemisphere AER continued to habituate in the presence of linguistically meaningful changes of the sound stimulus. With the linguistically irrelevant stimulus changes, AERs of both hemispheres continued to decrease in amplitude. This was interpreted as evidence of left-hemisphere perception of linguistically relevant stimuli. In contrast, the neonates did not show differential hemispheric AERs: across-boundary dishabituation resulted in an increment in response in both hemispheres, and within-boundary dishabituation resulted in the continued decrease of amplitude in both right and left hemispheres.

Hence, the neonates showed adultlike perception of the across-boundary changes. However, responses were bihemispheric rather than lateralized in the infant group, indicating that, when infants' lateralized AERs to speechlike stimuli are recorded, the responses are to acoustic rather than to phonetically meaningful cues. It is these nonlinguistic, acoustic mechanisms that are lateralized in the neonate.

In a later study, Molfese and Molfese (1979a) reported differential hemispheric AERs to voice onset time changes in neonates without the categorical discrimination across phoneme boundaries seen in adults and even in older infants. The older infants showed two specific components in the AER: a first factor representing variables of the right-hemisphere response to phonemic categories that had to be discriminated and a second factor common to both hemispheres and representing the ability to discriminate phonemic categories. Only the first component was observed in the neonates.

Molfese and Molfese (1979b) attempted to identify acoustic cues responsible for differential hemispheric responsiveness in early infancy. They found left-hemisphere ability to distinguish consonants differing in second-formant transitions containing normal-formant structure. A later-appearing AER component, reflecting the same ability but bihemispheric, was also noted.

In sum, the Molfeses have demonstrated that the newborn's and young infant's brain responds electrophysiologically to differences in speech stimuli and that there is some evidence of lateralization in cortical response. They have shown that newborns have a limited ability to discriminate acoustic cues and that older infants have an adultlike ability to utilize phonemically relevant cues categorially. However, some developmental linguists (e.g., Pisoni 1977) insist that infants, like neonates, rely on acoustic rather than phonemic cues. The Molfeses' studies of differential hemispheric AER patterns with systematic variations in the linguistic and acoustic nature of auditory stimuli provide the most direct evidence to date of some form of hemispheric specialization in language ability very early in infancy.

4.2 SEX DIFFERENCES

As with lateralization, the investigation of sex differences is plagued with problems of understanding and presents many unanswered questions. Is sex a categorical variable with mutually exclusive categories? Have any sex differences in the underlying neural substrate been found? Have neural sex differences in any way been related to psychological (dis)abilities, and how? Finally, how do neural and behavioral sex-related differences arise in development?

Sex-related differences that change during development have to be discriminated from more static sex-related differences in the adult. Recent reviews by J. Levy (1981) and McGlone (1977, 1980) present our current understanding of sex differences in the neuropsychological abilities of the adult. This section is concerned only with sex differences as they arise in early pre- and postnatal development; sex-related changes occurring at or after puberty are not discussed.

Neuropsychological differences between the sexes during development appear at first glance to be easy and convenient to study: groups of subjects of each sex can be compared by looking at their chromosomes, their brains, and their performance on specific behavioral tasks. However, such a comparative approach, while sometimes valuable, tends to focus attention away from determining the mechanisms for these differences. It must be kept in mind that there is typically more individual variation within a sex than between sexes.

Mechanisms of neuropsychological sex differences in development may range from genetic, hormonal, neural, and behavioral factors to differential socialization practices and sex roles. Although each of these factors has been suggested as a "cause" for sex differences, none of them alone can fully explain the findings. For these reasons, the study of sex differences in development has been confusing and perhaps misleading at times. The inclusion of a sex factor in many behavioral studies has to be carefully weighed.

Sex Differences in Neural Development

Sex can be defined at two basic levels: that of the chromosomes (**genetic differentiation**) and that of the sex organs and sexual characteristics (**gonadal differentiation**). Sex can be identified prenatally by examining the chromosomes; a **karyotype** displays the genes and tells us whether the embryo is male or female. Of the 23 pairs of chromosomes in humans, one pair (the **gonosomes**) specifies the sex of the individual; XX is the female, XY the male pattern. Sex is determined at fertilization since the ovum and sperm each carry half of the genetic material. The sex of the child depends upon the sex of the sperm because approximately half the time the sperm carries the X sex chromosome and half the time it carries the Y chromosome, while the ovum always contributes an X chromosome. At subsequent cell divisions, either the male (XY) or female (XX) pattern is passed on to all cells.

Up until about seven to eight weeks after fertilization, the gonads remain undifferentiated. The genetic male and the genetic female look alike. At this time, the male gonad becomes recognizable as testes; the female gonad does not differentiate into ovaries until about ten weeks after fertilization. Thereafter, the sex chromosomes have no known direct influence on subsequent sexual differentiation. External genitalia begin to develop during the ninth week as the Leydig cells appear in the testes and begin to secrete the male sex hormone **testosterone,** which is primarily under genetic control (MacKinnon 1979). Under this hormone's influence the external genitalia differentiate to form a penis and a scrotum. In contrast, the development of the female reproductive tract does not require hormonal stimulation. In the absence of testosterone, the external genitalia differentiate into those of the female. Female ovarian hormones (**estrogen,** for example) seem to have no effect at the early stage.

Several abnormalities are related to disorders in fetal sex differentiation. One has been studied extensively by Money and Ehrhardt (1972) and is called adrenogenital syndrome or **congenital adrenal hyperplasia.** The condition is transmitted in the autosomal recessive mode; both parents have to be carriers to produce the condition, in which an excessive amount of **androgen** is produced. In a genetic female with adrenogenital syndrome, there is a masculinization of the external genitalia while the internal reproductive organs remain female (Ehrhardt and Baker 1974). Treatment usually involves lifelong hormonal control and early surgical feminization of the external genitalia. A variant of this syndrome occurs in genetic males but has no noticeable effect on the genitalia. With early hormonal treatment, these boys appear normal; without treatment they experience premature pubertal development.

In another disorder, the **testicular feminization** or **androgen-insensitivity syndrome,** genetic males cannot appropriately utilize androgen. This defect results in a discrepancy between genetic and gonadal sex (XY) on the one hand and the external morphological sex appearance (female) on the other.

In **Turner's syndrome** (XO) the fetus is not exposed to any gonadal hormones during the early critical period. One of the sex chromosomes is missing, and the individual develops morphologically as a female.

As this brief introduction shows, fetal sex hormones have a profound effect on the development of sex-related characteristics. The next question is whether or not sex hormones also have an effect on neural development. The term used for the development of the two forms of a structure from an undifferentiated precursor is **dimorphism.** The question to be addressed is therefore, Is there a structural-chemical dimorphism in the brain?

HORMONES AND NEURAL DEVELOPMENT   Because sex differences have traditionally been seen as dichotomous and absolute, it was assumed that females produce only estrogens and males produce only testosterone. In actual fact, there is overlap and the hormones of both sexes are present in both men and women. Thus, the hormonal difference between the sexes has to do with the relative proportions as long as both types of hormones are present.

Hormones are known to influence the nervous system and its development (Reinisch 1974). Theoretically, they have two possible functions: (1) to act locally to activate a particular structure by influencing some of the functional properties of the neurons and (2) to help differentiate and organize the nervous system as a whole early in development by influencing nerve growth, neuronal circuitry, and brain architecture. These have been described as the **activational** and the **organizational hypothesis** (Arnold 1980, Goy 1970, Harlan et al. 1979).

From an evolutionary point of view, differentiating peripheral organs such as the testes or ovaries is of little interest unless there are differences in function and neural control as well, i.e., unless there are different functions for each of the gonads and also different neural centers controlling them.

> Normal differentiation of genital morphology entails a dimorphic sex difference in the arrangement of peripheral nerves of sex which, in turn, entails some degree of dimorphism in the representation of the periphery at the centrum of the central nervous system, that is to say, in the structures and pathways of the brain. (Money and Ehrhardt 1972, p. 8)

Evidence for the organizational hypothesis comes primarily from animal research. Hormonal messages governing the functions of the gonads are sent from the **pituitary gland,** which secretes hormones called **gonadotropins.** These hormones stimulate the ovary to operate cyclically (the menstrual cycle). The pituitary gland is controlled by portions of the hypothalamus, specifically the anterior and preoptic regions. The sexual dimorphism of these regions can be attributed to the prenatal masculinizing effect of androgen, which alters cell structure and function (Arnold 1980, MacKinnon 1979). Without androgen, these regions differentiate functionally as female. Thus, it is the male organism, again, that is changed.

One often overlooked interaction in studies of neural sex differences is that between sex hormone levels in the body and the number of sex hormone receptors available. There appear to be individual differences in both the number and the sensitivity of sex hormone receptors in the brain and in peripheral organs. This may cloud any relationship between level of sex hormone and functional activity of the brain.

With regard to brain structure, there is no evidence for sex differences in human neuronal circuitry or architecture (Hier 1981), although at all ages the average brain weight of males is about 10 per cent greater than that of females. The sex difference in brain size probably reflects a sex difference in neuronal size rather than neuronal number and therefore does not imply any sex differences in performance. In the rhesus monkey, however, Goldman and colleagues (1974) showed sex-dependent behavioral effects of cerebral cortical lesions during development. They found that male rhesus monkeys with orbital prefrontal lesions were impaired on behavioral tasks at ten weeks of age but similar deficits were not detected in females until 15 to 18 months of age. The results indicate earlier maturation of the orbital prefrontal areas in male monkeys, a sexual dimorphism in neural development.

Diamond (1981) found that, in male rats, the right cerebral cortex was thicker than the left from birth to old age; in female rats at the age of 90 days, the left cortex was thicker than the right, although this difference was not significant. Females whose ovaries were removed at birth developed a male pattern of hemispheric asymmetry.

So far, the differences reported by Goldman and by Diamond have not been replicated in humans. In fact, several studies have failed to find distinctive cerebral patterns for either sex (Chi et al. 1977). Hier (1981) concludes that there are as yet no known sex differences in human brain structure during development. J. Levy (1981), on the other hand, believes that generalization of the findings reported in monkeys and rats to other mammals, including humans, should be possible. In light of the behavioral evidence on sex differences, to be reviewed in the following section, Levy argues that the notion of human sexual dimorphism should be extended to brain development since there is no reason for such dimorphism to "occur for all portions of the body except the brain or that sexually dimorphic brains occur in all mammals except people" (p. 219).

Sex Differences in Behavior

The differences in behavior demonstrated between the sexes have been reviewed by R. C. Friedman et al. (1974), Hamburg (1974), and Maccoby and Jacklin (1974). We present a short summary of them here before considering the often conflicting evidence for theories of cerebral organization in relation to sex differences.

Burnstein et al. (1980) and Fairweather (1976) reached different conclusions after reviewing the current status of theories about psychological differentiation of the sexes: "There are few convincing sex differences, either overall or in interactions with (putative) functional localization" (Fairweather 1976, p. 231). "The existence of sex differences in cognitive functioning is clear, but further research is needed to elucidate the determinants of these differences" (Burstein et al. 1980, p. 289).

It is fairly well agreed that there are few, if any, major differences in motor abilities between the sexes. Nor have any sex differences in development been found in studies of activity level, vocalization, oral behaviors, auditory receptivity, and visual tracking (Korner 1973). General intellectual functioning as measured by IQ also usually fails to show sex differences, although two recent reports have stimulated renewed interest in this issue (Kaufman and Doppelt 1976, Wersh and Briere 1981). Studies of IQ differences in children, if they exist, are further obscured by the fact that the WISC-R, the most commonly used test, was deliberately constructed to avoid sex differences.

Sex-related differences in cognitive abilities appear most frequently and most consistently in the linguistic and spatial domains (Maccoby and Jacklin 1974). Specifically, girls tend to achieve higher scores on tests of verbal abilities and boys tend to achieve higher scores on tests of spatial abilities. The consistency of these findings, however, depends upon the ages studied. In the age range from 8 to 11 years, no consistent sex differences in verbal abilities can be demonstrated, but before age eight and after adolescence girls generally appear to outperform boys in measures of verbal skills (Burstein et al. 1980, Gaddes and Crockett 1975). The male superiority in tests of spatial ability, however, seems to show up in the age range from six years to adolescence (McGee 1979).

These differences are of course group differences. The distributions of the two sexes on measures of verbal and spatial ability overlap greatly.

Sex Differences in Cerebral Functional Organization

The question of whether there are sex-related differences in the degree and development of cerebral lateralization of cognitive functions has stirred considerable interest over the past decade. A critical look reveals much confusion and contradiction in this area.

Several researchers have proposed that there are sex differences in the development of cerebral lateralization and that they relate to differing behavioral capacities of the sexes. Buffery and Gray (1972, also Buffery 1976) argue that both speech and spatial skills become completely lateralized in females but remain more bilateral in males since developmental studies indicate an earlier acquisition of language function in females. The underlying assumption is that, for optimal achievement to develop, it is better to have language represented in one hemisphere and spatial skills in both hemispheres. Hence, males are better at spatial skills and females are better at linguistic skills.

Essentially the opposite developmental pattern has been suggested by Levy and Reid (1978), who assert that males are more strongly lateralized for both spatial and verbal functions than females and that bilateral language representation is conducive to higher verbal ability. Carter-Saltzman (1979), Waber (1976, 1977, 1979a), and Witelson (1977) have presented similar theories. Waber assumes that early sexual maturation (the female pattern) is associated with weaker lateralization of functions and that late maturation (the male pattern) is associated with greater lateralization. Weak lateralization then would lead to greater verbal ability and stronger lateralization to greater spatial ability, consistent with the findings in our own current review. Using a dichaptic task (which requires tactile recognition of two different shapes or objects simultaneously with each hand) in children,

Witelson (1977c) found that males showed a right-hand channel superiority for tactile matching but females did not. From this she concluded that there is early right-hemisphere specialization for spatial ability in males but females retain bilateral representation during development.

Perhaps these two lateralization theories are contradictory partly because of the variety of laterality and cerebral organization measures used (Bryden 1979). Several other theories on sex differences in brain development tend to deemphasize the role of lateralization and to stress the importance of differential maturation rates between the sexes. Ounsted and Taylor (1972), for example, hypothesize that the Y chromosome slows the rate of maturation of the male and permits more exposure to the environment and a fuller expression of the genetic material, which eventually leads to sex-related differences in higher cortical functioning.

As mentioned above, Waber proposes that the sex-related differences in higher cortical functioning, expressed behaviorally as the sex differences in verbal and spatial ability, are due to differences in physical maturation rate. On the basis of this theory, she postulated that, regardless of sex, early maturers would do better on tests of verbal ability and late maturers would do better on tests of spatial ability. Her study did show that late-maturing individuals (based on Tanner scale ratings) of both sexes performed better than early maturers on tests of spatial ability, but the groups did not differ on tests of verbal ability. A crucial assumption, only indirectly addressed by Waber, is whether the earlier physical maturation of girls is related to earlier mental development.

McGuinness and Pribram (1979; see also Goleman 1978) present another neurobehavioral theory relating cerebral functional organization to differing abilities of the sexes. They suggest that there are sex differences in brain structure that arise when different levels of sex hormones act on the structures that underlie behavioral sex differences. Sex differences are evident in the **arousal** (amygdala-frontal lobe) **and readiness** (basal ganglia) **systems** of the brain. By this theory males, considered to be more manipulative, would have a spatial-mechanical aptitude through the readiness system. Females, considered to be more communicative, would have an auditory-verbal aptitude and would show greater flexibility in the control of hemispheric functions through the arousal system.

In addition to these general theories of neurobehavioral sex differences, there have been numerous reports of developmental sex differences in relation to cerebral organization. Research with identical and fraternal twins has indicated that spatial ability has a genetic component. Identical twins are significantly more similar than fraternal twins on tests of spatial ability (Vandenberg and Kuse 1979), which therefore appears to be linked to the X chromosome. The theory has been called the "**sex-linked major gene hypothesis.**" However, a recent critique (Boles 1980) shows that severe methodological difficulties in many of the studies render the hypothesis unsatisfactory.

In recent studies (Shucard et al. 1981), significant sex-dependent AER asymmetries in three-month-old infants presented with verbal and nonverbal auditory stimulation were found. Females showed greater AERs from the left hemisphere, and males produced greater right-hemisphere responses during both the verbal and the nonverbal presentations. The authors suggested that their results support the behavioral data on the presence of sex differences in cognitive functioning at an early age: the left hemisphere in female infants is more receptive to complex sensory input and hence is predisposed for language-related functions, whereas in male infants the right hemisphere is more receptive, which may be related to earlier development of spatial functions. Their results need to be replicated and extended to other responses.

The topic of sex differences in behavior during development and at the adult level has raised considerable interest over a number of decades. Only in recent years have attempts been made to relate these differences to differences in the structure and function of the brain. The results of these efforts provide a very limited amount of factual information relating to brain function and a considerable amount of often contradictory theories. While differences in the development of lateralization (which presumably become permanent functional differences of brain organization) remain mainly conjecture, proposed sex differences in the rate of maturation find at least some indirect support in evidence of differential physical maturation and in the ablation studies with rhesus monkeys described earlier. One is likely to agree with Burstein et al. (1980) that there are *some* demonstrated sex differences in cognitive and other behavioral functions but few "hard" explanations as to why they occur.

Developmental Disabilities and Sex Differences

Further understanding of sex-related differences in brain and behavior may be gained from research on sex differences in neuropsychological disabilities as related to specific developmental mechanisms. One of the most frequently studied disabilities now known to show a sex difference is developmental dyslexia, a disorder in acquiring the ability to read (Chap. 25). Until recently there was no consensus on differences in prevalence between the sexes. In a critical review, however, Finucci and Childs (1981) reached the conclusion that we now have enough epidemiological evidence to confirm that there really are more dyslexic boys than girls, as clinical observations indicate. They concluded that the mean boy/girl ratio is 5.1/1, although it is partly related to age of subjects. The dyslexic boys in their own study not only showed more severe disability but also tended to be slightly older than the dyslexic girls. When Finucci and Childs began to explore the sex differences, however, they found that females seemed to function better in the presence of a dyslexic deficit than males. Witelson (1977b) agrees that females show more plasticity in development. When severity was included as a factor, the sex difference decreased to a male/female ratio of 2/1.

Other developmental disabilities also show an increased prevalence in males: mental retardation (the sex ratios differ for particular forms, but males are almost always over-represented); hyperactivity; X-linked disorders, such as Lesch-Nyhan syndrome (an inability to metabolize nucleic acids in food because of an enzyme deficiency) and agenesis of the corpus callosum; and epilepsy (Mosley and Stan 1982). The male predominance in all these disorders led Mosley and Stan to develop further a general theory, already put forth by Taylor (1976), that during the early embryological phase of human sexual dimorphism the male is exposed to greater risk. Females have less range of variability in genetic expression than males because the hemizygous nature of the male sex chromosome pair (XY) increases genetic variability. Therefore, the male is represented with greater frequency among both the positive and the negative extremes of behavior, including intellectual functioning. Mosley and Stan's theory appears to contradict the evidence just presented and suggests that there are sex differences not only in the quantity but also in the quality of cognitive abilities.

4.3 GENERAL DEVELOPMENTAL THEORIES OF BRAIN ORGANIZATION

Two major theories of the development of cerebral organization have been articulated. The first, expanded by MacLean (1970), provides an evolutionary perspective based on comparative anatomy. The second derives from some of Luria's (1966, 1973) concepts concerning the ontogenesis of certain functional systems in the brain.

The Triune Brain: An Evolutionary Perspective

Drawing on comparative anatomy, neuroanatomy, neurochemistry, and evolutionary theory, MacLean (1970) proposed that the mammalian brain can be divided anatomically as well as conceptually into three hierarchical systems: a protoreptilian brain, a paleomammalian brain, and a neomammalian brain. Together, they form the **triune brain.**

The **protoreptilian brain** system is, in an evolutionary sense, the oldest; it consists of regions in the upper spinal cord, the midbrain, the diencephalon, and the basal ganglia. It plays a crucial role in many instinctive activities necessary for survival of the individual and the species. The **paleomammalian brain** system represents the next evolutionary step in that it has a role in the integration of emotional expression and self-awareness. It has the ability to override and suppress the more primitive protoreptilian brain. The limbic system is the primary neural system corresponding to the paleomammalian brain (Isaacson 1975). The **neomammalian brain** is represented by the neocortex. MacLean views the cortex as responsible for the nonemotional, integrative, fine-grain analysis of the external environment. In the highly developed left hemisphere of humans, this characteristic is represented by language, which gives humans the ability to reason and to think about future prospects. The neomammalian brain is able to override the other two systems.

Van der Vlugt (1979) recently elaborated the triune brain concept from the viewpoint of developmental neuropsychology (Table 4-1). He cites historical precedents of similar conceptualization of the nervous system and suggests, as MacLean does, that the triune brain can be a reasonable representation not only of the evolutionary but also of the ontogenetic development of the nervous system. He assumes that each developmental step depends on earlier steps and that later-developing structures subserve more refined and complex adaptive and integrative functions than earlier structures. With regard to abnormal influences on the development of the nervous system, Van der Vlugt suggests that different patterns of behavioral deficits are seen depending upon which level of the triune brain is affected.

Luria's Theory of the Development of Functional Systems

Alexander Luria, a Russian neuropsychologist whose concepts and methods have had a great influence on contemporary neuropsychology, developed

TABLE 4-1   Evolutionary Concepts of the Organization, Function, and Development of the Brain

Pavlov (1955)	Yakovlev and Lecours (1967)	Luria (1973)	MacLean (1970)	Isaacson (1974)	Van der Vlugt (1979)
Second signal system	Supralimbic zone	Programing, regulating, verifying mental activity	Neomammalian brain	Guru	Level III
Conditioned reflex	Paramedian or limbic zone	Obtaining, processing, storing information	Paleomammalian brain	Lethe	Level II
Unconditioned reflex	Median zone	Regulating tone or waking	Protoreptilian brain	Graven image	Level I

Source: van der Vlugt, 1979.

the major theoretical concept of the brain's "functional systems" (Luria 1966). By this he meant those interacting areas of the brain that mediate a given behavior. Luria's view differed from other neurobehavioral theories—localizationism and equipotentiality—in its stressing that no single area of the brain can be considered responsible for any particular behavior, nor do all areas of the brain contribute equally to all behaviors. In Luria's view, a number of brain regions are involved in a functional system for a given behavior. A corollary concept is "**pluripotentiality**," which suggests that any specific area of the brain can participate in a variety of functional systems. Luria also held that functional systems are not unique; different systems may be responsible for any given behavior, depending upon the availability of alternate systems.

As a didactic tool in understanding functional systems, Luria (1973) presented a model of functional units within the brain. In this model, all functional systems must involve three basic units of the brain because they all represent interactions of several areas (Table 4-2). These units are (1) the **arousal unit,** which consists of the reticular formation and related structures and effects cortical arousal and modulates input; (2) the **sensory input unit,** which consists of the posterior portions of the hemispheres and is responsible for the analysis of sensory input and cross-modal integration; and (3) **the output/planning unit** (mainly the frontal lobes), the highest functional level of the brain, which is responsible for planning and carrying out

TABLE 4-2   Luria's Theory of Functional System Development

Stage	Functional system involved	Brain area involved	Ages of development
1	Arousal unit	Reticular system and related structures	Birth to 12 months
2	Primary motor and sensory areas	Visual, auditory, somatosensory, and motor regions (calcarine, superior temporal, pre- and postcentral gyri)	Birth to 12 months
3	Secondary sensory and motor areas Cerebral dominance	Secondary sensory and motor regions (peristriate, parietal, temporal, and premotor regions)	Birth to 5 years
4	Tertiary sensory input area	Parietal lobes	5 to 8 years
5	Tertiary output/planning unit	Prefrontal lobes	12 to 24 years

Source: Golden 1981, p. 289.

behavior. The sensory input and output/planning units can be further divided into primary, secondary, and tertiary areas, which represent increasing levels of complexity and integration in information processing.

Luria (1973) also related his theory to the ontogenetic development of brain-behavior relations. In his "law of the hierarchical structure of cortical zones," he described how the relationships between primary, secondary, and tertiary cortical zones change in the course of development. "In the young child, the formation of properly working secondary zones could not take place without the integrity of the primary zones" (1973, p. 74). Only after the development of the secondary ("gnostic") zones can the "creation of major cognitive synthesis," i.e., the full development of the higher cortical zones, take place. These tertiary zones assume the dominant role in the adult.

Parallel to the hierarchical development of the three zones proceeds the development from the "maximal modal" specificity of the primary zones to the "supramodal" organizational and interpretive function of the tertiary zones. In addition, development in Luria's theory includes a "progressive lateralization of function": while the right and left primary zones have "identical roles" in the functioning of the individual, handedness and the development of speech require a functional organization and specificity that take place together with the development of the secondary and tertiary zones and "differ radically" between right and left sides.

The quality of the performance in any stage does not predict the quality of performance in subsequent stages. Because psychological functions dependent upon tertiary areas of the input or output units do not develop until later in childhood or adolescence, obvious differences between the child and the adult in these skills are predicted.

Luria has elaborated in particular the increasing regulatory role of language in the development of the child. While the young infant has only a basic capacity to express itself by motor movements, crying, and facial expressions ("first signal system"), the young child begins to accompany its actions with verbal expressions and gradually develops a "second signal system." As the tertiary zones of the brain mature, language becomes more developed and the accompanying motor actions are no longer necessary. Language also need no longer be expressed, but becomes internalized; it mediates and regulates human behavior. Luria places the beginning of this third, mature stage at the approximate age of six years.

II

METHODOLOGICAL AND CONCEPTUAL ISSUES IN DEVELOPMENTAL NEUROPSYCHOLOGY

5

Methodological Concerns in Developmental Neuropsychology

This chapter addresses several concerns in research methodology and design that investigators in developmental neuropsychology encounter during the planning, execution, and interpretation of an investigation. The focus is on (1) sampling, (2) data-collection instrument (or test), (3) internal and external validity, (4) statistical analysis, (5) developmental research designs, and (6) replication. These areas encompass many of the issues that challenge an investigator. How should a sample be obtained? What instrument(s) should be used to collect data from this sample? What design is relevant and cost-effective for this investigation? What control groups are necessary to deal with the influence of factors that may co-relate with the factors of interest? What is the proper statistical analysis to determine the significance of measured group differences? Can the obtained findings be replicated with new samples? Finally, what conclusions can be drawn from the findings obtained?

It is beyond the scope of this chapter to provide more than a brief review of these issues (see Campbell and Stanley 1963, Cook and Campbell 1979, R. J. Harris 1975, Horton 1978, Winer 1971). Specific developmental methods have been introduced by Achenbach (1978, 1979), Baltes et al. (1977), and Friedrich (1972), as well as by Nesselroade and Reese (1973) and Nesselroade and Baltes (1979) in more advanced books. Methodological issues specific to neuropsychology have so far received only an initial examination (e.g., Parsons and Prigatano 1978).

5.1 SAMPLING OF SUBJECTS

The research questions posed by the investigator require the definition of the population(s) to be studied, e.g., brain-damaged children, adolescents afflicted with cerebral palsy, premature offspring of lower-class mothers in urban settings. Since it is impossible to collect data from all members of a population, samples must be drawn. **External validity** reflects the extent to which results can be generalized from the sample back to the defined population.

In some instances, a single *case study* and a *single-subject investigation* can be a powerful method of presenting information. Most of the germinal conceptions in neuropsychology were stimulated by case reports, especially for rarer forms of brain disorders. Information gathered about a single case can be of direct clinical or of heuristic, i.e., hypothesis-generating, value (Shallice 1979). In a truly **random sample** every member of the "parent" population has an equal chance of being chosen as a sample subject (Blalock and Blalock 1968). The extent to which a sample is not representative of the population reflects the amount of *sampling error* in the study. In many populations, obtaining a truly random sample of individuals may be as elusive a task as testing the entire population. A truly random sample of 12-year-olds, for example, would require a census tract data base to select from. Yet even this might not truly represent the population of 12-year-olds because it includes only those 12-year-olds whose parents or legal guardians are able or willing to file census statements.

Generalization to the population of interest is limited if variables such as familial income or education, subject accessibility, and severity of injury can influence the variables of interest. In addition, samples with developmental disorders (e.g., rubella, acquired postnatal brain injury) may differ not only with respect to etiology, course of disease process (progressive or static), and location of lesion but also with age of onset. For example, the effects of congenital rubella differ depending on fetal age at exposure; as do the effects of early-life anoxic episodes.

Modifications of strictly random sampling techniques may be used when an investigator wishes to control for variables that may influence the results. Matched groups or stratified random samples can be used in developmental research to balance for the factors of age, sex, and socioeconomic status. Overmatching may restrict the composition of the population to such an extent that the generalizations and inferences made are uninteresting or misleading. Additional restrictions in sampling (e.g., relying on volunteers, screening potential subjects, testing in only one of several economic groups or geographic locations) may lead to a deliberate or unknown redefinition of the population under study. For example, what may begin as a study of linguistic deficits in brain-damaged children in general may, in effect, end up as a study limited to brain-damaged children of affluent parents in university-affiliated, well-staffed, urban hospitals.

Experimental inferential analyses (as distinct from correlational descriptive analyses) attempt to manipulate levels of independent variables and view their influence on the dependent variable(s), to allow causal inferences. Subjects need to be *randomly assigned* to the levels of the manipulated variables to minimize any potential pre-existing group differences that could challenge the internal validity of the study. This type of design is rare in developmental neuropsychology, with the exception of intervention studies, because the researcher usually has neither direct control over the levels of the independent variable (e.g., severity of neuropathology or age) nor the opportunity to randomly assign subjects to treatment. Instead, neuropsychological investigations commonly rely on existing subject attributes (i.e., **attribute variables**) to define the levels of the independent variables, e.g., choosing subjects with naturally occurring CNS lesions left or right lateralized, and conduct a correlational examination. In a **correlational design,** the co-relation between one variable and another is examined. Merely because one variable is positively or negatively co-related with another does not mean that the one causes the other; other, unmeasured variables may be influencing both variables to bring about the obtained correlations.

Other issues of concern regarding sampling of subjects in developmental research include (1) changes in the parent population over time that lessen the generalizability of the results from the original sample and (2) selective subject survival (i.e., biological and experimental attrition for other reasons).

In developmental research, generalization from a sample back to the population of interest can be complicated by the fact that the population itself undergoes changes as a function of ontogenetic or cohort changes. An example of a plausible cohort change is the differences in obstetric care and technology available for a neonatal cohort in 1934 and in 1984. Victims of perinatal damage who would have died at or soon after birth in 1934 have a much greater chance of survival in 1984. This difference in survival rate may potentially contribute to differences in the characteristics of neonates observed at these two times. Cohort changes may be educational, economic, medical, social, or cultural; they are relevant only to the extent that they are related to differences in the behaviors under investigation.

Selective subject survival refers to attrition incurred over the course of an investigation because subjects refuse to continue an experiment, move away, are lost to follow-up, die, become ill or disabled, etc. Members of a brain-damaged group might be less able to complete a test session than members of a healthy control group; normal preschool children may be less cooperative and attentive than elementary school children. If this selective attrition is observed during the study, it is imperative to determine how the remaining sample differs from the full original sample before inferences are made (Droege 1971).

5.2 TEST INSTRUMENT

Data-collection instruments should be standardized, reliable, and valid for the age level at which they are used. These criteria are basic psychometric properties for which professional standards exist (American Psychological Association 1977).

Briefly, a **standardized test instrument** is one that is consistent in administration and format for all subjects and for all examiners. For example, if one subject completes the instrument in a quiet room while another does so in a very noisy room or if examiners differ greatly in the coaching they give subjects, then extra variability or **measurement error** will occur, which clouds the subject's true scores. Standardization is not attained without some cost. If, for example, a test is standardized to be given only in quiet settings with each subject relaxed, it might be difficult, if not impossible, to generalize the findings about that behavior to noisy or anxiety-provoking settings. This reciprocal relationship between standardization and generalization also affects the validity of research findings, as discussed below. Standardization criteria for a test instrument must be followed if comparisons with the test's normative data are made, e.g., with intelligence and cognitive tests such as the WISC-R or McCarthy scales. The collection of normative data, of course, raises the problems already discussed in the section on sampling of subjects.

The **reliability** of a measurement instrument is reflected in its internal consistency and in the consistency of its measurement over time. An **internally consistent instrument** is one in which all the individual items equally contribute to the measurement of the concept or ability the test is designed to assess. Individual-item analysis and split-half, or random-half, analyses of the test items determine the degree to which the test is internally consistent. A reliable data-collection instrument produces similar results when a subject is tested more than once over a period of time short enough so that the underlying skill, ability, or attribute will not have changed. Reliable tests will not yield precisely identical results on different occasions, but the differences between occasions should be small.

A *valid* test instrument is one that measures what it is intended to measure, i.e., it should meet an operational definition of the concept of interest. Three types of **validity**—content validity, construct validity, and predictive, or criterion, validity—can be demonstrated. **Content validity** refers to the adequacy of the items composing the test. Simply, do these items reflect an adequate sampling from the domain of behaviors to be measured? If, for example, a test of reading ability is composed of single-word items but not of phrases or sentences, then its validity as a test of reading ability may be questioned; in terms of content validity, such a test may be more adequately described as a test of single-word recognition. **Construct validity** is typically demonstrated by investigating the correlation of a new test with an established test of known validity that assesses the same concept or ability. **Predictive, or criterion, validity** refers to the ability of a test to validly discriminate individuals into relevant groups, for example, the discrimination between dyslexic readers and normal readers or the predictive discrimination of children at risk for later academic problems from those not at risk.

Standardization, reliability, and validity are especially difficult in the many developmental studies that cover a wide age span. Instrument standardization is difficult, for example, if two-, six-, and ten-year-old subjects are to be examined. If the same test is to be used for all three groups, then it may prove too difficult (i.e., it shows a **floor effect**) for the youngest subjects and exceptionally easy (i.e., a **ceiling effect**) for the oldest subjects. If different tests are used for each age, then changes in the concept or ability under investigation attributed to age may be a function of the different test instruments used and not a true age difference. In addition, confounds due to differences in attentional capacity, linguistic capability, or other factors not directly related to the measurement construct may mitigate against successful data collection. Even if the same test can be administered in standard and reliable fashion at different ages, the possibility that the structure of the underlying ability, aptitude, or attribute might change as a function of age may call the validity of the measurement instrument into question unless it has been validated at each age.

5.3 INTERNAL AND EXTERNAL VALIDITY

Internal validity refers to the degree to which the investigator can legitimately claim that observed differences between groups of subjects truly can be interpreted in terms of the research hypothesis. If other interpretations are more plausible or more parsimonious, then the validity of the researcher's claim is seriously threatened. The use of a *control group* (or several control groups) provides information on variables that may make the research finding ambiguous and helps to maintain internal validity. The possible threats to internal validity and recommended procedures for minimizing them have been discussed in detail by Campbell and Stanley (1963).

One threat to internal validity is the maturation of the subject(s). Ambiguity precludes an internally valid interpretation of an observed relationship between controlled variables of interest if maturational (endogenous) changes cannot be properly disentangled. For example, the naturally occurring, gradual recovery or compensation of function following brain damage may be independent of, yet coexisting with, systematic rehabilitation. Changes occurring over the treatment period may be attributed to the treatment when, in reality, they were due to a natural restitution of ability.

Uncontrolled environmental influences on subjects concurrent with the controlled independent variable may invalidate results. Conclusions from a 1980 cross-sectional study dealing with the outcome of prematurity in five- and ten-year-olds, for example, may be invalid because systematic differences in perinatal interventive care have occurred between the births of the two groups. Internal validity can also be jeopardized if repeating a test influences performance on a subsequent administration. Solomon and Lessac (1968) have presented a design to disentangle treatment effects from the effects of previous testing.

Sample-selection bias is a further threat to internal validity itself or when compounded with the problems of subject maturation, environmental change, or retesting. The remedies for this bias, random sampling and random assignment, usually cannot be used in developmental neuropsychological research. However, careful subject selection and assignment may at least partially avoid selection bias.

The test instrument or its use may also jeopardize the validity of interpretations, for example, because of fluctuations in the accuracy of timing or the progressively more ragged appearance of stimuli from an often-used visual perceptual task.

External validity reflects the degree to which the results of an investigation can legitimately be generalized to the larger population of interest. If the findings are idiosyncratically tied to the sample, they have purely descriptive rather than inferential value. The main consideration in examining external validity has traditionally been in terms of the subjects from which data have been gathered, i.e., Bracht and Glass's (1968) "population validity," although levels of treatment, measurement instruments, test settings, experimenters, etc., i.e., Bracht and Glass's "ecological validity," are also important. For example, data collected in a laboratory or clinical setting cannot be fully generalized to behavior in a more naturalistic milieu. Ecological validity in developmental research has been discussed in detail by Bronfenbrenner (1977).

5.4 STATISTICAL ANALYSIS

Depending upon the hypotheses under investigation, a study may use either a univariate or a multivariate statistical paradigm to analyze the significance of collected data. The choice depends on whether investigators wish to focus on the effect of a measured or manipulated variable or whether they wish to study the relationships defined by patterns among several measured variables. A **univariate** statistical paradigm involves one dependent variable and one or several independent variables that are individually and serially either manipulative or attributional in nature. **Multivariate statistical paradigms** involve more than a single dependent variable and one or several manipulative or attributional independent variables. For example, if the relationship between one measure of spelling ability and age, sex, and intellectual level is the focus of investigation, then a univariate paradigm is applicable. If, however, several discrete types of spelling errors are to be related to age, sex, and intellectual level, then a multivariate design is appropriate. Univariate and multivariate designs require specific statistical techniques: t-tests, analysis of variance, multiple regression, and nonparametric statistics are common univariate statistical tests; multiple analysis of variance, factor analysis, discriminant function analysis, and multidimensional scaling and profile analysis are common multivariate tests.

Given the complexity of neuropsychological development, generalizations from the outcome of studies using a univariate paradigm may be of limited usefulness. As noted by Baltes et al. (1977), many behaviors are controlled not by a single variable but by many interdependent variables. Multivariate paradigms allow the investigator to focus on several variables and their interdependence, i.e., a network of relationships.

Exactly how one should analyze change has been a controversial topic in developmental methodology for many years. Achenbach's text (1978) provides an introduction to this topic (see also Cronbach and Furby 1970, Frederiksen and Rotondo 1979, Nesselroade et al. 1980, Nunnally 1973). One principal issue in this discussion is **regression toward the mean:** an individual who obtains an extreme score on a measure tends to obtain a score closer to average on a second testing of the measure. When a population of individuals is tested and a normal distribution is obtained, the probability of obtaining extreme scores is lower than the probability of obtaining less extreme scores. It is common for a group of individuals to be selected from a population for further study based upon their extreme (poor or good) performance on a test measure. The group's subsequent mean score tends to be closer to the population mean. This "apparent effect" may be observed even in the absence of a deliberate treatment effect (Baltes et al. 1977, Nesselroade et al. 1980). A further problem in assessing change is that typical change scores (e.g., posttest minus pretest) do not take into account the influence of measurement errors on each data-collecting occasion (Nunnally 1973).

5.5 DEVELOPMENTAL RESEARCH DESIGNS

A variety of time-ordered research designs permit the investigator to examine the relationships between variables over time. The designs differ with respect to the control exerted over threats to internal and external validity and in cost efficiency (Fig. 5-1). The more elaborate designs are most appropriate for the study of normal development and have been rarely used with abnormal or clinical populations.

A **cross-sectional design** focuses on the relation between variables or attributes when measurement is taken only once. The three types relevant in neuropsychology are prevalence, retrospective, and prospective study designs.

Prevalence studies investigate the presence, absence, and/or level of an existing attribute in different population subgroups (e.g., age groups, brain-damaged versus non-brain-damaged groups). For example, a group of children with cerebral palsy and a suitable control group may be studied to determine the prevalence of visual anomalies or a group of language-impaired children may be compared with a suitable control group with respect to occurrence of middle-ear disease. Comparing the performance of

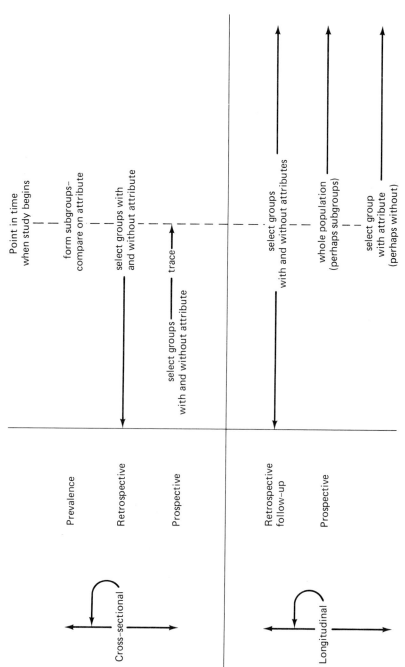

FIGURE 5-1   Time-ordered cross-sectional and longitudinal research designs.

children of different ages on a task is a common use of this design in developmental psychology.

In **retrospective cross-sectional** studies, a group is defined by a particular attribute (e.g., congenital malformations) and a suitable control group without this attribute is established. Histories are then investigated to determine the frequency of occurrence of a preceding attribute variable in each group. For example, a group of children with malformations and a suitable control group without malformations can be established. The investigator can then determine whether or not the mothers of these children took a particular drug during pregnancy.

In **prospective cross-sectional** (also called retro-follow-up) studies, data from the subjects' history are used to identify a group for which a certain attribute occurred previously and a suitable control group without the attribute. The selected subjects are then located and assessed to determine the frequency of occurrence of an attribute or variable. For example, an investigator may go through hospital records and establish a group of children born to mothers taking a particular drug during pregnancy and a control group of children born at the same time whose mothers did not take that drug. These children will then be located and assessed for a specific psychological or physical deficit.

Longitudinal designs involve the measurement of the relationship between variables or attributes at different times. Two types of longitudinal designs are retrospective follow-up (also called nonconcurrent) and prospective (also called concurrent, forward-looking, follow-up).

In **retrospective follow-up** design, a group with an attribute and a suitable control group without the attribute are identified and histories are taken. The design is similar to the cross-sectional retrospective design except that here both groups are reassessed at periodic intervals rather than only once. For example, a group of learning-disabled schoolchildren and a suitable control group may be identified and historical information concerning pre-, peri-, and postnatal events obtained. These children may then be assessed at regular intervals throughout their academic careers.

Prospective longitudinal designs may use a general population sample or select specific groups from the population. If a general population sample is used, an entire sample is measured on a particular variable or set of variables and then followed over time. For example, the Collaborative Perinatal Project (Broman et al. 1975) used this design to investigate the relations between adverse conditions surrounding birth and subsequent neurological and cognitive deficits in infancy and childhood. Data were collected on mothers admitted for prenatal care in 12 university-affiliated hospitals (1) during prenatal visits, (2) at admission for delivery, and (3) during labor and delivery. The children born to these mothers were examined as neonates and at specific intervals through age eight.

Alternatively, specific groups who are at risk or have been exposed to a particular factor and a suitable control group may be selected and followed over time. Identifying children who showed different degrees of jaundice at birth and assessing their cognitive abilities at specific intervals throughout childhood represents an application of this design.

The major advantage of the retrospective design is one of economy. Information is obtained quickly from available data. The retrospective design may be the only feasible approach when studying rare diseases. Examining the five clinically referred persons out of one million with a rare disorder would be much more practical than collecting data on a million persons in an effort to identify these five. One major disadvantage of retrospective designs is the problem of **backward contingency probabilities** (Gottfried 1973): the selected sample of subjects is an unknown proportion of the affected population and therefore does not represent the true frequency of such individuals in the population. In the example of malformed children and the relationship to drugs taken by the mothers during pregnancy, there may actually be a number of mothers who took the drug and whose children were not malformed. In a retrospective sampling design, this would not be detected and only an indirect estimate of risk could be provided.

Other potential sources of bias include incomplete or inaccurate historical information and attrition before testing due to the attribute. Knowledge of the present attribute (e.g., congenital malformation) may affect the recollection of facts concerning the events surrounding birth, a selection bias first noted in hospital studies by Berkson at the Mayo Clinic (**Berksonian bias**). In a neuropsychology clinic, such bias may arise if only learning-disabled children known to have sustained early brain injury are referred for assessment. Generalization of findings to the general population of learning-disabled children would not be possible.

Prospective designs provide more direct evidence of risk and are most valuable when specific hypotheses have already been developed from previous studies using retrospective designs. Subjective bias involved in identifying the initial attributes is decreased with the use of a prospective design. However, prospective designs are time-consuming and difficult to execute and are inefficient for studying rare attributes. They are also not suitable for exploratory research where the examiner may wish to look at a large number of factors of doubtful significance (retrospective designs are more feasible for this purpose).

Studies using a cross-sectional design are easier, quicker, and less expensive to conduct. However, they lack necessary controls for internal and external validity. For example, when age has been used to divide a population into groups, an assumption has been made that, if the behavior of younger and older children from the same population is being measured, say, the behavior of the older child is an indication of how the younger will eventually behave. This assumption is faulty since it is not possible to determine whether other influences, such as year of birth (cohort effects), may be affecting the results. The year or decade in which a person was born may affect performance, and this suggests that the developmental course of the particular cohort may differ from that of cohort groups born earlier or later. For example, the cohort effect has been implicated in discrepancies between cross-sectional and longitudinal studies of IQ over time. The influence of cohort effects increases as the time span of the investigation lengthens.

Longitudinal designs give a direct estimate of intraindividual changes and interindividual differences. However, these designs lack controls for the effect of repeat testing and other threats to internal validity. They are restricted in external validity since only one cohort is studied. Longitudinal designs are also vulnerable to the effects of attrition, which may be related to the subject characteristics and thus bias the remaining subjects further.

The *time-lag design* was developed specifically to identify cultural-historical effects and compare subjects from different cohorts when they reach a given age. For example, an investigator may wish to compare children born in four different years when they reach 11 years of age. One disadvantage of this design is that it confounds possible differences in cohorts with differences in year of measurement (Achenbach 1978).

In order to avoid the confounding of age, cohort, and time-of-study effects, sophisticated designs have been developed to control these variables explicitly through the use of sequential extensions of the three traditional designs—cross-sectional sequential, longitudinal sequential, and time-lag sequential.

Cross-sectional sequential designs involve samples from several birth cohorts assessed at successive times. That is, new samples are drawn from each cohort for each set of observations. The major advantage of this approach is that it does not require the retaining of the same subjects from one observation period to the next; therefore the effects of attrition and initial selection for stability do not threaten the validity (Achenbach 1978). The major disadvantage of this design is that changes in individuals cannot be identified over time; only the average change in functions can be determined. Baltes et al. (1977) noted that "cross-sectional sequences require fairly strict assumptions about linearity and additivity if inferences about average change functions are to be useful and valid" (p. 135). Another disadvantage of this type of design lies in uncontrollable random fluctuations in sampling.

Longitudinal sequential designs compare samples from several birth cohorts over the same longitudinal period. The major advantage of this design is the amount of information collected, which allows cross-sectional comparisons of cohorts at any point in the study, comparisons of longitudinal course of development in each cohort over the course of the study, and time-lag comparisons as subjects reach a particular age in successive years. This design also makes it possible to obtain longitudinal data on relatively long periods of development in less time than it takes the development to occur (Achenbach 1978) and allows the investigator to determine whether changes in behavior are attributable to cultural-historical changes, age changes, or an interaction of the two. As with all longitudinal designs, attrition may affect the results.

Time-lag sequential designs entail taking observations on two or more samples from each cohort as they reach two or more ages in different years. This design yields information specifically related to the effects of cultural-historical changes with fewer observations than other designs. However, the design is vulnerable to uncontrollable random fluctuations in sampling from the same cohort.

Baltes et al. (1977) noted that a greater degree of internal validity could be accomplished when cross-sectional and longitudinal sequences are used simultaneously. The authors recommended (1) that sequential data are best used for descriptions of intraindividual changes in various cohorts and (2) that explanatory interpretations of observed changes and interindividual differences in change be left to subsequent or parallel research.

Klausmeier and Allen (1978) used a time-lag sequential design in studying the cognitive development of children. Children at four grade levels were tested each year for four years. Control groups were incorporated into the design to evaluate possible cohort and retest effects for the groups studied longitudinally. Two cohort control groups of the same age as the groups under study, one born a year later and one born two years later, were established, as well as two retest control groups of the same age. Each of the retest control groups was tested only once. One group served as a control for the cohort control group that had been assessed twice, and one group served as a control for the groups studied longitudinally over four years. Table 5-1 illustrates this sophisticated research design.

5.6 REPLICATION

An "elemental principle of competent research" is the *replication* of findings (Kessen 1960). Unfortunately, replication is not a commonplace practice in most areas of psychological investigation, including developmental neuropsychology. A replication study can determine the reliability of findings, for example, whether sociocultural changes over time influenced findings previously established; it also allows generalizations, for example, the generality or cross-validation of an obtained finding (D. W. Smith 1970). Hence the goals of the replication study are to answer the following questions. Can the original investigator or an independent investigator following the information provided by the original investigator replicate the results of the original study? Have social, cultural, economic, medical, etc., changes in the population made previous findings obsolete or misleading?

TABLE 5-1 Design of a Combined Longitudinal and Cross-Sectional Study

| Grade in school each year of measurement | | | | N in 1976 | Control group designation |
1973	1974	1975	1976		
K →	1 →	2 →	3	62	Longitudinal Block A
		1 →	2	23–26	Cohort Control 1
			1	33	Cohort Control 2
		2		34–40	Retest Control 1
			3	32–40	Retest Control 2
3 →	4 →	5 →	6	77	Longitudinal Block B
		4 →	5	36–37	Cohort Control 1
			4	34–36	Cohort Control 2
		5		34–40	Retest Control 1
			6	37–40	Retest Control 2
6 →	7 →	8 →	9	80	Longitudinal Block C
		7 →	8	32	Cohort Control 1
			7	35	Cohort Control 2
		8		33–40	Retest Control 1
			9	37–40	Retest Control 2
9 →	10 →	11 →	12	73	Longitudinal Block D
		10 →	11	32–33	Cohort Control 1
			10	38	Cohort Control 2
		11		33–40	Retest Control 1
			12	34–40	Retest Control 2

Source: Klausmeier and Allen 1978.

Are the findings generalizable to a new set of subjects, test items, test settings, etc.? In sum, replication is a powerful tester for determining the relevance of an investigation and for weeding out findings that may show significance by pure chance or may have become obsolete.

6

Critical Periods and Plasticity

At first glance the concepts of critical periods and plasticity appear to be opposites, one suggesting rigidity, the other flexibility. On closer scrutiny, however, the ideas are not incompatible. At some developmental stages the organism is more receptive or vulnerable to environmental influence than at other stages, and it is at these times that the labels "critical" and "sensitive" are applied. The ability of the CNS to change in response to these environmental influences is referred to as **"plasticity."**

6.1 CRITICAL PERIODS

Definitions and Criteria

Essentially, the critical period is the time between the emergence anatomically or functionally of a given biobehavioral system and its maturation. The system may be affected in this emergent but immature state (for better or worse) by exogenous stimuli, and this effect can be permanent should the system "harden" to maturity. (Colombo 1982, p. 263)

The concept of critical periods has its origins in experimental embryology. Working on the effects of inorganic compounds on the development of Fundulus eggs, Stockard (1921) first thought that the development of one-eyed fishes was caused specifically by magnesium ion. Further experiments showed that similar malformations could be produced by other inorganic chemicals administered at appropriate times during development. Although the concept has been attributed to Stockard, he himself gives credit to Dareste for originating the basic idea 30 years earlier. Stockard, and later Child (1941), went on to specify that the more rapidly growing tissues are most sensitive to interference (Denneberg 1968, J. P. Scott 1962). In line with this early work, the concept of critical periods in development refers to stages of maximum sensitivity to exogenous stimuli.

The criteria for a critical period include (1) an identifiable onset and terminus; (2) an intrinsic component, i.e., the organism's sensitivity must be triggered by some maturational event; and (3) an extrinsic component, i.e., an external stimulus to which the organism is sensitive (Nash 1978).

The main areas of critical-period research have been visual development in the cat, imprinting in precocial birds, and canine socialization. (For a comprehensive bibliography in these areas, see Colombo 1982.) In these studies the period begins not with a sudden change but rather with a gradual rise in sensitivity to the critical stimulus. This increase in sensitivity reaches a plateau that can last from hours to days and years, depending on the behavior under investigation. The increase is in part a reflection of biological maturation, but it may also be triggered or extended by external stimuli. For example, Garey and Pettigraw (1974) noted that synaptic vesicles in the feline visual cortex could be reduced by limiting visual input.

The termination of a critical period may also be gradual but is generally less so than the onset. It remains controversial whether the critical period ends as a result of exogenous or endogenous factors, but current data suggest that biological factors probably set an outer limit on the period.

The intrinsic component consists of the neurobiological changes that underlie the sensitivity to stimuli. Most critical periods are paralleled by periods of rapid development. In mammalian visual development, the critical periods for binocular vision correspond to the postnatal development of the visual cortex (age 4 to 12 weeks in the cat, the first 9 weeks in the rhesus monkey, and the first 3 years in humans), when cells compete for cortical synapses (Colombo 1982).

The extrinsic component consists of the critical stimuli or events that can influence an organism's development. In some cases the nature of the extrinsic factor remains nonspecific. Lenneberg (1967) argued that a child must be exposed to language before age 14 if language is to be acquired and used. In contrast, such specific stimuli as exposure to light and ocular movement are critical in the development of cortical binocularity (R. D. Freeman and Bonds 1979, Hubel and Wiesel 1965).

Critical Periods During Prenatal Development

At the cellular level there is some support for the critical-period hypothesis. For example, in his study of the nerve fibers that connect the retina and the optic tectum in the frog, Jacobson (1978) was able to specify the exact point in development at which a disruption of the prespecified connections is irreversible. During the early stages of development, the optic nerve can be severed and the eye inverted but the nerve will regenerate and the eye will develop normally. At larval stage 31 and beyond, inversion of the eye causes the frog to have permanently inverted vision. Sperry (1963) attributed this developmental process to the biochemical specificity, or chemospecificity, acquired by each retinal ganglion cell.

There is also a great deal of gross embryological support for the hypothesis. **Teratogens,** i.e., agents capable of producing a deformed fetus, if introduced at particular times, produce a range of congenital anomalies. The organ systems most affected are those that show maximum cellular growth at the time of teratogenic introduction. Those systems that have either passed or not yet reached the rapid-growth stage are spared (Hamburger 1954). During the fertilization and implantation period in humans, which lasts from conception to 17 days gestation, toxic agents can interfere with all cells and result in death. The embryonic period from 18 to 55 days is the time of organ differentiation and characteristically shows extreme sensitivity to teratogenic agents. The outcome of exposure to toxic agents during this period produces both functional and morphological deficits.

Several principles of teratology require emphasis:

1. The critical period for teratogenesis is the phase of organ differentiation, corresponding approximately to the first trimester.
2. Susceptibility to teratogens, however, depends on the genotype of the conceptus, resulting in different effects in different species.
3. A variety of different teratogens may produce the same malformation.
4. A variety of malformations may result from a single teratogen.
5. Manifestations of deviant development are dose-dependent.

The developmental defects arising from teratogenic influences include developmental arrest; **agenesis,** or absence, of an organ; **hyperplasia,** or abnormal increase in cell numbers; and aberrant development. Teratogenic agents that cause abnormalities during the embryonic stage include infections, drugs, environmental pollutants, and metabolic deficiencies, which are described in detail in Chapter 10. Best known among the infections are syphilis, toxoplasmosis, rubella, cytomegalovirus, and herpesvirus—the STORCH agents. Among drugs, thalidomide is infamous for producing phocomelia, a shortening of the limbs. Studies have shown that the critical period for phocomelic defects occurs between 20 to 40 days after conception. Tetracycline has been implicated as causing eighth (auditory) nerve damage and multiple skeletal anomalies. Alcohol abuse during pregnancy has been correlated with microcephaly, cardiac defects, growth retardation, and developmental delay (Howard and Hill 1979).

Among the various environmental pollutants associated with gross abnormalities, mercury, DDT, carbon monoxide, and lead have been studied most extensively. Finally, radiation injury in the embryo or fetus has been recognized for some time and depends largely on age at time of exposure. If the exposure takes place in the first one or two weeks, resorption of the conceptus is probable (Wald 1979). Between the second and sixth weeks, the effect is on the particular organ undergoing development at that time. With increasing gestational age, more subtle generalized effects may occur, leading to deficits in growth and development. Human anomalies reported to have been induced by irradiation include microcephaly, hydrocephaly, mental deficiency, blindness, and spina bifida. Dobbing (1968b) noted a relationship between maternal proximity to the center of the Hiroshima atomic bomb explosion, gestational age of less than 15 weeks, and the incidence of microcephaly and mental retardation.

The relationship between severity and number of malformations and teratogenic dosage is fairly well established. During fetal development, lasting from the fifty-sixth day to birth, the fetus becomes less susceptible to gross malformations, and the primary effect of exposure to noxious environmental influences during this period is reduction in cell size and number (Howard and Hill 1979). Recently, attention has focused on the relationship between subteratogenic or marginally teratogenic doses and development. A dose-response relationship has been hypothesized (R. E. Butcher et al. 1975) and is illustrated in Fig. 6-1. The center curve describes the increase in number of gross malformations associated with large teratogenic doses during a period of rapid growth in the CNS. The right-hand curve describes a similar relationship for embryo-lethal effects. The left-hand curve suggests that, in addition to embryo-lethal and teratogenic effects, a given dose of a CNS teratogen may also produce functional impairments, including possible learning impairment or abnormal activity patterns.

The idea that behavioral deficits may result from low doses of teratogens during fetal development finds support in the animal research of Dobbing

FIGURE 6-1   Dose-response relationships for agents teratogenic to the central nervous system (R. E. Butcher et al. 1975).

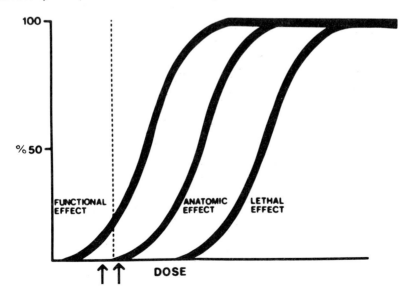

(1968a), Hicks and D'Amoto (1966), and Hutchings et al. (1975). For instance, excess vitamin A in fetal rats can produce motor disturbances and behavioral patterns resembling those of children with minimal brain dysfunction. Whether this can occur in humans is not yet known.

Dobbing asserts that there is a vulnerable, rather than critical, period at the time of rapid brain growth in humans, beginning at approximately 25 weeks of gestational age. During this period maturation of axonal and dendritic growth, glial multiplication, myelination, and growth in size take place (Fig. 6-2). An experiment with malnourished rats has been used to test the hypothesis (Dobbing 1968a). Restriction on growth during this period retards development and reduces the ultimate size of the brain. In behavioral terms, deficits of function rather than anomalies appear. The testing of Dobbing's hypothesis is far from complete and has involved experimental work on animals and observational studies with human populations at risk. Results indicate subtle behavioral deficits in learning ability. Although species such as the rat show distinct fetal development periods similar to humans and can be used for animal model studies (e.g., I. Fish and Winick

FIGURE 6-2   Concentration of cholesterol per unit of fresh weight in whole brain, forebrain, cerebellum, and stem during growth (Dobbing and Sands 1973).

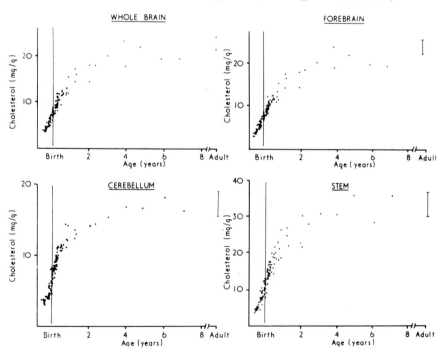

1969, Winick and Noble 1966), generalizations across species and inferences about consequences in the human fetus remain speculative at best.

Critical Periods in Postnatal Development

Although the concept of critical periods is well established in embryological terms and in many cases can be precisely defined, the issue of whether the concept has equal validity in behavioral and psychological terms after birth has raised considerable debate.

Traces of the critical-period hypothesis have been found in Freud's notion of the origin of human neuroses in early infancy and in his belief that early infancy is an especially sensitive period in development. The early work of Lorenz in 1937 (Lorenz 1970) also emphasized the importance of critical periods in the formation of primary social bonds in birds (imprinting). Later, McGraw (1946) suggested a critical period for the learning of motor skills in infancy. The idea of critical periods was also promulgated by J. P. Scott (1958) to explain socialization in dogs. The concept of educational readiness and stage-dependent theories of development such as Piaget's imply a critical-period hypothesis (Connolly 1973). The hypothesis has been expanded to include three major aspects of postnatal development: (1) the effects of early experience; (2) the establishment of basic social relationships, in particular the formation of attachment; and (3) learning.

Critical Periods and Early Experience

Over the last 20 years, an extensive literature on the effects of early experience has accumulated (Newton and Levine 1968). Not only can genetically based characteristics be extensively modified by early experience, but early experiences are one of the principal sources of individual differences in behavior.

A review of sensory deprivation studies in animals suggests that there is a genuinely critical period during which suitable experiences must occur if the visual system is to function normally. Rearing laboratory animals in the dark results in neuroanatomical and neurochemical changes that lead to later defects in visuomotor coordination and degenerative changes in the retina, the lateral geniculate body of the thalamus, and the granular and supragranular layers of the visual cortex (Riesen 1975). There is a relationship between the time of onset and length of light deprivation and the severity of effects (Rosinski 1977). A few hours of light exposure after the first opening of the eyes reduces the neuroanatomical effects of subsequent visual deprivation (McVicker-Hunt 1979).

A relationship between specific environmental stimuli and physiological change has been demonstrated in experimental work with cats. Exposure to horizontal, vertical, or slanted lines alters cell response in the **lateral geniculate nuclei** and changes the shape of the cortical response (Hubel and Wiesel 1965, Rosinski 1977). If this procedure is carried out for only one eye, a shrinkage of cells in the corresponding lateral geniculate nucleus occurs but at the same time more cells are driven by the normal eye than would be found if binocular vision had not been interfered with (Cynader 1982, Hubel 1976). The critical period for such interference in kittens lasts from two to five weeks (Van Sluyters and Freeman 1977).

Clinical reports and psychophysical studies indicate that there is a similar sensitive period for the development of the human visual system sometime during the first two years and that susceptibility may continue up to four to five years. In anatomical studies of visually deprived dogs, cats, and monkeys, Hickey (1977) describes a period of susceptibility for the parvocellular layer (X cells) of the lateral geniculate nucleus that might extend through the first 12 months; the period of rapid growth occurs in the first six months. Secondly, Hickey suggests a period of susceptibility for the magnocellular layer (Y cells) of the lateral geniculate nucleus that might continue until the end of the second year; the period of most rapid growth occurs in the first 12 months. During development the X and Y cells may compete for synaptic space relaying to cortical cells. By maturing faster, the X cells may gain an advantage that would show up when the system is visually deprived. These mechanisms may play a role in the effects of deprivation on monocular and binocular vision.

Comparisons of how early experiential enrichment and/or deprivation affects brain development in experimental animals support the idea of a sensitive period in early development. The basic model has been to compare pet-reared or enriched conditions (EC) with cage-reared or isolated conditions (IC) as to both biochemical and morphological characteristics of the brain. In general, EC produce a brain that is heavier and thicker, especially in the occipital lobes (Bennett et al. 1964). Weight and thickness have proved to be a function of corresponding differences in dendritic volume, glial density, and size of nerve cell bodies (Greenough 1976).

Similar research paradigms of EC and IC conditions for laboratory-reared animals have also highlighted the importance of EC for improved performance (Cooper and Zubeck 1958, Dennenberg 1968, Forgays and Forgays 1952, Hebb 1949). Conversely, the debilitating consequences of IC appear to be long-lasting. Harlow and Harlow's (1965) famous studies demonstrated that monkeys reared from birth in social isolation are unable to mother successfully in adulthood. The results of most experimental animal studies that include measures of both CNS and behavioral variables support the view that the developing brain is sensitive to the effects of environmental deprivation.

Critical Periods for Basic Social Relationships

The notion of the effects of early environmental deprivation on animal brain structure and early learning has its counterpart in the study of basic social relations.

In human development, the view that maternal deprivation in the first few years of life, through institutionalization or hospitalization, leads to later maladaptive behavior was firmly expressed in the work of Spitz (1945) and Bowlby (1951). They hypothesized a critical period for the development of social bonds that lasted from birth into the preschool years. The estimated length of the critical period varies from author to author. Goldfarb (1943) assumed that the critical period for social bonding terminates at age 3. Bowlby's affectionless psychopaths were found to have been maternally deprived after the first six months, whereas Spitz's studies suggest that the first three months are critical. J. P. Scott (1958) set the critical period for the establishment of social relations even earlier: between four and six weeks. Dennenberg (1968) has suggested that the equivalent of successful use of an enriched environment for the human infant begins roughly at six months. Subsequent reviews of these studies by Orlansky (1949), Pinneau (1955), and Kagan et al. (1978) indicate that the early infancy period may be sensitive rather than critical to the development of social relationships.

The concept of the development of attachment, or filiative, behavior also includes a sensitive period during which infant and mother establish and confirm social relations (Ainsworth 1973). Klaus and Kennel (1976) suggested that the sensitive period for the establishment of social relations occurs during the immediate perinatal period. They attempted to show that mothers who were allowed to interact with their infants immediately after birth later showed more attachment. Bowlby and Ainsworth asserted that a lack of constant mother-infant contact during the first two years would render the children incapable of forming permanent, affectionate bonds. Others have argued that early experience may serve to "tune" the neuroendocrine system, altering the threshold and duration of emotional stress reactions (S. Levine and Mullins 1968).

Ethological studies of imprinting (Lorenz 1970, Moltz 1968) made it clear that, at least in some animals, there is a short critical period for the establishment of social ties. In birds this occurs 20 to 28 hours after hatching, and in dogs it occurs between three and nine weeks (J. P. Scott 1958). The human equivalent of imprinting according to Caldwell (1962) begins soon after birth and can be described as visual pursuit. Visual pursuit is initially based on discrimination and occurs in response to isolated stimuli characterizing the mother. Toward the end of the infant's learning period, responses to far more subtle cues and groups of cues occur in such a way that individuals not possessing the total group of cues are rejected, i.e., anxiety toward strangers arises. The critical period, in this case, is regarded as the length of the learning period required for the establishment of the discriminative filiative response. Such attachment to the mother is usually established between 6 and 9 months of age in human infants.

Critical Periods for Learning

The existence of critical periods for learning was first noticed in children rather than in animals. McGraw (1946) described varying periods for learning different motor activities that depended on the degree of opportunity and stimulation.

Of special interest to neuropsychologists is the concept of critical periods for language acquisition and its relation to cerebral lateralization, discussed in Chap. 4. According to Lenneberg (1967), natural language acquisition can occur only during the critical period that begins at age 2 years and ends around age 14. After puberty, the basic acquisition of language is unlikely to occur because of a loss of cerebral plasticity upon completion of the cerebral lateralization of language function.

Other researchers have questioned Lenneberg's model. Some argue that the development of lateralization is complete by the age of 5 years. While a critical period for language aquisition may exist, its neurological substrata are not necessarily tied to the development of lateralization (Krashen 1973, B. Milner 1975). Still others have placed the critical age for transfer of language functions to one hemisphere at the age of 1 year (Woods and Carey 1979), as discussed in Chap. 4. Kinsbourne (1976) asserted that lateralized functions exist from birth (invariant lateralization).

The case of Genie, an adolescent girl who was isolated for 11 years before she acquired a language, is the most outstanding test of the critical-period hypothesis for language so far. Genie emerged from isolation at the age of 13 years 9 months with no verbal abilities and was faced with the problem of acquiring a first language (Curtiss 1977). Despite this handicap, Genie has shown steady progress in language learning. Her speech is similar to that of normal children with an equivalent mental age. (At 16 years, her mental age was 5 years 8 months.) Her vocabulary is large, but she has difficulty in learning formal rules of language. It appears that Lenneberg's critical period for language learning should be regarded as a sensitive period.

Conceptual Issues

The critical-period concept has been subject to considerable confusion. One reason for this has been its application both to periods during which a specific type of stimulation or experience was beneficial for normal development and to periods during which the organism was susceptible to the harmful effects of noxious stimuli. Colombo (1982) has characterized the differences as need periods versus vulnerable periods. Fox (1970) recommended the use of the term "critical period" for times during which normal development needs to be triggered by stimuli and the term "sensitive period" for times during which the organism is especially vulnerable to harmful influences. Moltz (1973) used the term "contingent" instead of "critical" need and "noncontingent" instead of "sensitive." Unfortunately, none of these divisions serve a heuristically useful purpose since it has not been shown that the two types of periods have different biological bases.

Another conceptual issue relates to what is described as "continuation versus noncontinuation of plasticity" (Colombo 1982). In behavioral development, most examples of deprivation during critical periods show that the effects are followed by some behavioral recovery. Moltz (1973) suggested that critical periods after which the organism has the ability to recover be distinguished from periods after which no recovery is observed. Krashen (1973) proposed "strong" and "weak" forms of the critical-period hypothesis, depending on the amount of plasticity remaining in the developing system after the end of the period. Thus, Moltz and Krashen base their distinctions of critical-period phenomena on recovery from deprivation or adverse experience. Reports of recovery, however, have been behavioral rather than anatomical or physiological.

A third issue relates to the levels of assessment used to measure effect on critical periods. Effects are more clear-cut and time-bound when they are assessed biologically rather than behaviorally.

6.2 THE CONCEPT OF PLASTICITY

The term "plasticity" refers to the capacity of the CNS to adapt or change following environmental stimulation. Two major research issues dominate current discussions of plasticity. The first relates to the concept of developmental plasticity and is supported by studies involving the surgical alteration of neural connections in animals. The second focuses on neural plasticity and on the recovery of function in children and adults.

Developmental Plasticity

Surgical alteration of neural connections in laboratory-reared animals indicates that there is a neonatal period of plasticity. In contrast to the classical notion that afferent cells either degenerate or survive without afferentation after surgical lesions, recent research suggests that afferent cells may form new connections by a process called synaptic reorganization. This process forms the basis of the concept of neural plasticity (Cotman and Nieto-Sampedro 1982, Gazzaniga et al. 1979, Lynch 1974).

Three forms of synaptic reorganization have been observed: sprouting, spreading, and extension (Steward et al. 1973). Gazzaniga and his colleagues have described these three forms in lesion studies of the afferent system of the dentate gyrus in the hippocampus (Fig. 6-3). Sprouting of new axons increases the number of terminals in the normal dendritic area. Spreading is the development of terminals in new target areas. Extension refers to the termination of afferents on cells that are not the normal targets.

Other evidence to support the concept of developmental plasticity comes from animal brain surgery. By artificially manipulating environmental conditions, researchers have been able to show parallel anatomical, biochemical, and physiological changes in the nervous system. Reference has al-

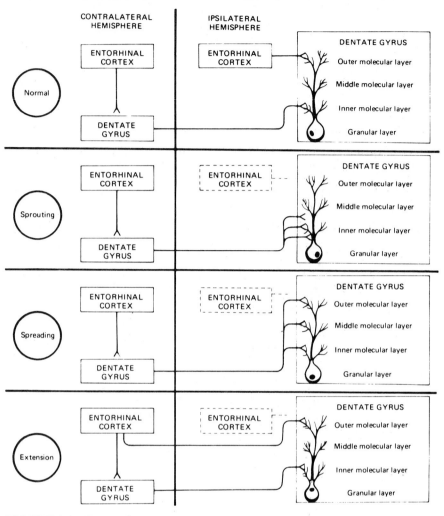

FIGURE 6-3   Types of synaptic reorganization (Gazzaniga et al. 1979).

ready been made to the effects of enriched and isolated conditions on brain weight and size. Hirsch and Jacobson (1975) noted other anatomical changes in the visual cortex of animals reared totally in the dark. These included decreases in the size of the neurons, the length of the dendrites of certain type of cells, and the number of synapses on the dendrites to other types of cells.

The experimental literature indicates that neural plasticity can be seen in:

1. Spared function. For example, the removal of the optic tectum in neonatal hamsters resulted in spared visual functioning in adulthood
   (G. E. Schneider 1974).
2. Maladaptive behavior. Schneider also showed that when the superior
   colliculus is lesioned on one side in neonatal hamsters, retinal projections spread to the remaining side and also to the contralateral tectum.
   As adults, these hamsters made inappropriate turning responses when
   presented with food in certain parts of the visual field.
3. Restoration of function. In the same series of experiments, Schneider
   showed that, when severed, the anomalcus connections to the lesioned
   superior colliculus result in the restoration of normal turning behavior
   (Gazzaniga et al. 1979).

Behavioral Plasticity

A central theme in the study of critical periods in brain development is that
the effects of disturbance are likely to be more profound and longer-lasting
for a growing brain than for a mature brain. Chemicals, drugs, infections,
and other factors may cause gross malformations in the developing brain,
whereas the same insults to the mature brain may produce no demonstra-
ble harm or only a transient effect. There are two exceptions to this. The
first is the greater resilience of the immature brain to hypoxia, which is
explained by its lower metabolic rate (R. O. Robinson 1981). The second
relates to the effects of mechanical disrupting events, such as trauma, infarction, local inflammation, and necrosis (death of tissue). Experimental
studies with animals and clinical reports on humans show that there is greater
functional recovery from these disrupting events if they occur in infancy.
One explanation is that the younger brain recovers better because of its
greater neuronal plasticity (Brunner and Altman 1974), but this view has
been a focus of debate for the last few years.

The mechanisms of recovery of function can be explained by a number
of models (Fig. 6-4), recently reviewed by Chelune and Edwards (1981) and
Finger and Stein (1982). The equipotentiality model of Lashley (1938) was
derived from studies with rats and attempted to account for recovery through
mass action of the remaining parts of the system, which maintain function
because of the inherent redundancy in brain systems.

Another common explanation of the recovery process is vicarious functioning. Munk (1881) suggested that functions lost after injury are taken over
by other areas of the brain, areas whose functions may be sacrificed to ful-
fill the role of the damaged area or areas that had been functionally dor-
mant. This idea is also used to explain the hypothesis of preferential immature plasticity. In young brains, cells are assumed to be less committed
to specific functions so that they can take over the functions of damaged
parts of the brain more easily (St. James-Roberts 1979).

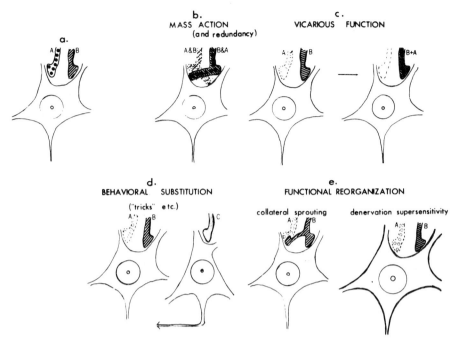

FIGURE 6-4   Models of recovery of function: (a) large neuron; (b) mass action; (c) vicarious function; (d) behavioral substitution; (e) functional reorganization (Goldberger, 1974).

Recovery has also been explained on the basis of "behavioral substitution," i.e., the use of similar neurophysiological processes to achieve the original end by different means (Goldberger 1974).

Denervation supersensitivity is another possible explanation for the synaptic reorganization that may underlie recovery (Stavraky 1961). Following denervation in a damaged area, the remaining fibers or postsynaptic processes may become supersensitive to residual neurotransmitters. It is possible that small amounts of neurotransmitters leaking from prelesion neurons could activate postlesion pathways. As a result, new synaptic connections and functional restoration might be achieved (Tsukahara 1981). The synapse renewal can be viewed as an extension of the "natural synapse turnover," which has been demonstrated for both the peripheral and various parts of the CNS in animals, especially in periods of hibernation or pregnancy and in response to environmental changes to increase or decrease specific activity (Rutledge et al. 1974, Thorbert et al. 1978).

Von Monakov (1911) formulated the concept of **diaschisis** to help explain recovery. He suggested that damage to one part of the nervous system deprives other areas of normal stimulation and leads to a state of shock. With recovery, the undamaged portions of the brain resume normal functioning. Some support for this theory from cerebral blood flow and metabolic studies has been reviewed by Hécaen and Albert (1978).

It is commonly assumed that age is a crucial factor in neuronal plasticity, though some investigators have recently challenged this view. Those who consider age an important variable argue that functional localization is poorly defined in the young infant. If there is enough unallocated reserve in the cortex, cognitive functions can be assumed by areas not traditionally serving this role, i.e., by vicarious functioning. The early experimental work of Kennard (1938) supported the notion of greater neural plasticity in infants. Her findings showed that unilateral lesions in the precentral (motor) cortex of newborn monkeys have minimal effects compared with the same lesions in adults. The contralateral and ipsilateral motor areas seem to take over for the damaged tissue. At the age of 2 months, the animals appeared undamaged in contrast to the adult monkeys, who were permanently hemiplegic. Later studies (Kennard 1942), however, showed that lesioned infant monkeys tested in adulthood had learning deficits, thus refuting the idea of full neural plasticity in infants.

The question of whether the immature brain is less vulnerable to injury was taken up again by Goldman (1974) and others (see Rakic and Goldman-Rakic 1982). Goldman showed that removal of the dorsolateral prefrontal cortex in both infant and adult monkeys led to different effects. Learning in the infant was unaffected, whereas the adult failed to learn. Follow-up of the infant monkeys, however, again demonstrated that learning deficits can emerge later. Goldman offered an alternative explanation to the idea of neuronal plasticity of the immature brain and suggested that selective parts of the cortex are preprogrammed for tasks that are taken up at different ages. She hypothesized that the dorsolateral prefrontal cortex is not used to solve delayed-response tasks in the infant monkey but develops that function later (R. O. Robinson 1981).

The concept of plasticity in the immature brain has been extensively applied to studies of language acquisition and hemispheric lateralization, particularly studies of infantile hemiplegia, hemispherectomy, and childhood aphasia. Careful scrutiny of these studies suggests that the degree of plasticity may be related to the site, nature, and severity of the injury.

Basser's (1962) work with hemiplegic subjects has been put forward to support the hypothesis of greater neural plasticity in infants. In this study of 102 children and adults with onset of hemiplegia in infancy, verbal performance was unaffected by the side of hemispheric damage and age at onset of hemiplegia. Equally optimistic results were reported by Obrador (1964), who described intact sensory motor functions, praxis, and language, no matter which hemisphere was preserved. In a comparison of residual function following hemispherectomy for tumors in adults and for intractable epilepsy in children, W. J. Gardner et al. (1955) noted greater deficits for adults.

Similar reports of lessened impact on young children following hemispherectomy were reported by Krynauw (1950), Cairns and Davisdon (1951) and Hillier (1954) (Chap. 17).

More recent studies by Isler (1971) showed serious neurological sequelae and motor, sensory, and intellectual deficits in a group of hemiplegic children. Annett (1973) found that 41 per cent of hemiplegic children with left hemispheric damage had special problems, compared with 15 per cent of children with right hemispheric damage. Language difficulties in complex tasks following left hemispherectomy were also reported by Dennis and Kohn (1975). In a study of clinical recovery from childhood aphasia using subtle language tests, Woods and Carey (1979) also demonstrated continuing language deficiencies in these children. In sum, recent studies have found only limited evidence for greater neuronal plasticity following early lesions in children.

7

Disconnection Syndromes

Just as dysfunction in a cortical region of cell bodies can lead to behavioral disturbance, so can lesions of connections between cortical regions. A **disconnection syndrome** is defined anatomically as "the effects of lesions of association pathways, either those that lie exclusively within a cerebral hemisphere or those that join the two halves of the brain" (Geschwind 1965, p. 242). Thus, a disconnection syndrome is the result of a lesion of either cortical association fibers, which connect cortical regions within a hemisphere, or commissural-interhemispheric fibers, which connect similar regions in the two hemispheres (Pandya 1975). The behavioral effects of such disconnections are relatively predictable when they occur after brain damage in adults (Dimond 1975, Geschwind 1970).

7.1 DISCONNECTION SYNDROMES IN ADULTS

The early history of the concept of disconnection syndromes has been reviewed by Dimond (1972b), Gazzaniga (1970), Geschwind (1965, 1970, 1975), and Joynt (1974). Wernicke (1874) introduced this concept when he predicted that an aphasic syndrome (conduction aphasia) could result from the disconnection of the sensory speech zone from the motor speech area by a single lesion in the left hemisphere. Déjerine (1892) first described definite symptoms resulting from a lesion of a commissural system, the corpus callosum, when he presented a case of **alexia** (loss of the ability to read) **without agraphia** (loss of the ability to write). The patient had a lesion in the left occipital lobe, blocking sight in the **right visual field (hemianopia),** and in the splenium of the corpus callosum. Dejerine interpreted this case as a disconnection of the speech area in the left hemisphere from the remaining right visual cortex. As a result, the patient could read correctly using the right visual cortex but not the left. However, the information from the right

105

visual cortex could not be transmitted to the speech area because the corpus callosum was damaged.

A few years later, Liepmann (1900–08) demonstrated in several patients
disconnections that led to disorders of voluntary movement (apraxias). In
1937 Trescher and Ford described a patient in whom the posterior half of
the corpus callosum was sectioned during the surgical removal of a colloid
cyst of the third cerebral ventricle. The resulting behavioral deficits, including loss of the ability to name letters placed in the left hand or read in
the left visual field (hemialexia), were attributed to a disconnection syndrome.

"Split-Brain" Studies

In 1940 Van Wagenen and Herren sectioned the corpus callosum, either
partially or fully, in ten patients for the relief of epileptic seizures. Their
reasoning was that this would stop the spread of the seizure across the
hemispheres through the corpus callosum. The surgery successfully limited
the seizures, and disturbances in behavior were minimal and temporary.
Akelaitis and his colleagues (1940–44) reported an extensive series of such
split-brain patients who showed little evidence of deficits in psychological
test performance or everyday behavior. The work of Akelaitis and Van
Wagenen, therefore, seemed to argue against lasting behavioral disconnection symptoms resulting from the commissurotomy.

The impetus for further study of disconnection effects came from animal
experiments conducted by Sperry and Myers in the 1950s (reviewed by
Sperry et al. 1969). They split both the optic chiasm and the cerebral commissures in cats and found that each of the two hemispheres could be trained
independently. However, they had to go to great lengths to obtain these
results. After splitting the chiasm and corpus callosum, they covered one
of the cat's eyes, thereby restricting visual input to only one hemisphere
since it could not be relayed either by the commissures or by the visual
system. They then presented certain discriminations to the cats, which were
learned almost normally. However, when subsequently the opposite eye
was covered to test for residual memory of the discriminations, no learning
could be demonstrated. In this way Sperry and Myers showed that the
hemispheres could apparently function independently of each other and
suggested that the normal role of the cerebral commissures is to transfer
information between hemispheres. Their vivid animal demonstration of disconnection symptoms resulting from a split corpus callosum forced a reexamination of corpus callosum sections in humans.

Two neurosurgeons, Bogen and Vogel, reported in 1962 the case of a
patient who underwent commissurotomy in a successful attempt to control
epileptic seizures (reviewed by Bogen 1979). Encouraged by the results,
they performed split-brain operations in other severely epileptic patients.
Sperry and his associates then began extensive psychological studies of these

patients. They developed new techniques, appropriate to humans, that allowed strict lateralization of visual and somesthetic stimuli to one hemisphere and demonstrated many of the disconnection effects predicted by the original theory, such as an inability to transfer certain types of information between the hemispheres (Sperry et al. 1969). Geschwind and Kaplan (1962) identified similar human disconnection symptoms in a patient with a tumor on the corpus callosum.

In 1965 Geschwind reviewed much of the early evidence for disconnection effects and presented the case for the use of anatomical knowledge in the prediction of symptoms resulting from fiber tract disruptions. His monograph has been influential in contemporary neuropsychology because it argues for a strict localizationist (or "connectionist") view of brain structure and function, a view not fully accepted by many neuropsychologists at that time and still debated.

Types of Disconnection Syndromes

Disconnection syndromes in adults can be divided into two major groups (Geschwind 1970): (1) those resulting from lesions of interhemispheric commissures, i.e., the corpus callosum and/or the anterior commissure, and (2) those resulting either from lesions of association pathways within one hemisphere or from a combination of lesions of association pathways with other lesions.

Commissural disconnection syndromes in adults usually result from surgical intervention, tumor, or interruption of the blood supply to the corpus callosum or immediately adjacent structures. The full syndrome includes (a) inability to match a stimulus object held in one hand to an object held in the other hand, (b) inability to match an object seen in one visual field to one seen in the other field, and (c) several disabilities restricted to the left side of the body related to the presence of speech in only one hemisphere, such as inability to carry out verbal commands with the left hand, inability to name objects placed in the left hand, and inability to write legibly with the left hand. These deficits have been consistently demonstrated in a number of patients and are interpreted as evidence that information is not transferred from one hemisphere to the other (Bogen 1979, Gazzaniga 1970). However, specialized tests are needed to demonstrate these deficits, and they are not seen in every patient (Trevarthen 1975). Quantitative differences in the ability to name by touch or on sight have been reported by Spreen et al. (1966), suggesting that the results of disconnection are not necessarily an all-or-none phenomenon.

Disconnection syndromes resulting from lesions in other association pathways have not been studied as extensively as the callosal syndromes. Two examples of the former type are alexia without agraphia (**pure word blindness**), which Dejerine first described, and conduction aphasia as originally postulated by Wernicke. Writing to dictation—spontaneously and by copying—is preserved in the former syndrome, but patients cannot read what they have written. A combination of lesions in the left occipital (visual) cortex and the splenium of the corpus callosum is usually found. Hence, the transfer of visual information (available only in the right hemisphere because of the left occipital lesion) to the reading (posterior language) area of the left hemisphere is disrupted.

In **conduction aphasia** the patient generally has normal or only mildly defective comprehension of written or spoken language and fluent though paraphasic speech (substituting or reversing phonemes, syllables, or whole words) with striking difficulty in repeating phrases spoken by the examiner (Damasio and Damasio 1980). The lesion spares Wernicke's area of the superior temporal region as well as Broca's area in the inferior frontal gyrus but typically involves the **arcuate fasciculus** (a fiber tract in the supramarginal gyrus) connecting these two areas (see Damasio and Damasio 1980 for other lesions). Since Wernicke's and Broca's areas are intact, language comprehension and speech output are both preserved. However, the pathway for speech running from Wernicke's area through the arcuate fasciculus to Broca's area is damaged, thus accounting for the aphasic aspects of speech as well as the peculiar defect in repetition.

7.2 COMMISSURAL DISCONNECTIONS IN CHILDREN

For a number of reasons—in particular, compensatory mechanisms and development—disconnection syndromes have not been adequately demonstrated in children. In reviewing behavioral effects of lesions of the connections between cortical areas in children, however, we shall follow the division into two types of disconnection syndromes, as we did for adults, to permit a comparison of the adult and childhood syndromes.

Surgical Disconnection

Commissurotomies for epilepsy are rarely performed in children. One report (Luessenhop et al. 1970) indicated that for three older children (two aged 3 years, one aged 7 years) the procedure was very effective in controlling seizures. A fourth child (age 4 months) continued to have seizures, possibly because they were bilateral in origin. The authors suggested that there were no obvious behavioral disconnection syndromes in these children, although subtle testing was not carried out. However, a tendency to neglect and even deny the left arm for several months after the surgery was noted in the seven year old.

Benes (1982) has reported preliminary results on the neurological and neuropsychological sequelae of transcallosal disconnection surgery in 15 children with a mean age of 10 years. The surgery was performed in most cases to remove a tumor located in the midline of the brain below the corpus callosum. The surgical approach therefore disconnected most of the commissural fibers. Benes did not use standardized psychometric tests to evaluate these cases postoperatively but does report several disconnection symptoms similar to those observed in the adult disconnection cases (Campbell et al. 1981). Following the operation, the patients were described as showing signs of tactile anomia and apraxia in the hand, as well as such other symptoms as hypokinesia and loss of recent memory. However, this brief report does not quantify the findings or state the number of children in whom these signs appeared.

Research on the effects of neonatal sectioning of the corpus callosum in young animals suggests that subtle disconnection signs are evident (Jeeves 1972), similar to those observed in the Benes (1982) study. A recent report by Geoffroy et al. (1983) reports that sectioning of the corpus callosum (rather than complete commissurotomy) was successful in controlling seizures in 14 children. The authors report that surgical morbidity was reduced and that electrophysiological and psychological function, especially memory, improved more than in reported cases of commissurotomy.

Agenesis of the Corpus Callosum

Agenesis of the corpus callosum is a condition in which the corpus callosum fails to develop properly (Slager et al. 1957). Though rare, callosal agenesis has been studied extensively by neurologists and neuropsychologists interested in disconnection effects in children (Grogono 1968, Harner 1977, Shapiro and Cohen 1973).

NEUROLOGICAL DATA   Callosal agenesis is thought to result from an arrest in the development of the primitive **commissural plate,** which forms in the second week of human fetal life (Dignan and Warkany 1977, Harner 1977, Loeser and Alvord 1968a, 1968b). Two main forms have been described: total agenesis, in which all the fibers of the corpus callosum are absent, and **partial agenesis,** in which some callosal fibers remain and develop anteriorly (Ettlinger 1977). The difference between the two is attributed to different timing in the arrest of development (Harner 1977, Loeser and Alvord 1968a). The cause of the arrest in development is thought to be mechanical, infectious, or possibly hereditary (Lynn et al. 1980).

Other defects often associated with callosal agenesis include those of midline CNS development, such as **holoprosencephaly** (failure to develop the cleavage of the prosencephalon), cysts of the septum pellucidum, and nonmidline CNS defects, such as **microcephaly,** a radial patterning of sulci in the hemispheres, and defective cortical lamination. These associated defects may sometimes be sufficient to explain the behavioral deficits of patients with callosal agenesis. The condition appears to produce a unique pattern of cerebral organization. Bossy (1970) and Stefanko and Shenk (1979) have demonstrated the occurrence of an extra bundle of longitudinal fibers **(Probst's bundle)** running in the medial wall of either or both hemispheres.

Loeser and Alvord (1968a) suggest that these fibers represent the decussating axons which normally would have crossed the midline as commissures but which under this condition terminate ipsilaterally. If this is the case, then callosal agenesis would represent a failure to develop the major interhemispheric connections rather than just an absence of the corpus callosum.

BEHAVIORAL STUDIES   Callosal agenesis in children allows tentative behavioral comparisons between disconnection syndromes in adults and children. Many behavioral studies of these children, often similar in form to adult split-brain studies, have been conducted. One obvious limitation of direct comparisons and of application to normal brain functioning lies in the pathological conditions of the patients; the split-brain data are based upon a neurologically abnormal population (epileptics) and the callosal agenesis patients often show accompanying neurological or behavioral deficits, such as low IQ and enlarged ventricles. Another limitation of such comparisons is that children born with incomplete commissures acquire behavioral patterns without these connections whereas adults with commissurotomy have a long history of development with intact connections. Hence, split-brain surgery and callosal agenesis are two very different situations. Much of the behavioral work with acallosal children has been summarized by Chiarello (1980) and A. D. Milner and Jeeves (1979).

Russell and Reitan (1955) studied a 19-year-old, mentally retarded acallosal girl with a number of psychological tests. They noted an inability to sustain focused attention on any task that required more than 10 seconds. The girl had trouble on a task involving bilateral transfer of learning from the dominant to the nondominant hand. She also had general visuomotor coordination problems.

Several psychological studies of acallosal children by Jeeves (1965a, 1965b, 1969, 1979) demonstrated deficits in bimanual coordination. This series of patients had below-average intelligence and impaired visuomotor coordination and were generally considered clumsy. They showed problems with bimanual coordination and slowing of **"crossed" reactions** (those involving interhemispheric transfer) compared with "uncrossed" reactions, as well as an inability to transfer movement aftereffects (Dixon and Jeeves 1970). Kinsbourne and Fisher (1971) could not corroborate these reaction-time differences in a 16-year-old boy with callosal agenesis. They suggested that the fact that Jeeves's subjects had both hands on the reaction-time key may have enhanced differences in the crossed condition because of response competition between the two hands. Thus the differences could have been, at least in part, an experimental artifact. Jeeves (1965b) and Reynolds and Jeeves (1974, 1977) countered that rather than looking for dramatic impairment of functioning in these patients, we should expect relative inefficiency.

Solursh and colleagues (1965) reported the case of a 14-year-old acallosal boy with an IQ of 107 whom they compared with ten control subjects on several psychological tasks. His initial learning of transfer from the contralateral to the ipsilateral hand on a tactual formboard was impaired, but his "overlearning" performance was not affected. He did show some other problems with integration of information across the midline: he could not tap correctly with one hand the same number of times he had tapped with the other hand, although he could identify objects by name and by pointing equally well with either hand. No deficits on a dichotic auditory task or with lateralized visual field presentations were found.

Lehman and Lampe (1970) studied nine cases of callosal agenesis, mainly with tactile tasks. They found that the patients were unimpaired on visual tasks but failed to show transfer of tactile maze learning, whereas controls had no difficulty on any of the three transfer tasks. Sheremata et al. (1973) failed to show any defect in interhemispheric transfer in a 51-year-old male acallosal patient.

In marked contrast to their findings with split-brain patients, Saul and Sperry (1968) reported normal test scores on a variety of measures for a 20-year-old college student with callosal agenesis. All of the cross-integration tasks were essentially normal. Dimond (1972a) noted that in this patient the anterior commissure was enlarged to 1.5 times its normal size, which may have aided cross-integration.

No auditory deficit was found in dichotic listening tasks given to acallosal patients by Bryden and Zurif (1970) and by Ettlinger et al. (1972). In a comprehensive series of studies, Ettlinger and colleagues (1972, 1974) could show no difference between agenesis and control groups on visual and tactile, crossed and uncrossed tasks. Their results are somewhat clouded, however, by the inclusion of both complete and partial callosal agenesis patients in their experimental group; these types of patients may differ in the extent of remaining abilities.

Several acallosal patients ranging in age from 19 to 30 years were tested by Ferriss and Dorsen (1975). Low intelligence and deficits in bimanual coordination, in transfer of kinesthetic learning, and in complex visuomotor performance were found. The usual laterality differences for language were absent. Ferriss and Dorsen suggested that in acallosal patients each hemisphere duplicates the functions of the other hemisphere in order to compensate for the loss of the corpus callosum.

Dennis (1976) gave two acallosal children a series of tactile discrimination tasks both for same- and for opposite-hand comparisons and contrasted them with two hydrocephalic and two normal control subjects. The children were asked whether one or two fingers had been touched with the eraser end of a pencil and, if it was two, how many fingers were between the fingers that had been touched. The tasks require both discrimination and accurate localization. In a second experiment, the children were asked to identify common objects, letters, and simple shapes as being the same or different, with the same or the opposite hand. They were then touched with a fairly thick nylon filament and asked which part (distal or proximal) of four fingers had been touched. Dennis found that acallosal patients were deficient in transfer of information from one hand to the other. However, they also had difficulty in identifying the locus of stimulation on the same hand even though they could discriminate one- and two-finger stimulation accurately with either hand. She suggested that subjects with callosal agenesis lack inhibitory activity normally mediated by the corpus callosum, which is necessary to acquire differentiated sensation and movement for each hand. Apparently, acallosal patients can compensate during interhemispheric transfer with their presumed alternate brain organization (i.e., a possibly bilateral functional development). However, they could not adequately differentiate sensations in the same hand. Using results of more sophisticated language tests, Dennis (1981) concluded that one behavioral function of the corpus callosum during development is to suppress ipsilateral information. This theory, based only on case studies, should be interpreted with some caution.

In a neuropsychological examination of two acallosal preschool-age children, M. Field et al. (1978) found low intelligence, impaired visuomotor coordination, and impaired bimanual coordination. One of the patients showed more disconnection symptoms than the other. Gott and Saul (1978) examined two 19-year-old acallosal patients with sensitive neuropsychological tests. The two patients did not demonstrate the major defects of cross-integration reported after commissurotomy. Pirozzolo et al. (1979) described a 60-year-old acallosal man with normal intelligence who showed no evidence of a disconnection syndrome.

More recent case reports include those of A. Martin (1981), Teeter and Hynd (1981), Sauerwein et al. (1981), and Lassonde et al. (1981). Sauerwein and his colleagues studied two siblings, an 18-year-old girl and a 10-year-old boy, who both showed total agenesis of the corpus callosum. They administered an extensive series of kinesthetic, somesthetic, and motor bimanual integration tasks and compared the results with those of matched controls. There were no differences between the acallosal and the control subjects on any of the transfer tasks; both acallosal subjects, however, were slow in bimanual operations. The authors suggested that, rather than assuming a bilateral organization of functions in these patients, increased use of ipsilateral and/or subcortical pathways should be considered as a more plausible explanation for the absence of disconnection symptoms.

A. Martin (1981) analyzed the visual processing skills of a 22-year-old male with callosal agenesis. This subject could name letters presented to the sides of the visual field better than he could localize them. Martin suggested that the anterior commissure could be capable of transferring information on the characteristics of such stimuli but that spatial information might be carried only by the posterior regions of the corpus callosum, which were absent in this patient.

In an extensive review of the cognitive functioning of 29 reported cases of agenesis of the corpus callosum, Chiarello (1980) addressed two basic questions: do acallosal subjects manifest split-brain symptoms and is the corpus callosum necessary for the establishment of lateralization? In answer to the first question, many behavioral studies indicate that, unlike commissurotomy cases, acallosal patients show very few symptoms of disconnection, but lasting impairment in visuo- or spatial-motor functioning often accompanies callosal agenesis. With regard to the second question, Chiarello concluded that there is no definite evidence that the corpus callosum is needed for lateralized development of functions, although it may play a role in satisfactory performance of some lateralized functions once they are established.

7.3 IMPLICATIONS

Disconnection syndromes are still to some extent a theoretical concept in developmental neuropsychology. Their presence in children cannot be demonstrated with certainty, even though cases of agenesis of the corpus callosum lend some support to the concept. Explanations for the failure to find disconnection syndromes in children generally invoke the concept of plasticity or reorganization of function (Chap. 6). In addition, several **compensatory mechanisms** have been suggested, particularly in regard to commissural disconnections (Chiarello 1980, Gott and Saul 1978, Jeeves 1979).

Among the proposed behavioral strategies is **cross-cueing.** This involves the subtle communication of information from one hemisphere to the other by a learned maneuver, such as tapping the object on the table, thereby sending auditory information to the other hemisphere. Gazzaniga (1970) describes several elegant examples of cross-cueing in his split-brain patients. Generally, such behavioral strategies do not satisfactorily account for the paucity of disconnection effects in children since one would expect improved performances (due to practice) over time. In a long-term follow-up of two acallosal patients, Jeeves (1979) showed that essentially the same pattern of disconnection deficits was present after 15 years.

Among the possibilities for reorganization of brain function that have been suggested are (a) bilateral representation of function in each hemisphere, i.e., **"equipotentiality"** (Ferriss and Dorsen 1975, Sperry 1970), (b) increased use and elaboration of ipsilateral pathways (Dennis 1976, Jeeves 1979, Reynolds and Jeeves 1977), and (c) increased use of noncallosal commissures, such as the anterior commissure (Ettlinger et al. 1972, 1974; Gott and Saul 1978; A. D. Milner and Jeeves 1979). While each of these neurological mechanisms could account, at least in part, for the lack of disconnection symptoms in children, none can explain all the varied findings satisfactorily. However, they are not mutually exclusive, and there could be individual differences in the cases that would make an explanation by one or the other mechanisms more satisfactory (Chiarello 1980).

III

DISORDERS OF
DEVELOPMENT
AND THEIR CONSEQUENCES

This part of the book deals with the link between neural development in early life and factors that interfere with it. Some of these factors, such as gross malnutrition of the mother, lack of breathing at birth (asphyxia), severe illness of the mother during pregnancy, or serious brain damage during birth, are obvious causes of developmental abnormalities; they often result in abortion or a stillborn child. Other factors, such as a mild infection of the mother during pregnancy or premature birth, are more subtle. Whether gross or subtle, however, these influences do not always lead to predictable consequences in impaired function of the child.

This section provides an overview of such factors along the lines established by epidemiologists and then examines in detail a few of the important ones whose effects on child development have been fairly well established. The description of even short-term sequelae is often difficult; the results of studies may be quite variable and at times contradictory. To take but one example: early descriptions of the **XYY male,** a clearly defined chromosomal disorder resulting from nondysjunction of the sex chromosome, suggested a definite association with an increased incidence of aggressive and violent criminality since the first studies that found such males with greater frequency in prison populations (Jacobs et al. 1965, Sandberg, 1963). This apparent demonstration of a well-defined relationship between chromosomal error and relatively complex behavioral consequences (as well as greater physical height) but without other disabling results was greeted with enthusiasm by a variety of researchers, especially in psychology and behavioral genetics. After more than a decade of research, a sobering review by D. R. Owen (1972) concluded that no consistent personality or behavioral characteristics can be predicted on the basis of the XYY complement if the effect of using highly selective prison populations is taken into account. Similar negative results were reported by Witkin et al. (1976) after a comprehensive study of 4139 tall young men in Denmark.

115

If relations between influences in early life and later psychological problems or behavioral abnormalities are to be demonstrated, we must rely on the methods of longitudinal research (Chap. 5) and critically evaluate existing long-term follow-up studies. Often this is not a yes-or-no matter but rather a question of exploring the interaction of numerous factors accompanying the growth of the individual. For instance, malnutrition during pregnancy usually exists alongside neglect, poor educational opportunities, an unsanitary environment, and poor health care. To focus single-mindedly on one factor and its effect on prenatal or neonatal neural development under such circumstances would be a mistake, yet it is necessary to carefully analyze each factor individually if we want to move beyond generalities.

8

Classification and Epidemiology

8.1. CLASSIFICATION

Classification systems for childhood disorders are of necessity designed for the convenience of the major disciplines involved. Psychiatrists use a system based on the psychiatric disorders of DSM-III (American Psychiatric Association 1980), psychologists and educators prefer a system designed along the lines of intellectual functioning and impairment, adaptive abilities, or personality characteristics, and for neurologists the neurological disorders are the primary focus. A recent panel on developmental neurological disorders (National Institute of Neurological and Communicative Disorders and Stroke 1979) used a mixed system. Generally, classification systems have coped with the priorities of different disciplines by developing a multiaxial system (Rutter et al. 1975a) that allows users to choose their own primary system while considering another system on a different axis in space.

One simple way to visualize such overlapping systems is to consider medical diagnosis as the horizontal dimension and degree of intellectual impairment as the vertical dimension. A given patient or group of patients could then be described in terms of both the horizontal and vertical axes. For example, ICD-9 (World Health Organization 1977) provides a major code, 31X, for intellectual status indicating the degree of mental retardation (310 borderline, 311 mild, 312 moderate, 313 severe, 314 profound) and then amplifies the major code by specifying the associated physical condition in an additional code following a period (e.g., 311.411 represents mild mental retardation with anencephaly). There is no limit to the number of additional axes that can be used. Such a multiaxial system was incorporated in DSM-III, ICD-9, and the *Manual on Terminology and Classification in Mental Retardation* (H. J. Grossman 1983). These three major classifications are designed to be compatible. The ICD-9 is by far the most detailed and comprehensive medical classification system available. Table

117

TABLE 8-1   Simplified AAMD Classification

.0 Infections and intoxications
   .01 Prenatal infection
   .02 Postnatal infection
   .03 Intoxication

.1 Trauma or physical agent
   .11 Prenatal injury
   .12 Mechanical injury at birth
   .13 Perinatal hypoxia
   .14 Postnatal hypoxia
   .15 Postnatal injury

.2 Metabolism or nutrition
   .21 Neuronal lipid storage diseases
   .22 Carbohydrate disorders
   .23 Amino acid disorders
   .24 Nucleotide disorders
   .25 Mineral disorders
   .26 Endocrine disorders
   .27 Nutritional disorders

.3 Gross brain disease (postnatal)
   .31 Neurocutaneous dysplasia
   .32 Tumors
   .33 Cerebral white matter, degenerative
   .34 Specific fiber tracts or neural groups, degenerative
   .35 Cerebrovascular system

.4 Unknown prenatal influences
   .41 Cerebral malformation
   .42 Craniofacial anomaly
   .43 Status dysraphicus
   .44 Hydrocephalus
   .45 Hydrancephaly

.5 Chromosomal abnormalities
   .50 A group chromosomes (1, 2, 3)
   .51 B group (4, 5)
      Examples: cri-du-chat syndrome, short-arm deletion 5
   .52 C group (6–12)
   .53 D group (13–15)
      Example: trisomy D
   .54 E group (16–18)
      Example: partial short-arm deletion 18
   .55 F group (19–20)
   .56 G group (21–22)
      Example: .560 trisomy G (Downs syndrome)
   .57 X chromosome
      Example: .570 Klinefelter's syndrome (XXY)
   .58 Y chromosome
      Example: .580 XYY syndrome

.6 Gestational disorders
   .61 Prematurity
   .62 Small for date (low birth weight)
   .63 Postmaturity

.7 Psychiatric disorders

.8 Environmental influence
   .81 Psychosocial disadvantage
   .82 Sensory deprivation

.9 Other conditions
   .91 Defects of special senses
   .98 Other conditions (unspecified)

Source: H. J. Grossman 1983.

8-1 presents an abbreviated summary of the Grossman system adopted by the American Association on Mental Deficiency (AAMD). This system is used in this book because it is designed to provide an overview of the main causes of mental impairment and is relatively brief and concise.

The AAMD system begins classification after the decimal point and has three significant digits. The first refers to the major physical or other condition of interest, the second to groups of disorders, and the third to a specific disorder.

The conditions under the first digit begin with physical diseases and insults that have well-established courses and effects on psychological development (.1 to .5) and end with psychiatric, environmental, and other factors that can produce intellectual deficits. It should be noted that environmental influences are strictly defined as psychosocial in nature. Malnutrition is defined as a nutritional disorder (.27) with the type of malnutrition, e.g., protein deficiency, specified by the third digit.

8.2 EPIDEMIOLOGY

Although data on the frequency of occurrence of the disorders included in the AAMD system are available, they come mainly from hospitals and institutions, so that only cases severe enough to require hospitalization or institutionalization are counted. Also, many diseases occur most frequently in Third World or newly industrialized countries where reliable epidemiological data are difficult to obtain. Moreover, such statistics do not necessarily follow the AAMD or ICD system but often use a classification system of their own. Table 8-2 presents some available statistics reorganized as following the AAMD classification. The first column is based on a complete survey of severely and profoundly retarded persons over age 10 in Quebec (McDonald 1973), the second relies on referrals to mental retardation clinics in the United States (DHEW 1973), and the third is based on a survey

TABLE 8-2   Frequency of Occurence of Childhood Disorders

	Severly retarded at age 10, %[a]	Clinics, %[b]	Institutions, %[c] First admission	Residents
.0 Infections and intoxications				
.01 Prenatal infection		2.1	6.6	5.6
.02 Postnatal infection	10	4.0		
.03 Intoxication		1.7	2.2	1.4
Hyperbilirubinemia	1.5	.8		
.1 Trauma or physical agent				
.11 Prenatal injury		1.4		
.12 Mechanical injury at birth	7	2.1		
.13 Perinatal hypoxia		5.3	10.8	8.4
.14 Postnatal hypoxia				
.15 Postnatal injury	1	2.5		
.2 Metabolism or nutrition				
.21 Neuronal lipid storage		.6		
.22 Carbohydrate disorders	21	.5		
.23 Amino acid disorders		.9		
.24 Nucleotide disorders			2.0	1.7
.25 Mineral disorders				
.26 Endocrine disorders		.4		
.27 Nutritional disorders		1.2		
.28 Other				

TABLE 8-2 Frequency of Occurence of Childhood Disorders *(continued)*

	Severly retarded at age 10, %[a]	Clinics, %[b]	Institutions, %[c]	
			First admission	Residents
.3 Gross brain disease (postnatal)				
.31 Neurocutaneous dysplasia		1.1		
.32 Tumors		.2	.6	.4
.33 Cerebral white matter				
.34 Specific fiber tracts				
.35 Cerebrovascular system				
.36 Unknown cause with structural reaction		10.1	15.6	5.9
.4 Unknown prenatal influence				
.41 Cerebral malformation		2.5		
.42 Craniofacial anomaly				
.43 Status dysraphicus		8.4	27.4	23.4
.44 Hydrocephalus				
.45 Hydrancephaly				
.49 Other prenatal causes		.82		
.5 Chromosomal abnormalities				
.50 A group chromosomes (1, 2, 3)				
.51 B group (4, 5)				
.52 C group (6–12)				
.53 D group (13–15)				
.54 E group (16–18)				
.55 F group (19–20)	23	7.8		
.56 G group (21–22)				
.57 X chromosome				
.58 Y Chromosome				
.6 Gestational disorders				
.61 Prematurity		5.3		
.62 Small for date	3			
.63 Postmaturity				
.7 Following psychiatric disorders				
.8 Environmental influences			29.1	35.7
.81 Psychosocial disadvantages				
.82 Sensory deprivation				
.88 Unknown cause for functional reaction		33.3		
.9 Other conditions				
.91 Defects of special senses				
.98 Other (unspecified)			5.6	17.6

[a] McDonald 1973. Frequencies based on severely and profoundly retarded in province of Quebec (IQ less than 50); 5.4/1000 of all live births.

[b] Department of Health, Education, and Welfare, 1973. Covers children served in mental retardation clinics.

[c] Department of Health, Education, and Welfare 1966. Covers all patients in institutions for the mentally handicapped in the United States.

TABLE 8-3   Average Annual Infant Mortality Rates for Selected Causes of Death by Age at Death and Color: United States 1965–1967

Cause of Death (7th Revision—International Classification of Disease)		Mortality rate per 100 000 live births									
		Infant			Neonatal			Postneonatal			
		Total	White	Nonwhite	Total	White	Nonwhite	Total	White	Nonwhite	
Infective and parasitis diseases	(001–138)	30.1	24.4	58.1	3.5	2.8	7.0	26.6	21.6	51.1	
Influenza and pneumonia, including pneumonia of newborn	(480–493, 763)	258.8	188.0	605.5	68.8	54.2	140.4	190.0	133.8	465.0	
All other diseases of respiratory system [a]	(470–475, 500–527)	61.3	48.1	126.1	5.4	4.7	8.7	55.9	43.3	117.4	
Gastritis and duodenitis, etc. [a]	(543, 571, 572, 764)	45.3	24.0	149.4	7.8	3.7	28.0	37.5	20.4	121.4	
All other diseases of digestive system	(530–542, 544–570, 573–587)	30.1	28.1	40.2	19.8	19.3	22.5	10.3	8.8	17.7	
Congenital malformations	(750–759)	342.4	350.3	303.3	227.5	237.7	177.8	114.8	112.6	125.5	
Birth injuries	(760, 761)	196.3	188.2	235.6	196.0	188.0	235.2	0.3	0.2	0.4[c]	
Intracranial and spinal injury at birth	(760)	63.1	55.7	99.4	63.1	55.7	99.4	[d]	[d]	[d]	
Other birth injury	(761)	133.2	132.5	136.3	132.9	132.3	135.8	0.3	0.2	0.4[c]	
Postnatal asphyxia and atelectasis	(762)	387.3	348.0	579.5	380.5	342.8	564.8	6.8	5.2	14.7	
Hemolytic disease of newborn	(770)	36.3	40.6	15.4	36.0	40.3	14.9	0.3	0.2[c]	0.5[c]	
Immaturity unqualified	(776)	363.4	302.6	660.9	361.5	301.7	654.1	1.9	0.9	6.9	
Neonatal disorders arising from certain diseases of mother during pregnancy, etc. [b]	(765–769, 771–774)	366.4	330.5	541.8	348.1	320.0	485.8	18.3	10.5	56.0	
Symptoms and ill-defined conditions	(780–793, 795)	70.1	40.0	217.4	19.5	8.9	71.2	50.6	31.1	146.3	
Accidents	(E800–E962)	84.2	68.8	159.5	10.6	8.1	22.4	73.6	60.6	137.1	
Residual	(140–468, 590–749, E963–E965)	92.3	81.4	145.4	27.8	26.0	36.8	64.4	55.4	108.6	
Certain diseases of early infancy	(760–776)	1426.0	1267.6	2200.8	1398.4	1250.4	2121.6	27.6	17.2	78.7	
All causes		2364.3	2062.9	3838.2	1712.8	1558.1	2469.6	651.4	504.8	1386.6	

[a]Includes gastritis and duodenitis; gastroenteritis and colitis, except ulcerative; chronic enteritis and ulcerative colitis; diarrhea of newborn.
[b]Includes neonatal disorders arising from certain diseases of mother during pregnancy; ill-defined diseases peculiar to early infancy; immaturity with mention of other subsidiary condition; and other diseases peculiar to early infancy not already shown. [c]Rate based on a frequency of less than 20 deaths. [d]Category not applicable.
Source: Department of Health, Education, and Welfare 1968.

of patients in mental institutions in the United States (DHEW 1966). The figures indicate the importance of each disorder in terms of need for public care and intervention, not of actual incidence. It is noticeable, for example, that the widely researched inherited metabolic disorders (such as phenylketonuria), for which medical science has developed reliable screening, diagnosis, and treatment methods, account for only a small fraction of the total, whereas the unknown-cause categories (unknown prenatal and environmental influences) without effective treatment accounts for more than 50 per cent of the total number of disorders. It is likely that the percentage of cases falling into the unknown-cause categories would be even higher if the general population incidence were known.

It should be remembered that incidence rates are based on live births only, i.e., on the surviving population affected by the disorder. The effect of spontaneous and induced abortions and of perinatal death is difficult to estimate. The Medical Research Council of Canada has published partial figures which suggest that survivors are only a small portion of those affected by many disorders. Downs syndrome, for example, is reported to have a frequency of 1.4 live births per thousand but a perinatal death rate of 3.3 and a spontaneous abortion (within 28 weeks of gestation) rate of 15 per thousand. For sex chromosome disorders, the rates are 0.22 per thousand live births, 1.2 for perinatal death, and 7.2 for spontaneous abortion. For children with structural abnormalities (AAMD category .4) the live birth rate is 0.25, the perinatal death rate 1.2, and the spontaneous abortion rate 1.1 per thousand (Kessner et al. 1973). Appropriate death rate figures for a variety of disorders can be seen in Table 8-3. Neonatal mortality in Canada

TABLE 8-4   Causes of Neonatal Death in 1094 Autopsies

| | Weight at birth, grams | | | |
| | Whites, % | | Blacks, % | |
	<2500	>2500	<2500	>2500
Birth injuries	5.1	5.4	6.0	8.1
Sepsis	1.6	1.3	3.1	3.8
Pneumonia	8.0	18.1	15.9	23.7
Hyaline membrane disease	14.7	10.1	17.0	6.5
Erythroblastosis	9.0	8.7	1.3	0.5
Pulmonary hemorrhage	5.4	10.1	5.6	11.8
Subarachnoid hemorrage	4.5	4.7	6.7	4.8
Congenital malformation	24.4	41.6	15.0	8.0
Aspiration of amniotic fluid	35.9	43.6	34.9	42.5

Source: Niswanger and Gordon 1972.
Data based on 1094 autopsies. Total in excess of 100 per cent because more than one condition may be present in the same case.

dropped by more than 50 per cent between 1958 and 1977 (Lee et al. 1982). However, this improvement is almost entirely due to better survival of low-birth-weight infants as a result of improved perinatal medical care. The major causes of death in newborns are listed in Table 8-4.

These figures not only reflect the magnitude of problems related to pre-peri-, and postnatal development but also stress the need to study the early phases of development in normal and affected children and to make a detailed analysis of the neuropsychological deficits.

The discussion in the following chapters of specific factors in abnormal development is restricted to a few examples. This reflects in part our spotty knowledge of these conditions. It would be pointless to describe conditions that have been insufficiently studied and do not have a well-established link with psychological sequelae or to describe multiple examples having similar outcomes. Even within this selection, it will be obvious that clear-cut cause-effect relationships are the exception rather than the rule. Prediction of the exact consequences of exposure to these factors remains hazardous at best.

9

Genetic Disorders

This chapter deals with two major forms of **disorders** often both loosely described as **genetic** but differing widely in origin: inherited disorders, i.e., disorders involving genetic transmission, and chromosomal disorders, i.e., defective formation of the genetic material itself. Inherited disorders are presumed to be carried by certain genes or combinations of genes and are primarily disorders of metabolism (.2 in the AAMD system). Chromosomal disorders (AAMD category .5) form a distinct group of defects of the chromosomal configuration (karyotype), clearly recognizable in the laboratory, that result from unknown or suspected environmental influences. The two groups can overlap to a minor degree since some chromosomal defects may be inherited.

Both inherited and chromosomal disorders are part of the "genetic load" (G. R. Frazer 1962), which has several components: (a) the spontaneous mutation of genes and/or chromosomes, i.e., the extent to which a population is impaired because of recurrent mutations; (b) a genetic incompatibility between the parents that leads to reduced fitness or disorder; (c) genes predisposing to a certain disorder and already present in the population that are combined in sexual reproduction. Hence, the genetic load for defects is present in the population—as part of genetic variability—and cannot be entirely eliminated. "We can only strive to keep it to a minimum; the ideal homozygote will never be found" (G. R. Frazer 1962).

9.1 GENETICALLY TRANSMITTED DISORDERS

A full listing of genetically transmitted disorders would exceed the purpose of this chapter by far. McKusick (1975) provides a regularly updated catalog of genetic disorders (as well as physical and mental characteristics) that follow Mendelian rules of inheritance.

In Mendelian inheritance, **autosomal dominant, autosomal recessive,** and

124

X-linked transmission are distinguished. The term "autosomal dominant" refers to any transmission via chromosomes other than the sex chromosomes that requires only the gene from one parent for the occurrence of the disorder or trait in the offspring. Autosomal recessive transmission requires the recombination of two genes, one from each parent, for the trait or disorder to occur in offspring. X-linked transmission refers to any disorder affecting one sex selectively and hence presumably transmitted by a gene located on the sex chromosomes. Beyond these basic forms of single-factor transmission, inheritance through the interaction of several genes (**polygenic**), inheritance of genetic predisposition (which may or may not lead to the disorder later in life), and inheritance based on single or multiple genes whose expression depends on environmental influences (interactive) have been described.

The most important of the genetic disorders of early development affect metabolism. More than 100 different forms have been described. As Table 9-1 indicates, groupings are usually made on the basis of what specific substance cannot be properly metabolized (e.g., .21 neuronal lipid storage disorder; .22 carbohydrate disorders) or which endocrine function is affected (.26 endocrine disorders). In most cases, the genetic transmission is auto-

TABLE 9-1   Inborn Errors of Metabolism Detected by Screening of Infants Born in Massachusetts Between 1967 and 1973

Disorder	Number screened	Number found	Presumed incidence
Phenylketonuria	1 012 017	66	1:15 000
Hyperphenylalaninemia	1 012 017	60	1:17 000
MSUD	872 660	5	1:175 000
Galactosemia (classical)	588 827	5	1:120 000
Homocystinuria (with hypermethioninemia)	480 271	3	1:160 000
Tyrosinemia (permanent)	438 907	0	—
Iminoglycinuria	350 176	37(?)	1:9000(?)
Cystinuria	350 176	23	1:15 000
Hartnup disease	350 176	22	1:16 000
Histidinemia	350 176	20	1:18 000
Argininosuccinic aciduria	350 176	5	1:70 000
Cystathioninuria	350 176	3	1:120 000
Hyperglycinemia (nonketotic)	350 176	2	1:175 000
Propionic acidemia	350 176	1	<1:300 000
Hyperlysinemia	350 176	1	<1:300 000
Hyperornithinemia	350 176	1	<1:300 000
Fanconi syndrome	350 176	1	<1:300 000
Rickets, vitimin D-dependent (with hyperaminoaciduria)	350 176	1	<1:300 000

Source: Wortis 1980.

somal recessive. Most of these disorders have been discovered fairly recently. Once the substance that cannot be metabolized is known, treatment by proper diet becomes possible. During the last two decades, methods of diagnosis and dietary treatment have developed rapidly (Prensky 1975).

Phenylketonuria

Phenylketonuria (PKU) is a well-known disorder of amino acid metabolism. Discovered by Folling in 1934, it has an autosomal recessive mode of transmission. An enzyme, phenalanine hydroxylase, that normally oxidizes the protein phenylalanine to tyrosine in the liver is altered in PKU and does not function properly. As a result, phenylalanine accumulates in many parts of the body and acts as a toxin to impede development, especially of nerve tissue. Autopsies on persons with PKU showed defective myelination with an excessive number of oligodendrocytes and astrocytes (Knox 1960). The early observation of an overflow of phenylalanine through the kidneys (with an excessive green coloring by phenylpyruvic acid in the urine and a distinctive odor) led to the possibility of detecting the disorder in newborns.

The estimated frequency of PKU at birth is 1 per 18 000 (Tischler and Lowry 1978). Since carriers of a recessive disorder would have to be 300 times more numerous than those actually affected by the disease, approximately 1.3 per cent of the population would be expected to be carriers of one gene for PKU (heterozygotes). The clinical effects described below were by no means uniform in children with detected PKU; further biochemical analyses showed that what appeared to be a single entity may have to be divided into several enzyme mutations and levels of severity (some of which may not require dietary treatment at all).

The clinical picture of the untreated child includes severe mental retardation, decreased attention span, and lack of responsiveness to the environment. Neurologically, these children suffer from seizures, spasticity, hyperactive reflexes, and tremors (Jervis 1963) as well as abnormal EEG patterns. Affected persons are shorter than average and have a small head; light hair, eyes, and skin; and a tendency to develop dermatitis (because the lacking amino acid is involved in pigmentation), though all of these findings are rarely present in a single individual.

Early clinical studies concentrated on the intelligence deficit. Berman et al. (1961) found that treated PKU children were more intelligent than their untreated siblings but inferior to matched control subjects with similar neurological findings. This discrepancy in IQ tended to decelerate with age after treatment was started. Koch et al. (1964) reported similar findings, suggesting that treatment should be started as early in life as possible. Later studies followed up different variants of PKU. Berman and Ford (1970) separated 33 classical PKU cases with blood phenylalanine levels higher than 20 milligrams per 100 cubic centimeters from 24 children with 6 to 9.99 milligrams (variant form) and 7 with less than 4 milligrams (transient variant form). All had been treated promptly. The mean IQ of the total group was 97, that of the variant form children was 111, and that of the transient variant form children was 102. Compared with other family members, the variant and the transient variant forms showed no IQ loss but the classical group showed an 11.5-point IQ drop. This study suggests some decrement in intelligence in classical PKU despite treatment. In untreated cases IQs were usually reported to be well below 50.

Anderson (1975) also reported three different levels of response to increased levels of phenylalanine, suggesting differences in enzyme systems, in the nervous system response to metabolic alterations, and probably in mutations at the major genetic locus as well. In the Collaborative Perinatal Study, similar results were found in 167 PKU cases: with treatment carried out between birth and 6 years of age, neither of the two low phenylalanine blood levels was found to be damaging (Williamson et al. 1981). The neurological status of these children was essentially normal. Average IQ at age 4 was 93, which represented a small but statistically significant difference relative to sex- and age-matched siblings (mean IQ 99). At age 6, the average IQ was 98 for 132 children remaining in the study compared with 103 for matched siblings. Treatment was designed so that half the group (randomly assigned) was intended to maintain a phenylalanine level below 5.4 mg/ml, the other half between 5.5 and 9.9 mg. No IQ differences between the two treatment groups were found. In an attempt to determine the variables most important for outcome IQ, a stepwise regression analysis was done on both treatment variables (phenylalanine measurements and days of exposure to high levels of phenylalanine before treatment was started) and nontreatment variables (e.g., mother's IQ, father's years of schooling, family coping pattern, father's age). Three important factors emerged: (a) mother's IQ ($r = .499$), (b) age when first treated ($r = .327$), and (c) how well parents adhered to dietary regimen ($r = .400$).

Relatively simple and effective screening methods have essentially eliminated cases of untreated PKU in most developed countries. The question of whether rigorous dietary treatment for children with low phenylalanine blood levels may be harmful (because important proteins are removed from the diet) has led to modifications in treatment (Hanley et al. 1970).

Another effect of PKU described in the earlier literature is "unpleasant" behavior. Untreated children were not friendly, placid, or happy; rather they were described as restless, anxious, jerky, tearful, hyperactive, irritable, and sometimes destructive, with uncontrollable temper tantrums, night terrors, and occasionally noisy psychotic episodes (S. W. Wright and Tarjan 1957).

Studies of the specific nature of PKU-related mental deficiency are rare since larger groups of children with PKU are not readily available to be contrasted with other retarded children. Chamove et al. (1973) simulated the condition in rhesus monkeys by feeding them a diet high in amino acids.

They found permanent mental retardation if the diet was fed either pre-natally or for 3, 6, or 12 months postnatally, suggesting that the damage occurs quite early in life. A second study, by Chamove and Molinaro (1978), explored the PKU-related behavior in more detail. Using a food-motivated operant situation, the authors described a "primary frustration reaction to reward that is an energizing emotional response." This excessive and dis-ruptive emotional response to nonreinforcement was similar to the behav-ior of monkeys with frontal brain lesions. The authors call this "an emotion-ality interpretation of the PKU learning deficit" and speculate that the PKU damage is most pronounced in the frontal lobes since this tends to be the last part of the brain to fully myelinate. Hence, extended to humans, one could call this a frontal lobe damage hypothesis to explain the behavior of PKU children.

Partial confirmation of the animal research can be found in a study by Stevenson et al. (1979) in which Rutter's rating scales for teachers and par-ents were used to measure deviance of a neurotic and antisocial type in 99 early-treated PKU children and 197 IQ- and age-matched controls. Twenty-four per cent of the PKU children were identified by their parents and 40 per cent by their teachers (as compared with 20 per cent of the control group) as having either type of behavior problem. Neurotic deviance ratings were found in 31 per cent of the PKU boys and 15 per cent of the PKU girls; 24 per cent of the boys and 13 per cent of the girls were classified as antiso-cial. Of the controls, 24 per cent of the boys and 10 per cent of the girls were classified as neurotic and 12 per cent of the boys and 13 per cent of girls as antisocial.

The subjects were treated PKU children with a mean IQ of 89.7 in males and 83.2 in females. Among girls, the neurotic behavior was more often found in those with IQs below 70. In the higher-IQ ranges, no significant differences between PKU and control groups were noted. Stevenson and collaborators commented that the PKU children had the highest behavioral deviance rate among the groups studied with the exception of children with multiple lesions above the brain stem, who had similar rates. They specu-lated that several factors may be responsible for this high rate:

1. A direct effect of the raised blood phenylalanine levels on brain cell me-tabolism
2. The effect of raised phenylalanine blood levels on brain growth and de-velopment in early life
3. Psychological effects of the prolonged abnormal diet on both the child and the family
4. A genetic mechanism linking PKU vulnerability to psychiatric distur-bances

The length of time for which dietary restrictions are necessary is still a topic of debate. In London, A. Smith et al. (1978) followed 52 PKU children between the ages of 5 and 15 who were returned to a normal diet. Twenty-six of these children had been on the restrictive diet since before the age of 4 months and 26 had begun treatment later. Following the return to a normal diet, a significant decline in mean IQ of five to nine points was observed. Schmid-Rüter (1977) in Germany followed 22 early-treated and 17 late-treated PKU patients after a relaxed diet was instituted but did not find a decline in overall IQ. However, the early-treated group in both studies showed a progressive decline. The late-treated groups showed no further decline after discontinuation of the restricted diet.

As a result of these studies, the recommendation that the special diet be discontinued at age 8 was altered to call for a moderate diet after age 8 to avoid the effects of rising phenylalanine levels, which may occur even then. The importance of the variants of PKU in relation to intellectual deterioration and the need for dietary treatment should be taken into account.

9.2 CHROMOSOMAL DISORDERS

A great many **chromosomal abnormalities** have been described. Table 9-2 presents a partial list of the most frequently occurring syndromes. Basically, they represent an unexplained failure of chromosomes to develop properly (**chromosomal dysgenesis**) during the formation of the oocyte or spermatocyte or during conception and germination, resulting in an irreversibly abnormal chromosome makeup in the embryo. Major forms are (a) the presence of extra chromosomes, for example, in trisomy three chromosomes of a particular type are present instead of two; (b) **translocation,** i.e., mismatched chromosome pairs or portions of a chromosome in the fertilized ovum; and (c) structural abnormalities involving partial or complete deletion of a part of the chromosome, e.g., short arm deletion.

Many fetuses having chromosomal disorders abort spontaneously. Among live newborns, 1 out of 200 has a significant chromosomal abnormality; about one third of these affect the autosomes and two thirds the sex chromosomes. As shown in Fig. 9-1, many chromosomal abnormalities show a relationship to the age of the mother. Chromosomal errors are usually the result of **nondysjunction** (i.e., chromosome pairs may remain attached as two chromosomes in one of the oval cells during the final cell division while the other cell has no portion of the particular chromosome). A similar process may occur immediately after fertilization during the first few cell divisions; this results in some parts of the embryo having a normal complement of chromosomes while other parts have a trisomic complement, a condition described as **mosaicism.**

Chromosomal abnormalities almost invariably result in physical abnormalities. Most of these are easily detected in the newborn, although a strikingly high proportion (25 per cent) of children with Down's syndrome (tri-

TABLE 9-2:   Incidence of Chromosomal Errors in Consecutive Infants

Jacobs et al. (pooled data)		Berger (pooled data)	
Both sexes	Frequency	Autosomal trisomies	Frequency
Trisomy		13	1/7100
13	1/10 000	18	1/3700
18	1/10 000	21	1/670
21	1/1000		
	1/830		

Lubs and Ruddle: Number of chromosome abnormalities in 4500 consecutive newborns

Jacobs et al. (Males)	Frequency	Type of abnormality	Chromosomal abnormalities (No./1000)
Males			
XYY	1/1100	Translocations	1.37
XXY	1/1100	XXY	0.92
Other	1/1700	Trisomy G	0.69
	1/400	XYY	0.69
Females		XXX	0.69
XO	1/10 000	Trisomy D	0.23
XXX	1/1100	Trisomy E	0.23
Other	1/3300	XO	0.23
	1/770		
Euploid autosomal rearrangement Both sexes	1/520		
Anuploid autosomal rearrangement Both sexes	1/2000		
Sex chromosome male and female	1/500		
Autosomal trisomies	1/830		
Autosomal rearrangement	1/420		
	1/179		

Source: DeMyer 1975.

somy 21, also translocation 15/21 and mosaic form of trisomy) are unrecognized at birth.

Mental retardation is a common consequence of chromosomal disorders. The intelligence of Down's syndrome children can range from extremely low to IQs up to 70, but on average falls below an IQ of 50. Speculations about a cerebellar deficit in Down's syndrome suggested by Frith and Frith (1974) have so far found only modest support (Seyfort and Spreen 1979). A recent paper by Zekulin-Bartley (1981) reported a reversed hemispheric dominance for language as explored by dichotic listening experiments.

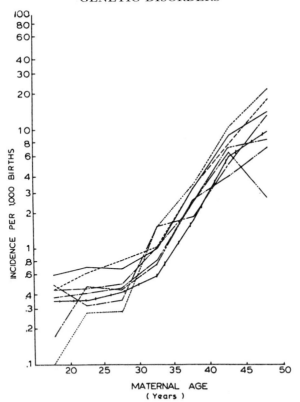

FIGURE 9-1   Incidence rates of Down's syndrome by maternal age at birth from selected studies, 1923–64 (Lilienfeld 1969).

Turner's Syndrome

First described by Turner in 1938, this example of chromosomal disorder drew attention not only because of its physical characteristics but also because of highly specific psychological abnormalities. The basic form of Turner's syndrome results from a missing sex chromosome (usually written as 45,XO) due to nondysjunction in the meiotic division of either parent or in the first meitotic division after fertilization. Hence, no relationship with maternal age has been found. Since the second sex chromosome determines the sex of the individual, Turner's syndrome infants are female. Mosaic forms have also been reported. The physical appearance is characteristic: small in stature (less than five feet tall), undeveloped or poorly developed primary sex characteristics, sexual dysfunction in puberty and adulthood, webbed neck, low posterior hairline, broad chest with widely spaced nipples, and a deformed bend of the forearm (deviating to the midline of the body in extended position and called cubitus valgus). Generally, mosaic individuals have fewer abnormalities. The structure of the brain has not been systematically studied, but there are usually no neurological abnormalities. Spontaneous abortions are quite frequent; in fact, it has been reported that 95 to 98 per cent of XO fetuses fail to survive (Hecht and MacFarlane 1969). Treatment with female hormones has had limited success in furthering sexual development during puberty, although sterility remains.

Turner's syndrome has attracted considerable interest in neuropsychology because of a cognitive impairment that was thought to be highly specific. While mental retardation is rare and only mild if it occurs, striking defects in the perception of form and space have been described. D. Alexander et al. (1966) found a mean IQ of 101 in a sample of 18 cases, but the verbal IQ was 112 on average while the performance IQ was only 81. Factor scores revealed specific disabilities on such Wechsler subtests as Digit Span and Arithmetic (factor: freedom from distractibility) and Block Design and Object Assembly (factor: perceptual organization, J. W. Shaffer 1962). The ability to draw human figures or reproduce geometric designs, map-reading skills, and word fluency usually are clearly defective; Turner's syndrome girls tend to have problems finding their way into and out of buildings or city districts. In a study of 67 Turner's syndrome females, ranging in age from 6 to 31 years and compared with matched controls, Garron (1977) found no increase in the incidence of mental deficiency (mean IQs 96 and 98, respectively) nor was intelligence related to the karyotype (XO or mosaic) or to the number or specific types of physical stigmata. Garron did confirm, however, that these subjects had specific difficulties in tasks requiring spatial and numerical abilities. On average, the performance IQ was 17 points lower than the verbal IQ.

Nyborg and Nielsen (1977) also reported poor scores on tests for the recognition of embedded figures, maze tasks, and the rod-and-frame test, which requires the subject to adjust a luminescent rod within a luminescent frame to the exact vertical position in a dark room; the frame may be tilted to varying degrees. The average error is about 6 degrees from true vertical, but Turner's syndrome females had an average of 12 degrees of error. The authors also reported that estrogen treatment tended to improve rod-and-frame test results.

These findings led to the speculation that the cognitive defect is based on a right hemisphere deficiency (Kolb and Heaton 1975), specifically the right parietal area (Money 1973). This interpretation is based on the view that spatial perception is more closely related to right hemisphere function; it does not explain the deficits in word fluency and the memory-for-rhythm test of Seashore (Silbert et al. 1977). Waber (1979b) conducted a comprehensive examination on 11 teenage to young adult women with Turner's syndrome and 11 controls matched for background, age, and overall IQ.

He found that the patient group performed significantly more poorly on tests of word fluency, perception of left and right, visuomotor coordination, visual memory, and motor learning. They also showed a higher incidence of left-ear advantage on the dichotic listening test, but their performance on other tests (including the perceptual organization factor on the Wechsler test, face recognition, a roadmap directional sense test, the spatial part of the California Test of Mental Maturity, and finger tapping) did not differ significantly from that of the control group. Waber concluded that it is questionable whether a specific defect in spatial ability exists. Rather than using a hemisphere-specific model, she prefers the interpretation that both cerebral hemispheres in the frontal and parietal areas may be involved in Turner's syndrome. Waber takes Luria's theoretical postion that "early alterations in brain development have a generalized rather than localized effect on brain function in later life." She also notes that the performance of Turner's syndrome girls resembles that of prepubertal children; hence the syndrome may reflect lack of pubertal changes or a maturational lag, since all the functions found impaired in patients improve markedly in normal children between the age of 6 and 10 years. Supporting evidence comes from Buchsbaum et al. (1974), who found in Turner's syndrome patients EEG immaturity similar to the EEG patterns of girls 6 to 9 years of age.

One specific finding of interest in Waber's study is the lack of ear lateralization in dichotic listening. Netley (1976) reported similar findings. Both authors suggest that sex hormones may be necessary for the lateralization of language to the left hemisphere. Some reports (Simpson 1976, Trunca 1980) suggest that Turner's syndrome women are socially immature, but it cannot be ruled out that this impression is simply based on the fact that they are short and sexually immature.

Further speculation centers around the possibility that Turner's syndrome may reflect an exaggerated "female" pattern of behavior since visuospatial skills have been reported to be more poorly developed in females generally (Wittig and Peterson 1979). Waber rejects this interpretation since many other nonspatial deficits are present. However, the findings in Turner's syndrome do raise the question of the role of the second X chromosome since this defect is obviously not related to survival. In terms of gender, Turner's syndrome females tend to present rather a neuter category, consistent with their genetic status. Gartler et al. (1973) suggest that the second X chromosome is important in many tissues for the first few cell divisions and that the lack of this chromosome may lead to irregular somatic growth that is reflected both in the physical abnormalities of Turner's syndrome women and in abnormal patterns of CNS development (Rovet and Netley 1982). The second X chromosome becomes inactive during later development in most parts of the body except for the ovaries.

10
Structural Abnormalities

This chapter deals with one major group of congenital defects, the **structural malformations** present at birth. These contrast with the congenital disorders involving physiological functions, such as metabolism, which are discussed in the preceding chapter. Structural abnormalities are usually of undetermined origin; hence H. J. Grossman (1977) refers to them under category .4 as caused by "unknown prenatal influence." One structural abnormality, agenesis of the corpus callosum, is discussed in Chap. 7 because of its impact on neuropsychological theory.

A group of structural abnormalities in which hands and feet are formed adjacent to the shoulders and hips (**phocomelias**) became notorious in the 1960s when about 15 000 babies were born with this malformation before thalidomide, a widely prescribed sleeping medication, was recognized as the teratogenic agent.

Not all malformations are evident upon physical examination at birth. It has been reported that two thirds of the malformations recognized at 12 months were not detected at birth (Myrianthopoulos and Chung 1974). An earlier study by R. McIntosh et al. (1954) indicated that only 4.3 per cent of all congenital malformations were recognized at birth despite the fact that, at 12 months, only 18.1 per cent remained undetected. Unrecognized malformations include some forms of hydrocephalus and microcephaly as well as minor neuroanatomical defects. Depending on the effect on an individual's life, some defects may be discovered only accidentally at autopsy (e.g., heteropia, misplaced groups of nerve cells). **Dandy-Walker syndrome,** which involves abnormal development of the posterior fossa and cerebellum and obstruction of the fourth ventricle, is often recognized during the first two years of life because of increased intracranial pressure, although it is usually not apparent prenatally or immediately after birth. Symptoms may, in fact, not appear until later in childhood and in some instances the condition may remain asymptomatic into adulthood (Lipton et al. 1978). Ultrasono-

134

graphic prenatal diagnosis has recently been reported as successful (Newman et al. 1982). Defects that are of neither medical nor cosmetic consequence (e.g., single palmar crease) have been termed "minor physical anomalies" (Waldrop et al. 1968, Table 10-1). Multiple minor malformations, however, tend to be associated with major malformations (D. J. Smith 1971).

TABLE 10-1 Minor Physical Anomalies and Their Significance in Scoring Weights

Anomaly	Significance
Head	
Fine, electric hair (very fine, does not comb down)	1–2
Two or more hair whorls near crown of head	0
Head circumference 1–1.5 standard deviations above norm	1–2
Eyes	
Epicanthus (vertical skin fold covering or partially covering lacrimal caruncle)	1–2
Hypertelorism (unusually wideset eyes) more than 32 mm according to norm for 7-year-old Caucasians)	1–2
Ears	
Low-seated ears (below line set by nose bridge and outer corner of eye)	1–2
Adherent ear lobes	1–2
Malformed ears	1
Soft and pliable ears (jellylike feel)	0
Mouth	
High-steeped palate (roof of mouth forming an angle rather than an arch)	1–2
Furrowed tongue (one or more deep grooves)	1
Tongue with smooth and rough spots (localized thickening of the epithelium)	1
Hands	
Inwardly curved fifth finger	1–2
Single transverse palmar crease	1
Feet	
Third toe longer than second	1–2
Partial webbing of two middle toes (webbing extending to the nearer toe joint)	1–2
Big gap between first and second toes (with flat base across gap at least the size of half the width of second toe)	1

Source: Waldrop and Halverson 1971.

10.1 STRUCTURAL ABNORMALITIES OF THE CENTRAL NERVOUS SYSTEM

Malformations of the CNS, particularly the brain itself, are naturally of primary importance in neuropsychological development (Pache 1969). The incidence of these abnormalities ranges from 2.5 to 3.0 per 1000 children under the age of 12 months (Table 10-2). Since spontaneous abortions are frequent with these disorders, the recorded incidence represents only a very small portion of the actual incidence. Table 10-2 includes only anencephaly and hydrocephaly, omitting many other brain malformations, such as the relatively frequent microcephaly (Fig. 10-1), and the many faults in development of the bones of the skull, face, and mouth (cranio-facial-oro syndromes), often including malformations of the fingers (digital syndromes).

The many syndromes combining structural abnormalities of the body and head are described in detail by D. W. Smith (1970), Holmes et al. (1972), and Duckett (1981). Many are classified as due to unknown prenatal influences and named after the authors first describing them. Distinctions are made between complete and partial lack of brain development (.411 anencephaly), disproportionately small brain development (.423 microcephaly, micropolygyria), and enlarged head development, often with hydrocephalus (.424 macrocephaly). Primary microcephaly is usually distinguished from secondary microcephaly as follows:

1. The rare, primary form is hereditary with autosomal recessive transmission (Figs. 10-2 and 10-3).
2. Other forms of microcephaly occur secondary to disorders of pregnancy or birth (Figs. 10-4 and 10-5) or associated with chromosomal disorders (e.g., cri-du-chat syndrome, short-arm deletion of a group 5 chromosome).

TABLE 10-2   Incidence of Anencephaly, Spina Bifida, and Hydrocephalus in Newborns

	WHO worldwide[a]	NINCDS[b] Whites	NINCDS[b] Blacks	Male/female ratio[c]
Disorder				
Anencephalus	1.05[d]	0.99	0.24	0.5
Hydrocephalus	0.87	1.4	1.3	NA
Spina bifida without hydrocephalus	0.55 ⎫	0.66	0.68	0.7
Spina bifida with hydrocephalus	0.26 ⎭			
Total	2.47	3.05	2.22	NA

[a] Stevenson et al. 1966.

[b] Myrianthopoulos and Chung 1974.

[c] Slater 1963.

[d] Values in first three columns are per 1000 births.

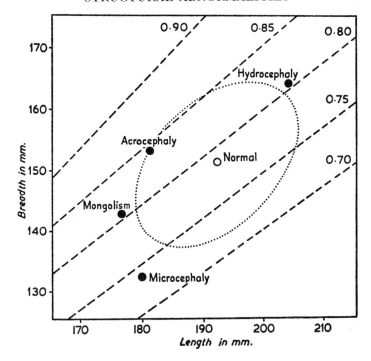

FIGURE 10-1   Mean head length and breadth in adult males (Penrose 1963).

Another group of conditions result from premature closure of some of the bones of the skull (.427 **craniostenosis**). Premature closure of the coronary bones results in a flat, short head (brachycephaly); early closure of the lateral bones results in asymmetric head shape; upward and forward extension of the head, face, and eyes (oxycephaly) results from early closure of all bony connections. Another malformation of importance is **status dysraphicus** (.43), incomplete closure of the membranes surrounding the brain and the spinal cord (the caudal neuropore; Fig. 2-1). Among the forms of this condition are meningoencephalocele (.431), a protrusion of the meningeal membranes and brain through a cranial defect, and meningomyelocele (.432), a protrusion of the spinal cord and its covering membranes through a defect in the vertebral column. Another major form of status dysraphicus that affects psychological development is **hydrocephalus** internus and externus (abnormal enlargement of the skull and the brain ventricles or subarachnoid space). The extent of the hydrocephalic condition is often described by Evan's ratio, defined as anterior horn width divided by internal skull breadth as determined in a CT scan (Fig. 10-6). In hydrancephaly, a special case of anencephaly, there is a failure of cortical development that does not include the lower temporal and occipital lobes as well as increased

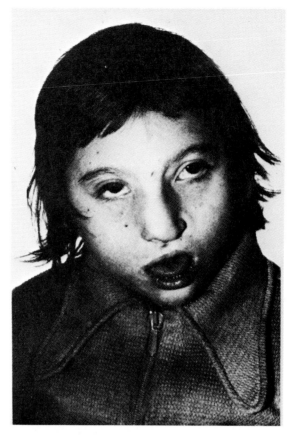

FIGURE 10-2   Microcephaly with damage to chromosome 13. Age 4.5 years; height 96 cm, head circumference 41 cm; cleft lip, jaw, and palate (Neuhaeuser et al. 1981).

cerebrospinal fluid (.45), multiple malformations (.46), and congenital single umbilical artery (.47). For a recent review of congenital neurological malformations, see Icenogle and Kaplan (1981).

10.2 ETIOLOGY

Although structural defects have been associated with some well-defined disorders (e.g., chromosomal abnormalities), the exact causes for most remain unknown. Basically, most CNS malformations are defects of the formation of the neural tube during the induction period (third and fourth weeks of gestation). A fault in the separation of the mesenchymal and neuroectodermal tissue disrupts the normal growth and fusion of the neuroectoderm (neural tube), at the same time often affecting proper bone development from mesenchymal tissue. Other abnormalities result from disorders of nerve cell migration and proliferation during the second through the sixth month of gestation.

What leads to the disorders is still open to speculation. Genetic factors are suggested by the fact that neural tube defects occur less frequently in males and in blacks and that the incidence rate tends to be higher in relatives of affected persons (Carter 1974). Fishman (1976) believes that a multifactorial genetic transmission can be assumed. Wide differences in frequency depending on geographical distribution (e.g., 4.5/1000 in Belfast versus 0.1/1000 in Bogota and Ljubljana) suggest both racial and nutritional factors. Among environmental factors, drugs, irradiation, and excessive intake of vitamins and even of tea, as well as withholding zinc from the mother's diet are related to increased incidence (National Institute of Neurological and Communicative Disorders and Stroke 1979, Table 10-3). A higher incidence among infants born during winter months, firstborns of very young mothers, and the youngest children of older mothers has been reported.

FIGURE 10-3   Tomography in micro-hydrocephaly of a 1-year-old child with postpartem hypoxia; enlargement of ventricular system and subarachnoid space (Neuhaeuser et al. 1981).

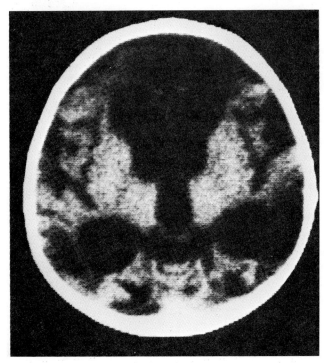

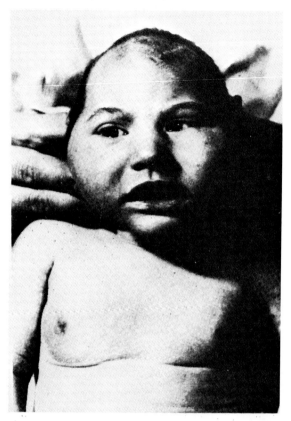

FIGURE 10-4   Microcephaly of exogenous prenatal origin. Hydrocephalus externus, cerebellar hypoplasia. Age 3 months, head circumf. 29 cm; generalized seizures, muscle hypertonus, normal karyogram (Neuhaeuser et al. 1981).

The relationship to maternal infections, especially the cytomegalovirus, is
discussed in Chap. 12.

Finally, it should be noted that retarded brain development in the fetus
affects the neuroendocrine balance. In particular, absence of the hypothalamus leads to lack of growth stimulation and, in addition, to failure to ac-
celerate labor; hence, the anencephalic or microcephalic fetus is likely to
be exposed to additional perinatal stress (Swaab et al. 1978). Except for major damaging infections, none of the genetic or environmental factors have
shown a direct causal relationship; they probably should be regarded as
contributing interactively to the etiology of structural defects.

10.3 DEVELOPMENT OF THE CHILD WITH
MENINGOMYELOCELE

The development of the newborn with a CNS anomaly depends upon the size and location of the defect, especially as it affects brain development. With anencephaly, early death is likely. Microcephaly, porencephaly, and hydrocephalus tend to be associated with developmental retardation, although the degree of retardation is highly variable. Meningomyelocele is chosen as an example here because of its special psychological interest.

Meningocele usually is evident as a sack-shaped bulge in the dorsal region, although in some instances it may be so small as to be undetectable by visual inspection and asymptomatic (spina bifida occulta). The defect is a herniation of the spinal cord and its membranes. It is often referred to as

TABLE 10-3 Known Causes of
Developmental Defects in Humans

Cause	Incidence, %
Known genetic transmission	20
Chromosomal aberration	3–5
Environmental causes	
Radiation	<1
Therapeutic	
Nuclear	
Infections	2–3
rubella virus	
cytomegalovirus	
herpesvirus hominis	
toxoplasma	
syphilis	
Maternal metabolic imbalance	1–2
endemic cretinism	
diabetes	
phenylketonuria	
virilizing tumors	
Drugs and environmental chemicals	2–3
androgenic hormone	
folic antagonists	
thalidomide	
organic mercury	
some hypoglycemics(?)	
some anticonvulsants	
Potentiative interactions	?
Unknown	65–70

Source: Wilson 1973.

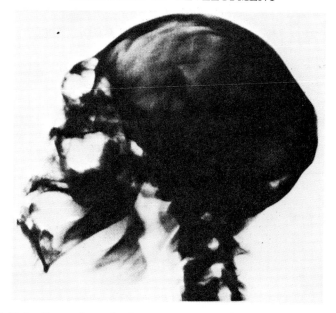

FIGURE 10-5   X-rays (lateral) of a 33-year-old patient with endogenous microcephaly. Height 162 cm, head circumference 45.3 cm (Neuhaeuser et al. 1981).

spina bifida because of the associated lack of closure of the vertebral lami-
nae normally covering the spinal canal. Spina bifida without meningocele
occurs fairly frequently (5 to 10 per cent of all newborns according to Scarff
and Fronczak 1981), but meningomyelocele is relatively rare (5 to 8 per
10 000 in Scandinavian surveys; Hagberg et al. 1963, Jansen 1978). If the
spinal cord tissue is bulging into the sack (meningomyelocele), paralysis may
occur depending on the location along the spinal cord. If located in the sac-
ral region, only bladder and bowel functions may be affected; if lumbar and
lower dorsal regions are involved, paraplegia and sensory loss usually follow. In rare instances, the defect occurs in the upper dorsal or cervical region and produces paralysis and sensory loss in all functions below that level.
Meningomyelocele is frequently accompanied by gross malformation of the
cerebral hemispheres. In all cases, risk of infection is high, although the
hernia may be closed surgically. Mental development depends, of course,
on the magnitude of the cerebral defect.

   Several other abnormalities are frequently associated with meningomyelocele: hydrocephalus occurs as a result of the partial closure of the cerebrospinal fluid ducts connecting the fourth ventricle and the subarachnoid
space; the cerebellum and the medulla protrude into the upper spinal canal
at the cervical level (Arnold-Chiari syndrome); the medulla shows an S-shaped
kinking; parts of the visual and auditory systems as well as some of the cor-

tical gyri remain underdeveloped; aberrant migration of cells during em-
bryogenesis results in clusters of nonfunctional neurons in many parts of
the brain (possibly producing epileptogenic foci).

Pregnancy is usually normal, but early detection by amniocentesis is
possible. Severely affected embryos frequently abort spontaneously. After
birth, the defect is usually closed to prevent infection and damage to the
herniated tissue; the hydrocephalus is shunted by insertion of a drainage
tube to relieve the pressure. Bottcher and colleagues (1978) reported significant reduction in ventricular size of 13 successfully shunted hydrocephalic children.

The subsequent development of children with meningomyelocele and
hydrocephalus has been widely studied. Intellectual functions usually remain at a mildly to moderately retarded level, IQ scores are commonly between 70 and 90 but range widely (Dennis et al. 1981, Lorber 1971, Tew
and Laurence 1972, 1975). As a group, such children tend to show impaired concentration and visuoperceptual difficulties (Miller and Sethi 1971).
Relatively good predictions about later achievement have been made as early
as the second year of life (Fishman and Palkes 1974).

Nielsen (1980) examined a series of 30 unselected meningomyelocele cases
in Denmark below the age of 18 months and attempted to follow them over

FIGURE 10-6   Intellectual performance (expressed as Evans' ratio) at time of investigation in 13 shunted hydrocephalic children (Bottcher 1978).

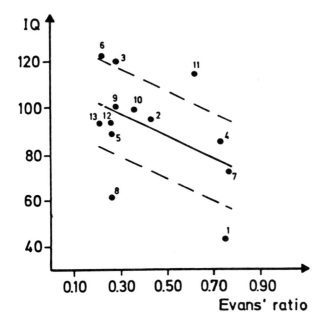

a five-year period. There were 19 girls and 11 boys in the sample. Only four did not require a shunt operation. At the age of 6 to 18 months, Cattell IQs ranged from 25 to 110 with a mean of 81; at age 3 years, the Minnesota Preschool Scale IQs ranged from 50 to 128 with a mean of 91; and at age 6 the WISC IQs ranged from 94 to 117 with a mean of 98 for the eight children remaining in the study. While these group differences may be influenced by sample attrition, those children who were retested on all occasions showed a definite gain in IQ level; correlations between measures ranged from .56 (between 6-month Cattell and 3-year Minnesota) to .84 (between 18-month Cattell and 3-year Minnesota). The authors interpreted the increase as the result of overcoming the early period of surgery with frequent, lengthy hospitalizations. Most studies found no significant sex difference in IQ scores, although Tew and Laurence (1972) found girls more retarded than boys. Shunt insertion tended to be associated with slower psychomotor development.

A recent study also reported lower IQ scores (mean 72) in 128 shunted children with meningomyelocele as compared with 39 nonshunted children (mean IQ 102). However, this difference was almost entirely attributable to the occurrence of CNS infections (ventriculitis) (McLone et al. 1982). Fruehauf (1976) followed 36 hydrocephalic children who were shunted during the first year of life. Retesting in the first grade (up to age 9) showed an increase in developmental quotients for 60 per cent of the children from quotients obtained during the first three years of life; 10 per cent showed a decrease. Children in a subgroup with significant gains had less severe brain damage and early shunting. The developmental quotient was computed from a variety of measures but rose mainly because of improved motor development (Ozeretzki Scale). The IQ remained stable over the years with a mean of 77 for the total group.

Surprisingly, many children with meningomyelocele acquire good verbal skills, although this has been characterized as an ability to learn words and speech at a superficial level. Hadenius and colleagues (1962) were the first to describe the verbal skills of meningomyelocele children as "**cocktail party syndrome**": a facility for chattering without knowing what they are talking about. Schwartz (1974) described such speech as having a "glib, chatty, superficial quality"; the children engage in irrelevant verbal production and may have higher verbal than performance IQ scores (Foltz and Shurtleff 1972). Considering the results of the Nielsen follow-up study discussed above, it is possible that cocktail party syndrome is the result of frequent hospitalizations and illness as well as of frequent physical handling because of paralysis, circumstances providing many more superficial child-adult interactions than retarded children with or without hydrocephalus would normally receive.

Children with hydrocephalus are also reported to show an "uneven growth of intelligence during childhood, with nonverbal intelligence developing less well than verbal intelligence" (Dennis et al. 1981). Dennis and colleagues propose a somewhat different explanation for the relatively good verbal intelligence of hydrocephalic children: although increased verbal stimulation and contact through handling may have a role, the important factor is the impaired development of the vertex and the occipital cortex, which blocks the cerebral aqueduct and results in visual abnormalities, motor deficits, and seizures. The child gains little visuospatial experience and thus develops poor nonverbal intelligence.

Very few reports on later development have been published. In a preliminary study of 119 young people, 89 with cerebral palsy, 30 with meningomyelocele with hydrocephalus, Anderson (1979) found that only 48 per cent were without marked or borderline psychological disorders compared with 85 per cent of a nonhandicapped control group. The incidence of psychological disorder was highest for meningomyelocele girls. The nature of the disorder was most frequently described as neurotic rather than conduct or mixed disorder (72, 15, and 5 per cent, respectively). Misery and depression, lack of self-confidence, self-consciousness, and fearfulness were most frequently mentioned. Ratings of the overall quality of life suggested that 41 per cent led an isolated and lonely life, 38 per cent had a very restricted social life, and only 21 per cent had satisfactory social lives (as compared with 93 per cent of the controls). Dependency on the family was high. Quality of life was closely related to severity of handicap.

10.4 PSYCHOLOGICAL DEVELOPMENT IN CHILDREN WITH OTHER ANOMALIES

Numerous studies of children with other CNS malformations, especially hydrocephalus, have been published. A general finding is the strong association between malformations on the one hand and the development of brain and intellect on the other.

Some debate has arisen about the association between minor physical anomalies—e.g., abnormal head circumference, highly arched palate, single palmar crease, abnormalities of toes and fingers—and the development of intelligence and occurrence of behavior problems. In school-aged boys, hyperactive, disruptive, impulsive behavior has been reported to be associated with the number of minor anomalies. In girls, an association with passivity, low activity level, withdrawal, and chronic anxiety has been noted (Waldrop and Goering 1971, Waldrop et al. 1976). Anomaly scores (based on the number and significance of physical anomalies) were also negatively correlated with IQ, although this was independent of the association with the inhibited behavior in girls.

Minor physical anomaly scores were also elevated in autistic and atypical children, and the degree of disturbance was associated with higher anomaly scores as well as lower IQ. In contrast, neurosis and learning disability in children showed less of an association with anomaly scores (Steg and Rapoport 1975). It is possible that even minor anomalies, though only of a cosmetic significance, may adversely affect the social interaction of the child and that both intelligence and behavior may be influenced as a result. However, the existence of subtle malformations or dysfunction of the brain in these children has not been ruled out.

11

Prematurity and Low Birth Weight

In 1949, a birth weight of 2500 grams or less was accepted by the World Health Organization as the single criterion of **prematurity. Birth weight** is easily measured and universally noted in records, whereas gestational age, the other main index of prematurity, is difficult to determine (Kopp and Parmelee 1979). Mortality and morbidity rates are highest for infants of low birth weight. Premature infants defined according to birth weight, however, constitute a heterogenous group that includes those with congenital abnormalities, those born of mothers of small stature, those born early whose weight is appropriate for age, and those born early who are clearly undernourished for age (Drillien 1964). When it became accepted that not all neonates of 2500 grams or less at birth are premature, the designation **low birth weight** was applied to them instead. With improvement in perinatal and neonatal care and reduced mortality rates, a need for differential diagnosis became increasingly clear, as did the importance of subgroups for understanding etiology, providing medical care, and making prognoses. In response to this need, the WHO in 1961 redefined prematurity to include infants with a birth weight 2500 grams or less who were born before 37 weeks gestation. Thus we have two criteria for prematurity: low birth weight and immaturity. Within this still broad definition, premature infants can be divided into two major subgroups: (a) infants born before 37 weeks whose weight is appropriate for gestational age, designated **preterm AGA,** and (b) infants born before 37 weeks whose weight is low for gestational age, designated **preterm SGA.** The latter are also called small-for-date infants (Eichorn 1979, Kopp and Parmelee 1979).

Cutting across the two major subgroups of premature infants is a third, more recently defined group, identified by **very low birth weight** (below 1500 grams) and referred to as **VLBW.** This heterogenous group includes infants born very early but at a weight appropriate for gestational age and infants who may be born either early or close to term but who suffer from

intrauterine growth retardation (IUGR), which is defined as birth weight falling below the 10th percentile for gestational age. The distinction between preterm AGA, preterm SGA, and VLBW is of more than academic interest because of differences in long-term outcome.

A widely used neurological assessment for the estimation of gestational age is the **Dubowitz scale** (Table 11-1, Figs. 11-1 to 11-4). This scoring system is based on ten neurological signs, related mainly to postures and primitive reflexes (Prechtl and Beintema 1964, Robinson 1966) and to 11 external criteria (Farr et al. 1966).

Despite the refinement of other measures to assess maturity (Dubowitz et al. 1970), birth weight remains a useful indicator, and many studies have focused on the sequelae of low birth weight alone instead of using a combination of criteria (Alm 1953, Caputo and Mandell 1970, Drillien 1964, Harper and Weiner 1965). Keller (1981) argues for a definition of prematurity that involves mortality rates, which are highly correlated with birth weight. Some studies are based on birth weight either below 2500 grams or below 1500 grams (De Hirsh et al. 1966, Knobloch et al. 1956), others

TABLE 11-1   The Dubowitz Scale

	Score
Neurological signs	
Posture	0–4
Square window	0–4
Ankle dorsiflexion	0–4
Arm recoil	0–2
Leg recoil	0–2
Popliteal angle	0–5
Heel to ear	0–4
Scarf sign	0–3
Head lag	0–3
Ventral suspension	0–4
External criteria	
Amount of edema	0–2
Skin texture	0–4
Skin color	0–3
Skin opacity of the trunk	0–4
Amount of lanugo (fluffy hair) over the back	0–4
Plantar creases (on sole of foot)	0–4
Nipple formation	0–3
Breast size	0–3
Ear form	0–3
Ear firmness	0–3
Genitals	0–2

Source: Dubowitz et al. 1970

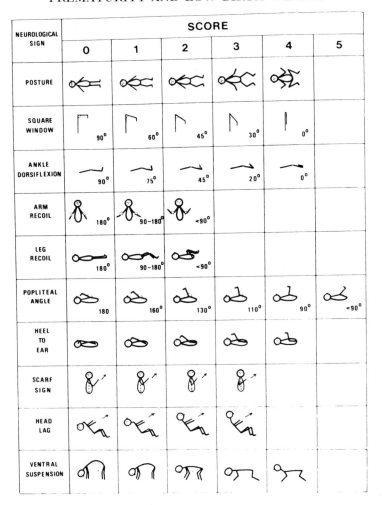

FIGURE 11-1 Scoring system for neurological criteria (Dubowitz et al. 1970). A total score greater than 70 corresponds to a gestational age of more than 43 weeks, of 50 to 39 weeks, and of 20 to 30 weeks gestational age.

on birth weight and gestational age (Kurtzberg et al. 1979), and still others on gestational age (Amiel-Tison 1980) or on a combination of age, weight, and body measurements (Caputo et al. 1981).

11.1 MAJOR RISK FACTORS ASSOCIATED WITH PREMATURITY

Approximately 5 to 8 per cent of all infants in North America and Europe are born before 37 weeks gestational age and have a birth weight of less than 2500 grams. About 1 per cent are born with very low birth weight

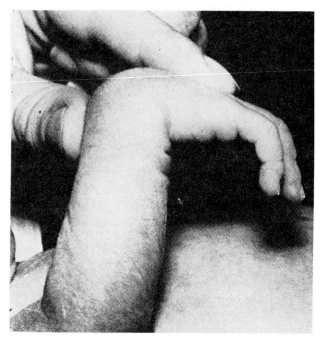

FIGURE 11-2   Technique for square window (Dubowitz et al. 1970).

FIGURE 11-3   Technique for popliteal angle (Dubowitz et al. 1970).

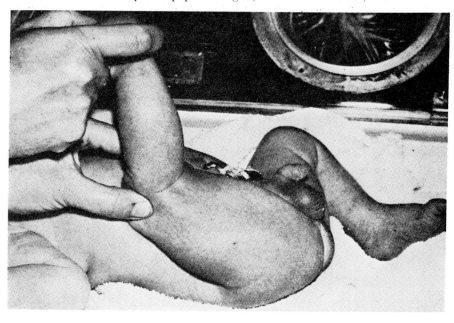

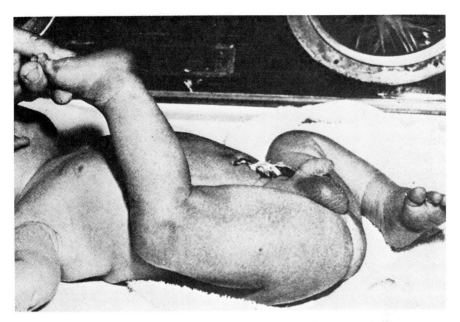

FIGURE 11-4   Technique for heel to ear maneuver (Dubowitz et al. 1970).

(Levene and Dubowitz 1982). In many cases the exact causes of prematurity are unclear, but numerous factors are implicated.

Individual risk factors contributing to prematurity include mother's age, birth order (parity), previous pregnancy history, family income and education, cigarette smoking, weight gain during pregnancy, and prepregnancy weight. Findings from the 1972 National Natality Survey in the United States (Placek 1977) show an increased rate of premature births among women younger than 20 years and older than 35 years of age. Bakketeig (1977) notes that the tendency to repeat preterm delivery accounts for 25 per cent of LBW infants among second births in Norway. In Canada, a previous preterm birth doubles the risk of having a LBW infant (Meyer et al. 1976). Income and education are inversely associated with the likelihood of prematurity (Garn et al. 1977), and smoking during the second half of pregnancy has been associated with a decrease of 200 grams in the average birth weight (Davies et al. 1976, Rush 1981). Rush's studies also suggest that the difference in birth weight is most pronounced in babies born to mothers in lower socioeconomic strata.

To examine the individual contribution of these risk factors to birth weight, Keller (1981) conducted a multiple regression analysis of data collected in a perinatal project. Table 11-2 illustrates the relative contribution of each variable. The most important factors are weight gain, prepregnancy weight, last prior birth weight, smoking and previous pregnancy outcome. It is in-

TABLE 11-2   Percentage of Variance in Birth Weight "Explained" by Various Factors Among Multiparous Women[a]

Factor	Variance explained	
	White (n = 8326)	Black (n = 10 723)
Weight gain	6.6	8.2
Prepregnancy weight	6.0	4.6
Last prior birth weight	6.0	4.6
Cigarettes/day	3.2	1.4
Previous pregnancy outcome	1.0	1.7
Parity (order of pregnancy)	0.3	0.4
Mother's age	0	0
Annual income	0.1	0.1
Height	0	0
Maternal diseases	0.2	0.4
Fetal attributes[b]	2.6	1.6
Complications of pregnancy and labor	7.3	6.5
Total explained variance (multiple R squared)	33.3	29.5

Source: Keller 1981.
[a] Based on linear regression analysis (Weiss and Jackson 1969).
[b] Includes sex, congenital malformations, and Coombs test for blood antibodies to detect erythroblastosis.

teresting to note that mother's age, parity, and income do not independently contribute much to the variance.

Three medical complications can be described as risk factors associated with prematurity: (a) toxemia, a hypertensive disease, (b) neonatal asphyxia, a lack of oxygen, and (c) neonatal hypoxia. In most cases, eight minutes is the upper limit of anoxia that the premature infant can tolerate. Infants surviving longer periods of asphyxia show varying degrees of brain injury (Werthmann 1981). Partial deprivation of oxygen (hypoxia) presents a more subtle but equally threatening hazard. If asphyxia is followed by abnormal behavior, such as apneic spells (disturbances of breathing), a syndrome of hypoxic-ischemic-encephalopathy may result (Robertson 1980). When hypoxic distress is not treated, small areas of brain circulation are closed down with permanent loss of function. The outcome can range from severe disabilities—including early seizures, spasticity, or hypotonia—to more subtle effects that are not evident until childhood (Werthmann 1981).

Respiratory problems are among the most common complications experienced by the preterm infant. Failure to breathe normally may be the result of immaturity, anoxia at birth, hemorrhage, or drug-induced respiratory depression (Rigatto and Brady 1972).

In summary, the premature infant is at risk for a series of conditions which, if left untreated, can seriously influence later development. Some researchers have attempted to quantify the risk contributed by these factors by developing screening systems and complication scales (Apgar 1953, Hines et al. 1980, Littman and Parmelee 1978, Prechtl 1968). The **Apgar scoring** technique is a quick and easy screening device used to identify the infant at risk. Infants can be rated at one, three, five, and ten minutes after birth on five signs (Table 11-3). A score of zero to two suggests severe hypoxia or depression, three to six moderate hypoxia or depression, and seven to ten a normal infant.

The risks associated with VLBW deserve special consideration. Warkany et al. (1961) used the term "intrauterine growth retardation" (IUGR) to describe infants who are small for gestational age. Most of these infants fall below the 3rd percentile for growth standards and weigh less than 1500 grams. Failure to grow is due to impaired fetal oxygen or nutrient transport or impaired exchange of metabolic waste, influenced by such maternal conditions as toxemia, smoking, drug and alcohol use, viral infections, structural features of the uterus, and placental or fetal abnormalities (Kopp and Parmalee 1979, Vorherr 1975). The VLBW infant is extremely susceptible to hypoglycemia, hypothermia, hypoxia, intracranial hemorrhage, and hypoxic-ischemic-encephalopathy. In mild cases of IUGR no fetal hypoxia during delivery may occur, but in severe cases resuscitation may be required. The issue of neurobehavioral sequelae, even without complicating factors, has been raised (Drillien 1972). Gruenwald's (1963) post-mortem studies, however, indicate that the lungs and liver may be more affected by IUGR than is brain size. Others suggest that VLBW may produce more subtle signs of brain damage (Kopp and Parmelee 1979). The gestational period during which growth retardation occurs may be of significance. In a

TABLE 11-3 Apgar Scoring

Sign	Score 0	Score 1	Score 2
Appearance (color)	Blue, pale	Body pink, limbs blue	All pink
Pulse (heart rate)	Absent	<100	>100
Grimace (irritability)	None	Grimace	Cry
Activity (muscle tone)	Limp	Some flexion of limbs	Active movement
Respiratory effort	None	Slow, irregular	Good strong cry

Source: Black 1972.

recent study, Parkinson et al. (1981) followed 60 SGA infants each of which had undergone serial ultrasound measures of head growth before birth. They found that children whose head growth had slowed before 34 weeks gestation were more likely to be of shorter stature at 4 years of age. Those who had slow head growth starting before 26 weeks gestation had lower developmental quotients at a four-year-follow-up and had difficulties with concentration, balance, and coordination at the six-year follow-up.

11.2 COMPARISONS BETWEEN LOW-RISK PREMATURE INFANTS AND FULL-TERM INFANTS

The neurobehavioral development of premature infants has been widely studied (Amiel-Tison 1968, Drillien 1964, Gesell and Armatruda 1945, Knobloch et al. 1956, Parmelee and Schulte 1970, Saint-Anne Dargassies 1966, Shirley 1938, Sigman et al. 1973). These studies, which compared full-term newborns at 40 weeks gestational age with preterm infants at 40 weeks conceptional age (i.e., gestational age plus age from birth), generally agree that the two groups show many similarities.

In contrast, another group of researchers suggest that the premature infant is maturationally advanced relative to the full-term newborn. Amiel-Tison (1980) provided evidence of an advance in neurological maturation of four weeks or more in 16 infants tested at gestational ages between 30 and 37 weeks. All infants were from pregnancies with recorded intrauterine stress. In general, most of the earlier studies agree that the behavior of the term infant at four weeks is equal to that of the preterm who has attained a corrected conceptional age of four weeks and that it is necessary to adjust for degree of prematurity because preterm infants appear to lag in development in the first 12 months.

More recent studies show that preterm infants at 40 weeks conceptual age have differences in neurobehavioral performance relative to full-term infants (for an extensive bibliography, see Ferrari et al. 1983). These differences include inferior performance of visual and auditory orienting, inferior motor performance, and state regulation.

Studies of sensory functioning in the preterm have demonstrated an uneveness of development. The fetal tactile, auditory, and visual systems are not equally developed at the time of preterm birth (Gottlieb 1971). The fetal tactile system develops first and is functional at 4 months of gestation (Hooker 1952). The fetal auditory system is not functional before 8 months of gestation (Parmelee 1981). The visual system continues to develop throughout pregnancy, and structural changes occur as late as 9 months of gestation (Mann 1969; Table 11-4). Some researchers argue that, because the normal environment for the developing sensory system is intrauterine, extrauterine conditions do not provide optimal support for development in preterm infants (Friedman et al. 1981). One would therefore expect the vi-

TABLE 11-4   Ontogenetic Sequence of Sensory Function in Neonates Whose Condition at Birth Is Normal After 265-Day Gestation

Function	Approx. day of onset	Type of evidence	Source
Tactile	Prenatal day 49	Behavior	Hooker 1952
		Histology	Humphrey 1964
Vestibular	Prenatal day 90–120	Behavior	Minkowski 1928
		Histology	Humphrey 1955, Langworthy 1933
Auditory	Prenatal day 210 or earlier	Behavior	Fleischer 1955
	Prenatal day 180 or earlier	Physiology and histology	Bredberg 1968
	Prenatal day 147 or earlier	Physiology	Weitzman and Graziani 1968
Visual	Prenatal day 180 or earlier	Physiology	Ellingson 1960
	Prenatal day 154 or earlier	Physiology	Engel 1964

Source: Gottlieb 1971.

sual system, which is not mature at preterm birth, to be most seriously affected by premature exposure to the extrauterine environment. Following this line of reasoning, the tactile system would not be affected by premature birth and the auditory system less affected than the visual. Results from a number of studies support this hypothesis (Caron and Caron 1981, Friedman et al. 1981, Parmelee 1981, Rose 1981, Siqueland 1981, White and Brackbill 1981).

Comparative studies of tactile processing in full-term infants and preterm infants with a mean conceptional age of 38 weeks show that the performance of the preterm infants, as measured by cardiac responsiveness, is only slightly deficient (Field et al. 1979, Rose et al. 1976). Studies of auditory processing describe preterm infants of less than 36 weeks conceptional age as less responsive (Als et al. 1979, Katona and Berenyi 1974).

The most marked differences between pre- and full-term infants have been found in visual processing. Fantz and Fagan (1975) reported a shorter attention span in preterm infants 10 weeks after delivery than in full-term infants five weeks after delivery. Sigman and Parmelee (1976) identified a preference for familiar rather than novel stimuli in preterm infants at 4 months corrected conceptional age. Using a visual recognition task, Rose (1981) found that preterm infants could not discriminate between the familiar and the novel until 12 months (corrected age) whereas full-term infants demonstrated such discriminations at 6 months. Caron and Caron (1981) studied the ability to process categorical information at 33 weeks conceptional age for both groups and found that preterm infants could respond only to changes in detail of stimuli whereas full-term infants could respond to changes in both detail and configuration. These studies suggest that the premature infant shows a less mature pattern of response with a delay in memory processing.

In trying to piece together the findings of experiments on sensory processing, one can conclude that the differences between pre- and full-term infants are minimal and that many of them disappear if adjustments are made for conceptional age. These differences are not evenly distributed across systems: more significant differences are found in visual than in auditory and tactile processing (Friedman et al. 1981). The lag or deficit in some areas of sensory processing can be explained as the result of exposure to the extrauterine environment before the sensory system completes maturation. Friedman et al. (1981) propose an inverse relationship between the degree of maturation of the sensory system at preterm birth and the impact it suffers as a result of exposure to the extrauterine environment. The evidence of uneven development in the premature infant and the hypothesis of maturational readiness fit well with Gottlieb's (1971) view on the development of sensory functions.

There have been several studies of supplemental **extrauterine stimulation,** including auditory (Katz 1971), tactile (Korner et al. 1975), and multimodal (Scarr-Salapatek and Williams 1973). Among the dependent variables have been growth measures, activity levels, performance on development assessments, visual orientation, and recognition memory. Most studies cite some benefits of supplemental stimulation, such as weight gain, increased activity level, improved visual and auditory responsivity, and better performance on developmental assessment scales, especially for motor development (Field 1980). Stimulation programs continued beyond hospital stay have also demonstrated sustained effects. Follow-up studies show better performance in exploratory behavior, parent-infant interaction, and long-term outcome (Heber and Garber 1975) and on the Bayley scales of infant development (Siqueland 1973, Sostek et al. 1979).

In summary, the evidence suggests that at 40 weeks conceptual age (a) the neurological and behavioral status of the premature infant without complications is generally similar to that of the full-term infant and (b) minor differences reflect an uneven development across sensory systems for the premature infant, particularly in visual and auditory orienting, motor performance, and state regulation. During the first year of life, subtle differences have been noted in visual recognition and memory. The differences are so small that they may fall within the variability of performance for the full-term range (Touwen 1980).

11.3 OUTCOME OF PREMATURITY

A synthesis of current research findings on outcome in premature infants is difficult because of the heterogeneity of the samples in published studies.

Premature infants differ in gestational age, birth weight, and adequacy of intrauterine growth for gestational age and in a plethora of possible complications, each with a number of different causes and outcomes. In addition, variations in experimental parameters, including different assessment and observation techniques, hamper comparisons within and between groups. Neurobehavioral findings are difficult to relate to underlying brain function in the newborn infant. Perinatal cerebral damage produces few characteristic effects that allow the localization of dysfunction (Kurtzberg et al. 1979). Equally important, the immature brain has the capacity for functional restoration in later development (Chap. 6). This restoration limits the degree to which neural damage occurring in early life remains apparent.

Neonatal neurological abnormalities are not necessarily predictive of later development, although Tronick and Brazelton (1975) argue that group prediction improves when neonatal behavioral data are included (Hunt 1981). However, low developmental test scores, which suggest behavioral delays, may not necessarily predict later performance. Some authors have reasoned that qualitative changes in the infant's behavior and skills are responsible for the poor prediction (McCall 1976). The association between early infant status and later intellectual outcome is complicated also by the mediating effects of the environment on growth (Drillien 1964, Knobloch and Pasamanick 1966, Sameroff and Chandler 1975). Except in cases of gross damage to brain structures in infancy, these mediating effects are potent and often control the outcome. While Knobloch and Pasamanick (1966) refer to a continuum of reproductive casualty triggered by prematurity, Sameroff and Chandler (1975), argue equally cogently for a continuum of caretaker causality, i.e., of the overriding effects of environment during infant development.

Paradoxically, many of the earlier studies that helped to record the outcome of prematurity and low birth weight have become less relevant because of changes in neonatal care. Current research is focused more on learning disabilities and social dysfunction, which may not be apparent until later childhood (Mitchell 1980).

Outcome Studies of Prematurity

In many of the earlier outcome studies of prematurity and low birth weight, the incidence of major handicap ranged from 10 to 40 per cent. In general, a major handicap precludes attendence at a normal school and is associated with an IQ below 70, definite cerebral palsy, and/or severe deafness or visual loss (Lancet 1980). A minor handicap is associated with an IQ below 84, slight hearing or visual defects, and early-childhood convulsive disorders that no longer require medication (Commey and Fitzhardinge 1979).

While older studies set the incidence of serious mental handicap as high as 40 per cent, the rate in present-day industrialized nations ranges from 5 to 15 per cent (Davies and Stewart 1975, Drillien 1972, Hagberg 1975). Today low birth weight (excluding VLBW) and preterm delivery are not a risk factor for severe impairment if the maternal, fetal, and placental systems have been functioning optimally and if the fetus or neonate does not experience complications. Unfortunately, a preterm delivery is often symptomatic of dysfunction in one of these systems, and there appears to be an increasing risk of medical complications with decreasing birth weight and with younger gestational age. Most findings are in agreement that premature infants in the upper range of low birth weight are minimally, if at all, intellectually impaired. Although full-term infants appear to score slightly higher on IQ tests, the mean score for premature groups is in the average range (Dann et al. 1974, De Hirsch et al. 1966, Francis-Williams and Davies 1974). In a ten-year follow up of 64 premature infants, Caputo et al. (1981) recorded a mean WISC-R of 100.3 for preterm and 108 for full-term infants. Their performance scales on the WISC-R and results on the Bender Gestalt, however, were significantly lower. The authors concluded that the premature infant demonstrates in later life a slight deficit in cognitive functioning that involves visually mediated, particularly visuomotor, functioning. Since very few of their subjects were not visually impaired and since there was no obvious neurological impairment, Caputo et al. (1981) further asserted that the visual-system deficit originates in the central nervous system and is based on subtle brain dysfunction or limited brain cell growth. An earlier study by De Hirsch et al. (1966), however, suggested that premature infants performed poorly in school because of a more global deficit that involved poor perceptual, motor, and linguistic abilities.

The long-term outcome of preterm birth of VLBW babies is a different picture. Despite improved survival, there is some disagreement regarding later development. Reports of VLBW babies during the early 1960s suggested a distressingly high incidence of serious mental and physical handicap. In a study of 69 subjects with birth weight below 1500 grams, Drillien (1958) reported 10 per cent ineducable, 18 per cent physically handicapped, and 18 per cent requiring remedial instruction. Altogether 49 per cent of infants below 1360 grams birth weight had visual handicaps. Drillien predicted that the survival of VLBW infants would be paralleled by an increase in incidence of handicap. Even more dramatic are Lubchenco et al.'s (1963) findings of visual handicap, cerebral palsy, or mental retardation in 63 per cent of their sample.

These early studies of VLBW infants noted impairments that have proved amenable to improved methods of delivery and neonatal care. Intensive neonatal care was pioneered in the 1960s, with encouraging, though inconsistent, results reported in the late 1960s and early 1970s. The prevention or treatment of birth trauma, birth asphyxia, hypoxia, hypothermia, hypoglycemia, and hyperbilirubinema has certainly improved the prognosis for VLBW babies. Table 11-5 (Commey and Fitzhardinge 1979) shows the comparative survival and outcome rates of infants with birth weight below 1501 grams.

TABLE 11-5 Incidence and Mortality of Major Neonatal Complications and Proportion Showing Handicap at 24-Month Follow-up

	Total	Mortality, %	Months followed	Handicapped, %
Total population[a]	109	26	71	49
Asphyxia	68	29	43	48
CNS depression on admission	48	48	25	76
Mechanical ventilation	46	39	28	46
Respiratory distress syndrome	26	46	14	57
Primary or late apnea	45	31	28	46
Seizures	20	65	7	57
Intracranial hemorrhage (clinical or autopsy diagnosis)	19	89	2	100
Meningitis	4	25	3	67
Hyperbilirubinemia needing exchange transfusion	19	26	14	71
Hypoglycemia	14	21	11	73
Necrotizing enterocholitis	6	33	4	0
None	25	0	22	36

Source: Commey and Fitzhardinge 1979.
[a]More than one complication may have occurred in the same infant.

Some impressive results come from University College Hospital, London (Lancet 1980, Rawlings et al. 1971, Reynolds 1974). In a five-year follow-up study, the UCH group found that approximately 90 per cent of the surviving VLBW infants were without handicap, 4 per cent had a physical disability, such as spastic diplegia or partial vision; and 4 per cent were mentally handicapped, with a mean IQ of below 72. Of the 85 children, only 10 per cent were below the 10th percentile for weight and below the 18th percentile for height. Robinson (1971) and Vohr et al. (1979) have reported similar results.

Less optimistic findings were published by an Australian research group that examined 158 VLBW infants in an eight-year follow-up study (Kitchen et al. 1979, 1980). Five per cent of the children were profoundly handicapped, IQ below 59; 10 per cent severely handicapped, IQ between 50 and 69; and 40 per cent significantly handicapped, IQ 70 to 84. Only 43 per cent showed minor or no handicaps and an IQ above 84. Of the total group, 50 children had some form of visual defect, four had cerebral palsy, six were receiving anticonvulsant medication, and six had sensorineural deafness.

A summary of ten recent studies shows similar survival rates, averaging about 58 per cent (Levene and Dubowitz 1982; Table 11-6). The incidence of major neurological handicap ranges from none in Coventry, England, to

TABLE 11-6 Summary of Survival and Outcome from Nine Follow-up Studies of Infants with Birth Weight ≤1500 Grams

Group	Time period of births	Survival rate, %	SGA, %	Inborn, %	Major CNS handicap	Significant cerebral palsy	Neonatal retardation (developmental quotient <80)	Age of assessment
Toronto (Fitzhardinge et al. 1976)	1970–73	48	47	0	33/75	14/75	35/75	>2 years
Sydney (Mercer et al. 1978)	1971–75	55	35[a]	100	11/88	2/88	8/88	Mean 4 years
Hammersmith, London (Jones et al. 1979)	1971–75	48	32	100	7/104	3/104	3/104	>23 months
Coventry (Hommers and Kendall, 1976)	1973–74	54	21	?	0/42	0/42	2/42	9–31 months
McMaster, Hamilton (Horwood et al. 1982)	1973–77	77[b]	?	100	21/134	—	—	1.5–6 years
Hamilton (Saigal et al. 1982)	1973–78	63	18	76	11/104[c]	24/104	9/104	2 years
Toronto (Fitzhardinge et al. 1978)	1974	66	19[a]	0	44/149[d]	13/149	40/149	>2 years
New York State (Knoblock et al. 1982)	1975–79	53	?	100	22/96	—	—	>1 year
Cleveland (Hack et al. 1979)	1975–76	65	26[a]	?	27/160	—	—	Mean 2 years
Melbourne (Kitchen et al. 1982)	1977–78	68	?	87	53/297	35/297	28/297[e]	>2 years

Source: Levene and Dubowitz 1982.
[a]Refers only to infants followed up.
[b]Only infants of birth weight 1000 to 1499 grams.
[c]30 per cent major CNS handicap in ventilated subgroup.
[d]53 per cent major handicap among infants with birth weight below 3rd centile for gestation.
[e]Number of infants with mental development index ≤68.

TABLE 11-7   Summary of Survival and Outcome of Infants with Birth Weight ≤1000 Grams from 11 Centers

Group	Time period of births	Survival rate, %	SGA, %	Inborn, %	Major CNS handicap	Significant cerebral palsy	Neonatal retardation (developmental quotient <80)	Age of assessment
University College Hospital, London (Stewart et al. 1977)	1966–74	32	?	47	2/27	1/27	2/27	>15 months
Sydney (Mercer et al. 1978)	1971–75	19	?	100	3/9	0/9	3/9	Mean 4 years
Los Angeles (Pomerance et al. 1978)	1973–75	40	?	45	9/27	?	8/27	1–3 years
Hamilton (Saigal et al. 1982)	1973–78	32	?	76	9/37	—	—	2 years
Toronto (Pape et al. 1978)	1974	47	33	0	13/43	2/43	9/43	>18 months
Illinois (Bhat et al. 1978)	1974–76	31	40	48	3/16	—	3/23	10–36 months
Pennsylvania (Kumar et al. 1980)	1974–77	26	5	100	2/50	—	2/50	?
Cleveland (Hack et al. 1979)	1975–76	40	?	?	7/32	—	—	Mean 2 years
New York State (Knoblock et al. 1982)	1975–79	20	?	100	5/9	—	—	>1 year
Syracuse, New York (Ruiz et al. 1981)	1976–78	34	18	45	10/38	4/33	6/28[a]	8–15 years
Columbia (Driscoll et al. 1982)	1977–78	48	38	56	7/23	2/23	3/23	18–36 months

Source: Levene and Dubowitz 1982.
[a] Number of infants with mental development index ≤68.

44 per cent in Toronto, Canada. The incidence in Toronto is due to the number of at-risk infants who arrive in poor condition from other centers. In addition, infants who are both SGA and preterm are at greater risk for adverse outcome. In these ten studies, 18 per cent suffered significant neurological handicap. Table 11-7 shows the survival and outcome of infants with birth weight below 1000 grams. Although the average survival rate is lower than for babies with weight above 1500 grams, the average incidence of major handicap is similar (about 22 per cent).

Few long-term follow-up studies have dealt with learning disabilities or behavioral problems. Francis-Williams and Davies (1974) compared preterm AGA infants with preterm SGA infants and found a difference in mean IQ of seven points in favor of the AGA infants. Although most VLBW infants were doing relatively well in school, they showed a high percentage of reading problems and immature drawings on the Bender Gestalt Test and their performance IQ was significantly below the verbal IQ. Drillien et al. (1980) reported that 60 per cent of VLBW infants who attended normal school had shown transient neurological signs in the first year of life and at age 7 years had poor scores on all measures used, including the WISC-R, Bender Gestalt, and school achievement tests. Those children who were able to attend normal school showed no evidence of intrauterine insult or perinatal complications and were neurologically normal (Drillien et al. 1980). In a study of 25 out of 45 long-term survivors with birthweight below 1000 grams, only seven were rated at or above grade level at age 10. Sixteen were attending a special education program (Nickel et al. 1982).

In summary, preterm birth and low birthweight do not normally place the child at risk for abnormal development. The outcome depends on the degree of prematurity, the severity of intrauterine growth retardation, and the socioeconomic level of the parents. The complications associated with prematurity during pregnancy, delivery, or the postnatal period increase the likelihood of an abnormal outcome. Poor neurobehavioral outcome is more likely if birthweight is less than 1500 grams, which in turn increases susceptibility to complications of medical procedures. During the early years, hazardous complications can be associated with developmental problems. Longer follow-up studies show, however, that environmental stimulation assumes increasing importance over time (Drillien 1964, Harper and Wiener 1965, Sameroff and Chandler 1975). There appears to be an interaction between degree and type of complications associated with prematurity, gestational age and weight at preterm birth, care-giving environment, and intellectual outcome.

12

Infections and Intoxications

Infectious organisms and intoxicants are two groups of the more than 800 teratogenic agents that may lead to structural or functional deviations in development. An annotated catalog of the complete list of agents is provided by Shepard et al. (1975). For a detailed discussion the reader is referred to E. M. Johnson and Kochlar (1983).

12.1 PRENATAL INFECTION

Infections affecting the CNS may be caused by bacteria, viruses, rickettsiae, fungi, protozoa, and helminths (R. T. Johnson 1982). During the prenatal period only those infectious agents that cross the placenta are of importance to the developing fetus. The clinical effects of severe prenatal infection have been known for a long time: severe retardation, convulsions, **chorioretinitis** (inflammation of the layer of eye tissue carrying blood vessels and retina), and micro- or hydrocephaly. More recently, the production of IgM, one of the immunoglobulins, has been used as an indicator as to whether or not an infection took place during the prenatal period. IgM does not pass the placenta but is produced by the fetus in response to infection and therefore can be used to survey the frequency of prenatal infection. By this measurement, 6 per cent of all living newborn infants are presumed to have had an intrauterine infection (W. DeMyer 1975). However, this figure does not include infections acquired from the mother's birth canal during birth or those acquired before the fifth to sixth month of pregnancy since the IgM levels do not respond to infections during these periods.

Only a small portion of maternal infections show clear-cut psychological consequences in the child. The best-known infections during pregnancy are the **storch** agents: syphilis (treponema pallidum), toxoplasma gondii (toxoplasmosis), rubella (German measles), cytomegalovirus (cytomegalic inclu-

163

sion disease, one of the many forms of the herpesvirus), and herpes simplex; together these account for about 20 per cent of all prenatal infections. The remaining 80 percent of infections are due to a variety of infectious agents, including mumps, hepatitis, chicken pox, and coxsackie-virus group B (Nahmias et al. 1976). The mechanism of damage to the fetus often remains unexplained and the effects on the future development of the child obscure. One reason for the lack of information is that many infections of the mother show only mild or no clinical signs and hence remain undetected. On the other hand, the infection may invade the cerebrospinal fluid and cause a narrowing (stenosis) of the cerebral aqueduct. This may lead to the development of a hydrocephalus in the infant, although at that time serological evidence of a viral infection can no longer be obtained. K. P. Johnson (1974) found, for example, that newborn hamsters inoculated with mumps and influenza viruses later developed malformations of the brain without evidence of a destructive inflammatory lesion.

Congenital Rubella

Since the first description of rubella effects on the embryo by Gregg in 1941, rubella infection has become perhaps the best known and most feared complication of pregnancy. If acquired before the thirteenth week, maternal rubella results in abnormalities in 50 per cent of the infants (Hardy 1973). It was thought that only infections during the first trimester of pregnancy posed a risk to the fetus, but more recent studies have shown that the risk extends well into the second trimester, though with diminishing severity (Hardy 1973, Ueda et al. 1979). A risk is even present if the maternal infection occurs after the last menstrual period but before conception, although in such cases the incidence of spontaneous abortion is very high (Ueda et al. 1979). Subclinical rubella occurs at least as often as the clinically apparent infection and poses the same amount of risk to the fetus (Knox et al. 1980). Maternal rubella infections may produce in the child rubella syndrome, the effects of which extend to many areas of function; mild disease; or an inapparent infection at birth. Even the latter, however, can lead to significant problems later in life. (Tables 12-1, 12-2, 12-3).

The clinical picture of rubella syndrome often includes low birth weight, meningoencephalitis, microcephaly, psychomotor and mental retardation, cataracts and pigmented retinopathy of the eye, and abnormalities of the heart and major blood vessels. Rubella epidemics have been recorded for some years, as in 1964, with fetus infections ranging from 4 to 30 per 1000 births. Since the introduction of the rubella vaccine, licensed in 1969, the incidence has dropped considerably.

A 9-to-12-year follow-up study of 29 nonretarded children who had congenital rubella suggests that an increasing number of manifestations not detected during infancy occur during childhood (Desmond et al. 1978). Among the 29 children, manifestations during the first two years of life included

TABLE 12-1:   Neurologic Abnormalities Noted in 32 of 64 Survivors of Meningitis Followed to 18 Months

Motor deficits		Other neurological abnormalities	
Tetraparesis	20	Hyperactivity and restlessness	16
With general spasticity	4	Hypotonic shoulder girdle	16
With hypotonia	9	Lateral rotation of feet	14
With spasticity of lower		Incoordination of swallowing	
extremities	4	mechanism	8
With athetosis	1	Strabismus (in infants without	
With asymmetric involve-		cataracts)	7
ment of upper extremities	1	Head retraction and back	
Paraparesis	2	arching	9
With spasticity	1	Hypertonicity on stimulation	8
With hypotonia	1	Stereotyped movements	12
		Abnormal associated move-	
Hemiparesis	2	ments	3
Monoparesis	2	Tremors	2
		Cutis marmorata	4
Severe motor delay	6	Apparent unawareness of envi-	
With hypotonia	5	ronment	8
With intermittent hyper-		Mental retardation (no prog-	
tonus	1	ress in adaptive behavior)	11

Source: Desmond et al. 1970.
Findings confined to 18 month examination.

TABLE 12-2   The Johns Hopkins Rubella Study: Fetal Outcome by Gestational Age at Time of Maternal Rubella

Completed weeks of gestation	No.	Died[a]		Survived				
		Fetal	Later	Defects			No defects	
				Severe	Moderate	Mild	? Normal	Normal
Preconception	5	2	2	1	—	—	—	—
0–4	23	2	4	11	6	—	—	—
5–8	28	2	1	7	9	7	1	1
9–12	14	—	—	3	3	7	1	—
13–16	10	1	1	2	3	1	2	—
17–20	7	1	—	1	—	2	1	3
21–30	11	—	—	1	2	2	2	4
31–45	4	—	—	—	—	1	2	1
	102	8	8	26	23	20	9	9

Source: Hardy 1973.
[a] Two additional deaths occurred between 4 and 5 years of age.

TABLE 12-3 The Johns Hopkins Rubella Study: Status of Surviving Children with Congenital Rubella at 4 to 5 Years of Age

Intelligence (IQ Score)	No.	Percent	H/O maternal rubella	Birth weight <2501 gm	Other abnormalities						
					Cardiac	Auditory	Visual	CNS	Other minor	Small head	None
Above average ≥110	20	11.7	13	3	7	15	1	3	6	11	4
Average 90–109	49	28.6	20	7	15	21	—	7	12	22	11
Low normal 75–89	31	18.1	14	12	14	17	4	10	9	20	1
Borderline 70–74	22	12.0	6	10	8	12	7	9	6	21	—
Defective <70	49	28.6	24	25	23	28	21	30	2	38	(1)
Total No.	171	—	77	57	67	93	33	59	35	112	16 + (1)
%		100.0	45	33	39	54	19	34	20	65	9

Source: Hardy 1973.
Distribution of defects in 171 children with congenital rubella by IQ score at 4 to 5 yr of age. The Stanford-Binet was used where possible. Other tests, such as the Merril Palmer, Leiter, and Cattell, were given where the child was deaf or otherwise unable to take the Binet.

abnormal muscle tone and reflexes (69 per cent), delays in motor development (66 per cent) feeding difficulties (48 per cent), and severe to profound hearing loss (79 per cent). Between 3 and 7 years of age, poor balance and motor incoordination (69 per cent) and such behavioral disturbances as short attention span, distractibility, perseveration, and emotional instability (66 per cent) were noted and hearing losses increased to 86 per cent. At age 9 to 12 years, 25 of the 29 children showed residual deficits, including learning problems (52 per cent) and deficits in tactile perception (41 per cent). The authors concluded that the primary problems of rubella children differ in each phase of childhood. The number of children with overt driven hyperkinesis was recorded as 66 per cent at age 3 but decreased to 17 per cent by age 9 to 12. Learning problems predominate in later years despite adequate measured intelligence (WISC-R IQ of 85 and higher). Feelings of isolation and low self-esteem were common. Fourteen of the children required a total communication program, including sign language, at school. Van Dijk (1982) presents similar results about the behavior and learning problems of 81 Australian rubella children with cataract and/or hearing impairment. Late-onset, progressive panencephalitis related to the original rubella infection, i.e., an infectious process affecting both the gray and the white matter of the brain, may occur as late as the second decade of life (Townsend et al. 1975, Weil et al. 1975).

Similar findings were reported by Chess et al. (1978) in a larger study group, 243 children with congenital rubella examined at age 2.5 to 5 years and followed up at age 8 to 9 years. In addition, they found mental retardation in 37 per cent, reactive behavior disorders in 15 per cent, behavior disorder in conjunction with neurological damage in 3.3 per cent, and autism in 7.4 per cent at the first examination. They stressed that autism is frequently associated with mental retardation and that all the autistic children were infected during the first trimester of pregnancy. Of the 210 children returning for reexamination at age 8 to 9, 25.7 per cent were mentally retarded; 18.1 per cent showed reactive behavior disorders, such as moodiness and rebelliousness; 12.4 per cent showed behavior disorder in conjunction with neurologic damage; 6.2 per cent autism; and 2.4 per cent neurotic behavior disorders. Thus, with increasing age, behavior problems rise in frequency as these children are exposed to the increased demands of school and society (Ziring 1977). Reviewing the 25-year outcome of 50 individuals who had congenital rubella, Menser et al. (1967) found that some degree of mental deficiency was present only in five and severe mental deficiency only in one case. Forty-seven had severe hearing loss, 26 had cataracts or chorioretinopathy, 11 congenital cardiovascular defects, and 40 speech defects. Despite evidence of chromosomal abnormalities in many infants with congenital rubella, 6 of the 11 married females had normal offspring. The authors pointed out that the socioeconomic adjustment of the group as a whole had been underestimated in previous assessments; only four of their subjects were unemployed. "The developmental potential of many patients had been assessed erroneously during the preschool period" (Menser et al. 1967, p. 1347).

The great variability in type and degree of psychological deficit has been ascribed to differences in the age of the fetus at the time the mother acquired the rubella infection. Yet very few systematic correlations between gestational age and symptoms or their severity have been clearly established. One study of outcome in relation to gestational age is illustrated in Tables 12-1 and 12-2 (Hardy 1973). In addition to gestational age, the physical condition of the mother, the amount of virus to which the fetus has been exposed, the virulence of the strain, and the immune response of both mother and fetus have been described as factors determining the effects of rubella infection during pregnancy.

Congenital Cytomegalovirus Infection

Among the many varieties of the herpesvirus (including herpes simplex, herpes zoster, and Epstein-Barr virus), cytomegalovirus (CMV) has been identified as one of the most common causes of intrauterine infection. Discovered in 1956, this virus is estimated to infect between 0.5 and 2.4 per cent of all newborns, although fewer than 5 per cent of those infected show clinical manifestations of the disease during infancy (S. E. Starr 1979). Since the infection remains subclinical in most adults as well, the maternal infection often remains undetected unless a serological examination is carried out.

The effects of invasion by the virus can be widespread, including enlargement of spleen and liver, intrauterine growth retardation, various congenital deformities, and damage to the developing visual and auditory system (R. T. Johnson 1977). After long-term follow-up, Pass et al. (1980) reported that, of 34 newborns with clinical evidence of infection and with the virus isolated from urine, 10 had died and all but 2 of the 23 patients remaining in the study showed evidence of CNS or auditory handicaps. Microcephaly was present in 70 per cent, mental retardation in 61 per cent, hearing loss in 30 per cent, neuromuscular disorder in 35 per cent, and chorioretinitis (optic atrophy) in 22 per cent of the children when seen at an average age of 4 years (ranging from 9 months to 14 years). These results are essentially in agreement with earlier studies by Starr et al. (1968) and W. Berenberg and Nankervis (1970).

There has been growing interest in children who are without clinical symptoms during the neonatal period and in whom the infection is not recognized. The virus has the capacity to survive and to replicate in the tissue for months or years after perinatal or intrauterine infection. Studies by Kumar et al. (1973) and by Melish and Hanshaw (1973) suggested that in 5 to 10 per cent of these asymptomatic cases, neurological symptoms may develop later. Reynolds et al. (1974) reported that, of 18 such children followed up to 5 or 6 years of age, more than half developed sensorineural hearing loss and there was a trend toward subnormal intelligence. Asymptomatic CMV infection has also been associated with school failure (Hanshaw et al. 1976).

The similarity between the long-term sequelae of CMV and of those of another prenatal infection, toxoplasma gondii virus, should be pointed out (Stagno 1980). C. B. Wilson and colleagues (1980) reported that 92 per cent of the children in a long-term follow-up study of toxoplasmosis during pregnancy showed late-developing effects, including a gradual decrease in IQ from an average of 97 to 74 over a five-year period.

12.2 POSTNATAL INFECTIONS

Most children are subject to numerous infections, only a few of which have more than a temporary effect on their well-being. Of concern here are those postnatal infections that have been shown to affect the development of the nervous system, especially if the infection involves brain tissue (**encephalitis**) or the membranes of the brain (meningitis). Well-known examples are measles, rubella (Townsend et al. 1982), and mumps. Some cases may be related to inoculation with serum or vaccines, others to autoimmune reactions.

Meningitis

Meningitis is the result of an inflammation resulting from infection by one of the numerous bacilli (e.g., meningococcus, pneumococcus, staphylococcus) that can invade the meninges via the middle ear, the paranasal sinuses, the bone of the skull, or the bloodstream. In the newborn, meningitis may be a complication of birth: premature rupture of the membranes may allow bacteria into the fetal environment. The clinical picture often emerges slowly, but at its peak often includes neck stiffness, clouding of consciousness, increased reflex activity, and seizures. Persisting defect is usually the result of damage to the blood supply (end arteries) provided by the meninges and damage to brain tissue because of swelling. The latter leaves nonfunctional (necrotic) tissue after the infection, usually more thickly at the base of the brain. Some blood vessels may become thrombosed and produce small infarctions, frequently affecting the brain as well (meningoencephalitis). The brain is swollen and shows ventricular dilation; cerebrospinal fluid ducts become obstructed. Abcesses of the infection into the brain are common.

The rapidly progressive and often fatal bacterial meningitis of the newborn (still fairly frequent, 1500 cases per year in the United States) is usually separated from the bacterial or viral meningitis occuring in older children and adults. Later in life, the clinical picture is often less obvious, though the destructive effects on brain tissue can be more pronounced.

Before the advent·of antibiotics, approximately 60 per cent of patients infected with bacterial meningitis suffered severe, permanent neurological damage; this figure has dropped to 30 per cent since then. In addition, about 20 per cent have significant difficulty with school work (Desmit 1955, Lawson et al. 1965, E. S. Smith 1954). Sell and coworkers (1972a, 1972b) reported that over 18 per cent of the children who had suffered from bacterial meningitis had lasting neurological sequelae, 7 per cent were mentally retarded, and others had impaired intelligence relative to siblings (Fig. 12-1). Following 88 children for at least one year after infection, Feigin and Dodge (1976) found that one died and nine were affected by hemiparesis or quadriparesis, though this cleared up in six of them within one year. Thirteen of the children had IQs between 80 and 90, and ten were below 80. Several authors noted clinically significant hearing defects in children after meningococcal meningitis.

Kresky et al. (1962) found high average intelligence but a marked dis-

FIGURE 12-1   Representation of IQ results of postmeningitis subjects compared with control sibling pairs (Sell et al. 1972b).

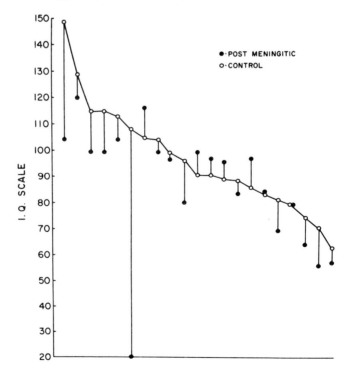

crepancy between verbal and performance parts of the WISC in many post-meningitis subjects. In addition, 20 per cent of their sample had school difficulties that could not be explained on the basis of IQ. Using a matched control group, L. Wright and Jimmerson (1971) examined 11 children approximately eight years after they had been hospitalized because of homophilus influenza meningitis at an age ranging from 4 months to 5.5 years. They found significant differences in full scale IQ, in verbal and performance IQ, and on ten Wechsler subscales, but not on the Bender-Gestalt test or on six Frostig test variables. Thus, their results indicate not a specific visuomotor impairment but rather a more general cognitive deficit.

12.3 INTOXICATIONS

Exposure of the mother during pregnancy or of the child after birth to any type of toxin may result in acute or chronic intoxication of the fetus or child and various forms of short- and long-term impairment during childhood. Among intoxications during pregnancy, **toxemia of pregnancy (gestosis)** is presumed to result from a variety of pathological conditions. These are essentially metabolic disturbances in the mother, which may lead to nausea, vomiting, gastric pains, headache, hypertension and edema (**preeclampsia**), sudden convulsions, and even coma (**eclampsia**).

As other maternal intoxications, bilirubinemia (**kernicterus**) due to blood-type incompatibility between mother and fetus and intoxication by carbon monoxide, mercury, lead, arsenic, quinine, and so on have been described (Rom 1976). The thalidomide tragedy focused attention on intoxications with prescribed and nonprescribed drugs (Stimmel 1982). The **fetal alcohol syndrome** in alcoholic mothers and in experimental animals (Abel 1981, Bond 1981, Golden et al. 1982, Graham-Clay 1983, Rosett and Sander 1979) and the possible teratogenic effects of smoking during pregnancy have also been studied in some detail. D. M. Ross and S. A. Ross (1976) reviewed studies relating maternal alcohol consumption and smoking with hyperactivity. While many of these effects have been known for a long time, it was usually assumed that the placenta functioned as a protective barrier and that all potentially toxic material would be filtered out. However, the protective function of the placenta is poorly understood; in fact, it is likely that the placenta may actually maintain an unusually high concentration of certain toxic elements, such as mercury. Deficiencies of certain trace elements, such as zinc and copper, may also have a damaging effect on the neurological development of the fetus.

Postnatally, various toxins tend to affect the developing organism adversely. Best known are the effects of lead and carbon monoxide poisoning. Anesthetics, hypnotics, and even mild exposure to various chemical neurotoxins, such as arsenic, strychnine and DDT, can have a toxic effect (Allen 1975).

Hyperbilirubinemia

Excessive formation and retention of bilirubin, the bile pigment formed in liver, spleen, and marrow, may be the result of failure in one or more steps of normal metabolism and excretion and may be related to the destruction of red blood cells. The accumulated bilirubin leads to the clinical picture of jaundice. High bilirubin levels are present in about 50 per cent of all newborns between the second and fourth days of life and vary depending on gestational age, birth weight, and many other factors, such as degree of hypoxia, drug ingestion, delayed cord clamping, and infection. A distinction between water-soluble (conjugated) and fat-soluble (nonconjugated) bilirubin levels is made since only the latter tends to be associated with increased risk to the newborn.

At high levels, kernicterus (nuclear jaundice) results in death or in severe nervous system damage in survivors. Damage is primarily the result of (1) depression of cell respiration and (2) impaired protein synthesis, primarily affecting neural tissue in areas of high susceptibility (basal ganglia, thalamus, hyppocampus, and brainstem nuclei) and in other areas of the CNS with a higher level of blood flow. The best-known cause of kernicterus is autoimmunization of the mother against one of the rh+ blood group factors. In this case antibodies (agglutamins) against red blood cells containing the rh+ factor are formed in the mother's blood system and may ultimately cross the placenta and destroy fetal red blood cells (erythroblastosis fetalis). In the past death during the first months of life occurred in 75 per cent of all infants, but this can usually be prevented now by blood exchange in the infant before birth. Infant mortality is now less than 5 per cent (Dekaban 1970). The danger of kernicterus in a firstborn child is quite low because sensitization of the mother builds up slowly, but it rises in subsequent pregnancies because of increased antibody formation. Injection with immune globulin during pregnancy markedly decreases the incidence of erythroblastosis fetalis.

This mechanism of the disorder presents a good example of the complex interaction of factors in intoxications. In this case, the brain defect results from an intoxication that is ultimately determined by genetic factors. Sequelae in survivors with bilirubin encephalopathy have been studied for some time. Snyder et al. (1945) found that, among an undifferentiated mentally retarded population, the incidence of rh incompatibility between parents was twice as high as in the normal population, suggesting, at least at that time, that the kernicterus remained unrecognized and untreated and results in mental retardation without specified causes and without gross physical abnormalities.

More recent studies indicate that the incidence of mental retardation, cerebral palsy, and other major handicaps after transfusion is very low (Bowman 1975, Gregg and Hutchinson 1969, Phibbs et al. 1971). In Bowman's study, 74 of 87 intrauterine transfusion survivors were completely normal on extended follow-up. If kernicterus does occur, gross physical disorders are common, including choreoathetosis, torsion spasms, localized hypertonicity with serious impairment of voluntary movements, grimacing, hearing and speech defects, and difficulty in chewing, swallowing, and maintaining eye fixation. Little improvement during the long-term development of these infants has been reported.

Further studies of hyperbilirubinemia have concentrated on the long-term effects of moderate elevations of bilirubin levels (physiological hyperbilirubinemia) in the newborn. The earliest effects are hypotonia and stupor, which may not be recognized. Severe hyperbilirubinemia of the newborn shows classical signs after the first year of life, including athetosis, deafness, paralysis of eye gaze, and mental deficiency. Boggs et al. (1967) found in an eight-month follow-up significantly lower motor scores on the Bayley Developmental Scales if bilirubin levels at birth exceeded 15 mg/100 ml. On autopsy of low-birth-weight infants who died from other causes, the typical yellow staining of the basal ganglia has been observed even if the bilirubin level was lower than 15 mg.

Since injury to the hypocampal areas may affect learning and retention, long-term studies with four- to eight-year-old children have focused on potential cognitive defects. Johnston et al. (1967) and Upadhyay (1971) found poor attention span, motor hyperacitivity, and poor motor coordination but no IQ deficit in children whose neonatal bilirubin level was greater than 20 mg, although a study by Robin et al. (1979) failed to confirm this result.

The breakdown into conjugated and nonconjugated bilirubin counts has been used only in recent follow-up studies. Johnson and Boggs (1974) found that cognitive impairment cannot be correlated with total bilirubin but that children with nonconjugated bilirubin levels of more than 15 mg showed deficits not only in fine motor integration but also in visual perception and expressive language.

Other Intoxications Before and After Birth

Many drugs administered to the mother can cross the placenta and affect the fetus. Those studied include the sedatives and hypnotics, local anesthetics (Dodson 1976), anticonvulsants, and alcohol (Hanson et al. 1976). Among the postnatal intoxications, chemical neurotoxins in industry and environment, such as lead, mercury, manganese, solvents, alkyl halides, organophosphates, and gases, have received considerable attention (Allen 1975, J. G. Wilson 1977).

Lead intoxication occurs when infants are exposed to lead-based paints and to dust, soil, and air with high lead content, usually in the vicinity of ore smelters, foundries, brass works, battery factories, printing operations, and other plants. Epidemic levels of lead absorption in approximately 2700 children near an ore smelter in El Paso, Texas, were reported by Landrigan et al. (1975). More recently, low-level lead intoxication from exhaust fumes in heavy traffic areas and other sources has been observed (Hankin et al. 1973, Needleman 1980, Needleman et al. 1974). Exposure is much more likely in relatively poor urban areas and hence is associated with low socioeconomic levels.

Lead intoxication affects virtually all tissue of the body and causes degeneration of nerve cells, neuronal loss, decreased myelination, and reactive gliosis. Necrosis of tissue can also occur because of occlusion of small blood vessels. Neural tissue involvement in acute intoxication is indicated by pallor, irritability, vomiting, deterioration of consciousness, seizures, and focal neurological signs. Survivors of acute encephalopathy usually show significant mental retardation. Long-term subclinical intoxication causes lead neuropathy with decreased reflexes, motor weakness, hypaesthesia, and reduced nerve conduction velocity. Children with sickle cell anemia, a hereditary disorder of hemoglobin, are especially vulnerable to lead neuropathy. In animal studies, raising the lead content of maternal milk has been shown to increase lead levels in the blood and brain tissue of the newborn. The rodents show increased motor activity, aggressiveness, tremor, and self-grooming (Golter and Michaelson 1975, Overmann 1977).

Lead poisoning during pregnancy has mainly been studied in severe cases (Angle and McIntire 1964, Palmisano et al. 1969). Hyperactivity in children is associated with increased blood levels of lead (David et al. 1972). Intelligence test scores are inversely related to lead blood levels (Beattie et al. 1975, Klein et al. 1974). Marlowe et al. (1983) found elevated lead and cadmium concentrations in a significantly higher proportion of hair samples from mild and borderline retarded children relative to levels in a control group of children in grades 7 to 12. Unfortunately, many studies are confounded with socioeconomic factors related to living in areas where lead exposure is likely. These same factors render many of the earlier studies of low-level lead exposure inconclusive (Lansdown et al. 1974, Rutter 1980).

13

Nutritional Disorders

Current estimates are that more than 1 billion people in today's world suffer from some degree of nutritional inadequacy. Most of these individuals are infants and young children in the developing world who suffer from **protein-calorie malnutrition,** a generic term for a wide spectrum of nutritional deficiencies that vary in type, timing, and severity. These deficiencies are distinct from the malnutrition that is a secondary symptom of medical conditions such as cystic fibrosis or genetically determined metabolic disorders such as phenylketonuria. Protein-calorie deficiencies are also distinct from deficiencies in specific vitamins (e.g., **vitamin A deficiency,** which is a primary cause of preventable blindness in infancy and childhood) or minerals (e.g., iron deficiency anemia, Leibel et al. 1979). These selective deficiencies usually occur in a diet that is otherwise adequate. If severe enough, a predominantly protein-deficient diet in the young child may present clinically as **kwashiorkor** and a predominantly calorie-deficient diet may present as **marasmus.** These two clinical syndromes are less commonplace, however, than severe combined deficiencies, sometimes called *marasmus-kwashiorkor*, and moderate though chronic *subclinical* protein, calorie, or combined deficiencies.

Both marasmus and kwashiorkor are postnatal nutritional syndromes. In Third World countries, the infant at risk for a nutritional deficiency has typically been subjected to direct prenatal stunting because of poor maternal nutrition and also to the influence of nutritional deficiencies spanning generations that have weakened the mother's ability to carry the fetus to term without difficulty. A poorly developed placenta and a very small pelvis interfering with fetal development are two examples of the influence of generations of malnutrition.

Such nutritional deficiencies rarely, if ever, occur as an isolated phenomenon. Usually, they are associated with inadequate medical facilities and care, increased risk of infection, insufficiencies in quality and quantity of

175

maternal care and environmental stimulation, poor education, and inadequate income. Any statements about the mental consequences of malnutrition need to be placed in the context of an early life of deprivation. This is particularly true in evaluating research if explicit control over the other deprivational factors is lacking.

The development of the CNS depends upon the availability of proper nutrients in adequate amounts to supply both the raw energy to fuel growth and the essential building blocks of growth at the biochemical level (Table 13-1). Proteins, carbohydrates, fats, water, minerals, and vitamins must be part of a balanced diet. For example, the human body cannot readily use fat-soluble vitamins if adequate supplies of fats are not also available from the diet.

When adequate amounts of nutrients are not available from the diet, they are initially drawn from biochemical stores accumulated in the body. If need persists, nutrients are catabolized from the body's cells and organs. If the deprivation is severe and prolonged, continued somatic wasting, coma, and death may occur. However, if an adult organism is moderately or even severely malnourished and then nutritionally rehabilitated and supplemented, weight gain ensues and few, if any, permanent anatomical or chemical changes are observed. Permanent neurological deficits are not usually observed when the duration of the protein-calorie deprivation occurs during adulthood. However, specific vitamin deficiencies can lead to permanent neurological damage and neuropsychological deficits. Wernicke-Korsakoff syndrome, for example, results in permanent memory deficits.

The developing organism does not have the same recuperative ability; once subjected to protein-calorie deficiencies and their **attendant milieu,** the infant or child may suffer permanent changes in both somatic and CNS status. Tissues that undergo the most rapid development during the deficiency are most vulnerable, which corresponds to the Dobbing hypothesis (e.g., Dobbing 1968b) of critical growth periods.

The primary concern of this chapter is the extent to which early-life nutritional deprivation influences functional abilities later on. Whether or not structural changes in the CNS actually mediate subsequent losses of function has been the subject of experimental work with animals, but few human studies have been reported.

13.1 PHYSICAL AND BIOCHEMICAL BRAIN ALTERATIONS

Prenatal Deficiency

The fetus has two buffers against inadequate nutrition: (1) direct nutrition from the consumption of food by the mother and (2) placental transfer of nutrients stored by the mother. It has been said that the fetus has a **para-**

sitic relationship with the mother, thriving fairly successfully to the detriment of the mother when she is moderately malnourished. However, this bit of science folklore has been contradicted by research indicating that the fetus does, in fact, suffer from insufficient maternal food intake.

It is difficult to determine the optimal level of nutrients needed for the normal development of the fetus because nutrients are ingested by the mother, not the fetus, so that the amounts that actually cross the placenta remain unknown (Zamenhof and van Marthens 1978). Furthermore, the precise quantities and qualities required by the fetus are not known. It was once assumed that fetal and maternal nutritional needs were identical, but fetal needs for amino acids unique to early life have placed this assumption into serious doubt. The fetus requires **glucose,** the main source of biochemical energy, which is stored as glycogen in the placenta and the fetal liver. These stores are important as short-term reserves in the organism's response to perinatal stress. The fetus also requires amino acids for protein synthesis; these are absorbed in the maternal small intestine from food proteins and cross the placenta to the fetus. Vitamins and essential fatty acids are required, but only in such small amounts that maternal stores can usually provide them regardless of the nutritional status of the mother. Since the fetus can extract minerals such as iron from the mother even when her daily intake is inadequate (Leader et al. 1981), it is not usually vulnerable to a prenatal mineral deficiency.

The importance of maternal biochemical stores as a defense against the

TABLE 13-1   Essential Human Nutrients

Carbohydrate		
Fat		
Protein		
Water		
Minerals		
Calcium	Iron	Cobalt
Phosphorus	Zinc	Chromium
Potassium	Selenium	Fluorine
Sulfur	Manganese	Silicon
Sodium	Copper	Vanadium
Chlorine	Iodine	Nickel
Magnesium	Molybdenum	Tin
Vitamins		
A	Riboflavin	
D	Niacin	
E	Pyroxidine	
K	Pantothenic acid	
C (ascorbic acid)	Folacin	
B6 (Thiamin)	B12	
Biotin		

consequences of fetal malnutrition during pregnancy was apparent in the **Hongerwinter** of 1944–45 in Holland, when maternal stores were able to partially or fully offset severe deficiencies of maternal nutrients during gestation (Z. Stein et al. 1975).

Severe malnutrition very early in pregnancy, i.e., during the period of rapid neuronal proliferation when the fetus is extremely vulnerable, usually results in a failure to maintain embryonic implantation and subsequent spontaneous abortion. Moderate malnutrition throughout a pregnancy or more severe deficiencies later in gestation usually allow the fetus to survive but lead to changes in the growth of both placenta and fetus. Winick (1976) reported that changes in the placenta accompany and usually precede changes in the fetus. For this reason, the placenta has proved to be useful in indirectly evaluating the types of changes presumed to occur in fetal tissue (e.g., Beaconsfield et al. 1980).

At birth, the most obvious clinical manifestation of prenatal malnutrition is small size for gestational age, indicating intrauterine growth failure due to maternal malnutrition, i.e., the type I growth failure in Brasel's (1974) terminology. Organ size and weight, including the brain, also are below normal. Unlike intrauterine growth failure due to placental insufficiency (Type II), where there is a good deal of brain "sparing" relative to other organs, there is a parallel influence on all body organs if the growth failure is attributable to inadequate maternal nutrition.

Reduction in gross brain weight with maternal deprivation has been demonstrated both experimentally in animals and clinically at autopsy. The weight reduction is attributable to reduction of cellular proliferation involving both neurons and glial cells. In humans, the reduction is chiefly glial. However, the number of microneurons, whose proliferation continues beyond the early peak period, is also reduced. Winick and Rosso (1969) and Zamenhof and van Marthens (1978) independently determined that the decrease in brain weight corresponds to about a 15 per cent reduction in brain cell number.

Postnatal Deficiency

Experimental evidence concerning the influence of nutritional deficiencies on postnatal brain development has generally been consistent with Dobbing's hypothesis: on-going development is impaired in those cell types, tissues, and regions that show a maximal rate of growth at the time of the nutritional deficiency. Once rapid growth of the CNS has ended and development has stabilized, protein-calorie malnutrition has little permanent influence on the status of the brain.

Significant decreases in nerve cell number are not observed when the organism has had adequate prenatal but inadequate postnatal nutrition. However, the number of glial cells may be permanently reduced as a consequence of early postnatal deprivation. The primary effect of postnatal nutritional deficiency is an overall reduction in the *size* of both neurons and glial cells. This is generally reversible when subsequent food intake provides adequate nutrition. The elaboration of neuronal processes may also be stunted: given the reduction of glial cells in both number and size, the extent of myelination in the brain is reduced, though the composition of the myelin is not grossly abnormal. In animal studies, the cerebellum shows greater reduction in cell number because the critical period for cell proliferation occurs later there than in the cerebrum or the brainstem.

Marasmus and kwashiorkor refer to the clinical manifestations of life-threatening malnutrition after birth. However, it is likely that in most cases some degree of prenatal maternal malnutrition also occurred. Postmortem examinations of the brains of marasmic infants as well as experimental studies indicate that there is a reduction in cell number and cell size rather than a particular pattern of neuropathology. The quantity of myelin is reduced, but, again, aberrations in myelin composition do not occur to any significant degree. Persistent alterations in auditory-evoked potentials as a consequence of marasmus, despite rehabilitation, have been reported (Barnet et al. 1978). In kwashiorkor, cell size is reduced, but the number of cells may be unaffected. In one study, the EEG of recovered kwashiorkor children differed from those of siblings and peers who did not suffer severe clinical malnutrition, as well as from those of a group of the same age who had no nutritional deficiencies of any kind. The abnormal EEGs revealed less alpha activity and more slow-wave activity, indicating neuronal alterations (Bartel et al. 1979). The brains of animals inadequately nourished during both prenatal and postnatal periods of rapid brain development show a greater cumulative stunting than those affected during either period alone. Winick (1976) reported a reduction of 60 per cent in brain weight in that situation compared with a reduction of approximately 15 per cent with either prenatal or postnatal deprivation alone (Fig. 13-1).

13.2 BEHAVIORAL ALTERATIONS

Consequences of nutritional deficiencies are examined by follow-up investigation of retrospectively or prospectively identified individuals who have suffered some degree of early-life nutritional deprivation. Causes cannot be directly investigated in the study population but must be inferred from human case studies and animal experiments. No study has combined both behavioral and later autopsy data from human patients with nutritional deficiencies. To provide the most relevant information, follow-up studies of children exposed to nutritional deficiencies should cover the breadth of neuropsychological functioning as well as provide information on adaptive, motivational, and social maturity. Unfortunately, no available study meets this ideal. Most examine the long-term consequences of malnutrition by using a global measure of intelligence, such as the Wechsler or Stanford-Bi-

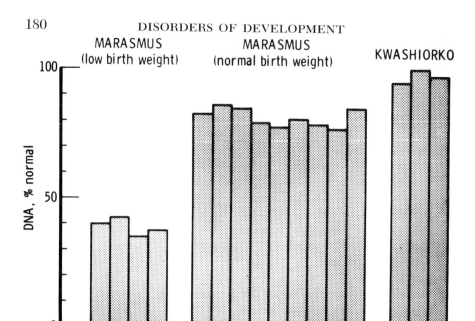

FIGURE 13-1   Comparison of brain cell numbers in marasmus, marasmus plus low birth weight, and kwashiorkor (Winick 1970).

net IQ scores. Others have sought to examine specific abilities, such as the development of cross-modal integrative capacities (i.e., identifying similarities and differences across senses) or language development. Groups that differ in nutritional history also differ in nutritional milieu, clouding any inferences of causality (Fig. 13-2).

As one solution to this perplexing difficulty, Cravioto and his associates (e.g., Cravioto and DeLicardie 1975) have done prospective research, collecting premorbid information about a large group of infants who subsequently may or may not become malnourished. A second approach has been to use animal (usually rat) models to study behavioral consequences just as they were used to study brain development. This approach has not been entirely successful because even in laboratory rats maternal care (Crnic 1976) and environmental stimulation (Levitsky and Barnes 1972) are potent early-life influences on later cognitive abilities.

In evaluating findings, the control groups used are important. They are usually matched for age and sex and include individual groups of siblings, neighbors, or members of the community with the same socioeconomic status (SES), as well as members of the community and of a neighboring community with a higher SES and minimal probability of suffering from nutritional deprivation. While the use of siblings is helpful in controlling family-child interactions and familial idiosyncrasies, it is very likely that siblings

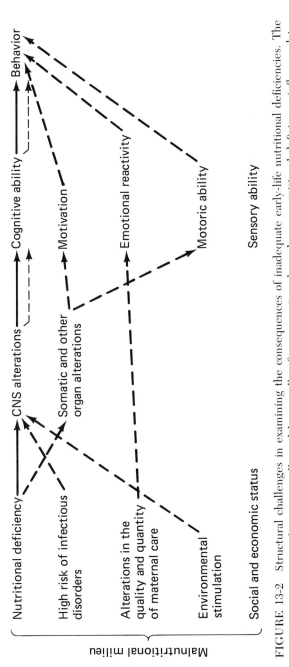

FIGURE 13-2 Structural challenges in examining the consequences of inadequate early-life nutritional deficiencies. The solid line represents what is typically and historically of concern, i.e., how does a nutritional deficiency influence later behavior? The additional variables are not exhaustive but are representative of the complicated array of variables that confront the researcher or clinician. As well, the alternative pathways (dashed lines) are just several examples of the underlying reality of what, at first glance, might appear to be altered behavior due to early-life nutritional status. For example, we know that environmental stimulation can offset the influences of nutritional deficiencies in early life (Levitsky and Barnes 1972) and can influence the CNS regardless of nutritional status. We also know, for example, that behavior can be influenced by early-life nutritional status via changes in muscular capacity influencing motor ability, again regardless of CNS influences.

also suffer from some degree of subclinical malnutrition. Comparisons between index and sibling groups may therefore underestimate the deficits (Hertzig et al. 1972).

Retrospective designs curtail the value of information gathered on the long-term consequences of early-life nutritional deficiencies. Relative to early-life nutritional status, a retrospective design cannot provide information about the premorbid status, standard medical diagnosis of the nutritional deficiency, and the percentage of the population of interest that died as a result of the deficiency. Retrospective studies of subclinical malnutrition are even less powerful because the presence of an early-life deficiency is only inferred from anthropometric measurements.

Marasmus Follow-up Studies

Marasmus typically is manifested during the first six months of life. The premarasmic child's low-calorie diet often is also low in protein. The marasmic infant shows a failure to grow, usually weighing less than 60 percent of the age-expected norm. In many cases, the marasmic infant has been stunted from conception because of the mother's insufficient nutritional and biochemical stores as well as the effects of nutritional deficiency endemic to her population for generations. The generational factor may have influenced, for example, the anatomy of her pelvic region and the efficiency of her digestive and metabolic systems.

Starvation of the infant is usually exacerbated by abrupt and premature weaning. Breast milk is frequently replaced by diluted, dirty, and infectious food. Muscle and organ wasting, loss of subcutaneous fat, and minimal hair growth are common, but swelling (edema) is absent. Marasmic infants are typically apathetic but become very irritable when handled. Without medical intervention, death from starvation compounded by infection is a common outcome. Successful nutritional rehabilitation can avert death, but usually the infant returns to an environment that continues to supply insufficient nutrition.

The literature examining the long-term consequences of marasmus is limited to retrospective investigations. The results of these studies have fairly consistently shown that marasmic infants perform significantly more poorly than controls on global measures of mental ability.

Cabak and Najdanvic (1965), for instance, tested 36 marasmic subjects (after successful rehabilitation in early life) when the subjects were between 7 and 14 years of age. The mean Binet-Simon IQ for this sample was 88. However, the lack of adequate control subjects matched for age, sex, and community experience leaves this finding open to dispute. In a more adequately controlled investigation, Brockman and Ricciuti (1971) examined the categorization behavior of marasmic infants after successful hospitalization and rehabilitation. A control group of children who were matched for age and sex and who did not show evidence of clinical malnutrition in early life was drawn from a day care center in an urban slum community. The previously malnourished infants performed less well on the task than the more adequately fed control group. McLaren and colleagues (1973) examined performance on the Stanford-Binet for groups of nutritionally stunted and control Lebanese children who were between 3 and 5 years of age at follow-up. Rehabilitated marasmic children, subclinically malnourished children, the siblings of both groups, and a control group matched for age and SES were tested. Global mean IQ values were lower by one standard deviation or more for the masasmic and subclinical groups.

In sum, infants who have suffered clinically diagnosed marasmus during the first year of life and have been rehabilitated show evidence of sizeable lasting mental deficits when examined at follow-up on global measures of intelligence.

Kwashiorkor Follow-Up Studies

Kwashiorkor usually appears between the first and third years of life. It is not observed in the early months of life because breast milk provides the infant with adequate protein and protection from infection. Kwashiorkor may begin to appear if the baby is weaned to a protein-deficient diet. The lack of adequate protein is compounded by severe diarrhea, which is reported for over 90 per cent of kwashiorkor cases (Gomez et al. 1955). Edema is a common feature of kwashiorkor, resulting in the typical image of the starving infant with a greatly bloated stomach, a moon-shaped face, and sparse, depigmented hair. The child is often apathetic, somnolent, and indifferent to its surroundings, producing intermittent periods of monotonous crying and/or echolalia. A low **serum albumin** (the main blood protein) level is characteristic of kwashiorkor.

Studies of children who have suffered kwashiorkor in infancy present more varied findings than those of the marasmic infant. Generally, deficits found after nutritional rehabilitation are less severe in kwashiorkor (see Pollit and Thompson 1977 for a detailed review).

Birch and colleagues (1971) examined Mexican children who were between 6 and 30 months of age and hospitalized because of diagnosed kwashiorkor and compared their performance with that of their nearest-aged sibling who did not show signs of a *clinical* nutritional deficiency. At follow-up, the children were between 6 and 13 years of age and had been out of hospital for at least three years. Full scale, verbal, and performance IQ scores were all significantly lower in the patient group than in the group of siblings. For example, the stunted group's mean full scale IQ was 68.5 and that for the siblings was 81.5. An analysis of the subtest scatter showed no specific deficiencies.

On the other hand, Bartel et al. (1977a, 1977b) and Evans et al. (1971) failed to find significant differences between groups of children who had a history of kwashiorkor and controls without evidence of clinical levels of malnutrition. Bartel et al. examined 31 children 5 to 14 years of age who had been diagnosed and treated for kwashiorkor by age 3. The performance of these children was contrasted with that of two control groups: nearest-age siblings and an age-matched group of peers from the same community. All three groups showed similar performance on all tasks—the tactual performance test, tactual form recognition, the categories test from the Halstead-Reitan battery and the WISC mazes task—but they differed on levels of alpha and slow-wave activity (Bartel et al. 1979). Evans et al. compared children who had a documented history of kwashiorkor with their adequately nourished siblings on the New South African Individual Scale of Intelligence and the Goodenough-Harris drawing task. The groups performed similarly on these tests.

Follow-Up Studies of Subclinical Nutritional Deficiency

Whereas studies of marasmus and kwashiorkor rely upon a medically diagnosed and documented early-life condition, the follow-up study of children with moderately inadequate nutrition has to rely on more indirect, anthropometric measures, such as size and weight for age. Despite this difficulty in classifying nutritional status, a carefully designed study by Cravioto et al. (1966) provided useful information about the cognitive consequences of subclinical deficiencies. The upper and lower quartiles for height in cross-sectional samples of 6 to 11 year olds from a poor rural and a high-SES urban community in Chile were chosen to determine cross-modal visual, kinesthetic, and haptic integrative capacity. In general, the high-SES urban group performed better on the tasks than the rural group. In the rural group, the lower height quartile (i.e., those who were likely to have suffered from early-life deficits) performed less well than the upper quartile, whereas in the urban-group quartile status was not related to cross-modal performances. The authors also examined the range of possible relations between early-life nutrition and later cognitive performances.

Other studies of subclinical malnutrition, discussed by Pollit and Thompson (1977), have explored the effect of nutritional and psychoeducational intervention programs on mental development. An investigation by McKay and colleagues (1978) found a narrowing of the differences between deprived and control children following treatment that combined nutrition, education, and health care. Zeskind and Ramey (1981) reported a similar amelioration of the effects of fetal malnourishment in a three-year follow-up. Recent studies reviewed by Ricciuti (1981) suggest, in fact, that under optimal rehabilitation conditions the long-term effects of subclinical malnutrition may be completely eliminated.

In an important prospective study, Cravioto and DeLicardie (1975) analyzed the relation between the conditions of a child's upbringing, especially nutrition, with the course of the child's physical growth, mental development, and learning. The setting of the study was a stable population in an agricultural community in southwestern Mexico. A census one year before the study cohort was born determined the similarity between the cohort's families and the community as a whole (population 5637). Eighty per cent of the villagers were under 35 years of age, reflecting the reduced life expectancy in the region. Most of the adults were seasonal agricultural laborers. Illiteracy was commonplace. Many households had substandard sanitary facilities. Malnutrition affected a large proportion of the village population and ranged from mild to clinically severe. The entire cohort born during a 12-month period in 1966 and 1967 was followed for seven years at dozens of data-gathering times. Demographic, nutritional, and social background data indicated that the families of the children in the study were representative of the community as a whole.

Of the 300 infants born during the 12 months, equal numbers were boys and girls. The mean birth weight was 2898 grams, with 12.3 per cent being below 2500 grams. The total first-year mortality rate was 6.4 per cent. During the first five years of life, 22 children were clinically diagnosed as suffering from severe malnutrition: fifteen were cases of kwashiorkor and 7 of marasmus. By the end of the first 38 months of life, 72 of the 276 (26 per cent) children surviving in the cohort showed growth failure relative to normative expectations, including 14 of the 19 clinically malnourished children. The first indication of growth failure in clinically malnourished children appeared an average of 7.7 months before the diagnosis of clinically severe malnutrition was made.

The 19 children with severe malnutrition before the age of 39 months were matched for gestational age, weight, and length at birth with children from the cohort who were not clinically malnourished but who probably suffered from some degree of nutritional deficit. A language "age" was determined for each child by the Gesell method, and the malnourished children showed poorer language development than their matched cohort mates. Early language development (e.g., babbling) was very similar for the two groups during the first year of life, when only one severe case of malnutrition had been diagnosed. As time passed and more children were recognized as suffering from malnutrition, differences in language development favorable to the control children became evident. The differences became more marked at each successive testing period.

In addition to the global measure of language development, a specific test of bipolar concept formation was administered on several occasions. The ability to recognize the difference between such concepts as big-little, in-out, and long-short was evaluated with this test. Testing at 26, 30, 34, 38, 42, 46, 50, 54, and 58 months indicated that the malnourished children had a poorer grasp of bipolar concepts than control subjects. The difference continued beyond the time of clinical recovery.

Family variables were examined in relation to test performance. Very little in the familial "macroenvironment" (a term used to refer to such variables as literacy, family size, and sanitation) correlated with test performance. Nor did age, height, weight, educational level, personal cleanliness, or sources of income account for a significant portion of the variability in test performance. The "**microenvironment**," however, was strongly associated with nutritional status. This basically represented the stimulation the child received at home, including stability of adult contact, vocal stimulation, need gratification, emotional climate, avoidance of restriction, breadth of experience, aspects of the physical environment, and available play materials. The strong association between nutritional status and microenvironment was present even at the age of 6 months, when only one infant was diagnosed as being severely malnourished. Cravioto and DeLicardie concluded that a deficit in the child's microenvironment was important in determining which children suffering from chronic, subclinical deficiencies will eventually develop a clinically diagnosable severe malnutrition. A follow-up by Cravioto and Arrieta (1979) showed that intensive infant stimulation at home was effective in the rehabilitation process.

A recent study by Galler et al. (1983a, 1983b) provided another detailed examination of 129 children between 5 and 11 years of age in Barbados who had been subjected to severe protein-calorie malnutrition during their first year of life. Compared with a matched control group, the malnourished children showed significantly lower IQ scores although socioeconomic differences between the two groups were not significantly associated with IQ differences. Teachers who rated the children without knowledge of their nutritional history indicated significantly more attentional deficits, reduced social skills, poorer physical appearance, and emotional instability for children in the study group than for controls. These behavioral characteristics were independent of IQ scores and more frequent in boys.

14

Anoxic Episodes

The maturing fetus and neonate are subject to alterations in the availability of oxygen and oxygenated blood during gestation, delivery, and the period immediately following birth. Maternal disease and cardiovascular difficulties, contractions of the uterus during delivery, the cutting of the umbilical cord, and numerous other conditions may interfere with normal oxygen supply. In most of these situations, the reduction in oxygen is relatively minor, transient, and amenable to natural physiological and metabolic compensation without risk of serious complications. However, a serious reduction in available oxygen (**hypoxia**) and termination of oxygen supply (**anoxia**) are not uncommon perinatal complications. A systemic reduction in oxygen level leads to decreased blood flow to local tissue, distinguished as ischemia and therefore sometimes called **anoxic ischemia.** These three terms are sometimes used interchangeably; we shall use "anoxic episode" as a general term. Anoxic episodes and their immediate consequences account for the greatest percentage of neurological difficulties encountered during the perinatal period. For example, they account for many of the convulsive disorders that occur in the neonatal period (A. Rose 1977).

An anoxic episode involves more than simply a drop in the amount of oxygen available. A decrease in available oxygen leads to a biochemical switch from the *aerobic* (i.e., occurring in oxygen) generation of energy to the less efficient anaerobic (in the absence of oxygen) generation and to a rapid depletion of the brain's very limited reserve of energy (in the form of adenosine triphosphate). An anoxic episode also results in the accumulation of biochemical waste products, such as carbon dioxide and lactic acid, generated anaerobically from spent energy supplies. These waste products are toxic and contribute to the neurological problems created by the anoxic episode.

An episode of anoxia can also lead to cardiac arrest and stagnation in the neonate's systemic blood circulation. Stagnated circulation increases the

187

vascular pressure, and this causes extravasation (leaking) of blood from circulatory vessels into the surrounding tissue. The result can be a very serious perinatal complication: intracranial hemorrhage. The brain is the organ most vulnerable to damage during an anoxic episode because it has a large and constant metabolic demand for oxygen and because neurons do not regenerate after cell death. The brain is also vulnerable to anoxia-induced vascular stagnation because of the proportionally large amount of blood flowing through it at any given time.

The period around birth is the time of greatest risk for an anoxic episode. Yet, it has also proved to be the period during which the organism can best react successfully, within limits. Since oxygen reduction is inherent in birth because of the pressure upon the placenta during delivery and because of the cutting of the cord, this resiliency is protective of the species in an evolutionary sense.

The premature infant is at especially high risk because it is essentially unprepared for birth. The premature infant simply is not ready to begin respiration and may require immediate intervention to avert asphyxiation. A complex surface-active substance in the lung, **surfactant,** is necessary for normal respiration (Notter and Shapiro 1981). Surfactant, which is composed predominantly of phospholipids, lowers the surface tension of lung tissue and allows respiration to occur. An adequate supply of surfactant has developed in the lungs by the time of a full-term birth but is not available in sufficient quantities for the premature. This condition is known as **respiratory distress syndrome** (RDS) or **hyaline membrane disease** (Avery and Mead 1959, Dabiri 1979). Until recently, when therapeutics became available, RDS was the leading cause of death in infants born before the thirty-seventh gestational week (Dabiri 1979).

Immediate and sustained intervention is necessary for babies with RDS. However, even intervention in such cases is hazardous. **Hyperoxia,** too much oxygen, has toxic consequences and may result in chronic lung disease and blindness due to retrolental fibroplasia (Stern 1973; see also Chap. 23). **Hypercarbia,** too much carbon dioxide waste product, coexists with the overabundance of oxygen and may also contribute to the observed toxic damage.

The long-term neurobehavioral sequelae in survivors of prenatal and perinatal anoxia have long been of interest to physicians and psychologists. Beginning with Little (1861), an anoxic episode during early life has been regarded as a primary determinant of both mental retardation and cerebral palsy. These clinical impressions stimulated empirical research, particularly during the 1950s and 1960s. Gottfried (1973) carefully reviewed the results of 24 major research studies up to the early 1970s. Since then, sophisticated long-term follow-up investigations have been completed.

14.1 CAUSES

When discussing anoxic episodes, it is useful to delineate three categories of causal factors according to time: (1) gestational, (2) parturitional, and (3) neonatal.

The gestational causes can be described as either maternal or placental. Maternal cardiac arrest, for instance, commonly leads to total oxygen deprivation in the fetus (Adamsons and Myers 1973). Maternal infectious diseases, diabetes mellitus, and toxemias all can reduce the oxygen available to the fetus. Severe anemia or bleeding in the mother is also a risk factor for a fetal anoxic episode. Disorders in the structure or function of the placenta, such as an infarction of placental tissue, may not permit adequate levels of oxygen to cross it and reach the fetus (Naeye 1977). If the mother is suffering from malnourishment, the placenta may be underdeveloped and therefore transport less than optimal amounts of oxygen to the fetus.

During parturition, abrupt fetal separation from the placenta, placental compression due to uterine hypertonicity, and placenta previa can reduce the availability of oxygen to the fetus. In **placenta previa** the fetus cannot be delivered normally because the placenta is partially or completely blocking the fetus's exit from the uterus. In this case, compression of the placenta may hinder the transport of oxygen to the fetus. An additional parturitional cause of an anoxic episode is traumatic brain injury. Perinatal brain trauma commonly includes the brainstem and may cause anoxic damage by interfering with CNS control over respiration and other vital systemic functions.

Gestation- and parturition-induced anoxic episodes often continue to have a negative influence on perinatal status after delivery and require immediate postnatal respiratory intervention. These newborns show clinical signs of oxygen deprivation (e.g., color change) and consistently low Apgar scores. However, the extent and severity of a prenatal anoxic episode is poorly indexed by these signs, even when the condition continues beyond birth. Thus an anoxic episode before birth is far more difficult to diagnose than a perinatal episode. However, the advent of nuclear magnetic resonance as a diagnostic technology (e.g., Partain et al. 1983) may provide for the in vivo diagnosis of prenatal anoxia as well as assess the location and extent of neuropathological damage. **Nuclear magnetic resonance** is a method of producing brain images and biochemical analyses of brain regions that is sensitive to, among other phenomena, acid-base changes in anoxically damaged brain tissue.

Immediately following birth, failure to begin respiration or subsequent apneic spells after the onset of breathing prevent environmental oxygen from reaching the neonate. The mechanisms that underlie initiation of respiration at birth are not completely understood and remain an active area of basic medical research (M. Purves 1974). Some of the factors that can interfere with normal respiratory activity are an incompetent or underdeveloped respiratory or circulatory system, traumatic injury to the CNS, traumatic injury to the lungs, and pneumonia. **Asphyxia neonaturum** is the traditional diagnostic label for a failure to begin respiration.

The consequences of an anoxic episode vary widely and depend upon such factors as cause, duration of the deprivation, age and developmental status at the time of deprivation, and, importantly, velocity of the reduction in oxygen level. In addition, secondary complications as a result of the episode are important when long-term outcome is examined. The child's prognosis, for example, may be especially poor if there is associated intraventricular hemorrhage or if neonatal seizures occur as a result of the anoxic episode.

14.2 DEFINING THE ANOXIC EPISODE

Several diagnostic difficulties are important in any evaluation of the neurobehavioral consequences of anoxia because the validity of a single-construct "anoxia" is untenable for any group analysis. Direct measures of anoxia, such as oxygen saturation and oxygen content in blood samples, normally vary so widely in early life as to be of little use in any long-term predictive sense (K. F. Graham et al. 1962). Even different perinatal measures of anoxia show less correlation among themselves than might be anticipated (Broman 1979). The definition of the anoxic episode could include not only the amount of time that the neonate does not breathe but also measurements of blood pressure, oxygen saturation, red blood cell count, blood sugar levels, and fluid/electrolyte balance.

It is apparent that various diagnostic groups with different prognoses are subsumed under the generic term "anoxia." The parameters of these groups are formed either deliberately in terms of etiology or "accidentally" because of limitations in the measuring instrument. Gottfried's (1973) critical analysis of the available follow-up literature provides a detailed discussion of some of these difficulties.

14.3 NEUROPATHOLOGY

Infants who survive an anoxic episode with gross CNS damage show variable patterns of neuropathology. The typical neurological consequence is **neuronal necrosis,** i.e., cell death. Necrosis is primarily, but not exclusively, located in cortical regions. Thalamic and brainstem necrosis has also been reported (Volpe 1976). Paradoxically, severely asphyxiated infants who die very soon after the perinatal episode do not show cellular damage because the many neuronal changes (e.g., loss of Nissl substance, nuclear pyknosis, hypertrophied astrocyte cells) begin to appear only 24 to 36 hours after the episode (Norman 1978).

In addition to these changes in the cell body, damage to the fibers that form CNS white matter also occurs as a consequence of the anoxic episode. **Periventricular leukomalacia,** for instance, is characterized by necrosis of white matter, principally that located in the regions adjacent to the anterior and the temporo-occipital horns of the lateral ventricles and in the corona radiata. This is a coagulation necrosis that is characterized by a loss of distinctiveness in cellular architecture and a homogenization of cellular components (Banker and Larroche 1962). The lesions appear as many small areas of coagulated, homogenized tissue surrounded by liquified areas, usually bilateral but not necessarily symmetrical. Periventricular leukomalacia occurs primarily in the premature infant who has suffered an anoxic episode (Volpe 1976). If the episode was a severe one, the leukomalacia may be complicated by a hemorrhagic inflow to the necrotic tissue (Hill et al. 1982).

Although this pathological condition was originally described in the mid-nineteenth century (Virchow 1867), Banker and Larroche (1962) provided the first detailed autopsy descriptions of periventricular leukomalacia, which they found in 20 per cent of their sample of severely oxygen-deprived babies. A decade later, Armstrong and Norman (1974) reported only one third that incidence. They attributed the difference to improvements in neonatal intensive care.

Another common pattern of anoxic neuropathology is the **watershed necrotic infarction** (Volpe 1976). These infarcts occur in "watershed" areas of the cerebral cortex and subcortical white matter, i.e., the boundary zone at the periphery of the outlying branches of the cerebral arteries. Because of their distance from the major arteries, watershed zones are most vulnerable to necrotic damage when there is a drop in arterial blood pressure and a loss of oxygenated blood.

Status marmoratus is a lesion of the basal ganglia that is sometimes observed in full-term babies who have suffered an anoxic episode (Volpe 1976). The major pathological features are neuronal loss, astrocytic gliosis, and increased myelination of astrocytes in the basal ganglia.

Towbin (1970, 1971) examined the neuropathological consequences of anoxia and anoxia-induced hemorrhage in 600 brains from both premature and full-term infants. Based on these studies, he proposed a three-stage anoxic process. The first stage is the anoxic episode itself; this results in systemic circulatory failure (stage two), which in turn causes local venous infarction (stage three). In the brain, systemic venous congestion increases venous pressure relative to the surrounding tissue. This tissue readily undergoes diffuse infarctional damage as the blood stagnates in the veins. Extravasation of the blood into surrounding tissue results in an intracerebral hemorrhage. However, the relationship between anoxia-induced venous stagnation and intraventricular hemorrhage has been examined and criticized by de Courten and Rabinowicz (1981), who argue that a more suitable explanation of the intraventricular hemorrhage is not the increased vascular pressure but decreased tissue pressure, as seen in dehydration.

Towbin's autopsy findings also revealed an important change in the locus of CNS damage depending on the infant's age at the time of the anoxic episode. Premature infants, particularly those between 22 and 35 weeks of gestational age, suffered cerebral infarctional damage in periventricular areas, which contain the residue of the germinal matrix. This residual matrix is the structurally weak tissue from which, earlier in development, brain cells began their migration to their permanent positions. The leaking of stagnated venous blood from this region into the lateral ventricles typically results in an intraventricular hemorrhage. Full-term infants, on the other hand, suffered diffuse cerebral cortical damage rather than periventricular damage because, by the time of term, the germinal matrix tissue has disintegrated and become insignificant. If hemorrhage occurred in full-term infants, extravasation of blood from the superficial, convex venous drainage system that spans the cerebral cortex was observed. Anoxia-induced hemorrhage was seen more frequently in premature infants than in full-term infants.

14.4 NEUROBEHAVIORAL CONSEQUENCES

Given the complexity and variability of anoxic episodes, it is difficult to generalize in a clinically useful manner about their long-term consequences. The possible consequences of an anoxic episode range from immediate death or gross neuropathology through various hypothetical subclinical lesions to the apparent absence of any mental and neurological sequelae.

Some generalizations, however, can be attempted. It was found in the Perinatal Collaborative Project that 22.8 per cent of infants who suffered intrauterine anoxia died during the perinatal period (Niswander et al. 1975). The percentage of neonatal deaths was higher (52 per cent) in an examination of infants who suffered very severe oxygen deprivation at birth (i.e., a delay of spontaneous respiration for at least 20 minutes and/or apparent stillbirth; H. Scott 1976). Dweck and colleagues (1974) reported an even higher death rate (31 of 51 cases) in infants with Apgar scores below 3 who required immediate intervention, and Mulligan and colleagues (1980) found a 44 per cent death rate among infants who required immediate intervention for at least 1 minute before the onset of spontaneous respiration.

The neurobehavioral sequelae in surviving infants vary depending upon the type of damage. Many of the nonprogressive motor deficits of childhood are apparently related to the occurrence of perinatal anoxic episodes (e.g., Crothers and Paine 1959). Neonates who suffer hypotonia following the anoxic episode have a poorer neurobehavioral prognosis than those who do not (Brown et al. 1974). According to Volpe (1976), the neurological consequences of periventricular leukomalacia may well include spastic diplegia, the most important motor deficit observed in prematurely born infants. Extrapyramidal disturbances, particularly choreoathetosis and rigidity, are associated with the basal ganglia damage that can occur in status marmoratus. Motor deficit, seizures, and mental retardation are all possible sequelae of cerebral necrosis, depending upon the locus and extent of cell death. Neonates with consistent Apgar scores of 3 or lower in the Perinatal Collaborative Project had a risk of developing cerebral palsy 162 times greater than that of infants whose Apgar scores were between 7 and 10 when measured 5 minutes after birth. More than one third of the surviving children with Apgar scores 3 or below at 20 minutes showed a motor disability at follow-up (K. Nelson and Ellenberg 1979). In the study by Mulligan et al. (1980) 18.5 per cent of survivors suffered from major neurological disorders at follow-up (e.g., spastic di-, quadri-, and hemiplegia); 9 per cent had milder neurological sequelae. Bilateral spastic paresis was the most common form of cerebral palsy observed. Neonatal seizures occured in all eight of the surviving children who had 20-minute Apgar socres of 3 or lower.

Infants who suffer an anoxic episode in early life are at greater risk for later mental retardation (Gottfried 1973). However, risk is not synonymous with occurrence: mental retardation is not an inevitable consequence of an early-life anoxic episode. The factors which influence the probability of occurrence are not well understood. Data from the Perinatal Collaborative Project indicate that mental retardation among children who had consistently low Apgar scores at birth is associated with cerebral palsy (Nelson and Ellenberg 1981a). Overt CNS damage accompanying an anoxic episode in early life increases the risk of mental retardation in later infancy and childhood (Broman 1979). Fifteen per cent of Mulligan et al.'s (1980) follow-up sample were intellectually impaired, although the median score of 108 on the Stanford-Binet intelligence test for the entire sample was in the higher-average range. All but one of the impaired children had associated neurological impairments. A recent 18-month follow-up of 62 full-term newborns treated for postasphyxial encephalopathy found major impairments in 47 per cent as reflected in Bayley DQ scores below 70. An additional 8 per cent had developmental quotients between 70 and 85. Hydrocephalus and spastic hemi-, quadra-, and diplegia were present in most of these cases (Fitzhardinge et al. 1981). The authors noted that CT scans taken during the first two weeks of life and at six months were highly predictive of outcome and served to specify the damage in these children.

Despite the high rates of death and frank neuropathology, many infants survive an anoxic episode with little, if any, medical sequelae. These infants have been the subject of many investigations to determine what, if any, learning or cognitive deficits they suffer. Gottfried's (1973) conclusions after reviewing the literature were that little specific information could be gleaned from the literature but that cognitive deficits after an anoxic episode are more prevalent in infants and preschoolers than in older children and adolescents.

There have been two large-scale longitudinal studies: the St. Louis prospective study conducted in the 1950s and 1960s by Graham, Corah, and colleagues (Corah et al. 1965, F. K. Graham et al. 1962) and the more recent Collaborative Perinatal Project (Broman 1979).

In the **St. Louis prospective study,** children who had suffered prenatal or postnatal anoxic episodes were assessed at 3 and 7 years of age along with a group of normal children matched for age, sex, race, and SES. The follow-up data included information concerning intellectual, neurological, anthropometric, conceptual, perceptual-motor, and personality status. At 3 years of age, the anoxic group performed significantly more poorly than the control group on all tests of cognitive functioning. These included the Stanford-Binet intelligence test and tests of concept formation and vocabulary. However, conceptual skills were more impaired than vocabulary skill. No impairment on perceptual-motor functioning was observed. The anoxic group contained more children with positive and suggestive neurological findings at follow-up than did the control group. The cognitive impairment was more severe in children who had a postnatal anoxic episode than in children with a prenatal episode. At 7 years of age, intelligence test differences between anoxic and control groups had dissipated to such a degree that the two groups were no longer significantly different in their performance. The only WISC subtest to differ significantly between the two groups was vocabulary. However, the anoxic group performed more poorly on tests of perceptual-motor functioning and perceptual attention than did the controls.

The Collaborative Perinatal Project indicated that an anoxic episode was a very weak predictor of later-life cognitive status. However, the anoxic group did show lower performances on cognitive tasks than did the nonanoxic controls at three ages; 8 months, 4 years, and 7 years. The differences between the groups were not very large and were more pronounced at 8 months than at 7 years. Unfortunately, both studies stopped soon after the children entered school, so that they provided no information on the development of academic and learning problems.

Recent follow-up studies have also addressed the outcome for specific anoxic subgroups. The literature on consequences of the respiratory distress syndrome, in particular, is growing (e.g., T. Field et al. 1979). Generally, groups of children with a history of this syndrome perform more poorly than children without this syndrome on tests such as the Bayley developmental scales.

In sum, an anoxic episode in early life is a very weak predictor of later childhood disability. The data of the Perinatal Project suggest that the episode per se accounts for only a small percentage of the observed variability in later intellectual and cognitive test performance. The St. Louis study, along with other literature, suggests that, although group differences may be apparent, inferences about the prognosis of individual children are highly tenuous. However, this weak predictive value is not unexpected given the wide range in causality, severity, and complications associated with an episode.

15

Brain Injury and Neoplasms

This chapter deals with certain types of early-life neurological damage, such as traumatic injuries to the brain and spinal cord during the stretching and molding of the fetus as it traverses and emerges from the birth canal. There is further risk of brain damage during the first few years of life as a result of head injuries due either to accidents or to child abuse. Finally, specific neurological diseases, such as brain tumors, though not very common in infancy, do occur and pose challenging problems for the neuropsychologist.

15.1 PERINATAL MECHANICAL DAMAGE

In addition to the occurrence of anoxic episodes, described in the previous chapter, the perinatal period is also a time of increased risk for CNS injury due to purely mechanical causes, such as stretching, compression, shearing, and twisting. These physical forces arise from the passage of the fetus through the birth canal and the final emergence of the neonate from the mother.

Figure 15-1 depicts the normal traverse and the requisite twists and turns of the fetus's head and body during labor. These complex events of vaginal delivery are associated with cranial molding and stretching as well as with rapid changes in the pressure impinging upon the fetus's head. The fetus's progress through the birth canal is difficult enough during a normal, uneventful delivery. However, it can easily become more difficult because of a wide variety of complicating factors, e.g., an inelastic birth canal that is physiologically not prepared for delivery of a premature infant, a large baby relative to the size of the birth canal, or fetal orientation during delivery that is not in the normal **vertex position** (i.e., head exiting from the birth canal first). The use of forceps (Fig. 15-2) to extract the neonate may cause fracturing of the skull and damage to underlying brain tissue.

A common cause for complications during delivery is the malpositioning

196

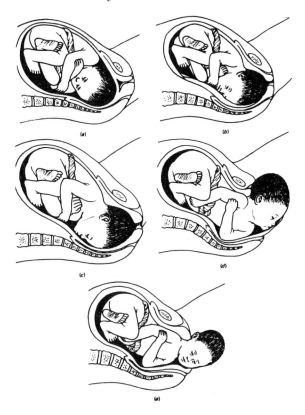

FIGURE 15-1   Mechanism of normal labor: (a) engagement, descent flexion, (b) internal rotation, (c) beginning extension, (d) completed extension, (e) external rotation (restitution) (Ross Clinical Education Aid 13, Ross Laboratories, Columbus, Ohio).

of the placenta or the fetus. Placenta previa is a condition in which the placenta blocks the passage for the fetus, and the continued pressure of the fetus against the placenta may curtail placental nutrients and oxygen. The **breech presentation** (i.e., buttocks first, head last) is a common malpositioning for the fetus and has been associated with increased mortality rates relative to nonbreach births (National Institutes of Health 1981).

A variety of fetal presenting positions immediately prior to labor can occur. In the normal vertex position, the cranium is the first part of the baby's body out of the mother. **Face presentations** twist the head away from the normal body axis. In the breech presentation (Fig. 15-3), the head is the last part of the baby's body to be removed from the mother, subjecting it to potentially more severe mechanical stresses for a longer period of time. An alternative type of delivery, **cesearean section,** is warranted when fetal

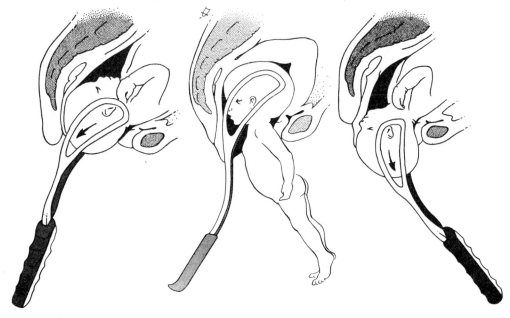

FIGURE 15-2   Forceps application: (a) in normal position, (b) in normal position showing change in force and direction, with aftercoming head (Oxorn 1980).

FIGURE 15-3   Lateral view of (a) face and (b) breech presentation (Oxorn 1980).

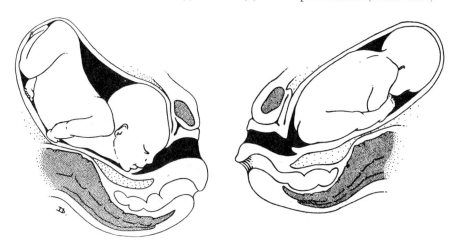

or placental malpositioning prevents a normal vaginal delivery: the fetus is surgically removed by incising through the uterus to prevent the serious injury, to neonate as well as mother, that might ensue during a complicated vaginal delivery (National Institutes of Health 1981).

The frequency with which mechanical injuries occur during birth has substantially decreased over the past half-century because of medical advances in obstetric diagnosis and care. These advances have not been solely technological but also include changes in our understanding of the complexity of the neonatal period. Because of obstetric advances, severe forms of perinatal mechanical injury are becoming rarer. Neonates who do sustain injuries are now immediately subjected to rigorous intensive care, which previously was unavailable. Care for the newborn has also become more sophisticated because of advances in diagnostic methods. Diagnostic imaging of the brain has become invaluable in the early diagnosis of intracranial hemorrhage, permitting immediate intervention for a specific diagnosis that previously might have been made only at autopsy (Cartwright et al. 1979). As fewer neonates succumb to severe perinatal damage and death, determining the nature of possible neuropsychological sequelae becomes more important because there will be larger pools of perinatal survivors.

Mechanical injury to the brain may result in two broad neurological conditions: intracranial hemorrhage and CNS tissue damage. Intracranial hemorrhage is the most common manifestation of perinatal CNS trauma and may cause further CNS tissue damage because increased intracranial pressure may displace brain tissue against the skull. Tissue damage may occur, however, in the absence of any hemorrhagic condition. Both may coexist in a wider complex of problems, including anoxic episodes and neonatal seizures, depending upon the severity of the infant's injury.

Hemorrhage

The extravasation of blood from intracranial blood vessels is a common consequence of perinatal mechanical injury. The major forms of perinatal hemorrhage are subdural, which may include a cerebral bleeding episode, a posterior fossa bleeding episode, or a small pial vein bleeding episode; subarachnoid; cerebellar; and periventricular. Hemorrhages typically bleed into the spaces between the meningeal layers overlying the brain; hence their names: subdural and subarachnoid hemorrhages. Peri- and intraventricular hemorrhages are discussed in Chap. 13. A cerebellar hemorrhage, like a periventricular hemorrhage, involves bleeding directly into nervous tissue. Perinatal intracranial hemorrhages usually arise from the large venous sinuses as well as from venous vessels, such as the vein of Galen. Figure 15-4 shows the superficial and deep venous systems of the brain.

A **subdural hemorrhage,** the discharge of blood into the subdural space, is particularly devastating. It is usually a consequence of trauma during full-term delivery, resulting from excessive molding of the head. The molding

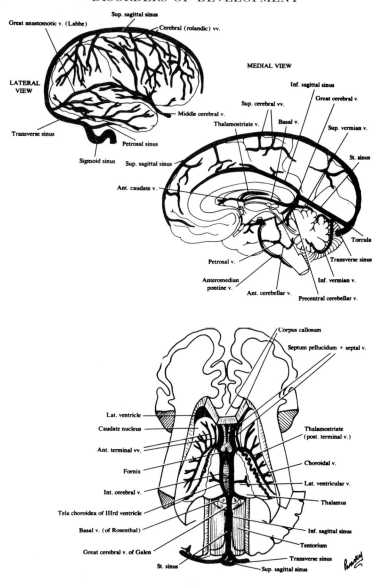

-123-

FIGURE 15-4   The superficial and deep venous sytem of the brain (Pansky and Allen 1980).

increases stress and strain on the meningeal structures, such as the tento-rium and the falx cerebri, and results in the tearing of these structures and nearby veins (Fig. 15-5). Blood from a subdural hemorrhage does not read-ily reabsorb into the bloodstream. In survivors, obstructive membranes

surround the bleed several weeks following the episode because of a proliferation of fibroblasts, which surround fluids (such as blood) that contain
large amounts of protein (Schurr 1969). These obstructions inhibit reab-
sorption.

There are several types of subdural hemorrhage. One form involves

FIGURE 15-5   Cutaway and coronal section of brain showing tentorium, falx, and
membranes (Pansky and Allen 1980).

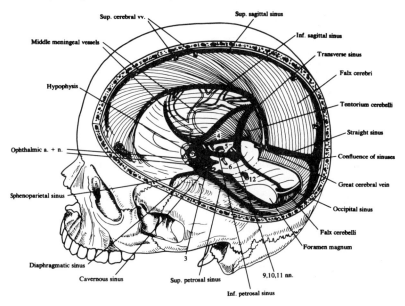

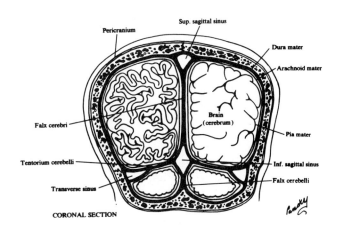

bleeding from the convex, bridging veins of the cerebral hemispheres entering the superior sagittal sinus. Another form involves bleeding from deep venous structures into the posterior fossa region, and another involves bleeding from small pial veins. Of the three types of subdural hemorrhage, the deep-structure bleed is by far the most critical.

Towbin (1969a) reported anatomical data on cerebral and posterior fossa extravasation. Cerebral subdural hemorrhage results in the discharge of blood over the convexity of the cerebral hemispheres. The veins that tear in this type of traumatic hemorrhage are the superficial bridging veins between the medial superior aspect of the cerebral hemispheres and the superior sagittal sinus. The bleeding results in a thin layer of blood over the entire cerebrum but is less dramatic in consequence than a posterior fossa bleed. Fifty to 80 per cent of survivors of a cerebral subdural hemorrhage are medically fit at follow-up. The remaining survivors may be left with focal cerebral signs and hydrocephalus (Volpe 1977).

A subdural hemorrhage into the surrounding posterior fossa region of the brain results from a tear at the junction of the falx cerebri and the tentorium, near the great vein of Galen. This form of bleeding is usually fatal within the first three days of life when it occurs at birth. The great vein of Galen is particularly susceptible to tearing because it is located between the two cerebral hemispheres, which maintain some mobility, and the fixed, passive vascular sinuses. While the head is being molded during delivery, the vein may kink and stretch with resultant occlusion of blood flow or rupture. In addition to the seriousness of a rupture per se, the accumulation of blood in the posterior fossa region causes compression of the brainstem and its displacement up against the skull. This compression has very serious, if not fatal, immediate consequences for normal homeostatic body functioning. Since the blood is not as easily reabsorbed, the hemorrhage remains and exerts continued pressure on the structures in that region of the cranium.

Another cause of a perinatal subdural hemorrhage is skull fracture (Ford 1960). Occasionally, a perinatal subdural hemorrhage does not become clinically evident until sometime during the first six months of life and is known as a *chronic* subdural hemorrhage (Natelson and Sayers 1973).

The overall outcome of subdural hemorrhage is very poor; death during the early neonatal period is common. In an 8- to 13-year follow-up of 42 infants with perinatal damage, Natelson and Sayers found that five of ten infants with a subdural hemorrhage died within a week of birth, four were mentally retarded at follow-up, and only one was within the normal range of mental abilities. An additional 13 infants showed a chronic subdural hemorrhage during the first six months of life which the authors felt was most likely related to mechanical injury suffered at birth. All 13 suffered from accompanying seizures. Only three of the 13 had normal IQs at follow-up. Whether or not the four nonretarded survivors suffered cognitive or learning difficulties cannot be ascertained from the data.

Norman (1978) discussed another type of subdural hemorrhage that is sometimes observed in large or postmature neonates who have suffered a traumatic birth. In these cases, continued bleeding from small pial veins is seen and results in an abrupt presentation of symptoms two to five days following birth.

A subarachnoid hemorrhage, the discharge of blood into the subarachnoid space, is currently the most common form of perinatal intracranial hemorrhage (Volpe 1977) and occurs predominantly in premature babies following breech delivery or in difficult term deliveries (Dekaban 1970). Subarachnoid bleeding in preterm infants is usually related to an accompanying anoxic episode; during a full-term delivery, it is related to mechanical injury. In these cases the bleeding arises from capillaries or from small meningeal vessels. The episodes are usually milder and less extensive than subdural bleeds (Cartwright et al. 1979). Bleeding is usually bilateral and occurs predominantly over the temporal lobes. One major result of subarachnoid hemorrhaging is hydrocephalus.

Volpe has delineated three syndromes of subarachnoid hemorrhage. The first group is composed primarily of preterm infants with minor hemorrhaging without major sequelae. The second group consists of full-term infants who have suffered a hemorrhage and show seizures very early in life. Finally, a smaller group of infants suffer massive bleeding with rapidly fatal consequences, probably due to the occurrence of both a traumatic injury and severe anoxia.

Historically, cerebellar hemorrhage has been recorded as an uncommon perinatal event sometimes seen in difficult term deliveries. However, more recent information indicates that this hemorrhage may occur with greater frequency in very premature (i.e., less than 28 weeks gestational age at birth) infants (Grunnet and Shields 1976). The cause of cerebellar hemorrhaging is not fully established because of the complex array of problems the very premature infant faces. Pape et al. (1975) attributed the hemorrhage to mechanical occipital skull deformities caused by the tight band used to hold supportive respiratory face masks in place. Grunnet and Shields suggested a more direct role of respiratory difficulties and minimized the role of mechanical trauma. Cerebellar hemorrhages show a variety of distributions of bleeding in the cerebellum, including total or partial bleeding into the cerebellar hemispheres. In the Grunnet and Shields sample, the cerebellar bleeds occurred together with periventricular bleeds and respiratory distress. The prognosis is poor; most infants who have been so diagnosed died soon after the bleed. Volpe (1977) cautioned, however, that cerebellar functioning should be carefully monitored in all small premature babies suffering any intracranial hemorrhage to determine whether subfatal cerebellar bleeds have occurred.

Tissue Damage

CNS structures, including the spinal cord, are subject to direct damage from perinatal mechanical influences. Such tissue damage as lacerations, contusions, and transections may be directly attributed to mechanical influences. Other injuries, such as brainstem compression and herniation, may occur secondary to hemorrhage.

Damage to the spinal cord may occur when there is increased mechanical stress during delivery. Mortality and morbidity data concerning spinal cord injuries that can be attributed to birth trauma are inconclusive because a complete spinal cord evaluation has not typically been a part of the neonatal autopsy. Also, the clinical course of survivors of perinatal spinal cord trauma may be easily confused with that of other syndromes, such as muscular dystrophy (Gresham 1975, Towbin 1969a). Severe spinal cord injuries due to mechanical stress, such as the complete transection of the cord, have significantly decreased in frequency due to better obstetric care. Cervical spinal cord transection may occur during forcible breech extraction because of the wide angulation of the baby's body and physical traction. DeSouza and Davis (1974) suggested that hypotonic, asphyxiated babies were at an especially high risk of severe spinal cord damage during delivery. Towbin (1969a) has examined less severe spinal cord mechanical injuries: meningeal, spinal nerve root, and focal spinal cord lesions. Such damage may be caused by stretching and pressure during delivery. Although spinal cord damage is very difficult to determine in the neonate, Towbin reported that the presence of an epidural hemorrhage in the spinal canal was the best indication that spinal cord damage had occurred. Of 170 autopsied cases of spinal cord damage, 16 showed severe damage and 14 showed more moderate damage.

The brainstem is particularly vulnerable to damage from perinatal mechanical stresses. The shape of the brainstem and its proximity to the **foramen magnum** (the opening at the base of the skull surrounding the brainstem) contributes to its vulnerability. Damage to the brainstem also raises immediate concern about the viability of the very delicate cranial nerves arising from and entering the CNS at the level of the brainstem. The types of damage are usually similar to those just described for the spinal cord; indeed, many times both the spinal cord and the brainstem are injured at the same time (Towbin 1969a). Damage to the brainstem is immediately life-threatening because of possible damage to homeostatic control centers, such as the medullary respiratory center. Cranial stretching or compression may result in brainstem and cranial nerve injuries. Laceration and herniation of the brainstem usually occur when it is compressed down against and through the foramen magnum at the base of the skull. Brainstem laceration may be the result of a direct mechanical cause or may be secondary to displacement by the increased pressure caused by hemorrhaging. The occipital bone near the foramen magnum may also lacerate the brainstem. Extensive brainstem damage was observed in six of Towbin's 430 brain autopsies, and more moderate injuries were observed in seven cases.

Cerebral damage caused by a mechanical injury that is not secondary to anoxia or hemorrhage is less common. One cause for mechanical cerebral trauma is skull fracture, often because of excessive forceps pressure when forceps delivery is deemed necessary. The typical perinatal skull fractures are localized depressions of the skull rather than an actual linear fracture. Parietotemporal regions are particularly vulnerable to localized skull depression. This depression, known as a **"ping pong ball" fracture,** may lead to cortical laceration beneath the fracture or a softening of the underlying tissue. Linear fractures are more commonly associated with cortical laceration as well as with meningeal lacerations, which may cause hemorrhage.

15.2 TRAUMATIC HEAD INJURY

Head injury can occur at any time in life, but the infant and young child are at especially high risk, particularly for nonpenetrating, closed-head injury. Closed-head injuries may occur when exploring toddlers fall down a flight of stairs or out of a window or when unrestrained infants in quickly stopping or colliding automobiles are thrown up against the dashboard or windshield.

Child abuse has received increasing attention over the past 20 years and occurs most frequently in the very young child and infant (R. M. Friedman et al. 1981). Gelles (1978) reported an extremely high incidence of child abuse in the widest sense of the word based on self-reports of 1146 parents of children aged 3 to 17. Of these, 58 per cent reported spanking and slapping; 40.5 per cent pushing, grabbing, and shoving; 13.4 per cent hitting with an object; 3.2 per cent kicking, biting, or hitting with a fist; and 1.3 per cent "beating up" with more than a single punch. In a survey of 140 children in two facilities for the retarded below 16 years of age, Buchanan and Oliver (1977) found that 3 per cent definitely and a possible maximum of 11 per cent probably had been rendered mentally handicapped by child abuse; in 24 per cent of the children neglect was considered a contributing factor. Other reported figures are lower, partly because abuse is defined by outcome and damage to the child rather than parental action (R. M. Friedman et al. 1981). Also, abuse decreases rapidly with age of the child.

Head injury may result in linear skull fracturing, cerebral concussion, lacerations, and contusions. Subdural and epidural hemorrhage are also common consequences of head injury. The investigation of the long-term mental consequences of infant head injury is typically part of more general studies of head injury in childhood. A full discussion of that literature is beyond the context of this part of the book. The long-term follow-up work by Klonoff and his associates (Klonoff and Low 1974, Klonoff and Paris 1974, Klonoff et al. 1969, 1977) and by Chadwick, Rutter, and their colleagues (Chadwick et al. 1981a, 1981b; Rutter et al. 1980) are exemplary programs of research. Jennett (1972), Boll and Barth (1981), and Levin et al. (1982) have provided reviews of the various medical and neuropsychological concerns that arise in cases of childhood head injury.

Despite the practical importance of understanding the consequences of head injuries in the first two years of life, studies of the consequences of damage sustained during this period have been relatively rare. Usually, examinations of early-life head injuries are limited to perinatal injuries, as discussed in the previous section. Otherwise, children with head injury and brain damage during this period are included in wider examinations of head injury spanning the entire period of childhood and early adolescence without systematic attention to the age factor, both at time of injury and at time of testing. Brink et al. (1970) found a direct relationship between length of coma following severe head injury and IQ at follow-up. Children in the younger age group (age 2 to 8 years) showed more severe deficits in intelligence test scores even though the length of coma was shorter than in the older group (9 to 18 years). Woods and Teuber (1973) and Teuber (1974) examined children whose head injuries occured from infancy through the preschool years (as manifested by the presence of a unilateral hemiplegia). They gave these children a set of cognitive tests in late childhood and early adolescence to determine the differential patterns of cognitive deficits that arise when the damage is located predominantly in either the right or the left hemisphere. They also examined the related issue of developmental plasticity of both hemispheres. The results indicated that, when the injury was located in the left hemisphere, children showed subsequent deficits in tests of both verbal and nonverbal skills relative to neurologically normal children. In contrast to what is commonly observed in adult left-hemisphere injury, however, aphasias were not prevalent.

Similarly, Levin and Eisenberg (1979) reported that verbal memory, as tested with a selective reminding test, was especially sensitive to closed-head injuries primarily affecting the left hemisphere. When damage was located in the child's right hemisphere, only nonverbal tasks were poorly performed. Levin and Eisenberg (1983) also reported that diffuse insult to the brain in children is more damaging than focal lesions. While children may often show complete recovery after focal lesions, diffuse lesions often show devastating effects in long-term follow-up. Studies that have examined head injuries sustained during infancy and the preschool period point to the importance of continued neurological well-being in early life in order for proper development of cognitive functioning. In five-year follow-up, Black et al. (1981) found that IQ test measures in these children improved slightly each year but that the results only "approached significance." Most authors agree that an understanding of the long-term effects of head injury in children requires systematic study of the age at onset and the age at testing and that such studies need to take into account the location, focal specificity, and extent of the lesion as well as the type and developmental complexity of the behavior under study (Boll and Barth 1981, Finger and Stein 1982, Levin et al. 1982).

15.3 NEOPLASTIC BRAIN PATHOLOGY

Childhood **neoplasms** (tumors) represent a small but important minority of the neurological cases seen most often in patients between 4 and 7 years of age. However, many childhood neoplasms do occur and are diagnosed during the first two years of life.

Table 15-1 shows some of the more frequent childhood neoplasms. At least 60 per cent of all childhood cerebral neoplasms (Koos and Miller 1971, Slooff and Slooff 1975) and at least 75 per cent of all intracranial tumors (Cushing 1927, Keith et al. 1949) are **gliomas,** i.e., glial cell tumors.

Recognizing a tumor in infancy and early childhood is difficult because many of the symptoms are general (e.g., headache, projectile vomiting, retinal swelling) and usually offer minimal cues for localization and differ-

TABLE 15-1   Selected Childhood Neoplasms

	Predominant site	Origin	Outcome	Per cent of all cerebral tumors	Connecticut Register 1935–74
Gliomas				60	
Astrocytoma	Cerebellum	Astrocytes			9
Medulloblastoma	Posterior fossa, often lateral to midline, spreads into ventricular system	Embryo's granular cells	One third survive 5 years without recurrence		30
Ependymona	Floor of 4th ventricle	Ependymal matrix	Consistent recurrence		16
Craniopharyngioma	Anterior	Congenital malformation	Visual problems, endocrine disorders, increased intracranial pressure; hydrocephalus during first 3 years of life		
Choroid Plexus Papilloma	Lateral ventricles, usually unilateral				
Meningioma		Meninges			13

ential diagnosis. The young child's inability to give accurate verbal information about symptoms further complicates this task. These difficulties may lengthen the time before diagnosis is made and intervention is attempted, both of which worsen prognosis. Common signs of tumor growth are hydrocephalus and increased intracranial pressure.

Survival and the probability of lasting deficits are determined chiefly by the histology of the tumor. **Benign tumors** have a relatively good prognosis, whereas **malignant tumors** have a very poor prognosis. Factors that may influence the prognosis include risks involved in surgical removal, the site of the growth, accessibility to surgical intervention, the importance of surrounding neural tissue, growth patterns, and the child's age. Gjerris (1976) found that survival rates were poorer for children with tumors during the first four years of life than for children with tumors in the second four years.

Children with tumors are a special challenge to the neuropsychologist, given both the tenuousness of their neurological condition and the seriousness of concurrent secondary medical problems. Determining the integrity of mental functioning before and after surgical intervention, the influences on cognitive ability of radiotherapy and chemotherapy, and, most important, useful prognostic statements concerning mental functioning are some of the tasks confronting the neuropsychologist.

Benign astrocytomas (grades I and II) are common among the childhood neoplasms, although relatively infrequent in incidence under the age of 2 years. An astrocytoma is a glioma that arises from the astrocyte cells of the CNS and forms cysts. One in five cerebral tumors are astrocytomas (Slooff and Slooff 1975). However, the predominant site for astrocytomas in childhood is in the cerebellum (DeLong and Adams 1975). Astrocytomas typically grow slowly and may produce epileptic reactions (Finkemeyer et al. 1975). The prognosis for them is favorable, although rarer cases with rapid and widespread tumor growth have a poorer prognosis. Malignant forms of astrocytoma (i.e., grades III and IV) are rare in childhood and have a poor prognosis.

Medulloblastomas are the most common and fastest-growing posterior fossa tumors in children. A medulloblastoma is regarded as an embryonal tumor that usually develops from the population of cells that proliferate in the first six to eight months of life to become the cerebellar granule cells. However, as with most tumors, the mechanism of the abnormal growth remains unknown. In a series of 68 children with medulloblastomas, the majority were observed to occur early in the first decade of life (Fig. 15-6).

The tumor is usually situated on the midline and infiltrates the ventricular system at the level of the fourth ventricle. Ventricular infiltration results in an obstructive hydrocephalus and permits these tumor cells to disseminate and seed throughout the entire neuraxis via the cerebrospinal fluid. Surgical removal of as much of the tumor as possible and subsequent radiotherapy of the entire neuraxis are vital.

The long-term prognosis for medulloblastoma is generally poor since

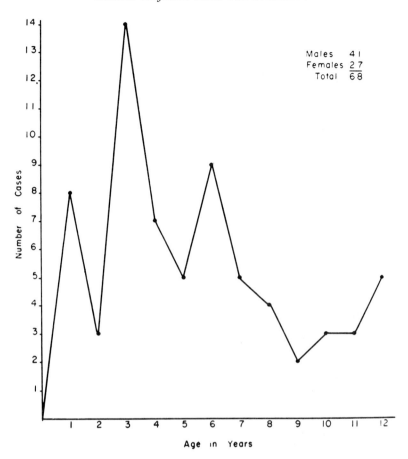

FIGURE 15-6   Age at time of hospitalization for 68 patients under 12 years of age presenting with medulloblastoma in posterior fossa (Ingraham and Matson 1954).

eventual regrowth is highly probable. In the Ingraham and Matson series, only 10 per cent survived for five years. However, higher survival rates have been reported during the past decade. N. McIntosh (1979), for example, reported a dramatic increase in the number of survivors five years after diagnosis and intervention in a 1970–74 sample relative to a 1965–69 sample. His study suggests that one third of the cases may survive five years without recurrent growth and that a very small minority may live for decades without any recurrence. Cook and Guthkelch (1983), writing experientially, report a 50 per cent chance of five-year survival for the patient who has received the best possible treatment. They conclude that this treatment includes transfer to a medical center that sees at least several medulloblastoma patients yearly, surgery to remove at least 80 per cent of the tumor, and whole neuraxis radiotherapy.

Cognitive deficits are common among survivors, which some authors attribute to the radiotherapy (Raimondi and Tomita 1979). Ellenberg (1982) presented serial neuropsychological assessments of two young medulloblastoma patients, both of whom showed some gains in cognitive skills with residual, persistent deficits in fine motor tasks, attention, and concentration.

Choroid plexus papillomas are benign neoplasms that occur predominantly in the first three years of life and tend to have a favorable prognosis. A majority of these tumors grow in one of the lateral ventricles, although some occur bilaterally. Slooff and Slooff (1975) reported a predominance of left-sided ventricular papillomas. Hydrocephalus is frequently observed in cases of choroid plexus papillomas (Laurence et al. 1961).

An **ependymoma** is a glioma that usually arises from the ependymal matrix on the floor of the fourth ventricle and extends laterally and inferiorly. Since this position makes complete surgical removal very unlikely, consistent recurrence following surgical extirpation makes the prognosis guarded at best.

A **craniopharyngioma** is a common supratentorial, nongliomatous cystic tumor that arises from a congenital malformation. Craniopharyngiomas are commonly found anteriorly in the brain, compressing and infringing upon the optic chiasm, the hypothalamus, and the third ventricle. This location leads to the commonly observed triad of symptoms consisting of visual problems, endocrinological disorders, and increased intracranial pressure due to the partial or total blockage of cerebrospinal fluid circulation. The endocrinological disorder may result in early growth retardation. Survival without major medical difficulties is common following successful removal of the growth; however, removal of a craniopharyngioma is sometimes hampered by its peripheral growth into poorly accessible yet vital surrounding regions. Galatzer et al. (1981) reported that the intellectual status of six children was in the normal range both prior to and following surgical intervention.

Epidemiological studies of childhood tumors are rare. One study by Farwell et al. (1978) reported on all neoplasms in the first 18 months of life recorded in the Connecticut Tumor Registry from 1935 to 1974. During that period, 54 tumors in infants were recorded. In all, 30 per cent were medulloblastomas, 16 per cent were ependymal growths, 13 per cent were meningeal growths (tumors arising from the meninges), and 9 per cent were astrocytomas. In terms of location, 44 per cent were located in the cerebellum, 37 per cent in the cerebrum, and 17 per cent in the brainstem. The average survival time was 43 months following diagnosis, which is a misleading figure today because the registry spanned different periods of medical technology and intervention. More complete introductory coverage of childhood neoplasms can be found in Matson (1969), DeLong and Adams (1975), Slooff and Slooff (1975), and Cohen and Duffer (1983).

16

Convulsive Disorders

16.1 THE NATURE OF CONVULSIVE DISORDERS

A common denominator for the set of disorders discussed in this chapter is that they involve the abnormal electric activity, or **discharge,** of cerebral neurons. The terms "convulsion," "seizure," and "epilepsy" are sometimes used synonymously but do not necessarily refer to the same phenomenon. For the sake of uniformity in this chapter, the term "convulsive disorder" is used when discussing abnormal discharges in brain cells. These electrical changes, extracellularly recorded as EEG paroxysms, are thought to be summations of synchronously developing depolarizations and hyperpolarizations in neurons (Goldensohn and Ward 1975). In simpler terms, the modulated balance of excitatory and inhibitory synaptic influences that are normally present in neurons are disturbed in an epileptogenic area of ganglion cells in the gray matter of the brain. A gigantic hyperpolarization spreads to other areas; the specific type of such spreading determines the timing, form, and distribution of the epileptic discharge and hence the clinical picture (Fig. 16-1).

The terms "convulsion," "seizure," "epilepsy," and "spasm" have also been used to define an abnormal cerebral discharge; however, these terms carry additional or different meaning as well. For example, the fact that a child has a convulsion or a seizure does not automatically imply the presence of epilepsy. A seizure may not always present itself clinically as a convulsion (i.e., abnormal motor activity), nor is a seizure the sole cause of a convulsion. Convulsions may also be caused by such nonseizure factors as breathholding spells or may be very closely mimicked, in early infancy, by an extremely jittery (though otherwise normal) baby. The disease process causing a convulsive disorder need not originate in the CNS but, as in the specific case of febrile seizures, may be extracerebral.

Epilepsy, at this point defined simply as recurrent and persisting seizure

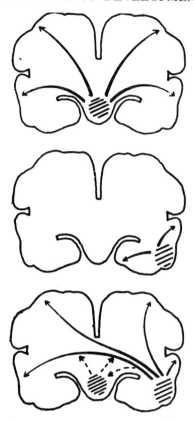

FIGURE 16-1   Types of epileptic seizures according to spreading of bioelectric activity: (a) primarily generalized seizures: grand mal (tonic or tonic-clonic seizures), petit mal (myclonic and astatic seizures, absences); (b) focal seizures of motor, sensory, or hypersentivity type, psychomotor seizures, adversive seizures; (c) generalized seizures of focal origin: grand mal (tonic or tonic-clonic seizures), minor seizures (not petit mal) with sudden dropping or sudden head, arm, or other body movements (Doose 1975).

activity, may occur at any time during the life of an individual. Most forms, however, tend to develop during the first years of life or during puberty and early adulthood. In addition to a brief description of the epilepsies, the main concern in this chapter is with the psychological correlates and sequelae in relation to time of onset and duration, as well as to the type, frequency, and origin of the convulsive disorders of early life.

In contrast to the convulsive disorders of infancy and childhood, epilepsy may be viewed as a long-ranging disturbance of the functioning of the individual rather than a disorder of development. Therefore, the topic overlaps to some extent with those discussed in Part IV. However, the many commonalities between early convulsive disorders and epilepsy suggest that they be treated jointly in this chapter.

In discussing convulsive disorders, it is important to understand that abnormal electric discharges of neurons are *symptoms*, rather than causes, of a disease. As with many isolated symptoms, the presence of a convulsion does not signify the existence of a single disease. Rather, the underlying cause of a convulsion may be one of numerous causal entities that may or may not be readily diagnosable (e.g., traumatic, metabolic, infectious, vascular, toxic). A relatively large percentage of convulsive disorders are caused by unknown factors and are labeled *idiopathic*. Unless properly treated, convulsions may lead to death or to further seizures independent of the underlying cause. How a seizure may "kindle," or increase the likelihood for, further seizures is an active area of current research. Kindling is an important issue when dealing with convulsive disorders in early life since animal-model research suggests that the immature brain is more susceptible to seizures than the adult brain (Moshe et al. 1982).

16.2 CONVULSIVE DISORDERS IN INFANCY AND CHILDHOOD

Convulsive disorders in infancy and childhood differ in many respects from those in adulthood. Perhaps most important, they occur far more frequently in individuals under the age of 15 than in adults and are considered by some authors to be a "disorder of childhood" differing in type and etiology from the adult disorders (Livingston 1972). Approximately 90 per cent of all epileptic patients develop their initial symptoms before the age of 20 (Livingston 1972). Unlike childhood convulsive disorders, the etiologies of convulsions in older individuals are more commonly symptomatic (i.e., they occur after brain trauma or in response to neoplastic or cerebrovascular disease, etc.). The types of behavioral manifestations seen in convulsive disorders also change over time.

Three common convulsive disorders observed in infancy and early childhood are neonatal seizures, infantile spasms, and febrile convulsions. The three (note the variability in names) are different age-specific medical diagnoses that vary widely in etiology and prognosis. Figure 16-2 shows a frequency distribution of the occurrence of each type of disorder. Neonatal seizures are bimodally distributed in the first week of life, infantile spasms are most frequent around the first half year of life, and febrile convulsions usually occur in later infancy and early childhood.

Neonatal Seizures

This form of convulsive disorder is the most frequent neonatal neurological emergency (A. Rose 1977). Neonatal seizures were documented in 0.5 per cent of the babies in the NIH Perinatal study (Holden et al. 1982). Feni-

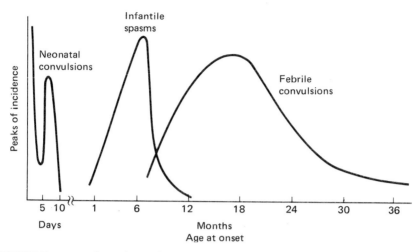

FIGURE 16-2   Chronology of epilepsy in infancy and early childhood (Brett 1975).

chel (1980) reported that premature infants have seizures 15 times more often than full-term babies and have a very high (approximately 90 per cent) mortality rate. Neonatal seizures usually occur as a result of serious neurological perinatal conditions, such as anoxic episodes or hemorrhaging. Owing to the relative immaturity of the synaptic connections and myelin coating, seizures with bilateral cortical involvement are rare in neonates because there is less capacity for spreading the electrical abnormality throughout the brain. Occasionally, "hemiconvulsions" are observed in which manifestations on one side very gradually change to the opposite side and then may or may not return to the original side. Neonatal seizures have immediate, negative effects on cerebral metabolism and on protein synthesis that may have long-lasting consequences (Volpe 1977).

There are two peak times for the occurrence of neonatal seizures: (1) the first and second day of life and (2) toward the end of the first week. Anoxia, intracranial bleeding, and hypoglycemia are common etiologies for seizures during the first peak, and simple hypocalcemia is the primary etiology for the second (A. Rose 1977). In the Perinatal study, 42 per cent of all documented cases of neonatal seizures occurred within the first 24 hours, 65 per cent by the end of day 2, and 87 per cent by the end of the first week of life (Holden et al. 1982).

The etiological agents of neonatal seizures are (1) perinatal anoxic episodes and mechanical trauma, (2) infections and malformations, (3) miscellanous factors, and (4) idiopathic etiology. Each accounts for roughly 25 per cent of the total incidence (Table 16-1). Many times, seizures develop unpredictably. Lombroso (1978), for example, found that neither the Apgar score nor the history of obstetrical complications had much predictive value for seizures. In Volpe's (1977) series, anoxic episodes were responsible for the greatest single percentage of neonatal seizures; others (e.g., Brown 1973) have found metabolic etiologies to be more prevalent. Aberrantly low levels of glucose (i.e., hypoglycemia) or calcium and inborn deficits of amino acid metabolism are particularly important in this regard.

The clinical manifestations of neonatal seizures vary. In many cases (particularly those involving premature infants), the clinical manifestations are extremely difficult to observe. The most frequent form has been defined as "subtle" or "minimal" because its clinical manifestations are easily overlooked. Volpe (1977) lists horizontal eye deviation, repetitive blinking or eyelid fluttering, oral-buccal-lingual movements, apnea, and pedaling or swimming limb movements as the most common manifestations of subtle neonatal seizures. However, tonic and clonic features are usually absent. Despite these subtle behavioral manifestations, the EEG in these cases is markedly abnormal.

Focal seizures are rare during the neonatal period; when they do occur, their etiology is typically a traumatic focal brain injury (Volpe 1977). Mul-

TABLE 16-1   Presumptive Etiologies in 239 Newborns with Seizures

Intracranial birth injury	36
Hypocalcemia	36
Hypoxia	26
Infections	22
Congenital CNS malformations	19
Hypoglycemia	14
Dysmaturity	13
Hypomagnesemia	4
Hypernatremia	4
Hyponatremia	1
Miscellaneous[a]	16
Cryptogenic	62
Total	253[b]

Source: A. Rose 1977.

[a]Includes five cases with strong family history of epilepsy, four cases of systemic sepsis, one sibship (2) and another case of pyridoxine dependency, one case of Leigh's disease, one case of undetermined leukodystrophy, one case of congenital heart disease, and one case of hemorrhagic disease of the newborn.

[b]In 14 patients, two or more etiologies were suspected.

tifocal or migratory convulsions are fairly common behavioral manifestions of neonatal seizures. Tonic seizures are more commonly seen in premature infants and are a sign of brain injury (Fenichel 1980). Apnea, upward eye deviation, and stiffening of the extended body are observed in these tonic seizures.

One of the more detailed follow-up investigations of neonatal seizures is the prospective Boston series (e.g., Lombroso 1978, A. Rose 1977) In this series, 265 full-term neonates who suffered from neonatal seizures were followed up at several points during their childhood. Two distinctly different prognostic groups were revealed at the five-year examination: those who were normal and those who were severely abnormal or had died. In the series, 52 per cent were normal, 20 per cent had died, and 28 per cent showed severely abnormal development, persisting neurological deficit, or continuing seizure activity. Prognosis was influenced by etiology, seizure type, and type of EEG abnormality. In some conditions, the etiology was clearly the most important consideration: simple hypocalcemia and subarachnoid hemorrhage were etiologies with good outcomes, whereas structural malformations and anoxic episodes carried poor prognoses (Tables 16-2 and 16-3). Outcome was not related to either seizure duration or severity, but the type of seizure had a definite influence. An especially poor prog-

TABLE 16-2   Relation of Etiologies to Abnormal Outcome Including Death

Etiology	Clinical outcome abnormal	Neurological sequelae		
		Seizures	Mental retardation (IQ<80)	Others	Predictability of mental retardation
Hypocalcemia					
Early onset	11	2	4	5	
Late onset	1	0	1	1	
Anoxia	21	8	18	13	Good
Intracranial injury					
Subarachnoid hemorrhage	2	0	2	1	
Contusion	2	2	0	1	
Ventricular hemorrhage	8	2	4	4	
Infection of CNS	14	5	8	4	
Hypoglycemia	9	7	9	5	Good
Congenital cerebral malformations	17	10	17	7	Good
Miscellaneous	14	5	2	0	
Unknown	20	14	10	11	

Source: Lombroso 1978.

TABLE 16-3 Relation of Etiologies to Clinical Outcome at Age 5 Years

Etiology	No. of cases	Dead	Clinical Outcome		Normal %	Predictability
			Abnormal	Normal		
Hypocalcemia						
Early onset	19	4	7	8	42	
Late onset	17	0	1	16	94	Good[a]
Anoxia	25	3	18	4	16	Good
Intracranial injury						
Subarachnoid hemorrhage	13	0	2	11	85	Good
Contusion	7	0	2	5	71	
Ventricular hemorrhage	8	4	4	0	0	Good
Infection of CNS	20	5	9	6	30	
Hypoglycemia	12	0	9	3	25	Good(?)
Congenital cerebral malformations	18	8	9	1	5	Good
Miscellaneous	19	1	13	5	68	
Unknown	52	5	15	32	62	
Total	210	30	89	91	43	

Source: Lombroso 1978.
[a]"Good" signifies a confidence level of between 0.1 and 4% and applies to predictions of both normal and abnormal outcome at age 5 years.

nosis was observed in children who suffered from the subtle form of neo-natal seizures. Poorly organized seizure patterns, such as myoclonic and tonic seizures, also had less favorable prognoses than those with focal and well-organized patterns.

The Perinatal study (Holden et al. 1980) provided follow-up information on 277 neonates who had suffered seizures. The mortality rate in the series was 34.7 per cent, with two thirds dying during the neonatal period. Death was associated with birth weight (there was an excessive number under 2500 grams and over 4000 grams in the series), gestational age, low five-minute Apgar score, number of days of seizure activity, and duration of seizure. When the seizure picture was complicated by apnea, the death rate rose to 60 per cent. Of the 181 survivors, 18.8 per cent were mentally retarded and 15.2 per cent showed borderline intellectual levels. Mental retardation was associated with cerebral palsy. At seven years, cerebral palsy was moderate or severe in 11.6 per cent of the sample and nonhandicapping in 2.2 per cent. Six per cent were diagnosed as cerebral palsied but died before the age of 7. Of the survivors, 22 per cent had subsequent afebrile seizures and 12.7 per cent were considered to be cases of active epilepsy.

Infantile Spasms (West's Syndrome)

Infantile spasms peak in occurrence between the fourth and sixth months of life (Chevrie and Aicardi 1978). This condition is also known as **West's syndrome,** named for a physician who, in the mid-1800s, reported a particularly severe type of seizures in his young son. **Infantile spasms** show three common clinical manifestation: the flexor spasm (the most common type, occurring in 70 per cent of cases), the nodding spasm (involving head movements), and the Blitzkrampf, or lightning, spasm (because it occurs extremely rapidly). A typical symptom triad involving spasms, severe mental retardation, and a markedly abnormal EEG was first described by Vazquez and Turner (1951). The EEG, studied in detail by Gibbs and Gibbs (1952), has been labeled *hypsarrhythmic* and shows random high-voltage slow waves and spikes spreading to all cortical areas (Fig. 16-3).

In roughly half the cases of West's syndrome, the spasms are preceded by other types of seizures, an indicator of a very poor prognosis. However, in idiopathic cases of infantile spasms, normal development is observed until the spasms occur. There is a 2:1 preponderance of males who suffer from infantile spasms but little familial incidence (Jeavons and Bower 1974).

There is a striking relationship in female children between West's syndrome and agenesis of the corpus callosum (Aicardi et al. 1965, Dennis and Bower 1972, Gastaut et al. 1978). Ocular anomalies (particularly involving the fundus) have been tied to infantile spasms with prenatal (as opposed to idopathic, perinatal, or postnatal) etiologies (Curatolo et al. 1981). A CT scan study of patients with West's syndrome revealed global cortical and subcortical atrophy, with particular involvement of the frontal and temporal lobes (Gastaut et al. 1978). Pneumoencephalography commonly reveals dilation of one or both lateral ventricles (Jeavons and Bower 1974), consistent with the findings of atrophy. **Agyria** (i.e., a smooth cortical surface) is frequently observed in cases coming to autopsy (Harper 1967).

In general, infants with West's syndrome have an extremely poor prognosis for mental development. In one of the best documented follow-up series of children with West's syndrome, Jeavons and Bower (1964) assessed the intelligence of survivors of infantile spasms with the Griffiths scale of mental abilities. Only three of 112 infants performed at a normal intellectual level at follow-up, and ten of the 112 were mildly subnormal; the majority (88 per cent) remained mentally retarded. A further follow-up at 5 to 14 years of age (Jeavons et al. 1970) found that 18 of the 98 children had died, many before age 4. Thirteen of the 98 children had made a full recovery, but most continued to convulse and 50 per cent had persistent neurological abnormalities (most commonly, spastic diplegia and quadriplegia). Recovery was related to the etiology of the spasms rather than to any treatment, such as steroid drug therapy. Children with spasms due to perinatal damage most commonly had persistent neurological abnormality, whereas idiopathic spasms and spasms due to early-life immunization procedures were

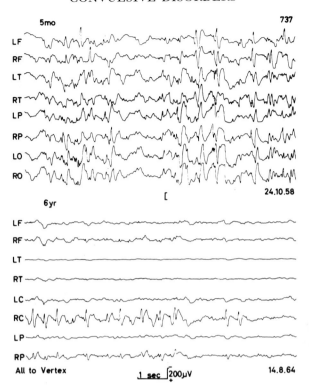

FIGURE 16-3   Hypsarrythmic brain activity: (upper) five-month old male with West syndrome and hypsarrhythmic EEG; (lower) same patient at age six years, with EEG now showing focal spike-wave activity as frequently seen in Lennox-Gestaut syndrome (Lou 1982).

associated with a better prognosis and with mental abilities in the normal range.

A later follow-up of 150 cases (presumably the previous 98 plus additional new cases) confirmed the earlier follow-up (Jeavons et al. 1973). In sum, the series indicated that the mental and neurological prognoses for children who suffered from infantile spasms was best either when the etiology was idiopathic or when the seizures followed from an immunization procedure. Roughly one third of the cases with these etiologies showed full recovery. However, in children with other etiologies, particularly those involving perinatal damage, a high death rate and persisting severe mental retardation in survivors were observed, regardless of therapeutic drug regimens. The absence of mental subnormality or other types of seizures at the time of the initial examination, and spasms that occurred for less than ten months, were also indicators of good recovery.

Another follow-up investigation reported by Chevrie and Aicardi (1977,

1978; Aicardi and Chevrie 1970) involved all forms of seizures occurring during the first year of life; the majority of the disorders (165 of 334) were infantile spasms. Of the 165, 9 per cent died by the time of follow-up, only 20 per cent were mentally normal, and 61 per cent were severely retarded. Death occurred most frequently in cases of infantile spasms with symptomatic etiology rather than idiopathic etiology. An investigation of the developmental histories of children with West's syndrome by Ohtahara et al. (1980) found that 59.3 per cent of 108 West's syndrome children continued to have seizures later in childhood; 85.9 per cent show slow spike and wave discharge along with characteristic seizure patterns (Lennox syndrome). The mental prognosis for cases that developed from West's into Lennox syndrome was particularly poor. Another aspect of the developmental course of surviving children is the increased prevalence of psychiatric disorders, particularly autistic behavior patterns (Riikonen and Amnell 1981).

Febrile Seizures

Approximately 2 to 5 per cent of all children between 6 months and 5 years of age have one or more febrile seizures, accounting for between one third to one half of all convulsive episodes in childhood. **Febrile seizures** occur soon after the onset of a febrile illness not directly affecting the CNS, usually three to six hours after the onset of the fever (Livingston 1972). However, febrile seizures can also be seen during the second or third day of an illness (Lennox-Buchstal 1973). Body temperature is usually at its peak at 39 to 40°C when the child seizes. Acute upper respiratory infection, tonsillitis, otitis media, and bronchial pneumonia are some common causes of a febrile seizure. The seizure is usually generalized and of short duration, though some may last for 20 minutes or longer. Males are more susceptible to febrile seizures than females. Most investigators believe that there is an inherited susceptibility to seize above a certain threshold of body temperature, with autosomal dominant transmission (Brazier and Coceani 1978).

Children who have a single febrile seizure have an excellent prognosis: there is little, if any, lasting neurological or mental deficit (NIH Consensus Conference 1980). The prognosis is less positive for children who have a febrile convulsion in conjunction with afebrile seizures, for those who have preexisting CNS abnormalities, or if the fever-inducing infection involves the CNS.

In a long-term follow-up, children who had febrile seizures were compared with their nearest-aged sibling on the WISC and WRAT tests of academic achievement at 7 years of age (Nelson and Ellenberg 1978, 1981). The mean full-scale IQ for the 431 febrile-group children, 93.0 (SD = 13.9), was not significantly different from the sibling group's mean IQ of 93.7 (SD = 12.8). WRAT performances, collected only from children with IQ above 90, did not indicate any group differences in spelling, arithmetic, and reading abilities.

16.3 EPILEPSY

Nature and Classification

The term **"epilepsy"** refers to persistently recurrent attacks, usually of the same type of seizures that are frequently accompanied by episodic and often chronic psychological changes and pathological activity in EEG. It has been estimated that 0.5 per cent of the total population suffers from one of the many forms of epilepsy. Prevalence of epilepsy in children has been estimated as 18.6/1000 (Rose et al. 1973). Only about 15 per cent of children with occasional seizures develop epilepsy. In addition, epilepsy may develop later in life, usually during late adolescence or early adulthood, as well as after brain lesions acquired later in life.

Penfield and Jasper (1954) suggested a seizure classification system (Tables 16-4a and 16-4b) organized on the basis of the origin of epileptic discharges. Table 16-5 shows the widely accepted international classification of epileptic seizures (Gastaut 1970) based on type of seizure. Almost all forms of epilepsy involve some type of abnormal motor activity, the classic form of a **generalized seizure** presenting in succession both hypertonic spastic states and clonic movements of the musculature. A distinction between *minor* seizures (which frequently start in childhood and adolescence), *focal* seizures, and *generalized* seizures is frequently made. Minor seizures include the **petit mal epilepsy,** with sudden states of unresponsiveness and disruption of activity, occasionally accompanied by nystagmic upward eye movements; minimal jerky movements in the arms; short, sudden movements of the head backwards; brief clouding of consciousness for a few seconds with dropping of head forward; brief lifting of legs and hands; and myoclonic seizures with sudden loss of muscle tone, dropping to the floor, jerky movements of arms and face musculature and oral automatisms. Frequent petit mal seizures are also described as pyknolepsia.

Focal seizures are limited to parts of the body, frequently on one half of the body, although they can spread and become secondarily generalized.

TABLE 16-4a   Seizure Classification

Type of seizure	Origin of epileptic discharge
Focal cerebral (symptomatic)	Hemispheric gray matter, usually cerebral cortex
Centrencephalic ("highest level")	Central integrating system of higher brainstem
Cerebral (unlocalized): not yet classified or result of extracerebral abnormality	Undiscovered or extracerebral cause

Source: Penfield and Jasper 1954.

TABLE 16-4b   Seizure Classification by Ictal Phenomena

Initial or most important phenomenon	*EEG pattern*
Focal Cortical Seizures	
Motor	Local unilateral spikes
Sensory	Sharp waves and rhythms
Autonomic	
Psychical	
Loss of concsiousness	
Automatism	
Centrencephalic Seizures	
Petit mal	3/sec wave and spike, primarily bifrontal
Myoclonic petit mal	Bilateral multiple spike and wave
Grand mal	Bilateral rapid rhythms
Petit mal automatism	3/sec wave and spike, primarily bifrontal
"Psychomotor automatisms"	4 to 6/sec rhythms, primarily bitemporal or frontotemporal

Source: Penfield and Jasper 1954.

Seizures of focal onset have their origin in various parts of the brain. If the precentral (motor) gyrus is involved, the symptoms of rigidity and clonic movements are confined to the opposite half of the body. Such elementary symptoms are called focal motor or **Jacksonian epilepsy.** Peculiar sensations (**auras**) frequently precede focal seizures. In psychomotor seizures these may be simple sensations of smell and taste but may be much more complex. Experiences may include the feeling of strangeness or of stretching or condensing of time, mood changes or outright hallucinations, followed by a limited clouding of consciousness with stereotyped movement sequences (e.g., chewing, smacking, swallowing, but also buttoning and unbuttoning the same button and similar patterns). Psychomotor seizures have been related specifically to temporal or frontal lobe damage and, in some cases, to specific damage in the area of the uncus (uncinate fits).

Generalized seizures often start with an initial shout, falling to the floor, turning of eyeballs upwards or to the side, lack of pupil reaction, and tonic tension of the musculature, followed by rhythmic, clonic jerking for one or two minutes and usually a period of comatose sleep. **Epileptic status** usually refers to grand mal seizures following each other rapidly so that consciousness does not fully return, but may occur occasionally with psychomotor seizures as well.

Etiology

While trauma has been considered as the primary cause of epilepsy, the full variety of pre-, peri-, and postnatal disorders—including disorders of metabolism, infections, and anoxic episodes—have also been considered. In addition, a genetic continuum of degree of susceptibility to epilepsy has been proposed. Annegers et al. (1982) found the risk of seizure disorders in relatives of patients with childhood-onset epilepsy to be 4.1 times as high as in the general population. Khan (1960) and other writers have attempted a distinction between structural epilepsies, starting early in life and accompanied by brain damage and mental retardation, and "functional" epilepsies of psychogenic origin, which do not ordinarily lead to brain damage or retardation. This distinction has been countered by the argument that the developing brain is more susceptible to repeated seizure activity, with result-

TABLE 16-5   International Classification of Epileptic Seizures

Partial seizures (beginning locally)
   Partial seizures with elementary symptoms (generally without impairment of consciousness)
      With motor symptoms (includes Jacksonian seizures)
      With special sensory or somatosensory symptoms
      With autonomic symptoms
      Compound forms

   Partial seizures with complex symptoms (generally with impairment of consciousness), temporal lobe or psychomotor seizures:
      With impairment of consciousness only
      With cognitive symptoms
      With affective symptoms
      With psychosensory symptoms
      With psychomotor symptoms (automatisms)
      Compound forms

   Partial seizures secondarily generalized

Generalized seizures (bilaterally symmetrical and without local onset)
   Absences (petit mal)
   Bilateral massive epileptic myoclonus
   Infantile spasms
   Clonic seizures
   Tonic seizures
   Tonic-clonic seizures (grand mal)
   Atonic seizures
   Akinetic seizures

Unilateral seizures (predominantly)

Unclassified epileptic seizures (due to incomplete data)

Source: Gastaut 1970.

ing cell death or at least inhibition of continuing enlargement and of the formation of more complex relationships between neurons. Hence the effect on intelligence may be more profound in children, invalidating the distinction between structural and functional epilepsy.

The fundamental mechanism that triggers seizures and causes epilepsy remains unknown. Reviewing several studies of epilepsy in humans, monkeys, and cats, Wada (1964, p. 452) concluded that focal cortical epileptogenic lesions form the basis for the development of (1) an acquired epileptic tendency with heightened brain excitability and progressive lowering ("kindling") of seizure threshold, (2) an independent and irreversible epileptogenic functional alteration of deep structures and homologous cortical areas, (3) changes in spontaneous behavior between seizures and in patterns of seizures, and (4) impaired learning ability unrelated to overt electrographic seizure at time of testing. Changes in sodium-potassium balance, in the availability of GABA (an inhibitory neurotransmitter; Morselli et al. 1981), and in other biochemical mechanisms have been identified (National Institute of Neurological and Communicative Diseases and Stroke 1979).

16.4 DEVELOPMENT DURING INFANCY AND CHILDHOOD

Considerable research has addressed the question of long-term development and outcome of children with epilepsy. As shown in the previous section, even with neonatal convulsive disorders only, prognosis is relatively poor. Children with recurrent seizures and epilepsy seem to run an even higher risk. In addition, the deleterious effects of continuing anticonvulsant medication must be considered in connection with long-term outcome. The neuropathological process underlying epilepsy is also closely related to outcome: with hypoxic-ischemic encephalopathy, normal development can be expected only in 10 to 20 per cent of these children; with survivors of subarachnoid hemorrhage, normal development can be found in 90 per cent; with intraventricular hemorrhage in 10 per cent; with hypocalcemia of early onset in 50 per cent; with hypocalcemia of late onset in 35 to 50 per cent; with bacterial meningitis in 20 to 50 per cent; and with developmental structural defect in none (National Institute of Neurological and Communicative Diseases and Stroke 1979).

Several studies have reported on the psychological performance, life adjustment, and numerous other characteristics of patients with recurrent epilepsy. An early survey of 400 noninstitutionalized adolescent and adult epileptics by Collins (1951) found a wide range of intelligence in epileptics, but for the group as a whole, averages were well below normal expectancy. Correlation with age of onset was positive, as expected, although correlation with duration was only marginal. Breaking subjects down into a constitutional (assumed genetic) and a brain-damaged group, Collins found the former quite superior to the latter, suggesting that epilepsy in itself may not have as serious a deleterious effect as previously assumed. Rather, epilepsy as a concomitant of brain damage is the major contributor to low intelligence. The author also notes that the nature of the disorder interferes with normal educational opportunities and hence the outcome may be influenced by environmental factors, such as educational opportunities, anxiety, and attitude. The difference between brain-damaged (symptomatic) and constitutional (idiopathic) epilepsy was present in children as well as adult patients (Fig. 16-4, Collins and Lennox 1947). There was also a striking difference between epileptics in institutions, those in outpatient clinics, and private patients.

Investigating the relation between seizure type and intelligence, Collins and Lennox (1947) found the poorest results in patients with both grand mal and psychomotor seizures and the best results in patients with petit mal only, with the second-highest IQ in children with psychomotor epilepsy (Table 16-6). Similar results were reported by Winfield (1947), Gudmundson (1966), and Freudenberg (1971). Milner (1954) ascribed a specific intellectual deficit to temporal lobe epilepsy, as did Taylor (1976). A detailed study by Freudenberg (1968) on 380 children and adolescents up to age 18 indicated that intelligence in children with prenatal damage is normal (IQ 90 to 110) only in 14.3 per cent and that 38.1 per cent of this group had severe retardation (IQ below 50). For birth trauma cases, 36.9 per cent had below-normal intelligence, but only 6.2 per cent had severe retarda-

FIGURE 16-4   Percentile curves of the IQs of institutional, clinic, and four groups of private patients (Collins 1951).

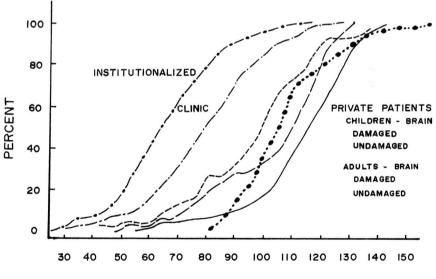

TABLE 16-6   Intelligence of Epileptic Patients

	Children (Stanford)		Adults (Bellevue)	
	Number	Average IQ	Number	Average IQ
Petit mal only	18	113.2	38	114.0
Psychomotor only	8	108.0	21	112.2
Grand mal only	36	105.3	114	112.0
Grand mal and petit mal	25	102.7	79	112.6
Grand mal and psychomotor	11	102.2	42	105.9

Source: Collins 1951.

tion. Similar results were found for children with cerebral damage during the first year of life (32.5 and 2.5 per cent, respectively); children with damage acquired later showed increasingly better intelligence, and 80 per cent of children damaged during the third year of life showed normal intelligence. Freudenberg notes that in two thirds of her children developmental delay was present even before the occurrence of seizures, suggesting that the intellectual deficit for the most part is probably not a secondary effect of seizures or of environmental factors. Although there can be a latency period of up to several years between cerebral damage and the beginning of seizures, the degree and extent of intellectual retardation were smaller the later the epilepsy became manifest for all types of seizures (Freudenberg 1968).

Angers (1963) investigated occupational placement and job performance for adult epileptics and stressed the working capabilities of these patients, suggesting that there is no typical epileptic. Mirsky et al. (1960) reported that focal (temporal lobe) epilepsy tended to impair memory more than generalized (nonfocal, diffuse, centrencephalic) epilepsy, with the reverse true for measures of attention. In studies of children, Holdsworth and Whitmore (1974) noted attentional problems in 42 per cent of epileptic children. In the adult, impairment of sustained, focused attention is quite common, even when the patient has normal intelligence (McDaniels and McDaniels 1976), with the exception of psychomotor epilepsy of unknown origin (Matthews and Klove 1967). A study of epileptic children by Stores et al (1978) examined the problems of activation, vigilance, attention, and distractibility by means of parent and teacher ratings as well as tests. In a comparison of 71 epileptic and 35 healthy control children, boys tended to show more inattention and motor hyperactivity and poorer concentration and perceptual accuracy. The authors ruled out medication effects and interpreted the sex difference as a result of the higher vulnerability of boys to epileptogenic lesions. A breakdown into four groups was made: (1) three per second spike and wave pattern, (2) irregular spike and wave pattern,

(3) right temporal focal spike discharge, and (4) left temporal focal spike discharge. Attentional function decreased in order from group 1 through 4, with boys with left temporal spike discharge showing the poorest performance. The results suggest that the left hemisphere in males is most vulnerable because of its relatively slower maturation (Remschmidt 1981). Hyperkinesis appears to accompany the inattention syndrome.

Freudenberg (1968) also reported poor performance on the Bender Gestalt test in epileptic children. Perceptual motor problems were common in all epileptic groups, although again most severe in symptomatic epilepsy. It was noted that even the least impaired pyknoleptic group showed significant deficits relative to controls. In relation to learning, Stores (1978) showed that epileptic boys had more reading problems than epileptic girls of the same age and socioeconomic environment. Again, children with focal epilepsy, and especially left temporal discharge, showed the most severe reading impairment, whereas those with right temporal discharge showed no difference from controls. In a study of 200 children with epilepsy, Whitehouse (1976) found that 70 per cent required special education and that even of the remaining 30 per cent "some still showed minor learning problems, enough to raise difficulties in classroom situations" (p. 23). Rodin and Rennick (1979) found a poor socioeconomic and occupational outook for epileptics, which they ascribed partly to inadequate schooling.

Reviewing reports of behavior problems in epileptic children, Remschmidt (1981) stressed that the type of problem is age-related. During infancy and early childhood, motor restlessness, aggressiveness, intolerance of frustration, increased sibling rivalry, and disorders in play behavior and in integration in social groups are common, whereas during school age cognitive deficits, problems of social integration, and isolation are predominant. These latter problems become more pronounced during puberty and adolescence, often complicated by personality alterations (lack of drive, psychomotor slowing, rigidity). It should be noted that many of the symptoms described by Remschmidt may be due at least in part to the anticonvulsant medication (e.g., motor restlessness with phenobarbital). At times, behavior problems may disappear entirely after a change in medication. Freudenberg (1971) found many reactive disorders—especially in cases of pyknolepsy—including depression, psychosomatic and sleep disorders, and anxiety, but rarely psychomotor retardation and personality alteration. Similar findings were reported by Stores (1978), Stores et al. (1978), and Gebelt (1971). Another reactive disorder frequently mentioned is increased emotional dependence on the mother and other important people in the child's life (Hartlage et al. 1972).

Whether or not there is a characteristic epileptic personality has been debated for some time (Tizard 1962). Studies of children with epilepsy show that personality alterations do not become apparent until puberty and that a relatively large number of adolescents do not show the classical syndrome or, for that matter, any striking personality alteration at all. If present, the hyperkinetic and rigid-sticky personality alterations mentioned above appear to be most frequent. In addition, persistence of affect is often mentioned; i.e., such adolescents, once irritated or angry, cannot channel their emotion and may lose control. An association between temporal lobe epilepsy and aggression and violence has been widely reported, although recent studies insist that it is not the temporal lobe damage but the damage to or dysfunction of the basal forebrain that may be associated with such behavior (Stevens and Hermann 1981).

Freudenberg (1968) demonstrated the relationship between personality alteration and intellectual defect (Fig. 16-5). The highest number of personality alterations were found with symptomatic grand mal seizures; alterations were least frequent in patients with petit mal and in patients with early onset of epilepsy. It must be remembered, however, that rigidity and perseveration as well as hyperactivity may not be direct consequences of the disorder itself but rather a coping mechanism developed by the epileptic in an attempt to maintain her or his emotional balance against increasing intellectual and social demands that she or he is unable to cope with. In this sense, Remschmidt (1972) viewed the behavioral changes as a balanc-

FIGURE 16-5   Proportion of 380 epileptic children with personality alteration and reactive disorders in relation to intelligence (Freudenberg 1968).

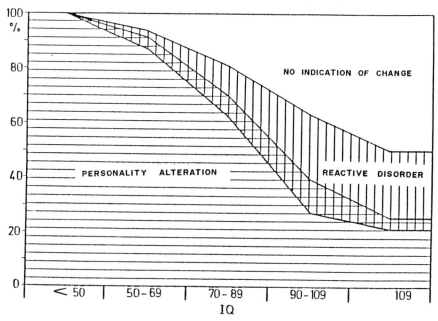

ing attempt with regression to a lower level of biological and psychosocial functioning.

In a review of psychotic disorders associated with epilepsy by Rentz (1980), psychoses were found to be rare but, if present, to manifest themselves between the ages of 7 and 14. Most of the psychoses were described as delirious psychosis with paranoia and hallucinations. Wolf and Forsythe (1978) list the following contributing factors: long duration of epilepsy without seizure-free periods, psychotic episodes in the history, abnormal psychosocial factors, disorders of intellect, poor perception and poor performance in school, and the use of certain antiepileptic medications. In addition, hallucinatory phenomena prior to the seizure (aura) and the disorientation following the seizure (postictal fugue) may directly contribute to the appearance of psychosis in epileptics.

17

Hemispherectomy

Much recent neuropsychological research has been concerned with the development of different functional capabilities in each hemisphere. The extreme situation, where one hemisphere is responsible for all brain regulation of physiological and behavioral functioning, is very rare. This chapter reviews a particular example of lateral dominance in which most of one cerebral hemisphere has been surgically removed. The main indications for this type of surgery are extensive invasion of the hemisphere by tumor, usually in adults, and infantile hemiplegia associated with neonatal convulsions. The operation is more accurately called *hemidecortication,* or removal of half of the cortex, since primarily cortical tissue is removed; the thalamus and striatum, as well as brainstem connections, usually remain. Often portions of the frontal and the occipital pole are also left in place to minimize the postoperative shift of the remaining hemisphere into the space left by the removed hemisphere (Verity et al. 1982). However, the terms "hemidecortication" and "hemispherectomy" are used interchangeably in the literature to refer to essentially the same surgical procedure.

Hemispherectomy is important to developmental neuropsychology because it may illuminate various aspects of the development of the cerebral hemispheres and their ability to recover from surgically imposed insults during childhood. Unfortunately, the available follow-up studies have not provided definitive answers, partly because of the infrequency of the operation, partly because the data reported have for the most part been incomplete and without standardized test results, and partly because of the paucity of long-term follow-up. Nevertheless, the available studies shed some light on the relation between hemispherectomy in adulthood and in childhood and on the differential hemispheric specialization during development. Extensive reviews have been written by Dimond (1972a) and by A. Smith (1974, Smith et al. 1972).

Hemispherectomy for the most part removes diseased tissue that is al-

230

ready nonfunctional. Hence, it is likely that the lesion itself has caused changes that predate the surgery. Improvement of function after hemispherectomy is found mainly because of successful reduction of seizure activity.

17.1 HEMISPHERECTOMY FOR TUMOR

Hemispherectomy for tumor is performed if one cerebral hemisphere is invaded by pathological tissue, such as by a malignant glioma, which occurs most frequently in adults and only rarely in children. The clinical picture following surgery is rather devastating. Many abilities normally subserved by the hemisphere are severely affected or lost. For example, a postoperative hemiplegia is invariably seen in adults. As with any malignant cerebral tumor, the possibility for recurrence of the tumor in other regions of the brain is high.

Because of the poor survival rate, few long-term follow-up studies of adult hemispherectomy patients have been conducted. The potential for follow-up is much greater if the hemispherectomy is performed on infantile hemiplegics (discussed in the next section).

The rationale for hemispherectomy in tumor cases was developed by Dandy (1928). He reasoned that, since each of the lobes of a hemisphere could be removed individually without dramatic impairment, it was logical to expect that the entire hemisphere (in his cases, the right hemisphere) could be removed with little future impairment. In his initial report of five cases of right hemispherectomy for tumor, Dandy noted no major effects on language, general intelligence, or personality. However, he did not have the results of detailed performance tests and the patients were not followed over time.

Zollinger (1935) reported the first case of a left hemispherectomy for tumor performed on an adult. He found, surprisingly after removal of so much cerebral tissue from the patient's dominant hemisphere, that many language abilities remained intact, including an elementary vocabulary. However, the patient died 17 days after the operation, and no formal tests were given to document the findings. During the next two decades, there were only a small number of similar ablations for tumors (reviewed by W. J. Gardner et al. 1955).

More detailed studies of hemispherectomy for tumor have been conducted since the 1960s. A. Smith and his colleagues (Burklund and Smith 1977; Smith 1966, 1969; Smith and Burklund 1966) presented several case reports of hemispherectomy for tumor in adults. In one case, a 47-year-old man who underwent a left (dominant) hemispherectomy for glioma was followed postoperatively and examined in detail with standardized tests. Immediately after the operation the patient showed a right hemiplegia, right hemianopia, and severe aphasia. During a seven-month follow-up, continuing recovery of language functions was observed. Smith (1966) concluded that the remaining right hemisphere makes some contribution to normal language performance, especially to receptive language. In 1969 Smith studied three cases of right (nondominant) hemispherectomy and found that all three patients showed specific nonlanguage deficits but no aphasia or other language disorder.

Based on these and past case reports, Smith (1969) compared the behavioral effects of right and left hemispherectomy for tumor in adults. He concluded that the left hemisphere plays a greater role than the right in speech, reading, and writing but not in verbal comprehension. He suggested that the right hemisphere is specialized primarily for nonverbal reasoning and visual ideational capacities, as evidenced by the marked impairment in these abilities following the removal of the nondominant hemisphere. Smith (1974) noted that hemispherectomy patients showed no evidence of other mental changes (psychosis, bizarre behavior, etc.) often associated with other cortical ablations.

Gott (1973a) studied one left and two right adult hemispherectomy cases. Using a general battery of neuropsychological tests, she demonstrated that following a hemispherectomy there is a memory defect, irrespective of side of operation. Specific lateralized deficits similar to those in previous reports were seen; the two right hemispherectomies showed greater nonverbal deficits, and the left hemispherectomy patient had greater verbal and language difficulties.

The systematic differences between right and left hemispherectomy reports in adults are consistent with the cerebral lateralization literature: massive removal of a cerebral hemisphere leads to hemisphere-specific deficits. Patients with a right hemispherectomy usually show left-side sensory and motor symptoms as well as disturbed nonverbal capacities while maintaining most language abilities. Patients with a left hemispherectomy show disturbed right-side sensory and motor functions and a severe disturbance in language. Because of the paucity of long-term follow-up studies, the issue of the "recovery" of lost abilities cannot be adequately addressed.

17.2 HEMISPHERECTOMY FOR INFANTILE HEMIPLEGIA AND STURGE-WEBER SYNDROME

The onset of **infantile hemiplegia**, unilateral paralysis in early childhood or infancy, is acute at or near birth in 75 per cent of cases (H. H. White 1961), is frequently preceded or followed by convulsions, and in many cases is associated with mental retardation or some degree of personality or behavioral disturbance. Although the clinical picture is similar in most cases, the pathological disturbance can arise from one of three factors:

1. Conditions present before birth or associated with birth, such as an anoxic episode or hemorrhage during labor

2. Conditions acquired after birth, usually a specific cerebral vascular disease, such as embolism associated with acute infectious diseases, or cortical trauma accompanied by hemorrhage

3. **Sturge-Weber disease,** in which a slow-growing tumor affects the blood vessels (angioma) in the area of the trigeminal nerve (innervating one half of the face and eye) and leads to inadequate blood supply to the brain, brain atrophy, and calcification, often accompanied by focal or generalized seizures, hemianopia, hemiplegia, and progressively poorer mental function (Hoffman et al. 1979)

The prognosis for infantile hemiplegia without intervention depends upon the amount of injury to the nervous system. However, the mortality rate is low (A. M. Kaplan 1958). The presence of convulsions makes the outlook less favorable because deterioration often occurs in such cases, presumably related to greater hemispheric damage. Treatment of infantile hemiplegia prior to 1950 was largely directed at control of seizures and correction of the physical deformities resulting from prolonged hemiplegia and spasticity. On the whole, results of treatment were not encouraging; many patients were institutionalized because of severe intractable seizures and behavior disorders as well as permanent hemiplegia.

Following Dandy's (1928) report of cerebral hemispherectomy in adults, McKenzie (1938) performed a hemidecortication in a young woman because of intractable epilepsy associated with spastic hemiplegia. Following the operation, the patient's seizures stopped and her general health and alertness improved but her hemiplegia remained unchanged. In 1945, Krynauw (1950) carried out 12 hemispherectomies for infantile hemiplegia over a five-year period. His patients ranged in age from 8 months to 21 years and included ten left hemispherectomies and two right hemispherectomies. In all except one of the patients, the injury occurred during the first ten months of life. Significant improvement in overall functioning was reported. None of the cases (including those with left hemispherectomy) showed impairment of speech as a consequence of the operation. No specific psychological documentation was presented. Krynauw argued that hemispheric dominance had "adjusted itself" before the operation as a result of the early neural injury (causing the hemiplegia) and that it was therefore the minor hemisphere that was removed in all cases.

Krynauw also specified that in all cases hemiplegia alone was not a sufficient indication for the operation. He insisted on the demonstration of unilateral cerebral disease either by air contrast studies or by the combination of a triad of symptoms: hemiplegia, seizures, and the presence of lowered intellectual functioning and/or uncontrolled emotional outbursts. Krynauw's favorable results established hemispherectomy as an acceptable and widely adopted form of treatment for certain cases of infantile hemiplegia.

17.3 PSYCHOLOGICAL OUTCOME OF HEMISPHERECTOMY FOR INFANTILE HEMIPLEGIA

The first studies of hemispherectomy to include psychological tests generally revealed good recovery of intellectual functions following the operation. Cairns and Davidson (1951) reported on three patients, two right-sided and one left-sided operation. All three patients showed general clinical improvement and an increase in intelligence test scores after the operation, with an average increase of about 20 IQ points. Munz and Tolor (1955) summarized the psychological test findings on four cases of hemispherectomy performed on patients between the ages of 14 and 24 years and stressed several important points: that there were unequal intervals between time of operation and psychological testing of the patients, that there was a lack of controls, and that postoperative follow-up periods were short. However, Munz and Tolor did consider the operations a success; the seizures stopped and there was no permanent increase in motor weakness. The patients were generally more pleasant and manageable but did show some personality changes, namely, increased feelings of morbidity and inadequacy. Munz and Tolor offer no reason for these personality changes. Although there were generally postoperative increases in IQ, Munz and Tolor stressed the importance of the premorbid intelligence level of the patient; only in cases with near-average preoperative intelligence, and presumably one hemisphere functioning normally, can significant increases in IQ be expected. Hence, the previous psychological make-up of the individual must be considered in evaluating hemispherectomy.

In an early summary of hemispherectomy results, W. J. Gardner et al. (1955) compared hemispherectomy for tumor in adults with that for infantile hemiplegia in children. The authors described a 29-year-old patient with infantile hemiplegia having a verbal IQ of 67 that rose to 78 when the patient was tested 37 days after right hemispherectomy and concluded that the deficits were much more devastating in adults. They suggested that the immature cortex of infantile hemiplegics can acquire functions planned for either hemisphere but, once a function has been established in the cortex, it cannot be "transferred."

During the 1960s and early 1970s, reviews and reports of larger series of hemispherectomy patients were presented, possible surgical pitfalls of the operation pointed out, and the long-term results of the operation questioned. A review by H. H. White (1961) of 269 cases from the world literature demonstrated an operative mortality of 6.6 per cent and a high rate of complications. White's review suggested that in the majority of cases overall improvement in functioning did result, including reduction of antisocial behavior. Carmichael (1966) expressed his disillusionment with results of the operation because of the inexplicable late complications occurring in otherwise healthy patients following surgery. Ignelzi and Bucy (1968), on the other hand, suggested that "practically all children suffering from this condition should have a cerebral hemidecortication" (p. 15) because of the remarkable clinical and psychological improvement.

P.J.E. Wilson (1970) attempted trying to reconcile the various postoperative findings and concluded that cerebral hemispherectomy in infantile cerebral disorder has a low operative mortality; the improvement in seizures and behavior disorder ranged from 70 to 90 per cent of patients. However, **morbidity** rates are high; the cardinal complication in 30 to 40 per cent of cases was subdural hemorrhage resulting in obstructive hydrocephalus of the remaining hemisphere. Wilson pointed out that surgical procedures to correct or minimize the complications were available, and therefore long-term postoperative complications remediable if not avoidable.

In a review of large-scale psychological studies, McFie (1961) criticized them for their failure to obtain pre- and posthemispherectomy indices of intellectual ability. He made repeated IQ measures of 34 hemispherectomized hemiplegic patients, ranging in age from birth to 5 years at the time of onset of hemiplegia and from 1 to 31 years at the time of hemispherectomy. Twenty-one cases had a right and 13 cases a left hemispherectomy. McFie compared the test scores of 28 of the cases with those of nine patients with partial hemispheric removal and found that the hemispherectomy patients displayed a greater increase in test scores following the operation. The IQ increase was found exclusively in patients with infantile hemiplegia onset during the first year of life. He found no significant difference in postoperative increase in scores between cases of left and right hemispherectomy in the infantile hemiplegia group and argued for a "critical period" for hemispherectomy recovery up to 1 year of age.

McFie found that the greatest improvement occurred in patients with normal EEGs in the remaining hemisphere. In contrast to earlier studies, McFie noted that the majority of patients showed a verbal intellectual deficit, in some cases dysphasia, irrespective of the hemisphere damaged. McFie attributed the results to a limit on the capacity of the remaining hemisphere to take on the normal function of both hemispheres, i.e., an **overloading** of the remaining hemisphere. St. James-Roberts (1979, 1981) reviewed McFie's classic study and noted several shortcomings: confounding of interage comparisons by differential status of the residual hemisphere, overdependence on unreliable IQ scores from young children, unequal distribution of three different psychometric tests across age groups, and inadequate control of recovery-period characteristics.

Basser (1962) investigated hemispherectomy with special reference to speech in 102 cases of hemiplegia of early onset; 48 cases had left hemisphere lesions, 54 had right hemisphere lesions, and hemispherectomy was performed in 35 cases. In 17 the left hemisphere was removed and in 18 cases the right. Basser considered whether the cerebral lesion was sustained before or after the onset of speech. He found that with regard to speech, hemispherectomy was beneficial in some cases but in the majority speech was unchanged. Basser concluded that speech was developed and maintained in the intact hemisphere and that in this respect the left and right hemispheres are "equipotential." One of Basser's major conclusions was that the verbal IQ of his patients remained unchanged irrespective of which hemisphere was removed. However, as St. James-Roberts (1979) pointed out, only 20 hemispherectomies were reported in detail and no verbal IQ scores were provided. Also, the IQs that were reported were generally low, indicating severe mental handicap and probably damage to the residual hemisphere. Basser did not use formal quantitative tests but merely provided short, descriptive phrases, such as "speech improved" or "dysphasic."

Griffith and Davidson (1966) presented the results of three patients with right hemispherectomy and eight patients with left hemispherectomy for infantile hemiplegia who were tested preoperatively, postoperatively, and 4 to 15 years later on standardized IQ tests. They found systematic differences in the effects of hemispherectomy on language functions but not on nonlanguage functions. Two right hemispherectomy patients had higher verbal than nonverbal abilities, and two left hemispherectomy patients had higher nonverbal than verbal skills. The authors suggested that the transfer of an ability from one hemisphere to the other after early brain damage may be incomplete and questioned whether the hemisphere removed was actually the nondominant hemisphere, as Krynauw had suggested.

Following P. J. E. Wilson's (1970) indications for hemispherectomy in infantile hemiplegics, the operation has been performed more selectively and with better morbidity outcome. Recent hemispherectomy research includes more detailed neuropsychological procedures and more careful case descriptions and controls. Several long-term follow-up studies have been published.

A series of studies by Dennis and colleagues (Dennis 1977, 1980a, 1980b; Dennis and Kohn 1975; Dennis and Whitaker 1976; Dennis et al. 1981; Kohn and Dennis 1974) focused on differences in the information-processing skills of left and right hemidecorticated infantile hemiplegics and Sturge-Weber patients, carefully matched for age at hemiplegia, age at hemidecortication, and verbal IQ. The authors demonstrated that right and left hemisphere differences cannot be attributed simply to gross verbal-nonverbal distinctions. Their tests compared specific linguistic capacities, such as syntax, between the two groups. Right hemidecorticates tend to be significantly better in the understanding or syntax than left hemidecorticates. Conversely, using right hemisphere visuospatial tasks, Dennis and collaborators found that left hemidecorticates are markedly superior in performance. These findings have been supported by other hemispherectomy studies (A. R. Damasio et al. 1975, Gott 1973b, Zaidel 1979, 1978) and imply that previous studies relied too much on single, gross measures of hemispheric performance (e.g., verbal IQ).

Another detailed report, by Netley (1972), compared the dichotic listening performance of 12 patients hemispherectomized for infantile hemiplegia and 12 matched controls. He found that congenitally injured patients performed differently than patients injured in infancy: the infantile injuries group recalled less material presented to the ear ipsilateral to the remaining hemisphere than the congenitally injured patients. Netley suggests that injury during the infantile period has a more permanent effect on the dichotic performance. Damasio et al. (1975) reported a case of right hemispherectomy performed on a woman of 20 who had suffered head trauma at age 5. They found improvement in left-sided sensory and motor performances over time, suggesting significant "adaptation," even in a mature brain. Zulch (1974) has noted, however, that much recovery may be due to strengthening of ipsilateral connections.

Verity et al. (1982) recently reported a follow-up study of eight infantile hemiplegics reviewed 3 to 16 years after hemispherectomy. They found that, although postoperative complications were frequent, the operation was followed by marked reduction in seizure frequency and improvement in behavior; there was little overall change in intellect or hemiplegia. Four of the patients showed borderline defective intelligence.

A study of considerable import reported by A. Smith and Sugar (1975) dealt with the long-term follow-up of a boy who showed cyanotic difficulties at birth, right hemiparesis at 5 months, and right-sided seizures at 3.8 years. A left hemispherectomy was performed at age 5.5. Postoperatively, EEG abnormalities disappeared from the remaining right hemisphere and the seizures ceased entirely. Before the operation the patient's mental age was reported to be 4.0 years with a speech defect but normal verbal comprehension. Four months after surgery he showed marked improvement; his mental age had risen to a value approximate to his chronological age and his speech had rapidly become normal. When tested three years later, his mental age was 7 years, 10 months, only slightly below his chronological age of 8 years, 8 months. In a first follow-up report, 15.5 years after the operation at the age of 21, a comprehensive battery of neuropsychological tests was given. On most of the tests, the patient scored in the average range. The WAIS verbal IQ (113; in the bright normal range) was 15 points higher than the performance IQ of 98. During re-examination with the same battery 5.5 years later at the age of 26.5, Smith and Sugar found that the patient had made even more remarkable progress—he was completing college and working in an executive position. The development of his intellectual and language capabilities was also reflected in his test scores: a WAIS full-scale IQ increase from 107 to 116; a slight increase in his performance IQ, from 98 to 102; and a large increase in his verbal IQ, from 113 to 126. Other tests documented similar above-average findings. Considering the demonstrated superior verbal abilities and average nonverbal, visuospatial capacities, it is difficult to conceive that this patient received a *left* hemispherectomy 21 years earlier!

To summarize, detailed recent reports of hemispherectomy for infantile hemiplegia, with the exception of Smith's case, seem to coincide more closely with the reports of hemispherectomy for tumor in adults than with the considerable earlier child hemispherectomy reports indicating highly optimistic functional "recovery" in children. It appears that these earlier reports did not use sensitive enough tests to detect hemisphere-specific deficits.

17.4 IMPLICATIONS OF THE HEMISPHERECTOMY REPORTS

Data from hemispherectomy reports have a bearing on two issues. (1) Assuming that lateralization is present in the young brain, recovery in infantile hemiplegics undergoing hemispherectomy has been interpreted as indicating the plasticity of the young brain, since some type of radical reorganization appears more likely than following adult hemispherectomy. (2) Given that there is some recovery following a hemispherectomy performed early in life, what is the effect of the removal of a cerebral hemisphere on the lateralized abilities represented in that hemisphere? Assuming no shift in functions from the removed to the remaining hemisphere, hemispherectomy appears to indicate that lateralization is not present early in infancy and that functions are represented in both hemispheres. This finding would support the concept of "equipotentiality" discussed in Sec. 4.1. We shall consider these two issues separately.

Plasticity

Isaacson (1975, 1976) has emphasized that hemispherectomy studies provide the only human experimental case analogous to animal lesion studies, in that both the tissue ablated and the substrate of remaining function are known. Hemispherectomy reports have been interpreted to show that the immature brain is "functionally plastic" (A. Smith 1974, Smith et al. 1972) in the sense that a function normally subserved by one cortical hemisphere may be transferred or relearned by the other hemisphere as long as damage to the original hemisphere occurs early in life. The adult-child comparisons seen in the early hemispherectomy reports tended to support this view in that they indicated greater recoverability and less vulnerability in the child's brain because fewer deficits were observed after the operation.

As discussed in Chap. 6, the groundwork for the belief in the diminished vulnerability of the immature brain was laid in animal work by Kennard in the late 1930s and early 1940s. Many experiments with animals confirmed that, when the behavioral effects of lesions differ according to the age at which they are inflicted, the difference is one of greater sparing of function for the earlier lesion (Teuber and Rudel 1971); this has been termed the **Kennard principle** (G. E. Schneider 1979). Many of the early hemispherectomy studies were interpreted as following this principle, for example, McFie's (1961) conclusions about juvenile versus congenital lesions. Differential recovery after hemispherectomy has even been used to determine the critical period of infant cortical plasticity. Based almost solely on hemispherectomy reports, this period has variously been set at 12 months (McFie 1961), 17 months (Netley 1972), 5 years (Krashen 1973), 12 years (Lenneberg 1967, based on Basser 1962), and 15 years (Obrador 1964) of age.

Most of the recent hemispherectomy studies, though, have not directly supported the Kennard principle; some, like Isaacson (1975) have rejected it completely. Dennis et al. in particular have argued that, with appropriate testing procedures, deficits similar to though less severe than those seen in adult tumor cases can be described in children. A comprehensive review by St. James-Roberts (1981) concluded that the hemispherectomy data fail to support the differential plasticity model. While some cases, notably Smith and Sugar's (1975) left hemispherectomy case, appear to provide direct evidence for the greater functional plasticity of the young brain, the bulk of the studies seem to provide no evidence for greater recovery from childhood lesions. (Indeed, there may be *less* recovery; see R. O. Robinson 1981.)

Lateralization and Equipotentiality

The data reviewed in Chap. 4 suggest that differential lateralization between the hemispheres occurs at an early age. The opposite concept, equipotentiality, maintains that both hemispheres ar equally capable of carrying out all cognitive functions in early life and that progressive lateralization occurs as the child grows older. During the equipotential period, variously estimated to end sometime between age 1 year and puberty, one hemisphere can fully compensate for loss of function in the other. Hemispherectomy data showing greater functional recovery in children were once thought to support the equipotentiality concept; however, recent hemispherectomy studies and the critique of the plasticity concept described above indicate just the opposite, namely, that differential specialization of the hemispheres is present very early in life. Thus, a left hemispherectomy in childhood will result in some type of linguistic impairment and a right hemispherectomy will result in some visuospatial deficit. Equipotentiality, or the similar concept of "safety (or duplication) in the nervous system" expressed by B. Campbell (1960), therefore does not appear to account for the effects of hemispherectomy.

In an attempt to reconcile the earlier reports of nervous system plasticity with the evidence suggesting specific deficits similar to the adult pattern of reciprocal specialization of the hemispheres, Teuber and Rudel (1967, 1971) discussed the "necessary cost" of early brain damage; by this term they implied that, following removal of large amounts of tissue, there is necessarily a diminished developmental capacity. As a specific example, Teuber suggested that, when language develops in the right hemisphere of children with left hemisphere lesions, it does so at the expense of the development of nonlanguage functions. Presumably, in a case of left hemispherectomy, language functions move into the intact right hemisphere and this results in a crowding effect in which a limit is imposed on the development of nonverbal functions. This crowding effect is very similar to McFie's (1961) notion of "overloading" a hemisphere. Smith (1974, Smith and Sugar 1975) noted, however, that the **crowding effect** can be explained more parsimoniously by assuming that the presence or absence of damage to the remaining hemisphere is the critical factor determining the extent of development for language and nonlanguage functions. Instead of the crowding concept, Smith (1974) proposed a developmental hierarchy in which language functions take precedence over reasoning functions. Language is therefore considered a more necessary ability in humans and is preserved first.

The timing of the "shift" in functions may or may not be related to the time of hemispherectomy. Since the operation is performed to remove diseased, largely nonfunctional tissue, a functional reorganization of the brain may occur well before surgery. In fact, no shift in functions need be assumed in congenital defects. In cases of perinatal or early infantile damage, it has been assumed that the diseased hemisphere may continue to function and in fact hinder the shift to the other hemisphere and that only through hemispherectomy will the healthy part of the brain be "released" to assume full functioning and to develop all the abilities it is capable of. Such considerations of timing do not affect the notions of crowding and developmental hierarchy discussed above but may explain the remarkable recovery in many cases after a considerable amount of cortical tissue has been removed.

IV

DISTURBANCES
OF NEUROBEHAVIORAL
FUNCTION

This part deals with childhood **disorders of function** that are frequently encountered in clinical practice, such as minimal brain dysfunction; motor disorders; epilepsy; attentional, visual, auditory, and language disorders; and deficits of cognition and learning.

R. J. Thompson and O'Quinn's (1979) developmental disabilities cube (Fig. 18-1) illustrates well the relationships between the major factors involved in disturbances of function. Whereas the first and second parts of this book deal with normal development, i.e., the time dimension of the cube, this third part concerns the etiological factors. The following chapters address what Thompson and O'Quinn call interdependent systems. The term is well chosen because any division into auditory, motor, visual, language, and other disorders must remain arbitrary to some extent. Considerable overlap exists in almost every individual afflicted with such disorders; pure disorders in any area are rare. Nevertheless, it seems desirable to deal with each area of function individually first, describing the disorders of that function and their relationship to neurological status and only then pointing out their commonality with other disorders.

Functional disorders resulting from perinatal and early-life events do not develop along rigid lines determined by etiology. The dysfunctional child is constantly interacting with other children and with adults in an environment that may help him or her learn to compensate and at least partially overcome the disabilities. Alternately, the child may lack the support needed and hence any deficit in functional abilities is compounded. Numerous failures where other children easily succeed, being excluded where peers happily play together, being viewed as deviant, and so on seem almost unavoidable for even the mildly handicapped child. Periods in hospitals and institutions not only disrupt normal development and the stimulation needed for growing up but may also create anxieties and frustrations far more severe than those experienced by the healthy child.

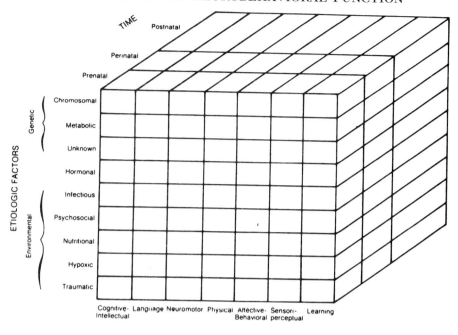

FIGURE 18-1 Developmental disabilities cube depicting the interaction of etiological factors occurring during development (R. J. Thompson and O'Quinn 1979).

For these reasons, emotional disorders are quite common in children with functional disabilities and are not necessarily related specifically to the etiology of the handicap. The last chapter in this part attempts to analyze this aspect of the disorders.

18

Minimal Brain Dysfunction

Minimal brain dysfunction (MBD) by definition overlaps into many areas. Although much of the early research on MBD focused on perceptual deficits, this would appear today almost a historical accident because many of the researchers were primarily interested in *gestalt* perception. Disorders of attention, of motor behavior, and of general activity level (hyperactivity) were mentioned in the early descriptions of MBD but became separate issues. Mental retardation, i.e., a general cognitive deficit, is frequently involved but up to the present has been deliberately excluded or at least deemphasized for two reasons: (1) to avoid the stigma of mental retardation and the assumed admission of general cognitive failure and (2) because mental retardation research with its traditional institutional affiliation has evolved in different directions and remains difficult to integrate. Our discussion of MBD follows this tradition and deemphasizes the role of attentional, motor, and general cognitive deficits and of hyperkinesis. Other conditions frequently related to MBD are poor impulse control, emotional abnormalities, and disorders of personal relationships (Bellak 1978). We return to these topics later in the book.

The concept of MBD remains highly debatable. It has been attacked by educators as useless or worse, as leading to self-fulfilling prophecies about the child, and by neurologists as producing "maximal neurological confusion" (Gomez 1967). The original term, "minimal brain damage," was discarded (MacKeith and Bax 1963), but the substitute term "minimal brain dysfunction" survives; several books and hundreds of papers on the subject appear almost every year (e.g., Rie and Rie 1980). We offer a redefinition from a developmental neuropsychological point of view and attempt to relate it to known and adequately demonstrated precursors and presumed causes. It should be noted that the term "MBD" has been used almost exclusively with school-age children; it is rarely applied to younger children and almost never to adults. Thus, it appears that from its very beginning the term has been intended to explain learning and behavior problems in children. In fact, even some recent publications treat the terms "MBD" and "learning disability" almost as synonyms (Millichap 1977).

18.1 THE CONCEPT OF MINIMAL BRAIN DYSFUNCTION

Detailed historical surveys have been published by Strother (1973) and by Kessler (1980). Reference to minor or residual damage can be found in studies of postencephalitic patients in the 1920s; in studies of children with head injury, birth trauma, and hyperactivity (Kahn and Kohen 1934); and in studies of specific learning problems (Hinshelwood 1917). With reference to mental deficiency, Lewis (1933) introduced the endogenous-exogenous distinction, referring to the general array of organic causes as exogenous, distinct from inherited or familial (subcultural) disorders. The term "brain-damaged child" became increasingly popular after publication of the influential papers by H. Werner and Strauss (1941, A. A. Strauss and Werner 1938) describing specific deficits in finger-schema and figure-ground perception based on physiological brain processes in the tradition of Gestalt psychology (for example, Koehler's 1920 book on "the physical Gestalten in resting and stationary states").

Most influential, however, were the books by A. A. Strauss and Lethinen (1947) on the psychopathology of brain-injured children and by Strauss and Kephart (1955) on its educational counterpart. In these books, the authors defined what was later named the **Strauss syndrome**: difficulty in figure-ground perception, abnormal distractibility, perseverative tendencies, conceptual rigidity, emotional liability, hyperactivity, and motor awkwardness. Strauss viewed this collection of disorders as a unitary syndrome in children resulting from brain damage of unspecified origin: "all brain lesions, wherever localized, are followed by a similar kind of disordered behavior" (Strauss and Lethinen 1947, p. 20). The hypothesis of the unitary nature of the syndrome has fueled controversy since localized lesions in the adult brain usually lead to highly distinctive and specific syndromes. Strauss's hypothesis refers, of course, to the fetal or infant brain, with its vastly different capacity for compensation during development; hence the effects of at least some forms of congenital damage may be viewed as more general than in adults and as leading to maturational delay or to a more generalized defect of unspecified range.

However, even this reasoning to justify Strauss's hypothesis has been refuted in light of the fact that some children show highly specific deficits (e.g., in language development, in hearing, or in auditory discrimination). Moreover, there have been identified many children with highly specific learning problems, especially in learning to read, who show few or none of the facets of the Strauss syndrome in the course of development. Birch (1964), Wortis (1957), and others have argued that even the child with only minimal indications of brain damage does not present the syndrome with any degree of regularity. "A whole group of people came to define brain-damaged individuals as a stereotype of hyperactive, distractable, perceptually disturbed children. Nothing could be farther from the truth" (Birch 1959).

The term "minimal brain damage" became popular as a result of a study of 500 premature and 492 full-term infants at the age of 40 weeks (Knobloch and Pasamanick 1966, Pasamanick and Knobloch 1960). It was noted that in the premature sample a wide range of cerebral damage could be demonstrated, from cerebral palsy to "minor but cleearly defined deviations from the neurological and behavioral developmental pattern" (p. 1384). The authors also noted that such minor deviations were frequently compensated by the age of 15 to 18 months, although some of them persisted well into the preschool period. Knobloch and Pasamanick proposed that such minor neurological deviation represented the least impaired end of a "**continuum of reproductive casualty.**"

Although the description of the MBD syndrome quickly gained popularity, offering a causal explanation of behavioral abnormalities frequently observed in children, reservations about its use were raised by both neurologists and psychologists. The neurologists' objection was to the inference of brain damage from what appeared to be primarily a behavioral description of the child. When neurological findings were reported, they were frequently ambiguous, difficult to elicit, and unreliable. These findings are often described as "**soft**" **neurological signs.** In 1962, the Oxford International Study Group on Child Neurology proposed the term "minimal brain dysfunction" rather than brain damage (MacKeith and Bax 1963). In the United States, a national task force attempted to clarify the concept (Clements 1966). The diagnostic use of neurological soft signs was criticized. Rutter et al. (1970a) suggested that we are dealing with three different groups of soft signs:

1. Signs that merely indicate developmental delay (e.g., motor incoordination, right-left orientation difficulties, extinction or suppression of sensory perception on simultaneous double tactile stimulation, speech and language delay) and are assumed to disappear with age. Such signs can be described only in relation to chronological and mental age. As already mentioned, Knobloch and Pasamanick's study found that minor developmental variations tend to disappear during the early years of childhood and that few persist to preschool age. Rutter's own study suggested that significant damage is required if psychological effects are to persist into school age.

2. Difficult-to-test signs, i.e., signs that are difficult to elicit and tend to have poor reliability in the neurological examination, e.g., slightly asymmetric reflexes or muscle tone, minimal athetosis, mild asymmetry of limb or skull or of motor function (hemiparesis). These signs are often a matter of degree since stronger degrees of asymmetry would clearly

be considered "hard" signs suggesting definite presence of brain damage.

3. Signs that may result not from pathological neurological conditions but from causes other than cortical damage (e.g., nystagmus, strabismus, tremor). In a recent review, Rutter (1982) agreed that, although subclinical signs may occur, the damage would have to be "rather severe and the result is not a homogenous syndrome" (p. 21).

Numerous different lists of signs have been presented. Clements (1966) lists 99 different symptoms including EEG abnormalities but also fluctuations in behavior, intellect, attention, activity level, impulse control, and affect. It should be remembered that soft signs remain just that; the presence of more than one soft sign does not make a hard sign. In other words, soft signs are not additive, even though in some studies the quantity of signs found has been used to infer a greater likelihood of actual brain damage rather than MBD. Minor EEG abnormalities (dysrhythmias) were widely used in early studies but were soon demonstrated to be of questionable value (Burnett and Struve 1970). More recently, attempting to demonstrate abnormalities with computed axial tomography, J. S. Thompson et al. (1980) found normal scans in all but two of 44 MBD children; one child showed agenesis of the corpus callosum and one a focal area of infarction. A series of studies attempting to demonstrate a delay of maturation by radiological bone age determination failed to find significant differrences between MBD and normal children, although six children showed a delay of more than two standard deviations and in general the variance within the MBD group was greater (Schlager et al. 1979).

The continuing inclusion of behavioral findings in lists of neurological signs of MBD has led to considerable confusion and, in fact, to complete rejection of the MBD concept by many psychologists. Although neurologists typically include a mental status examination in their reports, psychologists often express dissatisfaction with this practice. Moreover, a large number of studies coming primarily from the Gestalt theory camp (e.g., Ayres, Cruickshank, Frostig, Kephart) relied primarily or even exclusively on the behavioral aspects of the MBD syndrome. This leaves such studies open to the criticism that MBD is merely inferred and that the concept is based on circular reasoning. As a result, the universal use of MBD as a cause of childhood abnormalities and the inference of brain damage from behavioral symptoms has been abandoned by many authors and criticized as "empty and superfluous" (Satz and Fletcher 1979). The authors suggest that the term "should be discarded as illusory." Instead, they prefer to study specific syndromes of abnormalities (e.g. dyslexia, arithmetic disabilities) and their subforms without any inference of cause-effect relationships. For the educational researcher interested in learning-disabled children, environmental factors, such as home environment and stimulation; socioeconomic, racial, and ethnic factors; and educational intervention became the primary focus, far outweighing the potential influence of MBD on the development of the child. For a period of years, books on learning disabilities tended to reflect one of two extreme positions: an environmental or a congenital brain damage orientation. For example, Rhodes and Tracy (1974) deliberately contrasted several models of "child variance"—sociological, behavioral, psychodynamic, ecological, and countertheoretical—with a "biophysical" model (which comes closest to a model explaining childhood problems in terms of MBD). The material in these books was presented to 225 U.S. teachers and teaching instructors representing a broad sampling of university faculty members in education. Structured feedback from these sources indicated that the biophysical model was the least preferred and was considered the least influential on the thinking of the participants. Only recently have attempts at a reintegration of the two positions been attempted (Gaddes 1980, Hynd and Obrzut 1981).

18.2 ETIOLOGY

Minimal neurological abnormalities represent, by definition, the extreme upper end of the distribution of brain damage and overlap with the distribution of the normal, healthy child. In theory, any of the etiological factors described in Part III may be considered as possible causes. The impact of such damage is small enough to remain clinically obscure in the newborn and therefore even more elusive at a later age.

In most reports the MBD child is not recognized until school age and the diagnosis is based on the neurological status at the time of assessment. Etiology remains inferred and is often described simply as congenital, covering a wide variety of possible pre-, para-, and postnatal events. Schain (1968) points out that even the influential Kawi and Pasamanick (1958) study showed evidence of perinatal complications in only 37.6 per cent of the disabled sample as opposed to 21.5 per cent in controls. He argues that two genetic factors must be considered when the etiology of MBD is discussed: (a) autosomal inheritance of defects and (b) a genetically determined predisposition to MBD, i.e., an enhanced vulnerability to perinatal stress. Rutter (1982) describes the genetic syndrome notion as a possibility but adds that the claims so far "outrun the empirical findings that could justify them" (p. 21). In the most recent discussion of the subject, Stewart (1980) also refers to the interaction between genetic, perinatal, and constitutional factors, whereas H. P. Martin (1980) stresses the effects of nutrition, injury, and illness. Wender (1977) has proposed a genetic biochemical basis of MBD (irregularities of amine metabolism), especially with respect to hyperactivity. G. Weiss (1980), in her review of various potential etiological factors, concludes that the etiology of MBD is presently unknown and likely to be multifactorial and heterogenous: "No single etiology is sufficient to explain causation in MBD children" (p. 353). She points out that a disease entity of MBD could be supported only if a common etiological factor were found. However, behavioral studies as well as etiological studies suggest that no such entity exists.

Dykman and Ackerman (1976) attributed at least one form of the MBD/hyperactive syndrome to a possible frontal lobe dysfunction, namely, the impulsive patient who cannot sustain attention and is unable to evaluate and weigh different alternatives. Another type would be a "posterior" defect; in these children a sensory processing deficit in visual, auditory, or other sensory areas leads to inability to differentiate and input is constantly overloaded and confused. Focusing and scanning as two separate abilities would support a breakdown into subtypes. In addition, the authors distinguish dimensions of arousal and attention to arrive at four types based on an information processing model (including the frontal lobe types). Arousal is viewed as related to the reticular formation. A similar discussion of specific subtypes related to location of lesion has been presented by Prechtl (1978). These and other suggested subtypes remain, however, speculative at this time.

18.3 SOFT SIGNS AND BEHAVIORAL ABNORMALITIES

If we are to use the term "MBD" meaningfully, an attempt must be made to avoid confounding behavioral and neurological abnormalities (Denckla 1978). Even more important, it must be demonstrated that the presence of neurological findings (and especially of soft signs) has a meaningful effect on the future of the child. If, for example, soft signs are found with equal frequency in children with poor and with normal learning ability, then the presence of such signs may be regarded as fortuitous and of no practical consequence. Long-term outcome may be another criterion in deciding whether soft signs are meaningful or not. If it can be shown that outcome over a period of years is significantly better for children without such signs (all other factors being equal), then some meaningful prognostic significance can be attached to their presence regardless of whether such signs persist or not.

Unfortunately, research findings about these questions have been equivocal and contradictory. For example, Hertzig et al. (1969) studied 90 learning-disabled children and found that 29 per cent had classical (hard) neurological signs and 69 per cent had soft signs whereas only soft signs were present in 6 per cent of the controls. Although this study appears to present strong evidence for the importance of neurological signs in learning-disabled children, it should be noted that these children were in a special education facility and that admission was dependent on a confirmed diagnosis of brain damage. In contrast, R. M. Adams et al (1974) screened 368 regular fourth-grade children and found that soft signs were not related to whether the child was a normal learner, borderline, or learning-disabled as judged by their school records. Hence, some of the contradictions can be attributed to subject selection. In fact, neurological findings are rare in a cross section of poor learners in school but more frequent in selected samples from second- or third-line referral clinics. Since referral to such clinics usually is made only for persisting and severe problems, it seems possible that the neurological impairment is related to the severity of the learning problem. Other authors admit that an association between neurological signs and learning and behavior problems exists but question whether it is sufficiently strong to make any kind of prediction for the individual ("guilt by statistical association," Barlow 1975). Helper (1980), in a recent review of the subject, concludes that neurological soft signs elevate the "risk of psychopathy, lowered SES, antisocial behavior, and psychiatric contact, but total social and vocational incapacitation are evidently not the rule" (p. 110), and Small (1982) concludes that such children carry "an enormous negative prognostic burden" (p. 33).

Another, more theoretical question has been used as a criticism of the MBD hypothesis: If neurological soft signs are indeed age-linked, then they may signify no more than a maturational delay and can be assumed to disappear with time. Satz (1976) has discussed this interpretation of the **maturational lag hypothesis** and suggests that the child may overcome the problem later in life and that the MBD label is therefore inappropriate. This position is also stressed by Kinsbourne (1973), who states that "all indicators of MBD represent the normal state of affairs in younger children" (p. 272). In contrast, Rourke (1976) viewed MBD as a true deficit that may persist in a similar or modified form. The two contrasting interpretations predict differences in outcome and should be testable in longitudinal studies. Unfortunately, Satz's own longitudinal study covers only the period from kindergarten to grade 5, and Rourke's study focuses on 8 to 12 year olds. Hence the two studies are not directly comparable. It can be argued that an even longer follow-up period is required before the lag versus deficit argument can be settled.

Most studies of MBD start with the school-age child. Information about the origin of MBD is often inferred retrospectively and based on questioning of the mother. This leaves open the question of how many children underwent the same type of stress but did not show developmental problems. Kalverboer (1976, Kalverboer et al. 1975) addressed this question by exploring the effect of pre- and perinatal problems and of neurological findings in the neonatal period in relation to preschool neurological and behavioral characteristics of 147 children. Fifty per cent of these children had a normal newborn "optimality score"; the other half was "nonoptimal" (minor brain dysfunction risk). The global measure of integrity of the CNS in the neonate did not correlate significantly with the same measure at preschool age, although a subgroup of boys without complications during the interval between neonatal and preschool examination did show a small but significant correlation of .28, explaining approximately 9 per cent of the variance. Although this study suggests that indicators of MBD in the neonatal period are relatively unstable and have little predictive significance, it also showed a significant difference between preschool optimal and nonoptimal children in a free-field behavior observation, especially for boys and in nonstimulating situations. The Kalverboer study confirms a rather tenous association between early MBD signs and later childhood status. The author stresses the large variability of findings, which are somewhat reminiscent of the Graham studies (F. K. Graham et al. 1962, 1963) on the seven-year outcome of anoxia discussed earlier.

Hertzig (1981) followed up on 66 low-birth-weight children, including 13 with localizing and 20 with soft neurological signs. Children with soft signs sustained more complications at birth, whereas children with focal signs suffered more from postnatal complications. At 8 years of age, children with soft signs were more often found in special education settings or undergoing psychiatric evaluation than neurologically normal peers, although the difference between groups in IQ, reading, and arithmetic tests was not significant.

The association between soft signs and behavior at preschool and school age has also been investigated in several nonlongitudinal studies at different ages (Lucas et al. 1965, Paine et al. 1968). Most studies obtained equally tenuous findings about the association between MBD and behavioral abnormalities.

Multivariable studies of MBD children by Stevens et al. (1967) and Knights and Hinton (1969, Hinton and Knights 1971) suggest that such children are slower to respond, less able to follow verbal instructions, poorer in tone discrimination and tapping, with specific configurational patterns on the WISC intelligence test, but that "the pattern of abilities and deficits is not homogenous" (Knights and Hinton 1969) and that the deficits related to a particular symptom are varied. A recent study by Willems et al (1979) reported the results of 281 preschool boys and again concluded that "a few precise somatic anomalies, such as cryptochidia (retentio testes), squint, dysmorphias, and a history of low birth weight" are only slightly but significantly predictive when group comparisons with normal boys are made. The study also investigated psychological performance. Finger discrimination, attention span, and short-term and sequential memory were found highly significant in prediction; hand laterality, spatial orientation, and IQ (in the range above 70) were less predictive of group membership.

Paine et al. (1968) suggested that the lack of correlation is due to the failure to study patterns of abnormalities in individual children, which reflect "a complex matrix of underlying dimensions, some innate, some traumatic, and some psychosocial" (p. 517). As a first step toward the analysis of such patterns, Paine and colleagues factor-analyzed their results of 97

MBD children with a mean age of 8.4 years and suggested that at least two factors of neurological abnormality should be distinguished: a perceptual deficit and a motor incoordination factor. In addition to these two, the authors also reported an EEG and a reflex abnormalities factor. History was also divided into two factors: abnormal prenatal and abnormal perinatal; a third history factor suggested that birth order and maternal age might have to be treated as a separate dimension. On the side of the psychological (behavioral and educational) abnormalities related to MBD, a similar detailed division would seem to be indicated. This topic is addressed in Chap. 25.

Other nonlongitudinal studies have addressed the association of MBD neurological symptoms with clumsiness and other motor problems (Gubbay et al. 1965; Paine 1968, Prechtl and Stemmer 1962), visuomotor disability (M. W. Brenner et al. 1967), and behavior problems (Mordock and Bogan 1968). In the comparison of carefully selected clinic-referred groups, typically moderate group differences on all these variables can be found. Even in a comparison between 31 6 to 8-year-old learning-disabled children with questionable brain disorder (as inferred on the basis of a history of serious illness and trauma) and a learning-disabled control group without such history, significant differences, especially in motor and sensory test performance, were found (Tsushima and Towne 1977). The two groups could be discriminated on the basis of five such tests with an accuracy of 72.6 per cent. In a study of temperament, Carey et al. (1979) found among 61 clinically diagnosed MBD children a higher number of less adapted, less persistent, and more active children with negativistic behavior when compared to a control population. However, children in a hyperactive and in a learning disability control group were somewhat similar in temperament, suggesting that these behaviors are not necessarily unique to or characteristic of MBD.

18.4 LONGITUDINAL STUDIES

The objective of long-term longitudinal studies is not primarily to demonstrate differences between MBD and control groups at a given age but to determine whether such differences disappear with age or whether they may result in some long-term and possibly lifelong consequences for the individual. Such studies have been reviewed by Helper (1980) and by Spreen (1982). The results have usually shown a consistent picture with high risk of lasting deficits of functioning and poor adjustment in many respects (Dykman et al. 1973, D. Johnson and Neumann 1975, Kaste 1972, Kleinpeter and Göllnitz 1976), although some negative findings were also reported (Ackerman et al. 1977, Koppitz 1971).

A recent study by Spreen and collaborators (Denbigh 1979; Hern 1979; Spreen 1978a, 1981, 1983; Spreen and Lawriw 1980) reported a ten-year follow-up of 203 children originally referred to a neuropsychology clinic because of learning problems. On the basis of an independent neurological examination, the sample was broken down into three groups: brain damage, MBD, and learning problems without brain damage, and a control group of 52 normal learners was also studied. The four groups were reasonably well matched for age, sex, and SES. The majority of MBD outcome variables (assessed in a structured interview, from school records, and by a parent and a student inventory) presented significant differences between the four groups. These differences were typically linear, i.e., the learning-disabled children without neurological findings fared worse than the controls, the children with MBD showed poorer outcome than those without neurological impairment, and the brain-damaged group showed the poorest outcome of all. Areas of long-term adjustment studied included school and occupational achievement and personal and social adjustment. Inventories also reflected a consistent relationship between degree of neurological impairment and behavioral deviance and emotional adjustment. A striking sex difference emerged: females showed poorer emotional and social adjustment than males, and males showed more acting out behavior. The frequently claimed relationship between learning problems and MBD on the one hand and delinquency on the other could not be confirmed; it appeared, however, that the learning-disabled group without neurological impairment drew slightly more and somewhat more severe penalties in encounters with the police than the other groups. A current continuation of the project at a mean age of 25 suggests that both emotional disorders and occupational adjustment problems are more pronounced than they were at age 19.

The study appears to confirm the impact of MBD on long-term outcome and suggests that neurological impairment may be meaningfully treated as a continuum. It confirms Kaste's (1972) conclusion that in a long-term follow-up MBD subjects show "to an even more pronounced degree patterns which previously have been associated with cerebral dysfunction" (p. 1797) and that they did not "simply grow out of the problem or become more similar to other former patients with the passage of time." This partially contradicts the maturational lag hypothesis.

On the other hand, it must be remembered that these studies can describe the long-term outcome only of subjects identified during school age and that the results cannot be generalized to subjects in whom MBD was detected during the preschool or the postnatal period. Moreover, the effect of MBD (or of definite brain damage) must not be overinterpreted. Often, the presence of a mild handicap during early school age and the associated continuing school failure may create a broad generalizing effect on future academic achievement and on feelings of self-worth and social competence. Hence, the eventual long-term outcome represents the results of a continuing interaction between the actual deficit and numerous environmental variables as well as the endurance and toughness of the individual. Some studies show clearly that upper-class children educated in special private schools appear to have a better chance of overcoming the deficit. Here again, the effect of coming from a supportive, affluent home as well as the assistance in obtaining job training and jobs provided from such parental environment may be an important factor.

Another persistent factor influencing outcome is the general intellectual level of the child. This factor has been deemphasized in many studies. However, when it is included, children with lower IQ levels (though not mentally retarded) almost invariably show poorer response to treatment and poorer long-term outcome. Why such a treatment-by-intelligence interaction exists has not been adequately explained, although some obvious reasons, such as the ones discussed in the previous paragraph, may be primarily responsible.

19

Motor Disorders

Human behavior and all activity of the central nervous system can ultimately be expressed only by means of muscle action. In this chapter, we introduce briefly the basics of the motor system and then proceed to a description of the gross motor disorders, the fine motor disorders, and, eventually, the more complex disorders of movement, i.e., the apraxias.

19.1 THE MOTOR SYSTEM

The lowest level of motor control acting directly on muscles and viscera arises from the gray matter of the spinal cord. Motor action is merely reflexive at this level but capable of certain types of organized activity. The next level originates at the reticular formation of the brainstem. Axons from gray and white matter at this level (reticulospinal fibers) descend to the spinal cord and have a variety of functions, e.g., activation of motor cells, inhibition of reflex actions, and maintenance of muscular contraction and relaxation. If these fibers are destroyed, some excitatory mechanisms may become overly active, resulting in spasticity, and the inhibitory functions may become ineffective.

Another level of control originates in the basal ganglia and the cerebellum, with fibers extending to the brainstem reticular formation. These fibers are involved in the regulation and coordination of movement, balance, posture, timing, and so forth. The highest level of control extends from certain areas of the cortex, which in its fifth layer contains pyramidal cells that enter the white matter of the cerebral hemisphere and either relay excitation to subcortical levels or connect with direct pathways into the brainstem and the spinal cord. The lower the level of control, the more specific the action. Cortical control is least specific in its action on specific muscles, but it controls a great variety of combinations of muscle actions.

A division into lower and upper motor neurons is frequently made. Lower

254

motor neurons originate at the brainstem or spinal cord level and directly drive the muscles of the head and body; hence they are also called the final common pathway for all CNS activity. The connections between cortical motor areas or subcortical areas and the motor cells in the spinal cord are frequently called the upper motor neurons. Another distinction introduced in the first part of this book is that between the pyramidal system, providing direct voluntary control from cortex to muscle (Figure 19-1), and the extrapyramidal system, carrying control from the cortex but including a large variety of input at the subcortical level and providing specific mechanisms for the control of the final common pathway. The extrapyramidal system is highly interconnected; the basal ganglia, red nucleus, subthalamic nucleus, substantia nigra, and thalamus all participate. Many extrapyramidal pathways actually have projections running through the pyramids; only a small portion of the pyramidal cells actually projects into the precentral motor areas of the cortex. Hence the pyramidal-extrapyramidal distinction is somewhat misleading (E. Gardner 1968).

19.2 MOTOR DISORDERS

"Cerebral palsy" is a general term referring to the full spectrum of motor disorders after lesions at any level of motor control except those secondary to mental retardation or caused by progressive diseases (Molnar 1973). A description was given by Little (1861, Denhoff and Robinault 1960), whose paper led to general acceptance of the origin of the disorder (also described as Little's disease). Although the term originally referred only to disorders of the cerebrum, lesions at other levels were frequently included. Since cause and type of impairment are not specified in the term, it is currently used only in the generic sense.

Spasticity

Lesions at the cortical level or in its projections into the corticospinal tracts leave the appropriate muscles without voluntary control. The muscles remain resistant to active or passive movement, are often hypertonic, and show abnormally increased reflexes. The condition is usually described as spasticity. Mild or moderate forms of the disorder show clumsiness and weakness. The condition can be unilateral or bilateral, depending on the lesion. Spastic diplegia results from bilateral lesions of the cortex but is more likely to occur with lesions in the subcortical white matter near the lateral ventricles, affecting primarily the lower extremities (e.g., periventricular leucomalacia).

Paralysis

Paralysis (paresis) and weakness can occur with lesions at any level of the motor system. With lower-level lesions, strength and muscle tone are more

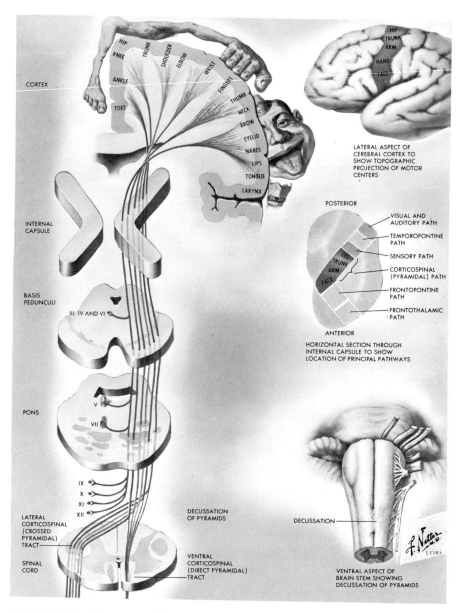

FIGURE 19-1   The pyramidal system (Netter 1962).

affected than dexterity; the opposite is the case with upper motor neuron lesions, when particularly fine motor ability is affected and muscle tone and reflex activity are increased but atrophy of the muscles is less pronounced.

Dystonia and athetosis

These terms refer to abnormal movements of the trunk and/or limbs; there is usually present a slow, spasmodic twisting that interferes with voluntary movements and may result in fixed body postures. The lesion is usually in the basal ganglia, which shows evidence of atrophy, cavitation, or marbling.

Chorea

Chorea refers to involuntary, irregular, jerky, and brisk movements, primarily affecting the limbs, face, jaw, and tongue. Choreatic movements often occur together with athetosis (choreoathetosis). The lesion is probably in the area of the basal ganglia (lateral to the motor pathways). In athetosis after kernicterus, the lesion is often more marked in the globus pallidus. However, for both chorea and athetosis the exact site of lesion is controversial. Both motor disorders are frequently symptoms of an imbalance of the relative activity of cholinergic and dopaminergic neurons and their receptors (Brain 1977).

Rigidity

In contrast to spasticity, rigidity (which is also associated with lesions in the area of the globus pallidus) shows an increased muscle tone. Both agonist and antagonist muscles contract simultaneously, producing stiffness. Rigid muscles are electrically active at rest, whereas spastic muscles are not.

Ataxia

This term refers to the inability to control the rate, range, force, and direction of movement adequately and is usually an indicator of dysfunction of the cerebellum and its afferent pathways. Balancing problems and difficulty in performing precise movements are common.

Tremor

Rhythmic oscillations of part of the body at rest or during activity is referred to as tremor. This condition may seriously interfere with the ability to perform precise movements. Lesions can be found at various levels. At the level of the pallidum, lesions may produce tremor at rest, primarily in the fingers and the head muscles. Tremor associated primarily with intentional movement indicates cerebellar lesions.

19.3 CAUSES OF MOTOR DISORDERS

Numerous causes of motor disorders have been identified, although in the individual case the etiology may remain speculative. Intrauterine damage by toxemia, infection, or antepartum hemorrhage and intoxication by fetal waste have all been described as possible causes. Insufficient supply of oxygen or nutrients across the placenta has also been cited. A major group of disorders result from problems during and immediately after birth. Risk factors include prematurity and low birth weight as predisposing factors, perinatal trauma, perinatal hemorrhage, kernicterus, hypoxic and ischemic events, and repeated convulsions during the neonatal period. Spasticity has also been associated with structural malformations, such as microgyria, porencephaly, and atrophy of one hemisphere, and with sclerotic lesions in one or more lobes of a hemisphere. Some forms of motor disorder in children (e.g., Friedreich's ataxia) are hereditary (Jabbari et al. 1983).

While the association between motor disorders and malformations is clearly demonstrated, the etiology remains speculative. In elucidating the cause of brain-structure abnormalities that occur prenatally, it is important to distinguish between an arrest or deviation of development and destructive lesions. The former might occur in relation to maternal exposure to drugs, infections such as rubella, and some viruses. The latter is more likely with cytomegalovirus, bacterial infections, and a maternal blood loss that causes a drop in fetal blood pressure. The nature of the structural abnormality may be related to the stage of development of the embryo or fetus at which the disrupting influence occurs. The stage of development can be estimated from examination of the brain. In some conditions, such as eclampsia and maternal hypertension, the effects on the fetus are not clearly defined. In others, the etiology may be described as multifactorial and includes an interaction with factors such as socioeconomic status and maternal weight.

Although many motor disorders are evident at birth and leave little room for diagnostic speculation, signs of spasticity may not show up until the end of the first year and minor weaknesses may not be evident until later. Dystonia, athetosis, and choreoathetosis are often not recognized until the second year of life. On the other hand, motor disorders of the newborn often improve markedly with age, suggesting that the developing nervous system is capable of compensating for small CNS lesions. Less obvious signs of motor disorder are a generally slow motor development, asymmetric postures and limb movements (including even an early strong hand preference), and the persistence of grasp, tonic neck, and Moro reflexes. The Moro reflex is elicited when the infant is left unsupported in the supine position and consists of flexing of the thighs and knees, fanning and clenching of the fingers, and outward spreading and then bringing together of the arms. These instinctive reflexes normally disappear after the age of 6 months.

Hypotonia and overly active reflexes also suggest persisting motor defects. Prechtl and Stemmer (1962) described a child's inability to hold its fingers quiet while stretching out its arms and keeping its eyes closed as a choreiform syndrome that may suggest minor damage to the basal ganglia or the cerebellum. Little information is available about early evidence for complex sensory-motor integration defects, dyspraxia, and similar problems found in early or late childhood.

19.4 ANIMAL STUDIES

In systematic studies on the effects of selective ablation of the motor areas in animals, unilateral and bilateral removal of motor and premotor areas in monkeys less than 4 weeks old did not immediately produce paresis. Where paresis developed later, it was much less severe than with similar lesions in adult animals (Kennard 1942). When neighboring areas were also ablated, the motor deficit in the young animal was aggravated, but this did not appear to affect the adult animals. Kennard interpreted this finding as a capacity for reorganization of the CNS, a capacity that slowly and progressively diminishes as the animal completes the second year of life. Sectioning the pyramidal tract (Lawrence and Hopkins 1972) and hemispherectomy in rats (Hicks and D'Amato 1970) led to similar findings.

The results obtained with ablation of the prefrontal motor association areas are mentioned in Chap. 3. Harlow et al. (1970) reported that sparing of function was directly related to the size of the lesion and age of the animal at time of surgery, although compensation of function was not found in animals older than 12 months. Goldman et al. (1970) introduced a distinction between the role of the dorsolateral cortex and that of the orbital prefrontal cortex and suggested that the recovery of function after early lesions depends on the maturation sequence of the structure. The dorsolateral cortex becomes functional only later in infancy; since it appears to be "uncommitted" earlier, it possesses the capacity to compensate for orbital lesions within certain limits of age. On the other hand, the orbital region cannot compensate for dorsolateral ablation even if such lesions are made as early as 1 month because it matures much earlier. If both areas are ablated, no recovery of function can occur. The studies involved the learning of alternating responses and delayed responses—a relatively complex behavior appropriate for the association cortex—and visual discrimination.

Hécaen and Albert (1978) speculated about the potential mechanisms of compensation for lesions in the immature brain. They list regeneration of tissue (including hypertrophy of the ipsilateral pyramid), formation of new connections, generation of abnormal axons provoked by chemical changes resulting from the lesion, and vicarious takeover of function; all of these contribute to the plasticity of the immature brain. The studies leave no question, however, that in spite of these compensatory mechanisms, recovery of function remains limited and more subtle forms of impairment persist.

19.5 STUDIES WITH CHILDREN

The incidence rate of motor disorders of any type in children has been estimated to range from 1 to 5.9 per 1000. Rutter et al. (1970a) reported an incidence of 2.0 to 2.5 per 1000 in school-age children. The overall incidence rate has declined to 1.6 during the last 27 years but remains unchanged at 12 per 1000 for surviving newborns with a birth weight of less than 2500 grams (Kudrjavcew et al. 1983). The estimated frequency of various types of motor disorder among children is shown in Table 19-1.

In studies of etiology, Malamud et al. (1964) found in postmortem examinations of 68 children with cerebral palsy that 35 per cent had indications of arrest or distortion of brain development during the prenatal period. Drillien (1974) found that 15 per cent of low-birth-weight children had either a major brain malformation or three or more minor ones. Half of these children showed moderate or severe neurological deficit at 1 to 3 years of age. Babson et al. (1975) reported that up to 40 per cent of CP infants and more than 75 per cent of children with spastic diplegia had low birth weight. Low birth weight hence remains the most important predisposing factor since it is frequently associated with subdural hemorrhage in the posterior fossa area or with epidural hemorrhage in the spinal cord and brainstem as a result of malpositioning during birth (Towbin 1970).

Of children with known intracranial hemorrhage, only 40 per cent appeared normal at an 11- to 20-month follow-up, 20 per cent had mild, and

TABLE 19-1   Classification by Sex and Type of Cerebral Palsy as Reported in the 1951 New Jersey Study

Type	Boys		Girls	
	Number	Per cent	Number	Per cent
Spastic	374	46.6	271	44.9
Athetoid	192	23.9	141	23.3
Rigidity	96	12.0	81	13.4
Ataxia	95	11.8	57	9.4
Tremor	10	1.2	17	2.8
Mixed cases	24	3.0	24	4.0
Rare cases	11	1.5	13	2.2
Total (1406)	802	100.0	604	100.0

Source: Hopkins et al. 1954.

40 per cent had moderate to severe motor defects (Krishnamoorthy et al. 1977). The same study also reported intracranial hemorrhage in 65 to 75 per cent of autopsied babies who showed respiratory distress at birth. The association of motor disorders with asphyxia has been confirmed in several studies: shock, breech birth, placental insufficiency, cesarean section, forceps, and other complications of birth were frequent. In a study by Brown et al. (1974), about half of the 94 infants with such complications either died or showed significant handicap. Even in children who appear normal during the first year of life, there may remain subtle defects that may show up on long-term follow-up as minimal brain dysfunction with or without subtle motor deficits.

Postnatal motor disorders are mainly the result of head trauma (including child abuse). Mealey (1975) reports that over 80 per cent of subdural hematomas occur during the first year of life. In a study of 80 infants suffering head trauma, 36 per cent of the injuries were a consequence of child abuse, 28 per cent resulted from "falls and blows," and 4 per cent were related to car accidents. Motor disorders have also been reported after bacterial meningitis, hemophilus influenza, immunization reaction, and other infections. A follow-up study by Feigin and Dodge (1976) showed that of 88 preschool children with bacterial meningitis, nine had hemiplegia or quadriplegia (although the paralysis persisted in only three children after one year) and two showed persisting ataxia. Hearing loss was also noted. The same study reported a risk for bacterial meningitis in children during the first five years of life as ranging from 1 in 400 to 1 in 2000. Again, it remains open whether more subtle sequelae persist in children who were apparently recovered at the one-year follow-up.

Motor disorders rarely occur in isolation. Frequently, tactile sensory loss is also present and highly correlated with cortical motor deficit, as shown by Laget et al. (1976) in a study of the somatosensory-evoked potential in 43 infants and children. Associated intellectual loss has frequently been observed (Feigin and Dodge 1976). The frequency distribution of IQ in a group of 140 children with infantile hemiplegia (Table 19-2) shows a significant shift toward the low end, although some children with superior intelligence were also present (Cruickshank et al. 1976). Mean IQs vary with type of paralysis (Table 19-3) and with type of motor disorder (Table 19-4). Even if subjects with an IQ lower than 80 are excluded, adult CP subjects still show a significantly poorer performance on tests of nonverbal intelligence, psychomotor speech, reproduction from memory, and visual memory but not in other tests of abstraction and retention (Cronhold and Schalling 1968).

In a detailed retrospective study, Annett (1973) used a British version of the Wechsler Intelligence Scale for children to examine 106 early-onset-hemiplegia children after they were 5 years old. The group was heterogeneous with regard to onset and cause. The mean IQ was approximately 80, with more than 60 per cent of the children scoring in the borderline or

TABLE 19-2   Levels of Intelligence in Three Samples of Cerebral Palsied Children

IQ level	Buffalo (n = 330)	New Jersey (n = 1000)	Birmingham (n = 354)
110 and above	4.5	6.9	4.0
90–109	23.0	21.6	20.1
70–89	22.5	22.7	26.8
50–69	22.5	20.4	22.9
0–49	27.5	28.4	22.3
Not yet assessable			3.9

Source: Cruickshank et al. 1976a.

average range (IQ greater than 70). Looking for correlates of general cognitive deficit, the author found lower IQs in children with greater physical disability, with recurrent seizure disorders, and with early onset of hemiplegia. Speech problems were more often found in children with late-onset hemiplegia, i.e., after the age of 44 months, but this finding obtained only for right hemiplegia. In left hemiplegia early onset was more often related to speech problems. In cases of unilateral hemiplegia the authors found no difference between verbal and performance IQ related to the side of hemiplegia, but in bilateral hemiplegia the performance IQ tended to be lower. Similar findings were reported by H. B. C. Reed and Reitan (1963) and by J. C. Reed and Reitan (1969). Exploring the role of familial lefthandedness, Annett found that in right hemiplegics without familial lefthandedness the verbal and performance IQs were more highly correlated with the motor speed of the affected hand than with the speed of the nonaffected hand; the opposite was true for other-handedness groups. The author concluded that children without familial sinistrality are more dependent on the left hemisphere. In children with familial left-handedness, Annett found more physical and intellectual disability except in left hemiplegic females, suggesting

TABLE 19-3   Comparison of Mean IQ and Standard Deviation in Subclassifications of Spasticity, Birmingham and New Jersey Groups

	Quadriplegia		Right hemisphere		Left hemisphere		Paraplegia	
	Birmingham	New Jersey	Birmingham	New Jersey	Birmingham	New Jersey	Birmingham	New Jersey
Mean IQ	50.2	57.39	76.8	74.73	77.9	79.73	74.3	76.76
SD	27.6	30.86	26.0	24.47	20.1	28.46	23.6	28.38
n	80	107	57	130	41	120	85	115
Not yet assessable	4		2		1		2	

Source: Cruickshank et al. 1976a.

TABLE 19-4   Comparison of Mean IQ and Standard Deviation, Birmingham and New Jersey Group, Birmingham Mixed Cases Omitted

	Spastic		Athetoid		Ataxic	
	Bir-mingham	New Jersey	Bir-mingham	New Jersey	Bir-mingham	New Jersey
Mean	67.9	71.94	67.6	72.60	63.3	54.96
SD	27.7	29.73	25.5	30.41	19.3	27.06
n	277	522	41	249	4	129
Not yet assessable	9	0	4	0	0	0

Source: Cruickshank et al. 1976a.

that perhaps cerebral organization and capability for compensation are different for this group.

Several studies have addressed the question of subtle motor disorders and other associated deficits in relation to clinical neurological findings. Teuber and Rudel (1967) in particular examined the long-term progress of lesion effects and found that immediate and definite clinical deficits in infancy tend to recede with time. For example, mirror movements after childhood hemiparesis tend to become less frequent between the ages of 6 and 16 years (Woods and Teuber 1978); the synkinesis consisted of unintentional movements with the other hand when the child was required to tap one finger against the thumb with one hand only. Teuber and Rudel stressed that other effects of the lesion sustained in childhood do not manifest themselves until adulthood. An example is the **Aubert task,** where the comparison of brain-damaged and normal children showed no differences but differences did emerge in adults. The Aubert task requires the adjustment of a luminous line to a vertical position while the body is tilted. It was also noted that this task was not related to level of intelligence.

That different types of motor activity and especially of fine motor skills are relatively independent of each other has been known for some time (Seashore et al. 1940). In a detailed study with ten brain-damaged and ten normal children for each age group between 6 and 12 years, Schilling (1970) confirmed that this diversity of relationships also holds in children for the six sets of tasks measured with the Oseretsky Test of Motor Development. The finding should be considered as a warning not to treat motor deficits as a unitary phenomenon. Instead, each type of motor activity has to be measured individually for a full assessment of the child's abilities. Wyke (1968) showed specific deficits for an arm-hand precision task, Steinwachs and Barmeyer (1952) showed deficits for several measures of writing grip pressure and writing time in adolescents with motor retardation. Boll and Reitan (1972) reported significant differences between congenitally brain-damaged and normal children on a variety of measures, including motor strength and speed and psychomotor skill as well as more perceptually based skills, such as finger localization, fingertip number writing, and tactile form recognition. Similar findings were also presented by Reitan (1971a, 1971b). **Motor impersistence** (inability to maintain eyes closed, tongue protruding, mouth open, lateral eye fixation on gaze, fixation of examiner's nose during confrontation testing) was also present in brain-damaged children, although no increase or decrease with age has been reported (Garfield 1964). A recent study by Klawans et al. (1982) ascribed to hypoxia at birth a progressive writing tremor in six patients that began between the ages of 8 and 54 years.

Difficulties in skilled movements (**apraxia**) have been studied extensively in adult patients (Heilman 1979), but few studies with children have been presented (De Negri 1967; Robaye 1967). Such disorders are usually investigated in studies of the clumsy child (Walton 1967). Classical apraxias appear to be rare and primarily the result of disconnection syndromes, whereas clumsiness may be the result of extrapyramidal and cerebellar lesions, i.e., may not meet the definition of apraxia at all. Some authors, however, have used the term loosely (Ayres 1965, Gaddes 1980) and included deficits in eye-hand accuracy, motor planning, gross motor planning, and finger identification as part of a developmental apraxia syndrome. M. W. Brenner et al. (1967) described a group of agnosic-apraxic children with significant impairment in manual skills, spatial judgment, spelling, arithmetic, and social adjustment.

Although several studies of disorders of relatively simple motor activity found little or no association with intellectual deficit, this dissociation does not hold for more complex motor tasks. Malpass (1963) has discussed this topic in detail. Groden (1969), in a study that included mentally retarded children, found correlations ranging from .51 to .68 between mental age on the one hand and motor skills, coordination, and complex reaction time tasks on the other, even when chronological age was partialled out. This finding is understandable since complex motor activity involves a considerable cognitive component.

20

Attentional Disorders and Hyperactivity

Attentional deficits characterize a number of childhood syndromes, including minimal brain dysfunction (MBD), learning disabilities, and hyperactivity. However, attempts to delineate these deficits are confounded by confusion in terminology. For example, MBD and hyperactivity are often used interchangeably when they may in fact refer to different syndromes. MBD children are defined as having neurochemical and neurophysiological dysfunction and perceptual or learning disabilities although this is not always associated with the hyperactive syndrome (Swidler and Walson 1979). On the other hand, hyperactivity has often been treated as part of the MBD syndrome despite statistical evidence to the contrary.

To clarify matters, many researchers have chosen to describe particular core-symptom patterns and avoid global labeling (D. M. Ross and S. A. Ross 1976, A. O. Ross and Pelham 1981; Table 20-1). This approach has revealed that attentional deficits constitute a primary symptom of the hyperactive syndrome (Douglas and Peters 1979). This chapter therefore focuses on the hyperactive syndrome to provide a context for understanding attentional deficits in children.

20.1 DEFINITION

The **hyperactive syndrome** refers to a constellation of symptoms, including overactivity or motor restlessness, distractibility, impulsivity, and short attention span (DSM III, Singh and Ling 1979), often accompanied by emotional immaturity, aggressiveness, and poor academic performance (Barkley 1981a, 1981b; Mash and Dalby 1979). The term "hyperactivity" is also used to refer to excessive restlessness and should be differentiated from the hyperactive syndrome, which incorporates the constellation of symptoms described above (Denckla and Heilman 1979). For purposes of this discus-

TABLE 20-1   Major Diagnostic Criteria of Attentional Deficit Disorder with Hyperactivity

---

Inattention: at least three of the following:
   Often fails to finish things
   Often does not seem to listen
   Easily distracted
   Has difficulty concentrating on tasks requiring sustained attention
   Has difficulty sticking to a play activity

Impulsivity: at least three of the following:
   Often acts before thinking
   Shifts excessively from one activity to another
   Has difficulty organizing work (this not being due to cognitive impairment)
   Needs a lot of supervision
   Frequently calls out in class
   Has difficulty awaiting turn in games or group situations

Hyperactivity: at least two of the following:
   Runs about or climbs on things excessively
   Has difficulty sitting still or fidgets excessively
   Has difficulty staying seated
   Moves about excessively during sleep
   Is always "on the go" or acts as if "driven by a motor"

Onset before age 7

Duration of at least six months

Not due to schizophrenia, affective disorder, or severe or profound mental retardation

---

Source: A. O. Ross and Pelham 1981.

sion, the term "hyperactivity" implies the syndrome unless otherwise stated.

Earlier terminology focused on overactivity as the primary symptom. More recently, however, attentional deficits have emerged as the central component of the syndrome (Douglas and Peters 1979). The recent renaming of the hyperactive syndrome as the "attentional deficit disorder" in DSM III reflects this shift in emphasis. Barkley (1981b, p. 14) defines the hyperactive syndrome as "a disorder of age-appropriate attention and rule-governed behavior (compliance, self-control, and problem solving) that arises in infancy or early childhood (before age 4), is pervasive in nature (cross-situational), and is not associated with gross sensory, motor, psychiatric or neurologic impairment or with mental retardation."

The characteristics of the syndrome have been poorly differentiated from normal behavior. Traits of high activity, distractibility, and short attention span exist in the general population. If 49 per cent of the population is by definition more active than the mean, how active must a child be to be considered hyperactive (Carey and McDevitt 1980)? Studies using clustering techniques suggest that hyperactivity is not a unitary syndrome but a loose association of symptoms. Subclassification of this heterogeneous group would clarify terminology and refine research endeavors (Ross and Ross 1976).

20.2 BEHAVIORAL CHARACTERISTICS OF THE HYPERACTIVE SYNDROME

Attention

In studying attentional deficits in hyperactive children, Douglas and her colleagues have hypothesized that "the major disability of hyperactive children is the inability to sustain attention and inhibit impulsive responding on tasks or in social situations that require focused, reflective, organized, and self-directed effort" (Douglas and Peters 1979, p. 173). The authors described the nature of the attentional deficit on the basis of distractibility and vigilance tasks (Sykes et al. 1971, 1972, 1973).

Classical studies of distractibility that investigated whether children can screen out task-irrelevant stimulation or potential distractors indicate that hyperactive children are no more vulnerable to extraneous stimuli than normal children. In addition, tests of incidental learning show no evidence that hyperactive children are more likely to process and remember task-irrelevant information than normal children (Douglas and Peters 1979).

The performance of hyperactive children on vigilance or sustained-attention tasks has been evaluated using the Continuous Performance Test (Rosvold et al. 1956). This task requires the subject to monitor a screen on which letters appear at regular intervals and to respond whenever a previously specified stimulus appears (Sykes et al. 1971) Hyperactive children made more errors of omission (fewer correct detections) and of commission (more incorrect responses), showed more rapid deterioration in performance than controls, and were less able to inhibit premature or repetitive responding, indicating poor impulse control (Sykes et al. 1971, 1973). Impairment in sustained attention is specific to tasks requiring prolonged attention; no impairment was observed on a Choice Reaction Time Test, which requires sustained attention only for brief periods. When performance on a self-paced attention task (Serial Reaction Test) was compared with that on an experimenter-paced or controlled task (CPT), hyperactive children were impaired on both tasks relative to controls; however, they did more poorly on the latter.

In one version of the simple reaction time tasks, a warning signal is followed by a preparatory interval that is terminated by the onset of a reaction signal. The results indicated that hyperactive children showed increased response latencies relative to normal children (Douglas and Peters 1979).

A study by Ullman et al. (1978) showed shorter attention span during free play; hyperactive children tended to be more inattentive and impulsive on vigilance tasks. Attentional deficits generalized across a variety of experimental tasks. The slower reaction time in children with poor ability to concentrate was accompanied by poor orientation and preparation response on the EEG (Gruenewald-Zuberbier et al. 1978). The EEG activity in hyperactive children shows a lower degree of activation than that of controls (Gruenewald-Zuberbier et al. 1975). In fact, the arousal response to tone became comparatively weaker in the course of the experiment. Similar results were obtained with studies of cortical-evoked potentials (reviewed in Stamm and Kreder 1979). This is interpreted as a "deficiency in sustained concentration of attention" (p. 157). Clinical EEG findings, on the other hand, have remained ambiguous. In a long-term follow-up study, G. Weiss and collaborators (1971) found a somewhat increased number of abnormal EEGs (42 per cent) in 6- to 13-year-old hyperactive children. Approximately the same number of abnormal EEGs was found at follow-up five years later. However, test-retest reliability of the EEG for the individual subject was low and EEG findings at age 10 and 15 were not related to measures of adult outcome (Hechtman et al. 1978). Steinhausen (1982) also reported 42.9 per cent abnormal EEGs in his sample, most of which were characterized as "maturation deficit." In a sample of 73 hyperkinetic children, the same author found 38.9 per cent abnormal EEGs (versus 29 per cent in normal controls), 26.9 per cent abnormal EEGs in conduct disorders, and 29 per cent in emotional disorders.

In conclusion, there is evidence of increased impulsivity and problems with sustained attention in hyperactive children. Douglas and Peters (1979) suggested that hyperactive children have a constitutional predisposition to poor impulse control and attentional problems, which in turn may contribute to impaired higher cognitive functions, i.e., problem-solving ability.

Motor Activity

The second major symptom of the hyperactive syndrome, increased **motor activity,** was studied by Ullman et al. (1978). Devices for measuring activity levels included grid-marked playrooms, wrist and ankle actometers (motion recorders), and stabilimetric chairs that record the child's movements while seated. Although conclusions are somewhat clouded by a short drug-washout period and the small number of subjects, group comparisons indicated that all measures of activity tended to discriminate the hyperactive from the control children. Hyperactive children showed generalized restlessness; increased activity was recorded regardless of the observational setting (free play, restricted play, movie-viewing, structured tasks).

It should be noted that measures of activity level failed to correlate with measures of attention in the hyperactive group; children who were inattentive did not necessarily show excessive restlessness. This indicates that the children were not homogeneous in their expression of behavioral symptoms.

20.3 INCIDENCE

Paine et al. (1968) found that the hyperactive syndrome occurs predominantly in boys, at an estimated male/female ratio of 9.1 to 4.1. Steinhausen (1982) even reports a 9 to 1 ratio. Estimates of the incidence in North America range from 1 to 13 per cent (Lambert et al. 1978, Trites 1979). In an attempt to reconcile the widely varying estimates of hyperactivity in children, a random sample of approximately 5000 children encompassing different socioeconomic and ethnic groups in the United States was tested. Approximately 5 per cent were considered to be hyperactive using at least one criterion, either parent, teacher, or physician reports, whereas approximately 1.2 per cent were identified as hyperactive using all three criteria.

British estimates of the incidence of hyperactivity among children are much lower. The Isle of Wight study identified only two cases of hyperactivity among 2199 children aged 10 and 11 years (Rutter et al. 1970b), whereas a much larger proportion was diagnosed as restless or overactive in association with a conduct or neurotic disorder. Such discrepancies underline the nonspecificity and variability in terminology.

20.4 ETIOLOGY

Historically, hyperactivity was thought to be caused by brain damage because many children were diagnosed with the syndrome following the epidemic of encephalitis lethargica after World War I (Kessler 1980). Popularization of the Strauss syndrome (A. A. Strauss and Kephart 1955) further contributed to the assumption of cerebral dysfunction. However, the comparison of the incidence of neurological soft signs in hyperactive and control children has failed to support an association between brain damage and hyperactivity (Rutter et al. 1970a, Werry et al. 1972). A recent report (Shaywitz et al. 1983) found no differences between attention deficit disorder and normal children on a variety of CT-scan measures.

Pasamanick and Knobloch (1960) related prematurity to later learning and behavioral problems and proposed that minimal brain damage represented the least impaired end of a continuum of reproductive casualty. Congenital risk factors were cited as a possible etiology for childhood hyperactivity (J. A. Johnson 1981, Rapoport and Ferguson 1981). However, further research failed to confirm that hyperactive children experience pre- and perinatal complications more frequently than normal children (Johnson 1981). An exception to this is the continuing controversy over the incidence of hyperactivity among low-birth-weight and premature infants discussed in Chap. 11. Some studies have reported an increased incidence (Alden et al. 1972, Francis-Williams and Davies 1974, Steinhausen 1982), whereas others suggest that the incidence in both populations is approximately the same (Simonds and Aston 1980).

Attempts have also been made to predict the behavioral outcome from prenatal and perinatal events. The Kauai study (Werner and Smith 1977, Werner et al. 1971) followed more than 1000 pregnancies prospectively for almost two decades, and the Collaborative Project of the National Institute of Neurologic Diseases and Strokes followed more than 50 000 pregnancies until age 7 years. The Kauai study revealed that perinatal stress by itself successfully predicted only severe disabilities, e.g., mental retardation or physical handicaps. The NINCDS study suggested that prenatal variables (e.g., maternal smoking or proteinuria during pregnancy) have some relationship to hyperactivity, low academic achievement, and neurological soft signs. However, the likelihood of these problems in the presence of these presumed damaging prenatal events increased only from 2 to 5 per cent (Nichols and Chen 1981). The two studies suggest a weak relationship with congenital risk factors.

A number of studies have found an association between minor physical anomalies of hands, feet, ears, face, and mouth with hyperactivity (Firestone et al. 1978, Rapoport and Quinn 1975, Waldrop and Halverson 1971, Waldrop et al. 1968). However, a follow-up study at the age of 3 years using teacher and parent questionnaires suggested that the relationship between anomalies and behavioral problems is weak and that the use of anomalies in isolation has only limited predictive usefulness (Burg et al. 1980).

In summary, results from these studies suggest that organic factors play only a minor role in the etiology of hyperactivity.

An underlying genetic component of the hyperactive syndrome, based on findings from both twin and adoption studies, has also been suggested (McMahon 1980, Stewart 1980). The biological parents of hyperactive children have been found to show an increased prevalence of psychiatric illness, including antisocial behavior, neurosis, suicide, alcoholism, sociopathy, and hysteria, as compared with parents of controls (Morrison and Stewart 1971, Satterfield et al. 1972, Wender 1971). Cantwell (1972, 1975) reported similar findings based on the psychiatric examination of a group of nonbiological parents of adopted hyperactive children and a group of biological parents of hyperactive children. The finding that hyperactive behavior in adoptees was associated with psychiatric problems in biological parents has since been confirmed by other investigators (Cadoret and Gath 1976, Cadoret et al. 1975, Morrison and Stewart 1973). Cantwell (1975) observed that hyperactivity occurred more often in biological first- and second-degree male relatives of hyperactive children than in relatives of control children. This increased incidence of hyperactivity in male biological relatives was seen as support for the genetic transmission of the hyperactive syndrome.

Data from a small sample of twins and siblings also provided evidence for a genetic component in hyperactivity. Safer (1973) reported a higher incidence of hyperactivity among full siblings of hyperactive children than among half siblings, and Lopez (1965) and Willerman (1973) found greater concordance of hyperactivity in identical twins than in fraternal twins. These findings lend some tentative support to the hypothesis that there are genetic determinants of hyperactivity. Unfortunately, many of the studies are limited by the small number of subjects involved or flawed in design and do not support the notion of the hyperactive syndrome as a "genetic entity" (Rutter 1982).

Environmental agents, such as lead poisoning (David et al. 1972, G. Weiner 1970) and radiation from television and fluorescent lights, have been suggested as causes of hyperactivity (Ott 1974), although the role of these agents has not been fully elucidated.

Feingold (1975) proposed that hyperactivity may result from the **toxic effect** of certain food additives or natural components of foods. To eliminate the disorder, he advocated a diet consisting of fresh meats and vegetables, milk, and homemade products and devoid of foods containing artificial colors and flavors. Early reports on the efficacy of this treatment were mainly anecdotal and suggested improvement in behavioral symptoms in some patients (A. Brenner 1977). More recent controlled investigations have generally been unable to demonstrate improvement in behavioral symptoms (Conners 1980, J. A. Johnson 1981, Mattes and Gittelman 1981, Williams and Cram 1978). Challenge doses of food coloring administered to children who were on the Feingold diet have produced only the occasional positive finding attributable to chance (Mattes and Gittelman 1981). A recent carefully designed double-blind study using two types of challenge doses with a group of children who were on an additive-free diet and another group who were on a strict phosphate-free diet showed completely negative results (Walther 1982). It appears that the relationship between food additives and hyperactivity cannot be confirmed.

Among other environmental factors, inadequate environmental stimulation (Tizard 1968), large family size and density, and social disadvantage were more frequent in families of hyperactive children (Rutter et al. 1970b). J. S. Miller (1978) studied family interaction patterns and proposed that hyperactivity is a reaction of the child to psychological disturbance in the family, including alcoholism, chronic anxiety, and recurrent maternal depression.

Stamm and Kreder (1979) suggested immaturity or late maturation of the **frontal lobes** as the etiological basis of hyperactivity. This immaturity or developmental lag results in an apparent motor, attentional, and behavioral dyscontrol observed in hyperactive children and is similar to the explanation proposed by Kinsbourne (1973) and by Satz (1976) as an explanation for MBD. The evidence for a frontal lobe developmental delay is inferred primarily from behavioral patterns.

Lastly, several theories of **biochemical dysfunction** in hyperactive children have emerged (Silbergeld 1977). A theory by Wender (1971) proposed that hyperactivity is the behavioral correlate of an imbalance in the functioning of two systems mediated by the catecholamine neurotransmitters, which determine the state of arousal and the level of activity and responsiveness. Wender proposed that the inhibitory mechanisms in the CNS are impaired in hyperactive children, resulting in a domination by the excitatory system. Bond (1981) suggested that a biochemical release from response inhibition as found in the fetal alcohol syndrome in animals may serve as a model for the causation of hyperkinetic behavior. It has also been proposed that the catecholaminergic neurotransmitter systems associated with excitation are overactive in hyperactive children (Kornetsky 1970, Silbergeld and Goldberg 1974) or that hyperactivity results from delays in biochemical development (Silbergeld 1977).

Animal experiments and biochemical studies of hyperactive children show little clear evidence to confirm or reject the proposed theories of neurochemical dysfunction in hyperactive children. Evidence for decreased dopaminergic activity in hyperactive children has been reported (Shaywitz et al. 1979a), although no substantial attempts have been made to integrate this evidence with theories of enhancement of excitability and neurodevelopmental immaturity.

More recently, attempts have been made to devise models that incorporate a multiplicity of **etiological factors** underlying hyperactivity. Kenny (1980) proposed an encompassing model containing seven interacting components: genetic predisposition, developmental lag, below-average intellectual and social skills, specific learning problems, disadvantaged environment (premature birth, nutritional deficiency, and poor social support and resources), emotional problems, and poor family relations. By combining some or all factors, different interactive etiological models of hyperactivity can be formed, each with different implications for treatment and management.

In summary, a number of etiologies have been proposed for the hyperactive syndrome. Historically, a tendency toward a unitary concept of the syndrome has prevailed. Researchers have sought genetic, biochemical, or environmental explanations for the disorder. However, more recent research suggests that many diverse factors may interact to produce the behavior. A multifactorial approach that more adequately reflects the complexity of the syndrome has been proposed.

20.5 DEVELOPMENT OF THE HYPERACTIVE CHILD

Studies of infants and young children reveal a series of typical behavioral symptoms thought to precede the hyperactive syndrome. Infants who consistently exhibit these behaviors are more likely to be diagnosed as hyperactive than those who do not. A composite of these behaviors during development was presented by Ross and Ross (1976). The infant's behavior is unpredictable; it may be crying or yelling one moment and calm the next. Crying is typically shrill and piercing, described as sounding like a siren or an animal in distress. The infant's personality is described as hypertonic, querulous, irritable, demanding, and unsatisfied. The infant is often very active and may exhibit advanced motor activity in the presence of normal growth and general development. Sleep patterns are reminiscent of the premature infant, with predominantly active or transitional sleep and only brief periods of quiet sleep.

The preschool hyperactive child often shows similar patterns of behavior: motor restlessness, lability in mood at times characterized by tantrums, poor sleep patterns, decreased frustration tolerance, and a short attention span. Speech development may be slow. Behavior in group settings is often aggressive or destructive. Rejection in peer social interactions may lead to low self-esteem.

Schleifer et al. (1975) observed nursery school behavior and found that hyperactive children were not differentiated from normal children on measures of motor activity and social behavior during free play situations. However, during structured play periods, when children were required to remain seated and participate in activities supervised by the teacher, hyperactive children were more often out of their chairs and more aggressive toward peers.

By school age, family and peer relations and school progress are all affected. Disruptive behavior, distractibility, poor sleep patterns, and low self-esteem are often in evidence. In addition, the hyperactive child often shows inadequate social skills. In school, poor work habits and problems with impulsivity and aggressiveness may be observed.

Assessment of the academic performance and cognitive abilities of hyperactive children in primary school reveals comparable IQ scores for hyperactive and control groups (Loney 1974, 1980). However, beginning in grade 3, WISC-R scores of hyperactive children are usually lower and more variable than those of control children (R. G. Miller et al. 1973, Palkes and Stewart 1972, Wikler et al. 1970). Unfortunately, it is difficult to interpret these results as valid estimates of cognitive ability because performance may be affected by poor work habits, short attention span, and poor self-concept.

20.6 DRUG THERAPY

Pharmacological treatment of hyperactivity has relied most heavily on stimulant drugs, most often Ritalin (methylphenidate hydrochloride) and Dexadrine (d-amphetamine). More recently, Cylert (pemoline) has been introduced because it shows fewer side effects (Singh and Ling 1979). Stimulant medication was first used in the 1930s for children with behavior and learning problems (Bradley 1937). By the 1950s, stimulants were widely used as treatment for hyperactivity. Recent studies indicate that approximately 2 per cent of all elementary school children in the United States receive stimulant medication for treatment of hyperactivity (Singh and Ling 1979).

Treatment studies indicate improvement of symptoms in about 75 per cent of hyperactive children (Steinberg et al. 1971, Weiss et al. 1979). Studies incorporating a placebo control, however, show up to 60 per cent improvement with placebo only. This finding underlines the importance of adequate experimental control in drug research (Millichap 1973).

It should be noted that only a subgroup of hyperactive children appears to be responsive to stimulants. At present, no reliable psychological or physiological indicators of those subjects who are drug-responsive have been described.

Research indicates that stimulant drugs cause the following behavioral effects in hyperactive children (Barkley 1981b):

1. Decreased activity
2. Decreased aggressive behavior and disruptiveness
3. Decreased impulsivity
4. Increased attention span and concentration
5. Improved compliance to adult demands

Activity

Stimulants reduce activity levels in hyperactive children, but results depend on the environmental setting in which the measures are taken (e.g., free play versus structured settings), the type of activity measured (wrist, ankle, locomotor), and the type of instrument used (actometers, pedometers, ultrasonic generators, grid-marked playrooms).

Seat restlessness and arm and ankle activity in structured settings were significantly reduced by stimulant medications (Barkley 1977). However, Barkley and Cunningham (1979) reported that gross motor activity (as measured by ankle and locomotor activity) was reduced only in structured situations; in large, free-field, informal settings, gross motor activity does not appear to change. Medication does not alter the amount of running, jumping, and climbing in hyperactive children.

Attention

Results from studies measuring different indices of attention support the role of stimulant treatment to improve attention in hyperactive children (Barkley and Cunningham 1979). Improvement in performance on a wide variety of measures of attention is attributed to an improved concentration span and inhibition of impulsive responding.

Behavioral Symptoms

Studies with rating scales administered to parents, teachers, and physicians, such as the Conners Symptom Questionnaire (Conners 1972), in general found improvement. For example, Conners et al. (1972) administered either stimulant medication or placebos to 81 children diagnosed as hyperactive. Parent, teacher, and clinician ratings obtained before treatment and at weekly intervals during treatment for eight weeks indicated significant improvement in behavioral symptoms at four and eight weeks, particularly in defiance, inattention, and hyperactivity as judged by teachers. Results with the Parent Rating Scale suggest improvement in conduct disorder, impulsivity, immaturity, and antisocial behavior. More recent studies indicate that, although all five sections of the Teacher Rating Scale are sensitive to stimulant drug treatment, the hyperactivity section shows the most reliable improvement (Barkley 1977).

Intelligence and Academic Performance

Barkley and Cunningham (1979) reviewed 17 short-term studies of the effect of stimulant drugs on academic performance in hyperactive children. When the results of the studies were combined, a crude estimate of the effects of stimulants on academic performance was obtained. Of the 52 dependent measures of achievement, 43 were not significantly improved by the stimulants. In cases where performance did improve, results were scattered and inconsistent. It was therefore concluded that improvements in performance were more related to enhanced attention resulting from drug treatment.

Studies using the WISC (Wechsler 1949) to assess the effect of stimulant medication on intellectual ability in hyperactive children found equivocal results; some studies report improvement in full-scale IQ, and others report changes in either verbal or performance IQ. Some authors have reported no significant changes in IQ. The inconsistency of findings suggests that basic intellectual or cognitive processes probably do not change significantly and that fluctuations in performances are related to improvement in concentration and attention (Barkley 1977).

In summary, the literature to date suggests that stimulants have no effect on intelligence or academic achievement but that the primary benefit of drug therapy is decreased activity and improved attention and concentration. The drug's usefulness is limited to short-term behavioral management, e.g., to decrease disruptiveness and impulsivity and improve compliance with adult demands.

20.7 LONG-TERM FOLLOW-UP

The long-term outcome of hyperactivity in children has been evaluated with respect to academic achievement and behavioral measures, and an effort has been made to determine whether children grow out of their hyperactivity. Studies typically evaluate the cognitive, behavioral, and social functioning of these children through childhood and adolescence and into adulthood.

Adolescence

Hyperactive children in adolescence do have cognitive, emotional, and social problems. In an eight- to ten-year follow-up study of 84 hyperactive children, Huessy et al. (1974) reported an increased risk for academic, emotional, and social problems. In this group, the school dropout rate was five times that of the general population and the institutionalization rate was 20 times greater. At the same time, overt hyperactivity appeared to decrease in a portion of these children. Mendelson et al. (1971) reported from a two- to five-year follow-up into adolescence that half the children showed moderate improvement, one quarter showed definite improvement, and one quarter remained unchanged.

The prospective follow-up studies at the Montreal Children's Hospital by G. Weiss and colleagues (1979) included children with long-term and sustained hyperactivity described by both parents and teachers. The initial age ranged from 6 to 13 years. The children had a WISC IQ of more than 84, no major brain damage, and no evidence of psychosis and were living at home with at least one parent. Referrals came from pediatric and psychiatric outpatient departments and from private pediatricians (Werry et al. 1964).

In a preliminary study, psychiatric referrals were excluded and the hyperactive group was matched with a control group. The mean ages were 8.8 years for the study group and 8.5 years for the controls. The hyperactive children showed increased motor activity, distractibility, poor frustration tolerance, sleep disturbances, motor incoordination, and social maladjustment (Werry et al. 1964). Sixty-four children were seen at an initial follow-up four to six years later (G. Weiss et al. 1971) at a mean age of 13.3 years (range 10 to 18 years). Behavioral symptoms, social adaptation, academic achievement, and cognitive and motor performance were evaluated. Overall, the authors concluded that the prognosis of this group as they matured into adolescence was relatively poor. Behavioral symptoms assessed with parent and teacher ratings showed that hyperactivity was no longer considered the chief complaint at follow-up. However, an analysis of the activity patterns of the hyperactive subjects revealed increased organized behavior unrelated to classroom activity; for example, they showed restlessness characterized by such activities as playing with pencils rather than the increased locomotion observed in younger hyperactive subjects. Distractibility remained a significant problem, although some improvement in concentration was observed. A similar pattern was found for aggressiveness.

The most common abnormal traits were emotional immaturity, lack of ambition, and inability to maintain goals. Low self-esteem was commonly observed and may relate to the experience of school failure (G. Weiss et al. 1978). Many showed poor social adjustment: 30 per cent were reported by their mothers to have no steady friends, 25 per cent showed acting-out behavior, and 10 per cent had been referred to courts. Twenty-five per cent had a history of antisocial or delinquent behavior, an increase over the previous assessment (Weiss et al. 1971). The authors concluded that at a five-year follow-up hyperactive subjects showed an inferior social and behavioral adjustment relative to normal adolescents.

Cognitive functioning assessed with the WISC showed a small increase in full-scale IQ from the initial evaluation to follow-up, and this was attributed to practice effects (pretest IQ = 103.6, follow-up = 106.9; Weiss et al. 1971). At the initial assessment, the hyperactive adolescents showed poorer performance on both the Lincoln-Oseretsky Motor Development Scale and the Goodenough Draw-a-Person Test. At follow-up, no change was observed in the Goodenough test but motor development scores were worse. In a later study of a subset of the hyperactive patients (n = 15) and matched controls (Hoy et al. 1978), the hyperactive group showed significantly lower scores on tests of visual-motor function, including the Bender Visual-Motor Gestalt Test. The analysis of individual Oseretsky items also indicated that the hyperactive group showed poorer performance on items measuring fine motor coordination.

Poor academic performance was present in 80 per cent of the hyperactive subjects. Only 20 per cent had not repeated at least one grade and were achieving at an average or above average level. Seventy per cent had repeated at least one grade (versus 15 per cent of the controls), and 30 per cent had repeated two or more grades. Ten per cent had been placed in special classes for varying periods, and 5 per cent had been expelled from school. Children who were successful in school at follow-up showed an initial mean IQ ten points higher than the rest of the group and a trend toward lower hyperactivity and distractibility scores at the initial assessment. However, poor intelligence is not the main factor involved in the academic failure of hyperactive children. Rather, uneven cognitive patterns, verbal difficulties, and poor self-esteem were considered to be important factors contributing to poor academic performance (Minde et al. 1971).

In a test of sustained attention, subjects tried to identify the letters in a series of orally presented words. A series of tests of stimulus-processing included visual scanning (Matching Figures Test), continuous auditory monitoring, and simultaneous monitoring of several information sources. Performance on all tests of sustained attention and stimulus-processing was significantly lower for the hyperactive group (Hoy et al. 1978). This group had more errors on multiple-choice tasks and more errors of commission on sustained attention tasks. The authors suggested that the hyperactive group analyzed stimuli at a more superficial level. No group differences on measures of distractibility were noted. The deficit on sustained-attention tasks was therefore attributed to attentional blocks or momentary lapses of attention (Sykes et al. 1971, 1973). It was also suggested that attentional and stimulus-processing deficits may translate into social problems because successful social interaction requires simultaneous monitoring of several information sources and in-depth processing of relevant stimuli, followed by selection and use of an appropriate social strategy. The authors concluded that attention and stimulus-processing deficits rather than overactivity and distractibility most clearly differentiate hyperactive subjects from controls during adolescence (Hoy et al. 1978).

Morrison (1980) studied the relationship between hyperactivity and delinquency in adolescents previously diagnosed as hyperactive and reported that a history of violence was four times as prevalent and arrests and convictions twice as frequent. Offord et al. (1979) divided a group of delinquent children into those with evidence of hyperactivity and those without. The hyperactive children displayed more antisocial symptoms, including recklessness, irresponsibility, fighting, and drug use. These behaviors also emerged at an earlier age than in other delinquents. The authors suggest that this subgroup of hyperactive delinquents is likely to have a poor prognosis for adulthood. It should be noted, however, that both studies were retrospective. Hence the relationship between hyperactive behavior in infancy and childhood and later delinquency remains ill-defined.

Adulthood

In an early study of the outcome of hyperactivity in adulthood, Laufer and Denhoff (1957) concluded from clinical observations that these children do not outgrow their symptoms but manifest increased psychopathology later in life. In a 25-year follow-up study by Menkes et al. (1967), 18 subjects were selected because of a childhood diagnosis of hyperactivity. Three subjects of this sample were still considered to be hyperactive at follow-up, and four had been institutionalized as psychotic. Of the 11 subjects examined neurologically, eight showed definite findings, one showed borderline results, and two were neurologically normal.

More recently, Borlund and Heckman (1976) compared a group of men diagnosed as hyperactive 20 to 25 years ago with their brothers. At follow-up, those diagnosed as hyperactive showed an excess of symptoms of hyperactivity, including restlessness, nervousness, impulsivity, and difficulty with temper. Despite similar levels of intelligence and education, the hyperactive group showed a lower socioeconomic status and more psychiatric problems, characterized by increased sociopathy, and social and marital problems. In a retrospective study, Morrison (1979) also reported that psychiatric patients who were formally diagnosed as hyperactive showed significantly more personality disorder, schizophrenia, sociopathy, alcoholism, and drug abuse than controls. A relationship between alcoholism and childhood hyperactivity has also been reported by Goodwin and collaborators (1975).

In a prospective study of the adjustment of hyperactive children in adulthood, Weiss and her colleagues reassessed their group of hyperactive children 10 years later at a mean age of 18.5, ranging from 17 to 24 years (Hechtman et al. 1976, G. Weiss et al. 1979). Seventy-five hyperactive subjects and 44 controls were contacted and agreed to participate. Thirty-five of the control subjects had also participated in the earlier five-year follow-up study. The results of biographical data, a psychiatric assessment, and the Brief Psychiatric Rating Scale (Overall and Gorham 1962) suggested that many of the hyperactive subjects continued to have some adjustment difficulties as young adults. One major characteristic of the group was impulsiveness, as demonstrated by an increased incidence of car accidents and change of residence as well as by impulsive responses during cognitive testing. A second enduring characteristic was restlessness; significantly more hyperactive subjects reported feeling restless during the interview and were observed as being restless.

Personality trait disorders were diagnosed significantly more often in the hyperactive group than in controls; the most frequent were impulsive and immature-dependent personality disorders. These disorders were considered to be "characterological" (versus clinical states) and did not prevent the subjects from functioning socially, attending school, or holding a job (Weiss et al. 1979). Two additional hyperactive subjects, however, were diagnosed as borderline psychotic.

Significantly more hyperactive subjects than controls rated their childhood as unhappy. This finding may relate to the previous observation of low self-esteem among hyperactive children. The hyperactive adults completed significantly fewer years of education than controls (10.5 versus 11.3), and the mean academic grade in high school was lower; significantly more subjects quit school because of poor achievement. Subjects in the hyperactive group also failed grades significantly more often and were more often expelled from school.

With regard to court referrals, there was a trend ($p<.07$) for more hyperactive young adults to have had more court referrals in the past five years, but no differences were found for the number and for the seriousness of offenses. Since there was no difference between groups during the last year of the follow-up, the authors interpreted this as suggesting a reduction in court appearances over time (Weiss et al. 1979). There was a similar trend for an increased percentage of hyperactive subjects to have used nonmedical drugs (mainly marijuana or hashish) in the previous five years but no difference between groups during the last year of the follow-up. There was no difference between groups regarding severity of drug use.

Job status and satisfaction of hyperactive young adults did not differ from that of controls. In a concurrent study (Weiss et al. 1978), rating scales to assess competence were sent to secondary schools and employers of the hyperactive and control subjects. Teachers rated hyperactive subjects to be inferior relative to controls on all items of the scale. However, no group difference on the employers' questionnaires was found. This discrepancy in findings may be explained by the many choices of work available and the increased freedom to change jobs and to select a satisfactory work environment.

In summary, the findings suggest that the hyperactive syndrome does not disappear over time, as shown by the presence of academic, emotional, and social problems on follow-up. Some symptoms observed in infancy and childhood persist, namely, restlessness, aggressiveness, emotional lability, and antisocial behavior. Impulsivity, distractibility and attentional problems were also observed consistently over time (D. M. Ross and S. A. Ross 1976, Weiss et al. 1971). Academic underachievement and low self-esteem emerged during adolescence and often persisted into adulthood. Increased delinquency, psychiatric disorders, and alcoholism were found in retrospective studies, but the major prospective study found only marginal evidence. The finding of comparable job status and job satisfaction among hyperactive adults and controls and of fewer court referrals than during adolescence may be interpreted as providing some evidence for improved long-term outcome.

21

Visual Disorders

Many hereditary and developmental disorders may affect the developing visual system. Depending on the site and extent of the damage, the resulting disorder may vary from absolute blindness, when there is not even light perception, to visual impairments identifiable only under special conditions (e.g., nightblindness).

Visual impairment may refer to any incapacitating loss or distortion of vision. The term "blindness" implies that the individual has no useful vision. The legal definition of blindness requires that visual acuity in both eyes with proper corrective lenses be 20/200 (6/60) or worse as measured with the Snellen chart or an equivalent test or that the field of vision in both eyes be restricted to less than 20 degrees. The prevalence of congenital blindness, including blindness acquired during the immediate postnatal period, has been reported to range from 1 to 8 per 10000 (Jan et al. 1977). Acquired blindness exists at approximately one quarter the rate of congenital blindness.

Pathology in various parts of the visual system may be manifest in similar ways; for example, visual field disturbances may result from lesions anywhere in the visual system, from the outer eye to the visual cortex. Some developmental disorders (e.g., rubella) exert diffuse effects in the visual system. Interference with initial reception of visual stimuli necessarily influences how information is processed.

Since impaired visual processing may result from damage to any part of the visual system, from the outer surface of the eye to the higher cortical brain structures, this discussion of visual disorders follows the pathway taken by the visual image. Figure 3-3 illustrates the **primary visual system.** Animal research has established the existence of a **secondary visual system** that projects from the retina to the pulvinar nucleus of the thalamus via the superior colliculus and terminates in the circumstriate, or visual association, areas. This second visual system appears to be involved in movements related to vision, such as orienting toward objects or obtaining information about space by moving the head, eyes, and body. The superior colliculus has been described as the primary area that correlates vestibular and proprioceptive inputs (Rapin 1982, Shebilske 1976). The two visual systems interact in visual functions, and damage to one system may potentially modify the activity of the other (Hécaen and Albert 1978). Evidence that the brainstem contributes to visual perception in humans has been found in adult commissurotomized patients, individuals who have undergone surgery to sever the bundle of nerve fibers connecting the two hemispheres (Trevarthen 1970). Although the processing in the right and left visual fields becomes independent after this type of surgery, separate moving visual stimuli presented to each visual half-field can be integrated by such patients.

21.1 DAMAGE IN THE PRIMARY VISUAL SYSTEM

Cornea and Lens

As outlined in Chap. 3, the visual image enters the eye via the cornea and lens and is received by receptors in the retina. The **cornea** and **lens** act as refractory mechanisms that focus the image clearly on the retina. If the focus of the image is behind the retina, **hyperopia** occurs; if the focus of the image lies in front of the retina, the term **myopia** applies. Infants are usually hyperoptic and attain a normal focus with growth of the eye (Harley and Lawrence 1977). If normal focus is not reached when the eye ceases to grow, the image projected onto the retina will be unclear. However, corrective lenses can usually provide near-normal acuity.

Damage to the cornea or lens leads to obstruction or distortion of image formation and diminished vision. Such damage may be the result of a variety of congenital or infantile disorders but is particularly associated with certain prenatal infections and nutritional deficiencies. For example, the eye may harbor live rubella virus for months or even years. Infection in the lens may result in unilateral or bilateral cataracts (Martyn 1975). Congenital glaucoma (clouding of the cornea) and transient nonglaucomatous corneal clouding also occur with congenital rubella syndrome. Inflammation of the cornea is frequent in congenital syphilis, which can persist in the eye for decades. Most ocular manifestations of congenital syphilis appear after the age of 5 or 6 years, although they may occur at any age (Chan 1975a).

Vitamin A deficiencies, whether caused by malnutrition or by diseases of the child or mother during pregnancy, may lead to lesions of the cornea. Vitamin B deficiencies also lead to severe corneal vascularization. Children suffering from kwashiorkor may manifest lens lesions, and corneal damage is evident just prior to death (Chan 1975b).

Retina

The **retina,** the site of the focused image, may be divided into the peripheral and the macular, or central, portion, which differ both structurally and functionally from each other. Peripheral vision and **scotopic vision**—the ability to perceive light, dark, and motion—are a function of the peripheral retina. Rod cells are the predominant nerve ending serving this purpose. **Central vision,** or sight directed at an object, and photopic vision, the ability to discriminate color, are a function of the macular retina. The cone cells are the predominant receptors for these functions.

Damage to the retina may reduce the ability to receive and transmit visual information, depending upon the site and magnitude of the retinal damage. Congenital and developmental disorders that result in damage to the retina include prenatal infections (e.g., rubella, syphilis) and nutritional deficits. An early symptom of retinal damage due to Vitamin A deficiency is **nightblindness,** or **nyctalopia,** which implies impaired rod function. **Retrolental fibroplasia** refers to an overgrowth of immature blood vessels from the retina into the vitreous humor behind the lens. These vessels outgrow the capacity to nourish themselves, and scar tissue develops and impairs retinal functioning. Retrolental fibroplasia has been linked to the administration of high concentrations of oxygen to low-birth-weight or premature infants (O'Neill 1980).

Optic Nerve

The **optic nerve** carries the visual information from the retina to the brain. Any damage to the nerve will result in impaired vision. The exact nature of the deficit depends on the extent of the damage. The outer fibers of the optic nerve carry information from the peripheral retina, and the inner fibers carry information from the macular retina. When only the outer fibers of the optic nerve are damaged, peripheral vision is affected. This limitation of vision has been termed **peripheral field restriction.** When the central portion of the nerve is affected, only central vision is affected, manifest as a **central scotoma** (blind spot). When the entire nerve is affected, the eye is blind. Optic nerve disorders may occur as a consequence of prenatal malformations, optic neuritis, or optic atrophy.

Optic nerve aplasia refers to a prenatal malformation in which the optic nerve and retinal vessels are completely absent. The eye is, of course, blind. A less severe form of optic nerve malformation is **optic nerve hypoplasia.** This congenital deficiency of the optic nerve fibers is generally attributed to a primary failure of the development of the retinal ganglion cells and their axons. This process begins approximately six weeks after conception, normally reaching the optic chiasm by the seventh week and the lateral geniculate body by the eighth week (Martyn 1975). Complete or partial failure of this process results in varying degrees of optic nerve hypoplasia.

Typically the consequence is an attendant abnormality of vision, ranging from complete blindness to peripheral field defects with spared central vision, depending on the severity, laterality, and symmetry of the condition.

Optic neuritis (inflammation of the optic nerve) and **optic nerve atrophy** (degeneration of the optic nerve fibers) are a consequence of many congenital and infantile developmental syndromes, including prenatal infections nutritional deficiencies, toxicity, or increased intracranial pressure.

Optic neuritis may result in temporary reduction of vision if the inflammation subsides or in permanent vision loss if the inflammation leads to optic nerve atrophy. For example, with congenital syphilis, the arachnoid sheath surrounding the optic nerve may be infiltrated by the virus and cause optic nerve edema in the acute stage and optic atrophy in the chronic stage. A variety of administered drugs may induce optic neuritis and/or optic nerve atrophy in infants (Chloramphenicol, phenothiazines, Quinine, Atoxyl), as may exposure to various toxins or poisons, such as lead, methyl alcohol, and carbon disulfide (Harley and Lawrence 1977).

Optic Chiasm

The optic nerve continues on toward the posterior areas of the brain and emerges on the floor of the middle fossa of the cranial cavity. At this point, anterior to the pituitary gland, the two optic nerves, one from each eye, meet and form the **optic chiasm.** Half of the fibers from each optic nerve cross over and project to the opposite hemisphere. Damage to the optic chiasm typically creates asymmetrical and usually binocular visual field defects, depending on the extent and exact position of the damage. For example, a **binasal hemianopia** (Fig. 3-3) may result from a lateral displacement of the chiasm by a tumor or aneurysm on the contralateral side of the chiasm, thus affecting the temporal fibers on both sides simultaneously. A **bitemporal hemianopia** (Fig. 3-3) occurs with lesions affecting the medial aspects of the chiasm. The most frequent cause of this type of chiasmal damage in children is a craniopharyngioma or optic glioma (tumor), although occasionally a dilated third ventricle may result in similar damage (Martyn 1975).

Optic tract

The **optic tracts** include fibers from the temporal half of the visual field of the eye on the same side (uncrossed fibers) and the nasal half of the visual field of the eye on the opposite side (crossed fibers). Damage to the optic tract usually results in hemianopia (half-field blindness), which is irregular unless the damage is total. With total damage, the result is a **homonymous hemianopia** affecting the same half-field of vision (either left or right) from both eyes (Fig. 3-3). Usually, central vision is spared but the entire peripheral visual field is lost. Many degenerative and demyelinating diseases (e.g.,

Tay-Sachs) affect the optic tracts as well as other portions of the visual system.

Lateral Geniculate Nucleus

The optic tracts terminate in the **lateral geniculate nuclei.** These bodies are relay stations that send visual information to the cortex and to other reflex centers in the brain that control eye movement and muscles in the eye (Harley and Lawrence 1977).

An important aspect of vision is **ocular motility.** Normal binocular vision depends on each eye's sending slightly different images to the higher cortical centers, where they are fused into a single percept. This fusion requires the coordinated simultaneous movement of the two eyes. Each extraocular muscle responsible for moving the eye must have the strength to contract and relax in conjunction with muscles of the other eye and other muscles of the same eye. The motor centers of the brain are involved in both reflexive (via the third, fourth, and sixth cranial nerves) and voluntary (via the left and right motor cortex of the frontal lobes) eye movements (Harley and Lawrence 1977). When the position of the body changes, involuntary reflex stimuli elicit movement of the eye muscles and thereby hold the perception of the world steady. Teuber (1966) used the term "**corollary discharge**" to identify this involuntary outflow of stimulation that prepares the visual system for changes in the visual image that are expected consequences of the intended movement. In the absence of corollary discharge, the external world would be experienced as unstable. As yet, no conclusive physiological mechanism responsible for this hypothesized reflex action has been identified (Hécaen and Albert 1978).

Impairment of ocular motility may be manifest in various ways. Extraocular muscle palsies are defects in individual ocular muscles resulting from impairment of the nuclear or infranuclear portion of the cranial nerves (in the subcortical structures of the brain, e.g., pons), of the neuromuscular junction, or of the muscle itself. Paired movement of the two eyes upward, downward, laterally, and in convergence and divergence are called **conjugate eye movement.** These may be impaired because of disorders of the supranuclear (i.e., cortical) centers or other pathways that govern the direction of both eyes in unison. **Nystagmus** is an involuntary rhythmical oscillation of one or both eyes in any or all fields of gaze (Martyn 1975). It may be defined further in terms of plane, amplitude, rate, or severity of prevalence in various direction of gaze. The oscillations may be of equal speed in each direction (pendular) or slow in one direction and rapid in the opposite (biphasic). **Strabismus** ("cross-eyedness" or heterotropia) is an abnormality in which one eye fixates its macula on the object of gaze while the other eye is directed elsewhere. It may be classified further as paralytic or nonparalytic and according to position (convergent versus divergent).

Impaired eye movement may result either in a lack of stereoscopic vision because the two images cannot be fused properly into a single percept or in **diplopia** (double vision). Diplopia, however, is not usually a problem in infants or very young children, as they tend to consciously suppress one image in order to avoid confusion (Harley and Lawrence 1977).

Disorders of ocular motility may result as a consequence of weak extraocular muscles or central nervous system abnormalities caused by trauma, anoxia, inflammation of the brain following various infections, compression of the cranial nerves by increased intracranial pressure, or the toxic effect of drugs. For example, lead poisoning may result in strabismus, and ingestion of some hormonal compounds, such as progesteronal steroids, may cause paralysis of the extraocular muscles. Abnormal eye movement may be seen in blind children, not because of muscle or central nervous system disorders per se but as a function of their blindness (i.e., lack of learned muscle control). For example, Martyn (1975) suggests that the pendular ocular nystagmus and strabismus present with congenital rubella are more commonly due to cataracts, glaucoma, optic nerve damage or high refractive error than a direct consequence of central nervous system disease. It has also been suggested that strabismus in infants, which sometimes goes unnoticed during the early months or years, may lead to reduced visual acuity that may be prevented by treatment (Lewerenz 1978).

Optic Radiation

The optic radiation emerges from the lateral geniculate nuclei, spreads in a fanlike fashion through the temporal lobes, and terminates in the middle layers of the primary visual cortex (area 17) of the two occipital lobes.

Damage in the optic radiation may lead to visual field defects. The entire visual half-field is not always affected, but a symmetrical quadrant loss may be evident for both eyes (Fig. 3-3). For example, damage to the lower geniculocalcarine fibers, which course forward into the temporal lobe (**Meyer's loop**), usually produces an upper **quadrantanopia**, a small upper-sector defect. Periodic visual hallucinations may also be manifest with damage to this area. Lesions of the optic radiation in the parietal lobe usually produce lower-quadrant field defects (Fig. 3-3).

Occipital Lobes

Damage to the occipital lobes may also produce contralateral visual field defects. Depending on the site and extent of damage, the defects may vary from small blind spots adjacent to central vision in both eyes (**homonymous paracentral scotoma**) to complete hemianopia. Such defects are usually caused by trauma or cerebrovascular disorders.

Damage to the occipital cortex may lead to **cerebral** or **cortical blindness**, a loss of vision in the presence of normal pupillary reflexes and without significant eye disease. Since pupillary responses are affected by pregeniculate lesions but not by postgeniculate lesions (Martyn 1975), the term "cortical blindness" refers to blindness resulting from any postgeniculate damage. Although cortical blindness in adults occurs mainly because of thrombosis of the vertebral and basilar arteries, which affects blood flow to the visual cortex (Symonds and McKenzie 1957), cortical blindness in children is often a consequence of hydrocephalus, meningitis, toxic or hypertensive encephalopathy, trauma, or diffuse demyelinating degenerative disease (Barnet et al. 1970, Duchowny et al. 1974, Martyn 1975).

Cortical blindness remains permanent more often in adults than in children. Almost all children with cortical blindness recover at least some visual function (Duchowny et al. 1974). Suggested underlying mechanisms contributing to cortical blindness include cellular ischemia (temporary deficiency of blood flow) as a result of hypotension, vasospasm, cerebral edema, thrombosis of cortical veins (Barnet et al. 1970), and focal ischemia of white matter (Tyler 1968).

Onset of recovery from cortical blindness may vary from hours to months. The typical course of recovery progresses from perception and tracking of light stimuli to perception of moving objects close to the eyes. Next, large, particularly brightly colored objects can be seen. Barnet et al. (1970) noted that at this stage visual hallucinations occasionally occur. Finally, visual acuity progressively improves, although visual cognitive and perceptual deficits may persist for a long time or remain permanently. Often the blindness is only one sign of more generalized structural brain damage, and refined visual-perceptual testing is hampered by profound mental retardation (Barnet et al. 1970, Jan et al. 1977).

Two of six children with cortical blindness examined by Barnet et al. (1970) denied their inability to see. This denial in adults with cortical blindness is termed **Anton's syndrome** or **anosognosia.**

Since visual-evoked responses (VER) originate in the occipital cortex, this electrophysiological technique may be of value in identifying visual disorders with a central origin. In addition, since this technique requires little active participation by the patient, it has proved useful for studying the development of visual behavior in infants and young children (e.g., Barnet et al. 1980).

The VER is the summed cortical response (sum of postsynaptic potentials) induced in occipital lobe neurons as a result of stimulus change. Both transient VERs, resulting from an isolated and abrupt stimulus change, such as a light flash, and steady-state VERs, i.e., regular, steady cyclical responses elicited by rapidly repeating stimuli, have been investigated. Short-latency VER components are thought to reflect activity of the primary visual pathway (Ciganek 1961, G. H. Rose 1971), whereas long-latency components reach the neocortex via the second visual system and terminate in the secondary visual centers with more diffuse cortical representation.

Abnormal electrocortical development has been noted in infants during the acute phase of severe protein malnutrition (e.g., Bartel, reported in Coursin 1974) and after kwashiorkor (e.g., Bartel et al. 1978). The VER deficit manifest in children five to ten years after hospitalization for kwashiorkor was restricted to the right hemisphere; this suggests either that permanent damage to the right hemisphere may be the consequence of early kwashiorkor or that the left hemisphere may overcome its maturational lag before the right hemisphere.

Reports on VERs in cases of cortical blindness, implying postgeniculate involvement, range from lack of response to completely normal responses (Bodis-Wollner et al. 1977, Frank and Torres 1979, Spehlmann et al. 1977). Some studies (Chisholm 1975, Crighel and Botex 1966, Koci and Sharbrough 1966, Medina et al. 1977) found a correlation between VERs and recovery of vision: both show gradual and parallel improvement during the recovery phase. However, Barnet et al. (1970) describe two children who, despite their blindness, show well-developed VERs. It is possible that this difference in findings may be related to the age of the patients since the previously reported cases were adults.

Persistence of VERs has been reported in two blind patients despite extensive bilateral damage to the visual areas of the brain (Spehlmann et al. 1977). Bodis-Wollner et al. (1977) examined a six-year-old boy who was left blind after an acute febrile illness at two years of age. Computerized tomography showed complete destruction of areas 18 and 19 in the right hemisphere but some preservation of tissue in these areas in the left hemisphere. Tissue corresponding to area 17 (striate cortex) and part of the optic radiation were also spared. VERs to both transient and steady-state stimuli were normal. It has been suggested that VERs may be present as long as the primary visual cortex is relatively intact but that functional vision may, at least in children, require the additional integrity of the secondary visual centers and their connections (Frank and Torres 1979).

Frank and Torres (1979) also noted that the presence of abnormal VERs is not incompatible with normal vision. Comparing a group of "cortically blind" children to an etiologically similar group of children with central nervous system disease but without visual symptoms, they found no significant differences in latency for any component of the VER.

Since the study of VERs in these clinical cases has not been useful in determining the status of visual functioning in children, the relationship between VERs and level of nervous system functioning remains unclear. However, it is possible that differences in etiology, extent of damage, and age of onset, if viewed in relation to the normal development of the visual system, may help explain these inconsistent results.

21.2 OTHER VISUAL DISORDERS

Other visual disorders may arise as a consequence of central nervous system disorder without specific locus. For example, transient episodes of vision loss or blurring may indicate central nervous system involvement. **Amblyopia** refers to temporary or permanent subnormal visual acuity ("dim vision") without ophthalmoscopically detectable retinal abnormality or afferent visual pathway disease, although it can occur secondary to insufficiency of blood supply from the basilar artery or secondary to pressure on the chiasm by a tumor (Poeck 1974). Generally, amblyopia implies a vision deficit due to sensory deprivation or inhibition occurring early in life (Martyn 1975). Distortions of visual perception in terms of form, contour, size, and movement (**metamorphopsias**) may occur. In adults, both localization and lateralization of lesion influence the form of the disturbance (Hécaen and Albert 1978). With lesions in the visual pathway, color vision may be impaired before form vision. True color vision impairment must be distinguished from **color agnosia** (the loss of the ability to recognize color) and from **amnestic color aphasia** (inability to recall or name colors), two conditions that may reflect cerebral affections that do not involve the perception of color radiations at all. Diplopia (double vision), though more often associated with eye movement disorders, may occur with increased intracranial pressure (e.g., tumors) or other neurological diseases (e.g., meningitis or neurodegenerative diseases).

Visual Processing and Its Disorders

Visual processing beyond detection and active scanning of the stimulus involves identification and analysis of salient visual cues, integration of these cues into a recognizable whole, tentative classification of the visual percept, and evaluation of the correctness of classification (which may entail alterations of classification). A variety of visually oriented tasks may be used for the assessment of these more complex **visual information processing** abilities. The tasks are subdivided into (1) spatial orientation, (2) visual discrimination, and (3) object recognition tasks (Chalfant and Scheffelin 1969) and differ with respect to degree of analysis, integration, and evaluation; they may include motor components as well. Disorders in visual processing are usually related to dysfunction of higher cortical centers.

Spatial orientation disorders may include left-right discrimination difficulty; reversal errors, such as in confusing the letters "b" and "d"; rotation errors, such as the inability to distinguish "p" from "d"; directional confusion in plotting a route or map from one place to another; difficulty in perceiving one's own body in space; or lack of attention to part of the spatial field. This last deficit, which has been termed **hemi-inattention** or **hemispatial neglect,** occurs independent of visual-field defects and may be manifest in a variety of ways, including failure to read words on one half of a page or to dress one half of the body.

Tasks of **visual discrimination** may involve selecting items on the basis of some salient characteristic, distinguishing an object presented in the context of a complex visual array, or identifying an object despite the fact that the total visual stimulus is not present. Rate, duration, and order of presentation on these tasks may influence performance and suggest different underlying visual processing disorders.

The failure to recognize objects despite intact visual capacity and the ability to discriminate parts of the object has been termed **visual agnosia.** While visual recognition of an object may be impaired, the object may be recognized through one of the other senses. The underlying disorder appears to involve synthesizing or integrating the discrete aspects of the stimulus into a unified whole. In adults, both occipital and frontal lobe lesions may lead to disorders of object recognition. With frontal lobe disorders a dysfunction of active investigation activity is more likely, whereas occipital disorders reflect deficits in synthesis and integration of visual stimuli (Luria 1966).

Failure to recognize faces has been singled out as **prosopagnosia,** which may refer to a highly specific process. Young infants tend to scan faces longer than any other visual object (Haith et al. 1977), and distinct developmental changes in these scanning habit have been described (Maurer and Salapatek 1976). Preferential responding to birdlike shapes has also been described in finches. Although the preference for scanning of faces may be determined mainly by its biological importance and social interaction, the encoding of such information may be a somewhat different neural process than the processing of visual information at a later age. The importance of the right occipitotemporal area for face recognition has been suggested by studies of patients with sectioning of the corpus callosum.

Alexia (the inability to appreciate the meaning of written words or musical or mathematical symbols) and **dyslexia** (denoting a partial rather than total impairment) are typically included among the visual processing disorders even though they are not directly related to damage in the visual system. The term **"developmental dyslexia"** is used to denote a congenital development disorder as opposed to the loss of ability resulting from injury to the nervous system. This topic is dealt with in a later chapter.

Many developmental disorders without gross damage may exert subtle effects on CNS functioning that are reflected in disturbances of visual processing. For example, Taub et al. (1977), in a prospective study, noted that children who were born prematurely had significantly lower performance IQs on the Wechsler Intelligence Scale for Children than full-term children in midchildhood. Tests requiring visually mediated behavior were particularly affected. In addition, performance on the Bender Visual Gestalt Test, which involves copying a variety of geometric shapes, was also poorer for prematurely born children. Taub et al. (1977) suggested that the visual system deficit associated with prematurity is based on subtle brain dysfunction or perhaps on a limitation of brain cell growth that the visual system may be more susceptible to than other parts of the nervous system.

Although assessment of the visual functioning of preterm infants during infancy has been limited by the lack of suitable assessment procedures, some research has been conducted involving both **optokinetic nystagmus** (OKN) and **preferential looking** (PL) techniques. OKN refers to involuntary eye movements that occur when a succession of similar objects passes across the visual field. The eye movements consist of (a) a slow phase in the same direction as the moving objects and (b) a fast phase, or jerk movement, back to the straight-ahead position. The latter occurs when the slow phase brings the eyes to the edge of the orbit. The objects moving across the field and the separation between them must be within the resolution capacity of the visual system or no OKN response will be elicited. The basic procedure (Gorman et al. 1957) involves placing the infant under a canopy-like apparatus that passes moving stripes 15 centimeters above the eyes. The narrowest stripe width that elicits an OKN response is then noted as an indicator of visual discrimination ability.

The PL procedure was developed by Fantz and Ordy (1959) for assessing vision in infants. The basic procedure is to place a patterned and an unpatterned stimulus in front of the infant for 20 seconds and then repeat the stimulation with the right-left positions of the stimuli reversed. The estimate of visual acuity is based on how long the eyes fixate on the stimuli and defined as the narrowest stripe width at which 75 per cent or more of the infants at that age show longer pattern than nonpattern fixations (Fantz et al. 1962). An age-related increase from birth is evident. The basic procedure has also been modified for the study of differential responses to stimuli such as color (Bornstein 1978, Teller 1981) complexity (Miranda 1970) and size and number (Fantz and Fagan 1975).

Studies using these techniques on preterm infants indicate that the visual system is functional at birth (Dubowitz 1979, Kiff and Lepard 1966). Even though some differential response to patterned visual stimuli can be elicited in all infants, including premature ones, the age from conception appears to be associated with responses to number and size of detail of stimuli; younger infants do not respond as well to patterns that differ only in small degrees along a given dimension (Miranda 1970).

The value of the PL procedure as a predictor of later neurological or mental deficits has been investigated. High-risk infants, many of them severely impaired, were rated as normal, suspect, or abnormal on the basis of their visual fixation performance in infancy. The results suggest that early deficits in visual processing are related to later mental status (Miranda et al. 1977). However, whether early deficits manifest in a less impaired group may be an adequate predictor of later subtle visual processing disorders remains to be explored.

It is not yet known how performance on visually oriented tasks in infants reflects involvement of different levels of the visual system. Fantz and Ordy (1959) suggested that the OKN is a subcortical reflex and does not involve cortical processing. Fantz et al. (1962) concluded that the capacity for complex pattern perception is present from birth, since infants attend more frequently to patterned than to nonpatterned stimuli. However, Bronson (1974) suggested that these findings may be merely a basic retinal processes mediated by a subcortical network, at least during the first month of life. More sophisticated neocortical-mediated mechanisms would be expected to contribute to the infants reactions from the second month onward. Bronson (1974) proposed that

> Rather than conceiving of postnatal change as reflecting a general improvement in the efficiency of a total system all of whose components are to some degree functional from birth, it seems more nearly correct to posit the emergence of a series of new capabilities corresponding to the progressive development of increasingly more sophisticated neural networks. (p. 887)

As discussed earlier, Bronson ascribed the visual responses elicited in the first month of life directly to the phylogenetically older second visual system. This system responds to directional loci of salient peripherally located stimuli and does not seem to be capable of complex pattern analysis. During the second and third months of life, more sophisticated responses begin to appear, reflecting the increased participation of the primary visual system. As memories accrue, visual behavior is no longer limited to the most salient aspects of a configuration and the infant becomes an internally directed, pattern-organizing individual. The process of postnatal visual development is viewed as the progressive encoding of increasingly complex aspects of the visual stimulus. This position implies that earlier visually oriented behaviors may differ qualitatively from later ones, rather than merely in relative efficiency.

Maurer and Terrill (1979) similarly suggested that two separate visual mechanisms explain the rapid improvement of visual function in the infant. The X pathway, which mediates fine acuity, maintains fixation, and analyzes patterns, relies on special types of cells in the retina and relays via the geniculate bodies to the cortex; the second, or Y, pathway mediates peripheral detection and perception of movement and flicker and contributes to scanning. Based on animal experiments, the authors propose that the X pathway is functional at birth and the Y pathway operates only to the superior colliculus level; the connection to the visual cortex is not functional until the second month of life.

21.3 THE DEVELOPMENT OF THE BLIND CHILD

Unless specially stimulated, blind children are likely to be delayed in motor, social, and sensory development. The blind child frequently begins to smile late, at five to six months of age instead of six weeks (D. G. Freeman 1964). Sitting unaided, crawling, and walking all occur with some delay unless the parents encourage and stimulate the child to perform these activities. Toilet training may be delayed, and feeding problems are common, especially in the child with additional impairment. If physical activity is not stimulated, muscle tone tends to be poor and musculature may develop improperly. The blind infant usually responds to sounds with inactivity and silence rather than with the anticipatory responses of the sighted infant. Elonen and Zwarensteyn (1964) suggested that this inactivity is the result of heightened attention to hear more effectively.

The blind child is usually more introverted and tends to use sensory exploration on its own body rather than on external objects and people. As a result, stereotyped behaviors of an autistic nature may develop. Fine (1968) found that 45 per cent of a sample of 2000 blind children had repetitive mannerisms, especially eye pressing, rocking, head nodding, hand flapping, and twirling movements. Ten per cent of partially sighted children also showed these tendencies. As the child learns to walk, is encouraged to explore objects, and is stimulated to engage in different activities, these autistic activities decrease.

Inactivity in the infant, delayed development, poor muscle tone, and persisting stereotyped behaviors in older blind children not infrequently lead to the false diagnosis of infantile autism or mental retardation. Unlike in the autistic or retarded child, these signs are reversible in blind children, provided the children are given additional stimulation.

The congenitally blind child is limited in some aspects of concept formation that depend on visual perception and in abstract concepts that make use of visual metaphors or analogies. Cognitive testing of blind children must be made with specifically designed tests, e.g., the Perkins Binet Test or the Blind Learning Aptitude Test. The current Wechsler Scales for Children may be used only if items dependent upon vision are eliminated and verbal scores are prorated. When compared with sighted children matched for total verbal IQ, blind children test low-average on comprehension and similarities and high-average on digit span and information on the verbal section of the WISC (Jan et al. 1977).

Although the blind child is thought to be more attentive to hearing and touch, there is no evidence that acuity in these senses is better. The use of echo to detect proximity of objects (echo location) develops naturally in some blind children and can be taught to older intelligent ones. Young blind children occasionally make a sharp, repetitive sound spontaneously in order to judge distances—another behavior that may be erroneously interpreted as a sign of infantile autism or other psychopathology (Jan et al. 1977).

21.4 HEMISPHERIC ASYMMETRY IN BLIND CHILDREN

Larsen and Hakonsen (1982) have advanced a new hypothesis regarding cerebral asymmetry in blind children. They noted that braille is more accurately read by the left hand (Heremelin and O'Connor 1971), presumably because of the higher demands of braille on the recognition of spatial patterns, a function that relies on right hemispheric specialization. The au-

thors argued that blind children would be more bilaterally organized because of the special cognitive strategies needed "to operate in their invisible
surroundings" (p. 197), namely, the need to develop detailed cognitive maps.
In an investigation of 36 congenitally blind children between the ages of 8
and 17 years, they found a lack of ear asymmetry on dichotic listening
whereas a matched control group showed the expected right-ear advantage.
The finding seems to support the notion of a bilateral organization of cognitive processing in blind children. The superior processing of braille with
the left hand is similar to the advantage of the left visual field in dot pattern
perception (Kimura 1969) and in the perception of the pictographic Kanji
signs in Japanese as opposed to the more alphabetic Kana symbols (Hatta
1977, Sasanuma and Monoi 1975). The latter also seems to relate to the
development of a more bilateral organization in Japanese subjects than in
British subjects for dichotic listening under special interference conditions
(Hatta and Dimond 1981).

22

Auditory Disorders

The auditory system in lower mammals primarily serves as a protective sense and is reflexive. The reflex action is controlled and coordinated by various centers in the brainstem (Barr 1972). The human cortex has larger areas for storage and processing of information arriving from the sensory organs (association areas), and this allows differential recognition, interpretation, and association of sounds with meanings. Most important, an intact auditory system allows the reception, sorting, and codifying of speech and thus permits verbal communication with others.

Auditory processing may be divided into levels of function, each potentially influencing the others (Galanter 1962, Hirsh 1966, Wood 1975). These functional levels include the ability to (1) detect auditory stimuli, (2) attend, both in terms of reflex action to sound and in terms of conscious focusing on the content and source of incoming stimuli, (3) discriminate between sounds and distinguish characteristics of sounds, such as frequency, intensity, and temporal sequence, (4) identify sounds previously heard so that meaning may be associated with them, (5) comprehend sounds by sorting and integrating them with other information in order to store and retain information, and (6) retrieve and restore the sounds for the formation of appropriate responses.

Detection of stimuli (auditory acuity) is a prerequisite for further auditory analysis. Rapid habituation to detected stimuli and the inability to suppress other incoming stimuli, either those from the other senses or irrelevant auditory stimuli may limit the ability to detect relevant auditory stimuli and interfere with further analysis. In addition, inability to respond appropriately to a previously heard stimulus, though possibly reflecting a detection problem, may in actuality reflect a problem of more complex forms of auditory analysis (e.g., storage or retrieval).

The anatomy and physiology of the auditory system (Fig. 3-1), from the receptor mechanisms of the inner ear to the auditory cortex, are highly complex with numerous possibilities for feedback controls and an abundance of synaptic connections within and among the neuronal groups. The role of many of the neuronal groups is poorly understood, and the ways in which these channels interact with each other and other areas of the brain are not clearly delineated (R. B. Eisenberg 1976). Extensive differences in structure and organization in individual nuclei exist, and transmission through the nuclei is associated with alterations of the signal parameters that reduce the correspondence between signals at successive levels. Above the level of the cochlear nucleus, all synapses are interconnected across the midline; hence information from each ear is projected to both sides of the brain. At the cortical level, a stronger signal is received from the contralateral ear and neural pathway and a weaker signal is received from the ipsilateral ear and neural pathway (Rosenzweig 1951). In addition, information from the cochlea may also reach the cortex by routes lying outside the classical auditory pathway (Eisenberg 1976).

22.1 DAMAGE IN THE AUDITORY SYSTEM

In general, detection of sound is primarily related to the integrity of the peripheral hearing mechanisms, whereas the more complex forms of auditory analysis are accomplished by more central areas of the auditory system. Many developmental disorders may effect the developing auditory system. Since auditory acuity and the more complex forms of auditory analysis develop at different rates (Fior 1972), auditory disorders related to damage within the auditory system during the course of development may be manifest at different ages and in different forms. The focus of study has been primarily on the many developmental disorders that result in profound auditory deficits. Subtle auditory disorders manifest at an early age usually come to clinical attention because of the resulting language disorders; until recently, evaluation techniques have not provided specific information concerning the nature of the underlying auditory deficit.

It is beyond the scope of this chapter to cover comprehensively all forms of developmental auditory pathology and related etiologies. Textbooks of otology, otolaryngology, and audiology (e.g., J. Katz 1972, R. Keith 1977, Lutman and Haggard 1983, Schuknecht 1974) describe all the forms of developmental auditory pathology and the etiological factors involved. Some of the auditory disorders associated with pathology in the three major anatomical divisions of the auditory system are described below.

Outer and Middle Ear

Auditory information from the external world is received by specialized sensory receptors that perceive fine, rapid movements in the inner ear (cochlea) via the outer (pinna) and middle ear. The outer ear collects a sound, and the middle ear primarily transmits and attenuates it. Abnormalities of the outer or middle ear that interfere with the conduction of sound into the cochlea may lead to **conductive hearing losses.** Most conductive hearing losses (acuity deficits) do not exceed 60 decibels and can be readily treated with a hearing aid.

Conductive hearing loss may result from blocking of the external meatus (channel into the ear) due to congenital malformations, accumulation of ear wax, tympanic membrane abnormalities (e.g., pressure or perforation) or from middle ear abnormalities due to congenital malformations or fractures at the base of the skull. However, the most common cause of conductive hearing loss in children is dysfunction or obstruction of the Eustachian tube, which results in **otitis media** (middle ear infections). If the infection is brief, the auditory consequences are trivial (Rapin 1975). However, recurrent or chronic otitis media is always accompanied by some degree of conductive hearing loss, which may be variable or episodic and results in a long-standing form of fluctuating auditory deprivation (Howie 1980). In addition to acuity deficits, related sequalae of chronic otitis media include (1) delays in the development of speech and language, (2) difficulty in the production of adequate speech, (3) deficits in auditory processing and receptive language skills, and (4) depressed IQ scores and academic skills.

Inner Ear and Eighth Cranial Nerve

Damage to the receptor apparatus of the cochlea (the organ of Corti) alters the sensory processes and reduces sound transmission to the auditory nervous system. Serious impariments of cochlear processes can lead secondarily to dysfunction of the auditory nerve (Gulick 1971). Abnormalities of the inner ear or the auditory nerve may result in **sensorineural hearing loss.** The severity of the acuity defects may range from profound deafness to mild hearing loss, present in both ears or unilaterally, and manifest as a sudden or fluctuating loss. The degree and extent of the hearing loss determine the presence of additional auditory processing deficits. For example, a child with a moderate hearing impairment may develop speech but with poor pronunciation of consonants whereas a child with a mild hearing impairment may have normal or only slightly impaired speech. Many developmental disorders, including viral infections, intoxications, demyelinating diseases, or concussion, may result in hearing loss as a consequence of cochlear or eighth nerve damage. For example, rubella infection during pregnancy frequently leads to sensorineural hearing loss of the child, most often if the infection occurs during the first trimester and least often if the infection occurs during the last trimester (M. Strauss and Davis 1973).

Ototoxic drugs (e.g., streptomycin, quinine, and chloroquine phosphate) ingested during pregnancy may cause deafness in the fetus by destroying neural elements of the inner ear or by causing extensive damage to the auricle and bone structures of the middle and inner ear (e.g., thalidomide)

(Hart and Naunton 1964, Jorgensen et al. 1964, Matz and Naunton 1968, G. C. Robinson and Cambon 1964, G. C. Robinson et al. 1963). In addition, several sulfa drugs, phenothiazines, methamphetamines, and tranquilizers and a wide array of other drugs (e.g., antidepressants, general anesthetics, nonbarbiturate anticonvulsants, and antihypertension agents) ingested during pregnancy have been linked to increased risks for sensorineural hearing loss in children (Lassman et al. 1980).

Retrospective studies of deaf children indicate that hearing impairments may be related to prematurity (Vernon 1976). However, preterm birth as such does not appear to affect the development of the hearing apparatus since differentiation of the cochlea is complete before the end of the second trimester. The assumption that duration of exposure to incubator noise is responsible for hearing loss in preterm infants has not been corroborated; rather, research indicates a strong correlation between the sum of perinatal risk factors and hearing loss (Schulte and Stennert 1978). Both anoxia (Wolfson et al. 1980) and intrapartum hemorrhage into the inner ear (Wong and Shah 1979) have been suggested as specific perinatal risk factors. Intrapartum hemorrhage into the inner ear may occur as a result of intrapartum injury or stress (e.g., forceps delivery). Blood released into the inner ear has a toxic effect on the organ of Corti, resulting in irreversible damage.

Postnatal infections (e.g., measles, mumps, bacterial meningitis) may also cause cochlear damage. The otological manifestations of congenital syphilis may occur early in childhood and result in severe bilateral hearing loss, although mild losses may occur later and even as late as the fifth decade of life (Wolfson et al. 1980). Tubercular meningitis may infiltrate and damage the sheath of the auditory nerve and the organ of Corti. In addition, drugs used in the treatment of tubercular meningitis (e.g., streptomycin, dihydrostreptomycin) and other drugs administered postnatally (e.g., neomycin, kanamycin) may be ototoxic. The effects of such drugs appear to be additive, and delayed hearing losses can occur (Strome 1977).

Subcortical Structures

Damage in the auditory system above the auditory nerve, including subcortical structures (i.e., cochlear nucleus, superior olivary complex, inferior colliculus, and medial geniculate body) and the auditory cortex, may also result in subtle to profound auditory impairment. Impairment may be temporary, e.g., in a postconcussion syndrome or after irridation of the temporal lobes, or permanent.

Although it has been possible to distinguish between conductive and sensorineural hearing impairments in children over 3 years of age, the assessment of hearing in the infant and the differentiation of hearing impairments with central origin have proved difficult. Recent developments in assessment have supplemented behavioral observations in the assessment of hearing in the infant and young child. The **Crib-o-gram** (Simmons 1975,

Simmons and Russ 1974) is an automated response unit that records the infant's startle responses to noise bursts and automatically samples activity level and scores it with reference to internally programmed criteria and complex algorithms. Electrophysiological recording of cochlear and eighth nerve activity (electrocochleography) and middle ear mechanisms (impedance measurements) with electrodes placed in the ear are also valuable additions to assessment. Heart rate audiometry (Schulman-Galambos and Galambos 1979), auditory-evoked responses (AER), and auditory brainstem responses (ABR) have been studied in human infants (Kaga and Tanaka 1980, Montandon et al. 1979, Ohlrich et al. 1978, A. Starr et al. 1977). However, B. A. Schneider et al. (1979) have pointed out that autonomic and electrophysiological measurements record attentional rather than hearing thresholds. The authors stress the need for using a variety of behavioral measures in infants and young children.

Auditory-evoked potentials (scalp-electrode recordings of the cortical responses) induced by auditory stimuli were described earlier in the discussion of hemispheric asymmetry (Chap. 4). **Auditory brainstem responses,** in contrast, are thought to measure sensory function in subcortical portions of the auditory pathway. Brainstem-evoked potentials are also recorded from scalp electrodes and consist of seven waves produced in the initial 10 milliseconds following a click or tone signal. The seven components presumably derive from sequential activation of the nuclei and pathways of the auditory system. Waves I, II, and III represent activity of the auditory nerve, cochlear nucleus, and superior olive, respectively, and waves IV and V represent activity of the inferior colliculus. The origins of waves VI and VII have not yet been established. Auditory brainstem responses can yield information about the status and development of auditory and neurological functioning in infants as well as locate damage in the auditory system. For example, when used in conjunction with behavioral audiometry in infants, ABRs can aid in determining whether or not an abnormally elevated behavioral response sensitivity reflects dysfunction above the level of the brainstem. If the deficit is above the level of the brainstem, ABRs will be normal. If the ABRs are abnormal, then a brainstem or peripheral lesion is implicated though central pathology can not be ruled out (Kaga and Tanaka 1980).

Information derived from both animal and human studies of preterm infants with kernicterus (Dublin 1951, Wolfson et al 1980) suggests that intrapartum asphyxia and anoxia may damage the cochlear nucleus (Dublin 1978, Hall 1964, Windle 1964). However, ABR research on kernicterus infants indicates that peripheral lesions are likely to be present, though concomitant brainstem and cortical pathology cannot be ruled out. Other reports on cases of kernicterus also support the notion that the hearing impairment is sensorineural (Schuknecht 1974).

Recent animal research has suggested that auditory deprivation induced by lack of environmental stimulation or by conductive hearing loss results in incomplete maturation of most auditory neurons of the brainstem: "There is a critical period for development of auditory brainstem nuclei. . . . Without adequate sound stimulation during this period, most brainstem auditory neurons do not fully develop (Webster and Webster 1979, p. 687). In light of ABR research that indicated that brainstem maturation in the human may continue into the second or third year of life (Kaga and Tanaka 1980), auditory deprivation during this period, regardless of cause, may have devastating consequences for the development of normal auditory processing. This finding is consistent with studies of the effects of chronic otitis media indicating that early hearing deficits adversely affect later central auditory functioning and supports the sensitive-period hypothesis of language acquisition.

Cortical Structures

The term "congenital auditory imperception" has been used to describe deafness originating from central rather than peripheral pathology. Although in some instances children with congenital auditory imperception do not respond to any sound consistently (S. Ward and McCartney 1978), more often some sounds do elicit responses but the child does not respond to spoken language. This disturbance of language appreciation is discussed further in Chap. 23.

Most research on the effects of pathological processes at various sites in the central auditory system has studied adult patients (Baru and Karaseva 1972). Lesions of subcortical and cortical areas of the auditory system in adults and children rarely affect acuity (Thatcher 1980), but the effects on complex auditory processing are a function of the nature of the auditory stimulus (e.g., speech, environmental sounds, melodies, rhythm), the temporal and spectral characteristics of the sounds (e.g., sound sequences, pitch), and aspects of the listening situation (e.g., monaural or binaural presentation, extraneous influences like noise and competing sounds, speaker characteristics).

In children, these more subtle disturbances of auditory processing have been referred to as auditory perceptual problems or auditory imperception but are best described as **central auditory processing disorders** (R. W. Keith 1981). Techniques available for the assessment of auditory processing in children include speech and sound discrimination tasks varying in one or more dimensions, auditory figure-ground selection, and sound localization (Chalfant and Scheffelin 1969, Myklebust 1954). More recently, techniques that involve modifications of the acoustic signal (e.g., frequency filtering of the speech signal, binaural fusion, competing messages, dichotic listening, synthetic sentences) have been developed (Beasley and Rintelmann 1979, J. Katz 1972). Most of these procedures are derived from methods for the assessment of medically related pathologies of the auditory system in adults.

Since peripheral hearing impairments may affect central processing, these measures are most useful when peripheral hearing is normal. Musiek and Geurkink (1980) described five children with learning difficulties referred for hearing assessments. In spite of normal audiograms, various types and degrees of auditory processing problems were detected on tests that included rapidly alternating speech, binaural fusion, low-pass filtered speech, competing sentences, staggered spondaic words, dichotic digits, and frequency patterns. One child exhibited a marked deficit of the left ear on the majority of the measures in addition to problems of space perception noted by teachers, parents, and the examiner during testing. Diffuse right hemisphere dysfunction was suspected.

The major causes of damage to the central auditory system are trauma (perinatal or postnatal), cerebrovascular disorders, and demyelinating or degenerative diseases. Abnormal cortical functioning as indicated by AERs have also been reported in malnourished infants for as long as one year after intervention. The greater abnormality of AERs in malnourished infants of short stature may represent the more devastating effects of chronic malnutrition (Barnet et al. 1978).

22.2 DEVELOPMENTAL PROBLEMS ASSOCIATED WITH AUDITORY DISORDERS

Depending on the nature of the lesion, **auditory disorders** are often accompanied by other sensory and motor deficits of varying degree and by cognitive impairment. Figure 22-1 shows the high rate of association with other handicaps found in 861 children with hearing loss in a sample of 2988 children (CEC Report 1980). The long-term effect of auditory disorders must therefore be viewed in the context of accompanying deficits.

Even auditory impairment without apparent accompanying disorders tends to have extensive consequences not limited to hearing and auditory processing alone but extending to other senses. A study by Vargha-Khadem (1982) noted a deficit in tactile recognition of letters and nonverbal shapes in a group of 16 prelingually deaf children. The most severe limitation imposed by deafness is the inability to acquire a formal verbal language (Rapin 1979). While lip-reading may be of some help and sign language can be learned with great proficiency, the communication with the majority of normal-hearing peers remains seriously disrupted. Formal language is frequently learned only when the child learns reading and writing and remains less than perfect. Schlesinger and Meadows (1972) showed that academic and language performance is aided by the early acquisition of a basic communication system, i.e., sign language. Deaf children of deaf parents who communicated with signs and gestures from infancy were found to be far superior to congenitally deaf children of hearing parents who did not use sign language. Chess et al. (1980) also reported rapid acceleration of

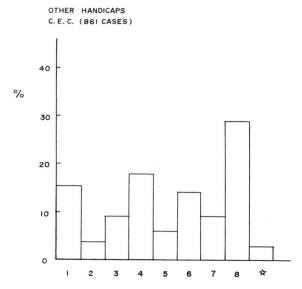

FIGURE 22-1   Distribution of additional disabilities in 861 out of 2988 children with hearing loss (CEC Report 1980).

academic and social functioning in children involved in a "total communication" program. IQ scores of deaf students on nonverbal intelligence tests, such as the Raven matrices (Goetzinger and Houchins 1969) and the performance part of the WISC (Vonderhaar and Chambers 1975), are not significantly different from those of hearing children. Subsequent to school, employment opportunities are severely limited. The emotional development of hearing-impaired children tends to be more normal than, for example, in blind children (Lou 1982); however, the incidence of emotional disorders is still higher than in normal children. This topic is discussed further in Chap. 26.

Children with central processing disorders face more subtle problems in their cognitive development (Aten and Davis 1968). In particular, school problems are common, and communication with others often remains impaired to some degree.

23

Language Disorders

Language, or verbal communication, is a crucial part of human behavior in society. Language permits the individual to communicate with others, a basic mechanism for social interaction. In addition, it provides the individual with a tool for thinking (Kendall 1966). Inadequate or failing language development may have far-reaching implications for a child's overall development as well as for specific behaviors involved in communicative transactions. In this chapter, several disorders of language are addressed and the broader implications of language disorders in relation to cognitive functioning discussed.

In considering manifestations of impaired language functioning in children, an appreciation of normal language acquisition is helpful in identifying and quantifying specific aspects of language disorder. Although a full discussion of normal language acquisition is beyond the scope of this chapter, it should be noted that a number of theories and approaches to its study are available. Some of these emphasize the linguistic aspects (e.g., phonemic, morphemic, syntactic, semantic), some emphasize the perceptual and cognitive bases of language acquisition (e.g., Vygotsky, Piaget), and others seek to explain linguistic development in terms of the development of more general cognitive structures (developmental psycholinguistics). In addition, differing emphasis has been placed on intrinsic and environmental factors involved in language acquisition. As yet, no definitive or complete model has emerged. However, it is important to realize that processes underlying the development of language depend on the existence and maintenance of both anatomical and physiological factors on the one hand and environmental ones (e.g., quality of early linguistic environment, parental and peer-group speech, amount and type of social interaction) on the other.

23.1 FORMS AND FREQUENCY OF LANGUAGE DISORDERS

Disturbances of language functioning may come to the attention of the clinician in a variety of forms. For example, a child may show a marked delay in beginning to speak or may exhibit persistent difficulty with speech comprehension, very restricted speech, persistent echolalia, or bizarre and inappropriate speech. Poor articulation and stuttering are probably even more frequent reasons for referral; however, these often temporary disorders of speech are usually not included in a discussion of disorders of language. Although there is no generally accepted terminology and classification system for language disorders, a basic distinction has been made based on whether the disorder represents a failure or delay in acquiring language or a complete loss or reduction in language capacity occurring subsequent to language acquisition. Marge (1972) defined these three categories as follows:

1. Failure to acquire language: children who at 4 years of age have not shown any sign of acquiring language (0.68 per cent)
2. Delayed language acquisition: children whose language acquisition level is below that attained by peers of the same age; the delay may occur in all components of language, only in one, or in a combination of the phonological, semantic, and syntactic aspects (6.2 per cent)
3. Acquired language disorder: children who had at some point in development acquired language and who subsequently suffered a complete loss or reduction of their capacity to use language (0.25 per cent)

Marge obtained estimates of prevalence of language difficulties among various handicapped populations. The overall prevalence among children in the United States at that time of 6.53 per cent of oral language disorders agrees closely with that reported by MacKeith and Rutter (1972) for the United Kingdom (6.7 per cent). Included in this estimate are mentally retarded children, children with emotional disorders, deaf and hard-of-hearing children, speech-handicapped children, and children with specific learning disabilities. Children who speak either a dialect or a foreign language and have experienced difficulties are not included. Type 2, the largest group, represents a wide range of difficulties, from mild articulation problems to serious difficulties with syntactic formulation. In contrast, Schulze and Teumer (1973/74) found in a sample of 2000 preschool and kindergarten children in Germany an incidence of language disorders of more than 44 per cent in the elementary grades. The discrepancy in reported incidence rate is primarily due to the inclusion of all minor speech and language defects (e.g., mild articulatory or stuttering problems) in the German survey, that is, a very broad definition of what constitutes a disorder.

Language delay as well as most other language disorders occurs approximately three to four times as often in boys as in girls (Satz 1982).

An additional distinction has been made between **congenital disorders of language,** referring to conditions in which neonatal brain damage or congenital defects result in language impairment, and **developmental disorders,** referring to language impairments occurring in children who have a family history of language disorders (Ingram 1959, 1960). Such developmental disorders have been explained on the basis of a hypothetical cerebral immaturity or developmental lag, originally proposed by Ewing (1930). They have also been observed in the context of generally defective cognitive competence, autism, and hyperkinesis.

23.2 DIFFERENTIAL DIAGNOSIS

A number of considerations help clarify the nature of language disorders and aid differential diagnosis (Table 23-1). If the disorder occurs in the absence of intellectual deficit and serious environmental deprivation, it is referred to as either **dysphasia** or aphasia, although dysphasia remains the preferred term for congenital disorders. Frequently, however, the language disorder occurs in the context of other, more pervasive disorders. For example, significant retardation of speech development is often seen in conjunction with deafness, mental retardation, and severe psychiatric disorders (e.g., infantile autism). Children who are intellectually subnormal often manifest retardation of a similar degree in motor, adaptive, and social

TABLE 23-1   Differential Diagnosis of Language Disorders in Childhood

Hearing loss
Oral-area sensory deficit
Aphasia
   Acquired
   Congenital
   Developmental
Dyslexia
   Acquired
   Developmental
Minimal brain dysfunction
Psychosis of childhood (including early infantile autism)
Nonpsychotic functional behavior disorders
Epilepsy
Mental retardation
Environmental deficits (sensory, emotional, and cultural deprivation; inadequate or incompetent instruction)
Normal variation

Source: Chase 1972.

aspects of development as well as in language development. Language acquisition by the retarded child tends to be delayed but follows basically the
same pattern as in children of normal intelligence. However, it is usually
accepted that some mentally retarded children also suffer from more specific forms of language disorders that could be classified as dysphasia (Benton 1964, Cromer 1978, Richardson 1972).

The language development of autistic children requires special differential diagnosis. Autistic children may show delayed or deviant language
development in addition to impaired social development, which is well below their intellectual level, and an insistence on sameness, as shown by stereotyped play patterns, abnormal preoccupations, or resistance to change.
Rutter (1978) notes that the pattern of language development and use in
autistic children is different from that of normal children and of children
with other language disorders. Autistic children fail to show much social
imitation (e.g., waving bye-bye). Frequently their patterns of babbling are
impaired or abnormal, their understanding of spoken language is limited,
and they lack gesture or mime. About 50 per cent of autistic children never
acquire speech, and those who do characteristically exhibit echolalia and
delayed reception of stereotyped phrases accompanied by I-you pronom-
inal reversals (Rutter 1978). Although there has been a tendency to consider the speech and language disturbance of autistic children as merely
one aspect of a broader, more complex disorder (Anthony 1958, M. A.
Cunningham 1968, de Hirsch 1967, Weiland and Legg 1964), it has been
argued that a central language disorder may well be the necessary and sufficient cause of behavioral characteristics in autistic and schizophrenic children and that the fundamental difference between these children and other
children with language disorders (e.g., dysphasic children) is the severity
of involvement (D. W. Churchill 1972). This notion is supported by Bartak
et al. (1975) and in a study by Morton-Evans and Hensley (1978) that found
that both dysphasic and autistic children had severe difficulty in associating
sounds with their visual counterparts in paired associate learning but that,
with training, dysphasic children overcame this deficit significantly faster
than autistic children.

A special case of language delay is presented in the Kasper Hauser syndrome (deprivation) as most recently studied in the case of "Genie" (Curtiss 1977). In this case gross environmental neglect and deprivation of language stimulation led to severe language delay. A somewhat similar situation
was reported for Luria and Yudovich's (1971) twins who "did not experience the necessity of using language to communicate with each other" (p.
105) and instead developed a substitute activity of practical pointing that
the authors described as "synpraxic speech." From a neuropsychological
perspective, such cases are of interest mainly in that they contribute to the
question of sensitive periods for language development as discussed in Chap.
6. Both Kasper Hauser and Genie gained a considerable amount of lan-

guage after deprivation ended as late as age 10 or 12 and an active language training program was started. The same applied to the twins after the age of five. The cases suggest that language aquisition during the first years of life may not be as critical as suggested by some authors (Lenneberg 1967), although in both case studies certain limitations in the development of more complex use of language appeared to emerge: "Her spontaneous speech was almost devoid of syntax, and communication was primarily single word production" (Curtiss et al. 1975).

Another consideration in clarifying the nature of language disorders is whether the primary problem is one of reception (understanding speech, decoding) or expression (expressing oneself in speech, encoding). The traditional clinical approach to the classification of language disorders on these dimensions is illustrated in Table 23-2. In practice, considerable overlap between comprehension and expression is found, as shown in a study of 315 children with difficulty in language learning by Martin (J.A.M. 1981; Table 23-3).

23.3 RECEPTIVE-EXPRESSIVE DISORDERS

Three types of receptive disorders or disorders of input (Rapin and Wilson 1978) may occur, depending on the level of receptive functions: (1) the auditory signal may not be detected, i.e., hearing loss (Menyuk 1977), (2) discrimination between auditory signals (i.e., of duration, pattern, or serial order) may not be made, and (3) semantic significance (or the decoding of the meaning of the phonological aspects of speech) of auditory symbols may not be established.

Discrimination ability may be affected differently depending on the type of auditory stimuli. For example, discrimination of speech may be impaired

TABLE 23-2 Classification of Organically Based Language Deficits

	Communicative functions						
	Decoding				Encoding		
Channel	Acuity	Discrimination	Association	Central processing	Association	Motor patterns	Discrete movements
Auditory	Deafness and hearing loss	Auditory agnosias	Auditory aphasias	Categorizing Problem solving Learning Storage and retrieval Language acquisition etc.	Oral aphasias	Oral apraxias	Oral paralyses
Visual	Blindness and visual loss	Visual agnosias	Visual aphasias		Manual aphasias	Manual apraxias	Manual paralyses

Source: Irwin et al. 1972.

TABLE 23-3   Overall Distribution of Verbal
Comprehension and Expression in 315 Language-
Impaired Children

Level of ability	Verbal comprehension	Verbal expression
Normal	108	54
Moderate impairment	60	58
Severe impairment	147	203
Total	315	315

Source: J.A.M. Martin 1981.

although the ability to discriminate environmental sounds remains intact. This condition has been described as **congenital word deafness** (Worster-Drought and Allen 1929a, 1929b) or **verbal auditory agnosia**. The term "auditory agnosia" has been applied to the total inability to differentiate all varieties of sound. In contrast, the term "**auditory imperception**" as used by Worster-Drought and Allen denotes an inability to differentiate speech sounds as well as some environmental sounds with impaired ability to imitate sounds, sing a tune, or show any natural response to rhythm. Receptive disorders are frequently accompanied by distorted speech since the speech-monitoring mechanism remains inadequate. Worster-Drought and Allen also noted the occurrence of frequent idiosyncratic speech containing neologisms; the authors described as "**idioglossia**" speech that remains largely unintelligible because of the large amount of idiosyncratic elements.

23.4   EXPRESSIVE DISORDERS

Three types of disorders of expression may be distinguished in accordance with the three types of production functions: (1) defects in the production of language occurring at the semantic level (with lexical and syntactic impoverishment) are referred to as expressive dysphasias, (2) defects at the motor level are referred to as apraxias, and (3) defects in discrete movements of the peripheral muscles (neuromotor control and coordination) are referred to as **dysarthrias**. Rapin and Wilson (1978) made an additional distinction between defective programming at the syntactic and the phonemic level. While the two levels of programming may not always be clearly separable, Yoss and Darley (1974) stressed that in some children syntax can be adequate and only the phonological output disturbed.

Motor pattern disorders affect the ability to speak in the absence of overt paralysis and have been termed **verbal dyspraxias** (Ferry et al. 1975, Yoss and Darley 1974) or **articulatory apraxias, apraxias of speech, apraxic dysarthrias,** or **cortical dysarthrias**. They occur in conjunction with intact ability to perform other purposeful movements of the oral musculature (e.g., blow out a match, whistle). Total inability to perform purposeful movements of the mouth and lower face in the absence of paralysis has been termed **oral** or **buccofacial apraxia.** A study of 60 patients with developmental verbal dyspraxia (Ferry et al. 1975) indicated absent or poorly intelligible ("dilapidated") speech that became worse when tested by increasingly more complex phonetic combinations. The authors report associated oral dyspraxia in more than half their patients and note that conventional speech therapy had been unsuccessful; spontaneous improvement occurred only up to the age of 6 years.

23.5 APPLICATION OF THE CLASSIFICATION SYSTEM

The approach to the traditional classification of language disorders described in the previous section—and also followed in a survey by Benton (1978)—is based to some extent on the study of disturbances of language in adult brain-damaged populations where relatively discrete forms of language impairment, as implied by the various dissociations, and no impairment of basic intelligence have been observed. Dissociations between these discrete forms of language impairment in adults have been associated with the clinical basis of the difficulty, i.e., specific focal brain lesions.

The application of this classification system to disturbances of language in children for the purpose of identifying specific groups of language disorders has not always been successful. In the adult brain damage interferes with well-established, organized functions, whereas in children functions are in the process of developing in a rapidly changing system. For example, it is expected that in children reception necessarily influences expressive output. In order to vocalize language sounds, it is necessary to receive both auditory input and feedback of one's own vocalizations. Lack of comprehension and feedback may reduce verbal output, thus interfering with the development of articulation skills (Milisen 1966). The fundamental differences between language disorders of adults with acquired brain damage and those seen in children have lead to a proliferation of terms designed to describe more adequately the childhood disorders (e.g., congenital or developmental dysphasia, word deafness with verbal apraxia, developmental or congenital auditory imperception). However, more neutral terms, such as specific developmental language disability and developmental language retardation, have also been used to avoid unintended implications regarding the essential nature of the underlying pathology as seen in adults.

Some authors (Ingram 1976, Zangwill 1978) have stressed the commonalities of childhood language disorders and the overlap between types. Eisenson (1968a) even emphasized in his "unitary explanation" that a "basic impairment in the necessary capacity for the analysis of speech signals and for the sequencing of temporal events" (p. 12) is an essential part of all developmental language disorders, especially dysphasia. On the other hand, some systematic breakdown into specific types is usually attempted. Menyuk (1978) emphasized that many language-distrubed children nevertheless follow a normal developmental sequence of language aquisition, though at a significantly slower pace. Deviant development patterns are rare. Menyuk stated that the nature of the basic problem changes with the changes in developmental needs over time; what may begin as a segmental and suprasegmental problem later appears as semantic and syntactic problems. She documented this developmental lag-change theory with experimental and observational evidence. Kerschensteiner and Hurber's (1975) case of a 23-year-old developmental aphasic also confirms the notion as far as acquisition of grammar is concerned; their patient showed language "quite comparable to the language of children from 3 to 6 (years old)" (p. 281), although his nonverbal (Raven test) IQ was 90. The authors described the language handicap as "incomplete maturation," especially for linguistic generalizations.

Rapin and Wilson (1978) proposed "multiple syndromes of developmental language disability," stressing that a single deficit cannot possibly account for the variety of observed disorders although current classification systems are insufficient or inadequate.

Although the value of adopting the adult classification system to children to ascertain the neurological locus of impairment is limited, the analysis and elucidation of receptive and expressive functions have proved useful for clarifying the nature of language disorders in children. For example, impaired auditory processing of normal speech has been hypothesized as the underlying cognitive deficit in children whose failure to acquire language is discordant with their nonverbal intelligence and peripheral hearing acuity (Eisenson 1968b). Several types of auditory processing deficits have been implicated in this regard: (1) impairment of storage capacity, especially in relation to grammatical complexity (Bliss and Peterson 1975); (2) impairment of speech sound discrimination; and (3) auditory inattention (Eisenson 1968a). In addition, other nonverbal aspects of auditory processing—such as impairment of sound localization, auditory rhythmical ability (P. Griffiths 1972, Kracke 1975), sequential perception (Eisenson 1968a, Lowe and Campbell 1965), and discrimination of rapidly changing acoustic information (Tallal 1978, Tallal and Piercy 1978, Tallal et al. 1980)—play a part in defining the exact nature of the language disorder. The assumption of a defect in serial order behavior in Lashley's (1951) sense has often been made (Aten and Davis 1968, Doehring 1968a). However, whether auditory processing deficits are to be viewed as (1) necessary causes of developmental language disorders, (2) sufficient but not necessary causes of developmental language disorders, (3) secondary to a primary defect of the linguistic system itself ("hierarchical structuring deficit," Cromer 1978) or even to a more general cognitive deficit (Rees 1973), or (4) concomitant with a linguistic deficit but not causally related to it (Tallal and Piercy 1978) is open to debate. As a case in point, a recent study by Ludlow et al. (1980) indicated that impairment of perception of temporal order may also be found in groups of children (patients with early Huntington's disease and hyperactive children) with normal language functions. The authors suggested that the deficit in temporal sequential perception may be better understood as reflecting general cognitive dysfunction.

On the basis of observations of "several hundred 6-year-old children described as dysphasic or with specific language disorders," J. M. Cooper and Griffiths (1978) developed a descriptive grouping in five categories that makes few assumptions about underlying deficits but instead concentrates on the evident forms of impairment:

1. Children without hearing loss but with little comprehension or use of speech. This group is described as bright and alert; they can express themselves in drawing, mime, and gesture.
2. Children with hearing loss. They may also show visual handicaps, may have a history of spasticity, and use mime and gestural communication; they are described as hyperactive and grossly immature.
3. Children with normal verbal comprehension but severely impoverished or absent verbal expression. Speech consists of short, simple, active declaratives. Often gross articulatory impairment as well as other motor impairment is present.
4. A group similar to group 3, but with late onset of relatively rapid speech development. Learning to read is often a problem, as is fine motor coordination, though the overall cognitive level is average or better.
5. Children who develop speech but use imitative, stereotyped, and irrelevant speech. Learning ability is even more severely affected. Behavior may frequently be obsessional and eccentric, though not necessarily disruptive. Relationships with other children are poor, but children in this group do relate to adults.

23.6 ACQUIRED LANGUAGE DISORDERS

Although acquired language disorders represent the smallest proportion of affected children, the study of these children has provided perhaps the most striking evidence concerning the complexities inherent in the study of the developing nervous system. The effects of cerebral lesions acquired during infancy and childhood on language functioning may differ markedly from lesions acquired during adulthood. For example, one notable clinical feature of the language of a child with acquired aphasia, in contrast to adult aphasics, is the reduction in the amount of speech produced regardless of the locus of lesion (Alajouanine and Lhermitte 1965, Guttman 1942, Karlin 1954, Rapin et al. 1977). In fact, it has been observed that the aphasic child may not only show reduced verbal output but may also be reluctant to communicate or exchange information by writing or using gesture (Alajouanine and Lhermitte 1965, Karlin 1954). Whereas dominant hemisphere involvement generally precipitates language disorders in adults, large brain lesions sustained early in life, even if treated by hemispherectomy, do not produce profound language impairment, regardless of the side of the brain involved. These findings and the observation that children recover language functions more rapidly than adults have been one major basis for theories about the ontogeny of cerebral dominance and of plasticity and critical periods for development of function, two key issues in developmental neuropsychology (Chaps. 4 and 6).

Dennis and Whitaker (1977) and Satz and Bullard-Bates (1981) reviewed the evidence on acquired aphasia in children and confirmed earlier suggestions for an initial equipotentiality of the two hemispheres for language. They concluded that this assumption holds only up to the age of approximately 1 year. While prior to this age right hemiplegia produces a 2 to 1 risk for language impairment, the frequency of aphasia associated with right hemiplegia increases dramatically after this age and by age 5 approximates the ratios found in adults. These findings are somewhat modified by studies of hemispherectomy reviewed by Ludlow (1979), which suggest that, although phonemic discrimination and lexicon may have an equal potential in the right and left hemisphere, the discrimination of complex syntactic material may be more seriously impaired by left hemispherectomy. This seems to suggest that the left hemisphere may "retain a nonredundant language behavior–syntactic complexity" (p. 185). Dennis (1980), in a review of hemispherectomy studies, stresses that the left hemisphere also "allows for the development of a set of semantic abilities not available to the right" (p. 183).

23.7 THE ORIGINS OF CHILDHOOD DYSPHASIA

Most language disorders related to hearing impairment are caused by pre- and postnatal infections affecting the organ of the auditory nerve rather than the brain itself. Language disorders of a higher level of auditory and central processing, on the other hand, have led to much speculation about their origin, although few actual studies are available. Some authors have suggested that abnormal hemispheric dominance and interhemispheric interaction or left hemisphere dysfunction may be responsible (Lebrun and Zangwill 1981a, Zaidel 1979). Hauser et al. (1975) reported an enlargement of the left temporal horn in the pneumoencephalogram of 15 out of 18 autistic children with language defect. Garvey and Mutton (1973) and Mutton and Lea (1980) reported (1) an increased occurrence of male sex chromosome trisomies (XXY and XYY) among children with specific speech and language delay and (2) depressed verbal and normal nonverbal IQ scores among Klinefelter syndrome (XXY) boys. The higher incidence in males has been explained in a polygenic reverse model by Decker and DeFries (1980, Decker 1982) that postulates that males have a lower threshold of liability to risk factors than girls. It follows from this model that affected females would be carrying more "risk genes" than males and that relatives of affected females would show a higher incidence of disorder than would be expected in the general population. This genetic risk model is of course not limited to language disorders but can be applied to others (e.g., autism, developmental dyslexia) as well.

Another series of related hypotheses about the causes of language disorders was first mentioned by Gellner (1959), who stated that subcortical lesions may be responsible for the lack of both language and cognitive development in retarded children. Subcortical lesions are also central to Matzker's (1958) theory of a binaural integration deficit in patients with a variety of disorders affecting language and to Rimland's (1964) notion of damage to the reticular activating system, proposed primarily as an explanation of autism. This notion was further elaborated by DesLauriers and Carlson (1969), based on Routtenberg's (1966) notion of two arousal systems (reticular and limbic). Since brainstem damage occurs frequently with hypoxic episodes during birth (Towbin 1970), a further exploration of these notions may be desirable.

Bilateral lesions of the central auditory system are most often postulated, both on the basis of the evidence concerning the normal plasticity of the infant brain (Rutter 1978) and the fact that the auditory pathways are crossed (O. Sugar 1952). It should be noted, however, that the plasticity hypothesis has been challenged, both on theoretical grounds of early hemispheric structural asymmetries assumed to be fundamental to language development and on the basis of the findings by Annett (1973) and by Rankin et al. (1981) that right hemiplegic children are inferior in speech production, vocabulary, and comprehension and syntax comprehension and formulation to a carefully matched group of left hemiplegic children. In a case study, Dennis (1980b) demonstrated the rapid recovery of language in a 9-year-old girl who had suffered a stroke involving the left anterior artery. On the basis of a detailed linguistic analysis, she stressed that major reorganizations that "change the fundamental organization not just of the output mechanics but of her language" (p. 66) had taken place. In support of the bilateral lesion hypothesis, M. A. Dalby (1975) presented the results of 87 pneumoencephalograms of children with developmental dysphasia and reported that in this group 26 children showed an enlarged left temporal horn, 6 an enlarged right temporal horn, and 14 enlargement on both sides. He concluded that medial temporal lobe structures are the most likely site of defect. In addition, there is some evidence to support the suggestion that bilateral involvement may be necessary to produce the severe receptive-expressive forms of language disorders seen in children.

Rapin et al. (1977) examined five children with "dense" deficits for decoding acoustic speech and profound impairments in oral speech. Three of these children exhibited bilateral cerebral dysfunction as inferred from bilateral epileptogenic discharges in the EEG. The other two were brothers with similar language difficulties. The onset of language deterioration in the older brother coincided with classic brief absences that were compatible with temporal-lobe discharge. The younger brother showed no seizure or EEG abnormality but exhibited a similar language deficit. It was suggested that the language disorders may not always reflect adventitious brain abnormality but may be genetic in some children. The authors also suggested that bilateral dysfunction must be suspected in children with a severe receptive language difficulty, whether congenital or acquired.

The only case reported in the literature of a child with a developmental language disorder who came to autopsy (Landau et al. 1960) also showed bilateral involvement. This boy had severe receptive and expressive language deficits and was initially thought to be deaf, although later audiograms indicated auditory acuity within the normal range. He learned to speak and understand within limits, but understanding was possible only if speech was presented to him slowly and with pauses between words. On autopsy, it was noted that he had old cystic infarcts involving the superior temporal gyrus bilaterally and severe retrograde degeneration on both medial geniculate bodies.

Although bilateral damage to the adult cochlea, eighth nerve, or cortical part of the auditory system would require rare and complicated combinations of lesions, a number of pre-, peri-, and postnatal diseases are capable of producing bilateral auditory system lesions. These include asphyxia neonatorum (Saxon 1961, Saxon and Ponce 1961, Windle 1971), kernicterus (Carhart 1967; Flower et al. 1966a, 1966b; Gerrard 1952; Goodhill 1950, 1956; Matkin and Carhart 1966), and maternal virus infections that involve the fetus, most notably rubella (Hardy 1968, 1973; Monif et al. 1966). Many of these diseases have been implicated as playing a role in the etiology of language disorders. For example, Goldstein et al. (1960), in a retrospective study, identified several etiological factors common to deaf and aphasic children (Table 23-4). In Table 23-5, the etiological factors have been reorganized to indicate which factors were predominantly associated with deafness or dysphasia in children. Only rubella and complications during pregnancy were associated in approximately the same proportions with both deafness and dysphasia. Mental retardation and early infantile autism also tended to be more frequently associated with these factors (Chase 1972). Athetosis has long been known to be strongly associated with language disorders in cerebral palsy (Achilles 1956). A study by Flower et al. (1966a, 1966b) compared groups of children with athetosis and hearing impairment (including kernicterus children) and with athetosis without hearing impairment. While language development was slowest in the hearing-impaired

TABLE 23-4 Etiological Classification of Deaf and Aphasic Children

	Deaf	Aphasic
Unknown	60	26
Prenatal		
Hereditary		
Hearing loss	12	3
Speech disorder, CNS disorder	0	6
Rubella of first trimester of pregnancy	10	7
Other congenital complications		
Historical data	9	4
Inferred from clinical evidence of brain damage	2	5
Rh, severe jaundice shortly after birth	0	4
Perinatal		
Complications of labor and birth	1	6
Postnatal		
Meningitis	9	1
Severe infection in infancy	11	1
Convulsive disorder	0	6

Source: R. Goldstein et al. 1960.

athetosis group, the authors failed to find a specific association between dysphasia and kernicterus, as suggested by R. Goldstein et al. (1960) and by Myklebust (1956).

De Ajuriaguerra et al. (1976) conducted a cross-sectional study of 40 and a longitudinal study of 17 developmentally aphasic children. In their cross-sectional study, the authors made a distinction between children with "restrained" expression, marked by the use of simple sentences, enumerative and descriptive narration, and little discrepancy between expression and comprehension, and a second group of "unrestrained" subjects whose speech was more voluble and who used complex sentences, variant word order, and generally incoherent narration and showed a large discrepancy between expression and comprehension. The majority of the children were

TABLE 23-5 Condensed Etiological Classification of Deaf and Aphasic Children

	Deaf	Aphasic
Meningitis, severe infection in infancy, family history of hearing loss	32	5
Maternal rubella, complications during pregnancy	19	11
Rh, complications of labor and birth, convulsive disorders, congenital brain abnormality, family history of speech or neurological disorder	3	27

Source: Goldstein et al. 1960.

normal in intelligence on the WISC, including its verbal part, but inadequate in information, vocabulary, and arithmetic. They also showed a deficit in spatial reasoning. Affective disorders tended to delay the onset of expressive language but were not related to severity of expressive or receptive deficit at a later age. The development of the 17 children followed longitudinally over a two-year period suggested that best progress was made by children who had the highest need to communicate and showed the least affective disorder; primarily, these children belonged to the "restrained" group. The authors concluded that developmental aphasia is not the same as a developmental language delay but that other factors must be taken into account and that such aphasia represents a particular form of disorganization of language during development with specific inability to acquire the structural or syntactic logic of language.

No long-term follow-up studies of children with various forms of congenital lesions that would further clarify the etiology of childhood dysphasia have been published. Among the many basic environmental influences during pregnancy investigated in the Collaborative Perinatal Study (LaBenz 1980), higher risks for sensorineural hearing loss in infants born to mothers who took certain drugs (sulfa drugs, phenothiazines, streptomycin, methamphetamine, and 17 different tranquilizers, as well as other drugs) was noted, but most other environmental factors played only a minimal role in the prediction of speech, hearing, and language deficit at age 3 or 8 years. Even weighted measures of these factors in a multiple regression analysis accounted for less than 8 per cent of the variance.

23.8 LANGUAGE DISORDERS IN RELATION TO COGNITION

While many language disorders in children occur together with cognitive deficits of similar severity, specific language disorders, by definition, assume normal intelligence and nonexceptional home background. Many of the children suffering from such disorders tend to remain language-handicapped; they are frequently resistant to speech therapy and also tend to be handicapped in reading and other school subjects (Zangwill 1978). As Benton (1978) described, however, the assumption of normal intelligence can be confirmed only by nonverbal intelligence tests. In studies with such tests, it has been found that, although nonverbal intelligence is in the normal range, it is usually lower than similar test scores for siblings and parents. If both expressive and receptive language are disturbed, a certain amount of deprivation even in a normal home environment is likely to occur. For example, the dysphasic boy described by Landau et al. (1960) showed a performance IQ of 78 at age 6; after three years of intensive training, the measured performance IQ was 98. Hence, Benton interprets the finding at age 6 as "pseudoretardation."

The relationship between language and cognition has been a subject of speculation, study, and theory formulation for many investigators. At first glance, the comparison with deaf children appears attractive: like children with specific language deficit, deaf children are deprived of verbal stimulation and tend to develop largely without oral speech; hence their intellectual development must proceed without the constant aid of verbal mediation that normal children are able to use. Yet, as Furth (1966) and others have shown, "thinking without language" is quite adequate in deaf children.

Deaf children also learn to read and to communicate by written language as well as by other communication systems (e.g., sign language). While a detailed review of these studies is not appropriate in the present context, it should be mentioned that concept formation in deaf children has been found to be approximately at the level expected on the basis of age as long as it involves new concepts (e.g., symmetry or sameness) whereas for other concepts, those that are overlearned by the use of language (e.g., opposites, learned by the frequent use of such verbal examples as high-low, up-down, big-small), normal children showed a distinct advantage. In fact, Furth and Youniss (1964) showed that deaf children learned better than normal children on tasks in which interference by implicit verbal responses was likely to occur. Deaf children also learned the temporal sequence of faces better than controls, but controls were better in remembering the temporal order of nonsense syllables (O'Connor and Hermelin 1973).

Unfortunately, the parallel with deaf children is suited only for a portion of children with specific language disability, namely, the types of disability listed in Table 23-3 as decoding problems. Presumably, the deaf child maintains the central processing ability for symbolic material, as witnessed by the aquisition of alternate means of communication and even lip reading. Hence, the discussion about the relationship between language and cognition focuses on the ability for central processing of language for cognition. If, as Table 23-3 implies, central processing is basic to categorizing, problem solving, learning, storage, and retrieval, then a disorder at this level must be considered as nearly identical to a severe cognitive deficit. On the other hand, if manipulating and processing of symbolic material is an ability that may be involved in, but is not basic to, all cognitive skills, then we would expect some but not all cognitive skills to be affected.

Luria (1966, Luria and Yudovich 1971) followed Pavlov in viewing the speech system as the highest regulator of human behavior, the "second signal system": "no single complex form of human mental activity can take place without the direct or indirect participation of speech" (p. 85). Bay (1962), consistent with his unitary view of brain function, also viewed concept formation as inseparably interwoven with language. A modifying role of language was assumed by Kuenne (1946). Kuenne, Milgram (1973) and others view language as a "verbal mediator" rather than as central to all cognitive activity. Verbal mediation assists and facilitates learning, problem solving, and concept formation. Finally, Reitan (1950) reported that he found little difference between the nonverbal intelligence test scores of aphasic and nonaphasic patients; he concluded that "language function is less important to complex thinking than has generally been presumed" (p. 375). More recent experiments have shown a defect in sequential perception and related cognitive activity in dysphasics (Kracke 1975), although an earlier study by Furth (1964) showed that sequence learning was not significantly more impaired in dysphasic children than in deaf children. One two-year follow-up study of eight developmentally aphasic boys at age 6 to 8 years found that they continued to be seriously deficient in auditory-vocal and oral-motor functioning and language comprehension but that they were equal to the normal control groups in visual-perceptual and visual-motor functioning (P. S. Weiner 1969). Spellacy and Black (1972) reported a mean Leiter scale (nonverbal) IQ of 99.4 for their younger language-impaired children (age 41 to 71 months), as contrasted with a Peabody picture vocabulary IQ of 75.8. The older groups (72 to 95 and 96 to 120 months), however, showed IQs of 75.8 and 73.9 even on the Leiter scale, whereas their PPVT IQs were 67.5 and 58.1, respectively. The findings suggest a deficiency even in nonverbal intelligence for the older children but less for the younger children. This conclusion remains tentative because this study was not longitudinal and did not use matched samples. A mild inferiority of dysphasic subjects in visuospatial functioning (Doehring 1960) and less habituation of the visual orienting response to new visual stimuli (Mackworth et al. 1973) have been observed. Children who at age 3 years still showed severe echolalia were found one year later to be significantly lower in IQ than those who had only mitigated echolalia even though the echolalia stage had disappeared at follow-up and even though the two groups were originally matched for IQ (Fay and Butler 1968). In other words, the question of whether a central processing deficit is crucial to cognitive activity still receives contradictory answers. Menyuk (1978), after a review of the experimental evidence, concluded that "the nautre of the specific task requirements may render language useful, nonuseful, or interfering in carrying out these tasks" (p. 69). Benton (1978) noted that several studies showed a strikingly large range of scores in dysphasic children. This suggests that perhaps a more detailed breakdown into types of language dysfunction may clarify the question in future experimentations. A study by McFie (1975) notes that, while the effects of lesions below the age of 10 years on intelligence and scholastic achievement were quite variable, left hemisphere lesions at any age tended to affect verbal long-term memory and span of apprehension quite consistently regardless of age at time of lesion. A recent study by Kimura (1981) also noted that, in several cases of deafness with CNS damage, signing ability was also impaired in cases of left-hemisphere-lesioned right-handers (interpreted as "manual apraxia").

23.9 OUTCOME OF CHILDHOOD LANGUAGE DISORDERS

With the exception of acquired aphasia in childhood, the long-term outcome of childhood language disorders presents a relatively poorly researched but generally bleak prospect. In general, outcome tends to be quite variable from case to case, and few distinctive predictive factors have been isolated.

For children who fail to develop language or who show severe delay in language aquisition, often accompanied by general cognitive handicap, language development usually proceeds in step with general mental development. While specific training procedures have been shown to be effective within a limited setting, generalization and long-term maintenance of responses acquired during training remain persistent problems (Ruder and Smith 1974) and show large variability among individuals. Such variability may represent the confounding of several factors, such as type and severity of brain damage and motivational, attentional, and general activity levels.

Children with specific language delay tend to show even more variability. Five children with congenital auditory imperception at age 1.4 to 3.4 years did not benefit either from early guidance with amplification perceptual training or from a synthetic approach; they showed, if anything, less, not more, interest in sound as they drew older (S. Ward and McCartney 1978). The authors reviewed other follow-up studies and confirmed that the long-term outlook for children with receptive language problems (but without deafness) is quite poor. Vetter et al. (1980) report from the large population of the Collaborative Perinatal Project that correlations between language measures at age 3 and at age 8 were between .00 and .43 for language comprehension, sentence complexity, and word identification. The same study (Darley and Fay 1980) also attempted an examination of the long-term predictive value of several perinatal stress measures, of family factors, of physical signs in newborns, and of eight-month Bayley Developmental Scale measures for the speech and language status at age 8 years. The at-birth variables contributed only 0.6 per cent of the variance (0.8 per cent if combined with the eight-month follow-up variables); adding the three-year indices to the prediction formula allowed as much as 11.5 per cent of the variance to be accounted for. In a study reported by Caputo et al. (1981), a group of preterm infants followed up to the age of 7 to 9.5 years also found only marginal relationships between measures of birth stress and language development unless the mother's IQ was added to the multiple regression equation. These findings provide a good indication of the large variability described by many authors in the past: some children show unexpected spurts in language development while others remain stagnant, and a majority shows a gradual but slow increase in language capability. Especially for children with severe comprehension deficit and autism, prognosis has to be considered extremely guarded.

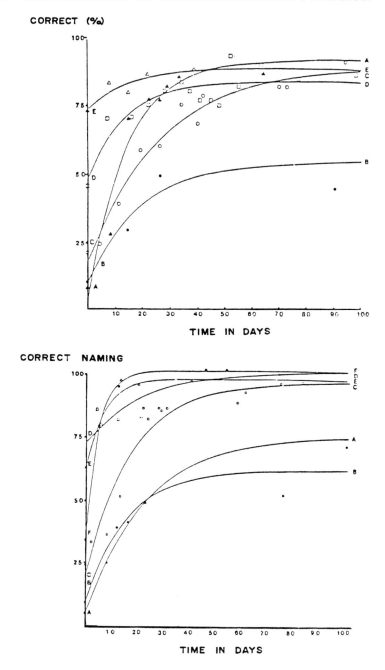

FIGURE 23-1 Exponential function of initial recovery from traumatic aphasia on the token test (above) and on picture naming (below) for individual patients between the ages of 10 and 17 Years (Niebergall et al. 1976).

More is known about the long-term outcome of acquired aphasia in childhood. Figure 23-1 shows the recovery rate for understanding sentences (token test) and for picture naming in several 10 to 17 year olds, indicating that even during late childhood and adolescence an exponential function of initial recovery during the first 100 days can be expected (Niebergall et al. 1976). Similar results were reported by Hécaen (1977) and others. Course and prognosis of acquired aphasia are of course dependent on etiology. Wenzel (1966) lists as poor prognostic indicators the factors of inflammatory disease, widespread damage, presence of epilepsy (J. A. Cooper and Ferry 1978), and severe EEG changes, whereas traumatic aphasia is usually considered as prognostically favorable (Remschmidt et al. 1980). Woods and Teuber (1978b) reported that, of 25 aphasic children age 2 to 15 years at onset, 21 showed full recovery after four years. In the four remaining cases, vascular etiology and epilepsy with hemiparesis were reported, although several of the younger children also had vascular lesions. Though frequently claimed, no clear-cut relationship between age at onset and degree of recovery can as yet be documented because of the confounding etiologic variables (Satz and Bullard-Bates 1981).

24

Cognitive Disorders

The term "**cognition**" covers a wide and ill-defined range of intellectual abilities, such as understanding language, remembering, thinking, and perceiving. Studies of cognitive development include such diverse topics as appreciating humor, learning the distinctive features of letters, and perceiving another person's unconscious motivation. Since many of these topics have yet to be investigated in a neuropsychological context and others are discussed separately in this book, the focus in this chapter is on the development of intelligence and intellectual handicap and on cognitive development and the cognitive characteristics of neurologically impaired children, e.g. their learning, memory, problem solving, reasoning, and concept formation. The development of the Down's syndrome child will be used as an example.

24.1 INTELLIGENCE

Though exploration of the dimensions of intelligent behavior has covered numerous abilities, conceptualized as factors of primary mental abilities by Thurstone (1938) and as a large number of factors in the famous cube model of Guilford (1956) with operations-content-product dimensions, most studies still treat intelligence as unitary or at least as a complex that can be described by one general factor, as first suggested by Spearman (1927). Another widely used breakdown, into fluid and crystallized intelligence (Cattell 1971), distinguishes between the capacity to find relationships, e.g., word fluency and psychomotor speed, and the sum of aquired abilities, e.g., space and verbal meaning (Table 24-1). Halstead (1947) and Hebb (1949) developed the concept of biological intelligence based on neuropsychological theory. Hebb also suggested a breakdown into two types of intelligence, similar to Cattell's fluid and crystallized intelligence: (a) problem solving and learning of new and unfamiliar material and (b) stored knowledge and

TABLE 24-1 Major Differences in Cattell's Factors of Intelligence

Fluid	Crystallized
Reaches its maximum early (age 14) and drops after age 20	Reaches maximum later (age 20?) and shows no decline with age
High correlation with rate of learning in new situations	Less correlated with rate of learning
Primarily constitutional and related to brain processes; varies with physiological conditions	Variance mainly related to cultural and environmental factors; consists of acquired habit systems and some specific cerebral substrates
Capacity reduced by brain damage	Total capacity reduced less by brain damage, but specific functions may be differentially affected
Difficult to distinguish in the structure of primary abilities	Leads to increasing development of primary abilities
In factor analysis, test loadings decrease only marginally during adulthood	Test loadings decrease in adulthood, especially with heterogeneous groups who specialize in different areas
Best measured in tests requiring speed in finding a response	Better measured with power tests without time limit and largely avoiding error of response factors

Source: Wewetzer 1972.

experience. Type (a) intelligence would be more likely compromised by brain damage than type (b). Most of these and similar breakdowns of cognitive abilities into major components based on empirical data and factor analytical studies are, however, rarely used in clinical practice. Instead, neuropsychological studies tend to have a pragmatic orientation toward cognition, one based on available tests with demonstrated usefulness in neurological populations. A breakdown into performance and verbal intelligence based on common sense and practical division of parts of a test rather than empirical demonstration is readily adopted if the available methods suggest it. However, many investigators rely solely on general IQ values, sometimes even without mentioning which particular method of assessment was used.

24.2 DEVELOPMENTAL HANDICAP

One reason for the popularity of the use of general IQ values is the concept of **developmental handicap** (DH), which suggests a general deficit of cognitive functions without specification of range and area of deficit or of mechanism or cause. The term replaces a series of now outdated historical equivalents (idiot, moron, imbecile; oligophrenia, mental deficiency, mental retardation). The long-standing popularity of such general designations of unspecified cognitive deficit rests on its assumed value for describing a section of the population that has difficulty in coping with the educational and, eventually, the social and economic demands of society. As a result, the population so designated varies in size with changes in society itself. Approximately 3 per cent of the population of Western societies today is usually described as DH (Spreen 1978a), although the size of *substantially* developmentally disabled population as defined by state disability plans in the United States is only 1.72 per cent of the general population (Jacobson and Janicki 1983).

Subdivisions of DH are usually made on the basis of deviations from the average IQ of 100, with mildly handicapped being 2 standard deviations, or an IQ between 69 and 55 on the Wechsler Intelligence Scale for Children; moderately handicapped being three standard deviations (IQ between 54 and 40); severely handicapped being four standard deviations (IQ between 39 and 25); and profoundly handicapped being five or more standard deviations (IQ below 25). For educational purposes a division into slow learners (IQ 75 to 85), educable (IQ 55 to 74), trainable (IQ 25 to 54), and custodial (IQ below 25) is frequently applied. While these subdivisions appear to have some merit for classification and general practical purposes, it is not always recognized that considerable variability in many cognitive skills exists within these subpopulations. Arguments against the use of the IQ measure as the sole indicator of an individual's capabilities have been raised for some time. Current definitions of DH include social adjustment as a second criterion for DH: "significantly subaverage general intellectual functioning existing concurrently with deficits in adaptive behavior, and manifested during the developmental period" (H. J. Grossman 1977). However, since adequate measures of adaptive behavior are relatively new and usually rely on reports from persons well familiar with the daily behavior of the individual, most professionals still rely on IQ measures as the sole criterion.

Both theorists of intelligence and developers of intelligence tests have been relatively unconcerned about neuropsychological issues, and neuropathological considerations have had little influence on their thinking. For example, Wechsler (1958) states, "It is probable that factors of the mind are to some extent physiologically and anatomically determined, but this is not a necessary condition for their acceptance."

24.3 ETIOLOGY

Investigations into the etiology of DH show that the full range of disorders described in Part III of this volume can be involved. In addition, mental development may be impaired as a result of sociocultural and psychological influences so that the cognitive status of an individual represents a mixture of influences in all these spheres. Moreover, the psychometric properties of any IQ measure follow a normal Gaussian distribution so that a certain proportion of DH may result from genetic variability of the trait. Dingman and Tarjan (1960) plotted the expected frequencies at the low end of the distribution against incidence statistics; the comparison yielded an apparent excess at the low end of the distribution (Fig. 24-1). A similar kind of excess was, incidentally, reported independently by Yule et al. (1974) for the distribution of measures of reading (i.e., an excess at the dyslexic end). While such comparisons of incidence and expected distribution statistics may be somewhat speculative and fraught with problems of sampling and the questionable validity of IQ measures in the low range, Dingman and Tarjan's explanation that the excess represents an additional distribution curve of pathological DH underlying the normal variability makes intuitive sense.

FIGURE 24-1   Frequency distribution of IQs assuming a total population of 210 million (Dingman and Tarjan 1960).

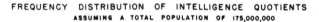

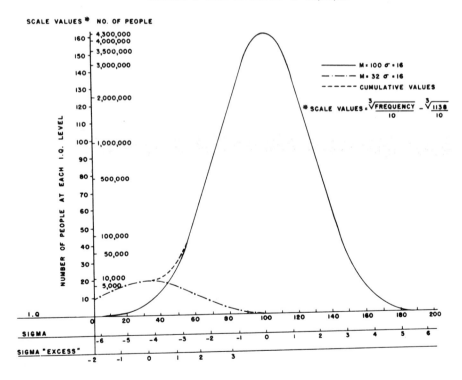

Such an explanation is also supported by the fact that profoundly intellectually handicapped persons almost invariably show evidence of severe neurological damage. Dingman and Tarjan's graph suggests, in fact, not only that pathological cognitive deficit shows its highest prevalence at the low end of the distribution but that it ranges well into the normal IQ area.

That neuropathology may be involved in a large number of children with DH has been confirmed in a number of studies. Salam and Adams (1975) reviewed advances in research on the pathology of DH with a traditional breakdown into areas of disorders of the germinal, embryonal, fetal, late uterine, parturitional, and postnatal periods. Neurological examinations show that, among moderately and severely handicapped children, only about 2.5 per cent (Malamud 1964b) are free of neurological findings, i.e., of structural malformations and other indications of CNS pathology. Autopsy findings of severely DH patients show a high incidence of malformations and other CNS pathology. Dekaban (1967) found that only 12.5 per cent of his series of autopsies were free of structured abnormalities. Davison (1977) reports that microcephaly is common in DH persons and that the cholinergic synaptic density may be low. Leisti and Iivanainen (1978) call attention to hypothalamic dysfunction in 12 of 15 DH subjects.

Moreover, as shown in Table 24-2, the incidence of devastating motor, sensory, and physical handicaps in profoundly handicapped children is extremely high, as is the incidence rate of abnormal EEGs and active seizures (Cleland 1979). With lesser degrees of DH the number of neuropathological findings diminishes, and among the mildly DH up to 70 per cent have been described as suffering from a psychosocial disadvantage (previously also called cultural-familial retardation), suggesting that in these cases DH exists as the result of poor environmental conditions and genetic endowment. It is also recognized that DH may follow psychiatric disorders, sensory depreviation, and sensory defect. Nevertheless, neuropathology has been found in a fair proportion of even mildly handicapped, and so the current discussion need not remain restricted to the severe and profound range of DH. Callaway (1973) has mustered an impressive summary of studies demonstrating the relationship between averaged evoked potentials and measures of intelligence. Other electrophysiological correlates are discussed by Karrer (1976).

The distinction between organic and psychosocial DH takes up much space in the DH literature and repeats to some extent the arguments for and against the notion of minimal brain dysfunction discussed in Chap. 18. Kohen-Raz (1977) lists retardation of more than four months in gross motor function and an increasing discrepancy between actual and expected mental level during the first 15 months of life as indicators of organic cognitive impairment. Such differences in developmental milestones, however, remain only superficial demarcations in the field, which was artificially created by the umbrella concept of DH itself. From the point of view of our current discussion, it would be more meaningful to follow the cognitive handicap of

TABLE 24-2 Observed Frequencies of Disability

| Combinations of conditions | Number and per cent of cases | | | | | | Est. cases in 100 M gen'l. pop. |
| | Age birth-21 | | Age 22 + | | All cases | | |
	n	%[a]	n	%	n	%	
Specific combinations of conditions							
Autism (AUT) only	348	0.024	36	0.001	384	0.009	9
Cerebral palsy (CP) only	602	0.048	383	0.013	985	0.023	24
Epilepsy (EP) only	307	0.021	384	0.013	691	0.016	17
Mental retardation (MR) only	8574	0.590	21 305	0.731	29 879	0.684	720
AUT, CP	5	0.001	0	0.000	5	0.000	0
AUT, EP	16	0.001	5	0.000	21	0.000	1
AUT, MR	532	0.037	174	0.006	706	0.016	17
CP, EP	83	0.006	55	0.002	138	0.003	3
CP, MR	1085	0.075	1531	0.053	2616	0.060	63
EP, MR	1897	0.128	4609	0.158	6506	0.149	157
AUT, CP, EP	0	0.000	0	0.000	0	0.000	0
AUT, CP, MR	13	0.001	5	0.000	18	0.000	0
AUT, EP, MR	81	0.006	35	0.001	116	0.003	3
CP, EP, MR	979	0.067	630	0.022	1609	0.037	39
AUT, CP, EP, MR	10	0.001	8	0.000	18	0.000	0
All cases	14 532		29 160		43 692		1053
Total instances of each condition							
Cases with AUT	1005	0.069	263	0.009	1268	0.029	31
Cases with CP	3400	0.233	2612	0.090	6012	0.138	145
Cases with EP	3373	0.232	5726	0.196	9099	0.208	219
Cases with MR	13 171	0.906	28 297	0.969	41 484	0.949	1000
Total conditions	20 949		36 898		57 863		1395
Conditions/case	1.44		1.29		1.32		

Source: Jacobson and Janicki 1983. [a]Column per cent of cases for specific combination reflects joint probability for occurrence within the survey population.

individual groups of children with specific disorders. However, because of the traditional subdivision, a brief discussion of some general findings for DH children is presented.

24.4 COGNITIVE CHARACTERISTICS OF THE ORGANICALLY IMPAIRED DH CHILD

Numerous attempts have been made to characterize the brain-damaged child as being distinct from children whose cognitive development is unimpaired or whose impairment is ascribed to sociocultural factors. Basic to such research are assumptions referring to disturbed or altered brain function that would produce a reduced or in some specified fashion altered cognitive performance. One major earlier theory of this type, the Strauss syndrome, proposed by a group of researchers coming from a Gestalt psychology orientation, has already been discussed. Another major theorist, Birch, proposed a less general notion of a child's cognitive change with brain damage, distinguishing between subtractive dysfunctions, i.e., simple loss or deficiency in one or more cognitive areas, and additive dysfunctions, which are accompanied by seizures, spasticity, perseveration, or perceptual distortion. Such behavioral changes were perceived as the result of active, ongoing distortions of the CNS processes (Birch and Diller 1959). A series of studies attempted to pinpoint the behavioral difficulties, proposing that the integration of input from more than one source was specifically impaired (Birch and Belmont 1965, Cravioto et al. 1967).

Another difference between brain-damaged and nonorganically handicapped children was the prolongation of critical inhibition after a response (Birch et al. 1965). A somewhat similar emphasis on the importance of the "stimulus trace" can be found in the earlier work of Ellis (1963). The stimulus trace, in Hebb's terms, is a brief reverberatory electrophysiological circuit in the brain that is triggered by a stimulus and ordinarily decays quickly but is responsible for the laying down of memory. Ellis proposed that such a trace would be both shorter in duration and lower in intensity in the DH child, a condition that would result in deficits in learning and retention. Birch's and Ellis's concepts are to some extent compatible: while Birch's prolonged inhibition was aimed at an explanation of perseverative behavior, poor cross-modal association, and sluggishness in thinking, Ellis's theory attempts to account for failures of short-term memory. Weak and short traces do not necessarily exclude the notion of prolonged inhibition after stimulation has taken place.

Research into both theories has not provided sufficient confirmation for the continued usefulness of either. In fact, cross-modal integration impairment has only rarely been found to be specifically impaired in brain-damaged children if their ability to do unimodal tasks is taken into account. As with most generalizations, the DH brain-damaged child is not a diagnostic entity but may, as Birch's notion of subtractive and additive deficits suggests, show a considerable variability from one individual to another.

More sophisticated studies have applied factor analysis to the investigation of differences between DH and normal children and between organically impaired DH children and those without indications of brain damage. Such studies usually extend the well-investigated notion of the developmental differentiation of **factor structure** as originally formulated by H. E. Garrett (1946): "abstract or symbol intelligence changes its organization as age increases, from a fairly unified and general ability to a more loosely organized group of abilities or factors."

The differentiation hypothesis has been investigated and at least partially confirmed mainly in the 6- to 18-year age range, although no agreement appears to exist about the exact nature of these changes (Reinert 1970). Differences in level of intelligence have been postulated to produce a delay in differentiation (Lienert 1961, Reinert et al. 1966) or, more likely, a different, not a more simplified, factor structure in DH persons (Baumeister and Bartlett 1962, I. B. Belmont et al. 1967, Ellis 1963, Lienert and Faber 1963). Such differences in structure have been described as the occurrence of additional factors, variously labeled as "speed" (Das et al. 1979) or "trace" (Ellis 1963), with loadings on such tests as arithmetic, digit span, coding, and block design of the Wechsler tests, lending at least partial support to the postulated stimulus trace or prolonged inhibition theories of changes in cognition.

Hebb's theory suggests that children depend much more on type (a) intelligence but adults can rely more on type (b)—stored knowledge and experience—for daily living. Finally, Wewetzer (1958) and Lienert (1961) proposed a **"genetic divergency hypothesis"** (Reinert et al. 1965) suggesting changes in intelligence structure for groups of subjects with the same age and increasing intelligence level analogous to subjects with increasing age. The change consists not only in the appearance of additional factors but also in the degree of intercorrelations: low-IQ subjects show higher correlations, more loadings on a general factor, higher commonalities, and higher intercorrelations between centroid factors. It should be remembered, however, that all these studies used the commonly available tests and hence are restricted in generalizations to the range of cognitive abilities sampled by such tests.

Considerations about the lateralization of cerebral lesions in at least some portion of organic DH children led to the speculation that either the verbal or the visuospatial abilities should be relatively more impaired. Hence a **verbal IQ–performance IQ "split"** on the WISC has been postulated for organically impaired DH children. The evidence for such a split in group studies has, however, remained unsatisfactory and contradictory (Filskov and Leli 1981). At least one study found no difference between 46 carefully matched pairs of brain-damaged and cultural-familial DH persons in measures of level and dispersion for the WISC tests (Spreen and Anderson 1966).

Halstead (1947) attempted to move away from the traditional intelligence concept by using the term **"biological intelligence"** for the basic coping and adaptive abilities of the organism; the concept was based on his studies of patients suffering primarily from frontal brain lesions. Halstead included measurements of time estimation, tapping, flicker frequency, and other tests that were not typically included in traditional intelligence testing. His theory of intelligence exerted little influence on the thinking of his contemporaries or on our current thinking. However, most of his tests became widely used because of the neurodiagnostic work of his student Reitan.

Several studies with the Halstead-Reitan battery of tests have been published to describe the difference between brain-damaged and normal children. Consistent with Halstead's and Hebb's theories, vocabulary was found to be the most sensitive test in separating brain-damaged children from matched normal controls (Boll 1974, H. B. Reed et al. 1965, Reitan 1974). The groups also differed in tests of concept formation, recognition of rhythms, and block design but not on tests of finger tapping, tactile form recognition, and similar perceptual and motor tasks. Boll (1972) concluded that brain-damaged children are conceptually rather than perceptually impaired, but this conclusion would appear to be a generalization of limited value since the differences on which it was based were relatively small and the variability in the brain-damaged group quite high. Denckla et al. (1980) reported a strong association between degree of neurological impairment and spatial orientation skills in 6- to 12-year-old children tested with route-drawing and route-walking tasks. A study by Meyer-Probst (1974) showed less effective strategies, decreased ability to verbalize, reduced learning advances, and poorer transfer of practice in concept-formation tasks for 60 children with mild cerebral lesions and normal intelligence. However, the study failed to show qualitative differences in the actual solutions or in the process of concept formation between subjects and controls. As Kinsbourne (1976) points out, "Children at a given mental age are really quite similar in the way they think, excluding only those at the lowest extreme of intelligence" (p. 563).

Wewetzer (1975) attempted to go beyond the broad genetic divergency hypothesis by investigating the factor structure of 132 brain-damaged and 186 control subjects matched for IQ. His results suggest an almost identical seven-factor solution for the two groups in the WISC and a variety of additional tests similar to those used by Strauss and by Reitan. While this study fails to confirm a divergency hypothesis (probably as a result of the restricted range of IQ, excluding the low range because of matching requirements), Wewetzer raised the question of whether the lack of homogeneity may also be the result of including subjects with widely differing etiology. He then proceeded to compare three types of brain-damaged children (postnatal traumatic cortical; postnatal cortical; and diffuse infection, perinatal diffuse hypoxia) and two types of controls (neurotics and normals) with 15 subjects in each group. A 17-variable discriminant function analysis produced 70 per cent correct classifications (Fig. 24-2). The F value was significant between all groups except between the traumatic and the hypoxic and between the traumatic and neurotic groups. The best discriminating variables were spatial motor performance (Bender Gestalt test) and figure-ground recognition, suggesting that perceptual components or disorders of depth and space perception were most crucial. Developmentally, however, it is possible that this deficit found in children of elementary and high school age may be preceded by a motor deficit at a younger age that affects perceptual functions later on.

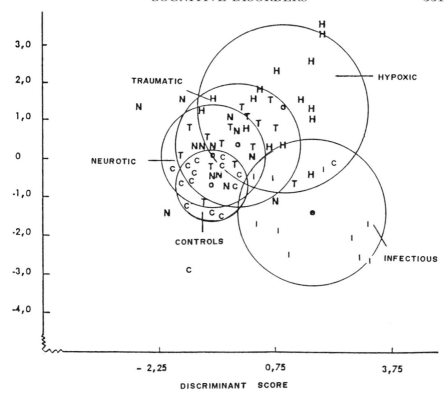

FIGURE 24-2   Graphic representation of a discriminant function analysis with 17 variables (Wewetzer 1975).

Sohns (1980) found what appears to be a more simplified factor structure in DH schoolchildren with seizures. In his study a three-factor solution for a series of tests was found, as opposed to a four-factor solution for a comparison group of generally DH subjects without seizures. His test battery included many visuoperceptual tests as well as nonverbal cognitive tests. Whether they had clinical seizures or not, children with indications of seizure activity in the EEG fared significantly worse on cognitive testing than children without EEG signs.

Das et al. (1979) also failed to find differences in factor structure between normal and learning-disabled and between normal and DH children; all three groups showed a simultaneous and a successive processing factor as well as a speed factor. In a recent study, Snart et al. (1982) attempted a breakdown into groups with different etiologies and again did not demonstrate differences in factor structure comparing brain-damaged children, Downs syndrome children, and children with uncertain etiology who were moderately impaired and not institutionalized.

In summary, investigations into the cognitive characteristics of the child with DH tend to find some support for a divergency of the factor structure of intelligence, although several studies failed to confirm this theory. The nature of the divergency has been postulated to lie primarily in a lack of fluid or biological intelligence, more specifically in deficits of complex information processing and of strategies for learning and retrieval. For brain-damaged children, perceptual and concept formation deficits, as well as a larger scatter between verbal and performance tasks, appear to be preeminent. Only one study has successfully differentiated the cognitive structure of children with differing etiologies. Further studies of this question would appear to represent a potentially useful and meaningful approach to the study of cognition in brain-damaged children.

24.5 THE DEVELOPMENT OF COGNITIVE FUNCTIONS IN DH CHILDREN

The hierarchical development of behavioral and intellectual functions (i.e., moving from concrete to abstract thinking) during infancy and childhood is to a large degree biologically determined. Little evidence has been found to indicate that this development can be accelerated unless the individual has the biological endowment to perform at that level (NINCDS 1979). However, the progression of the individual is dependent on many factors, and detailed studies of specific forms of impairment and specific environmental conditions are needed to explore these factors. At this time, few truly longitudinal studies of the long-term cognitive development of DH children are available. During infancy and early childhood, a tendency toward a decrease of cognitive ability has been noted, followed by a stabilization during puberty. A follow-up from age 2 to 7 showed more diversification after four years, with 25 per cent of the children retaining the same level of functioning, 30 per cent showing improvement, and almost 50 per cent showing decreased intellectual levels (Roesler 1971). A later study of 222 mildly handicapped children with early brain damage being followed from age 10 to 20 showed a reduction by ten IQ points in 11, an improvement by ten IQ points in 45, and no change in 15 (Roesler et al. 1976). Goodman and Cameron (1978) report a relatively high IQ constancy for the Bayley and the Stanford-Binet scales for DH children between the age of 2 and 7. Only the initial test score was related to etiology (neurological perinatal, chromosomal, metabolic problems, congenital anomalies, environmental neglect), but the "developmental rate, once determined, remains fairly constant" (Goodman 1977a, p. 209). Hence the author concluded that etiology has no bearing on the course of development. Goodman and Cameron note that the greatest amount of fluctuation can be found in the high-IQ (51–80) range. This fluctuation is similar to that of normal children and suggests a considerably higher growth potential for this range of DH. In general, the family environment is crucial in contributing to such changes and often determines whether the individual will be able to live independently as an adult or not. Institutional care has often been shown to have a detrimental effect, except for those DH persons who come from a very poor parental environment. Similarly, children of well-to-do parents who attend private school have shown better cognitive development (Helper 1980).

The Seattle study (Barnard and Douglas 1974) explored predictors of later cognitive development in DH children in a long-term follow-up project. Individual clinical factors obtained before the age of 2 were generally unsuccessful as predictors. However, a combination of various perinatal variables, including weeks of gestation, age of mother at birth, normal labor, diseases of pregnancy, infections during the second and third trimesters, age at first breath, age at first cry, birth weight, five-minute Apgar score, and highest level of bilirubin measured, allowed a modest predictive accuracy when used in a multivariate formula. In addition, maternal IQ and education, nutritional status of mother, and numerous environmental factors observed throughout childhood allowed a modest improvement of the predictive formula. This study and the Collaborative Perinatal Study on the same topic suggest that single specific predictor variables cannot be related to cognitive development with any degree of confidence. One study from the perinatal project, however, attempted to relate neurological findings at 8 months and at 8 years of age with cognitive development (Gold 1979). Children who were neurologically abnormal at the age of 8 months but normal at age 8 years tended to have specific difficulties with verbal cognitive tasks, whereas children who were neurologically normal at 8 months but neurologically deviant at age 8 years tended to show a global pattern of depressed cognitive competence.

Life-span developmental studies suggest that cognitive growth continues into the early 20s and, for higher IQ-level DH persons, even into the late 30s (Fisher and Zeaman 1970). In fact H. J. Butcher (1968) maintained that mental growth continues in DH subjects for a longer period than in normal individuals if continued training is provided. However, different limitations may apply to subjects with different etiologies. On the other hand, early decline has also been reported, at least in an institutionalized population. Growth curves (Fig. 24-3) suggest that a trend of higher initial growth and more pronounced decline is particularly evident at the mild and moderate levels of DH (Fisher and Zeaman 1970, Silverstein 1979), although Goodman (1977b) warned that this early decline may be an artifact of cross-sectional studies of institutionalized populations; those leaving the institution at any age tend to be the brightest. In a semi-longitudinal approach, the presumed decline changes to "regular increments, particularly in performance scores" (p. 203).

Several authors have speculated about the importance of the finding that DH populations tend to have a relatively high proportion of left-handers

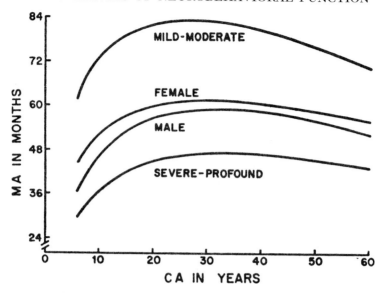

FIGURE 24-3   Fitted semi-longitudinal growth curves of intelligence for four groups of institutionalized mentally retarded subjects (Silverstein 1979).

(Gesell and Ames 1947, Touwen 1972). Hartlage and Lucas (1973) reported that right-handers in a population of minimal brain dysfunction children tend to fare prognostically better than mixed or left-handed subjects; their study relied on a retrospective follow-up of nearly 2000 grade 3 children. The authors noted that strongly left-handed children also tended to fare better than children with mixed handedness. The finding supports the notion of **"pathological handedness"** introduced by Satz (1977), which suggests that a relatively higher proportion of mixed handedness and left-handedness can be expected as a result of "switching" brain lateralization because of early insult to the brain. Since the genetic predisposition suggests right-handedness in the vast majority of the population, pathological left-handedness would be the result of brain damage in a child who is genetically right-handed. The hypothesis tends to be confirmed by studies of lateralization in DH persons.

24.6 COGNITIVE DEVELOPMENT OF THE DOWN'S SYNDROME CHILD

The cognitive development of the **Down's syndrome** (DS) child will be used as an example of one relatively homogenous group of children that has been studied perhaps more than any other group. The syndrome represents a lack of physical as well as psychological differentiation, a "pre-Gestalt" development (Wunderlich 1970). Gibson (1978) provided a complete review of the numerous studies about the psychological development of the DS child.

Several theories about the cerebral deficit of DS children have been proposed. Frith and Frith (1974) followed earlier studies by Benda (1960) and by Crome et al. (1966)—who found reduced weight of brain, brainstem, pons, medulla, and cerebellum in DS children—and developed the hypothesis of a cerebellar deficit in Down's syndrome. They suggested that such a deficit would explain problems of hypotonia of the muscles, motor coordination, and motor sequencing as well as problems of expressive language and articulation (Dodd 1976). Although the articulatory problems are well established (Smith 1975), studies of the cerebellar deficit hypothesis for language have so far produced contradictory results (Seyfort 1977). The finding by O'Connor and Hermelin (1962) that DS children show a specific retardation in tactile recognition does not directly support a theory of specific deficit in cerebellar functions, although partial support was provided by Seyfort and Spreen (1979), who showed that DS children did more poorly on a two-plate tapping task than an IQ-matched group of non-DS subjects.

Another hypothesis about the cerebral deficit in Down's syndrome, already mentioned in Chap. 9, suggests that there is delayed myelination, primarily in the development of the association cortex, i.e., in the frontal and superior temporal areas (Owens et al. 1971, Salam and Adams 1975). A shortened anterioposterior diameter of the brain, exposed insula, irregular sulci, and a narrow temporal gyrus have been described. This fits in with Hebb's (1949) notion that the greater the ratio of "associative" tissue to sensorimotor tissue in the brain, the greater the potential for cognitive complexity in the individual. Hebb noted that the first 24 months of life are the crucial time for the growth of associative tissue. This period coincides with Piaget's "sensorimotor" period, which in his view provides the experiential foundation for the establishment of more complex cognitive activity (see also the notion of growth spurts discussed in Chap. 2). The notion of an impairment of growth of associative tissue in Down's syndrome is also supported by behavioral studies (C. C. Cunningham 1979) and provides an attractive model for explaining the cognitive deficit of these children. From a psychometric point of view, Gibson (1978) concluded:

> The most favored psychometric abilities picture depicts Down's syndrome children as relatively high-scoring on tests loaded for rote memory, psychomotor, visual-motor, and nonconceptual components. Difficulty is experienced for MA-equated test material having significant abstract, symbolic, verbal, and recognition vocabulary content. The profile might be reliable for Down's syndrome but is not necessarily distinctive among the mental retardations. (p. 184)

The conclusion was further supported by a recent study of 377 DS subjects of a wide age range (4 to 56 years) by Silverstein and collaborators (1982). The authors found that five items of the Stanford-Binet Intelligence

Scale were typically performed better by DS subjects; all five required figural content and visual-motor abilities. On the other hand, DS children tended to be poorer on five items involving semantic content, social intelligence, general comprehension, judgment, and reasoning. Snart et al. (1982) also reported a deficit in an auditory sequential factor, including high-level auditory as well as verbal abilities. C. C. Cunningham and Mittler (1981) tested these conclusions in their study of 46 DS children with the Bayley scale of mental development; their findings suggest two relatively independent blocks of variables, which they interpret as representing "reaching and manipulation" (Piaget's primary circular reactions) and "relating objects, imitation, causality" (Piaget's coordination of secondary circular reactions). The authors concluded that the notion of an impairment of basic stages of development leading to deficits in the associative cognitive activity of the DS child must be tempered with caution because both factors appear to have been represented in their sample, at least at the age of testing (102 weeks).

Developmental delay in the DS child is usually noticed early; reaching of developmental milestones, such as sitting, standing, and walking, tends to be generally delayed. Most DS children do not exceed an IQ of 70, and the average is 40. However, cognitive development tends to correlate to some degree with intellectual status of the parents if the child remains at home during the first two years of life (Fig. 24-4) (F. C. Fraser and Sadovnik 1976). The highest levels of intelligence are reported for girls with mosaicism, although even this finding has not remained without contradiction. Whether the level of cognitive development is related to the number of physical abnormalities (**stigmata**) commonly found in Down's syndrome remains an unsettled question in spite of several investigations. Zeaman and House (1962) followed the cognitive development of DS children in a semilongitudinal study and noted that the IQ tends to drop by a few points each year until puberty (Fig. 24-5). Because of the relative constancy of this drop, they suggested that intelligence in Down's syndrome patients can be described by the formula

$$IQ = IQ/\log \text{ (age in years)}$$

Fisher and Zeaman (1970) extended this finding to DH generally. The shortest growth periods of intelligence were found for the severe and profound levels of DH.

This finding was confirmed in a study by Cunningham and Mittler (1981), who reported that their group of DS children started with a nearly average Bayley scale IQ that dropped rapidly during the first two years of life. Saxon and Witriol (1976) pinpointed the onset of developmental delay at the age of 4 to 6 months, "where most infants shift from subcortical to cortical control of behavior" (p. 45). It should be remembered that studies of intellectual development in DS children are based on groups of survivors since mortality is high and tends to affect selectively the most seriously impaired

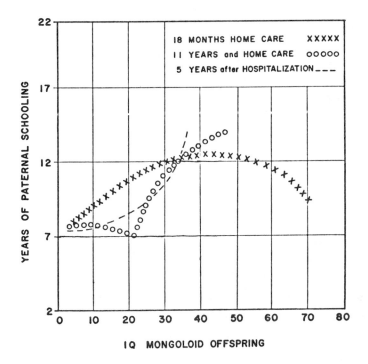

FIGURE 24-4 Distribution of Down's syndrome IQ and paternal academic achievement ($n = 141$) (Gibson 1967).

children. While improved medical care may have changed mortality rates to some degree, Warner (1935) reported that, by the age of 12.5 years, half of her sample had died, mostly because of heart disease frequently associated with Down's syndrome. The selective mortality should, in theory, favor an improving intellectual outcome. These considerations underline even more the decline of intelligence described above. J. A. Connolly (1978), however, warned that the decrease in cognitive abilities may in part reflect the effect of lack of extended educational opportunities and assumed deficit inferred from chromosomal and physical characteristics, which could be compensated for with the introduction of special school programs.

Schroth (1975) noted that DS children tend to show different levels of performance depending on what the task demands: in mechanical learning and primary retention tasks of the level 1 type according to Jensen's theory these children do fairly well, but on level 2 tasks requiring cognitive manipulations and insight they do worse than suggested by their overall IQ. This finding contrasts with the results in a group of DH children with similar degree of intelligence but without organic deficit, where no such difference was found. Such comparisons cannot be made, however, with groups

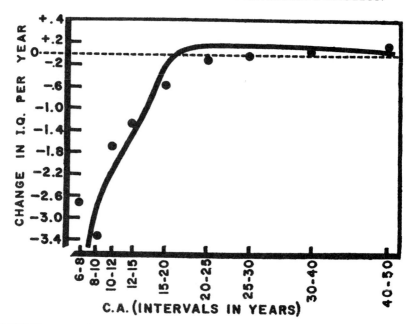

FIGURE 24-5   Change in IQ at different levels of chronological age in Down's syndrome. Note that most of the plotted points have negative values, indicating a decrease in IQ (Zeaman and House 1962).

of severely DH children since tasks for measurement of intelligence at that level are primarily of the level 1 type. Finally, DS children have been described as being exceptionally good at imitation and as having a good sense of rhythm and music, but little evidence has been found to support such notions (J. M. Belmont 1971).

The theory of early decline of cognitive abilities has been specifically claimed for Down's syndrome. Indirect confirmation for the theory has been provided by autopsy studies of older DS persons. Solitaire and Lamarche (1966) reported an early occurrence of deterioration of the type found in Alzheimer's disease; such deterioration was not present in the brains of other DH children of similar age. O'Hara (1972) also found in older DS patients plaques (cores of hollow fibers surrounded by deteriorating cell processes) and neurofibrillary tangles similar to those of Alzheimer's disease.

25

Learning Disabilities

Like all children, those with a history of neurological problems must face the challenge of school. For some, school entry may need to be delayed beyond the normal period because of hospitalization or remedial needs; for others, schooling may be limited to special education classes or special schools. What constitutes school readiness in children has been a long-standing topic of concern among educators and child psychologists. Kohen-Raz (1977), in his discussion of the psychobiological influences upon **school readiness,** has outlined three specific aspects: (1) intellectual maturity sufficient to handle the first-grade curriculum, (2) emotional emancipation from parents, leading to increased openness to interact with agents outside the family, and (3) control over affect and impulsiveness to the extent that the frustrations and demands of school can be dealt with. The child is considered prepared for school if these three conditions are met between the age of 5 to 7 years.

Upon entry into school a considerable proportion of children experience learning problems. For some, these problems arise because of sensory handicaps, such as extremely poor hearing or vision. A second group, described as developmentally handicapped, fails to acquire academic skills because of a general inability to learn. Other children develop problems due to deficient or improper instruction or poor or insufficient teaching. A fourth group is made up of those who, despite educational opportunity, are poorly motivated. Yet another group includes those who experienced brain damage in the pre- and perinatal periods and show learning problems. A final group includes children who are unable to make adequate progress despite intact senses, normal intelligence, proper instruction, and normal motivation. This last group has been designated as having **specific learning disabilities:**

> **"Learning disabilities"** is a generic term that refers to a heterogeneous group of disorders manifested by significant difficulties in the acquisition and use of

listening, speaking, reading, writing, reasoning, or mathematical abilities. These disorders are intrinsic to the individual and presumed to be due to central nervous system dysfunction (National Joint Committee for Learning Disabilities 1981).

Learning-disabled children constitute a considerable proportion (between 7 and 15 per cent) of the general school population (Gaddes 1976). Because of this high prevalence and because of interest in the presumed underlying mechanisms, this group of children has attracted considerable attention in the educational and neuropsychological literature (Knights and Bakker 1976). A distinction is usually made between specific disability in reading (dyslexia) and in arithmetic (dyscalculia), although considerable overlap between the two exists. This chapter retains the traditional division into dyslexia and dyscalculia and focuses mainly on patterns of deficit related to neuropsychological evidence and theory. The final sections discuss the school problems of the neurologically handicapped child in general.

25.1 DYSLEXIA

The term "**dyslexia**" has been applied to children who fail to acquire adequate reading skills, and the term "alexia" is used only for the impairment of already established reading skills after brain damage in adults. In 1968, the World Federation of Neurology defined developmental dyslexia as "a disorder manifested in difficulties in learning to read despite conventional instruction, adequate intelligence, and socio-economic cultural opportunity. It is dependent upon fundamental cognitive disabilities which are frequently of constitutional origin" (Critchley and Critchley 1978). This definition emphasizes the cognitive quality of the disorder and suggests that it results from essentially unknown factors rather than from any physical or structural defect of the brain. Dissatisfaction with the failure of this definition to include other forms of reading disability led to further subdivisions. **Primary, or specific, dyslexia** refers to a reading disability of constitutional origin and stresses possible subtle defects in cortical functions as described by Mattis (1978):

> Dyslexia is a diagnosis of atypical reading development as compared to other children of similar age, intelligence, instructional program, and sociocultural opportunity which, without intervention, is expected to persist and due to well-defined defect in any one of several specific higher cortical functions. (p. 54)

In contrast, **symptomatic dyslexia** describes reading disabilities resulting from early cerebral damage, such as perinatal brain damage or brain disease. **Secondary dyslexia** refers to reading disability resulting from environmental, emotional, and health factors (Quadfasel and Goodglass 1968). The total incidence of all forms of dyslexia combined has been estimated to be as high as 20 per cent in the United States.

Theoretical Background and Models

In one of the first descriptions of specific reading problems, Hinshelwood (1895) hypothesized that "visual word blindness," the inability to recognize words, resulted from damage to the visual memory center for words situated in the left angular gyrus. Morgan (1896) discussed the connection between acquired word blindness and problems of reading acquisition in children and suggested that a congenital form of word blindness could exist in otherwise intelligent children. The early concepts of reading disability were therefore based on case histories of acquired reading difficulties in brain-damaged adults. Several forms of alexia have been identified and reclassified by Benson and Geschwind (1969) (Table 25-1). The five major types of acquired reading disabilities are based on the disconnection hypothesis discussed in Chap. 7.

A third explanation of dyslexia was developed by H. Werner and Strauss (1940), who studied the differences between mentally retarded children with and without brain damage. They proposed that children who demonstrated the behavioral patterns of brain damage did have brain damage whether or not it was detectable by neurological techniques. Their proposed concept of minimal brain damage had the effect of grouping together children who showed different behaviors, such as dyslexia or hyperactivity.

Orton's theory (1925) suggested that dyslexia resulted from incomplete or mixed cerebral dominance. He proposed that it was not a deficiency in the center for visual images that caused reading problems but a lag in the development of the left hemisphere, dominant for language abilities. Because of this developmental lag, mirror images stored in the nondominant hemisphere were not suppressed and hence interfered with visual perception.

Current models of the relationship between the role of the brain and developmental dyslexia focus around the notion that brain maturation may be either defective or delayed in these children. The deficit model proposes that cerebral dysfunction underlies the inability to acquire appropriate reading skills. The maturational lag or delay model adopts a developmental outlook and proposes that cerebral maturation is delayed in dyslexic children.

Cognitive and Other Correlates of Dyslexia

The concept of dyslexia as a viable construct has been the focus of considerable debate (Benton 1975, Rutter 1969, Yule and Rutter 1976). Opinions have varied from the view that it constitutes a unique, unitary condition or that there are a number of reading disabilities each with its own specific set of characteristics and etiology to the view that reading disability is only part of a general pattern of learning disability.

Much of the early research focused on dyslexia as a single, presumably unitary disorder. In that research, a point along the series of events in-

TABLE 25-1 Summary of the Characteristics of Five Different Types of Reading Problems That Can Result from Brain Injuries to Adults with Previously Acquired Reading Skills

Type	Reading-related skills	Other language abilities	Nonlanguage abilities	Neurological dysfunction

Alexia without agraphia or aphasia (rare)	Impaired
	  Reading words and text
	Unimpaired
	  Reading letters
	  Writing
	  Letter naming
	  Oral spelling
	  Recognizing spelled words
		Sometimes impaired
		  Color naming
		  Calculation (no other language disorders)
			Unimpaired color matching and other abilities	Left medial occipital lobe *and* splenium of corpus callosum almost always from thrombosis involving the posterior cerebral artery

Alexia with agraphia and mild Wernicke's (fluent) aphasia	Impaired
	  Reading letters, words, and text (paralexia)
	  Letter naming
	  Writing
	  Oral spelling
	  Recognizing spelled words
		Mild impairment
		  Naming
		  Paraphasic substitutions
		  Calculation
			Sometimes impaired
			  Right-left orientation
			  Finger localization
			  Constructional skills
				Left angular gyrus from infarction, trauma, neoplasm, or arteriovenous malformation

Wernicke's (fluent) aphasia with alexia and agraphia	Impaired (secondary to aphasia)
	  Reading letters, words, and text
	  Writing
		Severe impairment
		  Comprehension and repetition of spoken language
		  Naming
		  Paraphasic substitutions
		Less impaired
		  Fluent (but paraphasic speech)
			Unimpaired	Left posterior superior temporal lobe from infarct or neoplasm

Broca's (nonfluent) aphasia with alexia and agraphia	Impaired
	  Letter reading
	  Letter naming
	  Writing
	  Oral spelling
	  Recognizing spelled words
	Less Impaired
	  Reading words and text
		Severe impairment
		  Nonfluent speech
		
		Less impaired
		  Listening comprehension
		  Naming
			Impaired
			  Eye movements
				Broca's area of frontal lobe from neoplasms and from infarctions involving anterior branch of middle cerebral artery

Visual agnosia (controversial)	Impaired
	  Reading letters, words, and text
	  Writing
		Unimpaired	Impaired
			  Visual perception and production of complex forms
				Right parietal lobe (?)

Source: Doehring et al. 1981.

volved in the extraction of meaning from print was selected and the performance of disabled readers was compared with that of a matched control group to discover a presumably unitary cause of reading disability (Doehring 1968b). In general, evidence from single-syndrome research suggested that at least some deficiencies in reading discrimination, phonological coding, or morphophonemic processing can be found; these deficits may be associated with abnormal, possibly genetically transmitted, left hemisphere functioning. The notion that reading disability in general is caused by deficiencies in visual attention, perception, or memory has been abandoned (Doehring et al. 1981).

Deficiencies in auditory processing that could interfere with the recoding from written to spoken language have been described as a primary deficit underlying reading disability (Doehring et al. 1981, Tallal 1980, F. R. Vellutino 1982, R. L. Vellutino 1979). Deficiencies in phonological processing have also been implicated. Liberman and Shankweiler (1979) suggested that some children are unable to extract phonemes from spoken words, a step that they argue is essential in learning to read. These children may also have problems in abstracting the phonological segments corresponding to printed letters (Doehring et al. 1981). Deficiencies in morphophonemic processing at the level of spoken language occur in some reading-disabled children; these children lack the skill to combine phonemes in order to form units of meaning (morphemes) (Vogel 1977). This deficit has been described as a lack of metalinguistic awareness.

Factor analytic research based on a model derived from Luria's (1966) theory and developed by Das et al. (1979) explored the cognitive structure of poor and average readers. Leong (1980, Downing and Leong 1982) demonstrated that, while poor readers were impaired on both the simultaneous and the successive processing factor, the difference was most pronounced in the successive factor. This factor represents a combination of tasks with a major component requiring sequential processing that has also been ascribed to left hemisphere cognitive abilities.

Current research favors Shankweiler's (1964) notion of a number of reading disability subtypes. Because different types of acquired reading disabilities have been found in adults, it seemed reasonable to assume that there could be more than one type of reading disability in children. Reading is also a complex act involving a number of component skills; it requires visual-perceptual skills involving discrimination of (1) closure, for example, between "o" and "c," (2) lines to curve transformation, for example, between "u" and "v," and (3) rotational transformation, for example, between "b," "d," "p," and "g." If these skills are defective, reading-disabled children may show difficulties with the discrimination and/or the orientation of letters. Sequencing skills are also needed, especially at the letter and semantic levels, to recognize the differences in, for example, "pan and nap," "cat chases mouse," and "mouse chases cat." Difficulties in serial thinking can be reflected in poor spelling and poor comprehension. The cross-modal transfer of information as an essential part of the reading process has been stressed by Benson (1981) and others. For example, writing to dictation demands that auditory input be translated into visual symbols. Reading is also a linguistic skill that requires the understanding of visual symbols used to convey meaning.

The many components of reading skills and the many different forms of dyslexia make it unlikely that a single focal lesion is responsible for all reading disabilities. Orton's (1937) cerebral dominance hypothesis has also found little support. In particular, Zangwill (1962) suggested that poorly developed cerebral dominance should result in a more general learning disorder, one that would include only a small subgroup of dyslexics. Among the deficits in nonreading skills that might cause reading disability, Birch (1962) suggested that inadequate maturation of perceptual systems could lead to reading problems. Disturbances in the development of visual perception as a primary cause of dyslexia was proposed by de Hirsch (1957), whereas D. J. Johnson and Myklebust (1967) distinguished between difficulties in visualizing and auditorizing. Doehring (1968b) found a group of reading-disabled children to be deficient on 31 nonreading measures.

Current theories of brain function, cognition, and language emphasize the complexity of these processes and stress their interactional, multifactorial role in reading (Downing and Leong 1982), which leads to a multiple-syndrome paradigm. Such a paradigm includes several different patterns of deficits in disabled readers.

Boder (1973) distinguished three types of reading disability based on the clinical-educational analysis of spelling and reading errors: a **dysphonetic reader,** which describes a child who shows little understanding of letter-sound relationships; a **dyseidetic type,** which describes an inability to read words as a whole; and a dysphonetic-dyseidetic (or alexic) type with problems in both areas. She found that of the 107 dyslexic children in her study, 63 per cent were dysphonetic, 9 per cent were dyseidetic, 22 per cent were alexic, and 6 per cent were of an undetermined type.

Denckla's (1979) types, also based on clinical reports, include a global mixed language disorder, an articulation-graphomotor type, an anomia-repetition disorder, a dysphonemic sequencing disorder, a verbal learning and memory disorder, and a correlational type in which reading was normal but low relative to IQ. The relationship between language, reading, and spelling is also stressed by Kirk (1982).

Myklebust (1978), again based on clinical studies, described an intermodal reading disability divided into auditory-intermodal and visual-intermodal dyslexia, as well as into inner-language dyslexia, auditory dyslexia, and visual-verbal agnosia. Pirozzolo (1979), on the other hand, describes only two types, an auditory-linguistic and a visual-spatial disorder.

A different approach to the study of subtypes is based on the multivariate analysis of a group of disabled readers. Mattis et al. (1975) identified three dyslexia syndromes in a multivariate grouping analysis: a language-disordered group, an articulation-graphomotor dyscoordination group, and a group with visual perceptual disorders. A cross-validation study with 400 children between the ages of 8 and 10 years confirmed this classification (Mattis 1978).

Doehring and Hoshko (1977) used the Q technique of factor analysis and combined the measurement of multiple nonreading skills with several reading skills. The design involved the analysis of the interaction of linguistic and neuropsychological deficits with reading skill deficits (Doehring et al. 1981). A battery of neuropsychological tests was administered to examine the extent to which neuropsychological deficit characterized each type of disability. Three types of reading disability were found: type O, slow oral word reading; type A, slow auditory-visual association of letters; and type S, slow auditory-visual association of words and syllables. Doehring's groups are strikingly similar to those found by Mattis, suggesting an emerging consensus of results from multivariate studies. Dysfunction in different cortical areas may be underlying each of these types.

A relatively rare from of reading disorder that does not fit into the usually observed groups should be mentioned: the *hyperlexic* child, who tends to outperform normal readers in word recognition (Silberberg and Silberberg 1972) in spite of general cognitive impairment. The performance of such children has been related to "visual information processing by the right hemisphere" (Cobrinik 1982), possibly as a result of left parietal lobe damage. The reading of such children seems to focus on the visual configuration rather than the phonetic and semantic content, comparable more to echolalia than meaningful reading. It frequently occurs in the presence of autism (Mehegan and Dreifuss 1972).

The Genetic Hypothesis

The notion that some forms of reading disability may be genetic has been raised since 1905 (C. J. Thomas 1905). The evidence includes family history or prevalence, the presence of reading disability in monozygotic and dizygotic twins, and the likelihood that a genetically determined reading disability will persist through a lifetime (Goldberg and Schiffman 1972, Hallgren 1950, Jorm 1979, Owen 1978, Sladen 1951).

The genetic basis of handedness has also been associated with dyslexia. Vernon (1971) claimed that left- or mixed handedness occurs more frequently in clinical cases of dyslexia. More recently, however, Yule and Rutter (1976) and Hardyck and Petrinovich (1977) have not found any association between handedness and dyslexia.

The argument for genetic involvement in dyslexia would be strengthened if the pattern of reading disability were found to be consistent within families. Following this line of reasoning, Omenn and Weber (1978) reported cases of similar dysphonetic spelling errors in some families. Finucci et al. (1976) found that 45 per cent of 75 first-degree relatives of dyslexics were affected, with significantly more males than females. While Finucci concluded that dyslexia is "genetically heterogeneous," Owen (1978) suggested that certain types of reading disability may be transmitted through multifactorial inheritance. In this case, a number of genes may contribute to the disability. The type and severity of the disability would be a function of genetic predisposition, environmental experiences, and the effectiveness of treatment. Hence, the mechanism of transmission would be quite similar to that suggested for cognitive disabilities, discussed in Chap. 24.

Dyslexia and Cerebral Asymmetry

Orton's (1937) theory that reading disability may be linked to atypical brain asymmetry has been investigated with dichotic-listening and visual half-field techniques in normal and impaired readers. It was expected that less lateralization of language in the left hemisphere would be reflected in a smaller right-ear or right visual half-field advantage. Dyslexics may also show abnormal lateral preference in the form of ambilaterality and left-handedness, crossed eye and crossed ear dominance (Bryden 1970), extreme right- or left-handedness, and discrepancies between lateral preference and performance (Kornmann et al. 1974). However, no consistent differences between good and poor readers have been found (Porac and Coren 1981, Satz 1976, Witelson 1976). Most recently, Wellman and Allen (1983) reported a higher incidence of inverted hand position during writing and drawing for 7- to 9-year-old poor readers, although their lateralization on dichotic listening and visual field experiments with verbal and visuospatial material did not differ significantly from that of good readers.

Bakker (1980) recorded visually evoked potentials from the right and left parietal areas of children with reading problems. His results suggested two types of dyslexic readers: L-type dyslexics are characterized by speech mediated by the left hemisphere but show a weak right hemisphere specialization for visual perception; L-type dyslexics read quickly, overlook the perceptual features of the script, and make substitution errors. P-type dyslexics show an overdevelopment of right hemisphere functions, as shown in visuospatial tasks, and a depression of the left hemisphere mediated linguistic capabilities; P-type dyslexics are sensitive to the perceptual features of script, read slowly, and make presuming errors.

Some anatomical evidence for a relationship between brain asymmetry and reading disability is reported by Hier et al. (1978). Computer-assisted brain scans were obtained for 24 developmentally dyslexic patients between the ages of 14 and 47 years. The width of the brain at the intersection of the parietal and occipital lobes on the right was wider than on the left in 42 percent (i.e., a reversal from the commonly found greater width of the left hemisphere), and 33 per cent of the subjects showed virtually no asymmetry. Heir et al. estimated that individuals with reversed brain asymmetry are at risk for reading disability five times greater than persons with normal asymmetry. The authors suggested that reversed cerebral asymmetry results in language lateralization to a hemisphere that is structurally less suited to support language. However, since brain lateralization is only one aspect of the neurological substrate for reading, it is likely that reversal of asymmetry interacts with other factors to produce reading disability.

The case history of acquired reading disability in a 6-year-old boy who underwent left temporal lobectomy revealed that, despite the lesion, speech remained strongly lateralized to the left hemisphere (D. Levine et al. 1981). The authors noted that some patients with developmental dyslexia may have dysfunction of the dominant left hemisphere rather than a reversal, delay, or incompleteness of language lateralization.

The disproportionately higher incidence of reading problems among boys has been known for some time (Ansara et al. 1981, Buffery 1976, Rourke 1978, Singer et al. 1968). Lansdell (1964) and Critchley and Critchley (1978) proposed that myelination rates for boys are generally delayed and that myelination is more rapid in the left hemisphere in girls and in the right hemisphere in boys. This has been supported in studies by Witelson (1977b) and by McGlone (1977). Differences in lateralization may be related to sex-linked recessive gene transmission (Aaron 1982). A study by Bakker et al. (1976) related ear advantage on a dichotic listening task to a word-naming test. The findings suggested that girls pass through the learning-to-read stages earlier than boys.

Neurodevelopmental Deficit Versus Delay Models of Dyslexia

Two contrasting models for the explanation of dyslexia on the basis of neurological development have been proposed. The deficit model considers dyslexia as the result of cerebral deficit, which may take the form of faulty hemispheric organization or of abnormal development of neural cells and connections. Benton (1974) noted that in order for brain damage to produce lasting and serious deficits it must be extensive. It follows then that the brain abnormality necessary to produce dyslexia cannot be thought of as minimal. J. T. Dalby (1979) noted that, given the magnitude of the population described as dyslexic, very few studies have reported neurological abnormalities in developmental dyslexics.

The neurodevelopmental delay model has found several different explanations. Some authors still accept Orton's theory that dyslexia is due to a delay in the establishment of cerebral dominance. Current research has shown, however, that, anatomically (Yeni-Komshian and Benson 1976), electroencephalographically (Gardiner and Walter 1977), and behaviorally (Caplan and Kinsbourne 1976), the beginnings of hemispheric specialization are present at or near birth.

Satz et al. (1974, 1978) stated that the delay underlying dyslexia occurs in the early sensory perceptual and later conceptual development and is caused by disorders of central processing. Satz's theory predicts that delays in those developmental skills that are in primary ascendance during the preschool period forecast problems in reading. However, neither reading nor the early perceptual-motor and oral language abilities are unitary abilities. Reading success depends on the interplay of a host of strengths and weaknesses related to the child's experiential and cultural background (Jansky 1978).

A neurodevelopmental delay model seems to imply that the child may eventually be able to develop these skills at a later age. Recent proponents of the delay model have modified this line of reasoning and asserted that further difficulties may persist during adolescence and later life because the learning history of the dyslexic child is affected (Denckla 1977). In fact, the adult outcome of reading disability, as far as it has been studied, appears to be quite poor not only for reading but also for general academic achievement as well as for personal, social, and occupational adjustment (Spreen 1982). Persistent dyslexia has also been observed in college students (Aaron 1982).

The issue of deficit or delay is akin to the nature-nurture controversy in that both factors exert considerable influence. A maturational lag could result in a neurological organization that remains deviant; a deficit, or brain damage, in children, which is rarely static, may result in delay. Also, children with brain damage may recover, but their catching up could be based on reorganized abilities of a different structure, not as an indication of a maturational lag. Current neuropsychological models of dyslexia are probably not sophisticated enough to accommodate the many different factors involved and to relate them to specific forms of dyslexia. In the case of acquired dyslexia, the reading disability is related to specific damage, most often in the left parietal-occipital area. In developmental dyslexia, the most important primary damaging event currently reported is anoxia, which often results in diffuse damage and which could manifest itself as a delay in the early stages of development (J. T. Dalby 1979).

25.2 WRITING AND ARITHMETIC DISORDERS

In addition to difficulty in learning to read, children may also have difficulty in producing written language or in performing mathematical tasks. Since writing and, to a certain extent, mathematics are dependent on the reception and comprehension of spoken and written language, many children with reading disorders will also experience difficulty with these other tasks. However, most dyslexia research does not report whether the children exhibited other learning problems. Some researchers have noted that only a small minority of children exhibit relatively specific learning problems. Recent studies (McAllister 1981, Tuokko 1982) showed that, in both clinic and school samples, as few as 7 per cent of learning-disabled children exhibited difficulty in learning to read when their learning of other subject material was adequate, and that only 5 per cent experienced difficulty with writing or arithmetic without difficulty in learning to read. Yet it has been suggested that the various patterns of learning problems represent different disorders that may be distinguishable on the basis of qualitative characteristics, associated cognitive weaknesses, and, perhaps, etiology (H. E. Nelson and Warrington 1976).

Writing Disorders

Writing as a means of self-expression is a highly integrative function involving language as well as perceptual and motor processes. Writing disorders have been described as primarily related to disturbance of the language system, of the visual and/or auditory perceptual system, or of the motor system necessary for structuring and forming letters.

A useful distinction has been made between writing and handwriting (Chalfant and Scheffelin 1969). Writing refers to the commitment of one's thoughts to a written idea; it involves the ideational (or propositional) use of language as well as the auditory and visual systems. Disturbances of any of these systems may interfere with the writing process. Handwriting, in contrast, refers to the motor aspects of writing. The term "**dysgraphia**" is often used to denote a disorder in handwriting: a child may have difficulty tracing shapes, using efficient strokes for forming letters, forming letters of appropriate size, or using a comfortable pressure in grasping (De Quiros and Schrager 1978). Some children may be able to produce well-formed letters but are extremely slow. Others may have difficulty in beginning to write or in completing a word.

A deficit in the skill to use fine motor movements of the hands and fingers has been suggested as the basis for dysgraphic disturbances (Orton 1937); this deficit may or may not extend to the learning of other new manual activity. K. Goldstein (1948) suggested that difficulty in remembering motor sequences for writing or the way in which letter shapes should be constructed may be involved.

Arithmetic Disorders

Arithmetic is the branch of mathematics that involves real numbers and their computations (Chalfant and Scheffelin 1969). The term "**dyscalculia**" is used to denote difficulties performing arithmetic operations, e.g., reading or writing of numbers or series of numbers, recognizing the categorical structure of numbers. Kosc (1974) considered developmental dyscalculia to be a complex disorder defined as "a structural disorder of mathematical abilities which has its origins in a genetic or congenital disorder of those parts of the brain that are the direct anatomico-physiological substrates of the maturation of the mathematical abilities adequate to age, without simultaneous disorder of general mental functions" (p. 47).

Developmental dyscalculia is differentiated from dyscalculia acquired after brain lesions and from acalculia (a complete failure of mathematical ability). Acquired calculation disturbances are most frequently related to posterior left hemisphere lesions (Grafman et al. 1982). Developmental dyscalculia has been further classified or characterized (Kosc 1974) as:

1. Verbal dyscalculia—disturbed ability to verbally designate mathematical terms and relations
2. Practognostic dyscalculia—disturbance of mathematical manipulations with real or pictured objects
3. Lexical dyscalculia—disability in reading mathematical symbols
4. Graphic dyscalculia—disturbance of the manipulation of mathematical symbols in writing
5. Ideognostic dyscalculia—disability in understanding mathematical ideas and relations and in doing mental computations
6. Operational dyscalculia—inability to carry out mathematical operations

These forms may occur in isolation or in combinations and are usually found with reading and/or writing disorders.

Other authors have classified the most salient features of errors made in calculation (e.g., spatial-temporal difficulties, including number reversals, number order reversals, and carrying out operations in the wrong sequence; mnestic failures, including difficulties remembering addition, subtraction, and multiplication tables). DeQuiros and Schrager (1978) suggested that, although dyscalculias may occur in isolation, they usually appear as symptoms of other clinical entities.

25.3 NEUROPSYCHOLOGICAL SIGNIFICANCE OF PATTERNS OF DEFICIT

Although developmental disorders of reading, writing, and arithmetic in children do not necessarily appear in the same form as acquired disorders in adults, the knowledge gained from the study of calculation disorders in brain-damaged adults has led to speculation about the possible organic bases of developmental problems. For example, in adults, dysgraphia and dyscalculia occurring in conjunction with right-left confusion and finger agnosia constitute the **Gerstmann syndrome,** which frequently has been associated with damage to the parietal lobe of the dominant hemisphere. The term **"developmental Gerstmann syndrome"** has been applied to denote the occurrence of several or all of these four behavioral deficits in children. Kinsbourne and Warrington (1963) described seven children with finger agnosia who, in every instance, exhibited two or more of the other elements of the Gerstmann syndrome. Both difficulty with spelling (five of the seven) and handwriting (four) were noted. Number concepts were not impaired, but difficulty with place value concepts was noted. The authors speculated that the underlying defect of the developmental Gerstmann syndrome is an inability to correctly order serial parts of a whole. Five of the seven children had sustained perinatal injury, but the neurological abnormalities found on examination appeared to reflect scattered disease rather than specific structural abnormality. Benson and Geschwind (1970) presented two "pure" cases of children who showed the full tetrad of the Gerstmann syndrome and preserved reading ability.

Spellacy and Peter (1978) examined two groups of seven dyscalculic children differing in reading ability (adequate versus impaired readers). None of the children showed deficits limited to the four elements of the developmental Gerstmann syndrome. Five children did show impairment on all four elements of the syndrome in addition to other deficits that were found among adequate and poor readers. The authors suggested that "since the presence or absence of the four Gerstmann behavioral elements does not describe a behaviorally homogeneous group, the value of the developmental Gerstmann syndrome as a behavioral description seems limited" (p. 202). No neurological examination was available for the children in this study. However, on the basis of the behavioral abnormalities exhibited by these children, bilateral involvement was proposed. Whether or not dominant parietal abnormality is indicated when all four elements of the syndrome are present in children remains an open question.

In an investigation of the neuropsychological significance of different patterns of reading, spelling, and arithmetic ability, H. E. Nelson and Warrington (1976) compared the types of spelling errors made by children with spelling as well as reading difficulty with those of children with spelling difficulty only. Children with spelling impairment only made significantly fewer phonetic errors than the reading- and spelling-impaired group; the spelling of the former was phonetically accurate, but they selected the wrong graphemes. Rourke (1978a) and Rourke and Finlayson (1978) examined qualitative and quantitative differences between two groups of 15 children matched for deficient arithmetic performance but differing with respect to achievement in reading and spelling. The group of children characterized by adequate word recognition and spelling but poor arithmetic ability exhibited defective visual perception and tactile perception and impaired psychomotor ability (Rourke and Finlayson 1978, Rourke and Strang 1978). Their arithmetic errors revealed that they attempted calculations in which they had little understanding of the task requirements (Rourke and Strang 1981). They also tended to misread mathematical signs and showed disorganized work and faulty alignment of rows and columns; occasionally entire steps in the calculation were omitted. The authors suggested that early impairment of sensory-motor experience may have lead to poor development of abstract conceptualization, which affected the basic understanding of mathematical operations. Children with poor word recognition and spelling skills but better arithmetic performance exhibited poor psycholinguistic abilities, but their visual perception, tactile perception, and sensorimotor coordination were well developed. These children avoided unfamiliar arithmetic operations. Errors usually reflected some difficulty in remembering arithmetic tables or steps in the procedure for solving a problem. Verbal memory impairment was raised as a possible underlying cognitive weakness affecting the arithmetic performance. Summarizing his findings, Rourke (1982) suggested that,

> the reading and spelling disability group exhibits performance that would be expected were they to be suffering from deficiencies in left hemisphere systems, whereas the arithmetic disability group exhibits performances that would be expected were they to be experiencing the untoward consequences of deficiencies in systems thought to be subserved by the right cerebral hemisphere. (p. 10)

25.4 SCHOOL PROBLEMS AND NEUROLOGICAL STRESS FACTORS AND IMPAIRMENT

Gordon et al. (1972) studied the learning styles used on two basic educational tasks by children attending metropolitan schools. The neurologically impaired children ($n = 85$) were either children with myelomeningocele and accompanying hydrocephalus or children with cerebral palsy. A group of 124 middle-class children and a group of 75 lower-class children of the same age but without neurological impairment were also examined. Although a statistical analysis and important sample attributes (such as IQ levels) were not reported, clear-cut quantitative and qualitative differences between the neurologically intact and the neurologically handicapped groups were evident. Teachers had to remain available for the brain-damaged children in order to obtain optimal performance. Even their optimal performance, however, was below that of control groups. The neurologically intact groups usually requested specific aid from the teacher on specific parts of the test, the middle-class group more directly than the lower-class group. For the brain-damaged children, the teacher's assistance was required to maintain attention, restructure the task, reduce frustration, and prevent illogical mistakes. The neurologically intact children, over the short term, benefited from occasional teacher assistance; fewer errors were made even if the teacher was not assisting. The brain-damaged group did not show independent gains in performance but usually returned to their initial haphazard, trial-and-error approach to the tasks.

Of 150 children who had suffered infantile seizures (West's syndrome), only 16 per cent were found to be educable in a normal school setting at follow-up 2 to 12 years after the onset of seizures (Jeavons and Harding 1975); of these, 10 per cent were educable in schools for the "educationally subnormal" and 18 per cent were attending basic skill training centers. The remaining 56 per cent either had died or were considered uneducable. None of the children for whom the seizures were directly attributable to perinatal causes were in regular school, 9 per cent were in schools for the education-ally subnormal, and 11 per cent were at training centers. Children with normal development and mentality before the onset of seizures fared better in school: 37 per cent were in a regular school and 36 per cent were ed-ucable at special schools and training centers.

In a comparison of children with a history of neurological deficit and their neurologically intact classmates in normal schools, Drillien (1961) found that the vast majority of very-low-birth-weight children performed more poorly. Children of very low birth weight, whether premature or not, were often up to six months behind children born at full term and of normal weight on all sections of the Wide Range Achievement Test: spelling, arithmetic, and single-word reading (Rubin et al. 1973). The low-birth-weight students also performed more poorly than their classmates on the Metropolition School Readiness Examination and repeated grades more often than the control subjects. The premature group performed slightly below the controls on these measures but better than low-birth-weight children.

Corah et al. (1965) compared teacher ratings of seven year olds with a history of early-life anoxia with ratings of children without history of neu-rological problems. Of the neurologically intact group, 34.2 per cent had above-average achievement, 43.6 per cent were average, and 22.2 per cent were below average. In the anoxic group, 31.9 per cent were above aver-age, 41.5 per cent were average, and 26.6 per cent were below average.

Holdsworth and Whitmore (1974) examined the school progress of 85 epileptic children and adolescents in rural British communities. For half of the sample the seizures started within the first five years of life, and 80 children were still on medication at the time of the study. Thirteen chil-dren had frequent seizure activity (defined as at least one seizure a month). Average to superior school progress was reported for 31.2 per cent, 53.1 per cent were "holding their own" at or below average levels, and 15.6 per cent were seriously falling behind their peers. Rates of failure were greater than among nonepileptic pupils. Six children were poor in all subjects, while most others showed relatively specific areas of weakness: reading (ten), writing (five), speech (four), spelling (two), memory (two), incoordination (ten). Of the 21 children who were doing well academically, five were very good in all subjects, three only in arts, six in oral work, two in mathematics and science, one in French, and four in physical education.

EEG abnormalities in learning-disabled children tend to be more fre-quent than in age-matched control groups of normal learners but tend to be nonspecific with respect to both the type of learning disability and the locus of EEG abnormality. The most recent studies involved as many as 32 parameters of the EEG analyzed with complex equations (John 1977). With these techniques, 48 per cent of a neurological "at risk" group, 46 per cent of a learning-disabled group, and 47 per cent of a group with specific learn-ing disability demonstrated EEG dysfunction in most recording areas (except the central areas bilaterally and the right frontal area), but only 4 and 2 per cent of two control groups showed such abnormalities (Ahn et al. 1980).

Single case reports dealing with the school performance and long-term outcome of children with early-life neurological problems may be informative. A. Thomas and Chess (1975) reported on Bert, a child who was born four weeks prematurely, weighed 2100 grams at birth, had difficulty breathing, and suffered anoxia during the first three days of his life. No other neurological complications occurred in infancy and childhood. Bert's motor functioning during the first six years of life was slow, clumsy, and uncoordinated. Language comprehension was good, but expression was very poor, particularly during the first four years. Intelligence was high-average at 4 and 6 years of age. He met the criteria for school readiness, and his early school progress was adequate, although he showed a persistent reversal of letters and numbers that interfered with written but not with oral arithmetic. By the age of 9, reading and arithmetic problems became even more noticeable in spite of continuing good performance in other subjects. In addition to reversals, Bert showed left-right confusion. These difficulties interfered with school performance, led to an aversion toward school, and strained interaction with his parents. Academic intervention at this time increased his basic reading and arithmetic skills; however, social and personality problems had become more prominent at the final follow-up.

These studies, selected from a larger body of group findings and case reports, suggest that children who suffered neurological disorders at birth or in infancy often cannot benefit from a standard school curriculum; even if they do remain in the regular classroom, learning difficulties are frequent. However, the variability from child to child is high.

25.5 SPECIFIC LEARNING DISABILITIES AND NEUROLOGICAL STRESS FACTORS AND IMPAIRMENT

Few prospective studies of the relationship between pre- and perinatal events and learning disabilities explore the relation between perinatal stress and specific learning disorders. Spreen (1978b) noted that, if the distinction between primary (congenital, no overt causes) and symptomatic (due to brain damage or dysfunction) forms of dyslexia is valid, one would expect to find differing neurobehavioral variables. Rourke (1978b) went further and stated that, if brain dysfunction interferes with reading acquisition, then it is necessary to investigate the relationship between reading acquisition and birth events that pose risk to normal brain development. So far, only a single autopsy report of a 12-year-old dyslexic boy has been published (Drake 1968). This case showed "anomalies in the convolutional pattern of the parietal lobes bilaterally. The pattern was disrupted by penetrating deep gyri that appeared disconnected. Related areas of the corpus callosum appeared thin" (p. 496).

Kawi and Pasamanick (1958) provided one of the earliest studies of the relationship between birth history and reading disorders. They found that 16 per cent of infants exposed to two or more complications during birth (especially fetal anoxia) had reading problems later in life. The authors suggested that a continuum of reproductive casualty arises from stress factors at birth and may extend from fetal death to behavior and learning problems. Gesell (Goldberg and Schiffman 1972) also suggested that unrecognized minimal birth injury could express itself in speech difficulty and later in reading problems.

Investigating the effect of mothers' smoking during pregnancy, N. R. Butler and Goldstein (1973) found that children of such mothers were four months behind in reading at the age of 7 years. Dunn and McBurney (1977) found significant differences in favor of nonsmokers' children in 14 of 48 psychological tests given at the age of 6.5 years.

Premature birth and reading disability were associated in a study by Kawi and Pasamanick (1958). However, when premature children without birth complications were compared with controls, there were no differences. De Hirsch et al. (1966) also found an association between prematurity and reading readiness but failed to equate their premature and full-term groups for IQ. Taub et al. (1977) found no differences in scholastic performance between prematures and controls at the ages of 7 and 9.5 years. They noted a weakness in perceptual organization among premature children that is probably overcome in later stages when verbal skills become more important (J. T. Dalby 1979). The many inconsistencies in the literature on prematurity and reading disability can be attributed to methodological differences (Caputo and Mandell 1970).

A retrospective study of several pre-, peri-, and postnatal variables by Lyle (1970) of 54 middle-class 6- to 12-year-old reading-retarded boys matched with 54 normal readers found two factors of reading performance: "freedom from perceptual and perceptual-motor distortions" (relating to letter and sequence reversal and memory for design errors) and "formal learning" (loading mostly on academic achievement and WISC intelligence test variables, such as arithmetic, digit span, information, and coding). The first factor was significantly predicted by birth variables, including birth injury, complications in utero, birth weight, short labor, and speech development at 6 and 24 months. The second factor was best predicted by postnatal developmental criteria. Lyle noted that low birth weight and toxemia of pregnancy were not related to later reading performance.

E. S. La Benz et al. (1980) looked at a large number of early predictors of deficits in reading, writing, and spelling in the context of the Collaborative Perinatal Project. The most reliable predictors were variables measured after the first year of life but included also birth weight, gestational age, neonatal distress, and complications of pregnancy and delivery; however, these variables were not predictive by themselves. The authors concluded that deficits in written communication are the result of multiple causes and that environmental and later developmental factors, particularly speech and language delay, play a more predictive role. On the other hand, some studies (Galante et al. 1972, A. C. Smith et al. 1972) demonstrated a correlation between reading disability and such minor deficits as unusual birth history, abnormal EEG, and soft neurological signs.

Balow et al. (1976) reviewed the relationship between perinatal events and reading disability and discussed problems of methodology, such as different outcomes studied and varying research designs. They concluded that the hypothesis that very low birth weight and certain pregnancy and birth complications (particularly anoxia) are related to impaired reading ability is adequately supported. However, the majority of studies of hypoxic children show more general learning deficits rather than dyslexia alone (Gottfried 1973, Sechzer et al. 1973). While neurological dysfunction in the newborn may play a role in dyslexia, the occurrence of such complications is neither a necessary nor a sufficient explanation for reading disability (Rourke 1978b). A retrospective study by Austin (1978) examined children between 6 and 16 years of age with dyslexia ($n = 48$) or dyscalculia ($n = 67$) who had an average IQ, no history of seizure disorders, cerebral palsy, hearing or visual loss and did not suffer from severe emotional disorder or environmental or cultural deprivation. Perinatal complications were found to be more frequent and more serious for children with dyscalculia (62 per cent) than for children with dyslexia (43 per cent) or for children without learning difficulty (7 per cent). Delays in the attainment of many developmental milestones were evident for children with dyscalculia, whereas dyslexic children were delayed only in the onset of speaking. Neurological soft signs and abnormal EEGs were also more frequent in the dyscalculic group than in the dyslexic group or the group with no learning disorders.

26

Emotional Disorders

This chapter discusses the major psychiatric disorders associated with developmental neurological deficit, the incidence and type of disorders found in children with existing developmental disorders, and the relationship between specific neurodevelopmental events and emotional and behavioral disorders. A final section addresses the relationship between impairment of language, hearing, and vision and associated psychopathology.

Childhood psychopathology may be divided into psychotic disorders, emotional disorders, and behavior disorders. **Psychotic disorders** are characterized by severe impairment of reality orientation, as found, for example, in infantile autism, schizophrenia, and the organic psychoses. **Emotional disorders** are those that are neither predominantly conduct nor psychotic disorders and include anxiety states, depression, phobic states, obsessive-compulsive disorders, hysteria, and conversion reaction (often referred to as neurotic disorders). *Behavior disorders* (also called **conduct disorders**) include aggressiveness, acting out, impulsiveness, overactivity, and antisocial behavior. The use of any of these terms implies psychopathology of sufficient severity to disrupt the day-to-day functioning of the child or of those around the child.

Psychopathology in children tends to be less differentiated than in adults. It is unusual in children to find a single specific disorder, such as severe obsession or depression, in isolation; more often they occur as part of a cluster of symptoms. Factor analytic studies show two basic factors in most psychiatric disturbances: the emotional disturbance factor, in which anxiety, depression, and somatic complaints predominate, and a conduct disorder factor, with attendant disobedience, disruptiveness, destructiveness, aggressiveness, and delinquency (Kolvin et al. 1971, S. Wolff 1971).

Children with neurological deficit show a raised incidence of psychiatric disorder of all types. Children suffering from the major psychotic disorders have a considerably higher rate of familial incidence, neurological impairment, and early childhood trauma than those with minor behavioral or emotional problems.

26.1 PSYCHIATRIC DISORDERS AND THEIR ASSOCIATION WITH NEURODEVELOPMENTAL DISORDERS

Infantile Autism

SYMPTOMS   **Infantile autism,** first recognized and described by Kanner (1943), begins before the age of 30 months. L. Eisenberg and Kanner (1956) identified two major signs that differentiate infantile autism from other disorders: (1) autism itself in the form of self-isolation and (2) "obsessive insistence on the preservation of sameness." Rutter (1978) identified three universal characteristics: failure to develop social relationships, language retardation, and compulsive or ritualistic behavior. Prevalence has been established at 4 in 10 000 children (Folstein and Rutter 1977).

The infant or child fails to develop social relations with other individuals, including the parents. The infant does not show affection for its parents, does not respond to attention or contact, and does not anticipate being picked up. Affection toward the parents often develops after a few years, but the child usually does not make friends with peers and shows a characteristic insensitivity and indifference when dealing with others.

A characteristic pattern of language disorder distinguishes infantile autism from developmental aphasia. Autistic children who do not develop language do not gesture to communicate and do not seem to understand gesture, in contrast to children with developmental aphasia, who frequently use and understand gesture. **Echolalia,** the repetition and mimicking of sounds or words, is common in autistic children but not in children with developmental aphasia. Another characteristic is the persistant reversal of the pronouns "I" and "you." Speech is monotonous and lacks expression. Impaired comprehension and poor formation of verbal concepts are common. Bartak et al. (1975) consider the severity of the language disorder as critical and "probably necessary for the development of autism" (p. 142).

Compulsive behaviors may include head-banging or rocking. Stereotyped movements are typical, and acute anxiety develops if movements are hindered; overactivity is common, changing to underactivity in adolescence. Attention span is short. When autistic children are dealing with other individuals, lack of eye contact is evident. In infancy, feeding difficulties are frequent; the older child is often preoccupied with one particular food. This need for sameness is also reflected in other behavior and ritualistic routines and in temper tantrums or acute anxiety if an attempt is made to change a routine, toy, food, or location.

Of all autistic children, 75 per cent are intellectually retarded, although visuospatial functions are usually normal (DeMyer 1974, Lotter 1967, Rutter and Lockyer 1967). One third of retarded autistic children develop epileptic seizures. Follow-ups during adolescence and adulthood show continuing problems in a large number of cases, although the type of psychopathology may change (Schopler and Mesibov 1981).

ETIOLOGY: GENETIC FACTORS The incidence rate in siblings of autistic children is 50 times higher than in the general population. However, incidence rates do not provide conclusive evidence of heritability because patterns of child rearing may be sufficient to account for the higher rate of occurrence in siblings. Folstein and Rutter (1977) studied 21 twin pairs, one of which showed autism. Eleven pairs were monozygotic (MZ), and ten pairs were dizygotic (DZ). Half of the autistic children were severely retarded, one quarter mildly or moderately retarded, and one quarter had normal intelligence. The male-female ratio was 3.4 to 1. When the twins of the originally selected autistic children were examined, the full syndrome of infantile autism was found in 4 of the 11 MZ pairs. Of the twins who were MZ but discordant, the nonautistic twin was in most cases cognitively impaired. None of the DZ twins showed concordance. In 6 of 17 autistic twins of the discordant pairs, evidence of brain injury at birth was found. The results suggest that a hereditary factor is not sufficient to produce autism; organic factors may play a contributory role.

A study of the twins' families revealed a history of affective disorders in four families, although schizophrenia was not found in any of the families. One nontwin sibling was also autistic. A history of speech delay in childhood was found for at least one parent in three of the families. The results were interpreted as indicative of a strong inherited predisposition for infantile autism in association with cerebral injury at birth. The lack of association with schizophrenia in the families suggests that the two syndromes are distinct, i.e., that autism is not an early form of schizophrenia.

ETIOLOGY: ORGANIC FACTORS Ornitz (1973) found more frequent perinatal complication in autistic children than in controls. He argued against a genetic etiology. In his opinion, Folstein and Rutter's (1977) concordance rate is too low to be considered significant. He observed that autistic individuals do not usually have children; hence a more likely explanation of autism would be early genetic damage caused by metabolic, traumatic, or infectious influences. Because both prenatal and postnatal influences might be etiologically related, organic rather than inherited factors are a more likely cause. Ornitz (1978) attempted to validate his hypothesis by examining 74 autistic children. He found that 23 per cent of the children had indications of major organic disorders, such as cerebral palsy, congenital rubella, and abnormal EEG. An additional 17.6 per cent also showed minor neurological disorders.

So far, no specific brain dysfunction or pathology has been associated with autism except for the general increase in observed neurological abnormalities. However, one study (Hauser et al. 1975) found an association between infantile autism and enlargement of the left temporal horn in the pneumoencephalogram. Fourteen of the 17 children in this study showed enlargement. The implication of a specific left-sided brain abnormality is consistent with the language problem of autistic children. Indirect confirmation was provided by Hoffmann and Prior (1982), who found a group of autistic children to be significantly poorer than children matched for chronological age and for mental age on left hemisphere tests, although they performed at their chronological age level on right hemisphere tests.

Chess (1971, 1977a, 1977b) examined 243 children with congenital rubella to observe the incidence of infantile autism. Ten of the children showed the complete syndrome of infantile autism, eight had partial autism, which was distinguished from the full syndrome if the child showed any recognition of another person. In a prospective study Chess reexamined the children at age 8 to 9 years. At this time, all 18 were still severely disordered, although Chess considered four to have recovered. These four children had not developed oral speech but could use sign language.

The incidence of infantile autism inferred from Chess's study for children with congenital rubella is 412 per 10 000 for the complete syndrome alone; the prevalence would be nearly twice as high if children with the partial syndrome were included. When compared with the prevalence in the general population, an association of the syndrome with congenital rubella seems evident. Chess did not address the incidence of other forms of psychopathology in the sample; one would expect a raised incidence of other types of psychopathology. Children with congenital rubella are likely to have the same predisposition for various forms of serious psychopathology as other children with organic disorders; it is unlikely that there is a *specific* relationship between autism and rubella.

PSYCHOSOCIAL FACTORS   The possibility that infantile autism is produced by the manner in which parents interact with their child has been considered from the time the syndrome was first recognized. Kanner (1949) originally hypothesized that parents of autistic children were cold, anxious, solitary, intelligent, and obsessive, although he conceded that these factors could provide only a partial explanation; the autistic quality of the child's behavior from birth on made it difficult to attribute the etiology entirely to parental influences. Goldfarb (1961) suggested that cold, rejecting, angry parents could precipitate autism in a genetically vulnerable infant. A study by Holroyd and McArthur (1976) that found that mothers of autistic children had more negative attitudes toward their children than mothers of Down's syndrome children was used to support the hypothesis.

In contrast, several studies did not find evidence of more than a slightly negative attitude of parents toward their autistic children compared with parents of normal children (M. DeMyer et al. 1972, McAdoo and DeMyer

1978, Pitfield and Oppenheim 1964, Rutter et al. 1970a). The negativity was attributed to a reaction of the parents toward a difficult, withdrawn, unresponsive, and rejecting child rather than as an unprovoked negativity that could generate autism. A study by Cox et al. (1975) found autism not related to parental personality attributes. To test the possibility that severe psychosocial stress precipitates infantile autism, Cox et al. (1975) compared 19 autistic boys with a group of boys with developmental receptive aphasia. All children had a normal nonverbal IQ and no overt neurological disorder. No significant differences were found between the two groups in the amount of stress suffered during the first two years of life, including events such as death of relatives, divorce of parents, financial status, health, and family relationships.

Children reared in conditions of extreme physical and emotional deprivation often show some of the features of autism in infancy. General development is retarded; the infant is passive, does not respond to human contact, does not maintain eye contact, smiles little, and shows repetitive behaviors, such as rocking or head banging (Spitz and Wolf 1946). However, unlike infantile autism, this condition seems to be completely reversible (McBride 1975).

PARENTAL PSYCHOPATHOLOGY   Unlike the parents of children with schizophrenia, parents of autistic children do not show a particularly high incidence of psychosis or other psychopathology. Kanner (1954) found no cases of schizophrenia among 200 parents of autistic children. Creak and Ini (1960) found schizophrenia in 2 out of 120 parents of autistic children. Lotter (1967) recorded only 1 psychotic parent among 60 autistic children. Kolvin et al. (1971) detected 1 case of schizoaffective disorder among 92 parents of autistic children but also found 6 parents with schizophrenia among 64 parents of children with late-onset schizophrenia.

Cantwell et al. (1978) concluded that the frequency of schizophrenia is not increased among parents of autistic children but that a marked increase in schizophrenia is found in parents of children whose psychosis begins in late childhood or adolescence. Controversy has existed throughout the history of the syndrome as to whether infantile autism is an early version of schizophrenia or whether it is a separate disorder. The difference in family prevalence of schizophrenia among children with autism supports the latter view.

Schizophrenia and Related Disorders

SYMPTOMS   Brief psychotic episodes may occur in childhood or adolescence in situations of extreme stress. However, the diagnosis of schizophrenia is reserved for a long-standing psychotic disorder with profound disturbances of thought, emotion, and behavior beginning after the age of 30 months (DSM III 1980).

Schizophrenia is distinguished from other psychoses principally by the type of thought disorder: speech ranges from looseness of associations in mild cases to total disorganization, referred to as "**word salad.**" Impoverished thought content with poor concept formation is evident. Delusions are common and reflect the disintegration of ego boundaries and lack of reality orientation, e.g., ideas of reference, thought intrusion, and ideas of persecution. Behavior may be bizarre with stereotyped, repetitive movements. Social inappropriateness and regression to earlier developmental stages are found. Withdrawal and other autistic tendencies are common. Affect is usually blunted, with absence of normal emotional responses to people and events; however, there may be episodes of euphoria or anger, the latter especially if the child is frustrated or provoked. Hallucinations, especially auditory, are not uncommon. The older the child, the more closely the pattern of schizophrenia resembles the adult syndrome. The prevalence rates for childhood and adult schizophrenia given in DSM III are 0.2 to 1 per cent in studies in Europe and Asia using a relatively narrow concept of schizophrenia. Higher rates (unspecified) are given for the United States. Yolles and Kramer (1969) reported a 3 per cent prevalence of schizophrenia using a broader North American definition of the disorder.

ETIOLOGY: GENETIC FACTORS   Kallman (1953) found among the total sample of patients in New York mental hospitals with schizophrenia 953 patients with a twin sibling, including 268 monozygotic twins. Assuming a prevalence of schizophrenia in the general population of 0.7 to 0.9 per cent, he found concordance rates of 14.2 per cent for ordinary siblings, 14.5 per cent for DZ twins, 86.2 per cent for MZ twins, and 91.5 per cent for MZ twins reared together. When both parents were schizophrenic, 68.1 per cent of the children were schizophrenic. Slater (1953) showed only a 76 per cent concordance rate among 41 MZ twins. Heston (1970), in a review of the evidence, pointed out that concordance rates can approach 100 per cent if the full range of the schizophrenic spectrum is included.

Kallman (1953) suggested transmission by a single recessive gene for schizophrenia. Homozygotes would develop the complete syndrome of schizophrenia, and heterozygotes with only a single recessive gene would show schizoid features but not the full syndrome. Heston (1970) proposed autosomal dominant transmission.

The heredity factor in schizophrenia thus appears to be established, although the details of genetic transmission have not been fully explored (Kety et al. 1983).

ETIOLOGY: ORGANIC FACTORS   The assumption that pathological cerebral processes account for at least some of the causes of schizophrenia does not preclude the possibility that genetic and psychosocial factors may also contribute or interact. Bender (1942) proposed that schizophrenia resulted from disordered neurological development: islands of primitive, poorly developed CNS organization occur together with areas of relatively normal development. According to this theory, areas subserving perception, body image, and certain aspects of cognition are affected, leading to acute anxiety in the child and poor adaptive ability, which in turn results in schizophrenia. The general neurological examination would be expected to show only soft neurological signs, such as hypotonia, choreiform movements, whirling movements, or persistence of the tonic neck reflex (Bender 1956). The association of schizophrenia with minimal brain dysfunction and genetic factors is also supported in a recent review by Bellak (1978).

A combined retrospective and prospective follow-up by O'Neal and Robins (1958) examined 248 children between the ages of 7 and 17 referred to a child guidance clinic because of severe behavioral or emotional problems. At that time, none of the cases were diagnosed as schizophrenic. After a follow-up period of 30 years, 10 per cent were schizophrenic and only 20 per cent were considered psychiatrically normal (called the "no-disease" group). The remaining patients had various personality, behavioral, and emotional disorders. Two groups were selected from the original sample for comparison: the no-disease and the schizophrenic group. In addition, a control group was chosen from public school records. When the histories at the time of the original examination in childhood for the schizophrenic and no-disease groups were compared, preschizophrenic children were found to have more infections in infancy, more physical handicaps, more hearing problems, more disfigurement, and, in boys, more feminine appearance. The preschizophrenic group also showed more acting-out behavior, pathological lying, difficulties in personal relationships, and overdependence on the mother. Developmentally, delay of walking and difficulties in feeding but not general developmental delay were different in the two groups (14 per cent of the schizophrenic group had been developmentally retarded compared with only 5 per cent of the no-disease group). Both groups had a high incidence of speech disorders and learning difficulties in school. Over 60 per cent of all the children were from homes having only one parent. Certain characteristics of thinking, such as paranoid ideation, bizarre ideas, ruminations, and obsessions, were found mainly among the preschizophrenic children.

O'Neal and Robins concluded that, even though all the children showed severely disturbed behavior at the time of the original referral, there were differences in the type of behavioral pathology between children who later would become schizophrenic and those who would show a more normal outcome. The early childhood histories also showed more severe infections and physical problems for the preschizophrenic group.

Similar to Bender, B. Fish (1957) hypothesized that children at risk for schizophrenia show **"pandevelopmental retardation"** in infancy: uneven and disordered development of motor function, sensation, and perception and poor integration of these functions. The predisposition for these irregular deficits was considered to be inherited. Fish proposed that schizophrenia in childhood represents a more severely disturbed group than adult-onset schizophrenia, characterized by greater incidence of neurological abnormalities. Moreover, the earlier the onset of schizophrenia, the more chronic and severe the schizophrenia in later life. Fish (1957) tested this hypothesis in a prospective study of 12 one-month-old children from a well-baby clinic in a mental hospital. The infants were examined for posture, muscle tone, reflexes, and sensory and perception processes and with the Gesell developmental testing. Three infants with indications of pandevelopmental retardation were predicted to be at risk for schizophrenia. Eight of the remaining children had minor abnormalities, such as perceptual deficits. Ten of the children were followed until age 18. By the age of 10, one of the children considered at risk was found to be schizophrenic and remained chronically schizophrenic at the age of 24. The other two children considered at risk had severe personality disorders resembling schizophrenia, characterized by disorders of thinking and identification but without sufficient psychotic features to be diagnosed as schizophrenia.

A second prospective study by B. Fish and Hagin (1973, Fish 1977) followed ten infants born in 1959 to mothers institutionalized for schizophrenia in state hospitals. Nine of the ten children showed severely uneven motor development and perceptual disabilities consistent with pandevelopmental retardation. Two children who had only minimally uneven development in infancy showed no psychiatric disorder at 10 years of age. The remaining eight children showed moderate to severe emotional or behavioral impairment at the age of 10 years. Most of the children were placed with adoptive parents or foster homes. One child spent most of her early childhood with her mother; this child became psychotic at the age of six and entered an institution. The seven remaining children showed schizoid-type personality disorders or neurotic disorders. Of particular interest was that the neurological signs of the children with psychopathology disappeared during the second year of life; only minor visual-motor deficits remained. None of the children with psychiatric disorder had a history of perinatal complications.

Fish (1977) concluded from these studies that severe to mild irregularity and retardation of physical growth, postural-motor, and visual-motor development are often followed by schizophrenia or by a schizoid-type personality disorder of corresponding severity. However, only for the more severely disordered cases could the outcome have been predicted by signs of pandevelopmental retardation.

Several studies have searched for organic correlates in groups of psychotic or purely schizophrenic children. Rutter (1965) found that one quarter of 63 psychotic children had a major neurological disorder, most often epilepsy; another quarter had "probable neurological disease." He considered that dysfunction in the language areas of the brain led to a degree of receptive aphasia; this, together with additional perceptual deficits, resulted in sensitivity to environmental stimuli and in turn to schizophrenic signs and symptoms. He admitted that this could be only a partial explanation because children with developmental aphasia do not necessarily become schizophrenic or autistic.

Other studies show similar rates of neurological abnormality in children with schizophrenia. Gittleman and Birch (1967) found neurological abnormalities in 19 per cent of 97 psychotic children including epilepsy, EEG abnormalities, choreiform movements, pathological reflexes, and myoclonic jerking. Luchins et al. (1983) noted that the percentage of persons showing reversed neuroanatomical asymmetry in the frontal and occipital areas (measured by CT scan) was significantly higher in schizophrenics than in the general population. Werry (1972) noted in a review that some studies did not control for IQ when comparing groups of psychotic children with controls. Since low intelligence is strongly associated with psychopathology, matching IQ for subjects and controls is essential in order to separate the specific relationship of organicity with psychopathology.

Manic-Depressive Psychosis

This disorder occurs rarely before puberty, although reactive depression is not uncommon even in early childhood (Achenbach 1982, Nissen 1982). J. D. Campbell (1952) reported that of 18 adolescents with manic-depressive psychosis only 3 developed the condition before puberty. The remaining 15 developed psychosis between the ages of 12 and 16 years.

No relationship with early cerebral damage or dysfunction has been observed (Fish 1977), although Nissen (1982) argues that pre-, peri-, or post-natal brain damage may be at least a participating factor in some forms of depression. However, no neurobehavioral signs predictive of later manic-depressive disorder have been found (Robbins 1966). The prevalence has been reported as 4 per 1000 (Kallman 1953), equally distributed between the sexes.

The etiology of manic-depressive psychosis appears to implicate inherited factors. Kallman (1953) proposed a dominant gene transmission with incomplete penetrance. Whether or not the disorder occurs can depend either on the presence of modifying genes or on environmental factors. Support for this hypothesis was gained by his twin study, which showed 100 per cent concordance for MZ twins, 25.5 per cent concordance for DZ twins, and 22.7 per cent for other siblings. Winokur and Tanna (1969) suggested dominant transmission linked to the sex chromosomes, but the evidence supporting these views is weak (McKusick 1975).

26.2 DEVELOPMENTAL NEUROLOGICAL DISORDERS AND THE RELATIONSHIP WITH EMOTIONAL BEHAVIOR DISORDERS

Prematurity and Low Birth Weight in Relation to Psychopathology

In several studies prematurity has been found to be associated with an increase in emotional and behavioral disorders in later childhood. However, this relationship is confounded with low socioeconomic status, illegitimacy, and poor maternal health (Chamberlain et al. 1976). In a prospective study by H. Robinson and N. Robinson (1965), the premature group appeared to have more behavior problems than would be expected in the general population, but when controls who were carefully matched for SES were chosen, the differences disappeared. The authors concluded that the social pathology associated with prematurity accounts for most of the children's psychopathology. Davie et al. (1972) studied all low-birth-weight children born during one week in 1958 in the United Kingdom and compared their social adjustment at the age of 7 with that of normal-birth-weight children. No significant differences in emotional and behavior disorders were found.

However, Drillien (1961, 1964) reported that in a prospective study infants with very low birth weight (below three pounds) showed a greatly increased incidence of behavior and emotional problems at school age. Seventy per cent of the children were described as hyperactive, restless, insecure, and having poor concentration. To a lesser extent, immaturity, anxiety, passivity, or aggressiveness were found. The majority of the children were neurologically impaired and showed sensory disability, epilepsy, or language retardation. It appears that the very-low-birth-weight child is especially vulnerable to emotional and behavioral disorder. This is consistent with the finding discussed in Chap. 11 that VLBW children are also at risk for generally retarded development and perceptual disorders.

In a prospective study 60 children were examined in utero by serial ultrasound measurement of head growth (**serial ultrasonic encephalometry**) (Parkinson et al. 1981). Forty-five small-for-date children born at a gestational age of at least 37 weeks were selected for follow-up. Birth weight was below the tenth percentile for the gestational age, adjusted for sex, birth order, mother's height, and mother's mid-pregnancy weight. Normal-weight babies were matched for age, sex, birth order, socioeconomic class, and race. No infant in either group had a history of intrauterine infection or of chromosomal or congenital anomaly at birth. The children were reexamined between 5 and 9 years of age, and teacher ratings of emotional and behavioral factors were obtained. The results showed that balance and coordination problems in childhood were more frequent if head growth slowed before the 26th week of pregnancy. Children whose head growth slowed before 34 weeks of gestation were shorter at age 4 independent of social class. The children most likely to have scholastic and behavior problems were boys whose head growth slowed before 34 weeks and after 26 weeks of gestation, particularly if they came from lower social classes. These boys were found to be clumsy, worried, fidgety, unadaptable, and unable to concentrate, while girls with the same slowness of head growth cried, bullied, and were irritable. Both sexes had more problems with reading, writing, drawing, and concentration. This carefully controlled study confirms the findings of Drillien's study.

The Relationship Between Perinatal Complications and Psychopathology

Pasamanick and Knobloch's (1960) retrospective study of psychiatrically disturbed children found a significant increase of birth complications; 40 per cent of the disturbed children also showed a hyperkinetic syndrome. However, most prospective studies have found no relationship between perinatal complications and emotional disorder. E. Werner and Smith (1977) found a relationship between perinatal complications and later behavioral and emotional status but noted that poor psychosocial status greatly increased the incidence and severity of psychopathology. No particular type of psychopathology could be singled out. S. Wolff (1970) examined retrospectively the perinatal history of 100 children with psychiatric disorders and found no differences for number or severity of perinatal complications compared with a control group matched for age, sex, and social class.

26.3 BRAIN INJURY AND PSYCHIATRIC SEQUELAE

Children who are at risk for psychiatric disorder because of disturbed family background and poor socioeconomic environment are also more likely to suffer head injuries (Harrington and Letemendia 1958, Rutter et al. 1970a). Manheimer and Mellinger (1967) suggested that these children were also more likely to be extroverted and risk-taking. D. Shaffer et al. (1975) and Rutter et al. (1975) found that children of unhappy marriages were three times as likely to have head injuries. These differences in the background of head injury must be taken into account in studies of the psychiatric sequelae of brain injury. However, most studies find a significant increase in the incidence of emotional and behavior disorder after head injury, even when these factors are controlled.

Brown et al. (1981) examined prospectively the incidence and type of psychiatric disturbance after head injury in two groups of children taken from consecutive hospital admissions after head injury. Twenty-eight children were placed in a severe group, defined by the presence of posttraumatic amnesia of one week or more following head injury. The mild head injury group included 29 children with posttraumatic amnesia of at least one hour and less than one week. A control group of 28 children hospitalized with orthopedic injuries was matched for psychosocial variables and age (range 5 to 18 years).

Psychological assessment, psychiatric rating of emotional and behavior status, and interviews and questionnaires with the parents were conducted immediately after the injury and after 4, 12, and 28 months. An estimate of preaccident adjustment and psychiatric status was made retrospectively. The severe head injury group suffered considerably more psychiatric disorder after the injury than either the mild head injury group or the orthopedic control group. One half of the severe brain injured group developed new psychiatric disorders after the injury, three times as often as did the mild injury and orthopedic control groups when nonblind raters were used. When a blind rater was used, some children were eliminated from a psychiatric diagnosis and the incidence reduced to between two and three times the incidence of the other two groups. The types of emotional and behavior disorders are shown in Tables 26-1 and 26-2. The most prominent disturbance attributable specifically to brain injury was a state of disinhibition found in five children, all in the severe head injury group; no disinhibition was found in the other two groups. In all cases, disinhibition occurred only after the head injury. The authors concluded that disinhibition

TABLE 26-1 Symptoms Specifically Attributable to Head Injury

Symptom	Attributable to head injury		P
	No ($n = 23$)[a]	Yes ($n = 18$)[a]	
Socially inapproriate behavior	8.7	55.5	0.003
Overtalkativeness	8.7	16.7	NS
Enuresis	13.0	27.8	NS
Slowness	0.0	16.7	NS
Overeating	4.3	16.7	NS
Stuttering	0.0	11.1	NS
Restlessness	47.8	11.1	0.026
Gross activity	34.8	16.7	NS
Fidgetiness	26.1	11.1	NS
Total activity assessment	43.5	16.7	NS
Relationship difficulty	69.6	38.9	NS
Tantrums	47.8	22.2	NS
Disobedience	34.8	16.7	NS
Stealing	26.1	0.0	0.045
Truanting	17.4	5.5	NS
Undereating	47.8	22.2	NS

	Mean	(S.D.)	Mean	(S.D.)	t	P
Gross activity score	1.13	(1.14)	0.67	(1.19)	1.26	NS
Restlessness score	1.52	(1.38)	0.50	(0.62)	2.91	<0.01
Fidgetiness score	0.78	(1.38)	0.33	(0.69)	1.75	NS
Total activity score	3.43	(2.81)	1.50	(2.45)	2.35	<0.05

Source: Brown et al. 1981.
[a]Values are percentage of all cases with disorders.

TABLE 26-2   Symptoms Specifically Attributable to Head
Injury

	Attributable to head injury	
	No (n = 23)[a]	Yes (n = 18)[a]
Headache	21.7	11.1
Other aches and pains	21.7	16.7
Eating problems	13.0	11.1
Sleeping problems	0.0	5.5
Fatiguibility	0.0	5.5
Encopresis	8.7	5.5
Other speech difficulty	8.7	16.7
Tics/mannerisms	8.7	16.7
Thumb-sucking	4.3	11.1
Nail-biting	34.8	27.8
Other habits	13.0	11.1
Peer relationship difficulties	4.3	12.5
Sib relationship difficulties	38.1	16.7
Mother relationship difficulties	26.1	16.7
Father relationship difficulties	21.0	13.3
Misery	34.8	27.8
Mood changes	21.7	27.8
Hypomania	4.3	0.0
Ruminations/compulsions	13.0	5.5
Specific fears	21.7	11.1
Destructiveness	13.0	16.7
Wandering from home	8.7	5.5
Impersistence	34.8	38.9
Affectional dependency rating (mean ± S.D.)	2.35 ± 2.23	2.78 ± 1.99

Source: Brown et al. 1981.
[a]Values are percentage of all cases with disorders.

was a specific sequel of severe head injury. The syndrome is characterized
by socially inappropriate behavior, social insensitivity, failure to follow social conventions, performing embarassing actions, and making inappropriate personal comments. Lack of reserve, overtalkativeness, poor hygiene, forgetfulness, and impulsiveness were also signs of this state. The
resemblance of the state to the frontal lobe syndrome in adults was noted.

Particularly associated with severe head injury was a tendency to eat to
excess, but this was found only at the two-year follow-up. Because of late
onset of overeating, the authors did not attribute this directly to the effect
of head injury. The spectrum of emotional and behavior disorders found in
the study was consistent with the incidence of psychiatric disorders in children in general. No particular diagnostic category, such as depression, was

more frequently associated with head injury. Three children showed a hyperkinetic syndrome immediately after the injury, but at the two-year follow-up, three additional children from the severe head injury group were also diagnosed as hyperkinetic. Two of them had shown a disinhibited state at the one-year follow-up. The authors concluded that only a very small number of head-injured children show hyperkinesis, which may be due to brain damage, but emphasized that if the syndrome occurs in isolation it cannot be taken as evidence that brain damage had occurred. More frequently, underactivity (rather than overactivity) was found as a particular correlate of severe brain injury.

Brown et al. (1981) explored whether any preinjury groups within the severe head injury group were especially predisposed to *new* psychiatric disorder. Children who had been given a "trivial or dubious psychiatric disorder" rating before the accident were found to be most likely to develop a new psychiatric disorder related to the injury. Children given a "no-disorder" rating before the injury were less likely to develop psychiatric disorder after the injury: over half of the children in the severe head injury group with trivial disorder before injury showed definite disorder at the one-year follow-up, and none of them received a zero rating for psychiatric disorder at that time. Of the children with a preinjury no-psychiatric-disorder rating, half received a zero psychiatric disorder rating at the one-year follow-up. Only four children in the preinjury no-psychiatric-disorder group showed a definite psychiatric disorder at one-year follow-up.

Thus increase in new psychiatric disorder is a function not only of head injury but also of preinjury personality and adjustment and the contributing factor of psychosocial adversity. The relationship between psychiatric disorder and head injury is less direct than between cognitive impairment and head injury. Mild head injury was not related to psychiatric outcome. The type of disorders found did not substantiate the brain damage syndrome of A. A. Strauss and Lehtinen (1947), characterized by hyperactivity and reduced attention span. Rather, disinhibition and reduced social sensitivity and control were most frequent. The late onset of hyperactivity in three children was interpreted as indirectly related to brain injury. Apart from these findings, a general increase in incidence of emotional or conduct disorder with approximately the same proportions as in the general child population was found.

26.4 ORGANIC BRAIN DISORDER AND PSYCHIATRIC SEQUELAE

Rutter et al. (1970a) examined psychiatric aspects of brain disorder in 3300 children. All children between the ages of 9 and 11 from the Isle of Wight were screened, using group testing and parent and teacher interviews. Mentally retarded children educated outside the school system and children who attended private schools (5.8 per cent of the total child population) were not included. Groups were selected for more intensive study, and organically impaired children of other age groups were added as follows:

A control group of 125 neurologically normal 9 to 10 year olds
A neurological disorder group, subdivided into
  Children with uncomplicated seizures
  Children with a definite structural lesion above the brainstem but without seizures
  Children with a lesion at or below the brainstem
  Children with a lesion above the brainstem and with seizures
A group of blind or deaf children
A non-neurological chronic physical disorders group (asthma, diabetes, heart disease)
A psychiatric disorder group

The children in the target groups were given neurological and psychiatric examinations and psychological testing. Interviews with the parents and the children's teachers were conducted and questionnaires regarding emotional, behavioral, and social adjustment were answered by parents and teachers.

The incidence of psychiatric disorder rose sharply with type of organic disorder. The prevalence of psychopathology for children with non-neurological physical disorders was 11.5 per cent. The general prevalence of psychiatric disorder among the school population of 10 to 11 year olds was 6.6 per cent. For children with uncomplicated epilepsy (seizures of unknown origin, or idiopathic epilepsy), the rate of psychopathology rose to 28.6 per cent. Children with lesions above the brainstem but without seizures showed 37.5 per cent psychiatric disorder. In children with a confirmed organic lesion above the brainstem with seizures, psychiatric disorder was found for 58.3 per cent (P. J. Graham 1971) (Table 26-3).

Although children with only physical handicaps may not appear to be more predisposed to diagnosable psychiatric disorder, it is a common clinical observation that they have low self-esteem and negative feelings, not only about the disability but about the attitudes of others toward them. Physical dependency on others, as well as considerable restriction of normal activities, requires emotional adjustment. Even if the child's family is thoughtful and careful in dealing with the child, it is not uncommon for others to deal with handicapped children unsensitively (Cruickshank et al. 1976b).

The finding that over half of the children with lesions above the brainstem and seizures showed psychiatric disorder indicates a particular vulnerability for psychopathology. The specific effect of a brain lesion was indicated by the finding that, in the study by Rutter et al., children with non-neurological physical disorders had an incidence of psychopathology close

TABLE 26-3   Psychiatric Disorders in Children Attending School

Diagnosis	Cases in general population (excluding neuro-epileptic children)	Cases of neuroepileptic children	
		With uncomplicated epilepsy	With lesions above brainstem with or without fits
Neurotic disorder	42	8	4
Antisocial or conduct disorder	41	6	3
Mixed disorder	26	3	4
Hyperkinetic syndrome	1	1	3
Psychosis	0	0	1
Other	1	0	1
Total cases	111	18	16
Total population in each group	2189	63	36

Source: Rutter et al. 1970a.

to average. The authors concluded that the high rate of psychiatric disorder in children with epilepsy cannot be attributed to the associated social difficulties often reported in epileptics because nonepileptic children with lesions above the brainstem showed an even higher incidence of psychopathology.

26.5 TYPE OF PSYCHOPATHOLOGY

Rutter et al. (1970a) found that the incidence of all psychiatric disorders was increased in children with neurological disorders (Table 26-3). Children with an organic lesion above the brainstem and associated seizures had the highest susceptibility to psychiatric disorder. No particular form of brain damage was found to be predisposing for a specific psychiatric diagnosis, although a trend toward hypoactivity was observed in some children. This relationship was also found by Schulman et al. (1965) and by Brown et al. (1981).

The results are also confirmed by a study (Seidel et al. 1975) that suggested that the incidence of psychiatric disorders is twice as high in children with cerebral pathology than in children with physical handicaps without cerebral involvement. The groups in Seidel et al.'s study were comparable in degree of physical handicap so that both suffered the same degree of motor and sensory deficit as well as visibility of handicap. As did Rutter, these authors concluded that the increased incidence of psychopathology was clearly a function of cerebral pathology.

Teachers' ratings of children with brain disorders revealed more restlessness and fidgetiness, poorer concentration, greater irritability, and more fighting than in the general population (Rutter et al. 1970a). However, examination of the data suggested that these behaviors were more a function of psychiatric disorder than of brain dysfunction because they were characteristic of many children with emotional and conduct disorders generally. However, children with brain pathology tended to be rated by their teachers as poorer in concentration than normal children irrespective of the presence of psychiatric disorder.

Reduced motor activity was noticed in 21 per cent of the children with brain disorder and psychopathology but only in 3 per cent of the children with psychopathology but without brain disorder.

In contrast to the overrepresentation of boys with psychiatric disorder in the general population, the incidence of psychiatric disorder for children with neurological disorder was equal for boys and girls.

26.6 LANGUAGE AND READING DISORDERS AND PSYCHOPATHOLOGY

The Isle of Wight study found that reading retardation was strongly associated with psychiatric disorder in both brain disorder and nonorganic disorder groups. The association was even more pronounced than the well-established relationship between IQ and psychiatric disorder (Rutter et al. 1970a). In another report, Rutter et al. (1970b) found that conduct disorders are more closely related to specific reading problems than are emotional disorders. One quarter of the children with specific reading retardation showed antisocial behavior. Conversely, one third of the children with conduct disorders were reading-retarded, compared with 4 per cent of the general school-age population. Clark (1970) reported similar findings. Rutter et al. (1970b) concluded from an analysis of individual behavior items and the specific forms of reading difficulties that antisocial retarded readers had more in common with "pure" retarded readers and less with "pure" antisocial children. It is possible therefore that the conduct disorder arises as a consequence of the reading difficulties, i.e., that the reduction in self-esteem from school failure engenders behavior problems. Social factors and family support are also highly influential. Similar findings were reported by Varlaam (1974).

Cantwell et al. (1980) examined 100 children between 2 and 13 years of age consecutively referred to a speech and hearing clinic and found that 53 were given a psychiatric diagnosis according to DSM III criteria (Table 26-4). The two most common disorders were attention deficit and oppositional behavior. Regrouped into broad categories of emotional or conduct disorder, 37 children fell into the conduct disorder category and 13 into the emotional disorder category. One child showed infantile autism. A recent

TABLE 26-4   Psychiatric Diagnoses in 100 Children Referred to a Speech and Hearing Clinic

Diagnosis	Number of occurrences
No mental disorder	47
Attention deficit disorder, with hyperactivity	17
Oppositional disorder	13
Shyness disorder	7
Unspecified mental disorder	6
Separation anxiety disorder	3
Undersocialized conduct disorder, aggressive type	3
Mild mental retardation	3
Attentional deficit disorder, without hyperactivity	2
Overanxious disorder	2
Moderate mental retardation	2
Infantile autism	2
Intermittent depressive disorder	1
Undersocialized conduct disorder, unaggressive type	1
Stereotyped movement disorder	1

Source: Cantwell et al. 1980

extension of the study to a population of 600 children confirmed these results (Mattison 1983). In children with pure speech disorders, the incidence of psychiatric disorders was 34 per cent, with speech and language disorders 59 per cent, and with language disorders only 7 per cent. Language disorders were associated with psychiatric disorders, especially in the form of behavior problems. There was a trend of increased prevalence of psychiatric disorder in children with low IQ, low educational level of father, and poor psychosocial environment. Psychiatric disorder was also associated with other developmental disorders, such as enuresis; however, the clinical neurological examination showed no differences between the psychiatric and nonpsychiatric groups of language-disordered children.

The contribution of environmental factors is indicated by differences in behavior according to the type of school placement. C. P. Griffiths (1969) found that children with severe language disorders developed behavior problems after being transferred from special to regular schools. Seidel et al. (1975) noted that both psychiatric disorder and reading retardation were less frequent among crippled children attending special schools rather than regular schools. Rutter et al. (1976) reported that, when educationally handicapped children were placed in special schools, secondary behavior problems were less likely to develop.

26.7 SENSORY IMPAIRMENT

Two factors tend to be related to emotional or behavior problems in children. First, the cerebral pathology responsible for the sensory handicap may itself increase the incidence of psychopathology. This relationship would be expected to exist for children with central rather than peripheral causes of sensory loss. Second, the reaction of the child to a handicap that impairs communication and social relationships may cause secondary emotional problems.

Deafness

Few studies have compared groups of deaf and normal children in order to describe differences of adjustment, personality, and psychopathology. Rutter et al. (1970a) found psychiatric disturbance in blind and deaf children at an incidence rate of 15.4 per cent for all ages. This figure is not substantially higher than the 5 to 15 per cent incidence of psychiatric disorder for children of all ages in the general population. However, the deaf children were not divided into groups of central and peripheral, or primary or secondary, deafness; the small number of children involved may have precluded such an analysis.

M. Vernon (1967) examined 117 prematurely born, congenitally deaf children. Thirty-four were considered emotionally maladjusted to the extent that they were unable to function adequately in school. He noted that hyperactivity was more noticeable in children with overt neurological abnormalities. A second pattern found in other children was a schizoid type of disorder with hallucinations and homosexual behavior.

A descriptive study by Norden (1981) of deaf children in a kindergarten for the deaf addressed personality development. Based on clinical judgment, the author found that personality development was good if the children were allowed to use sign language freely and formal oral speech training was avoided. The author observed that the children developed emotional strengths that were unlikely to be gained if they had been reared in a milieu of hearing people. Further support for this position is given by Meadow (1968), who found that deaf children reared by deaf parents showed more maturity in terms of personality adjustment than children reared by hearing parents. Deaf children reared by deaf parents were better adjusted in terms of sociability, popularity, emotional responses, willingness to communicate with strangers, and lack of communicative frustration; they also showed better scholastic achievement.

Visual Impairment

The congenitally blind child frequently has additional handicaps. In a 30-year survey of all congenitally blind children in British Columbia, Jan et al. (1977) found that 74 per cent had other handicaps, such as mental retardation, hearing loss, congenital heart defects, epilepsy, and cerebral palsy. Half of the children with aquired blindness also suffered from an additional handicap. In general terms, a child is less likely to have additional impairment if the cause is limited to the eye. Among cortically blind children, however, severe mental retardation is common. Blindness from infections and toxins is usually associated with other impairments, e.g., excessive arterial oxygen resulting from the high incubator oxygen concentrations used in the 1950s. Congenital rubella affects the embryo more severely in the earlier stages of development; retardation, deafness, and heart defects are the most common accompanying deficits.

Blind infants do not respond to the face of the mother and are delayed in responding to her voice. This may lead to the mistaken diagnosis of autism in such children, especially since blind children tend habitually to explore their environment and their own body by pressing their eyeballs; waving their head from side to side; smelling food, objects, and people; gazing at a light source, and waving their hand in front of their eyes; this behavior has been described as blindism (A. Thomas and Chess 1980).

Few studies have compared the incidence of psychopathology in blind and sighted children. Rutter et al.'s Isle of Wight study (1970a) found only 15 blind children; from this number it is difficult to generalize about the comparative incidence of psychiatric disorder. The study reported an incidence of emotional disorders of 16.6 per cent; four of the children were retarded. Jan et al. (1977) studied a sample of blind children with interview techniques and questionnaires adapted from Rutter's work. The children were compared with controls from the regular school system, but so far the full range of findings has not been published.

Blind children appear to be better adjusted when attending schools for the blind than when integrated into regular schools. In regular schools with sighted children, the blind child tends to be isolated and often rejected by peers and constantly has to cope with the disability in a setting designed for the sighted. In a school with other blind children, good friendships develop and fewer behavioral or emotional problems are noted. Moreover, schools for the blind are geared to the specific educational needs of the blind, both academically and in terms of general living skills and environment (Magelby and Farley 1968).

Epilogue

This volume attempts to survey a field of considerable magnitude. Previous books and chapters dealing with the topic usually have been limited to a specific area of investigation, e.g., language disorders, aspects of treatment and of assessment, problems of pediatric management, neurobiology, neuropathology. The disorders of childhood, especially learning disorders and cerebral palsy, have found detailed attention in the past. Our attempt to bring many research findings and theories in different areas together was guided by the unifying theme that the biopsychological development of the child must be seen as a continuing process, that the effects of early stress and damage to the nervous system must be followed through to provide an assessment of outcome. In the course of this survey, it was difficult to resist the temptation to lose sight of this goal and to elaborate on the richness of theory and research in any one area. Adhering to this goal often meant deliberately restricting the range of discussion and omitting many peripheral aspects of investigation. For this reason, some chapters may appear brief or even superficial to the specialist.

Adult human neuropsychology has been guided by and developed simultaneously with adult neurology. An impressive amount of well-documented clinical observation, experimental study, and systematic clinical research has been documented in several major textbooks during the last decades. Developmental neuropsychology does not have the same tradition, nor is an easy translation of the work with adults into a developmental framework possible. Rather, developmental work has its origins in such related fields as pediatrics, embryology, and animal research. The application of the knowledge from these areas to psychology and particularly to neuropsychology has been slow.

Two major obstacles to the development of a coherent framework for developmental neuropsychology are

1. The constantly changing picture of the developing child with age. While some generalizations to the adult with a specific type of brain lesion can be made, the effects of lesions on children vary greatly with age. This book stresses that age includes not only infancy and childhood but the full prenatal period as well.

2. The constant interaction of the developing individual with the environment. The reader will recall studies of severely malnourished children living in abject poverty in rural parts of Mexico and contrast them with studies of learning-disabled children from affluent families attending a specialized private school. This range and the attendant range of available services and remediation efforts make generalizations to children even within a specific age group extremely difficult.

Considering these two factors, one might wonder whether drawing general conclusions about human developmental neuropsychology is not an impossible task. Should we not rather write a book that restricts itself to research with children of a specific age and with a homogeneous socioeconomic background? Although books dealing with the problems of the school-age, middle-class child do exist, an integration of the findings presented in them with the early pre- and postnatal development and with the precursors of middle-childhood problems has been lacking so far. If we are to go beyond these highly selected problems of highly selected populations, if we are to take the word "developmental" seriously, then an integration must be attempted. The risk of such an attempt became clear during the writing of this book: numerous gaps in our knowledge, numerous studies that do not allow firm conclusions, made it necessary to discuss contradictory or marginally significant results that had to be stated with repetitive qualifications.

Who will fill in the gaps? We are encouraged by the many ongoing and recently published studies, the increasing sophistication in the design of studies, of statistical analysis, and specifically of subject description, psychological measurement, and neurological background material. A few exemplary studies, particularly those from the Collaborative Perinatal Project, have even attempted the multivariate analysis of a large number of dependent and independent variables. If some results of such studies are less impressive for those of us who want clear-cut answers, if we learn, for example, that head circumference at age 1 year contributed $-.26$ (i.e., approximately 7 per cent of the total variance) to a discriminant function analysis between 7-year-old learning-disabled and control children (Nichols and Chan 1981), we should keep in mind that, in a study of 30 000 children and in the context of numerous other variables, this is indeed a significant finding that must be interpreted in the context of other interacting variables to achieve predictive significance.

Predictive significance in such studies, as well as in almost all other studies, remains a matter of probability. It is predictive only for the group, not for each individual—who has his or her own background, history, and development. Many times in this book we take refuge in the somewhat nebulous term "interactive" in describing the effects of particular prenatal, perinatal, or postnatal event. The term is not meant to be evasive; rather it refers to the fact that the genetic history, the socioeconomic history of the mother and father, the history of pregnancy, the numerous stress factors during pregnancy and birth all contribute to the state of the newborn and hence to the measurements taken at birth or during the first few months. After birth, family size, early infant experience and stimulation, and a host of other environmental factors continue to shape the individual. Childhood illnesses, bumps and falls, nutrition, early childhood education, physical care and treatment, among others, contribute to the making of the individual in middle childhood, the time when most childhood problems reach the clinical psychologist. It is not surprising then that only the major damaging events show a profound influence on the development of the child while most "minor" events contribute only mildly to the eventual outcome.

We have tried to trace both the major and the minor events occurring before, during, and after the birth. Future studies will no doubt further clarify their importance. However, they will remain inseparable from the numerous other concurrent or subsequent effects that may continue to affect the child, decrease in importance, or take on new magnitude if cumulative damaging factors impinge upon the child.

In addition to age and environmental factors, two more traditional concerns of clinical neuropsychology have to be considered:

1. What type of brain damage has occurred and what specific area of the CNS has been affected? While in postnatal injuries these questions can be answered almost as well as in adult neuropsychology, pre- and perinatal damage tends to be less localized and to affect larger, major parts of the CNS. In contrast to the adult, brain damage sustained by the infant raises additional questions of compensation and plasticity that make the outcome much less predictable than in the individual with a fully matured CNS.

2. The question as to what psychological functions are affected by damage to the CNS is likely to lead to more qualified and complex answers than in the adult. Many psychological functions examined in the adult, e.g., reading and writing, have not even developed in the young child to a point where they can be tested. Language may not be available except in rudimentary forms. Hence, the prediction of long-term outcome becomes a matter of probability that cannot be addressed unless a long-term follow-up is conducted. Retrospective studies of individuals with specific disorders of function tend to be fraught with problems since causes other than organic impairment must be ruled out. Furthermore, such

studies provide no answer to the question of how many children with a similar lesion developed normally or near-normally and hence do not appear in the sample for retrospective study.

The clinical neuropsychologist is well aware of these many interacting factors but in daily practice must make use of the tools available and interpret them as best he or she can. In assessing a handicapped infant, the developmental neuropsychologist may have only a few formal tests supplemented with observations of her or his own and with those of the parents and caregivers working with the child. This book is meant to provide not only a summary of our knowledge but also the background needed for such clinical work. It is also written for the neuropsychologist and other health care professionals working with older children to provide better insight into the conditions that preceded what they find in their clients and to provide a better understanding of these influences.

Acknowledgments

We would like to acknowledge permission to use Table 1-1 by Dr. Lund and Oxford University Press; Table 2-1 by Drs. Adams and Victor and McGraw Hill Book Co.; Table 2-2 by Dr. Lowrey and Year Book Medical Publishers; Table 2-3 by Dr. Dodge and C. V. Mosby Co.; Table 4-1 by Dr. van der Vlugt and Plenum Publishing Corp.; Table 4-2 by Dr. Golden and Grune & Stratton, Inc.; Table 5-1 Drs. Klausmeier and Allen and Academic Press; Table 8-1 by Dr. Grossman and the American Association on Mental Deficiency; Table 8-4 by Drs. Niswanger and Gordon and the U.S. Department of Health, Education and Welfare; Table 9-1 by Dr. Wortis and Grune Stratton, Inc.; Table 9-2 by Dr. de Myer and Raven Press; Table 10-1 by Dr. Halverson and Brunner/Mazel, Inc.; Table 10-3 by Dr. Wilson and Academic Press; Table 11-1 and Figures 11-1 to 11-4 by Dr. Dubowitz and C.V. Mosby Co.; Table 11-2 by Dr. Keller and Academic Press; Table 11-3 by Dr. Black and Butterworth, Ltd.; Table 11-4 by Dr. Gottlieb and Academic Press; Table 11-5 by Drs. Commey and Fitzhardinge and the Journal of Pediatrics; Table 11-6 and 11-7 by Drs. Levene and Dubowitz and the British Journal of Hospital Medicine; Table 12-1 by Dr. Desmond and Granada Publishing Ltd.; Tables 12-2 and 12-3 by Dr. Hardy and the Archives of Otolaryngology; Table 16-1 by Dr. Rose and Spectrum Press; Tables 16-2 and 16-3 by Dr. Lombroso and Spectrum Press; Table 16-5 by Dr. Gastaut and Epilepsia; Table 19-1 by Dr. Hopkins and the Council for Exceptional Children; Tables 19-2, 19-3 and 19-4 by Dr. Cruickshank and Syracuse University Press; Table 20-1 by Dr. Ross and Annual Reviews Inc.; Table 23-1 by Dr. Chase and Appleton-Century-Croft, Inc.; Table 23-2 by Dr. Irwin and Prentice-Hall, Inc.; Table 23-3 by Dr. Martin; Table 23-4 and 23-5 by Dr. Goldstein and the Annals of Otology, Rhinology and Laryngology; Table 24-1 by Wissenschaftliche Buchgesellschaft; Table 24-2 by Drs. Jacobson and Janicki and the American Association on Mental Deficiency; Table 25-1 by Dr. Doehring and Academic Press; Tables 26-1 and 26-2 by Dr. Brown and Psychological Medicine; Table 26-3 by Dr. Rutter and Lavenham Press; Table 26-4 by Dr. Cantwell and the Archives of General Psychiatry.

Figures 1-1 and 1-3 by Dr. Thompson and Harper and Row, Publishers; Figure 1-2 by Oxford University Press; Figures 1-4 and 1-5 by Dr. Jacobson and Plenum Press; Figures 1-6 and 3-5 by Drs. Sidman and Rakic and Elsevier/North-Holland Publishing Co.; Figure 1-7 by Dr. Rakic and the Journal of Comparative Neurology;

381

Figure 1-8 by Dr. Berry and Academic Press; Figure 1-9 by Drs. Davison and Peters and Charles C. Thomas, Publishers; Figure 1-10 by Dr. Lecours and Blackwell Scientific Publications Ltd.; Figures 2-1, 2-2, 2-4, 2-5 and 3-4 by Dr. Lemire and Harper & Row; Figure 2-6 by Dr. Nelhaus and the American Academy of Pediatrics; Figure 2-7 by Dr. Hagne and Almqvist & Wiksell Förlag, Stockholm; Figure 3-1 by Dr. Livson and Random House, Inc.; Figure 3-2 by Dr. Reinis and Charles C. Thomas, Publisher; Figure 3-3 by Drs. Noback and Demarest and McGraw-Hill Book Co.; Figure 4-1 by Dr. Geschwind and the American Association for the Advancement of Science; Figure 4-2 by Dr. Entus and Academic Press; Figure 6-1 by Dr. Butcher and Lawrence Erlbaum Associates, Inc.; Figure 6-2 by Dr. Dobbing and the British Medical Journal; Figure 6-3 by Dr. Gazzaniga and Harper and Row; Figure 6-4 by Dr. Goldberger and Academic Press; Figure 9-1 by Dr. Lilienfeld and the Johns Hopkins University Press; Figure 10-1 by Sidgwick and Jackson Ltd.; Figures 10-2 to 10-5 by Dr. Neuhäuser and Zeitschrift für die allgemeine Medizin; Figure 10-6 by Dr. Bottcher-Boas and Neuropaediatrie; Figure 12-1 by Dr. Sell and Pediatrics; Figure 13-1 by Dr. Winick and W.B. Saunders Co; Figure 15-1 by Dr. Clausen and McGraw-Hill Book Co.; Figures 15-2 and 15-3 by Dr. Oxorn and Appleton-Century-Croft; Figures 15-4 and 15-5 by Dr. Pansky and MacMillan Press; Figure 15-6 by Charles C. Thomas, Publisher; Figure 16-1 by Dr. Doose and Desitin, Hamburg; Figure 16-3 by Dr. Lou and Raven Press; Figure 16-5 by Dr. Freudenberg and Karger Verlag; Figure 18-1 by Dr. Thompson and Oxford University Press; Figure 19-1 by Dr. Netter and Ciba Pharmaceutical Co.; Figure 23-1 by Dr. Niebergall and Zeitschrift für klinische Psychologie; Figure 24-1 by Dr. Tarjan and the American Association on Mental Deficiency; Figure 24-2 by Hogrefe Verlag, Göttingen; Figure 24-3 by Dr. Silverstein and Psychological Reports; Figure 24-4 by Dr. Gibson and the American Association on Mental Deficiency; Figure 24-5 by Dr. Zeaman and the Society for Research in Child Development.

Full details of each source can be found in the references.

REFERENCES

Aaron, P.G., 1982. The neuropsychology of developmental dyslexia. In R.N. Malatesha and P.G. Aaron (eds.), *Reading Disorders: Varieties and Treatments*. New York: Academic Press.

Abel, E.L. (ed.), 1981. *Fetal Alcohol Syndrome*. Boca Raton, Fla.: CRC Press.

Achenbach, T.M., 1978. *Research in Developmental Psychology: Concepts, Strategies, Methods*. New York: Free Press.

Achenbach, T.M., 1979. Psychopathology of childhood: Research problems and issues. In S. Chess and A. Thomas (eds.), *Annual Progress in Child Psychiatry and Child Development*. New York: Brunner/Mazel.

Achenbach, T.M., 1982. Childhood depression: A review of research. In B.B. Lahey and A.E. Kazdin (eds.), *Advances in Clinical Child Psychology*, vol. 5. New York: Plenum Press.

Achilles, R.F., 1956. Communicative anomalies of individuals with cerebral palsy: Part 2: Analysis of communicative processes of 90 athetoids as compared with 61 other types of cerebral palsy. *Cerebral Palsy Review* **17**, 19.

Ackerman, P.T., Dykman, R.A., and Peters, J.E., 1977. Teenage status of hyperactive and nonhyperactive learning-disabled boys. *American Journal of Orthopsychiatry* **47**, 577.

Adams, R.D., and Victor, M., 1981. *Principles of Neurology*, 2d edn. New York: McGraw-Hill.

Adams, R.M., Kocsis, J.J., and Estes, R.E., 1974. Soft neurological signs in learning-disabled children and controls. *American Journal for Disturbed Children* **128**, 614.

Adamsons, K., and Myers, R., 1973. Perinatal asphyxia: Causes, detection and neurologic sequelae. *Pediatric Clinics of North America* **20**(2), 465.

Ahn, H., Baird, H., Trepetin, M., and Kaye, H., 1980. Developmental equations reflect brain dysfunctions. *Science* **210**, 1259.

Aicardi, L., Lefevre, J., and Lerique-Koechlin, A., 1965. A new syndrome: Spasms in flexion, callosal agensis, ocular abnormalities. *Electro-encephalography and Clinical Neurophysiology* **19**, 609.

Aicardie, J., and Chevrie, J.J., 1970. Convulsive status epilepticus in infants and children: A study of 239 cases. *Epilepsia* **11**, 187.

Ainsworth, M.D.S., 1973. The development of infant-mother attachment. In B.M. Caldwell and H.N. Ricciuti (eds), *Review of Child Development Research*, vol. 3. Chicago: University of Chicago Press.

Aladjouanine, T., and Lhermitte, F., 1965. Acquired aphasia in childhood. *Brain* **88**, 653.

Alden, E.R., Mendelkorn, T., Woodrum, D.E., Wennberg, R.P., Parks, C.R., and Hodson, W.A., 1972. Morbidity and mortality of infants weighing less than 1000 grams in an intensive care nursery. *Pediatrics* **50**, 40.

Alexander, D., Ehrhardt, A., and Money, J., 1966. Defective figure drawing, geometric and human, in Turner's syndrome. *Journal of Nervous and Mental Disease* **142**, 161.

Alexander, G.E., and Goldman, P.S., 1978. Functional development of the dorsolateral prefrontal cortex: An analysis using reversible cryogenic depression. *Brain Research* **143**, 233.

Allen, N., 1975. Chemical neurotoxins in industry and environment. In D.B. Tower (ed.), *The Nervous System*, vol. 2: *The Clinical Neurosciences*. New York: Raven.

Alm, I., 1975. The long-term prognosis for prematurely born children. *Acta Paedopsychiatrica (Stockholm)* **42**, suppl. 94.

Als, H., Lester, B., and Brazelton, T.B., 1979. Dynamics of the behavioural organization of the premature infant: A theoretical perspective. In T.M. Field, A.M. Sosteck, S. Goldberg, and H.H. Shumann (eds.), *Infants Born at Risk: Behaviour and Development*. New York: Spectrum.

Altman, J., 1967. Postnatal growth and differentiation of the mammalian brain, with implications for a morphological theory of memory. In G.C. Quarton, T. Melnechuk, and F.O. Schmitt (eds.), *The Neurosciences: A Study Program*. New York: Rockefeller University Press.

Altman, J., Brunner, R.L., and Bayer, S.A., 1973. The hippocampus and behavioral maturation. *Behavioral Biology* **8**, 557.

Altman, J., and Bulut, F.G., 1976. Organic maturation and the development of learning capacity. In M.R. Rosenzweig and E.L. Bennett (eds.), *Neural Mechanisms of Learning and Memory*. Cambridge, Mass.: MIT Press.

American Psychiatric Association, 1980. *Diagnostic and Statistical Manual of Mental Disorders*, 3rd edn. Washington: American Psychiatric Association.

American Psychological Association, 1977. *Standards for Educational and Psychological Tests*. Washington, D.C.: American Psychological Association.

Amiel-Tison, C., 1968. Neurological evaluation of the maturity of newborn infants. *Archives of Disease in Children* **43**, 89.

Amiel-Tison, C., 1980. Possible acceleration of neurological maturation following high-risk pregnancy. *American Journal of Obstetrics and Gynecology* **138**, 303.

Anderson, E., 1975. Genetic mechanisms in human behavioral development. In K.W. Schaie, V.E. Anderson, G.E. McClearn, and J. Money (eds.), *Developmental Human Behavior Genetics*. Lexington, Mass.: Lexington Books, p. 113.

Anderson, E., 1979. The psychological and social adjustment of adolescents with cerebral palsy or spina bifida and hydrocephalus. *International Journal of Rehabilitation Research* **2**, 245.

Angers, W.P., 1963. Patterns of abilities and capacities in the epileptic. *Journal of Genetic Psychology* **103**, 59.

Angle, C.R., and McIntire, M.S., 1964. Lead poisoning during pregnancy. *American Journal of Diseases of Children* **108**, 436.

Annegers, J.F., Hauser, W.A., Anderson, V.E., and Kurland, L.T., 1982. The risks of seizure disorders among relatives of patients with childhood onset epilepsy. *Neurology* **32**, 174.

Annett, M., 1970. Handedness, cerebral dominance and the growth of intelligence. In P. Satz and D.J. Bakker (eds.), *Specific Reading Disability*. Rotterdam: Rotterdam University Press.

Annett, M., 1973. Laterality of childhood hemiplegia and the growth of speech and intelligence. *Cortex* **9**, 4.

Anokhin, P.K., 1964. Systemogenesis as a general regulator of brain development. *Progress in Brain Research* **9**, 54.

Ansara, A., Geschwind, N., Galaburda, A., Albert, M., and Gartrell, N. (eds.), 1981. *Sex Differences in Dyslexia*. Towson, Md.: Orton Dyslexia Society.

Anthony, E.J., 1958. An experimental approach to the psychopathology of childhood autism. *British Journal of Medical Psychology* **31**, 211.

Apgar, V.A., 1953. Proposal for a new method of evaluation of the newborn infant. *Anesthesia and Analgesia, Current Researches* **22**, 260.

Apgar, V., 1962. Further observations on the newborn scoring system. *American Journal of Diseases of the Child* **104**, 419.

Armstrong, D., and Norman, M., 1974. Periventricular leukomalacia in neonates: Complications and sequelae. *Archives of Diseases in Childhood* **49**, 367.

Arnold, A.P., 1980. Sexual differences in the brain. *American Scientist* **68**, 165.

Aten, J., and Davis, J., 1968. Disturbances in the perception of auditory sequence in children with minimal cerebral dysfunction. *Journal of Speech and Hearing Research* **11**, 236.

Austin, V.L., 1978. Discriminant and descriptive analyses of neuropsychological electroencephalographic, perinatal and developmental history correlates of children with math or reading disability. *Dissertation Abstract International* **38** (11-B), 5554.

Avery, M.E., and Mead, J., 1959. Surface properties in relation to atelectasis and hyaline membrane disease. *American Journal of Diseases of Childhood* **97**, 517.

Ayres, A.J., 1965. Patterns of perceptual-motor dysfunction in children: A factor analytic study. *Perceptual and Motor Skills* **20**, 335.

Babson, S.G., Benson, R.C., Pernoll, M.L., and Benda, G.I., 1975. Management of High-Risk Pregnancy and Intensive Care of the Neonate. St. Louis: Mosby.

Bakker, D.J., 1980. Dyslexia: Hemispheric specific etiology. Paper presented at the Department of Psychology, University of Victoria.

Bakker, D.J., Teunissen, J., and Bosch, J., 1976. Development of laterality-reading patterns. In R.M. Knights and D.J. Bakker (eds.), *The Neuropsychology of Learning Disorders: Theoretical Approaches*. Baltimore: University Park Press.

Bakketeig, L.S., 1977. The risk of repeated preterm or low birth weight delivery. In D. Reed, and F. Stanley, (eds.), *The Epidemiology of Prematurity*. Baltimore: Urban and Schwarzenberg.

Balazs, R., 1979. Cerebellum: Certain features of its development and biochemistry. In M. Cuenod, G.W. Kreutzberg, and F. E. Bloom (eds.), *Development and Chemical Specificity of Neurons (Progress in Brain Research*, vol. 51). Amsterdam: Elsevier/North-Holland Biomedical Press.

Balow, B., Rubin, R., and Rosen, M.S., 1976. Prenatal events as precursors of reading disability. *Reading Research Quarterly* **11**, 36.

Baltes, P.B., and Nesselroade, J.R., 1970. Multivariate longitudinal and cross-sectional sequences for analyzing ontogenetic and generational change: A methodological note. *Developmental Psychology* **2**(2), 163.

Baltes, P.B., Reese, H.W., and Nesselroade, J.R., 1977. *Life-span Developmental Psychology: Introduction to Research Methods.* Monterey, Calif.: Brooks/Cole.

Banker, B.Q., and Larroche, J.C., 1962. Periventricular leukomalacia in infancy. *Archives of Neurology* **7**, 386.

Barkley, R.A., 1977. A review of stimulant drug research with hyperactive children. *Journal of Child Psychology and Psychiatry* **18**, 137.

Barkley, R.A., 1981a. Hyperactivity. In E.J. Mash and L.G. Terdal (eds.), *Behavioral Assessment of Childhood Disorders.* New York: Guilford.

Barkley, R.A., 1981b. *Hyperactive Children: A Handbook for Diagnosis and Treatment.* New York: Guilford.

Barkley, R.A., and Cunningham, C.E., 1979. Stimulant drugs and activity level in hyperactive children. *American Journal of Orthopsychiatry* **49**(3), 491.

Barlow, H.B., 1975. Visual experience and cortical development. *Nature* **258**, 199.

Barnard, K.E., and Douglas, H.B., (eds.), 1974. *Child Health Assessment.* Part 1: Literature Review. Bethesda, Md.: U.S. Department of Health, Education, and Welfare. (DHEW HRA 75-30).

Barnet, A.P., Friedman, S.I., Weiss, J.I., Ohlrich, E.S., Shanks, B., and Lodge, A., 1980. Visual evoked potential development in infancy and early childhood: A longitudinal study. *Electroencephalography and Clinical Neurophysiology* **49**, 476.

Barnet, A.P., Manson, J.I., and Wilner, E., 1970. Acute cerebral blindness in childhood. *Neurology* **20**, 1147.

Barnet, A.P., Weiss, I.P., Sotillio, M.V., Ohlrich, E.S., Shkurovich, Z., and Cravioto, J., 1978. Abnormal auditory evoked potentials in early infancy malnutrition. *Science* **201**, 450.

Barr, D.F., 1972. *Auditory Perceptual Disorders: An Introduction.* Springfield, Ill.: Thomas.

Bartak, L., Rutter, M., and Cox, A., 1975. A comparative study of infantile autism and specific receptive language disorder: I. The children. *British Journal of Psychiatry* **126**, 127.

Bartel, P.R., Burnett, L.S., Griesel, R.D., Freiman, I., Rosen, E.U., and Geefhuysen, J., 1978. The visual evoked potential in children after kwashiorkor. *South African Medical Journal* **54**, 857.

Bartel, P.R., Griesel, R.D., and Burnett, L.S., 1977a. *Long-term Effect of Kwashiokor on Psychomotor Ability.* Johannesburg: Council of Scientific and Industrial Research.

Bartel, P.R., Griesel, R.D., and Burnett, L.S., 1977b. *Psychometric Assessment of the Long-Term Effects of Kwashiokor.* Johannesburg: Council of Scientific and Industrial Research.

Bartel, P.R., Griesel, R.D., Freiman, I., Rosen, E.U., and Geefhuysen, J., 1979. Long-term effects of kwashiorkor on the electroencephalogram. *American Journal of Clinical Nutrition* **32**, 753.

Baru, A.V., and Karaseva, T.A., 1972. *The Brain and Hearing.* New York: Consultants Bureau.

Basser, L.S., 1962. Hemiplegia of early onset and the faculty of speech with special reference to the effects of hemispherectomy. *Brain* **85**, 427.

Baumeister, A.A., and Bartlett, C.J., 1962. A comparison of the factor structure of normals and retardates on the WISC. *American Journal of Mental Deficiency* **66**, 641.

Bay, E., 1962. Sprache und Denken. *Deutsche Medizinische Wochenschrift* **87**, 1845.

Beaconsfield, P., Birdwood, G., and Beaconsfield, R., 1980. The placenta. *Scientific American* **243(2)**, 95.

Beasley, D.S., and Rintelmann, A.K., 1979. Central auditory processing. In W.F. Rintelmann (ed.), *Hearing Assessment*. Baltimore: University Park Press.

Beattie, A.D., Moore, M.R., Goldberg, A., Finlayson, M.J.W., Mackie, E.M., Graham, J.F., McLaren, D.A., Murdock, R.M., and Stewart, G.T., 1975. Role of chronic low-level lead exposure in the etiology of mental retardation. *Lancet* **1**, 589.

Beck, E.C., and Dustman, R.E., 1975. Developmental electrophysiology of brain function as reflected by changes in the evoked response. In J.W. Prescott, M.S. Read, and D.B. Coursin (eds.), *Brain Function and Malnutrition: Neuropsychological Methods of Assessment*. New York: Wiley.

Bellak, L., 1978. *Psychiatric Aspects of Minimal Brain Dysfunction in Adults*. New York: Grune and Stratton.

Belmont, I.B., Birch, H.G., and Belmont, L., 1967. The organization of intelligence test performance in educable mentally subnormal children. *American Journal of Mental Deficiency* **71**, 969.

Belmont, J.M., 1971. Medical-behavioral research in retardation. In N.R. Ellis (ed.), *International Review of Research in Mental Retardation*, vol. 5. New York: Academic Press.

Benda, C.E., 1960. *The Child with Mongolism*. New York: Grune and Stratton.

Bender, L., 1942. Schizophrenia in childhood. *The Nervous Child* **1**, 138.

Bender, L., 1956. Schizophrenia in childhood: Its recognition, description and treatment. *American Journal of Orthopsychiatry* **26**, 499.

Benes, V., 1982. Sequelae of transcallosal surgery. *Child's Brain* **9**, 69.

Benjamins, J.A., and McKhann, G.M., 1976. Development, regeneration, and aging. In G.J. Siegel, R.W. Albers, R. Katzman, and B.W. Agranoff (eds.), *Basic Neurochemistry*, 2d edn. Boston: Little, Brown.

Bennett, E.L., Diamond, M.C., Krech, D., and Rosenzweig, M.R., 1964. Chemical and anatomical plasticity of the brain. *Science* **146**, 610.

Benson, D.F., 1981. The alexias. In G. Pirozzolo (ed.), *Neuropsychological Processes in Reading*. New York: Academic Press.

Benson, D.F., and Geschwind, N., 1969. The alexias. In P.J. Vinken and G.W. Bruyn (eds.), *Handbook of Clinical Neurology*, vol. 4. Amsterdam: North-Holland.

Benson, D.F., and Geschwind, N., 1970. Developmental Gerstmann syndrome. *Neurology* **20**, 293.

Benton, A.L., 1964. Developmental aphasia and brain damage. *Cortex* **1**, 40.

Benton, A.L., 1974. Clinical neuropsychology of childhood: An overview. In R.M. Reitan and L.A. Davison (eds.), *Clinical Neuropsychology: Current Status and Applications*. New York: Wiley.

Benton, A.L., 1975. Developmental dyslexia: Neurological aspects. In W.J. Friedlander (ed.), *Advances in Neurology*, vol. 7. New York: Raven Press.

Benton, A. L., 1978. The cognitive functioning of children with developmental dysphasia. In M.A. Wyke (ed.), *Developmental Dysphasia*. New York: Academic Press.

Benton, A.L., and Pearl, D., 1978. *Dyslexia: An Appraisal of Current Knowledge*. New York: Oxford University Press.

Berenberg, S.R. (ed.), 1977. *Brain: Fetal and Infant*. The Hague: Martinus Nijhoff.

Berenberg, W., and Nankervis, G., 1970. Long-term follow-up of cytomegalic inclusion disease in infancy. *Pediatrics* **37**, 403.

Berman, J.L., and Ford, R., 1970. Intelligence quotients and intelligence loss in patients with phenylketonuria and some variant states. *Journal of Pediatrics* **77**, 764.

Berman, J.L., Graham, F.K., Eichman, F.D., and Waisman, R.G., 1961. *Pediatrics* **28**, 924.

Berry, M., 1974. Development of the cerebral neocortex of the rat. In G. Gottlieb (ed.), *Studies on the Development of Behavior and the Nervous System*, vol. 2: *Aspects of Neurogenesis*. New York: Academic Press.

Berry, M., McConnell, P., and Sievers, J., 1980. Dendritic growth and the control of neuronal form. In R.K. Hunt (ed.), *Neural Development*, part I *(Current Topics in Developmental Biology*, vol. 15). New York: Academic Press.

Birch, H.G., 1959. Summary of conference. *American Journal of Mental Deficiency* **64**, 410.

Birch, H.G., 1962. Dyslexia and the maturation of visual function. In J. Money (ed.), *Reading Disability*. Baltimore: Johns Hopkins Press.

Birch, H.G. (ed.), 1964. *Brain Damage in Children: The Biological and Social Aspects*. Baltimore: Williams and Wilkins.

Birch, H.G., 1974. Some ways of viewing studies in behavioral development. In S.R. Berenberg, M. Caniaris, and N.P. Masse (eds.), *Pre- and Postnatal Development of the Brain*. Basel: S. Karger.

Birch, H.G., Belmont, I., and Carp, E., 1965. The prolongation of inhibition in brain-damaged patients. *Cortex* **1**, 397.

Birch, H.G., and Diller, L., 1959. Rorschach signs of organicity: A physiological basis for perceptual disturbances. *Journal of Projective Techniques* **23**, 184.

Birch, H., Pineiro, C., Alcalde, E., Toca, T., and Cravioto, J., 1971. Relation of kwashiorkor in early childhood and intelligence at school age. *Pediatric Research* **5**, 579.

Black, F., 1972. *Neonatal Emergencies and Other Problems*. London: Butterworth.

Black, P., Blumer, D., Wellner, A.M., Shepard, R.H., and Walker, A.E., 1981. Head trauma in children: Neurological behavioral and intellectual sequelae. In P. Black (ed.), *Brain Dysfunction in Children: Etiology, Diagnosis and Management*. New York: Raven Press.

Blakemore, C., 1975. Development of functional connections in the mammalian visual system. In M.A.B. Brazier (ed.), *Growth and Development of the Brain: Nutritional, Genetic, and Environmental factors*. New York: Raven Press.

Blalock, H.M., and Blalock, A.B., 1968. *Methodology in Social Research*. New York: McGraw-Hill.

Bliss, L.S., and Peterson, D.M., 1975. Performance of aphasic and nonaphasic children on a sentence repetition task. *Journal of Communication Disorders* **8**, 207.

Boder, E., 1973. Developmental dyslexia: A diagnostic approach based on three reading-spelling patterns. *Developmental Medicine and Child Neurology* **15**, 663.

Bodis-Wollner, I., Atkin, A., Raab, E., and Wolkstein, M., 1977. Visual association cortex and vision in man: Pattern evoked potentials in a blind boy. *Science* **198**, 629.

Bogen, J.E., 1979. The callosal syndrome. In K.M. Heilman and E. Valenstein (eds.), *Clinical Neuropsychology*. New York: Oxford University Press.

Boggs, T.R., Jr., Hardy, J.B., and Frazier, T.M., 1967. Correlation of neonatal serum total bilirubin concentrations and developmental status at eight months. *Journal of Pediatrics* **71**, 553.

Boles, D.B., 1980. X-linkage of spatial ability: A critical review. *Child Development* **51**, 625.

Boll, T.J.., 1972. Conceptual vs. perceptual vs. motor deficits in brain-damaged children. *Journal of Clinical Psychology* **28**, 157.

Boll, T.J., 1974. Behavioral correlates of cerebral damage in children age 9–14. In R.M. Reitan and L.A. Davison (eds.), *Clinical Neuropsychology: Current Status and Application*. Washington, D.C.: V.H. Winston.

Boll, T.J., and Barth, J.T., 1981. Neuropsychology of brain damage in children. In S. Filskov and T.J. Boll (eds.), *Handbook of Clinical Neuropsychology*. New York: Wiley.

Boll, T. J., and Reitan, R.M., 1972. Motor and tactile-perceptual deficits in brain-damaged children. *Perceptual and Motor Skills* **34**, 343.

Bond, N.W., 1981. Prenatal alcohol exposure in rodents: A review of its effects on offspring activity and learning ability. *Australian Journal of Psychology* **33**, 331.

Borlund, B.L., and Heckman, H.K., 1976. Hyperactive boys and their brothers. *Archives of General Psychiatry* **33**, 669.

Bornstein, M.H., 1978. Visual behavior of the young human infant: Relationship between chromatic and spatial perception and activity of underlying brain mechanisms. *Journal of Experimental Child Psychology* **26**, 174.

Bosma, J.F., 1975. Anatomic and physiologic development of the speech apparatus. In D.B. Tower (ed.), *The Human Nervous System*, vol. 3: *Human Communication and Its Disorders*. New York: Raven Press.

Bossy, J.G., 1970. Morphological study of a case of complete, isolated, and asymptomatic agenesis of the corpus callosum. *Archives d'Anatomie, d'Histologie et d'Embryologie* **53**, 289.

Bottcher, J., Jacobsen, S., Glydensted, C., Harmsen, A., and Gloerselt-Tarp, B., 1978. Intellectual development and brain size in 13 shunted hydrocephalic children. *Neuropaediatrie* **9**, 369.

Boulder Committee, 1970. Embryonic vertebrate central nervous system: Revised terminology. *Anatomical Record* **166**, 257.

Bower, T.G.R., 1977, *A Primer of Infant Development*. San Francisco: W.H. Freeman.

Bowlby, J., 1951. *Maternal Care and Mental Health*, Monograph No. 2. Geneva: World Health Organization.

Bowman, J.M., 1975. Rh erythroblastosis fetalis. In F.A. Oski, E.R. Jaffe, and P.A. Miescher. (eds.), *Current Problems in Pediatric Hematology*. New York: Grune and Stratton, p. 29.

Bracht, G.H., and Glass, G.V., 1968. The external validity of experiments. *American Educational Research Journal* **5**, 437.

Bradley, C., 1937. The behavior of children receiving benzedrine. *American Journal of Psychiatry* **94**, 577.

Brain, R., 1977. *Diseases of the Nervous System.* 8th ed., revised by J.W. Walton. New York: Oxford.

Brandt, I., 1979. Patterns of early neurological development. In F. Falkner and J.M. Tanner (eds.), *Human Growth,* vol. 3: *Neurobiology and Nutrition.* New York: Plenum Press.

Brasel, J., 1974. Cellular changes in intrauterine malnutrition. In M. Winick (ed.), *Nutrition and Fetal Development.* New York: Wiley.

Brazier, M.A.B., and Coceani, F. (eds.), 1978. *Brain Dysfunction in Infantile Febrile Convulsions* (International Brain Research Organization Monograph Series). New York, Raven Press.

Brenner, A., 1977. A study of the efficacy of the Feingold diet on hyperkinetic children. *Clinical Pediatrics* **16,** 652.

Brenner, M.W., Gillman, S., Zangwill, O., and Farrell, M., 1967. Visuo-motor disability in schoolchildren. *British Medical Journal* **4,** 259.

Brett, E.M., 1975. The prognosis of seizures in the first three years of life. *Epilepsia* **16,** 346.

Brink, J., Garrett, A., Hale, W., Woo-Sam, J. and Nickel, V., 1970. Recovery of motor and intellectual function in children sustaining severe head injuries. *Developmental Medicine and Child Neurology* **12,** 565.

Brockman, L., and Ricciuti, H., 1971. Severe protein calorie malnutrition and cognitive development in infancy and early childhood. *Developmental Psychology* **4,** 312.

Broman, S., 1979. Prenatal anoxia and cognitive development in early childhood. In T. Field, A. Sostek, S. Goldberg, and H. Shuman (eds.), *Infants Born at Risk.* New York: Spectrum Press, p. 29.

Broman, S.H., Nichols, P.L., and Kennedy, W.A., 1975. *Preschool IQ: Prenatal and Early Developmental Correlates.* Hillsdale, N.J.: Erlbaum.

Bronfenbrenner, U., 1977. Toward an experimental ecology of human development. *American Psychologist* **32,** 513.

Bronner-Fraser, M.E., and Cohen, A.M., 1980. The neural crest: what can it tell us about cell migration and determination? In R.K. Hunt (ed.), *Neural Development,* part I (*Current Topics in Developmental Biology,* vol. 15). New York: Academic Press.

Bronson, G., 1974. The postnatal growth of visual capacity. *Child Development* **45,** 873.

Brown, G., Chadwick, O., Shaffer, D., Rutter, M., and Traub, M., 1981. A prospective study of children with head injuries: III psychiatric sequelae. *Psychological Medicine* **11,** 63.

Brown, J.K., 1973. Convulsions in the neonatal period. *Developmental Medicine and Child Neurology* **15,** 823.

Brown, J.K., Purvis, R.J., Forfar, J.O., and Cockburn, F., 1974. Neurological aspects of perinatal asphyxia. *Developmental Medicine and Child Neurology* **16,** 567.

Brunner, R.L., and Altman, J., 1974. The effects of interference with the maturation of the cerebellum and hippocampus on the development of adult behavior. In D.G. Stein, J.J. Rosen, and N. Butters (eds.), *Plasticity and Recovery of Function in the Central Nervous System.* New York: Academic Press.

Bryden, M.P., 1970. Laterality effects in dichotic listening: Relations with handedness and reading ability in children. *Neuropsychologia* **8,** 443.

Bryden, M.P., 1979. Evidence for sex-related differences in cerebral organization. In M.A. Wittig and A.C. Petersen (eds.), *Sex-Related Differences in Cognitive Functioning: Developmental Issues*. New York: Academic Press.

Bryden, M.P., 1982. *Laterality: Functional Asymmetry in the Intact Brain*. New York: Academic Press.

Bryden, M.P., and Allard, F.A., 1981. Do auditory perceptual asymmetries develop? *Cortex* **17**, 313.

Bryden, M., and Zurif, E., 1970. Dichotic listening performance in a case of agenesis of the corpus callosum. *Neuropsychologia* **8**, 371.

Buchanan, A., and Oliver, J.E., 1977. Abuse and neglect as a cause of mental retardation: A study of 140 children admitted to subnormality hospitals in Wiltshire. *British Journal of Psychiatry* **131**, 458.

Buchsbaum, M., Henkin, R.I., and Christiansen, R.L., 1974. Age and sex differences in averaged evoked responses in a normal population with observations on patients with gonadal dysgenesis. *Electroencephalography and Clinical Neurophysiology* **37**, 137.

Buffery, A.W.H., 1976. Sex differences in the neuropsychological development of verbal and spatial skills. In R.M. Knights and D.J. Bakker (eds.), *The Neuropsychology of Learning Disorders: Theoretical Approaches*. Baltimore: University Park Press.

Buffery, A.W.H., and Gray, J.A., 1972. Sex differences in the development of spatial and linguistic skills In C. Ounsted and D.C. Taylor (eds.), *Gender Differences: Their Ontogeny and Significance*. Edinburgh: Churchill Livingstone.

Burg, C., Rapoport, J.I., Bartley, L.S., Quinn, D.O., and Timmins, P., 1980. Newborn minor physical anomalies and problem behaviour at age 3. *American Journal of Psychiatry* **137**, 791.

Burnett, L.L., and Struve, F.A., 1970. The value of EEG study in minimal brain dysfunction. *Journal of Clinical Psychology* **30**, 489.

Burnstein, B., Bank, L., and Jarvik, L.F., 1980. Sex differences in cognitive functioning: Evidence, determinants, implications. *Human Development* **23**, 289.

Butcher, H.J., 1968. *Human Intelligence*. London: Methuen.

Butcher, R.E., Hawver, K., Bubacher, T., and Scott, W., 1975. Behavioural effects from antenatal exposure to teratogens. In N.R. Ellis (ed.), *Aberrant Development in Infancy*. Hillsdale, N.J.: Lawrence Erlbaum.

Butler, N.R., and Goldstein, H., 1973. Smoking in pregnancy and subsequent child development. *British Medical Journal* **4**, 573.

Butler, S.R., and Glass, A., 1974. Asymmetries in the electroencephalogram associated with cerebral dominance. *Electroencephalography and Clinical Neurophysiology* **36**, 481.

Butterfield, E.C., and Cairns, G.F., 1974. Discussion summary on infant reception research. In R.L. Schiefelbusch and L.L. Lloyd (eds.), *Language Perspectives: Acquisition, Retardation and Intervention*. Baltimore: University Park Press.

Cabak, V., and Najdanvic, R., 1965. Effect of undernutrition in early life on physical and mental development. *Archives of Diseases in Childhood* **40**, 532.

Cadoret, R.J., Cunningham, L., Loftus, R., and Edwards, J., 1975. Studies of adoptees from psychiatrically disturbed biologic parents. II. Temperament, hyperactive, antisocial and developmental variables. *Journal of Pediatrics* **87**, 301.

Cadoret, R.J., and Gath, A., 1976. Biologic correlates of hyperactivity: Evidence for a genetic factor. Paper presented at the Annual Meeting of the Society for Life History Research in Psychopathology, Ft. Worth, October.

Cairns, H., and Davidson, M.A., 1951. Hemispherectomy in the treatment of infantile hemiplegia. *Lancet* **2**, 411.

Caldwell, B.M., 1962. The usefulness of the critical period hypothesis in the study of filiative behaviours. *Merrill-Palmer Quarterly of Behaviour and Development* **8**, 229.

Callaway, E., 1973. Connections between average evoked potentials and meaures of intelligence. *Archives of General Psychiatry* **29**, 553.

Campbell, A.L., Bogen, J.E., and Smith, A., 1981. Disorganization and reorganization of cognitive and sensorimotor functions in cerebral commissurotomy. *Brain* **104**, 493.

Campbell, B., 1960. The factor of safety in the nervous system. *Bulletin of the Los Angeles Neurological Societies* **23**, 109.

Campbell, D.T., and Stanley, J.C., 1963. Experimental and quasi-experimental designs for research. In N.L. Gage (ed.), *Handbook of Research on Teaching.* Chicago: Rand-McNally.

Campbell, J.D., 1952. Manic-depressive psychosis in children: Report of 18 cases. *Journal of Nervous and Mental Disorders* **116**, 424.

Cantwell, D.P., 1972. Psychiatric illness in families of hyperactive children. *Archives of General Psychiatry* **27**, 414.

Cantwell, D.P., 1975. Genetics of hyperactivity. *Journal of Child Psychology and Psychiatry* **16**, 261.

Cantwell, D.P., Baker, L., and Mattison, R.E., 1980. Psychiatric disorders in children with speech and language retardation. *Archives of General Psychiatry* **37** (4), 423.

Cantwell, D.P., Baker, L., and Rutter, M., 1978. Family factors in autism. In M. Rutter and E. Schopler (eds.), *Autism: Reappraisal of Concepts and Treatment.* New York: Plenum Press.

Caplan, P.G., and Kinsbourne, M., 1976. Baby drops the rattle: Asymmetry of duration of grasp by infants. *Child Development* **47**, 532.

Caputo, D., Goldstein, K.M., and Taub, H.B., 1981. Neonatal compromise and later psychological development: A 10-year longitudinal study. In S. L. Friedman and M. Sigman (eds.), *Preterm Birth and Psychological Development.* New York: Academic Press.

Caputo, D.V., and Mandell, W., 1970. Consequences of low birth weight. *Developmental Psychology* **3**, 363.

Carey, W.B., and McDevitt, S.C., 1980. Minimal brain dysfunction and hyperkinesis: A clinical viewpoint. *American Journal of Diseases of Children* **134**, 926.

Carey, W.B., McDevitt, S.C., and Baker, D., 1979. Minimal brain dysfunction and temperament. *Developmental Medicine and Child Neurology* **21**, 765.

Carhart, R., 1967. Lesions due to kernicterus. *Acta Otolaryn.* (Stockholm), suppl. 221, 5.

Carmichael, A.E., 1966. The current status of hemispherectomy for infantile hemiplegia. *Clinical Proceedings of the Children's Hospital, Washington, D.C.* **22**, 285.

Caron, A.J., and Caron, R.F., 1981. Processing of relational information on an index of infant risk. In S.L. Friedman and M. Sigman (eds.), *Preterm Birth and Psychological Development*. New York: Academic Press.

Carter, C.O., 1974. Clues to the etiology of neural tube malformations. *Developmental Medicine and Child Neurology* **16**, suppl. 32, 3.

Carter-Saltzman, L., 1979. Patterns of cognitive functioning in relation to handedness and sex-related differences. In M.A. Wittig and A.C. Petersen (eds.), *Sex-Related Differences in Cognitive Functioning: Developmental Issues*. New York: Academic Press.

Cartwright, G., Culbertson, K., Schreiner, R., and Garg, B., 1979. Changes in clinical presentation of term infants with intracranial hemorrhage. *Developmental Medicine and Child Neurology* **21**, 730.

Cattell, R.B., 1971. *Abilities: Their Structure, Growth and Action*. Boston: Houghton Mifflin.

Caviness, V.S., and Rakiac, P., 1978. Mechanisms of cortical development: A view from mutations in mice. *Annual Review of Neuroscience* **1**, 297.

CEC, 1980. *Childhood Deafness in the European Community*, EUR 6413. Luxembourg: Commission of the European Community.

Chadwick, O., Rutter, M., Brown, G., Shaffer, D., and Traub, M., 1981a. A prospective study of children with head injuries: II. Cognitive sequelae. *Psychological Medicine* **11**, 49.

Chadwick, O., Rutter, M., Shaffer, D., and Shrout, P.E., 1981b. A prospective study of children with head injuries: IV. Specific cognitive deficits. *Journal of Clinical Neuropsychology* **3**(2), 101.

Chalfant, J.C., and Scheffelin, M.A., 1969. *Central Processing Dysfunction in Children: A Review of Research*, NINDS Monograph No. 9. Bethesda, Md.: U.S. Department of Health, Education and Welfare.

Chamberlain, R., Chamberlain, C., Howlett, B., and Claireaux, A., 1976. *British Births*. vol. 1: *The First Week of Life*. London: Heinemann.

Chamove, A.S., Kerr, G.R., and Harlow, H.F., 1973. Learning monkeys fed elevated amino acid diets. *Journal of Medical Primatology* **2**, 223.

Chamove, A.S., and Molinaro, T.J., 1978. Monkey retarded learning analysis. *Journal of Mental Deficiency Research* **22**, 37.

Chan, G.H. Jr., 1975a. Drug-induced side effects. In R.D. Harley (ed.), *Pediatric Ophthalmology*. Philadelphia: Saunders.

Chan, G.H. Jr., 1975b. Nutritional deficiency disorders. In R.D. Harley (ed.), *Pediatric Ophthalmology*. Philadelphia: Saunders.

Chase, R.A., 1972. Neurological aspects of language disorders in children. In J. V. Irwin and M. Marge (eds.), *Principles of Childhood Language Disabilities*. New York: Appleton-Century-Crofts.

Chelune, G.J., and Edwards, P., 1981. Early brain lesions: Ontogenetic-environmental considerations. *Journal of Consulting and Clinical Psychology* **49**, 777.

Chess, S., 1971. Autism in children with congenital rubella. *Journal of Autism and Childhood Schizophrenia* **1**, 33.

Chess, S., 1977a. Follow-up report on autism in congenital rubella. *Journal of Autism and Childhood Schizophrenia* **7**(1), 69.

Chess, S., 1977b. Developmental theory revisited: Findings of a longitudinal study. *Canadian Journal of Psychiatry* **24**(2), 101.

Chess, S., Fernandez, P., and Korn, S., 1978. Behavioral consequences of congenital rubella. *Journal of Pediatrics* **93**, 699.

Chess, S., Fernandez, P., and Korn, S., 1980. The handicapped child and his family: Consonance and dissonance. *Journal of the American Academy of Child Psychiatry* **19**, 56.

Chevrie, J.J., and Aicardi, J., 1977. Convulsive disorders in the first year of life: Etiologic factors. *Epilepsia* **18**, 489.

Chevrie, J.J., and Aicardi, J., 1978. Convulsive disorders in the first year of life: Neurological and mental outcome and mortality. *Epilepsia* **19**, 67.

Chi, J.G., Dooling, E., and Gilles, F.H., 1977. Gyral development of the human brain. *Annals of Neurology* **1**, 86.

Chiarello, C., 1980. A house divided? Cognitive functioning with callosal agenesis. *Brain and Language* **11**(1), 128.

Child, C.M., 1941. *Patterns and Problems of Development.* Chicago: University of Chicago Press.

Chisholm, I.H., 1975. Cortical blindness on cranial arteritis. *British Journal of Ophthalmology* **59**, 332.

Churchill, D.W., 1972. The relation of infantile autism and early childhood schizophrenia to developmental language disorders of childhood. *Journal of Autism and Childhood Schizophrenia* **2**(2), 182.

Churchill, J.A., Inga, E., and Senf, R. (1962). The association of position at birth and handedness. *Pediatrics* **29**, 307.

Ciganek, L., 1961. The EEG response (evoked potential) to light stimulus in man. *Electroencephalography and Clinical Neurophysiology* **13**, 165.

Cicni, G., and Pellegrinetti, G., 1982. Lateralization of sensory and motor functions in human neonates. *Perceptual and Motor Skills* **54**, 1151.

Clark, M.M., 1970. Reading Difficulties in School. Harmondsworth, England: Penguin.

Clausen, J.P., Flook, M.H., Ford, B., Green, M.M., and Popiel, B.S., 1973. *Maternity Nursing Today.* New York: McGraw-Hill.

Cleland, C.C., 1979. *The Profoundly Mentally Retarded.* Englewood Cliffs, N.J.: Prentice-Hall.

Clements, S.D., 1966. *Minimal Brain Dysfunction in Children,* Monograph No. 3. Bethesda, Md.: U.S. National Institute of Neurological Disease and Blindness.

Clopton, B.M., 1981. Neurophysiological and anatomical aspects of auditory development. In R.N. Aslin, J.R. Alberts, and M.R. Petersen (eds.), *Development of Perception: Psychobiological Perspectives.* vol. 1: *Audition, Somatic Perception, and the Chemical Senses.* New York: Academic Press.

Cobrinik, L., 1982. The performance of hyperlexic children on an "incomplete words" task. *Neuropsychologia* **20**(5), 569.

Cohen, M.E., and Duffner, P.K., 1983. *Brain Tumors in Children: Principles of Diagnosis and Treatment* (International Review of Child Neurology Series). New York: Raven Press.

Collins, A.L., 1951. Epileptic intelligence. *Journal of Consulting Psychology* **15**, 393.

Collins, A.L., and Lennox, W.G., 1947. The intelligence of 300 private-patient epileptics. *Proceedings of the Association for Research in Nervous and Mental Diseases* **26**, 586.

Colombo, J., 1982. The critical-period concept: Research, methodology and theoretical issues. *Psychological Bulletin* **91**(2), 260.

Commey, J.O.H., and Fitzhardinge, P.M., 1979. Handicap in the preterm small-for-gestational-age infant. *Journal of Pediatrics* **94**, 779.

Commission of the European Community, 1980. *Childhood Deafness in the European Community*, EUR 6413. Luxembourg: CEC.

Conel, J., 1939–1967. *The Postnatal Development of the Human Cerebral Cortex*, vols. 1–8. Cambridge, Mass.: Harvard University Press.

Conners, C.K., 1972. Psychological effects of stimulant drugs in children with minimal brain dysfunction. *Pediatrics* **49**, 702.

Conners, C.K., 1980. *Food Additives and Hyperactive Children*. New York: Plenum Press.

Conners, C.K., Taylor, E., Meo, G., Kurtz, M.A., and Fournier, M., 1972. Magnesium pemoline and dextroamphetamine: A controlled study in children with minimal brain dysfunction. *Psychopharmacologica* **62**, 321.

Connolly, J.A., 1978. Intelligence levels of Down's syndrome children. *American Journal of Mental Deficiencies* **83**(2), 193.

Connolly, K., 1973. Learning and the concept of critical periods in infancy. In S. Chess and A. Thomas (eds.), *Annual Progress in Psychology and Child Development*. New York: Plenum Press.

Connolly, K.J., and Prechtl, H.F.R. (eds.), 1981. *Maturation and Development: Biological and Psychological Perspectives*. London: SIMP/Heineman.

Cook, B.R., and Guthkelch, A.N., 1983. Modern approaches to the treatment of medulloblastoma. *Developmental Medicine and Child Neurology* **25**, 245.

Cook, T.D., and Campbell, D.T., 1979. *Quasi-Experimentation: Design and Analysis Issues for Field Settings*. Boston: Houghton Mifflin.

Cooke, J., 1980. Early organization of the central nervous system: Form and pattern. In R.K. Hunt (ed.), *Neural Development*, part I (*Current Topics in Developmental Biology*, vol. 15). New York: Academic Press.

Cooper, J.A., and Ferry, P.C., 1978. Aquired auditory verbal agnosia and seizures in childhood. *Journal of Speech and Hearing Disorders* **43**, 176.

Cooper, J.M., and Griffiths, P., 1978. Treatment and prognosis. In M.A. Wyke (ed.), *Developmental Dysphasia*. New York: Academic Press.

Corah, N.L., Anthony, E.J., Painter, P., Stern, J., and Thurston, D., 1965. Effects of perinatal anoxia after seven years. *Psychological Monographs* **79** (whole no. 596).

Corner, M.A., Baker, R.E., Van de Poll, N.E., Swaab, D.F., and Uylings, H. B.M. (eds.), *Maturation of the Nervous System* (*Progress in Brain Research*, vol. 48). Amsterdam: Elsevier.

Coryell, J., and Michel, G., 1978. How supine postural preferences of infants can contribute toward the development of handedness. *Infant Behavior and Development* **1**, 245.

Cotman, C.W., and Banker, G.A., 1974. The making of a synapse. In S. Ehrenpreis and I.J. Kopin (eds.), *Review of Neuroscience*, vol. 1. New York: Raven Press.

Cotman, C.W., and Nieto-Sampedro, M., 1982. Brain function, synapse renewal, and plasticity. *Annual Review of Psychology* **33**, 371.

Coulombre, A.J., 1970. Development of the vertebrate motor system. In F.O.

Schmitt (ed.), *The Neurosciences: Second Study Program*. New York: Rocke-feller University Press.

Coursin, D.B., 1974. Electrophysiological studies in malnutrition. In J. Cravito, L. Hambraeus, and B. Vahlquist (eds.), *Early Malnutrition and Mental Develop-ment*. Uppsala: Swedish Nutrition Foundation.

Cowan, W.M., 1979. The development of the brain. *Scientific American* **241**(3), 112.

Cowan, W.M., Stanfield, B.B., and Kishi, K., 1980. The development of the den-tate gyrus. In R.K. Hunt (ed.), *Neural Development*, part I (*Current Topics in Developmental Biology*, vol. 15). New York: Academic Press.

Cox, A., Rutter, M., Newman, S., and Bartak, L., 1975. A comparative study of infantile autism and specific developmental receptive language disorder: II. Parental characteristics. *British Journal of Psychiatry* **126**, 146.

Craft, A., Shaw, D., and Cartlidge, N., 1972. Head injuries in children. *British Medical Journal* **4**, 200.

Cravioto, J., and Arrieta, R., 1979. Stimulation and mental development of mal-nourished infants. *Lancet* **2**(8148), 899.

Cravioto, J., Birch, H.G., and Gaona, C.E., 1967. Early malnutrition and auditory-visual integration in school-age children. *Journal of Special Education* **2**, 75.

Cravioto, J., and DeLicardie, E., 1975. Longitudinal study of language develop-ment in severely malnourished children. In G. Serban (ed.), *Nutrition and Mental Functions. Advances in Behavioral Biology* (vol. XIV). New York: Plenum Press.

Cravioto, J., DeLicardie, E., and Birch, H., 1966. Nutrition, growth, and neuro-integrative development: An experimental and ecologic study. *Pediatrics* **38**, 319.

Creak, M., and Ini, S., 1960. Families in psychotic children. *Journal of Child Psy-chology and Psychiatry* **1**, 156.

Crighel, E., and Botez, M.I., 1966. Photic evoked potentials in man in lesions of the occipital lobes. *Brain* **89**, 311.

Critchley, M., and Critchley, E.A., 1978. *Dyslexia Defined*. London: William Hei-nemann.

Crnic, L., 1976. Effects of infantile undernutrition on adult learning in rats: Meth-odological and design problems. *Psychological Bulletin* **85**, 715.

Crome, L., Cowie, V., and Slater, E., 1966. A statistical note on the cerebellar and brainstem weight in mongolism. *Journal of Mental Deficiency Research* **10**, 69.

Comer, R.F., 1978. The basis of childhood dysphasia: A linguistic approach. In M.A. Wyke (ed.), *Developmental Dysphasia*. New York: Academic Press.

Cronbach, L.J., and Furby, L., 1970. How we should measure "change"—or should we? *Psychological Bulletin* **74**, 68.

Cronholm, B., and Schalling, D., 1968. Cognitive tests performances in cerebrally palsied adults without mental retardation. *Acta Psychiatrica Scandinavica* **44**, 37.

Crothers, B., and Paine, R.S., 1959. *The Natural History of Cerebral Palsy*. Cam-bridge, Mass.: Harvard University Press. 1959.

Cruickshank, W.M., Hallahan, D.P., and Bice, H.V., 1976a. The evaluation of in-telligence. In W.M. Cruickshank (ed.), *Cerebral Palsy, A Developmental Dis-ability*, 3d ed. Syracuse, N.Y. Syracuse University Press,

Cruickshank, W.M., Hallahan, D.P., and Bice, H.V., 1976b. Personality and behavioral characteristics. In W.M. Cruickshank (ed.), *Cerebral Palsy: A Developmental Disability*. 3d revised ed. Syracuse, N.Y.: Syracuse University Press.

Cunningham, C.C., 1979. Aspects of early development in Down's syndrome infants. Ph.D. dissertation. University of Manchester, England.

Cunningham, C.C., and Mittler, P.J., 1981. Maturation, development and mental handicap. In K.J. Connolly and H.F.R. Prechtl (eds.), *Maturation and Development: Biological and Psychological Perspectives*. London: Heinemann.

Cunningham, D.F., 1892. *Contributions to the Surface Anatomy of the Cerebral Hemispheres*. Dublin: Royal Irish Academy.

Cunningham, M.A., 1968. A comparison of the language of psychotic and non-psychotic children who are mentally retarded. *Journal of Child Psychology and Psychiatry* **9**, 229.

Curatolo, P., Libutti, G., and Matricardi, M. 1981. Infantile spasms: A neuro-opthalmological study. *Developmental Medicine and Child Neurology* **23**, 449.

Curtiss, S., 1977. *Genie: A Psycholinguistic Study of a Modern-Day Wild Child*. New York: Academic Press.

Curtiss, S., Fromkin, V., Rigler, D., Rigler, M., and Krashen, S., 1975. An update on the linguistic development of Genie. In D.P. Dato (ed.), *Developmental Psycholinguistics: Theory and Applications*. Washington, D.C.: Georgetown University Press.

Cushing, H.W., 1927. The intracranial tumors of preadolescence. *American Journal of Disorders in Childhood* **33**, 551.

Cynader, M.S., Modifiability of visual cortex under sensory deprivation. *Neurosciences Research Program Bulletin* **20**, 549.

Dabiri, C., 1979. Respiratory distress syndrome. In T. Field, A. Sostek, S. Goldberg, and H. Shuman (eds.), *Infants Born at Risk*. New York: Spectrum Press.

Dalby, J.T., 1979. Deficit or delay: Neuropsychological models of developmental dyslexia. *Journal of Special Education* **13**, 239.

Dalby, M.A., 1975. Air studies in language-retarded children: Evidence of early lateralization of language function. Paper presented at First International Congress of Child Neurology, Toronto, October.

Damasio, A.R., Lima, A., and Damasio, H., 1975. Nervous function after right hemispherectomy. *Neurology* **25**, 89.

Damasio, H., and Damasio, A., 1980. The anatomical basis of conduction aphasia. *Brain* **103**, 337.

Dandy, W.E., 1928. Removal of right cerebral hemisphere for certain tumours with hemiplegia. *Journal of the American Medical Association* **90**, 823.

Dann, M., Levine, S.Z., and New, E.V., 1974. A long-term follow-up study of small premature infants. *Pediatrics* **33**, 945.

Darley, F.L., and Fay, W.H., 1980. Speech mechanism. In F.M. Lassman, R. O. Fisch, D.K. Vetter, and E.S. La Benz (eds.), *Early Correlates of Speech, Language, and Hearing*. Littleton, Mass.: PSG Publishing, p. 199.

Das, J.P., Kirby, J.R., and Jarman, R.F., 1979. *Simultaneous and Successive Cognitive Processes*. New York: Academic Press.

David, O., Clark, J., and Voeller, K., 1972. Lead and hyperactivity. *Lancet* **2**, 900.

Davie, R., Butler, N., and Goldstein, H., 1972. *From Birth to Seven: A Report of the National Child Developmental Study*. London: Longman.

Davies, D.P., Gray, O.P., and Ellwood, P.C. 1976. Cigarette smoking in pregnancy: Associations with maternal weight gain and fetal growth. *Lancet* **1**, 385.

Davies, P., and Stewart, A.L., 1975. Low birth-weight infants: Neurological sequelae and later intelligence. *British Medical Bulletin* **31**, 85.

Davis, A.E., and Wada, J., 1977. Hemispheric asymmetries in human infants: Spectral analysis of flash and click evoked potentials *Brain and Language* **4**, 23.

Davison, A.N., 1977. The biochemistry of brain development and mental retardation. *British Journal of Psychiatry* **131**, 565.

Davison, A.N., and Peters, A., 1970. *Myelination.* Springfield, Ill.: Charles C Thomas.

De Ajuriaguerra, J., Jaeggi, A., Guignard, F., Kocher, F., Maguard, M., Roth, S., and Schmid, E., 1976. The development and prognosis of dysphasia in children. In D.M. Morehead and A.E. Morehead (eds.), *Normal and Deficient Child Language.* Baltimore: University Park Press.

Decker, S.N., 1982. Reading disability: Is there a hereditary pattern? In R.N. Malatesha and L.C. Hartlage (eds.), *Neuropsychology and Cognition*, vol. 2. The Hague: Martinus Nijhoff.

Decker, S.N., and DeFries, J.C., 1980. Cognitive abilities in families with reading disabled children. *Journal of Learning Disabilities* **13**, 9.

De Courten, G.M., and Rabinowicz, T., 1981a. Analysis of 100 infant deaths with intraventricular hemorrhage: Brain weights and risk factors. *Developmental Medicine and Child Neurology* **23**(3), 287.

De Courten, G.M., and Rabinowicz, T., 1981b. Intraventricular hemorrhage in premature infants: Reappraisal and new hypothesis. *Developmental Medicine and Child Neurology* **23**(3), 389.

De Hirsch, K., 1957. Tests designed to discover potential reading difficulty. *American Journal of Orthopsychiatry* **27**, 566.

De Hirsch, K., 1967. Differential diagnosis between aphasic and schizophrenic language in children. *Journal of Speech and Hearing Disorders* **32**, 3.

De Hirsch, K., Jansky, J., and Langford, W.S., 1966. Comparisons between prematurely and maturely born children at three age levels. *American Journal of Orthopsychiatry* **36**, 616.

Dekaban, A., 1967. On clinical and epidemiological aspects of mental retardation. In G.A. Jervis (ed.), *Mental Retardation.* Springfield, Ill.: Charles C Thomas.

Dekaban, A., 1970. *Neurology of Early Childhood.* Baltimore: Williams and Wilkins.

DeLong, G.R., and Adams, R.D., 1975. Clinical aspects of tumors of the posterior fossa in childhood. In P.J. Vinken and G.W. Bruyn (eds.) *Handbook of Clinical Neurology.* Vol. 18: Tumours of the brain and skull, part III. Amsterdam: North-Holland.

DeMyer, M., Pontinis, W., Norton, J., Barton, S., Allen, J., and Steele, R., 1972. Parental practices and innate activity in autistic and brain damaged infants. *Journal of Autism and Childhood Schizophrenia* **2**, 49.

DeMyer, W., 1975. Congenital anomalies of the central nervous system. In D.B. Tower (ed.), *The Nervous System.* vol. 2: *The Clinical Neurosciences.* New York: Raven Press.

Denbigh, K., 1979. Neurological impairment and educational achievement: A follow-up of learning-disabled children. M.A. thesis, University of Victoria.

Denckla, M.B., 1977. Minimal brain dysfunction and dyslexia: Beyond diagnosis by exclusion. In M.E. Blaw, I. Rapin, and M. Kinsbourne (eds.), *Topics in Child Neurology.* New York: Spectrum.

Denckla, M.B., 1978. Minimal brain dysfunction. In J.S. Chall and A.F. Mirsky (eds.), *Education and the Brain.* Chicago: University of Chicago Press.

Denckla, M.B., 1979. Childhood learning disabilities. In K.M. Heilman and E. Valenstein (eds.), *Clinical Neuropsychology.* New York: Oxford University Press.

Denckla, M.B., and Heilman, K.M., 1979. The syndrome of hyperactivity. In K.M. Heilman and E. Valenstein (eds.), *Clinical Neuropsychology.* New York: Oxford University Press.

Denckla, M.B., Rudel, R.B., and Broman, M., 1978. Spatial orientation skills. In D. Caplan, (ed.), *Biological Studies of Mental Processes.* Cambridge, Mass., MIT Press.

Denhoff, E., and Robinault, I.P., 1960. *Cerebral Palsy and Related Disorders: A Developmental Approach to Dysfunction.* New York: McGraw-Hill.

Dennenberg, V.H., 1968. A consideration of the usefulness of the critical-period hypothesis as applied to the stimulation of rodents in infancy. In G. Newton- and S. Levine (eds)., *Early Experience and Behaviour.* Springfield, Ill.: Thomas.

Dennis, J., and Bower, B.D., 1972. The Aicardi syndrome. *Developmental Medicine and Child Neurology* **14**, 382.

Dennis, M., 1976. Impaired sensory and motor differentiation with corpus callosum agenesis: A lack of callosal inhibition during ontogeny? *Neuropsychologia* **14**, 455.

Dennis, M., 1977. Cerebral dominance in three forms of early brain disorder. In M.E. Blau, I. Rapin, and M. Kinsbourne (eds.), *Topics in Child Neurology.* New York: Spectrum.

Dennis, M., 1980a. Capacity and strategy for syntactic comprehension after left or right hemidecortication. *Brain and Language* **10**, 287.

Dennis, M., 1980b. Strokes in Childhood. I: communicative intent, expression, and comprehension after left hemisphere arteriopathy in a right-handed nine year old. In R.W. Rieber (ed.), *Language Development and Aphasia in Children.* New York: Academic Press.

Dennis, M., 1981. Language in a congenitally acallosal brain. *Brain and Language* **12**, 33.

Dennis, M., Fitz, C.R., Netley, C.T., Sugar, J., Harwood-Nash, D.C.F., Hendrick, E.B., Hoffman, H.J., and Humphreys, R.P., 1981. The intelligence of hydrocephalic children. *Archives of Neurology* **38**, 607.

Dennis, M., and Kohn, B., 1975. Comprehension of syntax in infantile hemiplegics after cerebral hemidecortication: Left-hemisphere superiority. *Brain and Language* **2**, 472.

Dennis, M., Lovett, M., and Wiegel-Crump, C.A., 1981. Written language acquisition after left or right hemidecortication in infancy. *Brain and Language* **12**, 54.

Dennis, M., and Whitaker, H.A., 1976. Language acquisition following hemidecortication: Linguistic superiority of the left over the right hemisphere. *Brain and Language* **3**, 404.

Dennis, M., and Whitaker, H.A., 1977. Hemispheric equipotentiality and language aquisition. In S.J. Segalowitz and F.A. Gruber (eds.), *Language Development and Neurological Theory*. New York: Academic Press.

Department of Health, Education, and Welfare, 1966. *Patients in Mental Institutions. I. Public Institutions for the Mentally Retarded*. Washington, D.C.: National Institute of Mental Health.

Department of Health, Education, and Welfare. 1968. *Vital Statistics of the United States for the Years 1965–1967*. Washington, D.C.: Government Printing Office.

Department of Health, Education, and Welfare, 1973. *Children Served in Mental Retardation Clinics.: Fiscal Year 1970–1972* Washington, D.C.: U.S. Government Printing Office.

DeQuiros, J.B., and Schrager, O.L., 1978. *Neuropsychological Fundamentals in Learning Disabilities*. San Rafael, Calif.: Academic Therapy Publications.

DesLauriers, A.M., and Carlson, C.F., 1969. *Your Child Is Asleep: Early Infantile Autism*. Homewood, Ill.: Dorsey Press.

Desmit, E., 1955. A follow-up study of 110 patients treated for purulent meningitis. *Archives of Diseases of Children* **30**, 415.

Desmond, W., Vermiand, W.M., Melnick, J.L., and Rawls, W.E., 1970. The early growth and development of infants with congenital rubella. In D. H. M. Woolam (ed.), *Advances in Teratology*, vol. 4. London: Logos Press.

Diagnostic and Statistical Manual of Mental Disorders, 1980 (3d edn.). Washington, D.C.: American Psychiatric Association.

Diamond, M.C., Dowling, G.A., and Johnson, R.E., 1981. Morphologic cerebral cortical asymmetry in male and female rats. *Experimental Neurology* **71**, 261.

DiBenedetta, C., Balaza, R., Gombos, G., and Porcellati, G. (eds.), 1980. *Multidisciplinary Approach to Brain Development (Developments in Neuroscience,* vol. 9). Amsterdam: Elsevier/North Holland.

Dignan, P. St. J., and Warkany, J., 1977. Congenital malformations: The corpus callosum. In J. Wortis (ed.), *Mental Retardation and Developmental Disabilities*, vol. IX. New York: Brunner/Mazel.

Dimond, S.J., 1972a. *The Double Brain*. Edinburgh: Churchill Livingstone, Chap. 5.

Dimond, S.J., 1972b. *The Double Brain*. Edinburgh: Churchill Livingstone, Chap. 4.

Dimond, S.J., 1975. The disconnection syndromes. In D. Williams (ed.), *Modern Trends in Neurology*, vol. 6. London: Butterworth.

Dimond, S., 1978. The infant brain. In S. Dimond (ed.), *Introducing Neuropsychology*. Springfield, Ill.: Charles C Thomas.

Dingman, H.F., and Tarjan, G., 1960. Mental retardation and the normal distribution curve. *American Journal of Mental Deficiency* **64**, 991.

Dixon, N.F., and Jeeves, M.A., 1970. The interhemispheric transfer of movement aftereffects: A comparison between acallosal and normal subjects. *Psychonomic Science*, **20**(4), 201.

Dobbing, J., 1968. Vulnerable periods in developing brain. In A. N. Davison and J. Dobbing (eds.), *Applied Neurochemistry*. Oxford: Blackwell.

Dobbing, J., 1975. Prenatal nutrition and neurological development. In N.A. Buchwald and M.A.B. Brazier (eds.), *Brain Mechanisms in Mental Retardation.* New York: Academic Press.

Dobbing, J., and Sands, J., 1973. Quantitative growth and development of human brain. *Archives of Disease in Childhood* **48**(1), 757.

Dobbing, J., and Smart, J.L., 1974. Vulnerability of developing brain and behaviour. *British Medical Bulletin* **30**, 164.

Dodd, B., 1976. A comparison of the phonological systems of mental-age-matched normal, severely subnormal and Down's syndrome children. *British Journal of Disorders of Communication* **11**, 27

Dodge, P., Prensky, A., and Feigin, R., 1975. *Nutrition and the Developing Nervous System.* St. Louis: C.V. Mosby.

Dodgson, M.C.H., 1962. *The Growing Brain: An Essay in Developmental Neurology.* Bristol, England: Wright.

Dodson, W.E., 1976. Neonatal drug intoxication: Local anesthetics. *Pediatric Clinic of North America* **23**, 399.

Doehring, D.G., 1960. Visual-spatial memory in aphasic children. *Journal of Speech and Hearing Research* **3**, 138.

Doehring, D.G., 1968a. Discrimination of simultaneous and successive tones. *Perception and Psychophysics* **3**, 293.

Doehring, D.G., 1968b. *Patterns of Impairment in Specific Reading Disability.* Bloomington, Ind.: Indiana University Press.

Doehring, D.G., and Hoshko, I.M., 1977. Classification of reading problems by the Q-technique of factor analysis. *Cortex* **13**, 281.

Doehring, D.G., Trites, R.L., Patel, P.G., and Fiedorowizc, C.A.M., 1981. *Reading Disabilities: The Interaction of Reading, Language and Neuropsychological Deficits.* New York: Academic Press.

Doose, H., 1975. *Zerebrale Anfälle im Kindesalter.* Hamburg: Desitin.

Douglas, V.I., and Peters, K.G., 1979. Toward a clearer definition of the attentional deficit of hyperactive children. In G.A. Hale and M. Lewis (eds.), *Attention and Cognitive Development.* New York: Plenum.

Downing, J., and Leong, C.K., 1982. *Psychology of Reading.* New York, Macmillan.

Drake, W. E., 1968. Clinical and pathological findings in a child with a developmental learning disability. *Journal of Learning Disabilities* **1**(9), 486.

Drillien, C.M. 1958. Growth and development in a group of children of very low birth weight. *Archives of Diseases in Childhood* **33**, 10.

Drillien, C.M., 1961. The incidence of mental and physical handicaps in school-age children of very low birth weight. *Pediatrics* **27**, 452.

Drillien, C.M., 1964. *The Growth and Development of the Prematurely Born Infant.* Baltimore: Williams and Wilkins.

Drillien, C.M., 1972. Aetiology and outcome in low-birth-weight infants. *Developmental Medicine and Child Neurology* **14**, 563.

Drillien, C.M., 1974. Prenatal and perinatal factors in etiology and outcome of low birth weight. *Clinics in Perinatology* **1**, 197.

Drillien, C.M., Thomson, A.J.M., and Burgoyre, K., 1980. Low-birth-weight children at early school age: A longitudinal study. *Developmental Medicine and Child Neurology* **22**, 26.

Droege, R.C., 1971. Effectiveness of follow-up techniques in large-scale longitudinal research. *Developmental Psychology* **5**, 27.

Dublin, W., 1951. Neurologic lesions of erythroblastosis fetalis in relation to nuclear deafness. *American Journal of Clinical Pathology* **21**, 935.

Dublin, W.B., 1978. The auditory pathology of anoxia. *Otolaryngology* **86**(1), 27.

Dubowitz, L.M.S., 1979. Study of visual function in the premature infant. *Child: Care, Health and Development* **5**, 399.

Dubowitz, L.M.S., Dubowitz, V., and Goldberg, C., 1970. Clinical assessment of gestational age in the newborn infant. *Journal of Pediatrics* **77**, 1.

Duchowny, M.S., Weiss, I.P., Majlessi, H., and Barnet, A.B., 1974. Visual evoked responses in childhood cortical blindness after head trauma and meningitis. *Neurology* **24**, 933.

Duckett, S., 1981. Neuropathological aspects: Congenital malformations. In P. Black (ed.), *Brain Dysfunction in Children*. New York: Raven Press.

Dunn, H.C., and McBurney, A.K., 1977. Cigarette smoking and the fetus and the child. *Pediatrics* **60**, 772.

Dweck, H., Higgins, W., Dorman, L., Saxon, S., Benton, J., and Cassady, G., 1974. Developmental sequelae in infants having suffered severe perinatal asphyxia. *American Journal of Obstetrics and Gynecology* **119**(6), 811.

Dykman, R.A., and Ackerman, P.T., 1976. The MBD problem: Attention, intention and information processing. In R.P. Anderson and C.G. Halcomb (eds.). *Learning Disability/Minimal Brain Dysfunction Syndrome*. Springfield, Ill.: Charles C Thomas.

Dykman, R.A., Peters, J.E., and Ackerman, P.T., 1973. Experimental approaches to the study of minimal brain dysfunction: A follow-up study. *Annals of the New York Academy of Sciences* **205**, 93.

Eeg-Olofsson, O., 1970. The development of the electroencephalogram in normal children and adolescents from the age of 1 through 21 years. *Acta Paediatrica Scandinavica* suppl., **208**, 4.

Ehrhardt, A.A., and Baker, S.W., 1974. Fetal androgens, human central nervous system differentiation, and behavior sex differences. In R.C. Friedman et al. (eds.), *Sex Differences in Behavior*. New York: Wiley.

Eichorn, D.H., 1979. Physical development: Current foci of research. In J.D. Osofsky (ed.), *Handbook of Infant Development*. New York: Wiley.

Eimas, P.D., 1974. Speech perception in early infancy. In I.B. Cohen and P. Salapatek (eds.), *Infant Perception*. New York: Academic Press.

Eimas, P.D., Siqueland, E.R., Jusczyk, P., and Vigorito, J., 1971. Speech perception in infants. *Science* **71**, 303.

Eimas, P.D., and Tartter, V.C., 1979. On the development of speech perception: Mechanisms and analogies. *Advances in Child Development and Behavior* **13**, 155.

Eisenberg, L., and Kanner, L., 1956. Childhood schizophrenia. *Americal Journal of Orthopsychiatry* **26**, 556.

Eisenberg, R.B., 1976. *Auditory Competence in Early Life*. Baltimore: University Park Press.

Eisenson, J., 1968a. Developmental aphasia (dyslogia): A postulation of a unitary concept of the disorder. *Cortex* **4**, 184.

Eisenson, J., 1968b. Developmental aphasia: A speculative view with therapeutic implications. *Journal of Speech and Hearing Disorders* **33**, 3.

Ellenberg, J.G., and Nelson, K., 1978. Febrile seizures and later intellectual performance. *Archives of Neurology* **35**, 17.

Ellenberg, L., 1982. Cognitive recovery in pediatric medulloblastoma patients following neurosurgery and radiation therapy. Paper presented at the Xth Annual Meeting of the International Neuropsychological Society, Pittsburgh, February.

Ellingson, R.J., 1964. Studies of the electrical activity of the developing human brain. In W.A. Himwich and H.E. Himwich (eds.), *The Developing Brain (Progress in Brain Research*, vol. 9). Amsterdam: Elsevier.

Ellingson, R.J., 1967. The study of brain electrical activity in infants. In L.P. Lipsitt and C.C. Spiker (eds.), *Advances in Child Development and Behavior*, vol. 3. New York: Academic Press.

Ellis, N.R. 1963. The stimulus trace and behavioral inadequacy. In N.R. Ellis (ed.), *Handbook of Mental Deficiency*. New York: McGraw-Hill.

Elonen, A.S., and Zwarensteyn, S.B., 1964. Appraisal of developmental lag in certain blind children. *Journal of Pediatrics* **65**, 599.

Entus, A.K., 1977. Hemispheric asymmetry in processing of dichotically presented speech and nonspeech stimuli by infants. In S.J. Segalowitz, and F.A. Gruber (eds.), *Language Development and Neurological Theory*. New York: Academic Press.

Epstein, H.T., 1974. Phrenoblysis: Special brain and mind growth periods. *Developmental Psychobiology* **7**, 207.

Epstein, H.T., 1978. Growth spurts during brain development: Implications for educational policy and practice. In J.S. Chall and A.F. Mirsky (eds.), *Education and the Brain*. Chicago: University of Chicago Press.

Espenschade, A.S., and Eckert, H.M., 1980. *Motor Development*, 2 ed. Columbus, Ohio: Charles E. Merrill.

Ettlinger, G., 1977. Agenesis of the corpus callosum. In P.J. Vinken and G.W. Bruyn (eds.), *Handbook of Clinical Neurology*, vol. 30. Amsterdam: North-Holland.

Ettlinger, G., Blakemore, C., Milner, A., and Wilson, J., 1972. Agenesis of the corpus callosum: A behavioral investigation. *Brain* **95**, 327.

Ettlinger, G., Blakemore, C., Milner, A., and Wilson, J., 1974. Agenesis of the corpus callosum: A further behavioral investigation. *Brain* **97**, 225.

Evans, D., Moodie, A., and Hansen, J., 1971. Kwashiorkor and intellectual development. *South African Medical Journal* **45**, 1413.

Ewing, A.W.G., 1930. *Aphasia in Childhood*. London: Oxford University Press.

Fairweather, H., 1976. Sex differences in cognition. *Cognition* **4**, 231.

Fantz, R.L., and Fagan, J.F., 1975. Visual attention to size and number of pattern details by term and preterm infants during the first six months. *Child Development* **46**, 3.

Fantz, R.L., and Ordy, J.M., 1959. A visual acuity test for infants under six months of age. *Psychological Record* **9**, 159.

Fantz, R.L., Ordy, J.M., and Udelf, M.S., 1962. Maturation of pattern vision in infants during the first six months. *Journal of Comparative Physiological Psychology* **55**(6), 907.

Farr, V., Mitchell, R.G., Neligan, G.A., and Parkin, J.M., 1966. The definition of newborn infant. *Developmental Medicine and Child Neurology* **8**, 507.

Farwell, J.R., Dohrmann, G.J., and Flannery, J.T., 1978. Intracranial neoplasms in infants. *Archives of Neurology* **35**, 533.

Fay, W.H., and Butler, B.V., 1968. Echolalia, IQ, and the developmental dichotomy of speech and language systems. *Journal of Speech and Hearing Research* **11**, 365.

Feigin, R.D., and Dodge, P.R., 1976. Bacterial meningitis: Newer concepts of pathophysiology and neurologic sequelae. *Pediatric Clinics of North America* **23**, 541.

Feingold, B.F., 1975. Hyperkinesis and learning disabilities linked to artificial food flavors and colors. *American Journal of Nursing* **75**, 797.

Fenichel, G.M., *Neonatal Neurology*. New York: Churchill Livingston.

Ferrari, F., Grosoli, M.V., Fontana, G., and Gravazutti, G.B., 1983. Neurobehavioral comparison of low risk preterm and fullterm infants at term conceptual age. *Developmental Medicine and Child Neurology* **25**, 720.

Ferris, G., and Dorsen, M., 1975. Agenesis of the corpus callosum. 1. Neuropsychological studies. *Cortex* **11**, 95.

Ferry, P.C., Hall, S.M., and Hicks, J.L., 1975. 'Dilapidated' speech: Developmental verbal dyspraxia. *Developmental Medicine and Child Neurology* **17**, 749.

Field, M., Ashton, R., and White, K., 1978. Agenesis of the corpus callosum: Report of two preschool children and review of the literature. *Developmental Medicine and Child Neurology* **20**, 47.

Field, T., 1960. Supplemental stimulation of preterm neonates. *Early Human Development* **413**, 301.

Field, T., Dempsey, J.R., and Shuman, H.H., 1979. Developmental assessments of infants surviving the respiratory distress syndrome. In T. Field, A. Sostek, S. Goldberg, and H.H. Shuman (eds.), *Infants Born at Risk*. New York: Spectrum.

Filskov, S.B., and Leli, D.A., 1981. Assessment of the individual in neuropsychological practice. In S.B. Filskov and T.J. Boll (eds.), *Handbook of Clinical Neuropsychology*. New York: Wiley.

Fine, S.R., 1968. *Blind and Partially Sighted Children*. Education Survey No. 4, Department of Education and Science. London: H.M. Stationery Office.

Finger, S., and Stein, D.G., 1982. *Brain Damage and Recovery: Research and Clinical Perspectives*. New York: Academic Press.

Finkemeyer, H., Pfingst, E., and Zulch, K. J., 1975. The astrocytomas of the cerebral hemispheres. In P.J. Vinken and G.W. Bruyn (eds.), *Handbook of Clinical Neurology*, Vol. 18. Amsterdam: North-Holland.

Finucci, J.M., 1978. Genetic considerations in dyslexia. In H.R. Myklebust (ed.), *Progress in Learning Disabilities*, vol. 4. New York: Grune and Stratton.

Finucci, J.M., and Childs, B., 1981. Are there really more dyslexic boys than girls? In A. Ansara et al. (eds.), *Sex Differences in Dyslexia*. Towson, Md.: Orton Dyslexia Society.

Fior, R., 1972. Physiological maturation of auditory function between 3 and 13 years of age. *Audiology* **11**, 317.

Firestone, P., Peters, S., Rivier, M., and Knights, R.M., 1978. Minor physical anomalies in hyperactive retarded and normal children and their families. *Journal of Child Psychology and Psychiatry* **19**, 155.

Fish, B., 1957. The detection of schizophrenia in infancy. *Journal of Nervous and Mental Disorders* **125**, 1.

Fish, B., 1977. Neurobiologic antecedents of schizophrenia in children. *Archives of General Psychiatry* **34**, 1297.

Fish, B., and Hagin, R., 1973. Visual-motor disorders in infants at risk for schizophrenia. *Archives of General Psychiatry* **28**, 900.

Fish, I., and Winick, M., 1969. Cellular growth in various regions of the developing rat brain. *Pediatric Research* **3**, 407.

Fisher, M., and Zeaman, D., 1970. Growth and decline of retardate intelligence. In N.R. Ellis (ed.), *International Review of Research in Mental Retardation*, vol. 4. New York: Academic Press.

Fishman, M.A., 1976. Recent clinical advances in the treatment of dysraphic states. *Pediatric Clinics of North America* **23**, 517.

Fishman, M.A. and Palkes, H.S., 1974. The validity of psychometric testing in children with congenital malformations of the central nervous system. *Developmental Medicine and Child Neurology* **16**, 180.

Fitzhardinge, P.M., Flodmark, O., Fitz, O.R., and Ashby, S., 1981. The prognostic value of computer tomography as an adjunct to assessment of the term infant with postasphyxial encephalopathy. *Journal of Pediatrics* **99**(5), 777.

Flechsig, P., 1901. Developmental (myelogenetic) localization of the cortex in human subjects. *Lancet* **2**, 1027.

Flower, R.M., Viehweg, R., and Ruzicka, W.R., 1961a. The communicative disorders of children with kernicterus athetosis: I. Auditory disorders. *Journal of Speech and Hearing Disorders* **31**, 41.

Flower, R.M., Viehweg, R., and Ruzicka, W.R., 1961b. The communicative disorders of children with kernicterus athetosis: II. Problems in language comprehension and use. *Journal of Speech and Hearing Disorders* **31**, 60.

Folstein, S., and Rutter, M., 1977. Genetic influences and infantile autism. *Nature* **265**, 726.

Foltz, E.L., and Shurtleff, D.B., 1972. Hydrocephalus treated in the early weeks of life. In *Symposium on Myelomeningocele*, American Academy of Orthopedic Surgeons. St. Louis: C.V. Mosby.

Ford, F.R., 1960. *Diseases of the Nervous System in Infancy, Childhood, and Adolescence.* Springfield, Ill: Charles C Thomas.

Fox, M.W., 1970. Overview and critique of stages and periods in canine development. *Developmental Psychobiology* **4**, 37.

Francis-Williams, J., and Davies, P.A., 1974. Very low birth weight and later intelligence. *Developmental Medicine and Child Neurology* **16**, 709.

Frank, V., and Torres, F., 1979. Visual evoked potentials in the evaluation of 'cortical blindness' in children. *Annals of Neurology* **6**, 126.

Fraser, F.C., and Sadovnick, A.D., 1976. Correlation of IQ in subjects with Down's syndrome and their parents and sibs. *Journal of Mental Deficiency Research* **20**, 179.

Frazer, G.R., 1962. Our genetical load: A review of some aspects of genetical variation. *Annals of Human Genetics* (London) **25**, 387.

Frederiksen, C.H., and Rotondo, J., 1979. Time series models and the study of longitudinal change. In J.R. Nesselroade and P.B. Baltes (eds.), *Longitudinal Research in the Study of Behavior and Development*. New York: Academic Press.

Freeman, D.G., 1964. Smiling in blind infants and the issue of innate vs. acquired. *Journal of Child Psychology* 5, 171.

Freeman, R.D., and Bonds, A.B., 1979. Cortical plasticity in monocularly deprived immobilized kittens depends on eye movements. *Science* 206, 1093.

Freudenberg, D., 1968. *Leistungs- und Verhaltensstörungen bei kindlichen Epilepsien*. Basel: Karger.

Freudenberg, D., 1971. Die Pyknolepsie des Kindesalters: Eine Psychodiagnostische Untersuchung. Dissertation. University of Freiburg, Germany.

Friedman, R.C., Richart, R.M., and Van de Wiele, R.L. (eds.), 1974. *Sex Differences in Behaviour*. New York: Wiley.

Friedman, R.M., Sandler, J., Hernandez, M., and Wolfe, D.A., 1981. Child abuse. In E.J. Mash and L.G. Terdal (eds.), *Behavioral Assessment of Childhood Disorders*. New York: Guilford.

Friedrich, D., 1972. *A Primer of Developmental Methodology*. Minneapolis: Burgess.

Frith, U., and Frith, C.D., 1974. Specific motor disabilities in Down's syndrome. *Journal of Child Psychology and Psychiatry* 15, 293.

Fruehauf, K., 1976. Ergebnisse psychologischer Laengsschnittuntersuchungen bei Kindern mit aktivem Hydrozephalus nach Shunt-Operation im ersten Lebensjahr. *Zeitschrift fuer Psychologie* 184, 505.

Furth, H.G., 1964. Sequence learning in aphasic and deaf children. *Journal of Speech and Hearing Disorders* 29, 171.

Furth, H.G., 1966. *Thinking Without Language*. New York: Free Press.

Furth, H.G., and Youniss, J., 1964. Color-object paired associates in deaf and hearing children with and without response competition. *Journal of Consulting Psychology* 28, 224.

Gaddes, W.H., 1976. Prevalence estimates and the need for definition of learning disabilities. In R.M. Knights and D.J. Bakker (eds.), *The Neuropsychology of Learning Disorders*. Baltimore: University Park Press.

Gaddes, W.H., 1980. *Learning Disabilities and Brain Function. A Neuropsychological Approach*. New York: Springer.

Gaddes, W.H., and Crockett, D.J., 1975. The Spreen-Benton aphasia test: normative data as a measure of normal language development. *Brain and Language* 2, 257.

Galaburda, A., Sanides, F., and Geschwind, N., 1978. Human brain: Cytoarchitectonic left-right asymmetries in the temporal speech region. *Archives of Neurology* 35, 812.

Galante, M.B., Flye, M.E., and Stephens, L.S., 1972. Cumulative minor deficits: A longitudinal study of the relation of physical factors to school achievement. *Journal of Learning Disabilities* 5, 75.

Galanter, E., 1962. Contemporary psychophysics. In R. Brown, E. Galanter, E. Hess, and G. Mandler (eds.), *New Directions in Psychology*. New York: Holt.

Galatzer, A., Nofar, E., Beit-Halachimi, N., Aran, D., Shalit, M., Roitman, A., and Laron, Z., 1981. Intellectual and psychosocial functions in children, adolescents, and young adults before and after operation for craniopharyngioma. *Child: Care, Health and Development* 7, 307.

Galin, D., Johnstone, J., Nakell, L., and Herron, J., 1979. Development of the capacity for tactile information transfer between hemispheres in normal children. *Science* **24**, 1330.

Gall, C., and Lynch, G., 1980. The regulation of fiber growth and synaptogenesis in the developing hippocampus. In R.K. Hunt (ed.), *Neural Development*, part I *(Current Topics in Developmental Biology*, vol. 15). New York: Academic Press.

Galler, J.R., Ramsey, F., Solimano, G., Lowell, W.E., and Mason, E., 1983a. The influence of early malnutrition on subsequent behavioral development. I. Degree of impairment in intellectual performance. *Journal of the American Academy of Child Psychiatry* **22**(1), 8.

Galler, J.R., Ramsey, F., Solimano, G., and Lowell, W.E., 1983b. The influence of early malnutrition on subsequent behavioral development. II. Classroom behavior. *Journal of the American Academy of Child Psychiatry* **22**(1), 16.

Gardiner, M.F., and Walter, D.C., 1977. Evidence of hemispheric specialization from infant EEG. In S. Harnad, R.W. Doty, L. Goldstein, J. Jaynes., and G. Krauthamer (eds.), *Lateralization in the Nervous System*. New York: Academic Press.

Gardner, E., 1968. *Fundamentals of Neurology*, 5th edn. Philadelphia: Saunders.

Gardner, W.J., Karnoch, I.J., McClure, C.C., and Gardner, A.K., 1955. Residual function following hemispherectomy for tumour and for infantile hemiplegia. *Brain* **78**, 487.

Garey, L.J., and Pettigrew, J.D., 1974. Ultrastructural changes in kitten visual cortex after environmental modification. *Brain Research* **66**, 165.

Garfield, J.C., Motor impersistence in normal and brain-damaged children. *Neurology* **14**, 623.

Garn, S.M., Shaw, H.A., and McCabe, K.D., 1977. Effects of socioeconomic status and race on weight-defined and gestational prematurity in the United States. In D. Reed, and F. Stanley (eds.), *The Epidemiology of Prematurity*. Baltimore: Urban and Schwarzenberg.

Garrett, H.E., 1946. A developmental theory of intelligence. *American Psychologist* **1**, 372.

Garron, D.C., 1977. Intelligence among persons with Turner's syndrome. *Behavioral Genetics* **7**(2), 105.

Garvey, M., and Mutton, D.E., 1973. Sex chromosome aberrations and speech development. *Archives of Disease in Childhood* **48**, 937.

Gastaut, H. 1970. Clinical and electroencephalographical classification of epileptic seizures. *Epilepsia* **11**, 102.

Gastaut, H., Gastaut, J.L., Regis, H., Bernard, R., Pinsard, N., Saint-Jaen, M., Roger, J., and Dravet, C., 1978. Computer tomography in the study of West's syndrome. *Developmental Medicine and Child Neurology* **20**, 21.

Gazzaniga, M.S., 1970. *The Bisected Brain*. New York: Appleton-Century-Crofts.

Gazzaniga, M.S., Steen, D., and Volpe, E.T., 1979. Principles of brain development. In M.S. Gazzaniga, D. Steen, and B.T. Volpe (eds.), *Functional Neuroscience*. New York: Harper and Row.

Gebelt, H., 1971. *Psychische und soziale Prognose der Epilepsie im Kindes und Jugendalter*. Leipzig: Barth.

Gelles, R.J., 1978. Violence toward children in the United States. *American Journal of Orthospychiatry* **48**, 580.

Gellner, L., 1959. *A Neurophysiological Concept of Mental Retardation and Its Educational Implications*. Chicago: Julian Levinson Foundation.

Geoffroy G., Lassonde, M., Delisle, F., and Décarie, M., 1983. Corpus callosotomy for control of intractable epilepsy in children. *Neurology* **33**, 891.

Gerrard, J., 1952. Kernicterus. *Brain* **75**, 526.

Geschwind, N., 1965. Disconnection syndromes in animals and man. *Brain* **88**, 237 and 585.

Geschwind, N., 1970. The clinical syndromes of the cortical connections. In D. Williams (ed.), *Modern Trends in Neurology*, vol. 5. London: Butterworth.

Geschwind, N., 1975. Le concept de disconnexion: L'histoire d'une idee banale mais importante. In F. Michel and B. Schott (eds.), *Les Syndromes de Disconnexion Calleuse chez l'Homme* (Colloque Internationale de Lyon, 1974). Lyon: Hopital Neurologique.

Geschwind, N., and Kaplan, E., 1962. A human cerebral deconnection syndrome. *Neurology* **12**, 675.

Geschwind, N., and Levitsky, W., 1968. Left-right asymmetries in the temporal speech region. *Science* **161**, 166.

Gesell, A., and Ames, L.B., 1947. The development of handedness. *Journal of Genetic Psychology* **70**, 155.

Gesell, A., and Armatruda, C.S., 1945. *The Embryology of Behaviour*. New York: Harper.

Gibbs, F.A., and Gibbs, E.C., 1952. *Atlas of Electroencephalography*, vol. 2. Cambridge, Mass.: Addison-Wesley.

Gibson, D., 1967. Intelligence in the mongoloid and his parent. *American Journal of Mental Deficiency* **71**, 1014.

Gibson, D., 1978. *Down's Syndrome: The Psychology of Mongolism*. Cambridge: Cambridge University Press.

Gittleman, M., and Birch, G., 1967. Childhood schizophrenia: Intellect, neurologic status, perinatal risk, prognosis and family pathology. *Archives of General Psychiatry* **17**, 16.

Gjerris, F., 1976. Clinical aspects and long-term prognosis of intracranial tumours in infancy and childhood. *Developmental Medicine and Child Neurology* **18**, 145.

Glanville, B., Best, C., and Levenson, R., 1977. A cardiac measure of cerebral asymmetry in infant auditory perception. *Developmental Psychology* **13**, 54.

Goetzinger, M.R., and Houchins, R.R., 1969. The 1947 Colored Raven's Progressive Matrices with deaf and hearing subjects. *American Annals of the Deaf* **114**(2), 95.

Gold, P., 1979. Suspected neurological impairment and cognitive abilities: A longitudinal study. *Psychological Reports* **45**, 215.

Goldberg, H.K., and Schiffman, G.B., 1972. *Dyslexia: Problems of Reading Disabilities*. New York: Grune and Stratton.

Goldberger, M.E., 1974. Recovery of movement after CNS lesions in monkeys. In D.G. Stein, J.J. Rosen, and N. Butters (eds.), *Plasticity and Recovery of Function in the Central Nervous System*. New York: Academic Press.

Golden, C.J., 1981. The Luria-Nebraska children's battery: Theory and formulation. In G.W. Hynd and J.E. Obrynt (eds.), *Neuropsychological Assessment and the School-Age Child: Issues and Procedures*. New York: Grune and Stratton.

Golden, N.L., Sokol, R.J., Kuhnert, B.R., and Bottoms, S., 1982. Maternal alcohol use and infant development. *Pediatrics* **70**, 656

.Goldensohn, E.S., and Ward, A.A., 1975. Pathogenesis of epileptic seizures. In D.B. Tower (ed.), *The Nervous System*, vol. 2, p. 249. New York: Raven Press.

Goldfarb, W., 1943. Infant rearing and problem behaviour. *American Journal of Orthopsychiatry* **13**, 249.

Goldfarb, W., 1961. The mutual impact of mother and child in childhood schizophrenia. *American Journal of Orthopsychiatry* **31**, 738.

Goldman, P.S., 1974. An alternative to developmental plasticity: Heterology of CNS structures in infants and adults. In D.G. Stein, J.F. Rosen, and N. Butters (eds.), *Plasticity and the Recovery of Function in the Central Nervous System.* New York: Academic Press.

Goldman, P.S., 1975. Age, sex, and experience as related to the neural basis of cognitive development. In N.A. Buchwald and M.A.B. Brazier (eds.), *Brain Mechanisms in Mental Retardation.* New York: Academic Press.

Goldman, P.S., 1976. Maturation of the mammalian nervous system and the ontogeny of behavior. In J.S. Rosenblatt, R.A. Hinde, E. Shaw, and C. Beer (eds.), *Advances in the Study of Behavior*, vol. 7. New York: Academic Press.

Goldman, P.S., Crawford, H.T., Stokes, L.P., Galkin, T.W., and Rosvold H.E., 1974. Sex-dependent behavioral effects of cerebral cortical lesions in the developing rhesus monkey. *Science* **186**, 540.

Goldman, P.S., and Lewis, M.E., 1978. Developmental biology of brain damage and experience. In C.W. Cotman (ed.), *Neuronal Plasticity.* New York: Raven Press.

Goldman, P.S., and Nauta, W.J.H., 1977. Columnar distribution of corticocortical fibers in the frontal association, limbic, and motor cortex of the developing rhesus monkey. *Brain Research* **122**, 393.

Goldman, P.S., and Rakic, P.T., 1979. Impact of the outside world upon the developing primate brain. *Bulletin of the Menninger Clinic* **43**(1), 2.

Goldman, P.S., Rosvold, H.E., and Mishkin, M., 1970. Evidence for behavioral impairments following prefrontal lobectomy in the infant monkey. *Journal of Comparative and Physiological Psychology* **70**,454.

Goldstein, K., 1948. *Language and Language Disturbance.* New York: Grune and Stratton.

Goldstein, R., Landau, W.M., and Kleffner, F.R., 1960. Neurological observations on a population of deaf and aphasic children. *Annals of Otology, Rhinology, and Laryngology* **69**, 757.

Goleman, D., 1978. Special abilities of the sexes: Do they begin in the brain? *Psychology Today*, p. 258.

Golter, M., and Michaelson, I.A., 1975. Growth, behavior and brain catecholamines in lead-exposed neonatal rats: A reappraisal. *Science* **187**, 359.

Gomez, F.R., Ramos-Galvan, R., Cravioto, J., and Frank, S. 1955. Kwashiorkorprotein malnutrition. *Advances in Pediatrics* **7**, 131.

Gomez, M.R., 1967. Minimal cerebral dysfunction (maximal neurological confusion). *Clinical Pediatrics* **6**, 589.

Goodhill, V., 1950. Nuclear deafness and the nerve deaf child: The importance of the Rh factor. *Transactions of the American Academy of Ophthalmology and Otolaryngology* **54**, 671.

Goodhill, V., 1956. Rh child: Deaf or "aphasic"? 1. Clinical pathologic aspects of kernicterus nuclear "deafness." *Journal of Speech and Hearing Disorders* **21**, 407.

Goodman, J.F., 1977a. Medical diagnosis and intelligence levels in young mentally retarded children. *Journal of Mental Deficiency Research* **21**, 205.

Goodman, J.F., 1977b. IQ decline in mentally retarded adults: A matter of fact or methodological flaw? *Journal of Mental Deficiency Research* **21**, 199.

Goodman, J.F., and Cameron, J., 1978. The meaning of IQ constancy in young retarded children. *Journal of Genetic Psychology* **132**, 109.

Goodwin, D.W., Schulsinger, F., Hermauben, L., Guze, S.B., and Winckur, G., 1975. Alcoholism and the hyperactive child syndrome. *Journal of Nervous and Mental Disease* **160**, 349.

Gordon, R., White, D., and Diller, L., 1972. Performance of neurologically impaired pre-school children with educational materials. *Exceptional Children* **38**(5), 428.

Gott, P.S., 1973a. Cognitive abilities following right or left hemispherectomy. *Cortex* **9**, 266.

Gott, P.S., 1973b. Language after dominant hemispherectomy. *Journal of Neurology, Neurosurgery, and Psychiatry* **36**, 1082.

Gott, P.S., and Saul, R.E., 1978. Agenesis of the corpus callosum: Limits of functional compensation. *Neurology* **28**, 1272.

Gottfried, A., 1973. Intellectual consequences of perinatal anoxia. *Psychological Bulletin* **80**, 231.

Gottlieb, G., 1971. Ontogenesis of sensory function in birds and mammals. In E. Tobach, L.R. Aronson, E. Shaw (eds.), *The Biopsychology of Development*. New York: Academic Press.

Gottlieb, G., 1976. Conceptions of prenatal development: Behavioral embryology. *Psychological Review* **83**, 215.

Goy, R. W., 1970. Early hormonal influences on the development of sexual and sex-related behavior. In F.O. Schmitt (ed.), *The Neurosciences, Second Study Program*. New York: Rockefeller University Press.

Grafman, J., Passafiume, D., Faglioni, P., and Boller, F., 1982. Calculation disturbances in adults with focal hemispheric damage. *Cortex* **18**, 37.

Graham, F.K., Ernhart, C.B., Craft, M., and Berman, P.M., 1963. Brain injury in the pre-school child: Some developmental considerations. *Performance of Normal Children. Psychological Monographs* **77**, 1.

Graham, F.K., Ernhart, C.B., Thurston, D., and Craft, M., 1962. Development three years after perinatal anoxia and other potentially damaging newborn experiences. *Psychological Monographs* **76** (whole no. 522).

Graham, P.J., 1971. Pathology in the brain and antisocial disorder. In J. Hellmuth (ed.), *Exceptional Infant*, vol. 2, New York: Brunner/Mazel.

Graham-Clay, S., 1983. Fetal alcohol syndrome: A review of current human research. *Canada's Mental Health*, June, p. 2.

Greenberg, R.P., 1982. Evoked potentials in the clinical neurosciences. *Journal of Neurosurgery* **56**, 1.

Greenough, W.T., 1976. Enduring brain effects of differential experience and training In M.R. Rosenzweig and E.I. Bennett (eds), *Neural Mechanisms of Learning and Memory*. Cambridge, Mass: MIT Press.

Gregg, G.S., and Hutchinson, D.L., 1969. Developmental characteristics of infants surviving fetal transfusion. *Journal of the American Medical Association* **209**, 1059.

Gregg, N.M., 1941. Congenital cataract following German measles in the mother. Transactions of the Ophthalmological Society of Australia **3**, 35.

Gresham, E.L., 1975. Birth trauma. *Pediatric Clinics of North America* **22**, 317.

Griffith, H., and Davidson, M., 1966. Long-term changes in intellect and behavior after hemispherectomy. *Journal of Neurology, Neurosurgery, and Psychiatry* **29**, 571.

Griffiths, C. P., 1969. A follow-up study of children with disorders of speech. *British Journal of Disorders of Communication* **4**, 46.

Griffiths, P., 1972. *Developmental Aphasia: An Introduction*. London: Invalid Children's Aid Association.

Groden, G., 1969. Relationships between intelligence, simple and complex motor proficiency. *American Journal of Mental Deficiency* **74**, 373.

Grogono, J., 1968. Children with agenesis of the corpus callosum. *Developmental Medicine and Child Neurology* **10**, 613.

Grossman, H.J. (ed.), 1983. *Manual on Terminology and Classification in Mental Retardation*, 4th edn. Washington, D.C.: American Association on Mental Deficiency.

Gruenewald- Zuberbier, E., Gruenwald, G., and Rasche, A., 1975. Hyperactive behavior and EEG arousal reactions in children. *Electroencephalography and Clinical Neurophysiology* **38**, 149.

Gruenewald-Zuberbier, E., Gruenwald, G., Rasche, A., and Netz, J., 1978. Contingent negative variation and alpha attenuation responses in children with different abilities to concentrate. *Electroencephalography and Clinical Neurophysiology* **44**, 37.

Gruenwald, P., 1963. Chronic fetal distress and placental insufficiency. *Biologia Neonatorum* **5**, 215.

Grunnet, M.L., and Shields, W.D., 1976. Cerebellar hemorrhage in the premature infant. *Journal of Pediatrics* **88**(4), 605.

Gubbay, S.S., Ellis, S., Walton, J.N., and Court, S.D.M., 1965. Clumsy children, a study of apraxic and agnosic defects in 21 children. *Brain* **88**, 295.

Gudmundsson, G., 1966. Epilepsy in Iceland. *Acta Neurologica Scandinavia*, suppl. 25.

Guilford, J.P., 1956. The structure of intellect. *Psychological Bulletin* **53**, 267.

Guttman, E., 1942. Aphasia in children. *Brain* **65**, 205.

Hadenius, A.M., Hagberg, B., Hyttnes-Bensch, K., and Sjogren, I., 1962. The natural prognosis of infantile hydrocephalus. *Acta Paediatrica* (Uppsala) **51**, 117.

Hagberg, B., 1975. Pre-, peri-, and postnatal prevention of major neuropediatric handicaps. *Neuropaediatrie* **6**, 331.

Hagberg, B., Sjogren, I., Bensch, K., and Hadenius, A.M., 1963. The incidence of infantile hydrocephalus in Sweden. *Acta Paediatrica Scandinavia* **52**, 588.

Hagne, I., 1968. Development of the waking EEG in normal infants during the first year of life. In P. Kellaway and I. Petersen (eds.), *Clinical Electrophysiology of Children*. Stockholm: Almqvist and Wiksell (New York: Grune and Stratton).

Hagne, I., 1972. Development of the EEG in normal infants during the first year of life. *Acta Paediatrica Scandinavia*, suppl. **232**, 5.

Hahn, M.E., Jensen, C., and Dudek, B.C., 1979. The role of development in the brain-behavior relationship. In M.E. Hahn, C. Jensen, and B.C. Dudek (eds.), *Development and Evolution of Brain Size: Behavioral Implications*. New York: Academic Press.

Hall, J.G., 1964. The cochlea and the cochlear nuclei in neonatal asphyxia. *Acta Otolaryngoclogica*, Suppl. 1.

Hallgren, B., 1950. Specific dyslexia (congenital word blindness): A clinical and genetic study. *Acta Psychiatrica et Neurologica Scandinavia*, suppl. 65.

Halstead, W.C., 1947. *Brain and Intelligence: A Quantitative Study of the Frontal Lobes*. Chicago: University of Chicago Press.

Hamburg, B.A., 1974. The psychobiology of sex differences: An evolutionary perspective. In R.C. Friedman et al. (eds.), *Sex Differences in Behaviour*. New York: Wiley.

Hamburger, V., 1954. Trends in experimental neuroembryology. In P. Weiss (ed.) *Biochemistry of the Developing Nervous System*. Chicago: University of Chicago Press.

Hankin, L., Heichel, G.H., and Botsfold, R.A., 1973. Lead poisoning from colored printing inks. *Clinical Pediatrics* 12, 654.

Hanley, W.B., Linsao, L., Davidson, W., and Moes, C.A.F., 1970. Malnutrition with early treatment of phenylketonuria. *Pediatric Research* 4, 318.

Hanshaw, J.B., Scheiner, A.P., Moxley, A.W., Gaev, L., Abel, V., and Scheiner, B., 1976. School failure and deafness after silent congenital cytomegalovirus infection. *New England Journal of Medicine* 295, 468.

Hanson, J.W., Jones, K.L., and Smith, D.W., 1976. Fetal alcohol syndrome: Experience with 41 patients. *Journal of the American Medical Association* 235, 1458.

Hardy, J. B., 1968. Viruses and the fetus. *Postgraduate Medicine* 43, 156.

Hardy, J.B., 1973. Clinical and developmental aspects of congenital rubella. *Archives of Otolaryngology* 98, 230.

Hardyck, C., and Petrinovich, L.F., 1977. Left-handedness. *Psychological Bulletin* 84, 385.

Harlan, R.E., Gordon, J.H., and Gorski, R.A., 1979. Sexual differentiation of the brain: Implications for neuroscience. In D.M. Schneider (ed.), *Reviews of Neuroscience*, vol. 4. New York: Raven Press.

Harley, R.K., and Lawrence, G.A., 1977. *Visual Impairments in the Schools*. Springfield, Ill.: Charles C Thomas.

Harlow, H.F., and Harlow, M.K., 1965. The affectional systems. In A.M. Schrier, H.F. Harlow, and F. Stollnitz (eds.), *Behavior of the Nonhuman Primates*, vol. 2. London: Academic Press.

Harlow, H.F., Thompson, C., Blomquist, A., and Schilte, K., 1970. Learning in Rhesus monkeys after varying amounts of prefrontal lobe destruction during infancy and adolescence. *Brain Research* 18, 343.

Harner, R.N., 1977. Agenesis of the corpus callosum and associated defects. In E.S. Goldensohn and S.H. Appel (eds.), *Scientific Approaches to Clinical Neurology*, vol. 1. Philadelphia: Lea and Febiger.

Harper, J.R., 1967. Infantile spasms associated with cerebral agyria. *Developmental Medicine and Child Neurology* 9, 460.

Harper, P.A., and Wiener, G., 1965. Sequelae of low birth weight. *Annual Review of Medicine* **16**, 405.

Harrington, J.A., and Letemendia, F.J., 1958. Persistent psychiatric disorders after head injuries in children. *Journal of Mental Science* **104**, 1205.

Harris, R.J., 1975. A primer of multivariate statistics. New York: Academic Press.

Hart, C.W., and Naunton, R.F., 1964. Ototoxicity of chloroquine phosphate. *Archives of Otolaryngology* **80**, 407.

Hartlage, L.C., Green, J.B., and Offutt, L. 1972. Dependency in epileptic children. *Epilepsia* **13**, 27.

Hartlage, L.C., and Lucas, D.G., 1973. *Mental Development of the Pediatric Patient*. Springfield, Ill.: Charles C Thomas.

Hatta, T., 1977. Recognition of Japanese kanji in the left and right visual fields. *Neuropsychologia* **15**, 685.

Hatta, T., and Dimond, S.J., 1981. The differential interference effects of environmental sounds on spoken speech in Japanese and British people. *Brain and Language* **13**, 241.

Hauser, S.L., DeLong, R., and Rosman, P. Pneumographic findings in the infantile autism syndrome (a correlation with temporal lobe disease). *Brain* **98**, 677.

Hebb, D.O., 1949. *The Organization of Behavior*. New York: Oxford University Press.

Heber, R., and Garber, H., 1975. The Milwaukee Project: A study of the use of family intervention to prevent cultural-familial mental retardation. In B.Z. Friedlander, G.M. Sterrit, and G.E. Kirk (eds.), *Exceptional Infant*, vol. 3, *Assessment and Intervention*. New York: Brunner/Mazel.

Hécaen, H., 1977. Language representation and brain development. In S.R. Berenberg (ed.), *Brain: Fetal and Infant*. The Hague: Martinus Nijhoff.

Hécaen, H., and Albert, M.L., 1978. *Human Neuropsychology*. New York: Wiley.

Hecht, F., and MacFarlane, J.P., 1969. Mosaicism in Turner's syndrome reflects the lethality of XO. *Lancet* **2**, 1197.

Hechtman, L., Weiss, G., Finklestein, J., Werner, A., and Benn, R., 1976. Hyperactives as young adults: Preliminary report. *Canadian Medical Association Journal* **115**, 625.

Hechtman, L., Weiss, G., and Metrakos, K., 1978. Hyperactive individuals as young adults: Current and longitudinal electroencephalographic evaluation and its relation to outcome. *Canadian Medical Association Journal* **118**, 919.

Hecox, K., 1975. Electrophysiological correlates of human auditory development. In L.B. Cohen and P. Salapatek (eds.), *Infant Perception: From Sensation to Cognition*, vol. 2. New York: Academic Press.

Heilman, K.M., 1979. The neuropsychological basis of skilled movement in man. In M.S. Gazzaniga (ed.), *Handbook of Behavioral Neurobiology*, vol. 2: *Neuropsychology*. New York: Plenum.

Helper, M.M., 1980. Follow-up of children with minimal brain dysfunctions: Outcomes and predictors. In H.E. Rie and E.D. Rie (eds.), *Handbook of Minimal Brain Dysfunctions: A Critical Review*. New York: Wiley.

Hern, A., 1979. Health and behavioral adjustment in later life for learning handicapped children with and without neurological impairment. M.A. thesis, University of Victoria.

Hertzig, M.E., 1981. Neurological 'soft' signs in low-birth-weight children. *Developmental Medicine and Child Neurology* **23**, 778.

Hertzig, M.E., Birch, H.G., Richardson, S.A., and Tizard, J., 1972. Intellectual levels of school children severely malnourished during the first two years of life. *Pediatrics* **49**, 814.

Hertzig, M.E., Bortner, M., and Birch, H.G., 1969. Neurologic findings in children educationally designated as "brain-damaged." *American Journal of Orthopsychiatry* **39**, 437.

Heston, L.L., 1970. The genetics of schizophrenia and schizoid disease. *Science* **167**, 249.

Hewitt, W., 1962. The development of the human corpus callosum. *Journal of Anatomy* **96**(3), 355.

Hickey, T.L., 1977. Postnatal development of the human lateral geniculate nucleus: Relationship to a critical period for the visual system. *Science* **198**, 836.

Hicks, S.P., and D'Amato, C.J., 1966. Effects of ionizing radiation on mammalian development. In D.H.M. Woollam (ed.), *Advances in Teratology*. London: Logos Press.

Hicks, S.P., and D'Amato, C.S., 1970. Motor-sensory and visual behavior after hemispherectomy in newborn and mature rats. *Experimental Neurology* **29**, 416.

Hier, D., Le May, M., Rosenberger, P., and Perls, V., 1978. Developmental dyslexia. *Archives of Neurology* **35**, 90.

Hier, D.B., 1981. Sex differences in brain structure. In A. Ansara et al. (eds.), *Sex Differences in Dyslexia*. Towson, Md.: Orton Dyslexia Society.

Hill, A., Melson, G.L., Clark, H.B., and Volpe, J.J., 1982. Hemorrhagic periventricular leukomalacia: Diagnosis by real-time ultrasound and correlation with autopsy findings. *Pediatrics* **69**(3), 282.

Hillier, W.F., 1954. Total left cerebral hemispherectomy for malignant glioma. *Neurology* **4**, 718.

Himwich, W.A. (ed.), 1970. *Developmental Neurobiology*. Springfield, Ill.: Charles C Thomas.

Himwich, W.A. (ed.), 1973. *Biochemistry of the Developing Brain*. New York: Dekker.

Himwich, W.A., 1975. Phylogeny and ontogeny of mammalian brain. In J.W. Prescott, M.S. Read, and D.B. Coursin (eds.), *Brain Function and Malnutrition: Neuropsychological Methods of Assessment*. New York: Wiley.

Hines, R.B., Minde, K., Marton, P., and Trehub, S., 1980. Behavioural development of premature infants: An ethological approach. *Developmental Medicine and Child Neurology* **22**, 623.

Hinshelwood, J., 1895. Word blindness and visual memory. *Lancet* **2**, 1564.

Hinshelwood, J., 1917. *Congenital Word Blindness*. London: H.K. Lewis.

Hinton, G.G., and Knights, R.M., 1971. Children with learning problems: Academic history, academic prediction and adjustment 3 years after assessment. *Exceptional Children* **37**, 513.

Hirsch, H.V.B., and Jacobson, M., 1975. The perfectible brain: Principles of neuronal development. In M.S. Gazzaniga and C. Blakemore (eds.), *Handbook of Psychobiology*. New York: Academic Press.

Hirsh, I., 1966. Audition in relation to perception of speech. In E. Carterette (ed.),

Brain Function. vol. 3: *Speech, Language and Communication.* Berkeley: University of California Press.

Hoffman, H.J., Hendrick, E.B., Dennis, M., and Armstrong, D., 1979. Hemispherectomy for Sturge-Weber syndrome. *Child's Brain* **5,** 223.

Hoffmann, W.L., and Prior, M.R., 1982. Neuropsychological dimensions of autism in children: A test of the hemispheric dysfunction hypothesis. *Journal of Clinical Neuropsychology* **4**(1), 27.

Holden, K.R., Freeman, J.M., and Mellits, E.D., 1980. Outcomes of infants with neonatal seizures. In J.A. Woda and J.K. Penny (eds.), *Advances in Epileptology: 10th Epilepsy International Symposium.* New York: Raven Press.

Holden, K.R., Mellits, E.D., and Freeman, J.M., 1982. Neonatal seizures: I. Correlation of prenatal and perinatal events with outcomes. *Pediatrics* **70,** 165.

Holdsworth, L.K., and Whitmore, K.A., 1974. Study of children attending ordinary schools. I: Their seizure patterns, progress and behavior at school. *Developmental Medicine and Child Neurology* **16**(6), 746.

Hollyday, M., 1980. Motoneuron histogenesis and the development of limb innervation. In R.K. Hunt (ed.), *Neural Development,* part I (*Current Topics in Developmental Biology,* vol. 15). New York: Academic Press.

Holmes, L. B., Moser, H. W., Halldorsen, S., Mack, C., Pant, S.S., and Matzilevich, B.M., 1972. *Mental Retardation: An Atlas of Diseases with Associated Physical Abnormalities.* New York: Macmillan.

Holroyd, J., and McArthur, D., 1976. Mental retardation and stress on the parents: A contrast between Down's syndrome and childhood autism. *American Journal of Mental Deficincey* **80,** 431.

Hooker, D., 1952. The prenatal origin of behaviour. Porter Lectures (series 18). Lawrence: University of Kansas Press.

Hopkins, T., Bice, V., and Colton, K.C., 1954. *Evaluation and Education of the Cerebral Palsied Child: New Jersey Study.* Washington, D.C.: International Council for Exceptional Children.

Horton, R.L., 1978. *The General Linear Model.* New York: McGraw-Hill.

Howard, F.M., and Hill, J.E., 1979. Drugs in pregnancy. *Obstetrical and Gynecological Survey* **34** (9), 643.

Howie, V. M., 1980. Developmental sequelae of chronic otitis media: A review. *Journal of Developmental and Behavioral Pediatrics* **1,** 34.

Hoy, E., Weiss, G., Minde, K., and Cohen, N., 1978. The hyperactive child at adolescence: Cognitive, emotional and social functioning. *Journal of Abnormal Child Psychology* **6,** 311.

Hubel, D.H., and Wiesel, T.N., 1965. Receptive fields of cells in striate cortex of very young visually inexperienced kittens. *Journal of Neurophysiology* **28,** 1041.

Huessy, H.R., Metoyer, M., and Townsend, M., 1974. Eight–ten year follow-up of 84 children treated for behavioural disorder in rural Vermont. *Acta Paedopsychiatrica* **10,** 230.

Humphrey, T., 1964. Some correlations between the apperance of human fetal reflexes and the development of the nervous system. In D.P. Purpura and J.P. Schade (eds.), *Growth and Maturation of the Brain (Progress in Brain Research,* vol. 4). Amsterdam: Elsevier.

Humphrey, T., 1970. The development of human fetal activity and its relation to postnatal behavior. In H.W. Reese and I.P. Lipsitt (eds.), *Advances in Child Development and Behavior*, vol. 5. New York: Academic Press.

Hunt, J.V., Predicting intellectual disorders in childhood for preterm infants with birth weight below 1501 grams. In S.L. Friedman and M. Sigman (eds.), *Preterm Birth and Psychological Development*. New York: Academic Press.

Hutchings, D.E., Gibbon, J., Gaston, J., and Vacca, L., 1975. Critical periods in fetal development: Differential effects on learning and development produced by maternal vitamin A excess. In N.R. Ellis (ed.), *Aberrant Development in Infancy*. Hillsdale, N.J.: Erlbaum.

Hynd, G.W., and Obrzut, J.E. (eds.), 1981. *Neuropsychological Assessment of the School-Age Child*. New York: Grune and Stratton.

Hynd, G.W., Obrzut, J.E., Weed, W., and Hynd, C., 1979. Development of cerebral dominance: Dichotic listening asymmetry in normal and learning-disabled children. *Journal of Experimental Child Psychology* **28**, 445.

Icenogle, D.A., and Kaplan, A.M., 1981. A reivew of congenital neurologic malformations. *Clinical Pediatrics* **20**, 565.

Ignelzi, R.J., and Bucy, P.C., 1968. Cerebral hemidecortication in the treatment of infantile cerebral hemiatrophy. *Journal of Nervous and Mental Diseases* **147**, 14.

Imbert, M., 1977. Developmental plasticity in the visual cortex. In S.R. Berenberg (ed.), *Brain: Fetal and Infant*. The Hague: Martinus Nijhoff.

Ingraham, F.D., and Matson, D.D., 1954. *Neurosurgery of Infancy and Childhood*. Springfield, Ill.: Charles C Thomas.

Ingram, T.T.S., 1959. Specific developmental disorders of speech in childhood. *Brain* **82**, 450.

Ingram, T.T.S., 1960. Pediatric aspects of specific developmental dysphasia, dyslexia and dysgraphia. *Cerebral Palsy Bulletin* **2**, 254.

Ingram, T.T.S., 1976. Speech disorders in childhood. In E.H. Lenneberg and E. Lenneberg (eds.), *Foundations of Language Development*, vol. 2. New York: Academic Press.

Irwin, J.V., Moore, J.M., and Rampp, D.L., 1972. Nonmedical diagnosis and evaluation. In J.V. Irwin and M. Marge (eds.), *Principles of Childhood Language Disabilities*. New York: Appleton-Century-Crofts.

Isaacson, R. (ed.), 1968. *The Neuropsychology of Development*. New York: Wiley.

Isaacson, R.L., 1975. The myth of recovery from early brain damage. In N.R. Ellis (ed.), *Aberrant Development in Infancy*. Hillsdale, N.J.: Erlbaum.

Isaacson, R.L., 1976. Recovery (?) from early brain damage. In T.D. Tjossen (ed.), *Intervention Strategies for High-Risk Infants and Young Children*. Baltimore: University Park Press.

Isler, W., 1971. Acute hemiplegia and hemisyndromes in childhood., *Clinics in Developmental Medicine*, 41/42. Philadelphia: Lippincott.

Jabbari, B., Schwartz, D.M., MacNeil, D.M., and Coker, S.B., 1983. Early abnormalities of brainstem auditory evoked potentials in Friedreich's ataxia: Evidence of primary brainstem dysfunction. *Neurology* **33**, 1071.

Jacobs, P.A., Brunton, M., and Melville, M.M., 1965. Aggressive behaviour, mental subnormality and the XXY male. *Nature* **208**, 1351.

Jacobson, J.W., and Janicki, M.P., 1983. Observed prevalence of multiple developmental disabilities. *Mental Retardation* **21**, 87.

Jacobson, M., 1975. Brain development in relation to language. In E.H. Lenneberg and E. Lenneberg (eds.), *Foundations of Language Development*, vol. 1. New York: Academic Press.

Jacobson, M., 1978. *Developmental Neurobiology*, 2d ed. New York: Plenum Press.

Jan, J.E., Freeman, R.D., and Scott, E.P., 1977. *Visual Impairment in Children and Adolescents*. New York: Grune and Stratton.

Jansen, J., 1978. Spina bifida: Epidemiological data from a pilot study. *Acta Neurologica Scandinavia* **57**, 193.

Jansky, J.J., 1978. A critical review of some developmental and predictive precursors of reading disabilities. In A.L. Benton and D. Pearl (eds.), *Dyslexia: An Appraisal of Current Knowledge*. New York: Oxford University Press.

Jeavons, P.M., Bower, B.D., and Dimitrakoudi, M., 1973. Long-term prognosis of 150 cases of West's syndrome. *Epilepsia* **14**, 153.

Jeavons, P.M., and Harding, G.F.A., 1975. Photosensitive epilepsy. A review of the literature and a study of 460 patients. *Clinics in Developmental Medicine*, no. 56. London: Heinemann.

Jeavons, P.M., Harper, J.R., and Bower, B.D., 1970. Long-term prognosis in infantile spasms. *Developmental Medicine and Child Neurology* **12**, 413.

Jeeves, M.A., 1965a. Agenesis of the corpus callosum: Physiopathological and clinical aspects. *Proceedings of the Australian Association of Neurologists* **3**, 41.

Jeeves, M.A., 1965b. Psychological studies of three cases of congenital agenesis of the corpus callosum. In G. Ettlinger (ed.), *Functions of the Corpus Callosum* (Ciba Foundation Study Group No. 20). London: J. & A. Churchill.

Jeeves, M.A., 1969. A comparison of interhemispheric transmission times in acallosals and normals. *Psychonomic Science* **16**(5), 245.

Jeeves, M.A., 1972. Further psychological studies of the effects of agenesis of the corpus callosum in man and neonatal sectioning of the corpus callosum in animals. In J. Cernacek and F. Podivinsky (eds.), *Cerebral Interhemispheric Relations*. Bratislava: Publishing House of the Slovak Academy of Sciences.

Jeeves, M.A., 1979. Some limits to interhemispheric integration in cases of callosal agenesis and partial commissurotomy. In I.S. Russell, M.W. Van Hof, and G. Berlucchi (eds.), *Structure and Function of Cerebral Commissures*. Baltimore: University Park Press.

Jeffrey, W.E., 1980. The developing brain and child development. In M.C. Wittrock (ed.), *The Brain and Psychology*. New York: Academic Press.

Jennett, B., 1972. Head injuries in children. *Developmental Medicine and Child Neurology* **14**, 137.

Jervis, G.A., 1963. The clinical picture. In F.L. Lyman (ed.), *Phenylketonuria*. Springfield, Ill.: Charles C Thomas.

John, E.R., 1977. *Functional Neuroscience*, vol. 2, *Neurometrics: Clinical Applications of Quantitative Electrophysiology*. Hillsdale, N.J.: Erlbaum.

Johnson, D.J., and Myklebust, H.R., 1967. *Learning Disabilities*. New York: Grune and Stratton.

Johnson, D., and Neumann, C., 1975. Multidisciplinary evaluation of learning and behavior problems in children: A follow-up study of 40 cases. *Journal of the American Osteopathic Association* **74**, 160.

Johnson, E.M., and Kochhar, D.M. (eds.), 1983. *Teratogenesis and Reproductive Toxicology*. New York: Springer.

Johnson, J.A., 1981. The etiology of hyperactivity. *Exceptional Children* **47**, 348.

Johnson, K.P., 1974. Viral infections of the developing nervous system. In R.A. Thompson and J.R. Green (eds.), *Advances in Neurology*, vol. 6. New York: Raven Press.

Johnson, L., and Boggs, T.R., 1974. Bilirubin-dependent brain damage: Incidence and indications for treatment. In G.B. Odell, R. Schaffer, and G. Simopoulos (eds.), *Phototherapy in the Newborn: An Overview*. Washington, D.C.: National Academy of Sciences.

Johnson, R.T., 1982. Viral Infections of the Nervous System. New York: Raven.

Johnson, R.T., 1977. Viral infections and brain development. In S.R. Berenberg (ed.), *Brain: Fetal and Infant*. The Hague: Martinus Nijhoff.

Johnston, R.N., and Wessells, N.K., 1980. Regulation of the elongating nerve fiber. In R.K. Hunt (ed.), *Neural Development*, part II (*Current Topics in Developmental Biology*, vol. 16). New York: Academic Press.

Johnston, W.H., Angara, V., Baumae, R., Hawke, W.A., Johnson, R.H., Keet, S., and Wood, M., 1967. Erythroblastosis fetalis and hyperbilirubinemia: A five-year follow-up with neurological, psychological and audiological evaluation. *Pediatrics* **39**, 88.

Jorgensen, M.B., Kristensen, H.K., and Buch, N.H., 1964. Thalidomide-induced aplasia of the inner ear. *Journal of Laryngology and Otology* **78**, 1095.

Jorm, A.F., 1979. The nature of the reading deficit in developmental dyslexia. *Cognition* **7**, 429.

Joseph, R., 1982. The neuropsychology of development: Hemispheric laterality, limbic language, and the origin of thought. *Journal of Clinical Psychology* **38**, 4.

Joynt, R.J., 1974. The corpus callosum: History of thought regarding its function. In M. Kinsbourne and W. Lynn Smith (eds.), *Hemispheric Disconnection and Cerebral Function*. Springfield, Ill.: Charles C Thomas.

Kaga, K., and Tanaka, Y., 1980. Auditory brainstem responses and behavioral audiometry: Developmental correlates. *Archives of Otolaryngology* **106**(9), 564.

Kagan, J., Kearsley, R.B., and Zelazo, P.R., 1978. *Infancy: Its Place in Human Development*. Cambridge, Mass.: Harvard University Press.

Kahn, E., and Cohen, L.H., 1934. Organic driveness: A brainstem syndrome and an experience. *New England Journal of Medicine* **210**, 748.

Kallman, F.J., 1953. *Heredity in Health and Mental Disorder*. New York: Norton.

Kalverboer, A.F., 1976. Neurobehavioral relationships in young children: Some remarks on concepts and methods. In R.M. Knights and D.J. Bakker (eds.), *The Neuropsychology of Learning Disorders*. Baltimore: University Park Press.

Kalverboer, A.F., Touwen, B.C.L., and Prechtl, H.F.R., 1975. Follow-up of infants at risk of minor brain dysfunction. *Annals of the New York Academy of Sciences* **205**, 173.

Kanner, L., 1943. Autistic disturbances of affective contact. *Nervous Child* **2**, 217.

Kanner, L., 1949. Problems of nosology and psychodynamics of early infantile autism. *American Journal of Orthopsychiatry* **19**, 416.

Kanner, L., 1954. To what extent is early infantile autism determined by constitutional inadequacies? *Proceedings of the Association for Research in Nervous and Mental Diseases* **33**, 378.

Kaplan, A.M., 1958. Hemispherectomy in children. *Journal of Pediatrics* **70**, 476.

Kappers, J.A., 1971. On the structure, development, and connections of the limbic system. In G.B.A. Stoelinga and J.J. Van der Werff ten Bosch (eds.), *Normal and Abnormal Development of Brain and Behavior*. Baltimore: Williams and Wilkins.

Karfunkel, P., 1974. The mechanisms of neural tube formation. *International Review of Cytology* **38**, 245.

Karlin, I.W., 1954. Aphasias in chilren. *American Journal of Disabled Children* **87**, 752.

Karrer, R., 1976. *Developmental Psychophysiology of Mental Retardation*. Springfield, Ill.: Charles C Thomas.

Kaste, C.M., 1972. A ten-year follow-up of children diagnosed in a child guidance clinic as having cerebral dysfunction. *Dissertation Abstracts International* **33** (4-B), 1797.

Katona, F., and Berenyi, M., 1974. Differential reactions and habituation to accoustical and visual stimuli in neonates. *Activitas Nervosa Superior* **16**, 305.

Katz, J., 1972. *Handbook of Clinical Audiology*. Baltimore: Williams and Wilkins.

Katz, V., 1975. Auditory stimulation and developmental behaviour of the premature infant. *Nursing Research* **20**, 196.

Kaufman, A.S., and Doppelet, J.E., 1976. Analysis of WISC-R standaridzation data in terms of stratification variables. *Child Development* **47**(1), 165.

Kawi, A.A., and Pasamanick, B., 1958. Association of factors of pregnancy with reading disorders in childhood. *Journal of the American Medical Association* **166**, 1420.

Keith, R., 1977. *Central Auditory Dysfunction*. New York: Grune and Stratton.

Keith, R.W. (ed.), 1981. *Central Auditory and Language Disorders in Children*. San Diego: College-Hill Press.

Keller, C.A., 1981. Epidemiological characteristics of preterm births. In S.I. Friedman and M. Sigman (eds.), *Preterm Birth and Psychological Development*. New York: Academic Press.

Kendall, D.C., 1966. Language and communication problems in children. In R.W. Rieber and R.S. Brubaker (eds.), *Speech Pathology*. Philadelphia: Lippincott.

Kennard, M.A., 1938. Reorganization of motor function in the cerebral cortex of monkeys deprived of motor and premotor areas in infancy. *Journal of Neurophysiology* **1**, 477.

Kennard, M.A., 1942. Cortical reorganization of motor function: Studies on a series of monkeys of various ages from infancy to maturity. *Archives of Neurology and Psychiatry* **8**, 227.

Kenny, T.J., 1980. Hyperactivity. In H.E. Rie and E.D. Rie (eds.), *Handbook of Minimal Brain Dysfunction*. New York: Wiley.

Kerschensteiner, M., and Huber, W., 1975. Grammatical impairment in developmental aphasia. *Cortex* **11**, 264.

Kessen, W., 1960. Research design in the study of developmental problems. In P.H. Mussen (ed.), *Handbook of Research Methods in Child Development*. New York: Wiley.

Kessler, J.W., 1980. History of minimal brain dysfunctions. In H.E. Rie and E.D. Rie (eds.), *Handbook of Minimal Brain Dysfunctions: A Critical View*. New York: Wiley.

Kessner, D.M., Singer, J., Kalk, C.E., and Schlesinger, E.R., 1973. Infant death: An analysis by maternal risk and health care. *Contrasts in Health Status*, vol. 1. Washington: National Academy of Sciences.

Kety, S.S., Rowland, L.P., Sidman, R.L., and Matthysse, S.W. (eds.), 1983. *Genetics of Neurological and Psychiatric Disorders.* (Association for Research in Nervous and Mental Disease Research Publications, vol. 60). New York: Academic Press.

Khan, R.Z., 1960. An etiological reclassification of epilepsy and its relation to mental retardation. *Epilepsia* **2**, 108.

Kiff, R.D., and Lepard, C., 1966. Visual response of premature infants. *Archives of Ophthalmology* **75**, 631.

Kimura, D., 1967. Functional asymmetries of the brain in dichotic listening. *Cortex* **3**, 163.

Kimura, D., 1969. Spatial localization in left and right visual fields. *Canadian Journal of Psychology* **23**, 445.

Kimura, D., 1981. Neural mechanisms in manual signing. *Sign Language Studies* **33**, 291.

Kinsbourne, M., 1973. Minimal brain dysfunction as a neurodevelopmental lag. *Annals of the New York Academy of Sciences* **205**, 268.

Kinsbourne, M., 1976a. The neuropsychological analysis of cognitive deficit. In R.G. Grenell and S. Gobay (eds.). *Biological Foundations of Psychiatry,* vol. 1. New York: Raven Press.

Kinsbourne, M., 1976b. The ontogeny of cerebral dominance. In R.W. Rieber (ed.), *The Neuropsychology of Language.* New York: Plenum Press.

Kinsbourne, M., and Fisher, M., 1971. Latency of uncrossed and of crossed reaction in callosal agenesis. *Neuropsychologia* **9**, 201.

Kinsbourne, M., and Hiscock, M., 1977. Does cerebral dominance develop? In S.J. Segalowitz and F.A. Gruber (eds.), *Language Development and Neurological Theory.* New York: Academic Press.

Kinsbourne, M., and Hiscock, M., 1978. Cerebral lateralization and cognitive development. In *Education and the Brain,* 77th yearbook of the National Society for the Study of Education.

Kinsbourne, M., and Warrington, E.K., 1963. The developmental Gerstmann syndrome. *Archives of Neurology* **8**, 490.

Kirk, U. (ed.), 1982. *Neuropsychology of Language, Reading, and Spelling.* New York: Academic Press.

Kitchen, W.H., Rickards, A., Ruan, M.M., McDougall, A.B., Billson, F.A., Keir, E.H., and Naylor, F.D., 1979. A longitudinal study of very-low-birth-weight infants. II: Results of controlled trials of intensive care and incidence of handicap. *Developmental Medicine and Child Neurology* 21 (5), 582.

Kitchen, W.H., Ryan, M.M., Rickards, A., McDougall, A.B., Billson, F.A., Keir, E.H., and Naylor, F.D., 1980. A longitudinal study of very-low-birth-weight infants. IV: An overview of performance at eight years of age. *Developmental Medicine and Child Neurology* **22**, 172.

Klaus, M.H., and Kennel, J.H., 1976. *Maternal-Infant Bonding.* St. Louis: C.V. Mosby.

Klausmeier, H.J., and Allen, P.S., 1978. Cognitive development of children and youth: A longitudinal study. New York: Academic Press.

Klawans, H.L., Glantz, R., Tanner C.M., and Goetz, C.G., 1982. Primary writing tremor: A selective action tremor. *Neurology* **32**, 203.

Klein, M.C., Sayre, J.W., and Kotok, D., 1974. Lead poisoning: Current status of the problem facing pediatricians. *American Journal of Diseases of Children* **127**, 805.

Kleinpeter, U., and Göllnitz, G., 1976. Achievement and adaptation disorders in brain-damaged children. *International Journal of Mental Health* **4**, 19.

Klonoff, B., and Low, M., 1974. Disordered brain function in young children and early adolescents: Neuropsychological and electroencephalographic correlates. In R. Reitan and L. Davison (eds.), *Clinical Neuropsychology: Current Status and Applications*. Washington, D.C.: Winston.

Klonoff, H., Low, M., and Clark C., 1977. Head injuries in children: A prospective five-year follow-up. *Journal of Neurology, Neurosurgery, and Psychiatry* **40**, 1211.

Klonoff, H., and Paris, R., 1974. Immediate, short-term and residual effects of acute head injuries in children: Neuropsychological and neurological correlates; in R. M. Reitan and L. A. Davison (eds.), *Clinical Neuropsychology: Current Status and Applications*. Washington, D.C.: Winston.

Klonoff, H., Robinson, G., and Thompson, G., 1969. Acute and chronic brain syndromes in children. *Developmental Medicine and Child Neurology* **11**, 198.

Knights, R.M., and Bakker, D.J. (eds.), 1976. *The Neuropsychology of Learning Disorders*. Baltimore: University Park Press.

Knights, R.M., and Hinton, G.G., 1969. Minimal brain dysfunction: Clinical and psychological test characteristics. *Academic Therapy* **4**, 265.

Knobloch, H., and Pasamanick, B., 1966. Prospective studies on the epidemiology of reproductive casuality: Methods, findings and some implications. *Merrill-Palmer Quarterly of Behaviour and Development* **12**, 27.

Knobloch, H., Rider, R.V., and Harper, P.A., 1956. Neuropsychiatric sequelae of prematurity. *Journal of the American Medical Association* **161**, 581.

Knox, G.E., Reynolds, D.W., and Alford, C., 1980. Perinatal infections caused by rubella, hepatitis B, cytomegalovirus, and herpes simplex. In E.J. Quilligan and N. Kretchmer, eds. *Fetal and Maternal Medicine*. New York: Wiley.

Knox, W.E., 1960. Phenylketonuria. In J.B. Stanbury, J.E. Wyngaarden, and D.S. Frederickson (eds.), *The Metabolic Basis of Inherited Disease*. New York: McGraw-Hill.

Koch, R., Fishler, K., Child, S., and Ragsdale, N., 1964. Clinical aspects of phenylketonuria. *Mental Retardation* **2**, 47.

Kohen-Raz, R., 1977. Psychobiological aspects of cognitive development in infancy. In R. Kohen-Raz (ed.), *Psychobiological Aspects of Cognitive Growth*. New York: Academic Press.

Köhler, W., 1920. *Die physischen Gestalten in Ruhe und im stationären Zustand*. Leipzig: Barth.

Kohn, B., and Dennis, M., 1974. Patterns of hemispheric specialization after hemidecortication for infantile hemiplegia. In M. Kinsbourne and W. L. Smith (eds.), *Hemispheric Disconnection and Cerebral Function*. Springfield, Ill.: Charles C Thomas.

Kolb, J.E., and Heaton, R.K., 1975. Lateralized neurologic deficits and psychopathology in a Turner syndrome patient. *Archives of General Psychiatry* **32**, 1198.

Kolvin, I., Ounsted, C., Richardson, L., and Garside, R., 1971. Studies in the childhood psychoses. III. The family and social background in childhood psychoses. *British Journal of Psychiatry* **118**, 396.

Koci, K.A., and Sharbrough, F.W., 1966. Electrophysiological findings in cortical blindness. *Electroencephalography and Clinical Neurophysiology* **20**, 260.

Koos, W.T., and Miller, M.H., 1971. *Intracranial Tumors of Children*. Stuttgart: Thieme.

Kopp, C.B., and Parmalee, A.H., 1979. Prenatal and perinatal influences on infant behavior. In J.D. Osofsky (ed.), *Handbook of Infant Development*. New York: Wiley-Interscience.

Koppitz, E.M., 1971. *Children with Learning Disabilities: A Five-Year Follow-Up Study*. New York: Grune and Stratton.

Korner, A.F., 1973. Sex differences in newborns with special reference to differences in the organization of human behavior. *American Journal of Child Psychology* **14**, 19.

Korner, A. F., Kraemer, H.C., Haffner, M.E., and Cosper, L.M., 1975. Effects of waterbed flotation on premature infants: A pilot study. *Pediatrics* **56**, 361.

Kornetsky, C., 1970. Psychoactive drugs in the immature organism. *Psychopharmacologia* **17**, 105.

Kornmann, R., Brauch, L., and Hils, U., Riemer, C., and Schwender, V., 1974. Praferenz-und Leistungsdominanz der Hande bei lernbehinderten Sonderschülern. *Zeitschrift fur Heilpädagogik* **25**, 147.

Kosc, L., 1974. Developmental dyscalculia. *Journal of Learning Disabilities* **7**, 165.

Kracke, I., 1975. Perception of rhythmic sequences by receptive asphasic and deaf children. *British Journal of Communication Disorders* **10**, 43.

Krashen, S.D., 1973. Lateralization, language learning, in the critical period: Some new evidence. *Language Learning* **23**(1), 63.

Krech, D., Crutchfield, R.S., and Livson, N., 1969. *Elements of Psychology*. New York: A. Knopf.

Kresky, B., Buchbinder, S., and Greenberg, I.M., 1962. The incidence of neurologic residua after recovery from bacterial meningitis. *Archives of Pediatrics*, **79**, 63.

Krishnamoorthy, K., Shannon, D., DeLong, G., Todres, I., and Davis, K., 1979. Neurologic sequelae in the survivors of neonatal intraventricular hemorrhage. *Pediatrics* **64**, 233.

Krynauw, R.A., 1950. Infantile hemiplegia treated by removing one cerebral hemisphere. *Journal of Neurology, Neurosurgery, and Psychiatry* **13**, 243.

Kudrjavcev, T., Schonberg, B.S., Kurland, L.T., and Groover, R.V., 1983. Cerebral palsy: Trends and changes in concurrent neonatal mortality, Rochester, Minn., 1950–1976. *Neurology* **33**, 1433.

Kuenne, M.K., 1946. Experimental investigation of the relation of language to transportation behavior in children. *Journal of Experimental Psychology* **36**, 471.

Kuhl, P.K., and Miller, J.D., 1975. Speech perception in the chinchilla: Voiced-voiceless distinctions in alveolar plosive consonants. *Science* **190**, 69.

Kumar, M.L., Nankervis, G.A., and Gold E., 1973. Inapparent congenital cytomegalovirus infection: A follow-up study. *New England Journal of Medicine* **288**, 1370.

Kurtzberg, D., Vaughan, H.G., Daum, C., Grellong, B.A., Albin, S., and Rotkin,

L., 1979. Neurobehavioural performance of low-birth-weight infants at 40 weeks conceptual age: Comparison with normal full-born infants. *Developmental Medicine and Child Neurology* **21**, 590.

La Benz, E.S., Swaiman, K.F., and Sullivan, A.R., 1980. Written communication: Reading, writing and spelling. In F.M. Lassman, R.O. Fisch, D.K. Vetter, and E.S. La Benz (eds.), *Early Correlates of Speech, Language and Hearing.* Littleton, Mass.: PSG Publishing.

Laget, P., Salbreux, R., Raimbault, J., d'Allest, A.M., and Mariani, J., 1976. Relationship between changes in somesthetic evoked responses and electroencephalographic findings in the child with hemiplegia. *Developmental Medicine and Child Neurology* **18**, 620.

Lambert, N., Sandoval, J., and Sassone, D., 1978. Prevalence of hyperactivity in elementary school children as a function of social system definers. *American Journal of Orthopsychiatry* **48**, 446.

Lancet. The fate of the baby under 1501 g at birth, 1980. *Lancet* **1**, 461.

Landau, W., Goldstein, R., and Kleffner, F., 1960. Congenital aphasia: A clinicopathologic study. *Neurology* **10**, 915.

Landrigan, P.J., Gehlbach, S.H., Rosenblum, B.F., Schoults, J.M., Candelaria, R.M., Barthel, W.F., Liddle, J.A., Smrek, A.L., Staehling, N.W., and Sanders, J., 1975. Epidemic lead absorption near an ore smelter. *New England Journal of Medicine* **292**, 123.

Langman, I., Webster, W., and Rodier, P., 1975. Morphological and behavioral abnormalities caused by insults to the CNS in the perinatal periods. In C.L. Berry and D.E. Poswillo (Eds.), *Teratology: Trends and Applications.* New York: Springer-Verlag.

Langworthy, O.R., 1933. Development of behavior patterns and myelinization of the nervous system in the human fetus and infant. Carnegie Institute of Washington Publ. No. 433: *Contributions to Embryology* **139**, 1.

Lanier, L.P., Dunn, A.J., and van Hartesveldt, C.J., 1976. Development of neurotransmitters and their function in brain. In S. Ehrenpreis and I.J. Kopin (eds.), *Reviews of Neuroscience*, vol. 2. New York: Raven Press.

Lansdell, H., 1964. Sex differences in hemispheric asymmetrics of the human brain. *Nature* **203**, 550.

Landsdown, R.G., Sheperd, J., Clayton, B.E., Delves, H.T., Graham, P.J., and Turner, W.C., 1974. Blood lead levels, behaviour, and intelligence: A population study. *Lancet* **1**, 538.

Larroche, J.C., 1967. Regional development of the brain in early life, Symposium UNESCO and WHO. Oxford: Blackwell.

Larsen, S., and Hakonsen, K., 1983. Absence of ear asymmetry in blind children on a dichotic listening task compared to sighted controls. *Brain and Language* **18**, 192.

Lashley, K.S., 1938. Factors limiting recovery after central nervous system lesions. *Journal of Nervous and Mental Disorders* **88**, 733.

Lashley, K.S., 1951. The problem of serial order in behavior. In L.A. Jeffres (ed.), *Cerebral Mechanisms in Behavior.* New York: Wiley.

Lassman, F.M., Fisch, R.O., Vetter, D.K., and LaBenz, E.S., 1980. *Early Correlates of Language Speech and Hearing.* Littleton, Mass.: ESG Publishing.

Lassonde, M.C., Lortie, J., Ptito, M., and Geoffroy, G., 1981. Hemispheric asymmetry in callosal agenesis as revealed by dichotic listening performance. *Neuropsychologia* **19**(3), 455.

Laufer, M., and Denhoff, E., 1957. Hyperkinetic behaviour syndrome in children. *Journal of Pediatrics* **50**, 463.

Laurence, K.M., Hoare, R.D., and Till, K., 1961. The diagnosis of the choroid plexus papilloma of the lateral ventricle. *Brain* **84**, 628.

Lawrence, D.G., and Hopkins, D.A., 1972. Developmental aspects of pyramidal motor control in the Rhesus monkey. *Brain Research* **40**, 117.

Lawson, D., Metcalfe, M., and Pampiglione, G., 1965. Meningitis in childhood. *British Medical Journal* **1**, 557.

Leader, A., Wong, K., and Deitel, M., 1981. Maternal nutrition in pregnancy: A review. *Canadian Medical Association Journal* **125**, 545.

Leary, P.M., 1978. The electroencephalogram in childhood. *South African Medical Journal* **53**, 197.

Lebrun, Y., and Zangwill, C., 1981. *Lateralization of language in the Child*. Lisse: Swets and Zeitlinger.

Lecours, A.R., 1975. Myelogenetic correlates of the development of speech and language. In E.H. Lenneberg and E. Lenneberg (eds.), *Foundations of Language Development*, vol. 1. New York: Academic Press.

LeDouarin, N., 1980. Migration and differentiation of neural crest cells. In R.K. Hunt (ed.), *Neural Development*, part II (*Current Topics in Developmental Biology*, vol. 16). New York: Academic Press.

Lee, K., Gartner, L.M., Paneth, N., and Tyler, L., 1982. Recent trends in neonatal mortality: The Canadian experience. *Canadian Medical Association Journal* **126**, 373.

Lehman, H.J., and Lampe, H., 1970. Observations on the interhemispheric transmission of information in nine patients with corpus callosum defect. *European Neurology* **4**, 129.

Leibel, R., Greenfield, D., and Pollitt, E., 1979. Biochemical and behavioral aspects of schizophrenia. *British Journal of Haematology* **41**(2), 145.

Leisti, S., and Iivanainen, M., 1978. Growth, hypothalamic function and brain ventricle size in mentally retarded subjects. *Journal of Mental Deficiency Research* **22**(1), 1.

Lemire, R.J., Loeser, J.D., Leech, R.W., and Alvord, E.C., 1975. *Normal and Abnormal Development of the Human Nervous System*. New York: Harper and Row.

Lenneberg, E.H., 1967. *Biological Foundations of Language*. New York: Wiley.

Lennox-Buchtal, M., 1973. Febrile convulsions: A reappraisal. *Electroencephalography and Clinical Neurophysiology* **32**, suppl. 1.

Leong, C.K., 1980. Cognitive patterns of "retarded" and below-average readers. *Contemporary Educational Psychology* **5**, 101.

Levene, M.I., and Dubowitz, L.M.S., 1982. Low-birth-weight babies long-term follow-up. *British Journal of Hospital Medicine* **24**, 487.

Levi-Montalcini, R., 1964. Events in the developing nervous system. In D.P. Purpura and J.P. Schade (eds.), *Growth and Maturation of the Brain* (*Process in Brain Research*, vol. 4). Amsterdam: Elsevier.

Levin, H.S., Benton, A.L., and Grossman, R.G., 1982. *Neurobehavioral Consequences of Closed Head Injury*. New York, Oxford University Press.

Levin, H.S., and Eisenberg, H.M., 1979. Neuropsychological impairmant after closed head injury in children and adolescents. *Journal of Pediatric Psychology* **4**, 389.

Levin, H.S., and Eisenberg, H., 1983. Recovery of memory and intellectual ability after head injury in children and adolescents: Sparing of function after early injury? Paper presented at the 11th meeting of the International Neuropsychological Society, Mexico City.

Levine, D., Hier, D.B., and Calvanio, R., 1981. Acquired learning disability for reading after left temporal lobe damage in childhood. *Neurology* **31**, 257.

Levine, S., and Mullins, R.F., 1968. Hormones in infancy. In G. Newton and S. Levine (eds.), *Early Experience and Behaviour*. Springfield, Ill.: Charles C Thomas.

Levitsky, D.A., and Barnes, R.H., 1972. Nutritional and environmental interactions in the behavioral development of the rat: Long-term effects. *Science* **176**, 68.

Levy, J., 1981. Lateralization and its implications for variation in development. In E.S. Gollin (ed.), *Developmental Plasticity: Behavioral and Biological Aspects of Variation in Development*. New York: Academic Press.

Levy, J., and Nagylaki, T., 1972. A model for the genetics of handedness. *Genetics* **72**, 117.

Levy, J., and Reid, M., 1978. Variations in cerebral organization as a function of handedness, hand posture in writing, and sex. *Journal of Experimental Psychology* (general) **107**, 119.

Lewerenz, D.C., 1978. Visual acuity and the developing visual system. *Journal of the American Optometry Association* **49**(10), 1155.

Lewis, E.O., 1933. Types of mental deficiency and their social significance. *Journal of Mental Science* **79**, 298.

Lewkowicz, D., Gardner, J., and Turkewitz, G., 1979. Lateral differences and head-turning responses to somesthetic stimulation in premature infants. *Developmental Psychobiology*, **12**, 607.

Liberman, I.Y., and Shankweiler, D., 1979. Speech, the alphabet, and teaching to read. In L.B. Resnick and P.A. Weaver (eds.), *Theory and Practise of Early Reading*, vol. 2. Hillsdale, N.J.: Erlbaum.

Liederman, J., and Coryell, J., 1982. The origin of left hand preference: Pathological and nonpathological influences. *Neuropsychologia* **20**(6), 721.

Liederman, J., and Kinsbourne, M., 1980. Rightward motor bias in newborns depends upon parental right-handedness, *Neuropsychologia* **18**, 579.

Lienert, G.A., 1961. Überprufung und genetische Interpretation der Divergenzhypothese von Wewetzer. *Vita Humana* **4**, 112.

Lienert, G.A., and Faber, C., 1963. Über die Faktorenstruktur des HAWIK auf verschiedenen Alters- und Intelligenzniveaus. *Diagnostica* **9**, 3.

Lilienfeld, A.M., (1969) Epidemiology of Mongolism. Baltimore: Johns Hopkins University Press.

Lipton, H.L., Preziosi, T.J., and Moses, H., 1978. Adult onset of Dandy-Walker syndrome. *Archives of Neurology* **35**, 672.

Little, W.J., 1861. On the influence of abnormal partuition, difficult labour, premature birth, and asphyxia neonatorum on the mental and physical condition of the child, especially in relation to deformities. *Lancet* October 19, p. 378.

Littman, B., and Parmalee, A.H., 1978. Medical correlates of infant development. *Pediatriacs* **61**, 470.

Livingston, S., 1972. Epilepsy in infancy, childhood and adolescence. In B. Wolman (ed.), *Manual of Child Psychopathology*. New York: McGraw-Hill.

Loeser, J.D., and Alvord, E.C., 1968a. Agenesis of the corpus callosum. *Brain* **91**, 553.

Loeser, J.D., and Alvord, E.C., 1968b. Clinicopathological correlations in agenesis of the corpus callosum. *Neurology* **18**, 745.

Lombroso, C.T., 1978. Convulsive disorders in newborns. In R.A. Thompson and J.R. Green (eds.), *Pediatric Neurology and Neurosurgery*. New York: Spectrum.

Loney, J., 1974. The intellectual functioning of hyperactive elementary school boys: A cross-sectional investigation. *American Journal of Orthopsychiatry* **44**, 754.

Loney, J., 1980. Hyperkinesis comes of age: What do we know and where should we go? *American Journal of Orthopsychiatry* **50**, 28.

Lopez, R., 1965. Hyperactivity in twins. *Canadian Psychiatric Association Journal* **10**, 421.

Lorber, J., 1971. Results of treatment of myelomeningocele. *Developmental Medicine and Child Neurology* **13**, 279.

Lorenz, K., 1970. *Studies in Animal and Human Behaviour*, vol. 1 (translated by R. Martin). London: Methuen.

Lotter, V., 1967. Epidemiology of autistic conditions in young children. II: Some characteristics of the parents and children. *Social Psychiatry* **1**, 163.

Lou, H.C., 1982. *Developmental Neurology*. New York: Raven Press.

Lowe, A.D., and Campbell, R.A., 1965. Temporal discrimination in aphasoid and normal children. *Journal of Speech and Hearing Research* **8**, 313.

Lowrey, G.H., 1978. *Growth and Development of Children*, 7th edn. Chicago: Year Book Publishers.

Lubchenco, L.O., Horner, F.A., Reed, L.H., Hix, I.E., Metcalf, D., Cohig, R., Elliott, H.C., and Bourg, M., 1963. Sequelae of premature birth. *American Journal of Diseases of Children* **106**, 101.

Lucas, A.R., Rodin, E.A., and Simson, C.B., 1965. Neurological assessment of children with early school problems. *Developmental Medicine and Child Neurology* **7**, 145.

Luchins, D.J., Weinberger, D.R., and Wyatt, R.J., 1983. Reversed cerebral asymmetry in schizophrenia. Paper presented at the 11th Annual Meeting of the International Neuropsychological Society, Mexico City.

Ludlow, C.L., 1979. Research directions and needs concerning the neurological bases of language disorders in children. In C.L. Ludlow and M.E. Doran-Quine (eds.), *The Neurological Bases of Language Disorders in Children: Methods and Directions for Research*, NIH Publication 79-440. Washington, D.C.: U.S. Department of Health, Education and Welfare.

Ludlow, C.L., Cudahy, E., Caine, E., Brown, E.L., and Bassich, C., 1980. Auditory processing deficits in the absence of language disorder. Paper presented at the Annual Meeting of the Academy of Aphasia, San Diego. 1980.

Luessenhop, A.J., de la Cruz, T.C., and Fenichel, G.M., 1970. Surgical disconnection of the cerebral hemispheres for intractable seizures: Results in infancy and childhood. *Journal of the American Medical Association* **213**(10), 1630.

Lund, R.D., 1978. *Development and Plasticity of the Brain: An Introduction.* New York: Oxford University Press.

Luria, A.R., 1966. *Higher Cortical Functions in Man,* 2d edn. New York: Basic Books.

Luria, A.R., 1973. *The Working Brain.* New York: Basic Books.

Luria, A.R., and Yudovich, F.I., 1971. *Speech and Development of Mental Processes in the Child: An Experimental Investigation.* Harmondsworth, England: Penguin.

Lutman, M.E., and Haggard, M.P. (eds.), 1983. *Hearing Science and Hearing Disorders.* New York: Academic Press.

Lyle, J.G., 1970. Certain antenatal, perinatal and developmental variables and reading retardation in middle-class boys. *Child Development* **41,** 481.

Lynch, G., 1974. The formation of new synaptic connections after brain damage and their possible role in recovery of function. *Neuroscience Research Progress Bulletin* **12,** 226.

Lynn, R.B., Buchanan, D.C., Fenichel, G.M., and Freemon, F.R., 1980. Agenesis of the corpus callosum. *Archives of Neurology* **37,** 444.

Maccoby, E.E., and Jacklin, C.N., 1974. *The Psychology of Sex Differences.* Stanford, Calif.: Stanford University Press, Chap. 3.

MacKeith, R., and Bax, M. (eds.), 1963. *Minimal Cerebral Dysfunction. Little Club Clinics in Developmental Medicine,* no. 10. London: Heinemann.

MacKeith, R.C., and Rutter, M., 1972. A note on the prevalence of speech and language disorders. In M. Rutter and J.A. Martin (eds.), *The Child with Delayed Speech.* London: Heinemann.

Mackinnon, P.C.B., 1979. Sexual differentiation of the brain. In F. Falkner and J.M. Tanner (eds.), *Human Growth,* vol. 3: *Neurobiology and Nutrition.* New York: Plenum Press.

Mackworth, N.H., Grandstaff, N.W., and Pribram, K.H., 1973. Orientation to pictorial novelty by speech-disordered children. *Neuropsychologia* **11,** 443.

MacLean, P.D., 1970. The triune brain, emotion, and scientific bias. In F.O. Schmitt (ed.), *The Neurosciences: Second Study Program.* New York: Rockefeller University Press.

Magelby, F. L., and Farley, O.W., 1968. *Education for Blind Children,* Research Bulletin 16. New York: American Foundation for the Blind.

Malamud, N., 1964a. Neuropathology. In H.A. Stevens and R. Heber (eds.), *Mental Retardation, a Review of Research.* Chicago: University of Chicago Press.

Malamud, N., Itabashi, H.H., Castor, J., and Messinger, H.B., 1964b. An etiologic and diagnostic study of cerebral palsy. *Journal of Pediatrics* **65,** 270.

Malpass, L.F., 1963. Motor skills in mental deficiency. In N.R. Ellis (ed.), *Handbook of Mental Deficiency.* New York: McGraw-Hill.

Manheimer, D.I., and Mellinger, G.D., 1967. Personality characteristics of the child accident repeater. *Child Development* **38,** 491.

Mann, I., 1969. *The Development of the Human Eye.* New York: Grune and Stratton.

Marge, M., 1972. The general problem of language disabilities in children. In J. V. Irwin and M. Marge (eds.), *Principles of Childhood Language Disabilities.* New York: Appleton-Century-Crofts.

Marin-Padilla, M., 1978. Dual origin of the mammalian neocortex and evolution of the cortical plate. *Anatomy and Embryology* **152**, 109.

Marlowe, M., Errera, J., and Jacobs, J., Increased lead and cadmium burdens among mentally retarded children and children with borderline intelligence. *American Journal of Mental Deficiency* **87**, 477.

Marshall, W.A., 1968. *Development of the Brain*. Edinburgh: Oliver and Boyd.

Martin, A., 1981. Visual processing in the acallosal brain: A clue to the differential functions of the anterior commissure and splenium. Presented at I.N.S., Atlanta, February.

Martin, H.P., 1980. Nutrition, injury, illness, and minimal brain dysfunction. In H.E. Rie, and E.D. Rie (eds.), *Handbook of Minimal Brain Dysfunction: A Critical View*. New York: Wiley.

Martin, J.A.M., 1981. *Voice, Speech and Language in the Child: Development and Disorder. Disorders of Human Communication*, vol. 4. New York: Springer.

Martyn, L.J., 1975. Pediatric neuroophthalmology. In R.D. Harley (ed.), *Pediatric Ophthalmology*. Philadelphia: Saunders.

Mash, E.J., and Dalby, J.T., 1979. Behavioural interventions for hyperactivity. In R.L. Trites (ed.), *Hyperactivity in Children: Etiology, Measurement and Treatment Implications*. Baltimore: University Park Press.

Matkin, N.D., and Carhart, R., 1966. Auditory profiles associated with Rh incompatibility. *Archives of Otolarygnology* (Chicago) **84**, 502.

Matson, D.D., 1969. *Neurosurgery of Infancy and Childhood*. Springfield, Ill.: Charles C Thomas.

Mattes, J.A., and Gittelman, R., 1981. Effects of artificial food colorings in children with hyperactive symptoms. *Archives of General Psychiatry* **38**, 414.

Matthews, C.G., and Kløve, H., 1967. Differential psychological performance in major motor, psychomotor, and mixed seizure classifications of known and unknown etiology. *Epilepsia* **8**, 117.

Mattis, S., 1978. Dyslexia syndromes: A working hypothesis that works. In A.L. Benton and D. Pearl (eds.), *Dyslexia: An Appraisal of Current Knowledge*. New York: Oxford University Press.

Mattis, S., French, J.H., and Rapin, I., 1975. Dyslexia in children and young adults: Three independent neuropsychological syndromes. *Developmental Medicine and Child Neurology* **17**, 150.

Mattison, R., 1983. The prevalence of psychiatric disorder in children with speech and language disorders. Paper presented at the 11th Annual Meeting of the International Neuropsychological Society, Mexico City.

Matz, G.J., and Naunton, R.F., 1968. Ototoxicity of chloroquine: An effect similar to quinine when administered to pregnant women. *Archives of Otolaryngology* **88**, 370.

Matzker, R., 1958. *Ein binauraler Hörsynthese-Test zum Nachweis zerebraler Hörstörungen*. Stuttgart: Thieme.

Maurer, D., and Salapatek, P., 1976. Developmental changes in the scanning of faces by young infants. *Child Development* **47**, 523.

Maurer, D., and Terrill, I., 1979. A physiological explanation of the infant's early visual development. *Canadian Journal of Psychology* **33**, 232.

McAdoo, G., and DeMyer, M.K., 1978. Personality characteristics of parents. In M. Rutter and E. Schopler (eds.), *Autism*. New York: Plenum Press.

McAllister, M., 1981. WISC characteristics of clinic-referred subgroups of disabled learners. Unpublished masters thesis, University of Victoria.

McBride, H.C.G., 1975. The isolation syndrome in childhood. Part 1: The syndrome and its diagnosis. *Developmental Medicine and Child Neurology* **17**, 198.

McCall, R.B., 1976. Toward an epigenetic conception of mental development in the first three years of life. In M. Lewis (ed.), *Origins of Intelligence: Infancy and Early Childhood*. New York: Plenum Press.

McDaniels, J.W., and McDaniels, M.L., 1976. Visual and auditory cognitive processing affected by epilepsy. *Behavioral Neuropsychiatry* **8**, 78.

McDonald, A.D., 1973. Severely retarded children in Quebec: Prevalence, causes and care. *American Journal of Mental Deficiency* **78**, 205.

McFie, J., 1961. The effects of hemispherectomy on intellectual functioning in cases of infantile hemiplegia. *Journal of Neurology, Neurosurgery, and Psychiatry* **24**, 240.

McFie, J., 1975. Brain injury in childhood and language development. In N. O'Connor (ed.), *Language, Cognitive Deficits, and Retardation*. London: Butterworth.

McGee, M.G., 1979. *Human Spatial Abilities: Sources of Sex Differences*. New York: Praeger.

McGeer, P.L., Eccles, J.C., and McGeer, E.G., 1978. *Molecular Neurobiology of the Mammalian Brain*. New York: Plenum Press.

McGlone, J., 1977. Sex differences in the cerebral organization of verbal functions in patients with unilateral brain lesions. *Brain* **100**(4), 775.

McGlone, J., 1980. Sex differences in human brain asymmetry: A critical survey. *Behavioral and Brain Sciences* **3**, 215.

McGraw, M.B., 1946. Maturation of behaviour. In L. Carmichael (ed.), *Manual of Child Psychology*. New York: Wiley.

McGuinness, D., and Pribram, K.H., 1979. The origins of sensory bias in the development of gender differences in perception and cognition. In M. Bortner (ed.), *Cognitive Growth and Development*. New York: Brunner/Mazel.

McGuinness, D., and Pribram, K.H., 1980. The neuropsychology of attention: Emotional and motivational controls. In M.C. Wittcock (ed.), *The Brain and Psychology*. New York: Academic Press.

McIntosh, N., 1979. Medulloblastoma: A changing prognosis? *Archives of Disease in Childhood* **54**, 200.

McIntosh, R., Meritt, K.K., Richards, M.R., Samuels, M.H., and Bellows, M.S., 1954. The incidence of congenital malformations: A study of 5964 pregnancies. *Pediatrics* **14**, 505.

McKay, H., Sinesterra, L., McKay, A., Gomez, H., and Lloreda, P., 1978. Improving cognitive ability in chronically deprived children. *Science* **200**, 270.

McKenzie, K.G., 1938. The present status of a patient who had the right cerebral hemisphere removed. *Journal of the American Medical Association* **111**, 168.

McKusick, V.A., 1975. *Mendelian Inheritance in Man: Catalogs of Autosomal Dominant, Autosomal Recessive, and X-Linked Phenotypes*, 5th edn. Baltimore: Johns Hopkins Press.

McLaren, D.S., Yaktin, U.S., Kanawati, A., Sabbagh, S., and Kadi, Z., 1973. The subsequent mental and physical development of rehabilitated marasmic infants. *Journal of Mental Deficiency Research* **17**, 273.

McLone, D., Czyzewski, D., Raimondi, A.J., and Sommers, R.C., 1982. Central nervous system infections as a limiting factor in the intelligence of children with myelomeningocele. *Pediatrics* **70**(3), 338.

McMahon, R.C., 1980. Genetic etiology in the hyperactive child syndrome: A critical review. *American Journal of Orthopsychiatry* **50**, 145.

McVicker-Hunt, J., 1979. Psychological development: Early experience. *Annual Review of Psychology* **36**, 103.

Meadow, K.P., 1968. Towards a developmental understanding of deafness. *Journal of Rehabilitation of the Deaf* **2**, 1.

Mealey, J., 1975. Infantile subdural hematomas. *Pediatric Clinics of North America* **22**, 433.

Medina, J., Chokroverty, S., and Rubino, F.A., 1977. Syndrome of agitated delirium and visual impairment: A manifestation of medial temporo-occipital infarction. *Journal of Neurology, Neurosurgery and Psychiatry* **40**, 861.

Mehegan, C.C., and Dreifuss, F.E., 1972. Hyperlexia: Exceptional reading ability in brain-damaged children. *Neurology* **22**, 1105.

Melekian, B., 1981. Lateralization in the human newborn at birth: Asymmetry of the stepping reflex. *Neuropsychologia* **19**, 707.

Melish, M.E., and Hanshaw, J.B., 1973. Congenital cytomegalovirus infection: Developmental progress of infants detected by routine screening. *American Journal of Diseases of Children* **126**, 190.

Melzack, R., 1969. The role of early experience in emotional arousal. *Annals of the New York Academy of Sciences* **159**, 721.

Mendelson, W., Johnson, W., and Stewart, M., 1971. Hyperactive children as teenagers: A follow-up study. *Journal of Nervous and Mental Diseases* **153**, 273.

Menkes, M.M., Rowe, J.S., and Menkes, J.H., 1967. A 25-year follow-up study on the hyperkinetic child with minimal brain dysfunction. *Pediatrics* **39**(3), 393.

Menser, M.A., Dods, L., and Harley, J.D., 1967. A 25-year follow-up of congenital rubella. *Lancet* **2**, 1347.

Menyuk, P., 1977. Effects of hearing loss on language acquisition in the babbling stage. In B.F. Jaffe (ed.), *Hearing Loss in Children*. Baltimore: University Park Press.

Menyuk, P., 1978. Linguistic problems in children with developmental dysphasia. In M.A. Wyke (ed.), *Developmental Dysphasia*. New York: Academic Press.

Meyer, M.B., Jones, B.S., and Tonascia, J.A., 1976. Perinatal events associated with maternal smoking during pregnancy. *American Journal of Epidemiology* **103**, 464.

Meyer, P., Paul Flechsig's system of myelogenetic cortical localization in the light of recent research in neuroanatomy and neurophysiology. *Canadian Journal of Neurological Sciences* **8**(1), 1 (part I) and **8**(2), 95 (part II).

Meyer-Probst, B., 1974. Über kognitive Leistungsveränderungen hirngeschädigter Kinder. *Zeitschrift für Psychologie* (Leipzig) **182**, 181.

Michel, G., 1981. Right-handedness: A consequence of infant supine head orientation preference. *Science* **212**, 685.

Michel, G., and Goodwin, R., 1979. Intrauterine birth position predicts newborn supine head position preferences. *Infant Behavior and Child Development* **2**, 29.

Milgram, N.A., 1973. Cognition and language in mental retardation: Distinctions and implications. In D.K. Routh (ed.), *The Experimental Psychology of Mental Retardation*. Chicago: Aldine.

Milisen, R., 1966. Articulatory problems. In R.W. Rieber and R.S. Brubaker (eds.), *Speech Pathology*. Philadelphia: Lippincott.

Miller, E., and Sethi, L., 1971. The effects of hydrocephalus on perception. *Developmental Medicine and Child Neurology*, suppl. 25, 77.

Miller, J.S., 1978. Hyperactive children: A ten-year study. *Pediatrics* **61,** 217.

Miller, R.G., Palkes, H.S., and Stewart, M.A., 1973. Hyperactive children in suburban elementary schools. *Child Psychiatry and Human Development* 4, 121.

Millichap, J.G., 1973. Drugs in the management of minimal brain dysfunction. *Annals of the New York Academy of Sciences* **205,** 321.

Millichap, J.G. (ed.), 1977. *Learning Disabilities and Related Disorders: Facts and Current Issues*. Chicago: Year Book Medical Publishers.

Milner, A.D., and Jeeves, M.A., 1979. A review of behavioural studies of agenesis of the corpus callosum. In I.S. Russell, M.W. Van Hof, and G. Berlucchi (eds.), *Structure and Function of Cerebral Commissures*. Baltimore: University Park Press.

Milner, B., 1954. Intellectual functions of the temporal lobes. *Psychological Bulletin* **51,** 42.

Milner, B., 1975. Psychological aspects of focal epilepsy and its neurological management. *Advances in Neurology* 8, 299.

Minde, K., Lewin, D., Weiss, G., Lavigueur, H., Douglas, V., and Sykes, E., 1971. The hyperactive child in elementary school: A five-year, controlled follow-up. *Exceptional Children* **38,** 215.

Minkowski, A., Larroche, J.C., Vignaud, L., Dreyfus-Brisac, C., and Dargassies, S.S., 1966. Development of the nervous system in early life. In F. Falkner (ed.), *Human Development*. Philadelphia: Saunders.

Miranda, S., 1970. Visual abilities and pattern preferences of premature infants and full-term neonates. *Journal of Experimental Child Psychology* **10,** 189.

Miranda, S.B., Hack, M., Fanta, R.L., Fanaroff, A.A., and Klaus, M.H., 1977. Neonatal pattern vision: A predictor of future mental performance? *Journal of Pediatrics* **91,** 642.

Mirsky, A.F., Primac, D.W., Marsan, C.A., Rosvold, H.E., and Stevens, J.R., 1960. A comparison of the psychological test performance of patients with focal and nonfocal epilepsy. *Experimental Neurology* **2,** 75.

Mitchell, R.G., 1980. Perinatal follow-up. *Developmental Medicine and Child Neurology* **22,** 1.

Molfese, D.L., 1977. Infant cerebral asymmetry. In Segalowitz, S.J., and Gruber, F.A., Eds., *Language Development and Neurological Theory*. New York: Academic Press.

Molfese, D.L., and Molfese, V.J., 1979a. Hemispheric and stimulus differences as reflected in the cortical responses of newborn infants to speech stimuli. *Developmental Psychology* **15,** 505.

Molfese, D.L., and Molfese, V.J., 1979b. VOT distinctions in infants: Learned or innate? In H. Whitaker and H. Whitaker (eds.), *Studies in Neurolinguistics*, vol 4. New York: Academic Press.

Molfese, D.L., Nunez, V., Seibert, S.M., and Ramanaiach, N.V., 1976. Cerebral asymmetry: Changes in factors affecting its development. In S.R. Harnad, H.D.

Stekilis and J.B. Lancaster (eds.), *Origins and Evolution of Language and Speech.* Annals of the New York Academy of Sciences **280**, 811.

Molnar, G.E., 1973. Clinical aspects of cerebral palsy. *Pediatric Annals* **2**, 10.

Moltz, H., 1968. An epigenetic interpretation of the imprinting phenomenon. In G. Newton and S. Levine (eds.), *Early Experience and Behavior.* Springfield, Ill.: Charles C Thomas.

Moltz, H., 1973. Some implications of the critical period hypothesis. *Annals of the New York Academy of Sciences* **223**, 144.

Money, J., 1973. Turner's syndrome and parietal lobe functions. *Cortex* **9**, 385.

Money, J., and Ehrhardt, A.A., 1972. *Man and Woman, Boy and Girl.* Baltimore: Johns Hopkins University Press.

Monif, G.R.G., Hardy, J.B., and Sever, J.L., 1966. Studies in congential rubella, Baltimore 1964–65. I. Epidemiologic and virologic. *Bulletin of Johns Hopkins Hospital* **118**, 85.

Montandon, P.B., Cao, M.H., Engel, R.T., and Grajau, T., 1979. Auditory nerve and brainstem responses in the newborn and in preschool children. *Acta Otolaryngologica* **87**, 279.

Moore, R.Y., 1977. The developmental organization of the fetal brain. In L. Gluck (ed.), *Intrauterine Asphyxia and the Developing Fetal Brain.* Chicago: Year Book Medical Publishers.

Moore, R.Y., Bjorklund, A., and Stenevi, U., 1974. Growth and plasticity of adrenergic neurons. In F.O. Schmitt and F.G. Worden (eds.), *The Neurosciences: Third Study Program.* Cambridge, Mass.: MIT Press.

Mordock, J.B., and Bogan, S., 1968. Wechsler patterns and symptomatic behaviors of children diagnosed as having minimal cerebral dysfunction. *Proceedings, 76th Annual Convention APA*, Washington, D.C.: American Psychological Association.

Morest, D.K., 1969. The growth of dendrites in the mammalian brain. *Zeitschrift für Anatomie und Entwicklungsgeschichte*, vol. 128, p. 290.

Morgan, M., 1977. Embryology and the inheritance of asymmetry, In S. Harnad, R. W. Doty, L. Goldstein, J. Jaynes and G. Krauthamer (eds.), *Lateralization in the Nervous System.* New York: Academic Press.

Morgan, W.P., 1896. A case of congenital word blindness. *British Medical Journal* **2**, 1378.

Morrison, J.R., 1979. Diagnosis of adult psychiatric patients with childhood hyperactivity. *American Journal of Psychiatry* **136**, 955.

Morrison, J.R., 1980. Childhood hyperactivity in an adult psychiatric population: Social factors. *Journal of Clinical Psychiatry* **41**, 40.

Morrison, J.R., and Stewart, M.A., 1971. A family study of the hyperactive syndrome. *Biological Psychiatry* **3**, 189.

Morrison, J.R., and Stewart, M.A., 1973. The psychiatric status of the legal families of adopted hyperactive children. *Archives of General Psychiatry* **28**, 888.

Morse, P.A., 1972. The discrimination of speech and nonspeech stimuli in early infancy. *Journal of Experimental Child Psychology* **14**, 477.

Morse, P.A., 1977. Infant speech perception. In D.A. Sanders (ed.), *Auditory Perception of Speech.* New York: Prentice Hall.

Morselli, P.L., Lloyd, K.G., Loscher, W., Meldrum, B., and Reynolds, E.H. (eds.), 1981. *Neurotransmitters, Seizures and Epilepsy.* New York: Raven Press.

Morton-Evans, A., and Hensley, R., 1978. Paired associate learning in early infantile autism and receptive developmental aphasia. *Journal of Autism and Childhood Schizophrenia* **8**, 61.

Moruzzi, G., and Magoun, H.W., 1949. Brainstem reticular formation and activation of the EEG. *Electroencephalography and Clinical Neurophysiology* **1**, 455.

Moshe, S.L., Albala, B.J., Ackermann, R.F., and Engel, J., 1982. Increased seizure susceptibility of the immature brain. *Neurology* **32**(2), A121.

Mosley, J.L., and Stan, E.A., 1982. Sex differences in intellectual and neurological disorders: Biogenic risk factors and male vulnerability, in I. Al-Issa (ed.), *Gender and Psychopathology*. New York: Academic Press.

Movshon, J.A., and Van Sluyters, R.C., 1981. Visual neural development. *Annual Review of Psychology*, **32**, 477.

Mulligan, J., Painter, M., O'Donoghue, P., MacDonald, H., Allen, A., and Taylor, P., 1980. Neonatal asphyxia. II. Neonatal mortality and long-term sequelae. *Journal of Pediatrics* **96**(5), 903.

Munk, H., 1881. *Über die Funktionen der Grosshirnrinde. Gesammelte Mitteilungen aus den Jahren 1877–1880*. Berlin: August Hirschwald.

Munz, A., and Tolor, A., 1955. Psychological effects of major cerebral excision: Intellectual and emotional changes following hemispherectomy. *Journal of Nervous and Mental Diseases* **14**, 438.

Musiek, F.E., and Geurkink, N.A., 1980. Auditory perceptual problems in children: Considerations for the otolaryngologist and audiologist. *Laryngoscope* **90**(6), 962.

Mutton, D.E., and Lea, J., 1980. Chromosome studies of children with specific speech and language delay. *Developmental Medicine and Child Neurology* **22**, 588.

Myklebust, H.R., 1954. *Auditory Disorders in Children*. New York: Grune and Stratton.

Myklebust, H.R., 1956. Rh child: Deaf or 'aphasic'? Some psychological considerations of the Rh child. *Journal of Speech and Hearing Disorders* **21**, 423.

Myklebust, H.R., 1978. Towards a science of dyslexology. In H.R. Myklebust (ed.), *Progress in Learning Disability*, vol. 4. New York: Grune and Stratton.

Myrianthopoulos, N.C., and Chung, C.S., 1974. Congenital malformations in singletons: Epidemiologic survey. *Birth Defects* **10**, 1.

Naeye, R.L., 1977. Placental infarction leading to fetal or neonatal death: A prospective study. *Obstetrics and Gynecology* **50**, 583.

Nahmias, A.J., Visintine, A.M., and Starr, S.E., 1976. Viral infections of the fetus and newborn. In W.L. Drew, (ed.), *Viral Infections: A Clinical Approach*. Philadelphia: Davis.

Nash, J., 1978. *Developmental Psychology: A Psychobiological Approach*. Englewood Cliffs, N.J.: Prentice-Hall.

Natelson, S., and Sayers, M., 1973. The fate of children sustaining severe head trauma during birth. *Pediatrics* **51**(2), 169.

National Institutes of Health, 1980. Febrile seizures: A consensus of their significance, evaluation, and treatment. *Pediatrics* **66**, 1009.

National Institutes of Health, 1981. *Cesearean Childbirth*. Washington, D.C.: NIH.

National Institute of Neurological and Communicative Disorders and Stroke, 1979. *Technical Document of the Panel on Developmental Neurological Disorders to the National Advisory Neurological and Communicative Disorders and Stroke Council.* Bethesda, Md.: U.S. Department of Health and Human Services.

National Joint Committee for Learning Disabilities, 1981. *Perspectives on Dyslexia.*

Needleman, H. (ed.), 1980. *Low-Level Lead Expsoure: The Clinical Implications of Current Research.* New York: Raven Press.

Needleman, H.L., Davidson, I., Sewell, E.M., and Shapiro, I.M., 1974. Subclinical lead exposure in Philadelphia schoolchildren. *New England Journal of Medicine* **290,** 245.

Nelhaus, G., 1968. Head circumference from birth to 18 years. *Pediatrics* **41**(1), 106.

Nelson, H.E., and Warrington, E.K., 1976. Developmental spelling retardation. In R.M. Knights and D.J. Bakker (eds.), *The Neuropsychology of Learning Disorders.* Baltimore: University Park Press.

Nelson, K., and Ellenberg, J.H., 1979. Neonatal signs as predictors of cerebral palsy. *Pediatrics* **64**(2), 225.

Nesselroade, J.R., and Baltes, P.B., 1979. *Longitudinal Research in the Study of Behavior and Development.* New York: Academic Press.

Nesselroade, J.R., and Reese, H.W., 1973. *Life-span Developmental Psychology: Methodological Issues.* New York: Academic Press.

Nesselroade, J.R., Stigler, S.M., and Baltes, P.B., 1980. Regression toward the mean and the study of change. *Psychological Bulletin* **88**(3), 622.

Netley, C., 1972. Dichotic listening performance of hemispherectomized patients. *Neuropsychologia* **10,** 233.

Netley, C., 1976. Dichotic listening of callosal agenesis and Turner's syndrome patients. In S.J. Segalowicz and F.A. Gruber (eds.), *Language Development and Neurological Theory.* New York: Academic Press.

Netter, F.H., 1962. The Ciba Collection of Medical Illustrations, Vol. 1: *Nervous System.* New York: Ciba Pharmaceutical.

Neuhäuser, G., Koch, G., and Schwanitz, G., 1981. Mikrozephalien. *Zeitschrift für die allgemeine Medizin* **57,** 1211.

Newman, G.C., Buschi, A.I., Sugg, N.K., Kelly, T.E., and Miller, J.Q., 1982. Dandy-Walker syndrome diagnosed in utero by ultrasonography. *Neurology* **32,** 180.

Newton, G., and Levine, S. (eds.), 1968. *Early Experience and Behaviour.* Springfield, Ill.: Charles C Thomas.

Nichols, P., and Chen, T., 1981. *Minimal Brain Dysfunction. A Prospective Study.* Hillsdale, N.J.: Erlbaum.

Nickel, R.E., Bennett, F.C., and Lamson, F.N., 1982. School performance of children with birth weights of 1000 grams or less. *American Journal of Diseases of Children* **136,** 105.

Niebergall, G., Remschmidt, H., and Lingelbach, B., 1976. Neuropsychologische Untersuchungen zur Rückbildung traumatisch verursachter Aphasien. *Zeitschrift für klinische Psychologie* **5,** 194.

Nielsen, H.H., 1980. A longitudinal study of the psychological aspects of myelomeningocele. *Scandinavian Journal of Psychology* **21,** 45.

Nissen, G., 1982. Depressionen im Kinder und Jugendalter. *Triangel* **21,** 77.

Niswander, K.R., and Gordon, M., 1972. *The Women and Thier Pregnancies.* Washington, D.C.: U.S. Department of Health, Education and Welfare, no. 73-379.

Niswander, K.R., Gordon, M., and Drage, J., 1975. The effect of intrauterine hypoxia on the child surviving to four years. *American Journal of Obstetrics and Gynecology* **121**, 892.

Noback, C.R., and Demerest, R.J., 1981. *The Human Nervous System*. New York: McGraw-Hill.

Norden, K., 1981. Learning processes and personality development in deaf children. *American Annals of the Deaf* **126**, 404.

Norman, M.G., 1978. Perinatal brain damage. *Perspectives in Pediatric Pathology* **4**, 41.

Notter, R.H., and Shapiro, D.L., 1981. Lung surfactant in an era of replacement therapy. *Pediatric* **68**(6), 781.

Nunnally, J.C., 1973. Research strategies and measurement methods for investigating human development. In J.R. Nesselroade and H.W. Reese (eds.), *Life-span Developmental Psychology: Methodological Issues*. New York: Academic Press.

Nyborg, H., and Nielsen, J., 1977. Sex chromosome abnormalities and cognitive performance. III. Field dependence, frame dependence, and failing development of perceptual stability in girls with Turner's syndrome. *Journal of Psychology* **96**, 205.

Obrador, S., 1964. Nervous integration after hemispherectomy in man. In G. Schaltenbrand and C.N. Woolsey (eds.), *Cerebral Localization and Organization*. Madison: University of Wisconsin Press.

O'Connor, N., and Hermelin, B., 1962. Visual and stereognostic shape recognition in normal children and mongol and nonmongol imbeciles. *Journal of Mental Deficiency Research* **6**, 63.

O'Connor, N., and Hermelin, B., 1973. Short-term memory for the order of pictures and syllables by deaf and hearing children. *Neuropsychologia* **11**, 437.

Offord, D.R., Sullivan, K., Allen, N., and Abrams, N., 1979. Delinquency and hyperactivity. *Journal of Nervous and Mental Disease* **167**, 734.

O'Hara, P.T., 1972. Electron microscopic study of the brain in Down's syndrome. *Brain* **95**, 681.

Ohlrich, E.S., Barnet, A.B., Weiss, I.P., and Shanks, B.L., 1978. Auditory evoked potential development in childhood: A longitudinal study. *Electroencephalography and Clinical Neurophysiology* **44**, 411.

Ohtahara, S., Yamatogi, Y., Ohtoska, Y., Oka, E., and Ishida, T., 1980. Prognosis of West syndrome and special reference to Lennox syndrome: A developmental study. In J.A. Woda and J.K. Penny (eds.), *Advances in Epileptology: 10th Epilepsy International Symposium*. New York: Raven Press.

Omenn, G.S., and Weber, B.A., 1978. Dyslexia: Search for phenotypic and genetic heterogenity. *American Journal of Medical Genetics* **1**, 333.

O'Neal, P., and Robins, L.N., Childhood patterns predictive of adult schizophrenia: A 30-year follow-up study. *American Journal of Psychiatry* **115**, 385.

O'Neill, J.F., 1980. The visually impaired child: Introduction. *Pediatric Annals* **9**(11), 412.

Oppenheim, R.W., 1981. Neuronal cell death and some related regressive phenomena during neurogenesis: A selective historical review and progress report. In W.M. Cowen (ed.), *Studies in Developmental Neurobiology*. New York: Oxford University Press.

Orlansky, H., 1949. Infant care and personality. *Psychological Bulletin* **46**, 1.

Ornitz, E.M., 1973. Childhood autism: A review of the clinical and experimental literature (Medical Progress). *California Medicine* **118**, 21.

Ornitz, E.M., 1978. Biological Homogeneity or Heterogeneity? In M. Rutter and E. Schopler (eds.), *Autism: A Reappraisal of Concepts and Treatment*. New York: Plenum Press.

Orton, S.T., 1925. Word-blindness in school children. *Archives of Neurology and Psychiatry* **14**, 582.

Orton, S., 1937. *Reading, Writing and Speech Problems in Children*. New York: Norton.

Ott, J., 1974. The eyes' dual function, part II. *Eye, Ear, Nose and Throat Monthly* **53**, 377.

Ounsted, C., and Taylor, D., 1972. The Y-chromosome message: A point of view. In C. Ounsted and D. Taylor (eds.), *Gender Differences: Their Ontogeny and Significance*. Edinburgh: Churchill Livingstone.

Overall, J.E., and Gorham, D.R., 1962. The brief psychiatric rating scale. *Psychological Reports*. **10**, 799.

Overmann, S.R., 1977. Behavioral effects of asymptomatic lead exposure during neonatal development in rats. *Toxicology and Applied Pharmacology* **41**, 459.

Owen, D.R., 1972. The 47, XYY male: A review. *Psychological Bulletin* **78**, 209.

Owen, F.W., 1978. Dyslexia: Genetic aspects. In A.L. Benton and D. Pearl (eds.), *Dyslexia: An Appraisal of Current Knowledge*. New York: Oxford University Press.

Owens, D., Dawson, J.C., and Losin, S., 1971. Alzheimer's disease in Down's syndrome. *American Journal of Mental Deficiency* **75**, 606.

Oxorn, H., 1980. *Human Labor and Birth*, 4th edn. New York: Appleton-Century-Crofts.

Pache, H.D., 1969. Missbildungen des Zentralnervensystems. In H. Opitz and F. Schmid (eds.), *Handbuch der Kinderheilkunde*, vol. 8. New York: Springer.

Paine, R.S., 1968. Syndromes of minimal cerebral damage. *Pediatric Clinics of North America* **15**, 779.

Paine, R.S., Werry, J.S., and Quay, H.C., 1968. A study of minimal cerebral dysfunction. *Developmental Medicine and Child Neurology* **10**, 505.

Palkes, H., and Stewart, M., 1972. Intellectual ability and performance of hyperactive children. *American Journal of Orthopsychiatry* **42**, 35.

Palmisano, P.A., Sneed, R.C., and Cassady, G., 1969. Untaxed whiskey and fetal lead exposure. *Journal of Pediatrics* **75**, 869.

Pandya, D.N., 1975. Interhemispheric connections in primates. In F. Michel and B. Schott (eds.), *Les Syndromes de Disconnexion Calleuse chez l'Homme* (Colloque Internationale de Lyon, 1974). Lyon: Hopital Neurologique.

Pansky, B., and Allen, D.J., 1980. *Review of Neuroscience*. New York: MacMillan.

Paoletti, R., and Davison, A.N. (eds.), 1971. *Chemistry and Brain Development*. New York: Plenum Press.

Pape, K., Armstrong, D., and Fitzhardinge, P., 1975. Intracerebellar hemorrhage as a possible complication of mask applied mechanical ventilation in the low-birth-weight infant. *Pediatric Research* **9**(4), 383.

Parkinson, C.E., Wallis, S., and Harvey, D., 1981. School achievement and behaviour of children who were small for date at birth. *Developmental Medicine and Child Neurology* **23**, 41.

Parmalee, A.H., 1981. Auditory function and neurological maturation in preterm infants. In S.L. Friedman and M. Sigman (eds.), *Preterm Birth and Psychological Development*. New York: Academic Press.

Parmelee, A.H., and Schulte, F.J., 1970. Developmental testing of preterm and small-for-date infants. *Pediatrics* **45**, 21.

Parsons, O.A., and Prigatano, G.P., 1978. Methodological considerations in clinical neuropsychological research. *Journal of Consulting and Clinical Psychology* **46**(4), 608.

Partain, C.L., James, A.E., Rollo, F.D., and Price, R.R. (eds.), 1983. *Nuclear Magnetic Resonance Imaging*. Philadelphia: W.B. Saunders.

Pasamanick, B., and Knobloch, H., 1960. Brain damage and reproductive casualty. *American Journal of Orthopsychiatry* **30**, 298.

Pass, R.F., Stagno, S., Myers, G.J., and Alford, C.A., 1980. Outcome of symptomatic congenital cytomegalovirus infection: Results of long-term longitudinal follow-up. *Pediatrics* **66**, 758.

Pease, D.C. (ed.), 1971. *Cellular Aspects of Neural Growth and Differentiation* (UCLA Forum in Medical Sciences No. 14). Los Angeles: University of California Press.

Peele, T.L., 1954. *The Neuroanatomical Basis for Clinical Neurology*. New York: McGraw-Hill.

Penfield, W., and Jasper, H., 1954. *Epilepsy and the Functional Anatomy of the Human Brain*. Boston: Little, Brown.

Penrose, L.S., 1963. *The Biology of Mental Defect*, 2d rev. edn. London: Sidgwick and Jackson.

Phibbs, R.H., Harvin, D., Jones, G., Talbot, C., Cohen, M., Crowther, D., and Tolley, W.H., 1971. Development of children who had received intrauterine transfusions. *Pediatrics* **47**, 689.

Pinneau, S.R., 1955. Reply to Dr. Spitz. *Psychological Bulletin* **52**, 459.

Pirozzolo, F., 1979. *The Neuropsychology of Developmental Reading Disorders*. New York: Praeger.

Pirozzolo, F.J., Pirozzolo, P.H., and Ziman, R.B., 1979. Neuropsychological assessment of callosal agenesis: Report of a case with normal intelligence and absence of the disconnection syndrome. *Clinical Neuropsychology* **1**(1), 13.

Pisoni, D.B., 1977. Identification and discrimination of the relative onset of two component tones: Implication for the perception of voicing in stops. *Journal of the Acoustical Society of America* **61**, 1352.

Pitfield, M., and Oppenheim, A., 1964. Child-rearing attitudes of mothers of psychotic children. *Journal of Child Psychology and Psychiatry* **5**, 51.

Placek, P., 1977. Maternal and infant health factors associated with low infant birth weight: Findings from the 1972 National Natality Survey. In D. Reed and F. Stanley (eds.), *The Epidemiology of Prematurity*. Baltimore: Urban and Schwarzenberg.

Poeck, K., 1974. *Neurologie, ein Lehrbuch für Studierende und Ärzte*, 3d edn. Heidelberg: Springer.

Pollitt, E., and Thompson, C., 1977. Protein-caloric malnutrition and behavior: A view from psychology. In R. Wurtman and J. Wurtman (eds.), *Nutrition and the Brain*, vol. II. New York: Raven Press.

Porac, C., and Coren, S., 1981. *Lateral Preference and Human Behavior*. New York: Springer.

Prechtl, H.F.R., 1968. Neurological findings in newborn infants after pre- and paranatal complications. In J.H.P. Jonxis, H.D. Vissez, and J.A. Troelsttra (eds.), *Dysmaturity and Prematurity*. Leiden: Drocse.

Prechtl, H.F.R., 1978. Minimal brain dysfunction syndrome and the plasticity of the nervous system. *Advances in Biological Psychiatry* (Basel) **1**, 96.

Prechtl, H.F.R., and Beintema, D., 1964. *The Neurological Examination of the Full-Term Newborn Infant*. Little Club Clinics in Developmental Medicine, no. 12. London: Spastics Society.

Prechtl, H.F.R., and Stemmer, C.J., 1962. The choreiform syndrome in children. *Developmental Medicine and Child Neurology* **4**, 119.

Prensky, A.L., 1975. Metabolic disorders of genetic origin: Disorders of amino, organic, and nucleic acids and carbohydrate metabolism. In D.B. Tower (ed.), *The Nervous System*. Vol. 2: *The Clinical Neurosciences*. New York: Raven Press.

Purpura, D.P., 1975a. Dendritic differentiation in human cerebral cortex: Normal and aberrant developmental patterns. In G.W. Kreutzberg (ed.), *Advances in Neurology*, vol. 12. New York: Raven Press.

Purpura, D.P., 1975b. Normal and aberrant neuronal development in the cerebral cortex of human fetus and young infant. In N.A. Buchwald and M.A.B. Brazier (eds.), *Brain Mechanisms in Mental Retardation*. New York: Academic Press.

Purpura, D.P., 1977. Developmental pathobiology of cortical neurons in immature human brain. In L. Gluck (ed.), *Intrauterine Asphyxia and the Developing Fetal Brain*. Chicago: Year Book Medical Publishers.

Purves, D., and Lichtman, J., 1980. Elimination of synapses in the developing nervous system. *Science* **210**, 153.

Purves, M., 1974. Onset of respiration at birth. *Archives of Diseases in Childhood* **49**, 333.

Quadfasel, F.A., and Goodglass, H., 1968. Specific reading disability and other specific disabilities. *Journal of Learning Disabilities* **1**, 590.

Rabinowicz, T., 1964. The cerebral cortex of the premature infant of the eighth month. In D.P. Purpura and J.P. Schade (eds.), *Growth and Maturation of the Brain* (Progress in Brain Research, vol. 4). Amsterdam: Elsevier.

Rabinowicz, T., 1974. Some aspects of the maturation of the human cerebral cortex. In S.R. Berenberg, M. Caniaris, and N.P. Masse (eds.), *Pre- and Postnatal Development of the Human Brain*. Basel: Karger.

Rabinowicz, T., 1979. The differentiate maturation of the human cerebral cortex. In F. Falkner and J.M. Tanner (eds.), *Human Growth*. Vol. 3: *Neurobiology and Nutrition*. New York: Plenum Press.

Raimondi, A.J., and Tomita, T., 1979. The disadvantages of prophylactic whole CNS postoperative radiation therapy for medulloblastoma. In P. Paoletti, G. Walker, and R. Knerich (eds.), *Multidisciplinary Aspects of Brain Tumor Therapy*. Amsterdam: Elsevier/North Holland.

Rakic, P., 1972. Migrating cells and radial fibers in the developing cerebral cortex of the rhesus monkey. *Journal of Comparative Neurology* **145**, 61.

Rakic, P., 1975a. Timing of major ontogenetic events in the visual cortex of the rhesus monkey. In N.A. Buchwald and M.A.B. Brazier (eds.), *Brain Mechanisms in Mental Retardation*. New York: Academic Press.

Rakic, P., 1975b. Cell migration and neuronal ectopias in the brain. *Birth Defects* (Original Article Series) **11**(7), 95.

Rakic, P., 1979a. Genetic and epigenetic determinants of local neuronal circuits in the mammalian central nervous system. In F.O. Schmitt and F.G. Worden (eds.), *The Neurosciences: Fourth Study Program.* Cambridge, Mass.: MIT Press.

Rakic, P., 1979b. Genesis of visual connections in the rhesus monkey. In R.D. Freeman (ed.), *Developmental Neurobiology of Vision.* New York: Plenum Press.

Rakic, P., 1981. Developmental events leading to laminar and areal organization of the neocortex. In F.O. Schmitt, F.G. Worden, G. Adelman, and S.G. Dennis (eds.), *The Organization of the Cerebral Cortex.* Cambridge, Mass.: MIT Press.

Rakic, P., and Goldman-Rakic, P.S. (eds.), 1982. Development and Modifiability of the Cerebral Cortex. *Neurosciences Research Program Bulletin* **20,** 429.

Rankin, J.M., Aram, D.M., and Horwitz, S.J., 1981. Language ability and right and left hemiplegic children. *Brain and Language* **14,** 292.

Rapin, I., 1975. Children with hearing impairment. In K.E. Swaiman and F.S. Wright (eds.), *The Practice of Pediatric Neurology.* St. Louis: Mosby.

Rapin, I., 1979. Effects of early blindness and deafness on cognition. In R. Katzman (ed.), *Congenital and Acquired Cognitive Disorders.* New York: Raven Press.

Rapin, I., 1982. *Children with Brain Dysfunction: Neurology, Cognition, Language, and Behavior.* New York: Raven Press.

Rapin, I., Mattis, S., Rowan, A.J., and Golden, G.G., 1977. Verbal auditory agnosia in children. *Developmental Medicine and Child Neurology* **19**(2), 192.

Rapin, I., and Wilson, B.C., 1978. Children with developmental language disability: Neurological aspects and assessment. In M.A. Wyke (ed.), *Developmental Dysphasia.* New York: Academic Press.

Rapoport, J.L., and Ferguson, H.B., 1981. Biological validation of the hyperkinetic syndrome. *Developmental Medicine and Child Neurology.* **23,** 667.

Rapoport, J.L., and Quinn, P.O., 1975. Minor physical anomalies (stigmata) and early developmental deviation: A major biologic subgroup of "hyperactive" children. *International Journal of Mental Health* **4,** 29.

Rawlings, G., Reynolds, E.O.R., Stewart, A.L., and Strang, L.B., 1971. Changing prognosis for infants of very low birth weight. *Lancet* **1,** 516.

Reed, H.B.C., and Reitan, R.M., 1963. Intelligence test performance of brain-damaged subjects with lateralized motor deficits. *Journal of Consulting Psychology* **27,** 102.

Reed, H.B., Reitan, R.M., and Kløve, H., 1965. Influence of cerebral lesions on psychological test performances of older children. *Journal of Consulting Psychology* **29,** 247.

Reed, J.C., and Reitan, R.M., 1969. Verbal and performance differences among brain-injured children with lateralized motor deficit. *Perceptual and Motor Skills* **29,** 747.

Rees, N.S., 1973. Auditory processing factors in language disorders: The view from Procrustes' bed. *Journal of Speech and Hearing Disorders* **38,** 304.

Reinert, G., 1970. Comparative factor analytic studies of intelligence through the human life-span. In L.R. Goulet and P. Baltes (eds.), *Life-span Developmental Psychology: Research and Theory.* New York: Academic Press.

Reinert, G., Baltes, P.B., and Schmidt, L.R., 1965. Kritik der Differenzierungshypothese der Intelligenz: Die Leistungsdifferenzierungshypothese. *Psychologische Forschung* **28,** 246.

Reinert, G., Baltes, P.B., and Schmidt, L.R., 1966. Kritik einer Kritik der Differenzierungshypothese der Intelligenz. *Zeitschrift für Experimentelle und Angewandte Psychologie* **13**, 602.

Reinis, S., and Goldman, J.M., 1980. *The Development of the Brain: Biological and Functional Perspectives.* Springfield, Ill.: Charles C Thomas.

Reinisch, J.M., 1974. Fetal hormones, the brain, and human sex differences: A heuristic, integrative review of the recent literature. *Archives of Sexual Behavior* **3**(1), 51.

Reitan, R.M., 1950. The significance of dysphasia for intelligence and adaptive abilities. *Journal of Psychology* **50**, 335.

Reitan, R.M., 1971a. Sensorimotor functions in brain-damaged and normal children of early school age. *Perceptual and Motor Skills* **33**, 655.

Reitan, R.M., 1971b. Trail-making test results for normal and brain-damaged children. *Perceptual and Motor Skills* **33**, 575.

Reitan, R.M., 1974. Psychological effects of cerebral lesions in children of early school age. In R.M. Reitan and L.A. Davison (eds.), *Clinical Neuropsychology: Current Status and Application.* Washington, D.C.: Winston.

Remschmidt, H., 1972. Experimentelle Untersuchungen zum Perseverationsverhalten von Epileptikern. *Archiv für Neurologie und Psychiatrie* **215**, 315.

Remschmidt, H., 1981. Neuropsychologische Befunde bei Epilepsien. In H. Remschmidt and M. Schmidt (eds.), *Neuropsychologie des Kindesalters.* Stuttgart: Enke.

Remschmidt, H., Niebergall, G., and Geyer, M. 1980. Neuropsychologische Untersuchungen zur Rückbildung von Aphasien. In H. Remschmidt and H. Stutte (eds.), *Neuropsychiatrische Folgen nach Schädel-Hirntrauma bei Kindern und Jugendlichen.* Berne: Huber.

Rentz, R., 1980. Epilepsie und Psychose. *Klinische Paediatrie* **46**, 415.

Reynolds, E.O.R., 1974. Improved prognosis for infants of very low birthweight. *Pediatrics* **54**, 724.

Reynolds, D.McQ., and Jeeves, M.A., 1974. Further studies of crossed and uncrossed pathway responding in callosal agenesis: Reply to Kinsbourne and Fisher. *Neuropsychologia* **12**, 287.

Reynolds, D.McQ., and Jeeves, M.A., 1977. Further studies of tactile perception and motor coordination in agenesis of the corpus callosum. *Cortex* **13**, 257.

Reynolds, D.W., Stagno, S., Stubbs, K.G., Dahle, A.J., Livingston, M.M., Saxon, S.S., and Alford, C.A., 1974. Inapparent congenital cytomegalovirus infection with elevated cord IgM levels: Causal relation with auditory and mental deficiency. *New England Journal of Medicine* **290**, 291.

Rhodes, W.C., and Tracy, M.I. (eds.), 1974. *A Study of Child Variance.* Ann Arbor: University of Michigan Press.

Ricciuti, H.N., 1981. Adverse environmental and nutritional influences on mental development: A perspective. *Journal of the American Dietetic Association* **79**, 115.

Richardson, S.O., 1972. Medical diagnosis and evaluation. In J.V. Irwin and M. Marge (eds.), *Principles of Childhood Language Disabilities.* New York: Appleton-Century-Crofts.

Richter, D., 1975. Neurochemical aspects of the growth and development of the brain. In M.A.B. Brazier (ed.), *Growth and Development of the Brain: Nutritional, Genetic, and Environmental Factors.* New York: Raven Press.

Rie, H.E., and Rie, E.D. (eds.), 1980. *Handbook of Minimal Brain Dysfunctions: A Critical View.* New York: Wiley.

Riesen, A.H., 1971. Problems in correlating behavioral and physiological development. In M.B. Sterman, D.J. McGinty, and A.M. Adinolfi (eds.), *Brain Development and Behavior.* New York: Academic Press.

Riesen, A.H., 1975. *The Developmental Neuropsychology of Sensory Deprivation.* New York: Academic Press.

Rigatto, H., and Brady, J.P., 1972. Periodic breathing and apnea in preterm infants. II. Hypoxia as a primary event. *Pediatrics* **50**, 219.

Riikonen, R., and Amnell, G., 1981. Psychiatric disorders in children with earlier infantile spasms. *Developmental Medicine and Child Neurology* **23**, 747.

Rimland, B., 1964. *Infantile Autism.* New York: Appleton-Century-Crofts.

Risser, A., 1981. Neonatal lateralization: Asymmetrical attainment and maintenance of head posture. University of Victoria, unpublished M.A. thesis.

Robin, R.A., Balow, B., and Fisch, R.O., 1979. Neonatal serum bilirubin levels related to cognitive development at ages four through seven years. *Journal of Pediatrics* **13**, 337.

Robins, L.N., 1966. *Deviant Children Grown Up.* Baltimore: Williams & Wilkins.

Robinson, G.C., Brummitt, J.R., and Miller, J.R., 1963. Hearing loss in infants and preschool children. II. Etiological considerations. *Pediatrics* **32**, 115.

Robinson, G.C., and Cambon, K.G., 1964. Hearing loss in infants of tuberculous mothers treated with streptomycin during pregnancy. *New England Journal of Medicine* **271**, 949.

Robinson, H., and Robinson, N., 1965. *The Mentally Retarded Child.* New York: McGraw-Hill, p. 148.

Robinson, R.J., 1966. Assessment of gestational age by neurological examination. *Archives of Diseases in Childhood* **41**, 437.

Robinson, R., 1971. The small-for-date baby. II. *British Medical Journal* **4**, 480.

Robinson, R.O., 1981. Equal recovery of child and adult brain? *Developmental Medicine and Child Neurology* **23**, 379.

Roesler, H.D., 1971. Mental development of minimal brain-damaged children. *Acta Paedopsychiatrica* **38**, 71.

Rom, W.N., 1976. Effects of lead on the female and reproduction: A review. *Mount Sinai Journal of Medicine* **43**, 542.

Rose, A., 1977. Neonatal seizures. In M. Blaw, I. Rapin, and M. Kinsbourne, (eds.), *Topics in Child Neurology.* New York: Spectrum Press.

Rose, D., 1980. Some functional correlates of the maturation of neural systems. In D. Caplan (ed.), *Biological Studies of Mental Processes.* Cambridge, Mass.: MIT Press.

Rose, G.H., 1971. Relationship of electrophysiological and behavioral indices of visual development in mammals. In M.B. Sterman, D.J. McGinty, and A.M. Adinolfi (eds.), *Brain Development and Behavior.* New York: Academic Press.

Rose, S.A., 1981. Lags in the cognitive competence of prematurely born infants. In S.L. Friedman and M. Sigman (eds.), *Preterm Birth and Psychological Development.* New York: Academic Press.

Rose, S.A., Schmidt, K., and Bridges, W.H., 1976. Cardiac and behavioural responsivity to tactile stimulation in premature and full-term infants. *Developmental Psychology* **12**, 311.

Rose, S.W., Penry, J.K., Markrush, D., Radloff, P., and Putnam, J.K., 1973. Prevalence of epilepsy in children. *Epilepsia* **14**, 133.

Rosenzweig, M.R., 1951. Representations of the two ears at the auditory cortex. *American Journal of Physiology* **167**, 147.

Rosett, H.L, and Sander, L.W., 1979. Effects of maternal drinking on neonatal morphology and state regulation. In J.D. Osofsky (ed.), *Handbook of Infant Development*. New York: Wiley.

Rosinski, R.R., 1977. *The Development of Visual Perception*. Santa Monica, Calif.: Goodyear.

Ross, A.O., and Pelham, W.E., 1981. Childhood Psychopathology. *Annual Review of Psychology* **32**, 243.

Ross, D.M., and Ross, S.A., 1976. Hyperactivity: *Research, theory and action*. New York: Wiley.

Ross Clinical Education Aid 13. Columbus, Ohio: Ross Laboratories.

Rosvold, H.E., Mirsky, A.F., Sarason, I., Bransome, E.D., and Beck, L.H., 1956. A continuous performance test of brain damage. *Journal of Consulting Psychology* **20**, 343.

Röther, D., and Thaut, C., 1976. Entwicklung und Rückbildung psychischer Störungen: Nachuntersuchung an geistig Behinderten. *Zeitschrift für Psychologie* **184**, 485.

Rourke, B.P., 1976. Reading retardation in children: Developmental lag or deficit? In R.M. Knights and D.J. Bakker (eds.), *The Neuropsychology of Learning Disorders*. Baltimore: University Park Press.

Rourke, B.P., 1978a. Reading, spelling and arithmetic disabilities: A neuropsychological perspective. In H. Myklebust (ed.), *Progress in Learning Disabilities*, vol. 4. New York: Grune and Stratton.

Rourke, B.P., 1978b. Neuropsychological research in reading retardation. In A.L. Benton and D. Pearl (eds.), *Dyslexia: An Appraisal of Current Knowledge*. New York: Oxford University Press.

Rourke, B.P., 1982. Central processing deficiencies in children: Toward a developmental neuropsychological model. *Journal of Clinical Neuropsychology* **4**, 1.

Rourke, B.P., and Finlayson, M.A.J., 1978. Neuropsychological significance of variations in patterns of academic performance: Verbal and visual-spatial abilities. *Journal of Abnormal Child Psychology* **6**, 121.

Rourke, B.P., and Strang, J.D., 1978. Neuropsychological significance of variations in patterns of academic performance: Motor, psychomotor, and tactile-perceptual abilities. *Journal of Pediatric Psychology* **3**, 62.

Rourke, B.P., and Strang, J.D., 1981. Subtypes of reading and arithmetic disabilities: A neuropsychological analysis. In M. Rutter (ed.), *Behavioral Syndromes of Brain Dysfunction in Children*. New York: Guilford.

Routtenberg, A., 1968. The two-arousal hypothesis: Reticular formation and limbic system. *Psychological Review* **75**, 51.

Rovet, J., and Netley, C., 1982. Processing deficits in Turner's Syndrome. *Developmental Psychology* **18**, 77.

Rubin, R.A., Rosenblatt, C., and Barlow, B., 1973. Psychological and educational sequelae of prematurity. *Pediatrics* **52**, 352.

Ruder, K.F., and Smith, M.D., 1974. Issues in language training. In R.L. Schiefelbusch and L.L. Lloyd (eds.), *Language Perspectives: Aquisition, Retardation, and Intervention*. Baltimore: University Park Press.

Rune, V., 1970. Acute head injuries in children. *Acta Paediatrica Scandinavica* suppl. 209.

Rush, D., 1981. Maternal smoking during pregnancy and child development. A review, and methodology for a new study of over 10000 representative five year olds in Great Britain. In *Proceedings of the Third Symposium on the Prevention of Handicapping Conditions of Prenatal and Perinatal Origin.* Edmonton: Alberta Social Services and Community Health.

Russell, J., and Reitan, R.M., 1955. Psychological abnormalities in agenesis of the corpus callosum. *Journal of Nervous and Mental Diseases* **121**, 205.

Rutledge, L.T., Wright, C., and Duncan, J., 1974. Morphological changes in pyramidal cells of mammalian neocortex associated with increased use. *Experimental Neurology* **44**, 209.

Rutter, M., 1965. The influence of organic and emotional factors in the origins, nature and outcome of child psychosis. *Developmental Medicine and Child Neurology* **7**, 518.

Rutter, M., 1969. The concept of dyslexia. In P. Wolff and R.C. MacKeith (eds.), *Planning for Better Learning, Clinics in Developmental Medicine*, no. 33, London: Simp/Heinemann.

Rutter, M., 1978. Diagnosis and definition of childhood autism. *Journal of Autism and Childhood Schizophrenia* **8**,(1), 139.

Rutter, M., 1980. Raised lead levels and impaired cognitive/behavioral functioning: A review of the evidence. *Developmental Medicine and Child Neurology* Suppl. 42, 1.

Rutter, M., 1982. Syndromes attributed to "minimal brain dysfunction" in childhood. *American Journal of Psychiatry* **139**(1), 21.

Rutter, M., Chadwick, C., Shaffer, D., and Brown, G., 1980. A prospective study of children with head injuries. I: Design and methods. *Psychological Medicine* **10**, 633.

Rutter, M., Graham, P., Chadwick, O., and Yule, W., 1976. Adolescent turmoil: Fact or fiction: *Journal of Child Psychology and Psychiatry* **17**, 35.

Rutter, M., Graham, P., and Yule, W., 1970a. *A Neuropsychiatric Study in Childhood.* London: Heinemann Medical Books.

Rutter, M., and Lockyer, L., 1967. A 5- to 15-year follow-up study of infantile psychosis. 1: Description of sample. *British Journal of Psychiatry* **113**, 1169.

Rutter, M., Shaffer, D., and Shepherd, M., 1975a. *A Multi-Axial Classification of Child Psychiatric Disorders: An Evaluation of a Proposal.* Geneva: World Health Organization.

Rutter, M., Tizard, J., and Whitmore, K. (eds.), 1970b. *Education, Health and Behavior.* London: Longmans, Green.

Safer, D.J., 1973. A familial factor in minimal brain dysfunction. *Behavioral Genetics* **3**, 175.

Saint-Anne Dargassies, S., 1966. Neurological maturation of the premature infants of 28 to 41 weeks gestational age. In F. Falkner (ed.), *Human Development.* Philadelphia: Saunders.

Salam, M.Z., and Adams, R.D., 1975. Research on the clinical expression and pathological basis of mental retardation. In D.B. Tower (ed.), *The Nervous System.* Vol. 2: *The Clinical Neurosciences.* New York: Raven Press.

Saling, M., 1979. Lateral differentiation of the human head-turning response: A replication. *Journal of Genetic Psychology* **135**, 307.

Sameroff, A.J., and Chandler, M.J., 1975. Reproductive risk and the continuum of care-taking casuality. In F.D. Horowitz (ed.), *Review of Child Development Research*, vol. 4. Chicago: University of Chicago Press.

Sandberg, A.A., 1963. XYY genotype: Report of a case in a male. *New England Journal of Medicine* **268**, 585.

Sasanuma, S., and Monoi, H., 1975. The syndrome of Golgi (word-meaning) aphasia: Selective impairment of Kanji processing. *Neurology* **25**, 627.

Satterfield, J.H., Cantwell, D.P., Lesser, L.I., and Podosin, R.L., 1972. Physiological studies of the hyperkinetic child. *American Journal of Psychiatry* **128**, 1418.

Satz, P., 1976. Cerebral dominance and reading disability: An old problem revisited. In R.M. Knights and D.J. Bakker (eds.), *The Neuropsychology of Learning Disorders*. Baltimore: University Park Press.

Satz, P., 1977. Laterality tests: An inferential problem. *Cortex* **13**, 208.

Satz, P., 1982. Sex differences: Clues or myths on genetic aspects of speech and language disorders. In C. Ludlow (ed.), *Genetic Aspects of Speech and Language Disorders*. New York: Academic Press.

Satz, P., and Bullard-Bates, C., 1981. Acquired aphasia in children. In M.T. Sarno (ed.), *Acquired Aphasia*. New York: Academic Press.

Satz, P., and Fletcher, J.M., 1980. Minimal brain dysfunction: An appraisal of research concepts and methods. In H.E. Rie and E.D. Rie (eds.), *Handbook of Minimal Brain Dysfunction*. New York: Wiley.

Satz, P., Fried, J., and Rudegair, R., 1974. *Differential Changes in the Acquisition of Developmental Skills in Children Who Later Become Dyslexic: A Three-Year Follow-Up: Recovery of Function*. New York: Academic Press.

Satz, P., Taylor, H.G., Friel, J., and Fletcher, J., 1978. Some developmental and predictive precursors of reading disabilities: A six-year follow-up. In A.L. Benton and D. Pearl (eds.), *Dyslexia: An Appraisal of Current Knowledge*. New York: Oxford University Press.

Sauerwein, H.C., Lassonde, M.C., Cardu, B., and Geoffroy, G., 1981. Interhemispheric integration of sensory and motor functions in agenesis of the corpus callosum. *Neuropsychologia* **19**(3), 445.

Saul, R.E., and Sperry, R.W., 1968. Absence of commissurotomy symptoms with agenesis of the corpus callosum. *Neurology* **18**, 307.

Saxen, L., 1980. Neural induction: Past, present, and future. In R.K. Hunt (ed.), *Neural Development*. Part I: *Current Topics in Developmental Biology*, vol. 15. New York: Academic Press.

Saxon, S.V., 1961. Differences in reactivity between asphyxial and normal rhesus monkeys. *Journal of Genetic Psychology* **99**, 283.

Saxon, S.V., and Ponce, C.G., 1961. Behavioral defects in monkeys asphyxiated during birth. *Experimental Neurology* **4**, 460.

Saxon, S., and Witriol, E., 1976. Down's syndrome and intellectual development. *Journal of Pediatric Psychology* **1**(3), 45.

Scarff, T.B., and Fronczak, S., 1981. Myelomengocele: A review and update. *Rehabilitation Literature* **42**, 143.

Scarr-Salapatek, S., and Williams, M., 1973. The effects of early stimulation on low-birth-weight infants. *Child Development* **44**, 94.

Schain, R.J., 1968. Minimal brain dysfunction in children: A neurological viewpoint. *Bulletin of the Los Angeles Neurological Society* **33**, 145.

Scheibel, M.E., and Scheibel, A.B., 1976. Some thoughts on the ontogeny of memory and learning. In M.R. Rosenzweig and E.L. Bennett (eds.), *Neural Mechanisms of Learning and Memory*. Cambridge, Mass.: MIT Press.

Scheibel, M.E., and Scheibel, A.B., 1977. Specific postnatal threats to brain development: Dendritic changes. In S.R. Berenberg (ed.), *Brain: Fetal and Infant*. The Hague: Martinus Nijhoff.

Schilling, F., 1970. Zur Aussagefähigkeit des Oseretzky-Tests bei normalen und hirngeschädigten Kindern. *Acta Paedopsychiatrica* **37**, 249.

Schlager, G., Newman, D.E., Dunn, H.G., Crichton, J.U., and Schulzer, M., 1979. Bone age in children with minimal brain dysfunction. *Developmental Medicine and Child Neurology* **21**, 41.

Schleifer, M., Weiss, G., Cohen, N., Elman, M., Cvejic, H., and Kruger, E., 1975. Hyperactivity in preschoolers and the effect of methylphenidate. *American Journal of Orthopsychiatry* **45**, 38.

Schlesinger, H., and Meadows, K., 1972. *Sound and Sign: Childhood Deafness and Mental Health*. Berkeley: University of California Press.

Schmid-Rüter, E., 1977. Phenylketonurie: Früherfassung und geistige Entwicklung. Pilotstudie an 89 phenylketonurischen Kindern mit Diätbeginn im ersten bis einschliesslich zwölften Lebensmonat. *Monatsschrift für Kinderheilkunde*, **125**, 479.

Schneider, B.A., Trehub, S.E., and Bull, D., 1979. The development of basic auditory processes in infants. *Canadian Journal of Psychology* **33**, 306.

Schneider, G.E., 1974. Anomalous axonal connections implicated in sparing and alteration of function after early lesions. In E. Eidelberg and D.G. Stein (eds.), Function recovery after lesions of the nervous system. *Neurosciences Research Program Bulletin* **12**(2), 222.

Schneider, G.E., 1979. Is it really better to have your brain lesion early? A revision of the "Kennard principle." *Neuropsychologia* **17**, 557.

Schopler, E., and Mesibov, G., 1981. *Autism in Adolescents and Adults*. New York: Plenum Press.

Schroth, M.L., 1975. The use of IQ as a measure of problem-solving ability with mongoloid and nonmongoloid retarded children. *Journal of Psychology* **91**, 49.

Schuknecht, H.F., 1974. *Pathology of the Ear*. Cambridge, Mass.: Harvard University Press.

Schulman, J.L., Kaspar, J.C., and Throne, F.M., 1965. *Brain Damage and Behaviour: A Clinical-Experimental Study*. Springfield, Ill.: Charles C Thomas.

Schulman-Galambos, C., and Galambos, R., 1979. Assessment of hearing. In T.M. Field, A.M. Sostek, S. Goldberg, and H.H. Shuman (eds.), *Infants at Risk, Behavior and Development*. New York: SP Medical and Scientific Books.

Schulte, F.J., and Stennert, E. 1978. Hearing defects in preterm infants. *Archives of Disease in Childhood* **53**, 269.

Schulze, A., and Teumer, J., 1973/74. Untersuchungen über Vorkommen und Häufigkeit von Sprachschädigungen im Vorschul- und Schulalter. *Die Sprachheilarbeit* **18**, 161, and **19**, 1.

Schurr, P., 1969. Subdural haematomas and effusions in infancy. *Developmental Medicine and Child Neurology* **11**, 108.

Schwartz, E.R., 1974. Characteristics of speech and language development in the child with myelomengocele and hydrocephalus. *Journal of Speech and Hearing Disorders* **39**, 465.

Scott, H., 1976. Outcome of very severe birth asphyxia. *Archives of Disease in Childhood* 51, 712.

Scott, J.P., 1958. Critical periods in the development of social behaviour in puppies. *Psychosomatic Medicine* 20, 42.

Scott, J.P., 1962. Critical periods in behavioural development. *Science* 138, 949.

Scott, J.P., Stewart, J.M., and DeGhett, V.J., 1974. Critical periods in the organization of systems. *Developmental Psychobiology* 7(6), 489.

Seashore, R.H., Buxton, C.E., and McCollom, I.N., 1940. Multiple factorial analysis of fine motor skills. *American Journal of Psychology* 53, 251.

Sechzer, J.A., Faro, M.D., and Windle, W.F., 1973. Studies of monkeys asphyxiated at birth: Implications for minimal cerebral dysfunction. *Seminars in Psychiatry* 5, 19.

Segalowitz, S.J., and Gruber, F.A. (eds.), 1977. Language Development and Neurological Theory. New York: Academic Press.

Seidel, U.P., Chadwick, O., and Rutter, M., 1975. Psychological disorders in crippled children: A comparative study of children with and without brain damage. *Developmental Medicine and Child Neurology* 17, 563.

Sell, S.H., Merrill, R.E., and Doyne, E.O. 1972a. Long-term sequelae of Homophilus influenzae meningitis. *Pediatrics* 49, 206.

Sell, S.H., Webb, W.W., and Pate, J.E., 1972b. Psychological sequelae to bacterial meningitis: Two controlled studies. *Pediatrics* 49, 212.

Selnes, O.A., and Whitaker, H.A., 1976. Morphological and functional development of the auditory system. In R.W. Rieber (ed.), *The Neuropsychology of Language*. New York, Plenum Press.

Seyfort, B.M.A., 1977. An investigation of syndrome specific language impairment in Down's anomaly. Ph.D. dissertation, University of Victoria.

Seyfort, B., and Spreen, O., 1979. Two-plated tapping performance by Down's syndrome and non-Down's syndrome retardates. *Journal of Child Psychology and Psychiatry* 20, 351.

Shaffer, D., Chadwick, O., and Rutter, M., 1975. Psychiatric outcome of localised head injury in children. In R. Porter and D. Fitzsimons (eds.), *Outcome of Severe Damage to the Central Nervous System*. Amsterdam: CIBA Foundation Symposium no. 34.

Shaffer, J.W., 1962. A specific cognitive defect observed in gonodal aplasia (Turner's syndrome). *Journal of Clinical Psychology* 18, 403.

Shallice, T., 1979. Case study approach in neuropsychological research. *Journal of Clinical Neuropsychology* 1, 183.

Shankweiler, D., 1964. Developmental dyslexia: A critique and review of recent evidence. *Cortex* 1, 53.

Shapiro, Y., and Cohen, T., 1973. Agenesis of the corpus callosum in two sisters. *Journal of Medical Genetics* 10, 266.

Shaywitz, B.A., Cohen, D.J., and Bowers, M.B., 1979a. CSF monoamine metabolites in children with minimal brain dysfunction: Evidence for alteration of brain DA. *Journal of Pediatrics* 90(1), 67.

Shaywitz, B.A., Shaywitz, S.E., Byrne, T., Cohen, D.J., and Rothman, S., 1983. Attention deficit disorder: Quantitative analysis of CT. *Neurology* 33, 1500.

Shebilske, W.L., 1976. Extraretinal information in corrective saccades and inflow versus outflow theories of visual direction constancy. *Vision Research* 16, 621.

Shepard, T.H., Miller, J.R., and Marois, D., 1975. *Methods for the Detection of Environmental Agents That Produce Congenital Defects.* New York: Elsevier.

Sheremata, W.A., Deonna, T.W., and Romanul, F.C.A., 1973. Agenesis of the corpus callosum and interhemispheric transfer of information. *Neurology* **23**(4), 390.

Shirley, M., 1938. Development of immature babies during their first two years. *Child Development* **9**, 347.

Shucard, J.L., Shucard, D.W., Cummins, K.R., and Campos, J.J., 1981. Auditory evoked potentials and sex-related differences in brain development. *Brain and Language* **13**, 91.

Sidman, R.L., 1970. Cell proliferation, migration and interaction in the developing mammalian central nervous system. In F.O. Schmitt (ed.), *The Neurosciences: Second Study Program.* New York: Rockefeller University Press.

Sidman, R.L., and Rakic, P., 1973. Neuronal migration, with special reference to developing human brain: A review. Brain Research **62**, 1.

Sigman, M., Kopp, C.B., Parmalee, A.H., and Jeffrey, W., 1973. Visual attention and neurological organisation in neonates. *Child Development* **44**, 461.

Sigman, M., and Parmelee, A.H., 1976. Visual preferences of four-month-old premature and full-term infants. *Child Development* **10**, 687.

Silberberg, N.E., and Silberberg, M.C., 1972. Hyperlexia: The other end of the continuum. *Journal of Special Education* **5**, 233.

Silbergeld, E.K., 1977. Neuropharmacology of hyperkinesis. *Current Developments in Psychopharmacology* **4**, 179.

Silbergeld, E.K., and Goldberg, A.M., 1974. Lead-induced behavioral dysfunction: An animal model of hyperactivity. *Experimental Neurology* **42**, 146.

Silbert, A.R., Wolff, P.H., and Lilienthal, J., 1977. Spatial and temporal processing in patients with Turner's syndrome. *Behavior Genetics* **7**, 11.

Silverstein, A.B., 1979. Mental growth from 6 to 60 in an institutionalized mentally retarded sample. *Psychological Reports* **45**, 643.

Silverstein, A.B., Legutki, G., Friedman, S.L., and Takayama, D.I., 1982. Performance of Down's syndrome individuals on the Stanford-Binet intelligence scale. *American Journal of Mental Deficiency* **86**, 548.

Simmons, F.B., 1975. Automated hearing screening for newborns: The crib-o-gram. In G.T. Mencher (ed.), *Early Identification of Hearing Loss.* Basel: Karger.

Simmons, F.B., and Russ, F.W., 1974. Automated hearing screening: The crib-o-gram. *Archives of Otolaryngology* **100**, 1.

Simonds, J.F., and Aston, L., 1980. Preterm birth, low birth weight and hyperkinetic behaviour in children. *Southern Medical Journal* **73**,1237.

Simpson, J.L., 1976. *Disorders of Sexual Differentiation.* New York: Academic Press.

Singer, J.E., Westphal, M., and Niswander, K.R., 1968. Sex differences in the incidence of neonatal abnormalities and abnormal performance of early childhood. *Child Development* **39**, 103.

Singh, V., and Ling, G.M., 1979. Amphetamines in the management of children's hyperkinesis. *Bulletin on Narcotics* **31**, 87.

Siqueland, E.R., 1973. Biological and experiential determinants of exploration in infancy. In L. Stone, H. Smith, and C. Murphy (eds.), *The Competent Infant.* New York: Basic Books.

Siqueland, E.R., 1981. Studies of visual recognition memory in preterm infants: Differences in development as a function of perinatal morbidity factors. In S.L.

Friedman and M. Sigman (eds.), *Preterm Birth and Psychological Development*. New York: Academic Press.

Sladen, B.K., 1971. Inheritance of dyslexia. *Bulletin of the Orton Society* **31**, 30.

Slager, U., Kelly, A., and Wagner, J., 1957. Congenital agenesis of the corpus callosum: Report of a case and review of the literature. *New England Journal of Medicine* **256**, 1171.

Slater, B.C., 1963. Epidemiology of congenital malformations. *Developmental Medicine and Child Neurology* **5**, 351.

Slater, E., 1953. *Psychotic and Neurotic Illnesses in Twins*. Medical Research Council Special Report Series no. 278. London.

Slooff, A.C., and Slooff, J.L., 1975. Supratentorial tumours in childhood. *Clinical Neurology and Neurosurgery* **78**, 187.

Small, L., 1982. *The Minimal Brain Dysfunctions: Diagnosis and Treatment*. New York: Free Press.

Smith, A., 1966. Speech and other functions after left (dominant) hemispherectomy. *Journal of Neurology, Neurosurgery, and Psychiatry* **29**, 467.

Smith, A., 1969. Nondominant hemispherectomy. *Neurology* **19**(5), 442.

Smith, A., 1974. Dominant and nondominant hemispherectomy. In M. Kinsbourne and W.L. Smith (eds.), *Hemispheric Disconnection and Cerebral Function*. Springfield, Ill.: Charles C Thomas.

Smith, A., and Burklund, C., 1966. Dominant hemispherectomy: Preliminanry report on neuropsychological sequelae. *Science* **153**, 1280.

Smith, A., and Sugar, O., 1975. Development of above-normal language and intelligence 21 years after left hemispherectomy. *Neurology* **25**, 813.

Smith, A., Walker, M.I., and Myers, G., 1978. Hemispherectomy and diaschisis: Rapid improvement in cerebral functions after right hemispherectomy in a six-year-old child. Paper presented at A.P.A., Toronto, September.

Smith, A.C., Flick, G.L., Ferriss, G.S., and Sellmann, A.H., 1972. Prediction of developmental outcome at seven years from prenatal, perinatal, and postnatal events. *Child Development* **43**, 495.

Smith, C.A., 1975. The inner ear: Its embryological development and microstructure. In D.B. Tower (ed.), *The Nervous System*. Vol. 3: *Human Communication and Its Disorders*. New York: Raven Press.

Smith, D.J., 1971. Minor malformations: Their relevance and significance. In E.B. Hook, D.T. Janerich, and I.H. Porter (eds.), *Monitoring, Birth Defects and Environment: The Problem of Surveillance*. New York: Academic Press.

Smith, D.W. and Jones, K.L., 1982. *Recognizable Patterns of Human Malformation*. Philadelphia: Saunders.

Smith, E.S., 1954. Purulent meningitis in infants and children. *Journal of Pediatrics* **45**, 425.

Snart, F., O'Grady, M., and Das, J.P., 1982. Cognitive processing by subgroups of moderately mentally retarded children. *American Journal of Mental Deficiency* **86**, 465.

Snyder, L.H., Schonfeld, M.D., and Offerman, E.M., 1945. A further note in the Rh factor and feeblemindedness. *Journal of Heredity* **36**, 334.

Sohns, G., 1980. Empirische Untersuchung zur visuellen Wahrnehmungsleistung von Behinderten, Hirngeschädigten, Anfallskranken, Kindern und Jugendlichen. Ph.D. Dissertation, University of Bielefeld.

Solitaire, G.B., and Lamarche, J.B., 1966. Alzheimer's disease and senile dementia as seen in mongoloids: Neuropathological observations. *American Journal of Mental Deficiency* **70**, 840.

Soloman, R.L., and Lessac, M.S., 1968. A control group design for experimental studies of developmental processes. *Psychological Bulletin* **70**, 145.

Solursh, L.P., Margulies, A., Ashem, B., and Stasiak, E., 1965. The relationship of agenesis of the corpus callosum to perception and learning. *Journal of Nervous and Mental Diseases* **141**, 180.

Sostek, A.M., Quinn, P.O., and Davitt, M.K., 1979. Behaviour, development and neurologic status of premature and full-term infants with varying medical complications. In T. Field, A.M. Sostrek, S. Goldberg, and H.H. Shuman (eds.), *Infants Born at Risk.* Washington, D.C.: Spectrum.

Spearman, C., 1927. *The Abilities of Man.* New York: Macmillan.

Spehlmann, R., 1981. *EEG Primer.* Amsterdam: Elsevier/North-Holland Biomedical Press, chap. 10.

Spehlmann, R., Gross, R.A., Ho, S.U., Leestma, J.E., and Norcross, K.A., 1977. Visual potentials and postmortem findings in a case of cortical blindness. *Annals of Neurology* **2**, 531

Spellacy, F., and Black, F.W., 1972. Intelligence assessment of language-impaired children by means of two nonverbal tests. *Journal of Clinical Psychology* **28**, 357

Spellacy, F., and Peter, B., 1978. Dyscalculia and elements of the developmental Gerstmann syndrome in school children. *Cortex* **14**, 197

Sperry, R.W., 1951. Mechanisms of neural maturation. In S.S. Stevens (ed.), *Handbook of Experimental Psychology.* New York: Wiley.

Sperry, R.W., 1959. The growth of nerve circuits. *Scientific American* **21**(5), 68

Sperry, R.W., 1963. Chemoaffinity in the orderly growth of nerve fibre patterns and connections. *Proceedings of the National Academy of Sciences* **50**, 703

Sperry, R.W., 1968. Plasticity of neural maturation. *Developmental Biology Supplement* **2**, 36.

Sperry, R.W., 1970. Perception in the absence of the neocortical commissures. *Research Publications, Association for Research in Nervous and Mental Diseases (Perception and Its Disorders)* **68**, 123

Sperry, R.W., 1971. How a developing brain gets itself properly wired for adaptive function. In E. Tobach, L.B. Aronson, and E. Shaw (eds.), *The Biopsychology of Development.* New York: Academic Press.

Sperry, R.W., Gazzaniga, M.S., and Bogen, J.E., 1969. Interhemispheric relationships: The neocortical commissures; syndromes of hemispheric disconnection. In P.J. Vinken and G.W. Bruyn (eds.), *Handbook of Clinical Neurology,* vol. 4. Amsterdam: North-Holland.

Spitz, R., and Wolf, K. M., 1946. Anaclitic depression: An enquiry into the genesis of psychiatric conditions in early childhood. *Psychoanalytic Study of the Child* **2**, 313

Spitz, R.A., 1945. Hospitalism: An enquiry into the genesis of psychiatric conditions in early childhood. *Psychoanalytic Study of the Child.* **1**, 53

Spreen, O., 1978a. *Geistige Behinderung.* Berlin: Springer.

Spreen, O, 1978b. The dyslexias: A discussion of neurobehavioural research. In A.L. Benton and D. Pearl (eds.), *Dyslexia: An Appraisal of Current Knowledge.* New York: Oxford University Press.

Spreen, O., 1981. The relationship between learning disability, neurological impairment and delinquency: Results of a follow-up study. *Journal of Nervous and Mental Disease* **169**, 791–799.

Spreen, O. 1982. Adult outcome of reading disorders. In R.N. Malatesha (ed.), *Reading Disorders: Varieties and Treatment.* New York: Academic Press.

Spreen, O., 1983. *Learning Disabled Children Growing Up*, phase II. Final report, Medical Research Council of Canada. University of Victoria.

Spreen, O., and Anderson, C.W.G., 1966. Sibling relationship and mental deficiency diagnosis as reflected in Wechsler test patterns. *American Journal of Mental Deficiency* **71**, 406

Spreen, O., Benton, A.L., and Van Allen, M., 1966. Dissociation of visual and tactile naming in anmestic aphasia. *Neurology* **16**, 807

Spreen, O., and Lawriw, I., 1980. Neuropsychological test results as predictors of outcome of learning handicap in late adolescence and early adulthood. Paper presented at the International Neuropsychological Society, San Francisco.

St. James-Roberts, I., 1979. Neurological plasticity, recovery from brain insult, and child development. In H.W. Reese and L.P. Lipsitt (eds.), *Advances in Child Development and Behavior*, vol. 14. New York: Academic Press.

St. James-Roberts, I., 1981. A reinterpretation of hemispherectomy data without functional plasticity of the brain. I: Intellectual functions. *Brain and Language* **13**, 31

Stagno, S., 1980. Congenital toxoplasmosis. *American Journal of Diseases of Children* **134**, 635

Stamm, J.S., and Kreder, S.V., 1979. Minimal brain dysfunction: Psychological and neurophysiological disorders in hyperkinetic children. In M.S. Gazzaniga, *Neuropsychology*, vol. 2 of *Handbook of Behavioral Neurology* (F.A. King, ed.). New York: Plenum Press.

Starr, A., Amlie, R. N., Martin, W. H., and Sanders, S., 1977. Development of auditory function in newborn infants revealed by auditory brainstem potentials. *Pediatrics* **60**, 831

Starr, A., Bart, R.D., and Gold, E., 1968. Inapparent cytomegalovirus infection. *New England Journal of Medicine* **1**, 665

Starr, S.E., 1979. Cytomegalovirus. *Pediatric Clinics of North America* **26**, 283.

Stavraky, G.W., 1961. *Supersensitivity Following Lesions of the Nervous System.* Toronto: University of Toronto Press.

Stefanko, S.Z., and Schenk, V.W.D., 1979. Anatomical aspects of agenesis of the corpus callosum in man. In I. S. Russell, M.W. Van Hof, and G. Berlucchi (eds.), *Structure and Function of Cerebral Commissures.* Baltimore: University Park Press.

Steg, J.P., and Rapoport, J.L., 1975. Minor physical anomalies in normal, neurotic, learning-disabled and severely disturbed children. *Journal of Autism and Childhood Schizophrenia* **5**, 299

Stein, Z., Susser, M., Saenger, G., and Marolla, F., 1975. *Famine and Human Development: The Dutch Hunger Winter of 1944–1945.* New York: Oxford University Press.

Steinberg, G., Troshinsky, C., and Steinberg, H., 1971. Dextroamphetamine responsive behavior disorders in school children. *American Journal of Psychiatry* **128**, 174.

Steinhausen, H.C., 1982. Das hyperkinetische Syndrom: Klinische Befunde und

Validataet der Diagnose. In H.C. Steinhausen (ed.), *Das konzentrationsge-störte und hyperaktive Kind*. Stuttgart: Kohlhammer.

Steinwachs, F., and Barmeyer, H., 1952. Die Beziehungen der Feinmotorik zu den puberalen Alters- und Reifungsgraden. *Zeitschrift der menschlichen Verer-bungs- und Konstitutionslehre* **31**, 174

Stern, L., 1973. The use and misuse of oxygen in the newborn infant. *Pediatric Clinics of North America* **20**(2), 447

Stevens, D.A., Boydstun, J.A., Dykman, R.A., Peters, J.E., and Sinton, D.W., 1967. Presumed minimal brain dysfunction in children. *Archives of General Psychiatry* **16**, 281

Stevens, J.R., and Hermann, B.P., 1981. Temporal lobe epilepsy, psychopathology, and violence: The state of the evidence. *Neurology* **31**, 1127

Stevenson, A.C., Johnston, H.A., Stewart, M.I., and Golding, D.R., *Congenital Malformations*. Bulletin, suppl. 34. Geneva: World Health Organization.

Stevenson, J.E., Hawcroft, J., Lobascher, M., Smith, I., Wolff, O.H., and Graham, P.J., 1979. Behavioural deviance in children with early treated phenyl-ketonuria. *Archives of Disease in Childhood* **54**, 14

Steward, O., Cotman, C.W., and Lynch, G.S., 1973. Reestablishment of electro-physiologically functional entorhinal cortical input to the dendate gyrus de-afferented by ipsilateral entorhinal lesions: Innervations by the contralateral entorhinal cortex. *Experimental Brain Research* **18**, 396

Stewart, M.A., 1980. Genetic perinatal and constitutional factors in MBD. In H.E. Rie and E.D. Rie (eds.), *Handbook of Minimal Brain Dysfunction*. New York: Wiley.

Stimmel, B. (ed.), 1982. *The Effects of Maternal Alcohol and Drug Abuse on the Newborn. Advances in Alcohol and Substances Abuse*, vol. 1, nos. 3 and 4. New York: Haworth Press.

Stockard, C.R., 1921. Developmental rate and structural expression: An experi-mental study of twins, double monsters and single deformities and their inter-action among embryonic organs during their origins and development. *Ameri-can Journal of Anatomy* **28**, 115.

Stores, G., 1978. School-children with epilepsy at risk for learning and behavior problems. *Developmental Medicine and Child Neurology* **20**, 502.

Stores, G., Hart J., and Piran, N., 1978. Inattentiveness in school children with epilepsy. *Epilepsia* **19**, 169.

Strauss, A.A., and Kephart, N.C., 1955. *Psychopathology and Education of the Brain Injured Child. Vol. 2: Progress in Theory and Practice*. New York: Grune and Stratton.

Strauss, A. A., and Lehtinen, L. E., *Psychopathology and Education of the Brain Injured Child*, vol. 1. New York: Grune and Stratton.

Strauss, A.A., and Werner, H., 1938. Deficiency in the finger schema in relation to arithmetic disability (finger agnosia and acalculia). *American Journal of Or-thopsychiatry* **8**, 719.

Strauss, E., 1982. Manual persistence in infancy. *Cortex* **18**, 319.

Strauss, M., and Davis, G. L., 1973. Viral diseases of the labyrinths: Review of the literature and discussion of the role of cytomegalovirus in congenital deafness. *Annals of Otology, Rhinology and Laryngology* **82**, 577.

Strome, M., 1977. Sudden and fluctuating hearing losses. In B. F. Jaffe (ed.), *Hearing Loss in Children*. Baltimore: University Park Press.

Strother, F.C., 1973. Minimal cerebral dysfunction: A historical overview. *Annals of the New York Academy of Sciences* **205**, 6.

Sugar, O., 1952. Congenital aphasia: An anatomical and physiological approach. *Journal of Speech and Hearing Disorders* **17**, 301.

Swaab, D.F., Boer, G.J., Boer, J., Van Leeuwen, F.W., and Visser, M., 1978. Fetal neuroendocrine mechanisms in development and partuition. In M.A. Corner, R.E. Baker, N.E. van de Poll, D.F. Swaab, and H.B.M. Uylings (eds.), *Maturation of the Nervous System: Progress in Brain Research*, vol. 48. Amsterdam: Elsevier.

Swidler, H.J., and Walson, P.D., 1979. Hyperactivity: A current assessment. *Journal of Family Practice* **9**, 601.

Sykes, D.H., Douglas, V.I., and Morgenstern, G., 1972. The effect of methylphenidate (Ritalin) on sustained attention in hyperactive children. *Psychopharmacology* **25**, 262.

Sykes, D.H., Douglas, V.I., and Morgenstern, G., 1973. Sustained attention in hyperactive children. *Journal of Child Psychology and Psychiatry* **14**, 213.

Sykes, D.H., Douglas, V.I., Weiss, G., and Minde, K.K., 1971. Attention in hyperactive children and the effect of methylphenidate (Ritalin). *Journal of Child Psychology and Psychiatry* **12**, 129.

Symonds, C., and McKenzie, I., 1957. Bilateral loss of vision from cerebral infarction. *Brain* **80**, 415.

Tallal, P., 1978. An experimental investigation of the role of auditory temporal processing in normal and disordered language development. In A. Caramazzo and E.B. Zurif (eds.), *Language Acquisition and Language Breakdown, Parallels and Divergencies*. Baltimore: Johns Hopkins University Press.

Tallal, P., 1980. Auditory temporal perception, phonics, and reading disabilities in children. *Brain and Language* **9**,182.

Tallal, P., and Piercy, M., 1978. Defects of auditory perception in children with developmental dysphasia. In M. A. Wyke (ed.), *Developmental Dysphasia*. London: Academic Press.

Tallal, P., Stark, R. E., Kallman, C., and Mellitis, D., 1980. Developmental dysphasia: Relation between acoustic processing deficits and verbal processing. *Neuropsychologia* **18**, 273.

Taub, H.B., Goldstein, K.M., and Caputo, D.V., 1977. Indices of neonatal prematurity as discriminators of development in middle childhood. *Child Development* **48**, 797.

Taylor, D.C., 1976. Developmental stratagems organizing intellectual skills: Evidence from studies of temporal lobectomy for epilepsy. In R.M. Knights and D.J. Bakker (eds.), *The Neuropsychology of Learning Disorders*. Baltimore: University Park Press.

Teeter, A., and Hynd, G.W., 1981. Agenesis of the corpus callosum: A developmental study during infancy. *Clinical Neuropsychology* **3**, 29.

Teller, D.Y., 1981. Color vision in infants. In R.N. Aslin, J.R. Alberts, and M.R. Petersen (eds.), *Development of Perception: Psychobiological Perspectives*, vol. 2. New York: Academic Press.

Teszner, D., Tzavaras, A., Gruner, J., and Hecáen, H., 1972. L'asymetrie droite-gauche du planum temporale: A propos de l'etude anatomique de 100 cerveaux. *Revue Neurologique* **126**, 444.

Teuber, H.L., 1966. The frontal lobes and their function: Further observations on rodents, carnivores, subhuman primates and man. *International Journal of Neurology* **5**, 282.

Teuber, H.L., and Rudel, R.C., 1967. Behavior after cerebral lesions in children and adults. *Developmental Medicine and Child Neurology* **4**,3.

Teuber, H.L., and Rudel, R.C., 1971. Spatial orientation in normal children and in children with early brain injury. *Neuropsychologia* **9**, 401.

Tew, B.J., and Laurence, K.M., 1972. The ability and attainments of spina bifida patients born in South Wales between 1956 and 1962. *Developmental Medicine and Child Neurology* **14**, suppl. 27, 124.

Tew B., and Laurence, K.M., 1975. The effects of hydrocephalus on intelligence, visual perception and school attainment. *Developmental Medicine and Child Neurology* **17**, 129.

Thatcher, R.W., 1980. Neurolinguistics: Theoretical and evolutionary perspectives. *Brain and Language* **11**, 235.

Thomas, A., and Chess, S., 1975. A longitudinal study of three brain-damaged children. *Archives of General Psychiatry* **32**, 457.

Thomas, A., and Chess, S., 1980. *The Dynamics of Psychological Development.* New York: Brunner/Mazel.

Thomas, C.J., 1905. Congenital word-blindness and its treatment. *Ophthalmoscope* **5**, 380.

Thompson, J.S., Ross, R.J., and Horwitz, S.J., 1980. The role of computed axial tomography in the child with minimal brain dysfunction. *Journal of Learning Disabilities* **13**, 334.

Thompson, R.F., 1967. *Foundations of Physiological Psychology.* New York: Harper and Row.

Thompson, R.J., and O'Quinn, A.N., 1979. *Developmental Disabilities: Etiologies, Manifestations, Diagnoses, and Treatments.* New York: Oxford.

Thorbert, G., Alm, P., Owman, C., Sjoeberg, N.-O., and Sporrong, B., 1978. Regional changes in structural and functional integrity of myometrical adrenergic nerves in pregnant guinea pigs and their relationship to the localization of the conceptus. *Acta Physiologica Scandinavia* **130**, 120.

Thornburg, H.D., 1982. *Development in Adolescence,* 2d edn. Monterey: Brooks/Cole.

Thurstone, L.L., 1938. *Primary Mental Abilities.* Chicago: University of Chicago Press.

Timiras, P.S., Vernadakis, A., and Sherwood, N.M., 1968. Development and plasticity of the nervous system. In N.S. Assali (ed.), *Biology of Gestation,* vol. II. New York: Academic Press.

Tischler, B., and Lowry, R.B., 1978. Phenylketonuria in British Columbia, Canada. *Monographs of Human Genetics* **9**, 102.

Tizard, B., 1962. The personality of epileptics: A discussion of the evidence. *Psychological Bulletin* **59**, 196.

Tizard, B., 1968. Observations of overactive imbecile children in uncontrolled environments. *American Journal of Mental Deficiency* **72**, 540.

Tobach, E., Aronson, L.R., and Shaw, E. (eds.), 1971. *The Biopsychology of Development.* New York: Academic Press.

Toepfer, C.F., 1980. Brain growth periodization data: Some suggestions for rethinking middle-grades education. *High School Journal* **63**, 222.

Touwen, B.C.L., 1972. Laterality and dominance. *Developmental Medicine and Child Neurology* **14**, 747.

Touwen, B.C.L., 1980. The preterm infant in the extrauterine environment: Implications for neurology. *Early Human Development* **413**, 287.

Towbin, A., 1969. Latent spinal cord and brainstem injury in newborn infants. *Developmental Medicine and Child Neurology* **11**, 54.

Towbin, A., 1970. Central nervous system damage in the human fetus and newborn infant. *American Journal of the Disabled Child* **119**, 529.

Towbin, A., 1971. Organic causes of minimal brain dysfunction: Perinatal origin of minimal cerebral lesions. *Journal of the American Medical Association* **217**(9), 1207.

Townsend, J.J., Baringer, J.R., Wolinsky, J.S., Malamud, N., Mednick, J.P., Panitch, H.S., Scott, R.A.T., Oshiro, L.S., and Cremer, N.E., 1975. Progressive rubella panencephalitis, late onset after congenital rubella. *New England Journal of Medicine* **292**, 990.

Townsend, J.J., Stroop, W.G., Baringer, J.R., Wolinsky, J.S., McKerrow, J.H., and Berg, B.O., 1982. Neuropathology of progressive rubella panencephalitis after childhood rubella. *Neurology* **32**, 185.

Trehub, S.E., 1973. Infant's sensitivity to vowel and tonal contrasts. *Developmental Psychology* **9**, 81.

Trehub, S.E., 1979. Reflections on the development of speech perception. *Canadian Journal of Psychology* **33**,(4), 368.

Trevarthen, C., 1970. Experimental evidence for a brainstem contribution to visual perception in man. *Brain Behavior and Evolution* **3**, 338.

Trevarthen, C.B., 1974. Cerebral embryology and the split brain. In M. Kinsbourne and W. L. Smith (eds.), *Hemispheric Disconnection and Cerebral Function*. Springfield, Ill.: Charles C Thomas.

Trevarthen, C., 1975. Psychological activities after forebrain commissurotomy in man: Concepts, and methodological hurdles in testing. In F. Michel and B. Schott (eds.), *Les Syndromes de Disconnexion Calleuse chez l'Homme* (Colloque Internationale de Lyon, 1974). Lyon: Hopital Neurologique.

Trevarthen, C., 1980. Neurological development and the growth of psychological functions. In J. Sants (ed.), *Developmental Psychology and Society*. New York: St. Martin's Press.

Trites, R.L. (ed.), 1979. *Hyperactivity in Children: Etiology, Measurement, and Treatment Implications*. Baltimore: University Park Press.

Tronick, E., and Brazelton, T.B., 1975. Clinical uses of the Brazelton neonatal behavioural assessment. In B.Z. Friedlander, G.M. Sterritt, and G.E. Kirk, (eds.), *Exceptional Infant: Assessment and Interventions*, vol. 3. New York: Brunner/Mazel.

Trunca, C., 1980. The chromosome syndromes. In J. Wortis, (ed.), *Mental Retardation and Developmental Disabilities: An Annual Review*, vol. 11. New York: Brunner/Mazel.

Tsukahara, N., 1981. Synaptic plasticity in the mammalian central nervous system. Annual Review of Neuroscience **4**, 351.

Tsushima, W.T., and Towne, W.S., 1977. Neuropsychological abilities of young children with questionable brain disorders. *Journal of Consulting and Clinical Psychology* **44**, 757.

Tuckko, H., 1982. Cognitive correlates of arithmetic performance in clinic-referred children. Ph.D. dissertation, University of Victoria.

Tupper, D.E., 1982. Behavioral correlates of the development of interhemispheric interaction in young children. Ph.D. dissertation, University of Victoria.

Turkewitz, G., and Birch, H., 1971. Neurobehavioral organization of the human newborn. In J. Hellmuth (ed.), *The Exceptional Infant: Studies in Abnormalities*, vol. 2. New York: Brunner/Mazel.

Turkewitz, T., and Birch, H., 1968. Relations between birth condition and neurobehavioral organization in the neonate. *Pediatric Research* **2**, 243.

Turner, H.H., 1938. A syndrome of infantilism, congenital webbed neck and cubitus valgus. *Endocrinology* **23**, 566.

Turner, O.A., 1948. Growth and development of cerebral cortical pattern in man. *Archives of Neurology and Psychiatry* **59**, 1.

Turner, O.A., 1950. Postnatal growth changes in the cortical surface area. *Archives of Neurology and Psychiatry* **64**, 378.

Tyler, H.R., 1968. Neurologic disorders in renal failure. *American Journal of Medicine* **44**, 734.

Ueda, K., Nishida, Y., Oshima, K., and Shephard, T., 1979. Congenital rubella syndrome: Correlation of gestational age at time of maternal rubella with type of defect. *Journal of Pediatrics* **94**, 763.

Ullman, D.B., Barkley, R.A., and Brown, H.W., 1978. The behavioral symptoms of hyperkinetic children who successfully responded to stimulant drug treatment. *American Journal of Orthopsychiatry* **48**, 425.

Upadhyay, Y., 1971. A longitudinal study of full-term neonates with hyperbilirubinemia to four ages of age. *Johns Hopkins Medical Journal* **128**, 273.

Vandenberg, S.G., and Kuse, A.R., 1979. Spatial ability: A critical review of the sex-linked major gene hypothesis. In M.A. Wittig and A.C. Petersen (eds.), *Sex-Related Differences in Cognitive Functioning: Developmental Issues*. New York: Academic Press.

Van der Vlugt, H., 1979. Aspects of normal and abnormal neuropsychological development. In M. S. Gazzaniga (ed.), *Neuropsychology* (vol. 2 *Handbook of Behavioral Neurobiology*). New York: Plenum Press.

Van Dijk, J., 1982. *Rubella Handicapped Children: The Effects of Bilateral Cataract and/or Hearing Impairment on Behaviour and Learning*. Liss, the Netherlands: Swets and Zeitlinger.

Van Duyne, H.J., 1982. The development of ear asymmetry related to cognitive growth and memory in children. In R.N. Malatesha and L.C. Hartlage (eds.), *Neuropsychology and Cognition*, vol. II. The Hague: Martinus Vyhoff.

Van Sluyters, R.C., and Freeman, R.D., 1977. The physiological effects of brief periods of monocular deprivation in very young kittens. *Neurosciences Abstracts* **3**, 433.

Vargha-Khadem, F., 1982. Hemispheric specialization for the processing of tactual stimuli in cogenitally deaf and hearing children. *Cortex* **18**, 277.

Vargha-Khadem, F., and Corballis, M.C., 1979. Cerebral asymmetry in infants. *Brain and Language* **8**, 1.

Varlaam, A., 1974. Educational attainment and behaviour at school. *Greater London Council Intelligence Quarterly* **29**, 29.

Vazquez, H.J., and Turner, M., 1951. Epilepsia en flexion generalizada. *Archives of Argentine Pediatrics* **35**, 111.

Vellutino, F.R., 1982. Childhood dyslexia: A language disorder. In H.R. Myklebust (ed.), *Progress in Learning Disabilities*. Vol. 5: *Language Disorders*. New York: Grune and Stratton.

Vellutino, R.L., 1979. *Dyslexia: Theory and Research*. Cambridge, Mass.: MIT Press.

Verity, C.M., Strauss, E.H., Moyes, P.D., Wada, J.A., Dunn, H.G., and Lapointe, J.S., 1982. Long-term follow-up after cerebral hemispherectomy: Neurophysiological, radiological, and psychological findings. *Neurology* **32**, 629.

Vernon, M.D., 1971. *Reading and Its Difficulties*. Cambridge: Cambridge University Press.

Vernon, M., 1976. Prematurity and deafness: The magnitude and nature of the problem among deaf children. *Exceptional Children* **36**, 289.

Vetter, D.K., Fay, W.H., and Winitz, H., 1980. Language. In F.M. Lassman, R.O. Fisch, D.K. Vetter, and E.S. La Benz (eds.), *Early Correlates of Speech, Language, and Hearing*. Littleton, Mass.: PSG Publishing.

Virchow, R., 1867. Zur pathologischen Anatomie des Gehirns: I. Congenitale Encephalitis und Myelitis. *Virchow's Archiv für Pathologische Anatomie und Physiologie für Klinische Medizin* **38**, 129.

Vogel, S., 1977. Morphological ability in normal and dyslexic children. *Journal of Learning Disabilities* **10**, 41.

Vohr, B.R., Oh, W., Rosenfield, A.G., and Lowett, R.M., 1979. The preterm small-for-gestational-age infant: A two-year follow-up study. *American Journal of Gynecology* **133**, 425.

Volpe, J., 1976. Perinatal hypoxic ischemic brain injury. *Pediatric Clinics of North America* **23**, 383.

Volpe, J.J., 1977. Neonatal intracranial hemorrhage: Pathophysiology, neuropathology, and clinical features. *Clinics in Perinatology* **4**(1), 77.

Von Bonin, G., 1962. Anatomical asymmetries of the cerebral hemispheres. In V.B. Mountcastle (ed.), *Interhemispheric Relations and Cerebral Dominance*. Baltimore: Johns Hopkins Press.

Vonderhaar, W.F., and Chambers, J.F., 1975. An examination of deaf students' Wechsler performance subtest scores. *American Annals of the Deaf* **120**(6), 540.

Von Economo, C., 1929. *The Cytoarchitechtonics of the Human Cerebral Cortex*. London: Oxford University Press.

Von Monakow, C., 1911. Lokalisation der Hirnfunktionen. *Journal für Psychologie und Neurologie* **17**, 185 (translated in von Bonin, G., *Some Papers on the Cerebral Cortex*. Springfield, Ill.: Charles C Thomas).

Vorherr, H., 1975. Placental insufficiency in relation to post-term pregnancy and fetal postmaturity. *American Journal of Obstetrics and Gynecology* **123**, 67.

Waber, D.P., 1976. Sex differences in cognition: A function of maturation rate? *Science* **192**, 572.

Waber, D.P., 1977. Sex differences in mental abilities, hemispheric lateralization and rate of physical growth at adolescence. *Developmental Psychology* **13** (1), 29.

Waber, D.P., 1979a. Cognitive abilities and sex-related variations in the maturation of cerebral cortical functions. In M.A. Wittig and A.C. Peterson (eds.), *Sex-*

related Differences in Cognitive Functioning: Developmental Issues. New York: Academic Press.

Waber, D.P., 1979b. Neuropsychological aspects of Turner's syndrome: *Developmental Medicine and Child Neurology* **21**, 58.

Wada, J.A., 1964. Longitudinal analysis of chronic epileptogenic brain process. In *Epileptology, Clinical and Basic Aspects.* Tokyo: Igaku Shoin.

Wada, J.A., Clark, R., and Hamm, A., 1975. Cerebral hemispheric asymmetry in humans. *Archives of Neurology* **32**, 239.

Wald, N., 1979. Radiation Injury. In P.B. Beeson, M.D. McDermott, and J.B. Wyngaarden, (eds.), *Cecil Textbook of Medicine,* vol. 1. Philadelphia: Saunders.

Waldrop, M.R., Bell, R.Q., and Goering, J.D., 1976. Minor physical anomalies and inhibited behavior in elementary school girls. *Journal of Child Psychology and Psychiatry* **17**, 113.

Waldrop, M.F., and Goering, J.D., 1971. Hyperactivity and minor physical anomalies in elementary school children. *American Journal of Orthopsychiatry* **41**, 602.

Waldrop, M., and Halverson, C.E., 1971. Minor physical anomalies and hyperactive behaviour in young children. In J. Hellmuth (ed.), *The Exceptional Infant.* New York: Brunner/Mazel.

Waldrop, M.F., Pedersen, F.A., and Bell, R.C., 1968. Minor physical abnormalities and behavior in preschool children. *Child Development* **39**, 391.

Wallace, R.B., Kaplan, R., and Werboff, J., 1977. Hippocampus and behavioral maturation. *International Journal of Neuroscience* **7**, 185.

Walther, B., 1982. Nahrungsphosphat und Verhaltensstörung im Kindesalter: Ergebnisse einer köntrollierten Diaetstudie. In H.C. Steinhausen (ed.), *Das konzentrations-gestörte und hyperaktive Kind.* Stuttgart: Kohlhammer.

Walton, J.N., 1967. The 'clumsy child' syndrome: Apraxia and agnosia of evolutive origin in childhood *Recenti Progressi in Medicina (Roma)* **43**, 490.

Ward, S., and McCartney, E., 1978. Congenital auditory imperception: A follow-up study. *British Journal of Disorders of Communication,* **13**(1)

Warkany, J., Monroe, B.B., and Sutherland, B.S., 1961. Intrauterine growth retardation. *American Journal of Diseases of Childhood* **102**, 249.

Warner, E.N., 1935. A survey of mongolism with a review of 100 cases. *Canadian Medical Association Journal* **33**, 495.

Webster, D. B., and Webster, M., 1978. Effects of neonatal conductive hearing loss on brainstem auditory nuclei. *Annals of Otolaryngology, Rhinology and Laryngology* **88**, 684.

Wechsler, D., 1949. Wechsler Intelligence Scale for Children Manual. New York: Psychological Corporation.

Wechsler, D., 1958. *The Measurement and Appraisal of Adult Intelligence.* New York: Psychological Corporation.

Weil, M.L., Itabashi, H.H., Cremer, N.E., Oshiro, L.S., Lennette, E.H., and Carnay, L., 1975. Chronic progressive panencephalitis due to rubella virus simulating subacute sclerosing panencephalitis. *New England Journal of Medicine* **292**, 994.

Weiland, I. H., and Legg, D. R., 1964. Formal speech characteristics as a diagnostic aid in childhood psychosis. *American Journal of Orthopsychiatry* **34**, 91.

Weiner, G., 1970. Varying psychological sequelae of lead ingestion in children. *Public Health Report* **85**, 19.

Weiner, P.S., 1969. The perceptual level of functioning of dysphasic children. *Cortex* **5**, 440.

Weiss, G., 1980. Critical diagnostic issues. In H.E. Rie, and E.D. Rie (eds.), *Handbook of Minimal Brain Dysfunction.* New York: Wiley.

Weiss, G., Hechtman, L., and Perlman, T., 1978. Hyperactives as young adults: School, employer, and self-rating scales obtained during ten-year follow-up evaluation. *American Journal of Orthopsychiatry* **48**, 438.

Weiss, G., Hechtman, L., Perlman, T., Hopkins, J., and Wener, A., 1979. Hyperactives as young adults: A controlled prospective ten-year follow-up of 75 children. *Archives of General Psychiatry* **36**, 675.

Weiss, G., Minde, K., Werry, J.S., Douglas, V., and Nemeth, E., 1971. Studies on the hyperactive child: Five-year follow-up. *Archives of General Psychiatry* **24**, 409.

Weiss, W., and Jackson, M., 1969. Maternal factors affecting birthweight. In *Perinatal Factors Affecting Human Development.* New York: Academic Press.

Wellman, M.M., and Allen, M., 1983. Variations in hand position, cerebral lateralization and reading ability among right-handed children. *Brain and Language* **18**, 277.

Wender, P.H., 1971. *Minimal brain dysfunction in children.* New York: Wiley Interscience.

Wender, P.H., 1977. Speculations concerning a possible biochemical basis of MBD. In J.G. Millichap (ed.), *Learning Disabilities and Related Disorders.* Chicago: Year Book Medical Publishers.

Wenzel, H., 1966 Die Aphasie im Kindesalter. Dissertation, Faculty of Medicine, University of Marburg.

Werner, E., and Smith, R., 1979. An epidemiological perspective on some antecedents and consequences of childhood mental health problems and learning disabilities. *American Academy of Child Psychiatry* **16**, 293.

Werner, H., and Strauss, A., 1940. Causal factors in low performance. *American Journal of Mental Deficiency* **45**, 213.

Werner, H., and Strauss, A., 1941. Pathology of figure-background relation in the child. *Journal of Abnormal and Social Psychology* **36**, 236.

Werry, J.S., 1972. Childhood Psychosis. In H.C. Quay and J.S. Werry (eds.), *Psychopathological Disorders of Childhood.* New York: Wiley.

Werry, J.S., Minde, K., Guzman, A., Weiss, G., Dogan, K., and Hoy, E., 1972. Studies on the hyperactive child. VII: Neurological status compared with neurotic and normal children. *American Journal of Orthopsychiatry* **42**, 441.

Werry, J.S., Weiss, G., and Douglas, V., 1964. Studies on the hyperactive child. I: Some preliminary findings. *Canadian Psychiatric Association Journal* **2**, 120.

Wersh, J., and Briere, J., 1981. WISC-R subtest variability in normal Canadian children and its relationship to sex, age and IQ. *Canadian Journal of Behavioural Science* **13**, 76.

Werthmann, M.W., 1981. Medical constraints to optimal psychological development of the preterm infant. In S.I. Friedman and M. Sigman (eds.), *Preterm Birth and Psychological Development.* New York: Academic Press.

Wewetzer, K.H., 1958. Zur Differenzierung der Leistungsstrukturen bei verschiedenen Intelligenzgraden. Report, 21. Congress of Deutsche Gesellschaft für Psychologie. Göttingen: Hogrefe.

Wewetzer, K.H., 1972. Intelligenz und Intelligenzmessung. Darmstadt: Wissenschaftliche Buchgesellschaft.

Wewetzer, K.H., 1975. Zur Differenzierung des organischen Psychosyndroms nach kindlichen Hirnschäden; Kurzbericht einer experimentellen Studie. *Diagnostica* **21**, 182.

White, H.H., 1961. Cerebral hemispherectomy in the treatment of infantile hemiplegia: Review of the literature and report of two cases. *Confinia Neurologica* **21**, 1.

White, K.D., and Brackbill, Y., 1981. Visual development in pre- and full-term infants: A review of chapters 12–15. In S.L. Friedman and M. Sigman (eds.), *Preterm Birth and Psychological Development*. New York: Academic Press.

White, S.H., 1970. Some general outlines of the matrix of developmental changes between five and seven years. *Bulletin of the Orton Society* **20**, 41.

Whitehouse, D., 1976. Behavior and learning problems in epileptic children. *Behavioral Neuropsychiatry* **7**, 23

Wikler, A., Dixon, J., and Parker, J. Jr., 1970. Brain function in problem children and controls: Psychometric, neurological and electroencephalographic comparison. *American Journal of Psychiatry* **127**, 634.

Willems, G., Noel, A., and Evrard, P., 1979. L'examen neuropediatrique des fonctions d'apprentissage chez l'enfant en age prescolaire. *Revue Francaise d'Hygiene et de Medicine Scolaire et Universitaire* **32**, 3.

Willerman, L., 1973. Activity level and hyperactivity in twins. *Child Development* **44**, 288.

Williams, J.I., and Cram, D.M., 1978. Diet in the management of hyperkinesis: A review of the tests of Feingold's hypotheses. *Canadian Psychiatric Association Journal* **23**, 241.

Williamson, M.L., Koch, R., Azen, C., and Chang, C., 1981. Correlates of intelligence test results in treated phenylketonuric children. *Pediatrics* **68**, 161.

Wilson, C.B., Remington, J.S., Stagno, S., and Reynolds, D.W., 1980. Development of adverse sequelae in children born with subclinical congenital toxoplasma infection. *Pediatrics* **66**, 767.

Wilson, J.G., 1973. *Environment and Birth Defects*. New York: Academic Press.

Wilson, J.G., 1977. Environmental Chemicals. In J.G. Wilson and F.C. Frazer (eds.), *Handbook of Teratology*, vol. 1. New York: Plenum Press.

Wilson, P.J.E., 1970. Cerebral hemispherectomy for infantile hemiplegia: A report of 50 cases. *Brain* **93**, 147.

Windle, W. F., 1964. Neurological deficits of asphyxia at birth of rhesus monkeys: Prevention and therapy. In P. Kellaway and I. Petersen (eds.), *Neurological and Electroencephalographic Correlative Studies in Infancy*. New York: Grune and Stratton.

Windle, W.F., 1971. Origin and early development of neural elements in the human brain. In E. Tobach, L. R. Aronsen, and E. Shaw (eds.), *The Biopsychology of Development*. New York: Academic Press.

Winer, B.J., 1971. Statistical principles in experimental design, 2d edn. New York: McGraw-Hill.

Winfield, D.L., 1950. Intellectual performance of cryptogenic epileptics, symptomatic epileptics, and posttraumatic encephalopaths. *Journal of Abnormal and Social Psychology* **45**, 336.

Winick, M., 1970. Cellular growth in intrauterine malnutrition. *Pediatric Clinics of North America* **17**, 69.

Winick, M., 1976. Malnutrition and brain development. New York: Oxford University Press.

Winick, M., and Noble, A., 1966. Cellular response in rats during malnutrition at various ages. *Journal of Nutrition* **89**, 300.

Winick, M., and Rosso, P., 1969. The effect of severe early malnutrition on cellular growth of human brain. *Pediatric Research* **3**, 181.

Winokur, G., and Tanna, V.L., 1969. Possible role of X-linked dominant factor in manic depressive disease. *Diseases of the Nervous System* **30**, 89.

Witelson, S.F., 1976. Abnormal right hemispheric specialization in developmental dyslexia. In R. Knights and D. Bakker (eds.), *The Neuropsychology of Learning Disorders*. Baltimore: University Park Press.

Witelson, S.F., 1977a. Neural and cognitive correlates of developmental dyslexia: age and sex differences. In C. Shagass, S. Gershan, and A.J. Friedhoff (eds.), *Psychopathology and Brain Dysfunction*. New York: Raven Press.

Witelson, S.F., 1977b. Early hemisphere specialization and interhemispheric plasticity: an empirical and theoretical review, in *Language Development and Neurological Theory* (S.J. Segalowitz and F.A. Gruber, eds.). New York: Academic Press.

Witelson, S.F., and Pallie, W., 1973. Left hemisphere specialization for language in the newborn: Neuroanatomical evidence of asymmetry. *Brain* **96**, 641.

Witkin, H.A., Mednick, S.A., Schulsinger, F., Bakkestrom, E., Christiansen, K.O., Goodenough, D.R., Hirschhorn, K., Lundsteen, C., Owen, D.R., Philip, J., Rubin, D.B., and Stocking, M., 1976. Criminality in XYY and XXY men. *Science* **193**, 547.

Wittig, M.A., and Petersen, A.C. (eds.), 1979. *Sex-Related Differences in Cognitive Functioning: Developmental Issues*. New York: Academic Press.

Wolf, S.M., and Forsythe, A., 1978. Behavior disturbance, phenobarbital, and febrile seizures. *Pediatrics* **61**, 728.

Wolff, J.R., 1978. Ontogenetic aspects of cortical architecture: Lamination. In M.A.B. Brazier and H. Petsche (eds.), *Architectonics of the Cerebral Cortex*. New York: Raven Press.

Wolff, S., 1970. Behavioral pathology of parents of disturbed children. In E.J. Anthony and C. Vioupernik (eds.), *The Child in His Family*, vol. 1. New York: Wiley.

Wolff, S., 1971. Dimensions and clusters of symptoms in disturbed children. *British Journal of Psychiatry* **118**, 421.

Wolfson, R.J., Aghamohamadi, A.M., and Berman, S.E., 1980. Disorders of hearing. In S. Gabel and M.T. Erickson (eds.), *Child Development and Developmental Disabilities*. Boston: Little, Brown.

Wong, D., and Shah, C.P., 1979. Identification of impaired hearing in early childhood. *Canadian Medical Association Journal* **121**, 529.

Wood, N.E., 1975. Assessment of auditory processing dysfunction. *Acta Symbolica* **6**, 113.

Woods, B.T., and Carey, S., 1979. Language deficits after apparent clinical recovery from childhood aphasia. *Annals of Neurology* **6**, 405.

Woods, B.T., and Teuber, H.I., 1978a. Mirror movements after childhood hemi-paresis. *Neurology* **28**, 1152.

Woods, B.T., and Teuber, H.L., 1978b. Changing patterns of childhood aphasia. *Annals of Neurology* **3**, 273.

Woolsey, T.A., Durham, D., Harris, R., Simons, D.J., and Valentino, K., 1981. Somatosensory development. In R.N. Aslin, J.R. Alberts, and M.R. Petersen (eds.), *Development of Perception: Psychological Perspectives.* Vol. I: *Audition, Somatic Perception and the Chemical Senses.* New York: Academic Press.

World Health Organization, 1977. *Manual of the International Statistical Classification of Diseases, Injuries and Causes of Death,* vols. 1 and 2. Geneva: World Health Organization.

Worster-Drought, C., and Allen, I.M., 1929a. Congenital auditory imperception (congenital word-deafness) with report of a case. *Journal of Neurology and Psychopathology* **9**, 193.

Worster-Drought, C., and Allen, I.M., 1929b. Congenital auditory imperception (congenital word-deafness): Investigation of a case by Head's method. *Journal of Neurology and Psychopathology* **9**, 289.

Wortis, J., 1957. A note on the concept of the 'brain injured' child. *American Journal of Mental Deficiency* **61**, 204.

Wortis, J. (ed.), 1980a. *Mental Retardation: An Annual Review,* vol. 11. New York: Grune and Stratton.

Wortis, J. (ed.), 1980b. *Mental Retardation and Developmental Disabilities: An Annual Review,* vol. 11, New York: Brunner/Mazel.

Wright, L., and Jimmerson, S., 1971. Intellectual sequelae of homophilus influenzae meningitis. *Journal of Abnormal Psychology* **77**, 181.

Wright, S.W., and Tarjan, G., 1957. Phenylketonuria. *American Journal of Diseases of Children* **93**, 405.

Wunderlich, C., 1970. *Das mongoloide Kind. Möglichkeiten der Erkennung und Betreuung.* Stuttgart: Enke.

Wyke, M.A., 1968. The effect of brain lesions in the performance of an arm-hand precision task. *Neuropsychologia* **6**, 125.

Yakovlev, P.I., 1962. Morphological criteria of growth and maturation of the nervous system in man. *Research Publications, Association for Research in Nervous and Mental Diseases* **39**, 3.

Yakovlev, P.I., and Lecours, A.-R., 1967. The myelogenetic cycles of regional maturation of the brain. In A. Minkowski (ed.), *Regional Development of the Brain in Early Life.* Oxford: Blackwell Scientific.

Yeni-Komshian, G.H., and Benson, D.A., 1976. Anatomical study of cerebral asymmetry in the temporal lobe of humans, chimpanzees and rhesus monkeys. *Science* **192**, 387.

Yolles, S.F., and Kramer, M., 1969. Vital Statistics. In L. Bellak and L. Loeb (eds.), *The Schizophrenic Syndrome.* New York: Grune and Stratton.

Young, G., 1977. Manual specialization in infancy: Implications for lateralization of brain functions. In S.G. Segalowitz and F.A. Gruber (eds.), *Language Development and Neurological Theory.* New York: Academic Press.

Yoss, K.A., and Darley, F.I., 1974. Developmental apraxia of speech in children with defective articulation. *Journal of Speech and Hearing Research* **17**, 399.

Yule, M., and Rutter, M., 1976. Epidemiology and social implications of specific reading retardation. In R.M. Knights and D.J. Bakker (eds.), *The Neuropsychology of Learning Disorders*. Baltimore: University Park Press.

Yule, W.M., Rutter, M., Berger, M., and Thompson, J., 1974. Over- and underachievement in reading: Distribution in the general population. *British Journal of Educational Psychology* **44**, 1.

Zaidel, E., 1978. Auditory language comprehension in the right hemisphere following cerebral commissurotomy and hemispherectomy: A comparison with child language and aphasia. In E. Zurif and A. Caramazza (eds.), *The Acquisition and Breakdown of Language: Parallels and Divergencies*. Baltimore: Johns Hopkins University Press.

Zaidel, E., 1979. The split and half brains as models of congenital language disability. In C.I. Ludlow and M.E. Doran-Quine (eds.), *The Neurological Bases of Language Disorders in Children: Methods and Directions for Research*, NIH Publication no. 79-440. Bethseda, Md.: U.S. Department of Health, Education and Welfare.

Zamenhof, S., and van Marthens, E., 1978. Nutritional influences on prenatal brain development. In G. Gottlieb (ed.), *Early Influences*, vol. IV. New York: Academic Press.

Zangwill, O.L., 1962. Dyslexia in relation to cerebral dominance. In J. Money (ed.), *Reading Disability*. Baltimore: Johns Hopkins Press.

Zangwill, O.L., 1978. The concept of developmental aphasia. In M.A. Wyke (ed.), *Developmental Aphasia*. New York: Academic Press.

Zeaman, D., and House, B.J., 1962. Mongoloid MA is proportional to LogCA. *Child Development*, **33**, 481.

Zekulin-Hartley, X. 1981. Hemispheric asymmetry in Down's syndrome children. *Canadian Journal of Behavioural Science* **13**(3), 210.

Zeskind, P.S., and Ramey, C.T., 1981. Preventing intellectual and interactional sequelae of fetal malnutrition: A longitudinal, transactional, and synergistic approach to development. *Child Development* **52**, 213.

Zimmer, J., 1978. Development of the hippocampus and fascia dentata: Morphological and histochemical aspects. In M.A. Corner, R. Baker, N.E. Van de Poll, D.F. Swaab, and H.E.M. Uylings (eds.), *Maturation of the Nervous System (Progress in Brain Research*, vol. 48). Amsterdam: Elsevier Scientific.

Ziring, P.R., 1977. Congenital rubella: The teenage years. *Pediatric Annals* **6**, 762.

Zollinger, R., 1935. Removal of left cerebral hemisphere: Report of a case. *Archives of Neurology and Psychiatry* **34**, 1055.

Zulch, K.J. 1974. Motor and sensory findings after hemispherectomy: Ipsi- or contralateral functions? *Clinical Neurology and Neurosurgery* **77**(1), 3.

INDEX

Page numbers in *italic type* indicate where terms have been defined or explained.

463